Problems in
European
Prehistory

To Jane

Problems in European Prehistory

A collection of 18 papers,
each with a new introduction
and bibliography, and
an original introductory essay by

COLIN RENFREW

Professor of Archaeology
University of Southampton

Edinburgh University Press

Edinburgh University Press
22 George Square, Edinburgh
ISBN 0 85224 355 3 (hardback)
0 85224 362 6 (paperback)
Printed in Great Britain by
R. & R. Clark Ltd, Edinburgh

CONTENTS

Acknowledgements vii

INTRODUCTION:
Problems in European Prehistory 1

1) Trade and Culture Process in European Prehistory 22

2) The Aegean and the West Mediterranean 43

3) The Characterisation of Obsidian and its Application to the Mediterranean Region (with J. R. Cann) 65

4) Cycladic Metallurgy and the Aegean Early Bronze Age (with an Appendix by J. A. Charles) 87

5) The Autonomy of the South-East European Copper Age (with Appendixes by J. A. Charles and J. Frierman) 137

6) The Tărtăria Tablets 180

7) Neolithic Trade Routes Realigned by Oxygen Isotope Analyses (with N. Shackleton) 183

8) Sitagroi, Radiocarbon and the Prehistory of South-East Europe 190

9) The Copper Age of Peninsular Italy and the Aegean (with R. Whitehouse) 202

10) Malta and the Calibrated Radiocarbon Chronology (with an Appendix by Jane M. Renfrew) 255

11) Colonialism and Megalithismus 262

12) Wessex without Mycenae 281

13) British Faience Beads Reconsidered (with R. G. Newton) 293

14) Wessex as a Social Question 304

15) Problems of the Radiocarbon Calendar and its Calibration (with R. M. Clark) 310

16) Tree-ring Calibration of Radiocarbon Dates and the Chronology of Ancient Egypt (with R. M. Clark) 326

17) The Tree-ring Calibration of Radiocarbon: An Archaeological Evaluation 338

18) Varna and the Social Context of Early Metallurgy 377

Index 389

ACKNOWLEDGEMENTS

I am grateful to Mr Archie Turnbull, Secretary to the Edinburgh University Press, for the invitation to publish this collection of essays relating to European prehistory. Particular thanks are due to my colleagues, co-authors of a number of the papers, who have generously allowed me to reprint them here: J. R. Cann ; J. A. Charles ; R. M. Clark ; J. Frierman ; R. G. Newton ; J. M. Renfrew ; N. J. Shackelton and R. D. Whitehouse. I owe each a much greater debt of gratitude for rewarding, enjoyable and often very stimulating collaboration in the first place.

The editors of the following journals where these papers were first published (the full references are all indicated below) have all kindly indicated approval of their inclusion here: *American Journal of Archaeology, Annual of the British School of Archaeology at Athens* (with the approval of the Management Committee), *Antiquity, Archaeometry, Current Anthropology* (and the University of Chicago Press), *Nature, Nestor, Proceedings of the Prehistoric Society.*

Trade and culture process in European prehistory (1969) *Current Anthropology 10*, 151–69. The characterization of obsidian and its application to the Mediterranean region (1964) *Proceedings of the Prehistoric Society 30*, 111–33. Cycladic metallurgy and the Aegean early bronze age (1967) *American Journal of Archaeology 71*, 2–26. The autonomy of the south-east European copper age (1969) *Proceedings of the Prehistoric Society 35*, 12–47. The Tărtăria tablets (1 December 1966) *Nestor*, 469–70. Neolithic trade routes realigned by oxygen isotope analyses (1970) *Nature 228*, 1062–5. Sitagroi, radiocarbon and the prehistory of south-east Europe (1971) *Antiquity 45*, 275–82. The copper age of peninsular Italy and the Aegean (1974) *Annual of the British School at Athens 69*, 343–90. Malta and the calibrated radiocarbon chronology (1972) *Antiquity 46*, 141–4. Colonialism and megalithismus (1967) *Antiquity 41*, 276–88. Wessex without Mycenae (1968) *Annual of the British School at Athens 63*, 277–85. British faience beads reconsidered (1970) *Antiquity 44*, 199–206. Wessex as a social question (1973) *Antiquity 47*, 221–3. Problems of the radiocarbon calendar and its calibration (1974) *Archaeometry 16*, 5-18. Tree-ring calibration of radiocarbon dates and the chronology of ancient Egypt (1973) *Nature 243*, 266–70. The tree-ring calibration of radiocarbon: an archaeological evaluation (1970) *Proceedings of the Prehistoric Society 36*, 280–311, Varna and the social context of early metallurgy (1978) *Antiquity 52*, 199–203.

Chapter 2 is taken from Chapter X ('The Cyclades and the West') of my doctoral dissertation, *The Neolithic and Early Bronze Age Cultures of the Cyclades and their External Relations*, University of Cambridge, 1965.

INTRODUCTION

Problems in European Prehistory

> The early Culture-History of Mankind is capable of being treated as an Inductive Science, by collecting and grouping facts. It is true that very little has as yet been done in this way . . . ; but the evidence has only to a very slight extent been got into a state to give definite results, and the whole argument is extremely uncertain and difficult: a fact which sufficiently accounts for writers on the Origin of Civilisation being able to tell us all about it, with that beautiful ease and confidence which belong to the speculative philosopher, whose course is but little obstructed by facts (E. B. Tylor 1870, 162).

European prehistory has been the subject of systematic and detailed investigation for almost one hundred and fifty years, and over that period an enormous volume of archaeological literature, based on extensive fieldwork and excavation across the entire continent, has built up. There is no doubt that Europe is, archaeologically speaking, the most intensively researched area of the earth, and the national museums in each country testify to the richness of the material data.

In general the wealth of finds is well matched by the quality of the research devoted to them. From the early and seminal writings of the Northern Antiquaries (notably Thomsen and Worsaae) and the meticulous excavations of Pitt-Rivers to the comprehensive modern corpus (for instance by Müller-Karpe) and the scale of a major excavation project, like those of Blegen in the Aegean or the state-organised programmes in eastern Europe, the information available has steadily increased.

Twenty years ago it seemed clear that the outlines of European prehistory were secure, and that the task of further research was to amplify and enrich a prehistoric narrative already sound in its essentials. So it was, for example, that in 1958, when opening a conference on the British iron age organised by the Council for British Archaeology, Hawkes was gratified by the degree of agreement between participants.

> This surely means—and I think we can be gratified all round—that in the dozen years since the C B A last caused a general survey to be put forward, or the twenty years since Childe was writing in *Prehistoric Communities*, we have taken our Iron Age studies through a process of expansion, and of revaluation, and yet have emerged still pretty well together (Hawkes 1959, 170).

Yet over the past fifteen years this view of a soundly-based structure, augmented by new discoveries as each was fitted into place, has been substantially transformed. Universally accepted assumptions have been called into question, modes of explanation assailed, chronological relationships disputed, and the very concepts of the researcher and the terms used to express them subjected to critical examination.

The essays in this volume, all published within the past decade and a half, have formed part of this critical scrutiny. Each relates specifically to prehistoric Europe, although of course these developments in European prehistory form part of a world-wide reassessment of approaches to the early human past. Together with such re-appraisals as Hodson's 'Reflections of the ABC of the British Iron Age' (Hodson 1960 ; 1964), Clark's 'The invasion hypothesis in British archaeology' (Clark 1966) and Snodgrass's reassessment of the Greek 'Dark Age' (Snodgrass 1971), they attempt a re-examination of several of the basic, unifying ideas of the hitherto well-established and traditional approach to the subject (see also Case and ApSimon 1969 ; Neustupny 1968).

The alteration in outlook has been so rapid over the past few years that Sterud (1973) has found it worthwhile to view the change as an example of the sort of paradigm shift described in Kuhn's *The Structure of Scientific Revolutions* (1962), and Neustupny (1971, 35) has written of a crisis in European archaeology.

It would be easy to see all of this as just one aspect of the emergence of a 'New Archaeology' (see Binford 1972 ; Clarke 1968 and 1972 ; Renfrew 1973a), as indeed in a sense it is. Yet it is also something more than this, just as it is considerably more than a response or reaction to the development of radiocarbon dating and the calibration of the radiocarbon time scale. For chapters 2 and 11 below, and the papers by Hodson and Clark cited above owe very little to radiocarbon dating. At the same time works whose explicit purpose was to give an outline of European prehistory based on radiocarbon dates (Ehrich 1965 ; Thomas 1967) have omitted to draw what today seem the obvious inferences, and have instead contrived to reconcile (albeit in a manner not always entirely convincing) the traditional narrative with the new radiocarbon dates.

The roots of the recent and profound shift in our outlook go very much deeper, back to that extraordinary ferment of intellectual activity which followed and (in the case of a few highly original thinkers such as Alfred Wallace, Herbert Spencer and Daniel Wilson) partly preceded the publication of Darwin's *Origin of Species.* As Glyn Daniel (1950) has stressed, that year 1859, which also saw the establishment of the Antiquity of Man, was the *annus mirabilis* for the study of prehistory.

The three decades which followed saw the emergence—and sometimes, the extinction—of many of the ideas which have re-surfaced over the past decade and a half to challenge the now orthodox position.

Since that time, over a century ago, the most influential student of European prehistory was Gordon Childe. Already in the Preface to the first edition in 1925 of his great work *The Dawn of European Civilisation* he expressed very well the problem which remains the principal preoccupation of the papers that follow here, even though their conclusions are radically different from his. He wrote (Childe 1925, xiii) in words which we can echo today:

> My theme is the foundation of European Civilisation as a peculiar and individual manifestation of the human spirit.
>
> But on this topic sharply opposed views are current. One school maintains that Western Civilisation only began in historic times after 1000 BC in a little corner of the Mediterranean and that its true prehistory is to be found not in Europe but in the Ancient East. On the other hand, some of my colleagues would discover the origin of all the

higher elements in human culture in Europe itself. I can subscribe to neither of these extreme views: the truth seems to me to lie between them. In such a field it would of course be presumptuous to pretend to have attained a final synthesis. I can but present in all due humility the results of an earnest attempt to survey the facts as a whole.

The Question of Independent Invention

The long dispute in European prehistory between the protagonists of migration as an explanation for innovation and those advocating independent invention goes back far before the nineteenth century. But it was not until that time that appreciable quantities of evidence were gathered to advance the subject beyond pure speculation (Daniel 1971).

Many original thinkers, such as Tylor and Morgan, recognised that:

> Such coincidences as these, when found in distant regions between whose inhabitants no intercourse is known to have taken place, are not to be lightly used as historical evidence of connexion. It is safest to ascribe them to independent invention, unless the coincidence passes the limits of ordinary probability (Tylor 1870, 175).

Morgan was the great exponent of human progress, a view which he sometimes expressed in a rather prescriptive form, opening him to the criticism of following a rather simplistic, unilineal view:

> It can now be asserted upon convincing evidence that savagery preceded barbarism in all the tribes of mankind, as barbarism is known to have preceded civilisation. The history of the human race is one in source, one in experience, one in progress (Morgan 1877, ix).

Yet his work was not lacking in sophistication, and his influence was immense, primarily through his impact upon Marx and on Engels (1884), and also, within European archaeology, upon Gordon Childe (1951). His view was that similar developments were to be expected in different areas, yet this did not exclude the possibility of explanation in terms of genetic affinity or of migration:

> It may be remarked finally that the experience of man has run in nearly uniform channels; that human necessities in similar conditions have been substantially the same; and that the operations of the mental principle have been uniform in virtue of the specific identity of the brain of all the races of mankind. This, however, is but a part of the explanation of uniformity in results. The germs of the principal institutions and arts of life were developed while man was still a savage. To a very great extent the experience of the subsequent periods of barbarism and of civilisation have been expended in the further development of these original conceptions. Wherever a connection can be traced on different continents between a present institution and a common germ, the derivation of the people themselves from a common stock is implied (Morgan 1877, 8).

These ideas of the early anthropologists implying the innate creativity of man, accept both the Darwinian concept of evolution and its counterpart, argued by Herbert Spencer, of social evolution. They naturally ran counter to religious dogma. For the concept of a unique divine creation could best be used to explain the very different conditions of man in the recent world by assuming the 'degeneration' of those peoples now in a state of savagery from an earlier and higher state, rather than the progress to civilisation of the more fortunate. In the words of Archbishop Whately, quoted by Tylor (1870, 163):

> For, all experience proves that men, left in the lowest, or even anything approaching to the lowest, degree of barbarism in which they can possibly subsist at all, never did and never can raise themselves unaided into a higher condition.

Yet, although the early anthropologists rightly ridiculed this doctrine of divine intervention, it should be remembered that, perhaps without exception, they would themselves today be stigmatised as racists, for their frequent assumption that there were prominent differences in the innate abilities of different races. For although Lubbock advocated independent invention:

> I have already expressed my belief that the simpler arts and implements have been independently invented by various tribes, and in different parts of the world (Lubbock 1865, 473),

yet his book is full of statements which the modern reader finds difficult to accept.

> Savages have often been likened to children, but so far as intelligence is concerned, a child of four years old is far superior (Lubbock 1865, 463) .... But after making every possible allowance for savages, it must be admitted that they are as inferior morally as well as in other respects to the more civilised races. There is indeed no atrocious crime, no vice recorded by any traveller, which might not be paralleled in Europe, but that which is with us the exception is with them the rule (ibid. 465). ... It is not too much to say that the horrible dread of unknown evil hangs like a thick cloud over savage life and embitters every pleasure (ibid. 472).

The underlying psychic unity of mankind, propounded as a general principle by Adolf Bastian (1860) was stressed by a number of archaeologists at this time, and their arguments are worth repeating here at length, because despite their plausibility they do not seem to have influenced the actual practice of European prehistory to any significant extent. As Westropp put it in his *Pre-Historic Phases* (1872, 115–17):

> The most remarkable feature in the early periods of man's history, is the almost identity—for it is more than a striking analogy—in the forms of implements of warfare, and tools used in countries the most widely apart. Man in all ages, and in all stages of his development, is a tool-making animal. His instincts and necessities lead him to fashion implements and tools suited to his requirements. However different in race, and dwelling however remotely apart, we find in him the same wants and necessities; the same natural instincts and spontaneous powers of suggestion, contributing their aid in ministering to the needs of his nature, which he shares in common with the whole human family. The same universal processes of mind and instinct will lead the Australian, the New Zealander, the Peruvian, the North American, the Scandinavian and the ancient Britain to fashion and shape a stone weapon to supply his necessities and requirements. ...

The weapons and implements devised and fashioned by man in each stage of his development, are almost identical in all countries; for it does not admit of doubt that men in a similar stage of civilisation will devise and invent similar and identical objects. As Dr Keller remarks, 'A similar state of civilisation always calls for similar wants, and then again for similar means to supply them, and consequently similar implements, for the different purposes of life.' This similarity affords strong evidence of the uniformity of the operations of instinct, and the suggestive principle in the mind of man, among all races, and in all ages.

Why then, in the face of these ringing assertions, has the practice of European archaeology, from Fergusson and Worsaae through Montelius and Childe up to our own time, been so very different? For there is no doubt that it *has* been different: the general principle enunciated above by Westropp is directly contradicted by Childe (1950, 9):

I assume that the major technological inventions and discoveries—the wheeled cart, the potter's wheel, intelligent copper smelting, the rotary quern, the scythe—were usually made but once and diffused from a single centre. In prehistoric archaelogy this seems to be a useful working hypothesis or heuristic principle unless there are found objective grounds against it. Where a given device or process is found at widely separated points in space and/or time, it challenges the archaeologist to look for intermediate links in the archaeological record. But where the record is reasonably complete and still discloses no links, then we must not manufacture them but frankly admit an exception to our general rule.

In general, however, even the diffusionists have been cautious of trans-Atlantic links, with the notable exception of Elliot Smith (1929) and his hyper-diffusionist colleagues (Perry 1935), not without their supporters in our own day. I shall conclude this section with another, slightly equivocal quotation from the same early period, reflecting the same hesitation, (or is it breadth of mind?) as that from Morgan. Here Fergusson (1872, 518) the author of *Rude Stone Monuments*, the pioneering comparative survey in prehistoric archaeology, which he devoted to megalithic monuments, compared those of Peru and of Europe:

No one will, I presume, contend that there was any direct communication between Europe and the west coast of South America before the time of Columbus. Yet there are similarities between the masonry of the Peruvian monuments and those of the Pelasgi in Greece and Tyrrheni in Italy which are most striking, and can only be accounted for, at present, on the assumption that nations in the same stage of civilisation, and using similar materials, arrive nearly at the same results. Perhaps we ought to add this, provided they have some taint of the same blood in their veins; and that, in this case, does not seem absolutely improbable.

Migration or Diffusion?

The initial debate, as we have seen, was between those explaining similarities in terms of the psychic unity of mankind—an old-fashioned term now, but an idea not very different in substance from the inspiration of contemporary structuralist anthropology—and the advocates of common racial origin brought about by migration. Within the field of European prehistory the latter view prevailed in almost every case.

Happily the racial component of migrationist thinking steadily diminished, until it was almost universally abandoned in a widespread revulsion against the National Socialism of Hitler in the 1930s and 1940s. As indicated in the next section, Gordon Childe as early as 1929 was able to distinguish between ethnic group and racial group, seeking to recognise the former archaeologically rather than the latter. But racial arguments were still used by Kossinna and his followers during the Second World War for their reconstruction of German prehistory. The seventh edition of *German Prehistory, an Eminently National Science* (Kossinna 1941) quotes the following words by the Führer and Reichskanzler:

> We are no more indebted to the Romans or the Greeks, to the Gauls or the Britons and to their contemporary successors for any cultural benefits than they are to us. We should be just as little ashamed of our ancestors as they are of theirs. Rather we could point out that already a thousand years before Rome was founded the Germans were at a high cultural level. With even greater justice, we could and must point out, as not only German but European prehistoric research proves, that almost all European peoples are Indo-German (Hitler 1934).

The principal discussion within European prehistory centered not on racial questions of this kind but instead on whether specific developments were the result of movements of significant numbers of people, or rather of 'influences' which 'diffused' from the higher centres of civilisation. As Leeds (1924, 600) spoke of his own position:

> With regard to the method of derivation, he does not postulate migration, but prefers to speak more generally of 'influence' or 'intercourse'.

Perhaps the two major issues in European prehistory, considered by all authors from Worsaae and Montelius to the present, were the origin of the collective chamber tombs, the 'megaliths', and the inception of European metallurgy.

Fergusson (1872, 508) in the first comprehensive survey of the megalith problem, concluded:

> From shortly before the Christian era, till the countries in which they are found became entirely and essentially Christian, the use of these monuments seems to have been continual, whenever a dolmen-building race—or in other words, a race with any trace of Turanian blood in their veins—continued to prevail.

His map, fig. 1, is perhaps the first of many in the field of European prehistory, where the movements of peoples, as reflected by similar artefacts or monuments, are indicated by far-reaching arrows.

The leading Scandinavian antiquary Worsaae (1886, 25–6) was every bit as firm:

> It is altogether inconceivable that races so rude and cut off from the rest of the world, as Denmark's primeval inhabitants, should have been in a better condition than other similarly situated peoples not merely at once and thoroughly to adopt a higher civilisation of alien origin, but even to carry it to a pitch of development elsewhere unknown. Even

Figure 1. The origin of the European Megalithic tombs as explained by migrations indicated by arrows on Fergusson's map from *Rude Stone Monuments* (1872).

apart from the eloquent contents of the stone graves, the mere consideration of their distribution, their huge structure, their mutual agreement and general exterior, both in other lands and in the North, lead us involuntarily to recognise that, just as in the West and South, they are derived directly or principally from new, powerful tribes pushing on more and more northwards.

It was, I think, one of the main achievements of Gordon Childe to translate these migrationist arguments into what he himself saw as a 'modified diffusionism', whereby the story of European prehistory, rather than a complicated sequence of actual movements was seen instead as a more gradual process, 'the irradiation of European barbarism by Oriental civilisation' (Childe 1957, 70). He was the first to see with great clarity, although Montelius had outlined similar arguments, that economic and social processes, including the development of a metal industry in response to the oriental demand for raw material, could account for many of the changes observed in the material record. The ultimate impetus for these changes would still have come from the Near East, but this did not always imply any long distance movements.

So, for instance, when considering the spread of monumental burial in neolithic Europe, he thought less of tribal movement than of religious influence. And the map with which Daniel accompanied his important article summarising the position (fig. 2 ; Daniel 1941, fig. 2) is intended to convey lines of influence, rather than the migrations indicated on Fergusson's earlier map. Yet there is no doubt that the initial and essential inspiration was seen as coming from the east Mediterranean. Such too was the almost unquestioned assumption for the origins of metallurgy. Both these positions are examined and rejected in the papers that follow.

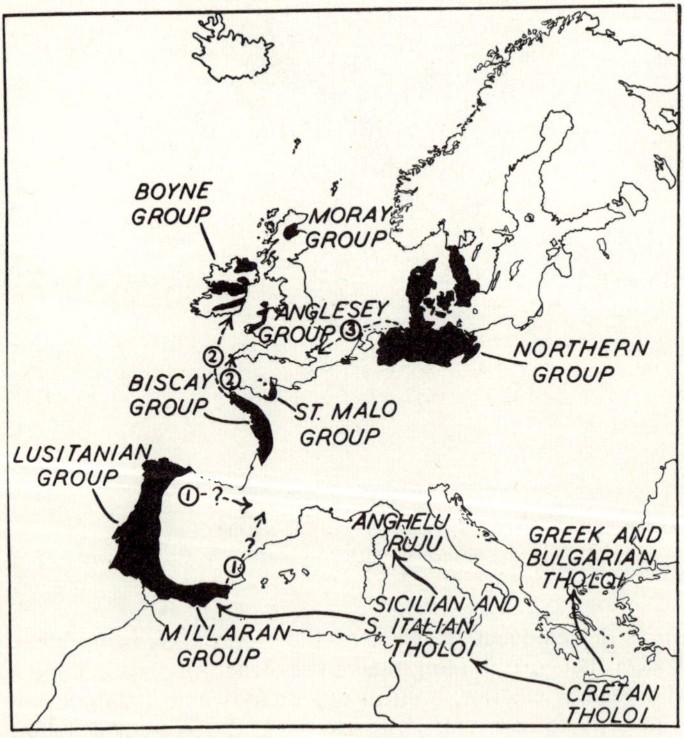

Figure 2. The origin of the European Megalithic tombs explained by a process of diffusion indicated by arrows on Daniel's map (1941).

Over the years, largely through the influence of Childe, most of the changes in Europe that were previously seen as the result of movements of peoples, came to be viewed instead as the result of the gradual diffusion of innovation. One exception to this, which will be considered in the next section, is offered by the widespread changes at the end of the neolithic period which Childe and others associated with the 'coming' of the Indo-Europeans. The other was the development in Iberia of copper metallurgy and of collective burial in built stone tombs.

Among the most influential early excavations in Europe were those conducted in south-east Spain by the Siret brothers (1887). The tombs, the metal objects and the small fortified townships such as Los Millares which they found persuaded them at first that they had discovered the western outposts of Phoenician traders. But later they allowed that the exotic, east Mediterranean influences might be earlier in date, and compiled (Siret 1913, fig. 6) a chart summarising the points of resemblance between the two areas (fig. 3). This view of a direct migration from the east Mediterranean was firmly endorsed by Gordon Childe, who suggested that the area of origin for the immigrant colonists might be the early bronze age Cycladic Islands of the Aegean. The case was re-stated with abundant detail by Blance (1961) and was almost universally accepted, so that Daniel and Evans (1967, 50) could write:

> It now seems virtually certain that some of these Aegean communities, perhaps the daring seafarers of some of the Cycladic islands, established colonies in the coastal regions of southern Spain and Portugal with a view to the exploitation of these resources. Remains of townships of strongly Aegean aspect have been found in both these regions which covered areas of up to 12½ acres and were defended by massive walls with semicircular bastions, like those at Chalandriani in Syros or at Lerna on the Greek mainland. . . . The new funerary architecture, perhaps influenced by the family tombs of the Aegean Early Bronze Age, had a notable effect on the indigenous tomb-building in Iberia, and the native cists and dolmens were developed into massive megalithic tombs of various kinds.

This view of Aegean colonies in Iberia implying a direct, long-distance movement of people, was and remained (e.g. Sangmeister 1977) central to the 'modified diffusionist' view of Iberian prehistory, and of European prehistory in general. In the chapters which follow it is rejected in its entirety.

Evolution and Monogenesis

Darwin's theory of natural selection was the major intellectual event in the life sciences during the nineteenth century. It soon came to dominate the thinking of many anthropologists, and remains influential, in a way no longer entirely constructive, at the present day. Of course it is generally accepted that what distinguishes the evolution of culture from that of the natural species is precisely man's ability to learn, and to inherit the acquired cultural characteristics of his parents and elders in a fashion more Lamarckian than Darwinian. But this has not inhibited the unthinking acceptance of the dangerous doctrine that 'like fits on to like' (Pitt-Rivers 1906, 19).

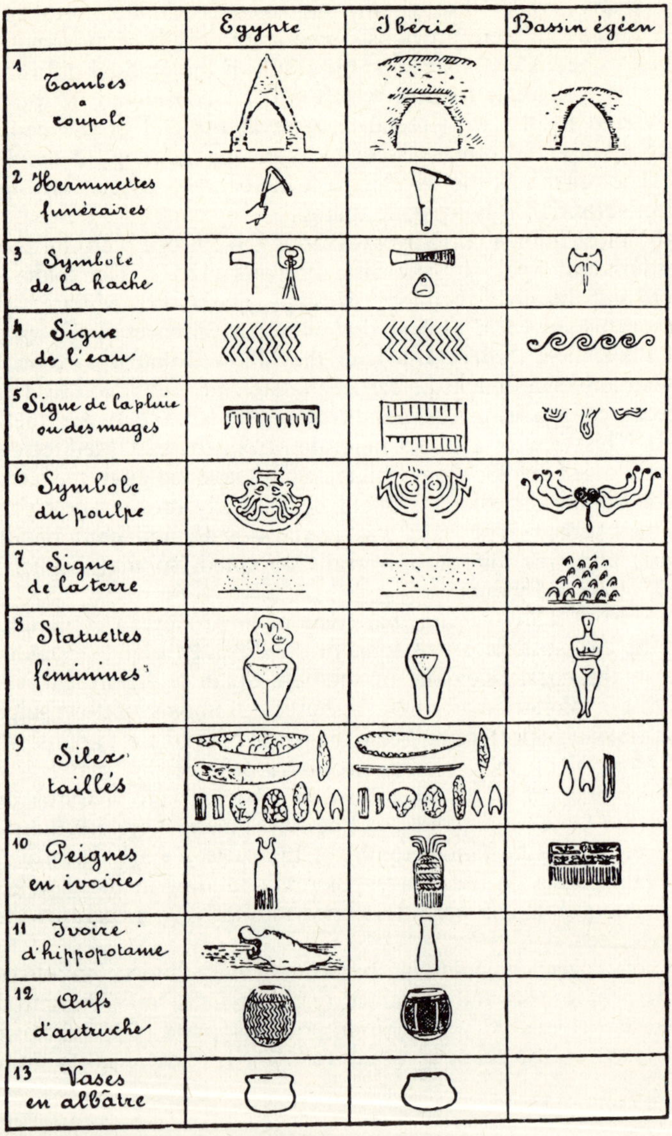

Figure 3. Comparisons between the Iberian Eneolithic, Egypt and the Aegean made by Louis Siret (1913) to sustain his theory of Phoenician colonisation.

The strong influence of Darwin is clearly reflected in the title of a study by John Evans (1875, 476), 'The Coinage of the Ancient Britons and Natural Selection'. In it he arranged the Celtic coinage in what today would be termed a typological succession (fig. 4), starting with the prototype, the gold stater of Philip of Macedon, hoping to show that evolution and human history were mutually relevant to the archaeologist:

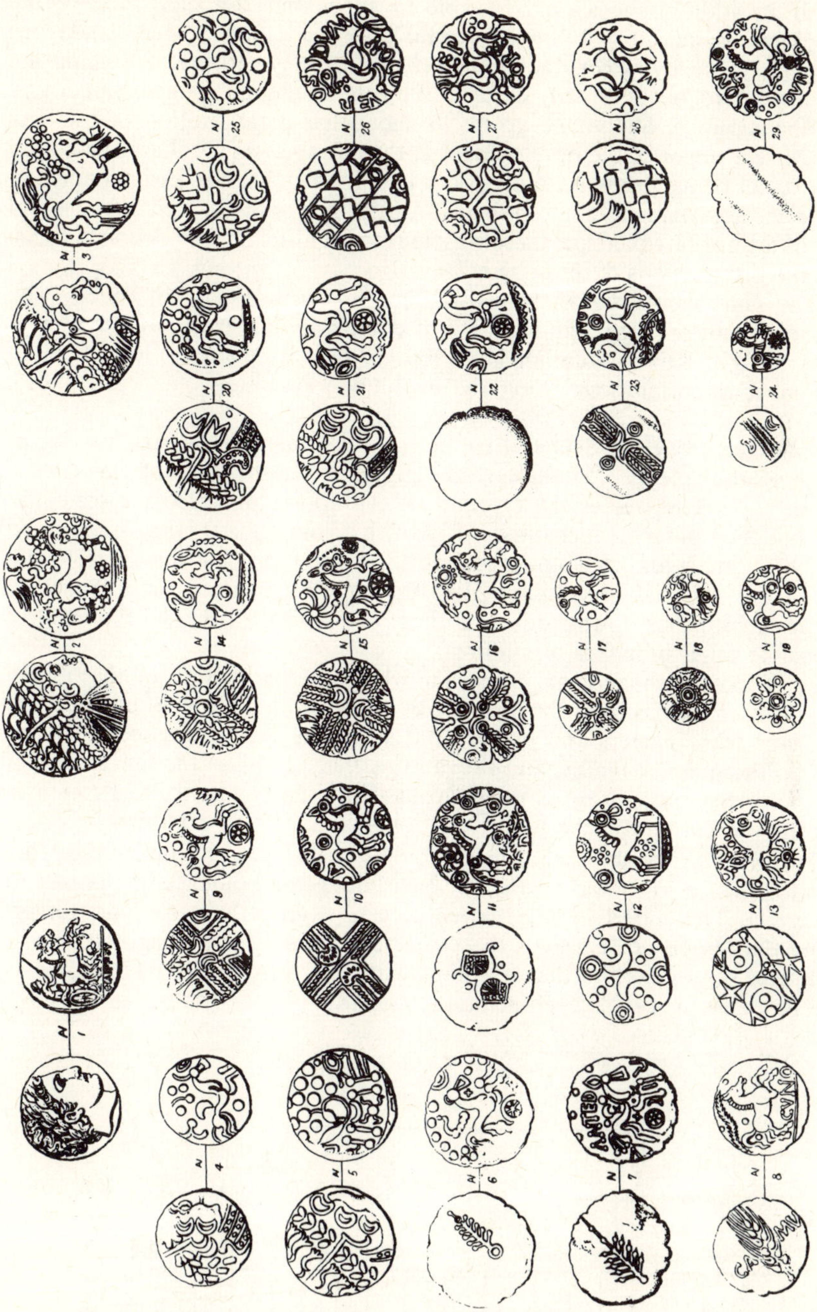

Figure 4. The impact of Darwinian evolution on archaeological thought: Sir John Evans's arrangement of the early British coinage (1875).

> If in addition he should be able to show that the succession of the types of the coins followed certain laws, to a great extent analogous with those by which the evolution of successive forms of organic life appear to be governed, the two subjects would no longer seem to be incongruous. Should he go on to show that a recognition of the successive stages of the development in the coinage was absolutely necessary for its being properly understood, and for placing the various coins in even approximately chronological order, it would be seen that instead of a want of coherence there was, in fact, an intimate connection between the two portions of the subject.

The same view became the central tenet in the work of Pitt-Rivers, who gathered and arranged the magnificent ethnographical collection of what is now the Pitt-Rivers Museum in Oxford to give it concrete illustration. In his most important essay 'On the evolution of culture', he wrote (1875, 520):

> We see from these facts that both growth and decay, the two component elements of evolution, are represented in the study of the material arts. . . . The tree is the type of all evolution: all trees are seedlings, but they differ in their mode of growth. Some like the beech and oak, throw their branches upwards, and these are typical of the development of the material arts; others, like the straight-stemmed pine, throw off their branches downwards, and these are typical of the development of some other branches of culture.
>
> There are huge gaps in our knowledge of the history of the human race, and it has been the pleasure of mankind in all ages to people these gaps with jugglers and bogies; but surely, if slowly, science will open up these desert places, and prove to us that, so far as the finite mind of man can reach, there is nothing but unbroken continuity to be seen in the present and in the past.

Pitt-Rivers meant these words literally: the way to understand the evolution of a form was to trace it back along the branches of the tree to its origin. The underlying idea, often used to express the basic unity underlying the *Origin of Species* is the cladistic or 'family tree' diagram (fig. 5).

Precisely this notion, that like goes with like, was used by Montelius as the basis for his typological method (1903, 16):

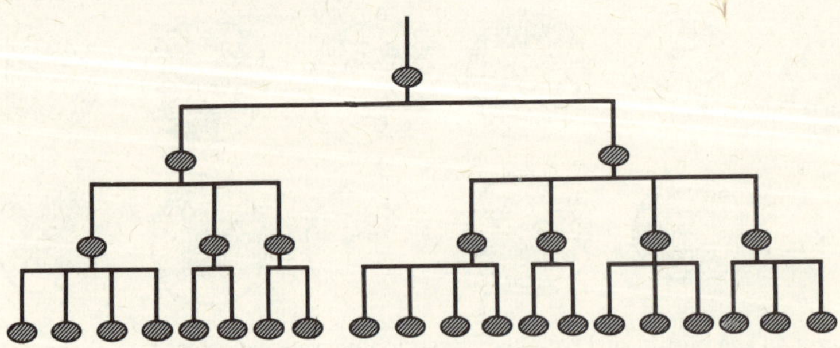

Figure 5. Cladistic diagram or family tree. Similarities in forms observed at a given time (lowest level) explained by monogenesis: the descent from a single common ancestor.

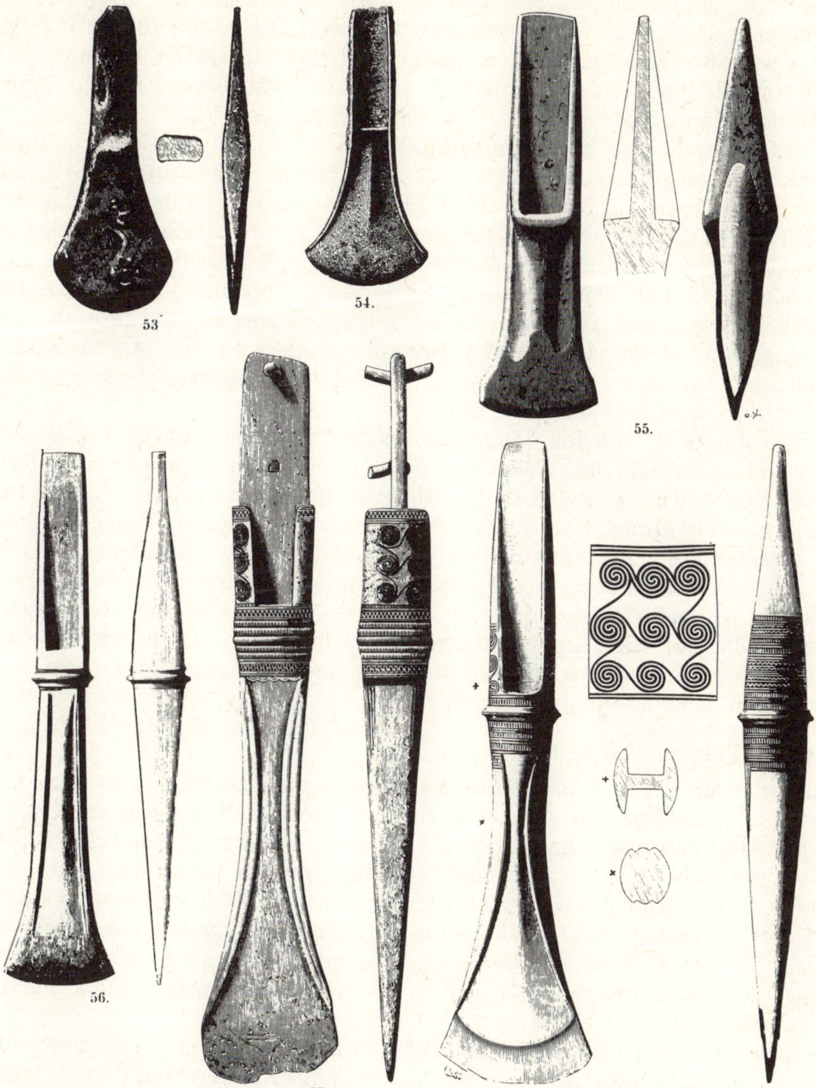

Figure 6. 'Like fits on to like.' The evolutionary ideas of Pitt-Rivers were embodied in the 'typological method' of Montelius, exemplified by the bronze axes of Sweden (1903).

> Die wichtigsten Serien der Waffen, Geräthe, Schmucksachen und Gefässe nebst ihren Ornamenten habe ich jede für sich geprüft, um den Gang der Entwicklung—so zu sagen die Genealogie—kennen zu lernen und zu erfahren, in welcher Ordnung die Typen, nach ihren eigenen Kriterien beurtheilt, auf einander gefolgt sind.

Thus it became enshrined as a principle in archaeological theory that the genealogy of objects could be established by inspecting them and by arranging them in an appropriate order, so that like goes with like (fig. 6). This was also the basis of the 'seriation' procedure devised by Petrie (1899; see Kendall 1969) and of comparable methods devised in the United States (Robinson and Brainerd 1951; Clarke 1962; Gelfand 1971).

But in each case the argument rests on an analogy between cultural evolution and organic evolution, first spelt out by Evans and Pitt-Rivers. The same procedure is followed by biologists today, who develop cladistic diagrams or 'cladograms', whereby natural forms are arranged in terms of coefficients of similarity (Sokal 1966; Sokal and Sneath 1963; Doran and Hodson 1975): the entire discipline of numerical taxonomy rests upon this basis. It is assumed, and for organic evolution is generally the case, that an arrangement in terms of phenotypes approximates to one of genotypes: that is to say that a plausible order in terms of similarity is close to the genetic order of unfolding evolution.

But if this is true for organic evolution, it is emphatically not so for cultural evolution, not unless the assumption of monogenesis is valid: that is to say, unless it can be known and assumed beforehand that all the objects being arranged *do* have a common origin. The typological method is essentially a diffusionist method, allowing no place for independent invention, or for parallel or convergent evolution. Its use in European prehistory, without a proper appreciation of these limitations, has been largely responsible for the recent confusion which has followed the rejection of diffusionist assumptions and the adoption in many cases of independent invention as an alternative hypothesis.

Culture, People and Language

In the early years of this century European prehistory developed, in the wake of Montelius, into what sometimes seemed a rather sterile exercise in typological ordering. Chronological sequences, like that of Reinecke, which were perfectly valid for the single localised area in which they were developed, were applied over much wider regions—it is still common to speak of the 'Hallstatt period' in the south-east Balkans. Nor has the advent of the computer in itself improved the situation: typological seriation, even when conducted by computer, can be no more valid than the monogenetic assumptions which sustain it.

It was Gordon Childe who, in 1929, introduced an important new emphasis, introducing to archaeology the concepts of culture and culture area. As he later summarised his views (1950, 2):

> A culture is defined as an assemblage of artefacts that recur repeatedly associated together in dwellings of the same kind and with burials by the same rite. The arbitrary peculiarities of implements, weapons, ornaments, houses, burial rites and ritual objects are assumed to be the concrete expression of common social traditions that bind together the people. And sometimes we can see the whole complex move about; that must signify a folk movement.

There is no doubt that the careful work of Childe and his successors, using this concept, added greatly to the detailed knowledge of the material evidence, systematically classified with respect to space and time. For whereas the typological method used only a temporal dimension, the concept of culture laid proper weight upon questions of distribution in space. In some ways it was the inception of a spatial approach in archaeology (see Renfrew 1974, 12).

But the agreeably logical sequence:

Recurrent Assemblage →Culture →People →Folk Movement

is open to question at each stage.

In the first place, the so-called 'cultures' of the prehistoric archaeologist are often artefacts of their own devising. I have explained elsewhere (Renfrew 1978) how the pattern of research naturally leads to the naming of such assemblages, and their separation from others on the grounds of 'similarity' or the lack of it, in a manner often completely arbitrary and depending upon the sequence of discovery.

Secondly, even when a recurrent assemblage with well defined boundaries can be established, it is often far from clear what its proposed counterpart concept of 'folk' or 'people', which Childe postulates, would actually mean. The concept of the 'tribe' has been critically re-examined by anthropologists (Helm 1968) and is certainly no sure foundation on which to build.

But I think it may be possible to suggest why Childe found this interpretive framework so useful and attractive, although his other writings, such as *Social Evolution* (1951) and *Man Makes Himself* (1936) took a much more positive approach towards the dynamics of culture change. The secret lies, I think, in the third step, the potential use of the archaeological data, to reconstruct folk movements, and hence to the difficult question of prehistoric language change.

Gordon Childe came initially to archaeology with a strong interest in languages, and I believe he set himself the task of solving by archaeological means, the long-standing problem of the origin of the Indo-Europeans. His first published article (Childe 1915) attempted this task for prehistoric Greece, identifying 'Minyan ware' with the coming of the Indo-Europeans, and his second book *The Aryans* (1926) attempted to use the material he had gathered for *The Dawn of European Civilisation* (1925) to undertake the same task on a pan-European basis. He later by implication repudiated *The Aryans,* never referring to it in his later writings, finding I imagine that its title brought him too close for comfort to Kossinna and his ilk. But it should of course be stressed that as the nature of racist archaeology emerged, Childe became one of its fiercest critics, and already in 1929 he was distinguishing between racial and ethnic inferences.

Childe returned to the Indo-European question for the last time in *Prehistoric Migrations in Europe* (1950). Earlier he had attempted an equation between the Indo-Europeans and the Beaker and Battle-Axe peoples of the European final neolithic. This view has been taken up and notably extended by Gimbutas in her monumental work (1965, 23):

> The period examined in this book lies between the two great westward expansions of the inhabitants of the steppe: the Kurgan people whom I consider Proto-Indo-Europeans in the last quarter of the third millennium BC and the Scythians at the end of the eighth century BC.

In *Prehistoric Migrations* Childe selected a later possibility than this for his first Indo-Europeans. (1950, 219):

> Hence all the Indo-European speaking peoples of temperate Europe can be connected directly or indirectly with the Urnfield cultures of the Late Bronze Age. If these be due to an invading aristocracy, the latter are the last migrants who could possibly have introduced Indo-European speech into Europe. I do not assert that they did, nor even that there was a migration at all. I have merely advanced that as a possible hypothesis.

In my own view the probabilities are strongly against so late a date as this, indeed against so late a date as that chosen by Gimbutas: if we are looking for very widespread and fundamental movements of people, the obvious place to consider is the inception of the European neolithic itself (Renfrew 1973b). But I have not chosen to include the article developing that view in this volume of collected papers, not merely because it is speculative (which would clearly not single it out for exclusion), but because I believe that the attempt to mould European prehistory into a shape where it can give a convincing answer to these linguistic problems has generally resulted in distortion and confusion. At the root of that confusion, perhaps, is the problem of monogenesis briefly discussed in the last section. I do not believe that there was ever a single, proto-Indo-European language restricted to a small Indo-European 'homeland'. Monogenesis may yet be revealed as a concept as dangerous when applied to language as it is for human culture.

Linguistic problems, I believe, may have made 'culture' a particularly convenient term. But Harris (1968, 374–7) has shown that the notion of 'culture area' in American anthropology is an essentially diffusionist one, and such proved to be the outcome of Childe's application of the *Kulturkreis* idea to European prehistory. The concept of culture in European prehistory, like that of 'phase' in the Midwestern Taxonomic System, no longer seems an appropriate approach to the description of human societies or polities.

Contact and Culture Process

Both the manipulation of artefacts into typological series ('seriation') and their division into hypothetical spatio-temporal entities ('cultures') must be rejected as meaningful explanatory procedures. Each, however, within appropriate limits and with the explicit formulation of the underlying assumptions, can be a perfectly acceptable mode of analysis: seriation within a limited area will remain a good approach to relative chronology, and naming by 'cultures' will continue to be a convenient shorthand, just as we still for convenience sometimes use terms like 'neolithic' or 'bronze age', which now likewise hold no explanatory content or potential.

Some of the alternative lines of investigation have long been with us. Grahame Clark's ecological approach, with the plotting of archaeological finds spatially, and their correlation with climatic and vegetational zones (Clark 1952, fig. 1) is at least as 'geographical' as the culture area approach, and leads on to much more fruitful consideration of the interrelationship between man and his environment, the focus of much contemporary research.

Gordon Childe himself, in his *Social Evolution* (1951) initiated a direction of study which is now being followed vigorously by archaeologists concerned with the definition and recognition of early social structure.

One of the most immediately fruitful techniques of study, developed in recent years, has been the characterisation of materials—the recognition of characteristics identifying their place of origin—and hence the documentation of culture contact on the basis of hard evidence, rather than on supposed similarities of form. Some of the papers in this volume report early efforts in this direction, and the discipline of archaeometry is now applying an increasing battery of scientific aids with this purpose. The application of the natural sciences to archaeology has been one of the most important developments in the field in recent years, and the examples of characterisation and radiometric dating given here are just a few among the very numerous examples which could now be quoted.

Characterisation is a fruitful undertaking also since the evidence of contact which it reveals generally indicates trade or exchange. The significance of such contact will often be as much of an economic and social nature as for the flow of new ideas and innovations which it allows to diffuse from outside. This outlook is outlined in the paper which follows this introduction.

Trade, however, is only one subsystem in the overall culture system, and its importance in itself should not be exaggerated. Instead the thrust of much contemporary work is to grasp how the different subsystems of the culture system articulate together to determine the course of future change (Renfrew 1972, chapters 2, 3 and 21 ; Clarke 1968, ch. 2 ; Plog 1974).

The papers which follow scarcely begin (and certainly do not accomplish) such a task. It will require the combined efforts of many European prehistorians, drawing on the experience of archaeologists in the world at large, if substantial progress is to be made. But the necessary first step is to recognise that there is indeed such a task to be accomplished, and that the seemingly very coherent and persuasive picture of European prehistory built up in the century or more up to around the year 1960 is deficient in a number of respects.

Some of those deficiencies are examined in detail in the papers which follow. I have tried above, by looking back into the origins of the discipline, and at the basis for some of the early assumptions, to show how they arose. The first need is to recognise these unjustified assumptions more clearly for what they are, and to offer alternative hypotheses to stand beside them or replace them.

The factual basis which we as archaeologists have to work with in Europe is unusually rich, so that it has already proved possible to test some of the alternatives by direct comparison with the data. Here we have been fortunate that radiocarbon dating and its improvement by dendrochronological calibration have been available to help us. The method has offered a decisive chronological test which in some cases decides unequivocally in favour of one possibility and against another. This is a rare situation in archaeology. And it is perhaps only in European archaeology, where the traditional chronologies were already before the radiocarbon era very clearly formulated, that the method has been able to act in this way as a test offering a choice between hypotheses, rather than simply as a first chronological structure *in terra incognita.*

Yet while radiocarbon offers this power of discrimination, allowing us to use the material evidence for other purposes than merely chronological (and hence, paradoxically, reducing the interest of such chronological questions) it cannot help resolve the more basic issues. Many of these were clearly seen and identified by Gordon Childe, although some of the conclusions which he reached can now be seen as erroneous. As I have tried to show, many of them have much earlier roots. In some cases, indeed, the seemingly coherent framework of 'modified diffusionism' constructed in the earlier part of this century actually served to obscure the areas where fundamental research was needed.

Innovation remains the least understood phenomenon in European prehistory, perhaps in culture history in general. Under what circumstances are inventions made, and in what conditions are they widely adopted? Sometimes contact with neighbouring groups offers the opportunity for the flow of information (including the basic technological detail of the invention). Sometimes such contact has economic and social consequences which themselves favour local invention and the subsequent widespread adoption of innovation. Sometimes however when such contact occurs, its impact on development is nonetheless minimal, and such innovations as are adopted derive from the internal dynamic of the society itself. These are problems which have not been seriously addressed nor contemplated, without diffusionist and monogenetic preconceptions, for almost a century. We have to go back to the fathers of anthropology to find them clearly posed, although not often adequately answered. Today we may be more ready to consider sympathetically such basic concepts as the psychic unity of mankind and the innate equality of races. But unfortunately to assert that all men are born equal does little to advance research, or to explain for us the wide divergences in the historical patterns which we seek to understand.

This is not the occasion to attempt to give an answer to these questions. But, as this volume seeks to show, they do exist and they must some day receive more serious consideration than in recent decades.

I will conclude this essay as I began, with a quotation from Edward B. Tylor. It contains an assertion whose merits a century of European prehistoric research contrived to obscure, and then, more recently, to reveal anew. Despite the much greater mass of archaeological data now available, archaeological theory still gives us little of substance to add to this simple, indeed perhaps somewhat naive statement, which (despite racialist overtones, to be pardoned in a writer more than a century ago) still has force today. That this should be so is a challenge: a challenge to use the rich data of European archaeology not only to describe but, casting aside outmoded preconceptions, to explain.

> In the first place, the facts collected seem to favour the view that the wide differences in the civilisation and mental state of the various races of mankind are rather differences of development than of origin, rather of degree than of kind. . . . And wherever the occurrence of any art or knowledge in two places can be confidently ascribed to independent invention, as for instance, when we find the dwellers in the ancient lake-

habitations of Switzerland, and the modern New Zealanders, adopting a like construction in their curious fabrics of tied bundles of fibre, the similar step thus made in different times and places tends to prove the similarity of the minds that made it. . . .

Considered from this and other points of view, this uniform development of the lower civilisation is a matter of great interest. . . . We might reasonably expect that men of like minds, when placed under widely different circumstances of country, climate, vegetable and animal life and so forth, should develop very various phenomena of civilisation, and we even know by evidence that they actually do so ; but nevertheless it strikingly illustrates the extent of mental uniformity among mankind that it is really difficult to find, among a list of twenty items of art or knowledge, custom or superstition, taken at random from a description of any uncivilised race, a single one to which something closely analogous may not be found elsewhere among some other race, unlike the first in physical characters, and living thousands of miles off (Tylor 1870, 370–2).

BIBLIOGRAPHY

Bastian, A. (1860) *Der Mensch in der Geschichte*. Leipzig: O. Wigand.

Binford, L. R. (1972) *An Archaeological Perspective*. New York: Seminar Press.

Blance, B. (1961) Early bronze age colonists in Iberia. *Antiquity* 35, 192–202.

Case, H. and ApSimon, A. (1969) The neolithic and early bronze ages in the north of Ireland. *Ulster J. Archaeol.* 32, 3–72.

Childe, V. G. (1915) On the date and origin of Minyan ware. *J. Hell. Stud.* 35, 196.

Childe, V. G. (1925) *The Dawn of European Civilisation*. London: Kegan Paul.

Childe, V. G. (1926) *The Aryans*. London: Routledge.

Childe, V. G. (1929) *The Danube in Prehistory*. Oxford: Clarendon.

Childe, V. G. (1936) *Man Makes Himself*. London: Watts.

Childe, V. G. (1950) *Prehistoric Migration in Europe*. Oslo (Instituttet for Sammenlignende Kulturforskning, Series A, Forelesninger xx).

Childe, V. G. (1951) *Social Evolution*. London: Watts.

Childe, V. G. (1957) Retrospect, *Antiquity* 32, 69–74.

Clark, J. G. D. (1952) *Prehistoric Europe, the Economic Basis*. London: Methuen.

Clark, J. G. D. (1966) The invasion hypothesis in British archaeology, *Antiquity* 40, 172–89.

Clarke, D. L. (1962) Matrix analysis and archaeology with particular reference to British Beaker pottery. *Proc. Prehist. Soc.* 28, 371–82.

Clarke, D. L. (1968) *Analytical Archaeology*. London: Methuen.

Clarke, D. L. (ed.) (1972) *Models in Archaeology*. London: Methuen.

Daniel, G. E. (1941) The dual nature of the megalithic colonisation of prehistoric Europe. *Proc. Prehist. Soc.* 7, 1–49.

Daniel, G. E. (1950) *A Hundred Years of Archaeology*. London: Duckworth.

Daniel, G. E. (1971) From Worsaae to Childe, the models of prehistory. *Proc. Prehist. Soc.* 38, 140–53.

Daniel, G. E. and Evans, J. D. (1967) The western Mediterranean, in *Cambridge Ancient History* (2nd edition) II, ch. 37. Cambridge: University Press.

Doran, J. E. and Hodson, F. R. (1975) *Mathematics and Computers in Archaeology*. Edinburgh: University Press.

Ehrich, R. W. (ed.) (1965) *Chronologies in Old World Archaeology*. Chicago: University Press.

Elliot Smith, G. (1929) *The Migrations of Early Culture*. Manchester: University Press.

Engels, F. (1884) *The Origin of the Family, Private Property and the State*. Moscow: Foreign Languages Publishing House (1954 edition).

Evans, J. (1875) The coinage of the Ancient Britons and Natural Selection. *Proc. Roy. Inst. G. B.* 7, 476–87.

Fergusson, J. (1872) *Rude Stone Monuments in All Countries, Their Age and Uses.* London: Murray.

Gelfand, A. E. (1971) Seriation methods for archaeological materials. *American Antiquity* 36, 263–74.

Gimbutas, M. (1964) *Bronze Age Cultures in Central and Eastern Europe.* The Hague: Mouton.

Harris, M. (1968) *The Rise of Anthropological Theory.* London: Routledge.

Hawkes, C. F. C. (1959) The A B C of the British Iron Age. *Antiquity* 33, 170–82.

Helm, J. (ed.) (1968) *Essays on the Problems of the Tribe.* Washington: American Ethnological Society.

Hitler, A. (1934) Speech delivered in Karlsruhe, quoted in Kossinna 1941, iii.

Hodson, F. R. (1960) Reflections on the A B C of the British Iron Age, *Antiquity* 34, 318–19.

Hodson, F. R. (1964) Cultural grouping within the British pre-Roman Iron Age. *Proc. Prehist. Soc.* 30, 99–110.

Kendall, D. G. (1969) Some problems and methods in statistical archaeology. *World Archaeol.* 1, 68–76.

Kossinna, G. (1941) *Die deutsche Vorgeschichte, eine hervorragend nationale Wissenschaft* (8th edition). Leipzig: J. A. Barth Verlag.

Kuhn, T. S. (1962) *The Structure of Scientific Revolution.* Chicago: University Press.

Leeds, E. T. (1924) The Western Mediterranean. *Cambridge Ancient History,* I, ch. 21. Cambridge: University Press.

Lubbock, J. (1865) *Pre-Historic Times.* London: Williams and Norgate.

Montelius, O. (1885) Sur la chronologie de l'âge du bronze. *Om tidsbestämning inom bronsaldern med särskildt afseenda pa Skandinavien.* Stockholm.

Montelius, O. (1903) *Die älteren Kulturperioden in Europa,* I. *die Methode.* Stockholm.

Neustupny, E. (1968) Absolute chronology of the neolithic and aeneolithic periods of central and south-eastern Europe. *Slov. Archaeol.* 16, 19–56.

Neustupny, E. (1971) Whither archaeology? *Antiquity* 45, 34–9.

Morgan, L. H. (1877) *Ancient Society.* New York: World Publishing.

Perry, W. J. (1935) *The Primordial Ocean.* London: Methuen.

Petrie, W. M. F. (1899) Sequences in prehistoric remains. *J. Anthrop. Inst.* 29, 295–301.

Pitt-Rivers, A. L. F. (1875) On the evolution of culture. *Proc. Roy. Inst. G. B.* 7, 496–520 (Under the author's signature A. Lane-Fox).

Pitt-Rivers, A. L. F. (1906) *The Evolution of Culture and other Essays by the late Lt.-Gen. A. Lane-Fox Pitt-Rivers,* J. L. Myres (ed.). Oxford: University Press.

Plog, F. T. (1974) *The Study of Prehistoric Change.* New York: Academic Press.

Renfrew, C. (1972) *The Emergence of Civilisation, the Cyclades and the Aegean in the Third Millennium B.C.* London: Methuen.

Renfrew, C. (ed.) (1973a) *The explanation of Culture Change, Models in Archaeology.* London: Duckworth.

Renfrew, C. (1973b) Problems in the general correlation of archaeological and linguistic strata, in Crossland, R. A. and Birchall, A. (eds.), *Bronze Age Migrations in the Aegean.* London: Duckworth, 263–75.

Renfrew, C. (ed.) (1974) *British Prehistory, a New Outline.* London: Duckworth.

Renfrew, C. (1978) Space, time and polity, in Friedman, J. and Rowlands, R. (eds.), *The Evolution of Social Systems.* London: Duckworth, 89–112.

Robinson, W. S. and Brainerd, G. W. (1951) A method for chronologically ordering archaeological deposits. *Amer. Antiq.* 16, 293–313.

Sangmeister, E. and Schubart, H. (1977), Zambujal, eine befestigte Siedlung der Kupferzeit in Portugal, *Antike Welt* 8, no. 3, 23–34.

Siret, H. and L. (1887) *Les Premiers Ages du métal dans le sud-est de l'Espagne.* Paris.

Siret, L. (1913) *Questions de chronologie et d'ethnographie ibériques.* Paris: Paul Geuthner.

Snodgrass, A. M. (1971) *The Dark Age of Greece.* Edinburgh: University Press.

Sokal, R. R. (1966) Numerical taxonomy. *Sci. Amer.* 215, 106–16.

Sokal, R. R. and Sneath, P. H. A. (1963) *Principles of Numerical Taxonomy*. San Francisco: Freeman.

Sterud, G. (1973) A paradigmatic view of prehistory, in Renfrew, C. (ed.), *The Explanation of Culture Change, Models in Prehistory*. London: Duckworth, 3–17.

Thomas, H. L. (1967) *Near Eastern, Mediterranean and European Chronology*. Lund (Studies in Mediterranean Archaeology 17).

Tylor, E. B. (1870) *Researches into the Early History of Mankind*. London: John Murray (2nd edition ; 1st edition 1865).

Westropp, H. M. (1872) *Pre-History Phases*. London: Bell and Daldy.

Wilson, D. (1851) *The Archaeology and Prehistoric Annals of Scotland*. Edinburgh.

Worsaae, J. J. A. (1886) *The Pre-History of the North*. London: Trübner.

1) Trade and Culture Process in European Prehistory

The importance of trade for the understanding of early culture change has been increasingly stressed over the decade since this paper was written, and the field is well summarised in two collective volumes (Sabloff and Lamberg-Karlovsky 1975 ; Earle and Ericson 1977). The thrust of recent work has been to see evidence of exchanges as an indicator of social as well as economic significance, and the distinctions drawn by Karl Polanyi and his collaborators between reciprocity, redistribution and market exchange (Polanyi, Arensberg and Pearson 1957) have been widely followed. Recently, however, Adams (1974) has re-asserted the importance of the profit motive in non-state societies which lack a well-organised system of markets.

The technical means available for the characterisation of archaeological materials, well reviewed by Tite (1972), have become more sensitive, with an increasing emphasis upon neutron-activation analysis. Explicit taxonomic methods to search for significant groups among the data from chemical or trace-element analysis are now widely used. The methods of locational analysis are frequently employed to search for spatial patterning. A recent volume of studies on trade and exchange of pottery edited by Peacock (1977) utilises some of these approaches.

It is important not to view in isolation the role which increasing trade can play in favouring social and economic development. Instead the mutual interactions between the different subsystems of society, summarised in fig. 2 below, should be stressed (see Renfrew 1972, ch. 2, 3 and 21). Among important recent studies, where the role of trade is examined in relation to other social and economic developments in the society, are those of Flannery (1968), Rowlands (1971) and Pires-Ferreira (1975). Work on the iron age of Europe is now developing similar ideas and applying them to understanding the development towards urban society in north Europe at that time.

BIBLIOGRAPHY

Adams, R. M. (1974) Anthropological perspectives on ancient trade. *Curr. Anthrop.* 15, 239–58.

Earle, T. K. and Ericson, J. A. (eds.) (1977) *Exchange Systems in Prehistory.* New York: Academic Press.

Flannery, K. V. (1968) The Olmec and the Valley of Oaxaca: a model for inter-regional interaction in Formative times, in Benson, E. P. (ed.), *Dumbarton Oaks Conference on the Olmec.* Washington, 79–110.

Peacock, D. P. S. (ed.) (1977) *Pottery and Early Commerce.* London: Academic Press.

Pires-Ferreira, J. W. (1975) *Formative Mesoamerican Exchange Networks with Special Reference to the Valley of Oaxaca* (Memoirs of the Museum of Anthropology, University of Michigan, No. 7), Ann Arbor.

Polanyi, K., Arensberg, C. M. and Pearson, H. W. (eds.) (1957) *Trade and Market in the Early Empires.* New York: Free Press.

Renfrew, C. (1972) *The Emergence of Civilisation, the Cyclades and the Aegean in the Third Millennium BC.* London: Methuen.

Rowlands, M. J. (1971) The archaeological interpretation of prehistoric metalworking. *World Archaeol.* 3, 210–24.

Sabloff, J. and Lamberg-Karlovsky, C. C. (eds.) (1975) *Ancient Civilisation and Trade.* Albuquerque: University of New Mexico Press.

Tite, M. S. (1972) *Methods of Physical Examination in Archaeology.* London: Academic Press.

TRADE AND CULTURE PROCESS IN EUROPEAN PREHISTORY

Trade is one of the activities of prehistoric man which has received much less attention than it deserves. Its particular and sometimes crucial importance lies in a dual status: as the indicator for us today that intercultural contact was taking place, and as a prime motive, among prehistoric groups for such contact. In this paper an attempt is made to indicate the unique opportunities which a study of trade holds for the understanding of culture change. The examples and discussion are limited in scope to European and Near Eastern prehistory, but the underlying principles are general ones and should bear upon the prehistory of any region.

The first point, trade as an indicator of contact, implies a proof that trade (or at least the transport of goods from one region to another) was taking place. In the past, identification of unique products has sometimes been made on the basis of simple inspection. Lapis lazuli, Polish banded flint, Grand Pressigny flint, and Olonetz slate (Clark, 1952, 246–47) are examples of raw materials which can very probably be assigned to a limited source area on the grounds of visual inspection alone. To these well-known cases can be added, for example, African ostrich egg shell and ivory in early Iberia (Renfrew 1967*a*). Amber (sources in northern Europe, Iberia southern France, Sicily, Rumania, and points east) and *Spondylus* shell (available in the Adriatic and perhaps the Black Sea as well as the Aegean), however, are commodities whose significance may have been misinterpreted in the past (de Navarro 1925; Clark 1952, 242, 263). A proper interpretation depends upon the scientific characterisation of the material.

Trade as a motive for contact, and the entire question of intercultural contact in the New World as well as the Old, is wrapped in confusion. There has been little serious discussion of prehistoric trade mechanisms and virtually no attempt to set up the facts on a quantitative basis. Finally there has been little attention to the role of trade, an important element in economic growth, as a causative factor in cultural change within given regions.

The present paper, in seeking to open up discussion on the role of trade in culture contact and culture development, has three central points to make:

1. Much of our thinking on the subject of cultural change in the prehistory of Europe and beyond is outdated and inadequate. Too much emphasis has been placed on supposed invasions and diffusion from 'higher centres of civilisation' and insufficient on the economic and social development of what may have been, for many purposes, essentially independent systems. The evidence for supposed outside influences must be re-examined and an attempt made to understand the factors which work towards change within society.

2. If the explanation for an observed change in the prehistoric record is generally to be sought within the community or culture rather than outside it, this implies an understanding, preferably in quantitative terms, of various

factors or systems, particularly economic systems, which operate within the cultures. Trade is only one such factor, but one of the easiest to evaluate.

It is here suggested that the economic importance of trade in European prehistory has been misinterpreted in several ways. There has been a tendency to overdramatise the scope and range of trade in early periods ; to see traders and prospectors from Sumer influencing the development of prehistoric Europe, and Mycenaean princes sending their emissaries to the barbarian North. These romantic ideas of early tele-commerce, where a civilised region colonises, at least economically, a less advanced one, have tended to obscure the real and very important role which trade seems to have played in developing the economic life within particular cultural areas, progressing and growing quite independently of outside influence. Also obscured has been the fact that trade, as an agent in communication, and hence in establishing areas of cultural and material exchange, had a cultural significance which long preceded its economic one.

3. Trade cannot be assumed ; it has to be proved. For instance, the amber trade between the Baltic and the Aegean in the Mycenaean period, the cornerstone of many a theory and of chronologies, may yet prove to be a myth. Again, the popular notion of a metal trade between Iberia and the Aegean in the 3rd millennium BC, supposedly a cause of Iberian development and even of the whole phenomenon of the European megaliths, could well be without foundation. A considerable range of scientific techniques is now available for the characterisation of materials and the determination of their sources, so that the foreign nature of a traded commodity need no longer be in dispute. If such determinations can be linked with an estimate of the quantities involved (and factors of preservation make an obvious difficulty), we shall be in possession of prehistoric trade statistics. Already the subsistence of any prehistoric society can be known to us, with a little trouble, on a quantitative basis. With a quantitative knowledge of its trade also, we shall come much closer to an understanding of the factors which may work towards stability or change in the society.

Before proceeding further, however, it is important to explain the meaning which is here attached to the term 'trade'. Although for early historic times the existence of full-time professional traders can sometimes be documented, it can certainly not be assumed for prehistoric societies. Professional trade and commerce was probably absent from most prehistoric communities. 'Trade' is therefore to be understood in its widest sense: the reciprocal traffic, exchange, or movement of materials or goods through peaceful human agency. The reciprocity cannot always be demonstrated, but it can often be assumed, when booty, tribute, or tax seem unlikely. At least it makes clear that the goods must change hands ; this I take to be the crucial defining feature. When goods are given, unless they are given under duress or as 'unsolicited gifts', something is received in return. This need not imply a commercial transaction, but simply a mutually satisfactory exchange—a process which can be repeated several times for the same commodities. The full-time trader, a non-producing middleman deriving his livelihood or sustenance entirely from these exchanges, is often the product of more recent and more advanced societies. For this reason ethnographic parallels have to be used with extreme care, and comparisons between prehistoric colonisations and trade and those of European commerce in the world during or since the Middle Ages are of doubtful validity. Thus when the terms 'commodity', 'profit', or 'surplus' are used below, they are not intended to imply commercial transactions or economic structures like those of our own time. Evidently different levels and modes of economic organisation are served by different kinds of trade. To define the word too rigorously or narrowly is to exclude the wide variety of transactions and exchanges which are the subject of the inquiry.

In the first section which follows, the vague and conflicting models in current use in the study of prehistory, both in Europe and beyond, for the explication of culture change are briefly cited. The second section surveys in outline some of the methods of characterisation now available for the scientific documentation of cultural contact. The third section mentions some of the scattered and incomplete attempts which have been made in Europe at the quantitative assessment of archaeological materials from an economic standpoint. Finally, one test case is considered where, contrary to current standard opinion, trade within a region, rather than influence from outside, seems to have been a major factor in the significant change of the way of life from 'pure Neolithic' to 'urban'.

Models for Cultural Change

THE INVASIONIST MODEL

The invasionist/migrationist model, when applied to a particular case, will suggest that an apparently rapid and marked change in culture is explicable by the arrival of a new group of people (Daniel 1962, 82). To give modern instances of the application of this model—which is obviously an entirely valid one in some instances—it is not necessary to take extreme cases. Sir Grafton Elliot Smith's notion of wandering Egyptians (Elliot Smith 1929) responsible for the origin and development of all civilisations everywhere is today a curiosity hardly worth attacking. The idea that the transition in Britain to a Neolithic way of life (Piggott 1954) is an instance of invasion-change, is today widely accepted, although later British developments are subject to considerable controversy (Clark 1966, 172). Again, the earliest Neolithic settlements in southeastern Europe are generally regarded as belonging to an intrusive population, although Rodden (1965, 86) has discussed other possibilities.

Most such instances, however, are less acceptable. It has been held that the Aegean Early Bronze Age was introduced from the southeast, financed by Mesopotamian capital (Childe 1957, 19–21), and several scholars suggest an invasion at this time (Haley and Blegen 1928 ; Weinberg 1965*b*, 302–4). The situation is here complicated by linguistic arguments, but the evidence for outside influence is, in fact, very tenuous (Renfrew 1964) ; often the invasion is assumed rather than demonstrated. The Iberian Chalcolithic, and sometimes all of the European megaliths in addition, have been considered the product of colonisation, and similar views are often propounded for the southeastern European Chalcolithic also (Blance 1961 ; Popovitch 1965). A diffusionist theory is sometimes preferred in these cases but rarely is the mechanism of the supposed transmission considered.

Very rarely is any systematic attempt made to consider how an invasion would emerge in the archaeological record, or how further relevant evidence could be elicited. A new pottery style, e.g. 'Minyan' ware in Middle Helladic Greece, is often accepted as enough; or a widespread destruction, such as befell the Late Minoan 1B settlements of Minoan Crete. The ease with which these views can be abandoned for another dramatic and perhaps equally suspect theory (for example, the Santorini catastrophe as the causc of the Minoan destructions and decline) is symptomatic of the uncertain state of our thinking.

THE DIFFUSIONIST MODEL

The diffusionist model holds that changes observed in a society are brought about by strong influences from a 'higher culture', without the significant transfer of population. (The term 'diffusion' in its broader sense sometimes includes migration also). Gordon Childe was the arch-diffusionist in recent European archaeological thinking; of his book *The Dawn of European Civilisation,* he wrote (Childe 1956*a*, 70), 'The sole unifying theme was the irradiation of European barbarism by Oriental civilisation. . . .' Of course, he was in a different class altogether from the now ludicrous Kossinna or Elliot Smith. To him, the 'secondary and tertiary civilisations' of Europe were the product of 'economic imperialism' on the part of the 'primary civilisations' of the Near East (Childe 1956*b*, 176–77). Axiomatic to such a view is 'the useful heuristic hypothesis that each invention has been made but once', and with its aid, Childe was able to fit the prehistory of Europe into a diffusionist mould. So pervasive is its influence that few prehistorians today can contemplate equably the possibility that metallurgy may have originated independently in Iberia and the Balkans as well as in the Near East.

The problem of distinguishing the products of diffusion from those of independent invention is of course a very old one (Galton 1889), and it has been reviewed several times recently (e.g Rowe 1966). In much of European prehistory, and especially in the Bronze Age, the diffusionist model implicitly underlies and supports the very framework of the cultural succession itself, the supposedly factual data on which further conclusions are based.

THE EVOLUTIONIST MODEL

The evolutionist model seeks to illuminate a development in one place or period by comparing it with a supposedly similar development elsewhere. It is felt that the process of viewing the different developments jointly as products of the working (as yet unexplained in detail) of multi-linear evolution has some explanatory power. Of course the old prescriptive Three Ages, like Morgan's seven-point scale of Savagery, Barbarism, and Civilisation, have been widely abandoned, and few would try to make all civilisations jump through so narrow an evolutionist hoop. Nonetheless some anthropologists seek to retain the notion of some universal cultural causality and law. Steward (1949) drew up a system of developmental regularities of early civilisations (Formative, Regional Florescence, Initial Conquest, Dark Ages, Cyclical Conquests, etc.), while a similar system (Lithic, Archaic, Formative, Classic, Postclassic) is widely used by American archaeologists today (Willey and Phillips 1958). Steward himself precluded criticism of this kind of theorising with a pre-emptive strike:

'theories are not destroyed by facts—they are replaced by new theories'. It is relevant to ask just what explanative power the multilinear evolution hypothesis in fact has to command. When the development of two remote and presumably independent societies shows features which are in some ways analogous, the similarity is explained as the product of multilinear evolution ; but often this appeal to the superorganic implies no more than the 'general truth' that independent societies often develop through apparently similar sequential stages. The 'explanation' in such a case consists of reiteration of the data which it is supposed to explain : it is tautologous.

These grand, prescriptive, and sometimes inaccurate generalisations of multilinear evolution are not often based on any very detailed understanding of the factors underlying changes in the more complex societies, although Steward was himself a pioneer in such studies among hunting bands. We are not ready for them ; the first need is to know more of the way specific prehistoric societies developed and changed.

THE CULTURE-PROCESS MODEL

A recent development in American archaeology has been the insistence that culture or cultures cannot usefully be studied as units, as in the above three cases, but must be regarded rather as aggregates of systems, each of which varies independently. Such systems must be studied in isolation in order to contribute to an understanding of the whole. Binford (1965, 203) has criticised, with justice, an outlook, largely shared by European prehistorians, in which cultures are indivisible units and 'culture influence' is a term which can meaningfully be applied to the culture, and changes in culture, as a whole. He has stigmatised this as the 'aquatic view of culture', where archaeologists think and speak rather vaguely in terms of a 'culture stream' and, as well as providing some stimulating and controversial case studies, he has urged them to isolate and study particular systems.

Because the study of particular systems corresponds so well to the way archaeologists, with their research focus on ecosystems and human adaptions to them, are in fact working today, it promises to be particularly useful. It is no longer possible today to view a culture change, such as for instance the origin of urban settlement in the Early Bronze 2 Aegean, simply as the adoption of a new set of artefacts, with a different pottery assemblage, brought in from some ill-defined centre of migration. The interior workings of the society, particularly its economic subsystems, have to be understood. The material cultural assemblage is not likely to change significantly without a change in these subsystems, whether in agriculture, stock-rearing, fishing, or other subsistence occupations, in metallurgy, trade, or social organisation.

Systems of trade or exchange form only one component in the aggregate of systems which constitute a culture, but they play an important, and particularly complex role. Among its multiple functions, trade works (*a*) as a source of wealth to the trader and to the community, since efficient or favourable exchange can encourage the production of, or produce, a surplus ; (*b*) towards specialised and hence more efficient production ; (*c*) to promote contact between communities and the interchange of ideas through personal contact ; and (*d*) to create new demand and ultimately the production of new commodities (e.g. silk in the Classical world or metal in prehistoric Europe). The last two factors always operate towards change rather than conservatively; thus trade facilities change through the reception of outside ideas.

These functions have deliberately been phrased in terms applicable equally to modern commerce. They certainly do not imply, however, the existence of modern commerce. None of them is restricted to commercial transactions, and all can be seen at work, for instance, in the Aegean of the 3rd millennium BC, the Chalcolithic of Iberia, and probably the Wessex culture of the British Early Bronze Age. Not all of them need operate in any one case—perhaps only the third applies to the obsidian trade in the Near East in the 8th millennium BC. Nevertheless, when culture change is the subject of inquiry, trade should usually be considered in the first instance.

The Investigation of Trading Systems

Trade is of two kinds; of material commodities whose natural distribution is limited (e.g. salt, tin, amber, wine, opium, etc.) and of products which, through superior know-how or other economic factors, are most efficiently produced in a limited area (e.g. Hittite iron, slaves, Swiss cuckoo-clocks). In prehistoric times the first kind was more common, for despite Childe's insistence on the economic imperialism of the skilled Sumerians, there is only sporadic evidence for a trade in commodities where manufacturing skills was the primary factor until the export of Greek vases to Etruria and Etruscan jugs to the Celts. It follows, therefore, that prehistoric trade objects are to be recognised by their material more often than by their style.

A good example is the Egyptian stone bowls of Early Minoan Crete, whose stylistic evaluation has led to disagreement, while petrological examination is often conclusive. Again, the frequent use of ivory in Crete at that time documents contact, probably with Syria, while the design alone of the seals and other ivory objects would be open to stylistic argument.

The considerable battery of scientific methods available for the characterisation study of materials now includes examination by the following techniques:[1] simple inspection (materials of unique appearance, e.g. lapis lazuli, ostrich egg); petrological examination of thin section (e.g. stone tools, pottery, etc.); optical spectroscopy (e.g. pottery, metals, obsidian, faience, etc.); X-ray fluorescence (e.g. metals, obsidian, glass, jade, etc.); neutron activation (e.g. metals, pottery, obsidian, etc.); β-ray back-scatter (e.g. glass, glaze); infra-red absorption (e.g. amber); cathode-luminescence (e.g. marble); X-ray diffraction (e.g. jade, emery). Of importance too are various methods of dating the formation of materials, which can aid in their characterisation, e.g. determination of the isotopic composition of lead by mass spectrometer, or fission-track dating of obsidian.

The possibilities and difficulties encountered with several of these commodities are of particular interest:

Amber. The well-known pattern of an amber trade from the Baltic to the Mediterranean may yet be disrupted by a more careful consideration of the problem, setting aside the old and inaccurate succinic acid determinations and taking into account other sources throughout Europe (Beck *et al.*

1965). Conclusions of considerable importance for the chronology and interpretation of the Central European Bronze Age are based upon this amber trade, and its validation (or modification) is an urgent need in European prehistory.

Jade. The strange mystery of the source of the Breton/British axes, evidently traded in considerable quantity, remains unsolved, despite very detailed examination by W. Campbell Smith (1965). The investigation as so far conducted, however, is clearly along lines which will lead to an eventual solution: the absence of local sources is puzzling, but one feels that they must one day be discovered, probably in Brittany. Again, the results are of great importance for prehistoric trade, and this is a good example of an investigation, not yet complete, which promises exciting conclusions.

Copper. Several attempts have been made, by trace-element analysis, to pinpoint the sources of the copper used in the European Early Bronze Age to produce specific objects. The literature is now a vast one, and many thousands of analyses have been conducted (e.g. Junghans, Schroder, and Sangmeister 1960), but there have been several valid criticisms of the logic and statistical validity of the interpretative methods used (Butler and Van der Waals 1964). The value of the analyses for the understanding of early technology is undoubted, and within a limited region the technique can provide very valuable information (cf. Pittioni 1959). It seems, however, that variation in the trace-element composition of the ores within a given region and uncertainties and variation in the smelting methods employed make the attribution to a single source exceedingly difficult.

Obsidian. Recent work on obsidian has allowed the establishing of trade patterns in the Near East back to the 8th millennium BC, with more isolated finds of earlier date (Renfrew, Dixon, and Cann 1966). These patterns of contact, from the earliest Neolithic period, are significant for the development and dissemination of the Neolithic way of life in the three 'nuclear' regions of the Near East. The method is applicable in America, Australasia, and Africa, as much as in Europe and the Near East.

Pottery. Very impressive work has been carried out, both by petrological examination of thin sections and by trace-element analysis, in tracing imported potsherds back to their region of manufacture (Catling, Richards, and Blin-Stoyle 1963; Bennyhoff and Heizer 1965). This seems one of the most promising points of research development for the study of trade.

Successful documentation of a trading pattern in commodities such as these, even if established on a quantitative basis, does not, of course, adequately describe the trading system. All trade is a two-way process. Unfortunately the reciprocal trade, which may have a different pattern of its own, is often less clearly documented in the archaeological record. In most cases, even when a distribution pattern of objects travelling in the other direction can be established, the actual equation of the two commodities, and a fortiori any notion of their relative value, is hypothetical. At present we are forced to rely on recent anthropological analogies (Herskovits 1952, 155–56; Clark 1965) or to imagine a simpler form of the systems which are documented for the early empires (Polanyi, Arensberg, and Pearson 1965; Oppenheim 1954; Mallowan 1965).

Quantitative Evaluation of Economic Data

The quantitative evaluation of archaeological materials is a relatively new development. Most of the work hitherto undertaken (e.g. that of Robinson and Brainerd, Tugby, Doran and Hodson, Sackett, Clarke, Dempsey and Baumhoff, Kuzura, Mead and Dixon, and Hole and Shaw) [2] has been devoted to typological and taxonomic ends: the ordering of artefacts for chronological or taxonomic purposes. A separate and fascinating development is the classification of artefacts to reach conclusions bearing on social organisation (e.g. the work of Deetz (1965) and of Hill (1966). Rather similar in procedure is the recent interesting attempt to distinguish functional (and thus economic) groups in Palaeolithic assemblages (Binford and Binford 1966).

All these take as their starting point certain taxonomic features of the artefactual material. The quantitative analysis of non-artefactual material, as undertaken notably by Heizer[3] and by Meighan (1959) in the USA, especially in conjunction with the ecological outlook well exemplified by Hole and Flannery (1967),[4] offers a more direct insight into the economic factors at work. In Britain, E. S. Higgs has been influential in this direction (Higgs, Vita-Finzi, Harris, and Fagg 1967 ; cf. Higham 1967).

As an example of which I have personal knowledge, I would like to report a quantitative study of the animal remains from two excavation areas of the Neolithic site of Saliagos in the Cyclades (Evans and Renfrew 1968). Here the calculation of the meat weights (see Table 1) [5] transformed the understanding of the site (cf. Shawcross 1967). The relatively small size of the tunny fish vertebrae, which contributed only a very small fraction of the

Table 1. Calculated meat weights of various species represented at the neolithic site of Saliagos in the Cyclades

	Cliff 17, Pit A			Square N 3		
	Min. no.* of animals	Meat wt† kg	Meat wt %	Min. no. of animals	Meat wt kg	Meat wt %
Sheep/goat	17	490	6·6	22	640	19·1
Bovine	1	210	2·8	6	1,260	38·2
Pig	4	180	2·5	10	450	13·6
Tunny	48	6,500	87·9	7	950	28·5
Limpet (*Patella*)	1,900	6·5		1,970	6·9	
Top shell (*Monodonta*)	340	0·4	0·01	650	0·7	0·03
Murex	140	0·7		216	1·8	
Cockle (*Cerastoderma*)	45	0.1		53	0.1	

* Minimum numbers calculated for livestock on the number of humeri found, for tunny on the number of vertebrae, 39 vertebrae per fish. Cephalapod remains were considered insufficient to allow of their incorporation in the table.

† Meat weight for livestock is taken as half modern liveweight; meat weight for tunny is taken as 135 kg, a rough average for fish of length 0·6 to 1·8 m.

osteological material recovered, entirely masked the huge proportion of the meat weight which they represent. With this unexpected result, the marine location of the site, and of others of the same culture, takes on a new significance. The appearance of the tanged point of obsidian as the principal type of the lithic assemblage at these sites can also be reinterpreted. Seen as an arrowhead, the dominance of this point was puzzling, since virtually no wild animals were represented in the faunal remains ; but interpreted as the prong of a fishing spear or leister, it suggests the great importance of the seasonal tunny slaughter which, as elsewhere in the Mediterranean today, must have been the major economic event of the year during the life of the settlement.

So far, the economic approach in prehistory has very successfully focused attention upon the function, rather than just the form, of artefacts of organic as well as inorganic materials (Clark 1952). There have been very few quantitative, rather than merely qualitative, considerations, however, and those which have been made deal, like the above, with food residues. The enormous impact upon archaeological research which one can foresee for the quantitative understanding of archaeological residues (from coprolites to entire mounds) has not yet been felt.

The quantitative study of imported materials will one day be a basic approach in the study of trade. At present, however, there is pitifully little quantitative work to set beside the growing body of information bearing on food production in subsistence communities. Snodgrass recently evaluated, by means of an elegant table, the date of the real impact of iron metallurgy in northern Greece (Snodgrass 1965, 231). Stone and Thomas (1956), working with faience beads, and Hooker (1967), with Mycenaean pottery in Egypt, have usefully considered the *quantities* of imported material rather than simply its presence, but these studies, while adding significantly to our knowledge, are exceedingly simple compilations. They are only the pathfinders for what should be a whole new approach to the problem of economic development, trade, and cultural contact.

Obsidian has proved a very convenient material for the quantitative study of trade. In the first place, its point of origin can usually now be determined. Secondly, on most prehistoric sites, chipped stone is very abundant, so that even when obsidian is, relatively speaking, rare, enough pieces may yet be found to make statistical treatment possible. The data on the Early Neolithic obsidian finds in the Zagros area of the Near East (see Tables 2–4) make

Table 2. The proportion of grey obsidian (group 1*g*) at early neolithic sites in the Zagros area*

	Deh Luran area				
	Bus Mordeh	Ali Kosh	Mohammad Jaffar	Sarab	Jarmo
Total in sample	196	578	367	498	683
No. of Group 1*g* pieces	0	72	107	82	251
% Group 1*g*	0	12·4	29·4	16·8	35·7

* Approximate dates for the sites are as follows: Bus Mordeh 7000 BC, Ali Kosh 6500 BC, Mohammed Jaffar 6000 BC, Sarab and Jarmo 6500 BC.

Table 3. Variation in quantities of obsidian present at early neolithic sites in the Zagros area

	Deh Luran area				
	Bus Mordeh	Ali Kosh	Mohammad Jaffar	Sarab	Jarmo
Vol. excavated (cu. m)	70	144	165	50	2,700
Total chipped stone	19,574	23,231	23,934	40,864	93,239
Chipped stone/cu. m	279	162	144	817	34*
Obsidian/cu. m	2·8	4·0	2·2	14·5	14·3
% obsidian/total stone	1·0	2·5	1·6	1·8	42·0
Mean weight of obsidian fragments (gm)	0·30	0·41	0·39	0·53	0·2

* The small amount of chipped stone per cubic meter at Jarmo is probably explained by the large volume of building debris, from *tauf* walls, at this site.

Table 4. Total calculated weights of obsidian at early neolithic sites in the Zagros area

	Deh Luran area				
	Bus Mordeh	Ali Kosh	Mohammad Jaffar	Sarab	Jarmo
No. of pieces in sample	196	578	367	723	39,211
Sample as fraction of total site	1/338	1/338	1/135	1/50	1/25
Size of site (cu. m)	24,000	49,000	22,000	2,500	68,000
Total calculated weight of obsidian (kg)	20	80	19	18	196

a very suitable subject for discussion (Hole, Flannery, and Neely 1968). Characterisation study establishes that no obsidian was reaching the Zagros area from central Anatolia at this time; the obsidian found is of groups 4*c* and 1*g*, from two different sources in eastern Anatolia. The following features are noteworthy: (1) The proportion of obsidian falls off to the south, away from the sources. (2) Little or no group 1*g* obsidian reached Deh Luran in the earliest, Bus Mordeh, phase. (3) In the Deh Luran area, the chipped stone industry possibly diminishes at the end of the Bus Mordeh phase, although the obsidian component increases both relatively and absolutely. (4) The increase in proportion at the end of the Bus Mordeh phase correlates with an increase in the mean weight of fragments. This may be due to a functional or culturally determined change, rather than to a simple increase in abundance, since the mean weight does not decrease greatly when obsidian becomes rarer again in the succeeding, Mohammad Jaffar, phase. (5) The very approximate calculations allow an estimate of the total weight of obsidian contained at the sites. At first sight the totals do not appear large; but it must be taken into consideration that there were no pack animals at the time and transport was by river or by human agency alone.

This example of a quantitative consideration of trade at an early date is, of course, a very simple one, but it leads directly to a more sophisticated

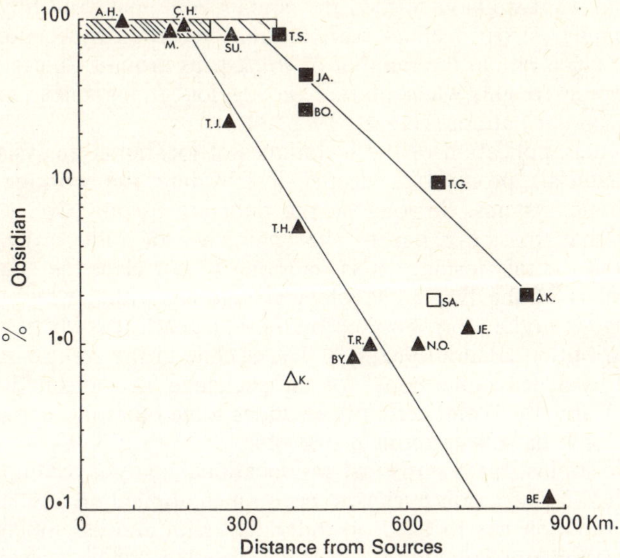

Figure 1. Percentage of obsidian in the total chipped stone industry, plotted on a logarithmic scale against distance from source, for Early Neolithic sites in the Near East, *c.* 6500 to *c.* 5000 BC. Triangles indicate sites in central Anatolia and the Levant (supplied by central Anatolian sources), squares those in the Zegros area of Iraq and western Iran (supplied by eastern Anatolian sources). Shaded areas indicate the supply zones; the straight lines show the approximately exponential fall-off in the contact zones.

analysis on a larger geographical scale. The fall-off in the proportion of obsidian in the total chipped stone industry, as the distance of the sites from the sources increases, has already been mentioned. Plotted on a graph this seemed so marked as to warrant replotting with the axis for '% Obsidian' (in the total lithic assemblage) on a logarithmic scale (fig. 1). Sites indicated by squares lie along the Zagros range of Iran and Iraq, and were obtaining their obsidian from sources in eastern Anatolia, as trace element analysis has shown (Renfrew, Dixon, and Cann 1966). Those indicated by triangles lie in central Anatolia and the Levant, and obtained their obsidian from the central Anatolian sources. The figures are discussed in detail in a more recent paper (Renfrew, Dixon, and Cann 1968).

For present purposes, the details of this trade in the 7th and 6th millennia BC are less significant than the pattern established. In each case, within a distance of about 300 km. from the source—delimiting a region which I have called the supply zone—sites were well supplied with obsidian, which formed more than 80% of their lithic assemblage. Outside the supply zone the percentage falls off steeply. If all the points fell in a straight line, the fall-off would be exponential with distance *from the edge of the supply zone.* As the points do not form a perfect line, in both cases it may be more appropriate to see the fall-off as proportional to the fourth or fifth power of the distance from the supply zone. In any case, the pattern is very striking. This fall-off in what we have termed the contact zone may fruitfully be compared with similar sharp declines with distance recorded by economic geographers. The lapse rate in the number of truck trips around Chicago or of world ocean-going freight, when plotted on log/log or log/linear axes, gives a strikingly similar pattern (Haggett 1965, 34).

It is clear that the application of the techniques of locational analysis to archaeological materials promises a deeper insight into the working of prehistoric economic systems. So long as the data are quantitative, their limited accuracy may not be a bar to the emergence of valid order-of-magnitude patterns. In this instance it is tempting to correlate the supply zones with the locus of the two archaeological cultures within which the natural sources lie—a notion corroborated by the independent study of tool typology and distribution (Bialor 1962, 43). The decline in the contact zone can be simulated by at least one model for the exchange mechanism (Renfrew, Dixon, and Cann 1968) and certainly excludes some other mechanisms which might otherwise have been thought plausible.

So far, the more sophisticated statistical and locational analysis techniques have not, other than for seriation purposes, been much applied on any large areal scale, and attention has focused on individual sites and assemblages. The study of an abundant commodity, such as obsidian, which is widely (although not uniformly) distributed through individual sites, and among sites in a given region, is clearly an easy task compared with some. For finds of a more sporadic nature, some sort of sampling procedure might be applied to combat the irregularities in archaeological preservation.[6]

These figures are prehistoric trade statistics ; we know where the material was coming from, in what quantity, and when. In the 7th millennium BC, the obsidian trade was probably not of great economic significance ; but if a similar approach could be applied to different commodities, and later periods, when the volume of trade was greater, our understanding of prehistoric economic processes would take on an entirely new dimension.

Trade and Urbanisation

Hitherto, as probably for some time to come, the detailed quantitative study of a complete regional economic or trading system has not been possible. A qualitative approach with the same objectives seems useful as an interim measure. The example presented here may help in the understanding of urbanisation in general. It has often been argued that urbanisation can only take place in very centralised societies (priest/king autocracy), or under their influence. I have come to the conclusion that the early development of Aegean civilisation did not come about in this way, although by the great Palace periods in Crete and Mycenae centralisation was certainly a basic factor in the economy.

In the discussion which follows, the term 'urbanisation' is used in a different sense from 'civilisation'. Both are intended to contrast with the essentially self-sufficient life of the earlier Neolithic village communities of Europe, such as the Danubian I settlements or the farmers of the Sesklo culture of Thessaly. 'Civilisation' is used in the now-conventional way—implying, as in Clyde Kluckholn's definition, at least two of the three following features: writing, ceremonial or religious centres, and settlements with a population greater than 5,000. If palaces are considered as representing ceremonial centres, one may properly speak of a Minoan-Mycenaean civilisation using this definition, even though settlement size was not large. The idea of civilisation without cities is likewise widely accepted for the Early Dynastic kingdom of Egypt and the Maya civilisation. 'Urbanisation', as used here, relates to towns as 'civilisation' generally relates to cities. In the 3rd millennium, Aegean towns like Troy or Phylakopi were not necessarily larger than the earlier Neolithic villages. Most of them, however, had stone-built houses, fortifications, a flourishing metal technology, some evidence of social stratification, and several new indications of wealth. In this sense they are towns, and we may speak of 'urbanisation' in the absence of any new or more acceptable word. Those to whom 'urbanisation' automatically implies the great cities of the Near East would perhaps prefer the terms 'proto-urban' and 'proto-urbanisation' for a settlement like Troy II, which was only about two acres (one hectare) in area. In such a case it will be sufficient to substitute 'proto-urban' for 'urban' in what follows: it is simply a question of definition of terms.

Urbanisation in the Aegean seems to have been the result neither of the development of a centralised autocracy, nor of significant influences from outside. It is my suggestion that a sudden and marked increase in trade was the principal causal factor, bringing in its wake new wealth, new craft specialisations, new weapons and defensive needs, and increased communication between maritime settlements in the Aegean. The transformation of a village subsistence economy into an urban society took place very rapidly, and there is no evidence of a marked increase in population at the same time (although a population increase before this transformation, at the very beginning of the Early Bronze Age, seems possible).

In the outline which follows, an attempt is made to explain this transformation in terms of culture process, notably the expansion of trade. It is suggested that neither migration nor diffusion from outside the Aegean was a significant factor. Nor would multilinear evolution be a valid explanation, for the process of urbanisation in the Aegean was evidently different in kind from the process in the Near East, where irrigation and very high population density were important factors, rather than an independent example of the same basic process.

During the Neolithic period in the Aegean, up to about 3000 BC, the largest and most prosperous settlements appear to have been the tell sites of the flat alluvial plains, especially of Thessaly, Macedonia, and Boeotia. Numerous Neolithic sites are known from southern Greece, Crete, and the Cycladic islands, but with the exception of Knossos they do not compare in size or apparent prosperity with those further north. The artefactual assemblages of these sites—Sesklo and Dimini are the most famous—include pottery, both plain and painted, chipped stone, stone axes and other tools, a few stone bowls, figurines, spindle whorls and 'stamp seals' of clay, and bone tools (Weinberg 1965*a*). Obsidian from Melos was the chief known trading commodity (Renfrew, Cann, and Dixon 1965). Ceramic similarities between sites are close enough to indicate some transmission of ideas, but until characterisation studies have been undertaken, it will not be possible to assert that pottery was actually traded between communities. Essentially these appear to have been independent farming settlements, with obsidian as the only indication of, or motive for, contact.

The Early Bronze Age sees the development of a new settlement pattern. The increase in the number of settlements in Crete, the Cyclades, and southern Greece has been correlated with a supposed influx of population at this time, a theory for which there seems little evidence (Renfrew 1964). Very possibly it is to be explained rather by the development of Mediterranean polyculture farming, based on the olive and vine as well as the Neolithic cereals, such as is practised in the same areas today. From the present point of view, however, it is not so much the population distribution which is significant as the development in culture. By the end of the Early Bronze Age,[7] the Aegean cultures of Crete, the Cyclades, southern Greece, and western Anatolia are on the path to civilisation. (Neither elaborate palaces with frescoes, drainage, and other advanced features nor writing appear, however, until the Middle Bronze Age, so it would be wrong to speak of a full civilisation at this time.) Admittedly the settlements are not very much larger than those of the Neolithic period ; but in the Aegean Late Bronze Age civilisations themselves, the settlements are still exceedingly small compared with the Sumerian cities. If settlement size alone were the criterion, we could not speak of a Minoan or a Mycenaean civilisation.

The emergent factor in the Aegean Early Bronze Age, of the later 3rd millennium BC, is an increase in the *intensity* of the cultural life—in the variety and richness of the artefacts found and in the sophistication of the crafts which they imply. Stone-built fortifications are seen at a large number of sites, including Troy, Chalandriani, Lerna, and so forth. Metallurgy becomes widespread, with the manufacture of tools, weapons, personal adornments, and luxury goods (gold and silver vessels). Personal ownership may be indicated by the use of seals in Crete and possibly by the discovery of clay sealings in Lerna. The beautiful stone sculptures of the Cycladic islands reach 1.5 m. in height, and stone bowls are common there and in Crete. A taste for luxury materials develops, especially in Crete (ivory, coloured stones), and the dead are buried with care and accompanied with rich personal goods either in cist graves (the Cyclades) or in communal built tombs (Crete). The much wider range of artefacts is what separates these cultures of the Early Bronze Age from those of the Neolithic, whose way of life appears to have remained essentially unchanged over 3,000 years.[8] This richness links them to the civilisations of the Late Bronze Age and leads me to think in terms of *urbanisation* at this time, although their small towns (Troy, Phylakopi) are not necessarily larger than the Neolithic villages.

Although in the Near East, and to some extent in the Americas, it has been common to link irrigation with the development of civilisation, it does not follow that an increase in the efficiency of food production is an essential component of such development. The rather straight-forward view that increase in leisure, afforded by greater agricultural efficiency, allows specialisation and leads to civilisation is not universally true. Many primitive communities have ample leisure, and agricultural efficiency is only one of the basic components of civilisation. More important are new needs, the trades to fulfil them, and the concomitant development in organisation. It is here suggested that these can lead towards civilisation without either a newly increased efficiency in food production or an increase in population.

The new needs here cited are documented by the development and ubiquity of the crafts and occupations of prehistoric societies which do not directly facilitate the food quest. These include town planning, palaces and temples, decorative metallurgy and ceramics, and indeed most of the manifestations of urbanisation and civilisation. In Crete and certain other early civilisations, these are accompanied by an increasingly centralised social organisation, but neither by irrigation agriculture nor by a striking increase in population. I suggest indeed that urbanisation and civilisation are not to be gauged by population increase or improved farming efficiency, since efficient and improved subsistence is presumably a goal of all human societies. Urbanisation and civilisation represent an increase in the *range* of environmental factors over which man exercises control. The most important of these environmental factors is man himself, and it is no coincidence that most civilisations show not only complex social organisation but also an elaborate procedure to regulate the relationship between man and the gods, both before and after death. It is easy to overlook that what seems pointless superstition today was then a very practical concern ; religion was a complicated and expensive technology designed to control man's environment or to influence it favourably.

All this is relevant here because there is a very close correlation between this 'culture intensification' in the Aegean, the inception of metallurgy, and the development of trade. Most of the new features indicated appear in the Early Bronze 2 period, not in the Early Bronze 1, throughout the Aegean. So does metallurgy. So does a wide network of trade: Early Helladic pottery is found in the Cyclades and western Anatolia, Anatolian two-handled 'depas' cups in southern Greece and the Cyclades, and Cycladic marble folded-arm figurines in southern Greece and Crete.

For reasons presented elsewhere (Renfrew 1967*b*), I believe that metallurgy may have originated independently in the Aegean ; but whether or not the basic technique (of smelting and casting copper) was local is irrelevant, since its development (alloying to make bronze, tool type, weapon types) certainly was. The development seems to have been a rapid one in all the regions around 2500 BC. The correlation between the metallurgical development and the growth of trade is striking. The explanation is, I believe, that for the first time there was a commodity worth trading, and on a large scale. For the first time trading became profitable.

The obsidian trade may never have been very significant economically, although culturally it did bring about contact. The quantities involved are small. With the appearance of a material which could transform crafts (as shown by flat and shaft-hole axes) and warfare (witness many daggers and spearheads), the situation changed dramatically. Perhaps the finished objects were traded first from a few more advanced metallurgical centres, such as Thermi and Chalandriani. Local metallurgical industries certainly grew up, however, and supply of the raw material must have been a pressing concern, although not until the Late Bronze Age is it documented by finds of ingots.

In the Early Bronze 2 period, therefore, the local development of metallurgy must have set up a demand throughout the Aegean for metal artefacts, a demand which could not always be satisfied locally in each region. Trade for the first time played a major economic role. This increase in trade and in contact produced, and is reflected by, the widespread distribution in the Aegean of recognisably local products. The ceramic types for the first time begin to follow metal prototypes. Unfortunately, the place of origin of these traded objects has not been established by any characterisation study (a study of marble has given negative conclusions), but the Anatolian inception of the 'depas' cup and the Cycladic one of the folded-arm figurine is universally accepted.

Metal was an obvious form of wealth, more notably so than stone in Neolithic times, and the development of fortification may be related to this and to the increase in seafaring. In any case, the intensification of culture at this time has as two causative factors the economic upsurge produced by the invention and production of a new commodity and the striking increase in communications within the Aegean. These were certainly more important than any increase in agricultural efficiency and population[9] brought about by the introduction of metal tools.

It would obviously be desirable to set up this explanation in quantitative terms, although this would be difficult at present. Clearly, too, the various systems at work require closer definition: trade may be conceived as constituting one economic system within a single community, within a given culture (or 'tradition'), or within the whole of the Aegean contact zone (or 'interaction sphere'). New concepts are required, for we are no longer dealing with essentially subsistence economies where the functioning of a system can be viewed as an almost automatic process depending on feedback from a very limited number of factors. Society in transition from subsistence community to urban settlement has reached a stage of complexity in which the variables are inconveniently numerous. New ways of handling these will have to be devised. The simplified (and perhaps naively primitive) representation of the network of interrelated factors given in figure 2 at least indicates that several forces are now relevant which were not so at an earlier stage. Trade is only one of these, but obviously a crucial one. The factors listed are those which can be documented for the later-3rd-millennium Aegean on the basis of the archaeological evidence. To this extent—despite the somewhat cabalistic appearance of the diagram—they are not hypothetical, although other valid factors could perhaps be found. Although constructed for the Aegean, the diagram suggests applications in other regions. There remains the need, however, to structure the variables in a more coherent and less arbitrary way, and until this can be done the explanation will remain a rather rudimentary and descriptive one.

Many of these factors, of course, are implicit in the further development to city life and civilisation. There one expects to find, in addition to increased community size, evidence of some centralised or civic direction facilitated by the use of writing for commercial purposes. The media of public and artistic expression are correspondingly more impressive in scale. The urban communities of the Aegean Early Bronze Age may be regarded as intermediate between the village communities of the Neolithic and the Minoan-Mycenaean civilisation, and they show, at an early stage of development, many of the new economic systems on which the latter depended.

If such an explanation be adopted for urbanisation, and indeed for civili-

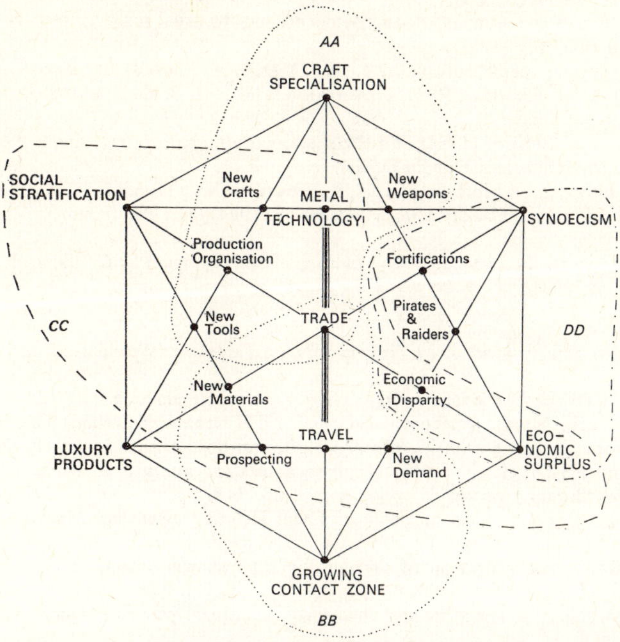

Figure 2. Urbanisation in the Aegean: the interrelationship of some of the new factors generated by the inception of metallurgy and the expansion of trade in the 3rd millenium BC. Alternatively, the points may be regarded as elements within severally overlapping *sets* (delineated by broken lines): set AA, industrial system; set BB, communications system; set CC, non-agricultural wealth; set DD, defence.

sation in the Aegean, the need for significant influence from 'higher cultures' in Egypt or Sumer, let alone any invasion of civilised or skilled migrants, disappears. It is my belief that a similar pattern of events will emerge in Iberia when the chronology of the Copper and Bronze Ages there is better understood (Renfrew 1967*a*). There is probably no need, and certainly little evidence, to link the development of urban centres, such as Los Millares or Vila Nova de São Pedro, with civilising influences from the Aegean.

'Savages', said Lord Raglan, 'never invent or discover anything.' I am sure, on the contrary, that they are inventing all the time, and that trade is one of the key factors enabling these inventions to contribute to economic progress and cultural development. [1969]

NOTES

The first draft of this paper was read at the Research Seminar in Anthropology and Related Subjects at the Institute of Archaeology, University of London, on November 7, 1967. I am grateful to Lewis Binford, George Dalton, and Frank Hole for helpful comments on the original text.

[1] Many of these methods are described in the periodical *Archaeometry;* see also Aitken (1961, 156–75) and Lucas (1962).

[2] See bibliography by Doran (1967); also Cowgill (1967), Soudsky (1967), and Hole and Shaw (1967).

[3] For bibliography, see Heizer (1960) and Cook and Heizer (1965).

[4] For the application of the concept of microenvironment to areal research in prehistory, see Coe and Flannery (1967).

[5] Compiled using species identifications by I. M. Clegg, I. A. Kinnes, and E. S. Higgs (mammalian fauna), J. M. Renfrew, P. H. Greenwood, and P. J. Whitehead (fish), and N. J. Shackleton (molluscs).

[6] See the discussion by Binford (1964) and the sustained application to a single site by Binford, Binford, Whallon and Hardin (1966.)

[7] A brief survey with a good bibliography is given by Weinberg (1965*a*).

[8] For a general account, see Caskey (1964), Vermeule (1964), and Pendlebury (1939).

[9] The idea is contrary to the views of many culture historians, such as Childe and White (see White 1959, 293).

BIBLIOGRAPHY

Adams, R. M. (1966) *The Evolution of Urban Society*. London: Weidenfeld and Nicolson.

Aitken, M. J. (1961) *Physics in Archaeology*. New York: Interscience.

Beck, C. W., Wilbur, E., Meret, S., Kossove, E. L., and Kermani, K. (1965) The infrared spectra of amber and the identification of Baltic amber. *Archaeometry* 8, 96.

Bennyhoff, J. A. and Heizer, R. F. (1965) Neutron activation analysis of some Cuicuilco and Teotihuacan pottery. *Amer. Antiq.* 30, 348.

Bialor, P. (1962) The chipped stone industry of Catal Huyuk. *Anatolian Studies* 12, 67.

Binford, L. R. (1964) A consideration of archaeological research design. *Amer. Antiq.* 29, 425–41.

——(1965) Archaeological systematics and the study of culture process. *Amer. Antiq.* 31, 203–10.

Binford, L. R. and Binford, S. R. (1966) A preliminary analysis of functional variability in the Mousterian of Levallois facies, in *Recent studies in palaeoanthropology* (eds Clark, J. D. and Howell, F. C.) pp. 238-95. *Amer. Anthrop.* 68 (2), part 2.

Binford, L. R., Binford, S. R., Whallon, R. C. and Hardin, M.A. (1966) *Archaeology at Hatchery West, Carlyle, Illinois*. Southern Illinois Museum Archaeological Salvage Report no. 25.

Blance, B. (1961) Early Bronze Age colonists in Iberia. *Antiq.* 35, 195.

Braidwood, R. J. and Howe, B. (1960) *Prehistoric Investigations in Iraqi Kurdistan*. Chicago: University of Chicago Press.

Butler, J. J. and Van der Waals, J. D. (1964) Metal analysis. SAM I and European prehistory. *Helinium* 4.

Caskey, J. L. (1964) Greece, Crete and the Aegean Islands in the Early Bronze Age, in *Cambridge Ancient History* 1, chap. 26. Cambridge: Cambridge University Press.

Catling, H. W., Richards, E. E. and Blin-Stoyle, A. E. (1963) Composition and provenance of Mycenaean and Minoan pottery. *Annu. Brit. School Archaeol. Athens* 57, 94.

Childe, V. G. (1925) *The Dawn of European Civilisation*. London: Kegan Paul.

——(1929) *The Danube in Prehistory*. Oxford: Clarendon Press.

——(1939) The Orient and Europe. *Amer. J. Archaeol.* 44, 10–26.

——(1950) The urban revolution. *Town Plann. Rev.* 21, 3.

——(1952) *New Light on the Most Ancient East*. London: Routledge and Kegan Paul.

——(1956*a*) Retrospect. *Antiq.* 32, 70–4.

——(1956*b*) *Man Makes Himself*. London: Watts.

——(1956*c*) *Piecing Together the Past*. London: Routledge and Kegan Paul.

——(1957) *The Dawn of European Civilisation*. 6th edition. London: Routledge and Kegan Paul.

Clark, J. G. D. (1952) *Prehistoric Europe, the Economic Basis*. London: Methuen.

——(1965) Traffic in stone axes and adze blades. *Econ. Hist. Rev.* 18, 1–28.

——(1966) The invasion hypothesis in British prehistory. *Antiq.* 40, 172–89.

Coe, M. D. and Flannery, K. V. (1967) *Early Cultures and Human Ecology in south coastal Guatemala*. Smithsonian Contributions to Anthropology no. 3.

Cook, S. F. and Heizer, R. F. (1965) *Studies in the Chemical Analysis of Archaeological Sites.* Berkeley and Los Angeles: University of California Press.

Cowgill, G. L. (1967) Computer applications in archaeology. *Computers and the Humanities* 2, 17.

Daniel, G. E. (1962) *The Idea of Prehistory*. London: Watts.

Deetz, J. (1965) *The Dynamics of Stylistic Change in Arikara Ceramics.* Illinois Studies in Anthropology, No. 4. Urbana: University of Illinois Press.

Dixon, J. E., Cann, J. R. and Renfrew, C. (1968) Obsidian and the origins of trade. *Scie. Amer.* 218, 38.

Doran, J. E. (1967) Electronic computers and archaeology. Paper presented to the Research Seminar in Archaeology, Institute of Archaeology, London, January, 1967.

Elliot Smith, G. (1929) *The Migration of Early Cultures.* Manchester: University of Manchester Press.

Evans J. D. (1964) Excavations in the Neolithic Settlement of Knossos. *Annu. Brit. School Archaeol. Athens* 59, 132.

Evans, J. D. and Renfrew, C. (1968) *Excavations at Saliagos near Antiparos.* London: British School of Archaeology at Athens and Thames and Hudson.

Galton, F. (1889) Comment on E. B. Tylor's 'On a method of investigating the development of institutions ; applied to laws of marriage and descent.' *J. R. Anthropo. Inst.* 18, 272.

Haggett, P. (1965) *Locational Analysis in Human Geography*. London: Edward Arnold.

Haley, J. B. and Blegen, C. W. (1928) The coming of the Greeks. *Amer. J. Archaeol.* 32, 141–54.

Heizer, R. F. (1960) Physical analysis of habitation residues. Heizer, F. F. and Cook, S. F. *The Application of Quantitative Methods in Archaeology*. Chicago: Quadrangle Books.

Herskovits, M. J. (1952) *Economic Anthropology*. New York: W. W. Norton.

Higgs, E. S., Vita-Finzi, C., Harris, D. R. and Fagg, A. E. (1967) The climate, environment and industries of Stone Age Greece. Part 3. *Proc. Prehist. Soc.* 33, 1–29.

Higham, C. W. (1967) Stock rearing as a cultural factor in prehistoric Europe. *Proc. Prehist. Soc.* 33, 84–106.

Hill, J. N. (1966) A prehistoric community in eastern Arizona. *Southwest. J. Anthropol.* 22, 9–30.

Hole, F. and Flannery, K. V. (1967) The prehistory of southwestern Iran: A preliminary report. *Proc. Prehist. Soc.* 33, 147.

Hole, F., Flannery, K. V. and Neely, J. A. (1968) *Prehistory and Human Ecology of the Deh Luran Plain.* Smithsonian Contributions to Anthropology. Washington: Smithsonian Institution.

Hole, F. and Shaw, M. (1967) *Computer Analysis and Chronological Seriation.* Rice University Studies 53 (3).

Hooker, J. T. (1967) The Mycenaean Siege Rhyton and the question of Egyptian influence. *Amer. J. Archaeol.* 71, 269–81.

Junghans, S., Schroder, M. and Sangmeister, E. (1960) *Metallanalysen kupferzeitlicher und frühbronzezeitlicher Bodenfunde aus Europa.* Berlin: Mann.

Lucas, A. (1962) *Ancient Egyptian Materials and Industries.* London: Edward Arnold.

Malinowski, B. (1960) *A Scientific Theory of Culture and Other Essays.* New York: Oxford University Press.

Mallowan, M. E. L. (1965) The mechanisms of trade in Western Asia. *Iran* 3, 1–7.

Meighan, C. W. (1959) The Little Harbour site, Catalina Island: An example of ecological interpretation in archaeology. *Amer. Antiq.* 24, 383.

Navarro, J. M. de (1925) Prehistoric routes between Northern Europe and Italy defined by the amber trade. *Geog. J.* 66, 481.

Oppenheim, L. (1954) The seafaring merchants of Ur. *J. Amer. Orient. Soc.* 74, 6.

Pendlebury, J. D. (1939) *The Archaeology of Crete.* London: Methuen.

Piggott, S. (1954) *Neolithic Cultures of the British Isles.* Cambridge: Cambridge University Press.

Pittioni, R. (1959) Zweck und Ziel spektralanalytischer Untersuchungen für die Vorgeschichte des Kupferbergwescens. *Archaeol. Austr.* 26.

Polanyi, K., Arsenberg, C. M. and Pearson, H. W., Ed. (1965) *Trade and Market in the Early Empires*. New York: The Free Press.

Renfrew, C. (1964) Crete and the Cyclades before Rhadamanthus. *Kret. Chron.* 18, 107.

——(1966*a*) Rumania find of 4,000-year-old tablets; Europe as possible cradle of writing. *The Times* (London), December 2.

——(1966*b*) The Tartaria tablets, *Nestor,* December, p. 469–70.

——(1967*a*) Colonialism and Megalithismus. *Antiq.* 41, 276–88.

——(1967*b*) Cycladic metallurgy and the Aegean Early Bronze Age. *Amer. J. Archaeol.* 71, 1–20.

——(1969) The autonomy of the south-east European Copper Age. *Proc. Prehist. Soc.* 35, 12–47.

Renfrew, C., Cann, J. R. and Dixon, J. E. (1965) Obsidian in the Aegean. *Annu. Brit. School Archaeol. Athens* 60, 225.

Renfrew, C., Dixon, J. E. and Cann, J. R. (1966) Obsidian and early cultural contact in the Near East. *Proc. Prehist. Soc.* 32, 30.

——(1968) Patterns of trade: Further analyses of Near Eastern obsidians. *Proc. Prehist. Soc.* 34, 319–31.

Rodden, R. J. (1965) An early Neolithic village in Greece. *Scie. Amer.* 213, 86.

Rowe, J. A. (1966) Diffusionism and archaeology. *Amer. Antiq.* 31, 334–37.

Shawcross, W. (1967) An investigation of prehistoric diet and economy on a coastal site at Galatea Bay, New Zealand. *Proc. Prehist. Soc.* 33, 107.

Smith, W. C. (1965) The distribution of jade axes in Europe with a supplement to the catalogue of those of the British Isles. *Proc. Prehist. Soc.* 31, 25–33.

Snodgrass, A. H. (1965) Barbarian Europe and early Iron Age Greece. *Proc. Prehist. Soc.* 31, 229–40.

Soudsky, B. (1967) *Principles of Automatic Data Treatment Applied on Neolithic Pottery*. Prague: Czechoslovak Academy of Sciences.

Steward, J. H. (1949) Cultural causality and law: A trial formulation of the development of early civilisations. *Amer. Anthropologist* 51, 1–27.

——(1955) *Theory of Cultural Change*. Urbana: University of Illinois Press.

Stone, J. P. S. and Thomas, L. C. (1956) The use and distribution of faience beads in the Near East and in prehistoric Europe. *Proc. Prehist. Soc.* 22, 59.

Vermeule, E. (1964) *Greece in the Bronze Age*. Chicago: University of Chicago Press.

Vlassa, N. (1963) Chronology in Transylvania. *Dacia* 7, 485–94.

Weinberg, S. S. (1965*a*) The Stone Age in the Aegean, in *Cambridge Ancient History* 1, chap. 10. Cambridge: Cambridge University Press.

——(1965*b*) The Aegean in the Stone and Early Bronze Ages in *Chronologies in Old World Archaeology,* Ehrich, R. W. (ed.) pp. 258–320. Chicago: University of Chicago Press.

White, L. A. (1959) *The Evolution of Culture*. New York: McGraw-Hill.

Wild, J. P. (1966) Papyrus in pre-Roman Britain. *Antiq.* 40, 139–41.

Willey, G. R. and Phillips, P. (1958) *Method and Theory in American Archaeology*. Chicago: University of Chicago Press.

Wittfogel, K. A. (1959) *Oriental Despotism, a Comparative Study of Total Power*. New Haven: Yale University Press.

2) The Aegean and the West Mediterranean

Even before the systematic application of radiocarbon dating to the West Mediterranean, and certainly before the calibration of the radiocarbon time scale, the deficiencies of the traditional view of the prehistory of the area were beginning to become apparent. The theory of the arrival of colonists from the Aegean in Italy, Malta or Iberia could be seriously questioned. So too could the assumption that the Butmir culture and its neighbours in western Jugoslavia were in direct maritime contact with the Aegean.

This chapter, which is printed substantially without alteration from my doctoral dissertation in 1965, sets out these deficiencies and does so without leaning very heavily on radiocarbon and without reference to the calibration, which had not yet been established. The arguments were later presented, in rather different form, with reference only to Iberia and with mention of the calibration, in a paper published in 1967 (chapter 11). But the presentation here, as a *jeu d'esprit*, of the case *for* the colonies followed by the arguments for the preferred alternative does highlight some of the issues.

The case for substantial east Mediterranean influence on the west, was reiterated by Daniel and Evans (1967) in their chapter for the revised Cambridge Ancient History, where they accept direct Aegean contact with Spain. Their position may profitably be compared with the more independent view of Leeds (1924) in the comparable chapter for the first edition of the same work. It should be noted too that a decade ago a number of scholars seeking to employ radiocarbon dating (e.g. Brown 1965 ; Thomas 1967) were continuing to argue along traditional lines of interpretation. Indeed some authors (e.g. Höckmann 1977) do so today.

BIBLIOGRAPHY

Brown, D. F. (1965) The chronology of the northwestern Mediterranean, in Ehrich, R. W. (ed.), *Chronologies in Old World Archaeology*. Chicago: University Press, 321–42.

Daniel, G. E. and Evans, J. D. (1967) The Western Mediterranean, in *Cambridge Ancient History* II, chapter 37. Cambridge University Press (2nd edition).

Höckmann, O. (1977) The Cyclades and the West Mediterranean, in Thimme, J., Getz-Preziosi, P. and Otto, B. (eds.), *Art and Culture of the Cyclades*. Karlsruhe: C. F. Müller, 163–72.

Leeds, E. T. (1924) The Western Mediterranean, in *Cambridge Ancient History* I, chapter 21. Cambridge University Press (1st edition).

Thomas, H. L. (1967) *Near Eastern, Mediterranean and European Chronology* (Studies in Mediterranean Archaeology 17). Lund.

THE AEGEAN AND THE WEST MEDITERRANEAN

The question of cultural relations between the Aegean and the West Mediterranean is one of the most difficult in the whole of European archaeology today. It is not that evidence is lacking, for Sicily, Malta and Sardinia and the Spanish tombs have all been the subject of systematic modern research and documentation, which is at last being carried forward for the long neglected peninsula of Southern Italy. On the contrary, parallels and comparisons have been made by so many people and for so long that there can be no two regions anywhere whose interrelations have been so comprehensively argued. And indeed it is precisely this which makes the difficulty, for the problem is no longer of spotting similarities, but of evaluating or rejecting those which have been presented.

It is a task for which we have no real criteria to guide us. Childe's 'heuristic hypothesis' that each invention has been made but once (Childe 1956, 145) certainly produces results. But without careful qualification it is so general and inclusive as to be virtually without value.

Indeed the history of archaeology itself in this respect is a depressingly cautionary one. Already in the fifteenth century the pattern was established of seeking always, for the origin of a rich and advanced 'barbaric' culture recently raised from 'savagery', the influence of one of the Ancient Civilisations. So Trojan Brutus migrated to Britain, and so too began the long journeys of the Lost Tribes. These of course disclose the influence of biblical historiography, where peoples may either migrate or stay where they are, never developing culturally without some outside intervention. It is here that the notion of 'prehistoric migrations' was born, and was richly sustained in the nineteenth century by classical scholarship. Thus Herodotus writes of Tyrrhenus leading the Rasena from Lydia to Etruria, and Thucydides of the Dorians sweeping unheralded into Greece and of Ionians leaving it for Anatolian shores. It was natural therefore for early excavators to fit their finds to such a framework. In this way one had the rich prehistoric cultures of Spain brought by Phoenicians (Siret 1913, 53 and pl. 1); and the hand of Mycenaean or Egyptian craftsmen was detected in the temples of Malta and the tombs of Spain.

It is easy of course, when choosing an object from the millennia of Spanish or Maltese prehistory, to find a parallel for it somewhere in the long and varied culture sequence of the Aegean. But more adequate chronology has forced the archaeologist to abandon some of the most attractive of these, such as the direct Mycenaean origin of the Spanish 'tholoi'. Childe indeed soon abandoned his early insistence on the importance of the Mediterranean in cultural transmission (seen in the first edition of *The Dawn*) and insisted rather on the role of the Danube. And even here, although there are still many problems awaiting clarification, it seems that the theory was in large measure wrong: the influence of Troy on Vinča—its basic chronological tenet—is just not chronologically feasible.

One enters the discussion encumbered by traditions of interpretation that are no longer entirely acceptable. I am personally very sceptical of many of the claims that are put forward for Aegean contact with the West. The earliest really sure and indubitable imports to the West seem to be the fragments of Middle Helladic matt-painted ware to Monte Sallia in Sicily and Filicudi in the Lipari Islands (Taylour 1958, pl. 16, 1 and 1, 1). Before this time nothing so characteristic, whether artefact or raw material, can be identified with certainty as originating in the Aegean.

Of course there are many similarities, and a good prima facie case for contact can be made out. Miss Blance has done so recently in her systematic and cogent article on early Iberia (1961). But to judge this case systematically is a difficult task. For within a single area similarities can often and with reason be taken to imply contact: the folded-arm figurines or Trojan cups in the Aegean are acceptable in this way, as probably the West Mediterranean rock-cut tombs such as those of Alcaide in Spain and Thapsos in Sicily with their stepped door frames. Yet to link these at once with the rather different tombs of Phylakopi, Manika or Athens would be incautious. Equally one may doubt the validity of a map showing the folded-arm figurine of the Aegean and the rather different marble figurines of Sardinia (Bray 1963) as part of the same distribution. They might indeed be connected, but the differences are so great as to make the danger of superimposing separate distributions a very real one.

The division of the Cycladic sequence into cultures and the recognition of a Cycladic Neolithic throws fresh light on some of the possible connections. It is not possible to go into these matters in great detail here, and for obvious reasons the discussion must be limited to the Cycladic aspect of the Aegean cultures. After a brief examination of the nautical feasibility of these rather distant contacts, the case for Cycladic relations with Dalmatia is considered ; other Balkan areas being included for convenience. The Italian peninsula and neighbouring islands are then very briefly discussed. Finally, in order to examine just how far the same evidence is open to different interpretations, Spain is approached from two opposing viewpoints. A positive 'colonialist' view is first presented followed by a more sceptical account of the evidence. It should be stressed that this exercise, perhaps something of a reductio ad absurdum, does not imply disrespect for Miss Blance's work, which by its lucid presentation of the Iberian material has greatly advanced our knowledge. Perhaps however it is useful to demonstrate how very tentative our conclusions in this matter must be.

Cycladic Shipping

The governing factor in maritime trade or colonisation is the shipping available. And in the Cyclades we are fortunate in having an exceptionally fine series of illustrations for the period. The frying pans of Syros (pl. 1c ; Tsountas 1899, fig. 16–22 ; Zervos 1957, pl. 204, 218, 219, 223) undoubtedly give the clearest picture of early sea-going ships in Europe, perhaps in the world. They were powered with oars, and did not have sails.

In the matter of their construction a considerable controversy has sprung up as to which end was the bow. At first sight one would expect the fish mascot to face forwards, and Tsountas took the view therefore that the higher end was the prow. In this he was followed by Evans (1921–35, II, 240 and 438) who considered the projection at the lower end to be a fixed rudder. But a number of scholars including Edgar (in Atkinson et al. 1904, 91), Dussaud, Sovoronos and Koster (quoted in Marinatos 1933, 182) have taken the opposite view. They hold that the poop is the highest part of the ship, and the projection at the other end a sort of spur or ram which was common on Greek and Phoenician vessels, and apparently seen already in Melos in Mycenaean times (op. cit. fig. 10).

In support of the latter view is the high stern, identified through the steering oar, on a sherd from Phylakopi I (pl. 1b). The curved line of the stern suggests, however, that this may be a different kind of craft altogether.

New evidence has come to light to support the recent clear restatement of the high prow theory given by Hutchinson (1962, 92). The Ashmolean in Oxford has three model boats of lead, apparently from a cist grave of the Keros-Syros culture, and found with two folded-arm figurines (pl. 1d). They have not previously been illustrated, and it may be that the curious choice of material caused their authenticity to be doubted. The abundant evidence for the working of lead at this time is however a good confirmation that they are genuine.

These useful models clearly represent the same craft as are seen on the frying pans: the form is now admirably documented. It is clear that the higher end is the bow, and the more gently angled stern portion corresponds closely to that seen on the frying pans (pl. 1c ; Tsountas 1899, fig. 17, 21). That this type of ship was in use also on the Mainland is shown by an incised sherd from Orchomenos (Kunze 1934, pl. XXIX, 3)—the apparent masts are probably unrelated incisions. Nothing so sophisticated is seen in Crete at this time, but the models from Palaikastro and Mochlos (Seager 1912, fig. 48, 31) are of similar form.

It seems that the sail was a slightly later innovation: the mast is first seen on a Middle Minoan seal (Marinatos 1933, pl. XV and XVII, 32) where the shape of the vessel is much the same. This too is the craft seen on the painted sherd from Phylakopi (pl. 1a) probably from the First City. Mr Hutchinson sees in the adaptation of the sail in the Aegean the influence of the 'Byblos ship' (1962, 93), and to similar influence may be due the introduction of the curved prow and poop which became dominant in Middle Minoan times (cf. pl. 1b).

The ship with which we are dealing is therefore not a sailing ship. Its size could be judged approximately if we know the number of oars by use of the *interscalmium*, the distance from oar to oar in Classical times, now estimated at five feet. Professor Marinatos in considering the matter (1933, 191) has concluded that because as many as 26 oars are sometimes shown on the frying pans, their representation there is purely a token one. But there are several more careful renderings with a dozen oars on each side, and it seems reasonable therefore to think in terms of a vessel some 20 metres in length.

This craft is far more easily handled than a sailing ship: until recently there were pirate ships in the Aegean, all of this type. Indeed the earliest mention in the Classics of piracy (Thucydides I, 4) tells of Minos ridding the islands of pirates, and the Cyclades have probably a continuous tradition in that calling of several millennia. (The appearance of fortifications in the Keros-Syros culture could well be due to pirate raids.) Professor Marinatos (1963, 162) has pointed out that 'at definite periods of the year navigation in definite directions is not very difficult, and open-sea sailing is less dangerous than coastal; small vessels are preferable to larger ones since one can take to the oars and find a quick refuge in an anchorage at times when a larger ship, governed only by wind, would perish'. The crossing from Greece to Italy would take only a few days, and already during the night, he suggests, the flames from Etna would be visible to guide the helmsman.

So we cannot doubt that in Early Bronze Age times the means at least were available to make the journey west from the Cyclades. In the words of Dante's Odysseus:

ma misi me per l'alto mare aperto,
sol con un legno e con quelle compagna
picciola, della qual non fui deserto.
L'un lito e l'altro vidi infin la Spagna,
fin nel Morrocco e l'isola de' Sardi,
e l'altre che quel mare intorno bagna.

Jugoslavia and the Balkans

In the Cyclades themselves there is surprisingly little that might be considered of Balkan origin, other than the spiral itself. The schematic figurine from Saliagos (pl. 4d) and the male from Kephala have already been mentioned, together with the possibility that the tanged arrowheads are linked with the Danilo culture of the Dalmatian coast. Of some interest too is the anthropomorphic vase of marble in the Ashmolean Museum (pl. 4f) which in view of its form and decoration is distinctly reminiscent of some of the anthropomorphic vases of the Balkans, especially of Hungary, as Professor Evans has pointed out. The vessels of the Baden Pecel culture, for example (Kalicz 1963, 43 and pl. II), may be of about the same date. But at present it is the only object in the Cyclades which stands out from its context as displaying a rather non-Cycladic taste. The figurines and arrowheads, in contrast, are completely at home in the islands, despite their Balkan parallels.

There are several forms, chiefly figurines, in the Balkans themselves for which Cycladic influence has been or might be suggested. In Rumania the seated figurines of Hamangia (pl. 4a, background; Berciu, 1961, fig. 275–7) have been compared with the Keros musician, and could equally be set beside the seated Teke figurine (pl. 4b). But seated figurines are known equally from Çatal Hüyük and Hacilar, and from elsewhere in the Balkans, and it seems scarcely necessary to connect them all. Nor would the use of Spondylus (pl. 4e) or of marble (pl. 4a) in the Hamangia and Salcutsa cultures, be taken as of much significance, were it not for the similarities in some of the standing figurines of marble (pl. 2a and b). The schematic ones of bone (pl. 4c; Georgiev and Angelov 1957, fig. 60) were widespread at the same time. Carbon-14 dates (cf. Mellaart 1960; dates are c. 150 years older after correction for new half-life) suggest that they are earlier than the Cycladic figurines. The marble ones are not all from good contexts, but the most 'Cycladic' of all (pl. 2a; Georgiev 1962, fig. 8) was securely stratified in the Gumelnitsa levels at Azmashka Moghila in Bulgaria. Although the great variety of figurines in Bulgaria especially (Ziomecki 1957) makes it possible that these are of local origin, the rather close similarities in posture, including the folded-arm position, make it impossible to rule out a Cycladic influence. Unfortunately the head of the figurine is missing, and it may well have had the typically Bulgarian pierced ears (pl. 2b) which are not seen in Cycladic figurines. The complete absence of Cycladic influence in the North Aegean makes any direct connection seem rather unlikely.

In Jugoslavia, the old chronological arguments about Vinča have not yet been satisfactorily settled, despite the reasoning based by Mellaart (1960) on C-14 determination. The parallel most vigorously argued (Garašanin 1961, 277) is the pedestal jar from Vinča (Garašanin 1958, pl. 3, 7) which does indeed have similarities with examples from Syros and particularly Amorgos (Zervos 1957, pl. 77). These can now be placed securely in the Keros-Syros culture, so that there is great chronological disparity. In any case the magnitude of the distance and the simplicity of the form would lead one to reject, albeit tentatively, such a comparison.

The striking and unusual parallels between the Danilo and Elateia coal scuttles has already been discussed and indeed accepted because of the complex and peculiar nature of the form. This in turn leads one to allow of a possible link in the arrowheads of Danilo and Butmir with those of Elateia and Saliagos. It would seem then that the stage is set for an acceptance too of relations in the spiral decoration (pl. 3) of the two areas.

There are no pottery relief spirals in the Cyclades, however. The running spirals there are found exclusively on frying pans of the Kampos type (incised) or steatite vases of the Keros-Syros culture (relief). So much has at times been made of this single trait (e.g. by Grbic 1957, pl. 47, IV), that it is difficult to look at the matter objectively. The hard facts are, however, that Butmir, although later than Danilo, is still to be related to the period of Vinča-Pločnik (Benac 1961, 58) and must be a millennium earlier than the Keros-Syros culture on a C-14 chronology. The spiral is a motif found still earlier in the Danilo culture also (pl. 3b) and has a range of form in that area exceeding anything met with in the Cyclades. Cycladic influence in the direction of Butmir must be ruled right out. The spirals of the Keros-Syros culture were presumably influenced by those of the Louros frying pans, and it is scarcely necessary either to derive them from Butmir. And indeed there are no intermediate parallels of relief spirals to indicate the path of the landlocked Butmir spirals on their triumphal march south (cf. Schachermeyr 1955, 122).

Similar claims of Cycladic contact have been made for the Dalmatian island of Hvar (Novak 1959) but the nearest parallel there is a cylindrical pyxis with hatched triangles (Mirosaljevic 1950–1, pl. V) which is different from Cycladic examples, and the case for Aegean contact has perhaps been exaggerated. Yet although one can present typological, distributional and chronological arguments against these connections, we have no criteria for actually disproving them, and can do no more at present than regard all these suggestions with a hostile but impotent scepticism.

Italy and the Islands

Malta. The evidence for Cycladic contact with Malta is at first attractive, but very strong chronological objections emerge when many of the suggested parallels are examined. And it may be said that the tradition of acceptance for Aegean parallels, mentioned earlier, persists even though it is now not possible to derive the temples from outside, and the spirals prove older than those of Mycenae.

One newly discovered parallel is very striking: the clay head of the Red Skorba phase (pl. 5a), found unstratified at Skorba by Dr Trump. It compares interestingly with the heads of Kephala and the Athenian Agora (pl. 5b and c) although lacking the prominence at the back of the head and the traces of ears. The C-14 date of 3380 BC (uncorrected 3225 ± 150 BC) for the Red Skorba deposit means that it may be contemporary with the Kephala cemetery. The sceptic might well argue that the four bodies found at Skorba (Trump 1963, fig. 9), with their protruding buttocks do not resemble the Cycladic ones at all, and thus that the similarities in the heads are fortuitous. But it is scarcely permissible to argue from the form of the later marble figurines in the Cyclades what that of the earlier clay ones at Kephala would be, and the matter must be left open.

Trading connections at this time with Lipari and Pantelleria are amply demonstrated by the lumps of obsidian found at Skorba (Trump 1963) which have proved on analysis to come from these sources (Cann and Renfrew 1964). But while the figurine might be held to indicate a Cycladic connection, the simple and undecorated bone tube of the Grey Skorba period (Trump 1963, fig. 4) surely cannot do so, for it is nearly a millennium earlier than those of Syros and Naxos, or of the Levant (Maier 1961, 294).

It could be argued too that the 'fiddle figurine' of the Ggantija period (Evans 1959, pl. 80) is not sufficiently close to the Cycladic ones in type or date for a link to be plausible. Rather more positively, the suggested relationship between the fat figurines of the Tarxien phase (pl. 5d and g) and those of the Early Neolithic of Greece (pl. 5e and f)—but not necessarily the Cyclades—may be held in question. Parallels could be found also for the reclining figurine (Evans 1959, pl. 57). Yet the fat figurine is surely sufficiently general a form to fall outside Childe's 'each invention has been made but once' dictum. Certainly the purchase of a fine figurine of Greek type from a Maltese dealer (Evans 1963, figs. 1–2) is highly suggestive, but the chronological difficulties seem insuperable. The Red Skorba figure must antedate the Tarxien one by centuries, and is itself surely a millennium at least earlier than the Greek fat figurines.

The Greek examples have been discussed earlier, and while the seated form has been considered a Cycladic type (Weinberg 1951), the fat standing form of marble is surely more at home on the Mainland. There are no attested finds in the Cyclades while several are known on the Mainland, including examples from Sparta, Aegina (two), Avaritsa in Thessaly and a recent find from Alepotrypa in the south-west Pelponnese (Daux 1961, 724, fig. 5). It would be difficult to suggest a typology from the Greek figurines to the Tarxien period ones with the more schematic Red Skorba form as an intermediate stage. And it seems unlikely that the fat form would persist for nearly two millennia, for part of the time alongside the more simple form.

If the figurines, temples and spirals were set aside, the evidence for contact with the Aegean world would be scanty indeed. However the Middle Helladic contacts with Sicily must have been preceded by influences such as those bringing the bossed bone plaques. In the earliest phases the appearance of the 'Impressed Ware' farmers must obviously indicate an incursion, but probably from Sicily in the first instance, whatever their further ancestry. After that there are few other signs of Aegean influence other than the Zebbug menhir and perhaps the appearance of rock-cut tombs in the same phase, until the Tarxien Cemetery period when ceramic similarities became more notably abundant. Thus while it would be impossible to argue the question of Aegean contacts adequately in so short a space, the Cycladic ones at least must be held in doubt.

Sardinia. The recent progress in Sardinian prehistory (Bray 1963 ; Guido 1964) has made impossible the old double link with the Aegean of domus de janas and nuraghi taken together. Although at first sight some of the nuraghi complexes (pl. 6d) would compare well with Panermos in Naxos (pl. 6e) there would seem to be a difference in date of nearly a millennium, while the rock-cut tomb is really as much a Western Mediterranean as an Aegean phenomenon.

The case for Minoan contacts with Crete, which are principally later than the Early Minoan period, has been made by Bray (1963). He lays weight also on the similarities between the marble figurines of Sardinia and the Cyclades. The marble of the Sardinian ones is said to be local however. It must be admitted that there are striking similarities (pl. 6a) in the treatment of the face and breasts. Yet the arrangement of the arms, with the hole at the elbows, the rudimentary treatment of the legs, and the frequently large size, separates them from the Cycladic ones. If there really was a Cycladic influence at work at the inception of this Sardinian form, one would hope sooner or later to find in Sardinia something rather closer to the Cycladic prototype. Until such evidence can be found, the case can perhaps be regarded as not proven.

Italy. The Chalcolithic of Italy shows similarities with the Aegean in rather the same way as does Iberia. The midrib daggers of the Rinaldone culture (Childe 1957, 241) seem chiefly to have a tang (pl. 7c) and are thus distinct from those of Crete and the Cyclades, which they otherwise resemble.

There are also ceramic forms of some interest. From the cemetery of rock-cut tombs at Gaudo near Paestum (Sestieri 1946) which resemble in form those of Euboia, come various suggestive shapes including what amounts to a duck vase, as well as a midrib dagger. The cemetery of Ponte S. Pietro in Tuscany produced a bowl with pattern burnish (pl. 8c) as well as suspension pots which could conceivably be related to those of Pelos. These resemblances with the Aegean, both in the decorative technique and the form of the pottery and in the metal types, are really as close as anything seen in Spain. It is surprising therefore that more has not been made of them, for the possible Greek origin of the earlier painted wares has been firmly advanced. So too have the claims of Lipari for Aegean contact (Cavalier 1960), but apart from the one-handled cup in the Piano Quartera culture, reminiscent of the Aegean E.B. 2 form, these do not become very persuasive until Middle Helladic times.

Indeed the position of Italy with respect to Greece makes it a far more likely recipient of Aegean influences than Spain. But despite all the possibilities which these parallels suggest, it is disappointing that nothing more positively convincing has been found. It would need better evidence than this before contact in the Chalcolithic period between Italy and the Cyclades could be accepted.

Iberia

The Case for 'Colonies'. The very rich nature of the Spanish Copper Age and its predecessors has long suggested to archaeologists inspiration from the Aegean area. That Cycladic mariners would be capable of such a journey was shown above, and that they did so in the Early Bronze Age is suggested by the finds of Phylakopi I beaked jugs at Marseilles and Addaya (Bossert 1954, pl. 16, 2–3). And we know from the evidence of Anatolian obsidian at Jericho (Cann and Renfrew 1964) that journeys over long distances were made even in Preceramic Neolithic times when there was sufficient motive.

The earliest Neolithic of Spain, the Impressed Ware culture, is a West Mediterranean spread of probable Greek origin, and already in Almerian times we can see signs of direct Aegean influence. The defining characteristics of Blance's non-indigenous group (1961, 192) are bifacially worked arrowheads, stone axes, flat idols of bone or stone, amphorae and round tombs. The case for contact has been greatly strengthened by the discovery of a Cycladic Neolithic. The stone flat idols of the Grotta-Pelos culture (pl. 7d) now have an antecedent in bone from Saliagos (pl. 4d) which may be compared with Almerian examples. The principal feature of the Saliagos culture is the bifacially flaked tanged arrowhead and its appearance in Almeria is clearly of significance. Of great importance too is the discovery at Kephala of round tombs sometimes with several burials, which invite comparison with the Almerian ones. Stone axes are known at both Kephala and Saliagos. These comparisons suggest a rather early date for the Almerian culture, certainly well before Blance's 2700, but this seems reasonable on other grounds.

This first wave of Aegean influence is followed in the Bronze Age by direct colonisation. This term is taken to imply settlement in an alien environment by traders from the Aegean, who remained in contact with the homeland. The fortifications of Los Millares, Vila Nova de São Pedro (pl. 6f) Zambujal and now Lébous in France may be compared with Chalandriani, and especially the newly discovered Panermos (pl. 6e and g). Both these sites, like the Iberian ones, were concerned with the practice of metallurgy. It may be that the Iberian settlements were founded at different times from different parent cities: Mesas de Asta with its pattern burnish ware (pl. 8a) could be a rather early foundation, perhaps from Tigani in Samos. Vila Nova de São Pedro, with its incised 'Import Ware', which corresponds so closely with Pelos pottery would be a little later.

Other significant links may be the bone pins of Vila Nova de São Pedro (do Poço and Sangmeister 1956, pl. 16) especially the bird-headed ones, painted ware, the mother goddess idea, and of course the tholos tomb. Although this is surely earlier than the Mycenaean examples, the evolution from the early Cretan tholos to the Mycenaean has been advocated by Hood (1960, 176) and influences must have reached Iberia during this process. The rock-cut tomb is a later development, showing similar and continuing contact.

Most significant of all, perhaps, is the beginning of metallurgy in Iberia, for the search for raw materials was probably the basic reason for Cycladic contact with Spain. The midrib daggers of Los Millares Tomb 57 and Alcalà Tomb 3 (pl. 7c) shows similarities with the Amorgos ones, and the bivalve mould used for the Alcalà daggers is surely a sign of Aegean influence ; its use died out in the succeeding Beaker period.

The rather isolated nature of the colonies themselves, where these exotic types tend to be concentrated gives general support to the argument. It seems likely that Iberia was the area from which the Aegean beliefs and burial customs were transmitted to Western Europe. The colonies in Iberia are only one aspect of the considerable influence which the Aegean exercised at this time in the West Mediterranean.

Doubts on the 'Colonies'. The above section presents the conventional evidence for the 'colonies', together with some new arguments arising from the Cycladic Neolithic discoveries. And it is a difficult case to criticise, not so much perhaps because it is a particularly strong one, but since there are no clear or established criteria available for judging such arguments, however flimsy they might in fact be.

There are three trends in the argument which can be singled out. The first is a willingness to accept as corroborative evidence, supporting a case put forward on other grounds, flimsy parallels which standing on their own would not command respect. The important daggers (pl. 7c) do not in fact compare very closely with the Amorgos or Cretan midrib daggers, which are pierced with rivet holes and not fitted with a handle by means of nicks at the neck. There is no real similarity between Iberian and Aegean painted wares. Above all, the 'Import Ware' of Vila Nova de São Pedro (pl. 7a), far from being a rarity from overseas, is essentially the defining characteristic of the Portuguese 'colonial' Chalcolithic: it is certainly known from more sites in Portugal than there are Pelos Group cemeteries in the Cyclades. Moreover it is not identical to the Cycladic wares, and has been shown by petrological examination to be of local Portuguese manufacture. That the excavators of Vila Nova de Sao Pedro should have named this local pottery 'Import Ware' is symptomatic of the committed approach sometimes adopted towards this problem.

It should be noted too that the credentials of both the Marseilles (Benoît 1956, 12 and 17) and Addaya (Almagro 1940, 117) beaked jugs have been convincingly discredited. Both must be products of the early plundering of the Phylakopi tombs in the nineteenth century.

The second vagueness is chronological. It may reasonably be asserted that much of the evidence on which the colonial theory is based depends itself on a sorting of the material into colonial and non-colonial, a somewhat circular process. In Portugal the 'Import Ware' is found in almost every case in association with Beaker material. Beakers have been found mixed with the supposed primary colonist material at many important sites. At Mesas de Asta they are found mixed with pattern burnish ware (Guerrerro 1945, 39), they turn up in Los Millares I (Leisner 1943, 459), and at Vila Nova de São Pedro, although apparently stratified above the 'Import Ware', they may be contemporary with the construction of the defensive wall (do Poço and Sangmeister 1956, 222). They may be the result of a later intrusion in every case, but this is by no means certain, for in the Portuguese rock-cut tombs Beakers are the dominant ceramic find. The Iberian relative chronology is simply not yet adequately established. When it is, it will be possible to question such inconsistencies in the argument as supposed Pelos type 'Import Ware' being found at Vila Nova de São Pedro with Syros type bird-headed pins and fortifications, or as the destruction of the fortification wall at Los Millares at a date (2460 BC, corrected) when those of Lerna and Chalandhriani had not yet been built.

The third and most critical vagueness is in the selection of significant traits. The pottery has not yet been systematically considered or subjected to comparison as a complex, and the Almerian and Los Millares wares just do not show obvious Aegean affinities. The most numerous and striking objects of religious significance in the Los Millares and Portuguese material are the decorated bone phalanges and schist plaques respectively, for which nothing comparable can be found in the Aegean. And even the flat figurines of Almeria and Los Millares show a far greater variety (Leisner 1945, pl. 178–9) than is to be seen in the Cyclades.

The possibilities of local originality seem consistently underrated. In the Almerian culture the arrowhead forms include concave based examples (op. cit. 433) and various other types not seen in the Aegean: one is in face of a vigorous local tradition. A North African origin for this is also a distinct possibility (cf. Santa Olalla 1944, pl. CXVII and CLXIII). It may be doubted on a priori grounds also whether one has to derive burial in a constructed tomb of circular form from outside. Admittedly some of the flat idols do show similarities with Cycladic ones, but there seems just no way of deciding whether they are the product of outside influence or of the iconographically inventive spirit which produced the later range of figurations. It seems difficult therefore to refute conclusively the theory of Aegean influence on the Almerians, but it may well be doubted. To regard the matter as proved would surely be premature.

For the Chalcolithic of Iberia the doubts are more numerous. The strongest argument in favour of colonisation would be the metallurgical one, and there is as yet no other explanation for the use of the bivalve mould, as seen at Alcalà. Yet one cannot conceive of any reason for Cycladic colonists to set up in Iberia: copper was available in the Aegean, and the use of tin—which might have provided sufficient motive—was not then known in Spain, as analyses have shown (Junghans, Schröder and Sangmeister 1960, nos. 297, 737, 825). But an economic or trading motive is surely the only conceivable one, for it is doubtful whether the pressure of population was sufficiently great in the Cyclades in the third millennium to allow of the Lebensraum explanation which might be brought forward to explain the colonisation of Thasos or Cyrene from the Cyclades in Archaic Greek times.

The fortifications too seem significant, but to put the matter bluntly, is there any more reason why they should originate in the Aegean than in Iberia? The E.B. 2 period in the Aegean begins around 2500 BC, yet the collapse of the wall at Los Millares is dated to about this time by C-14, earlier therefore than the construction of the supposed Aegean prototypes.

The chronological problem in Iberia is indeed one of the most difficult ones. For the theory holds that all the imported traits at a colony were brought in a fairly short space of time by the colonists. Yet if the walls, the daggers (in the Cyclades these are later than the Syros settlement) and the tholos tombs in Iberia all belong together, they must surely be later there than the tombs in Brittany. The question of the chamber tombs of Iberia is of great interest in itself, and the Aegean influence theory has virtually collapsed through the various chronological inconsistencies: the direction of influence could even be reversed (Piggott 1953). But in any case, although this is not perhaps always sufficiently emphasised, the most impressive feature of the Spanish tholoi is the passage itself, which is always covered and sometimes of great length. It bears no relation to the Mycenaean dromos, for given a chamber tomb some kind of entry is inevitable, while the earliest Aegean round graves were not provided with an entrance passage at all.

It is not possible to examine here in detail the various parallels that have been drawn. But many of the most forceful arguments seem to depend on vaguenesses and chronological inconsistencies that are very disquieting. It would seem as easy to see colonists in Chalcolithic Italy as in Spain. And indeed the similarities between the Spanish (pl. 8a) and Italian (pl. 8c) pattern burnish wares has already been pointed out by Evans (1957, 60). If it is necessary to derive such a wide variety of Iberian features from outside, a great many—such as collective burial, pattern burnish and painted ware, and midrib daggers—could as easily be Italian as Cycladic. There seems little reason to derive the Spanish forms from so far, or from one single source. Just as the Argar culture of the Spanish Bronze Age is properly regarded as a local fusion of a great variety of outside influences, so the Chalcolithic should be seen not as the result of direct colonisation but of local ingenuity, stimulated perhaps from outside at different times and in different ways.

But it is really too early yet to suggest even vague conclusions of that kind. The overwhelming methodological difficulty is that we have no criteria at all for rejecting parallels once they have been put forward. Personne ne dispose. Until these can be evolved it would seem wiser to hold in doubt the question of Aegean influence on the Iberian Neolithic and Chalcolithic. Although such influence seems possible and indeed plausible, there is no reason why the Iberians should not have produced themselves most or all of the forms in use in Chalcolithic times. [1965]

BIBLIOGRAPHY

Almagro, M. (1940) El hallazgo de la ria de Heulva y el final de la edad del bronce en el Occidente de Europe. *Ampurias* 2, 117.

Atkinson, T. D., Bosanquet, R. C., Edgar, C. C., Evans, A. J., Hogarth, D. G. and Mackenzie, D. (1904) *Excavations at Phylakopi in Melos.* Society for the Promotion of Hellenic Studies Occasional Paper No. 4.

Benac, A. (1961) Studien zur Stein- und Kupferzeit im nordwestlichen Balkan. *42. Bericht der Römisch-Germanischen Kommision,* 1.

Benoît, F. (1956) La Constitution du Musée Borely et les fraudes archéologiques des fouilles de Marseille. *Provence Hist.* 6, 1.

Berciu, D. (1961) *Contributii la Problemele Neoliticului in Rominia in Lumina Noilor Cercetari.*

Blance, B. (1961) Early Bronze Age colonists in Iberia. *Antiq.* 35, 192.

Bossert, E.-M. (1953) Zur Datierung der Gräber von Arkesine auf Amorgos. *Festschrift für Peter Goessler,* 23.

Bray, W. (1963) The Ozieri culture of Sardinia. *Riv. Sci. Preist.* 18, 155.

Cann, J. R. and Renfrew, C. (1964) The characterisation of obsidian and its application to the Mediterranean region. *Proc. Prehist. Soc.* 30, 111.
Cavalier, M. (1960) Les Cultures préhistoriques des Iles Eoliennes. *Bull. Corr. Hell.* 84, 319.
Childe, V. G. (1965) *Piecing Together the Past.*
Childe, V. G. (1957) *The Dawn of European Civilisation.*
Daux, C. (1962) Chronique des fouilles. *Bull. Corr. Hell.* 86.
Evans, A. J. (1921–35) *The Palace of Minos at Knossos* I–IV.
Evans, J. D. (1957) Two phases of prehistoric settlement in the western Mediterranean. *Annu. Rep. Insti. Archaeol.* Vol. 13, 49.
Evans, J. D. (1959) *Malta.*
Evans, J. D. (1963) A statuette bought in Malta and its implications. *Bosch-Gimpera Festschrift.*
Garašanin, M. V. (1958) Neolithikum und Bronzezeit in Serbien und Makedonien. *39. Bericht der Römisch-Germanischen Kommission.*
Garašanin, M. V. (1961) The Neolithic in Anatolia and the Balkans. *Antiq.* 35, 276.
Georgiev, G. (1962) Azmashka Moghila near Stara Zagora. *Archeol.* (Sofia) Vol. 4, 39.
Georgiev, G. and Angelov, N. (1957) Ausgrabungen des Siedlungshügel bei Russe. *Bull. Inst. Archéol. Bulgare* 21, 41.
Grbic, M. (1957) Preclassical pottery in the central Balkans. *Amer. J. Archaeol.* 61, 137.
Guerrero, M. E. (1945) Excavaciones de Asta Regia. *Acta Arqueol. Hispan.* III.
Guido, M. (1964) *Sardinia.*
Hood, M. S. F. (1960) Tholos tombs of the Aegean. *Antiq.* 35, 166.
Hutchison, R. W. (1962) *Prehistoric Crete.*
Junghans, S., Schröder, M. and Sangmeister, E. (1960) *Metallanalysen kupferzeitlicher und frühbronzezeitlicher Bodenfunde aus Europa.*
Kalicz, N. (1963) *Die Peceler (Baden) Kultur und Anatolien.*
Kunze, E. (1934) *Orchomenos* III.
Leisner, G. and V. (1943) *Megalithgräber der Iberischen Halbinsel, Der Süden.*
Maier, R. A. (1961) Neolitische Tierknochen-Idole und Tierknochen-Anhänger Europas. *42. Bericht der Römisch-Germanischen Kommission.*
Marinatos, S. (1933) La marine créto-mycénienne. *Bull. de Corr. Hell.* 57, 170.
Marinatos, S. (1963) The Minoan-Mycenaean civilisation and its influence on the Mediterranean and on Europe. *Atti del VI. Congr. Internaz. Sci. Preist. e Protoist.* Vol. 1, 161.
Mellaart, J. (1960) Anatolia and the Balkans. *Antiq.* 24, 270.
Mirosaljevic, V. (1950–1) Une découverte de culture helladique dans la grotte de Pokrivenik sur l'ile de Hvar. *Bull. Archeol. e Stor. Dalmata* 53, 123.
Novak, G. (1959) Problems and chronology of the finds in the Cave of Grabak. *Archaeol. Jugoslav.* 3, 11.
Piggott, S. (1953) The tholos tomb in Iberia. *Antiq.* 28, 137.
do Poço, A. and Sangmeister, E. (1956) Vila Nova de São Pedro, eine befestigte Siedlung der Kupferzeit in Portugal. *Germania* 34, 211.
Santa Olalla, J. M. (1944) El Sahara anteislámico. *Acta Argueol. Hispan.* II.
Schachermeyr, F. (1955) *Die älteste Kulturen Griechenlands.*
Seager, R. B. (1912) *Excavations in the Island of Mochlos.*
Sestieri, P. C. (1946) La necropoli preistorica di Paestum. *Riv. Sci. Preist.* 1, 244.
Siret, L. (1913) *Questions de chronologie et d'ethnographie ibériques.*
Taylour, W. D. (1958) *Mycenaean Pottery in Italy.*
Trump, D. (1963) Skorba: Malta's Earliest Temple. *Illust. London News,* 14th September 1963.
Tsountas, C. (1899) Kykladika II. *Archaeol. Ephem.* 1899.
Weinberg, S. S. (1951) Neolithic Figurines and Aegean Interrelations. *Amer. J. Archaeol.* 55, 121.
Weinberg, S. S. (1962) Excavations at Prehistoric Elateia 1959. *Hesperia* 29.
Zervos, C. (1957) *L'Art des Cyclades du début à la fin de l'âge du bronze.*
Ziomecki, J. (1957) Plastyka figuralna z Bulgarii w epoce neolitu i eneolitu. *Archaeol.* (Warsaw) 9, 35.

NOTES TO THE PLATES

1. Early Cycladic shipping. c. 2300 BC.
(a) and (b) from the First City, Phylakopi, Melos (National Museum, Athens); (c) incised 'frying pan' from the Chalandriani cemetery, Syros (National Museum, Athens). Photo Peter Clayton; (d) lead boat model from Naxos (Ashmolean Museum, Oxford).

2. Marble figurines from Bulgaria and the Aegean.
(a) From the copper age levels, Tell Azmak, Bulgaria (Stara Zagora Museum). After Georgiev; (b) from copper age levels at various sites in Bulgaria (Archaeological Museum, Sofia); (c) folded Arm Figurine from the early bronze age of the Cycladic islands, Greece (National Gallery, Budapest, no. 4709). Ht. 24 cm. Photo National Gallery, Budapest.

3. Spirals from Jugoslavia and the Cyclades.
(a) Relief spirals on pottery from Butmir (after Radminsky); (b) incised decoration on pottery from Danilo (after Korošec); (c) Pyxis of chlorite schist from Early Cycladic grave on Naxos (National Museum, Athens). Ht. 7 cm. After Zervos.

4. Objects from Rumania and the Aegean.
(a) Marble bowl from the Salcutsa culture, with pottery figurines of the Hamangia culture from Cernavoda in the background (Archaeological Museum, Bucharest); (b) Early Minoan seated marble figurine from Teke, Crete (Archaeological Museum, Herakleion); (c) bone figurines of the Salcutsa culture (Archaeological Museum, Bucharest); (d) bone figurine of the Saliagos culture from Antiparos, Greece (Paros Museum); (e) bracelet of the shell *Spondylus gaederopus* and shell necklaces of the Hamangia culture (Constantsa Museum); (f) marble vessel from the early bronze age of the Cyclades (Ashmolean Museum, Oxford).

5. Figurines from Malta and the Aegean.
(a) Clay figurine head of the Red Skorba phase from Skorba, Malta (National Museum, Malta). Photo David Trump; (b) clay figurine head from the Kephala cemetery, Kea, Cycladic Islands. Photo J. L. Caskey; (c) late neolithic clay figurine head from the Agora, Athens (Agora Museum). Photo Agora; (d) limestone statues of the Tarxien phase from Hagar Qim, Malta. Ht. 49 cm (National Museum, Malta); (e) marble figurine from the Greek neolithic, supposedly from Amorgos. Ht. 9 cm (Ashmolean Museum, Oxford). Museum photo; (f) seated marble figurine of the Greek neolithic from Patissia near Athens. Ht. 12 cm (Ashmolean Museum, Oxford). Museum photo; (g) limestone seated statue of the Tarxien phase from Hagar Qim, Malta. Ht. 23 cm (National Museum, Malta).

6. Figurines and fortifications from the West Mediterranean and the Aegean.
(a) Figurine from Porto Ferro, Sardinia (after Zervos); (b) Early Cycladic marble figurine (British Museum); (c) Early Cycladic marble figurine from Syros (Athens, National Museum); (d) the fortified settlement at Barumini, Sardinia (after Zervos); (e) the fortified Early Cycladic settlement at Panermos, Naxos; (f) the fortifications at Vila Nova de São Pedro, Portugal (after do Poço and Sangmeister); (g) the Early Cycladic fortifications at Chalandriani, Syros.

7. Objects from the Cyclades, Italy and Iberia.
(a) Incised 'import ware' sherd from Vila Nova de São Pedro (after Blance); (b) incised Early Cycladic pyxis from Melos (Ashmolean Museum, Oxford); (c) copper age daggers from the Rinaldone culture of Italy (right) and from Tomb 3 at Alcalà, Spain (left). After Peet and Leisner; (d) early Cycladic schematic marble figurine (Ashmolean Museum, Oxford); (e) figurines of the Almeria culture, Spain (after Leisner).

8. Pottery from Italy, Iberia and the Aegean.
(a) Pattern burnish ware from Mesas de Asta (after Guerrero); (b) pattern burnish sherds from Phase VIII at Emborio, Chios (by courtesy of Mr M. S. F. Hood and the British School of Archaeology at Athens); (c) pots of the Rinaldone culture with pattern burnish from Ponte S. Petro, Tuscany (after Laviosa-Zambotti); (d) early Cycladic duck-vase from Phylakopi, Melos (Ashmolean Museum, Oxford); (e) Askos from the cemetery at Gaudo near Paestum, Italy (after Laviosa-Zambotti).

Plate 1. Early Cycladic ships *c.* 2300 BC: representations on pottery, and a lead ship model.

Plate 2. Marble figurines from the Bulgarian Copper Age (a and b) and from the Cycladic Early Bronze Age (c).

Plate 3. Spiral decoration from the Early Bronze Age of the Cycladic Islands (c) and the Jugoslav Neolithic (a and b).

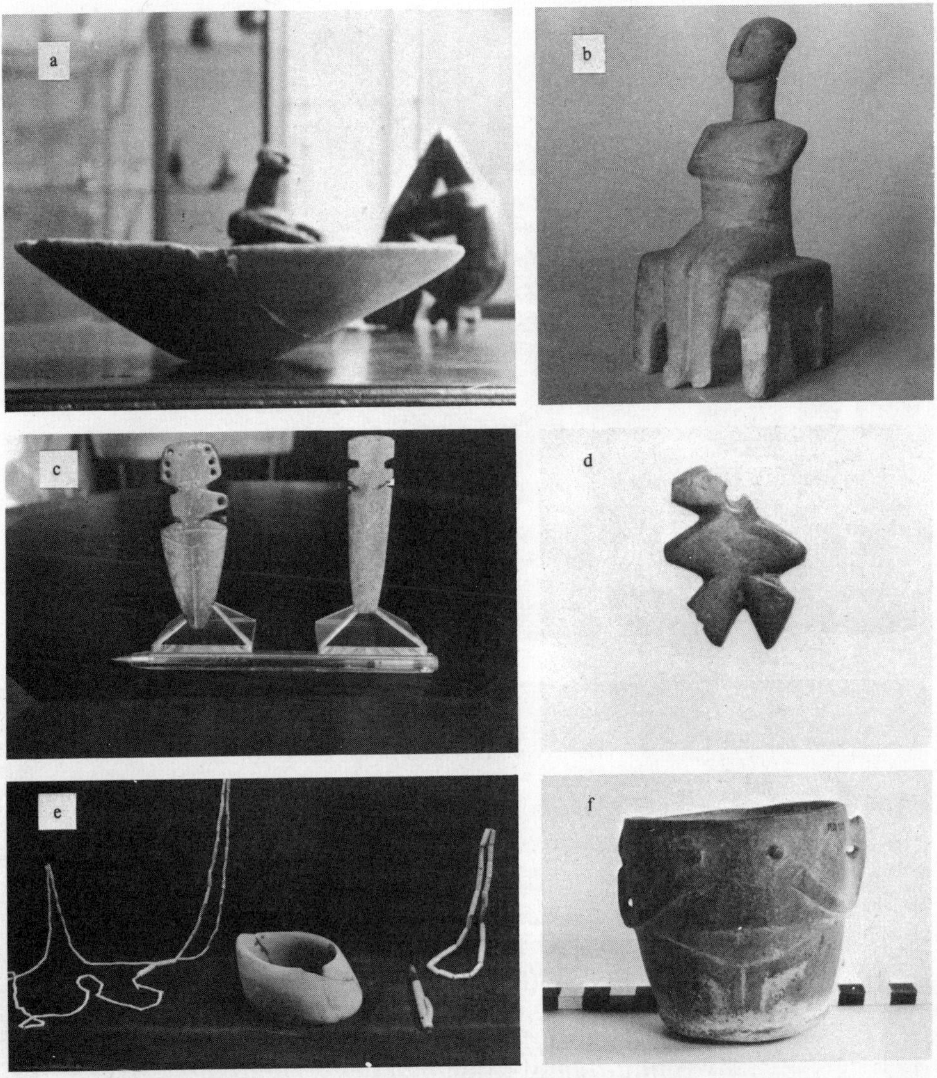

Plate 4. Figurines, marble objects and ornaments from the Neolithic and Copper Age of Romania (*left*) and from the Aegean (*right*).

Plate 5. Figurines from Malta (a, d, g) and from the Aegean (b, c, e, f).

Plate 6. Figurines and fortifications in the West Mediterranean (a and d, Sardinia; f, Portugal) and in the Aegean.

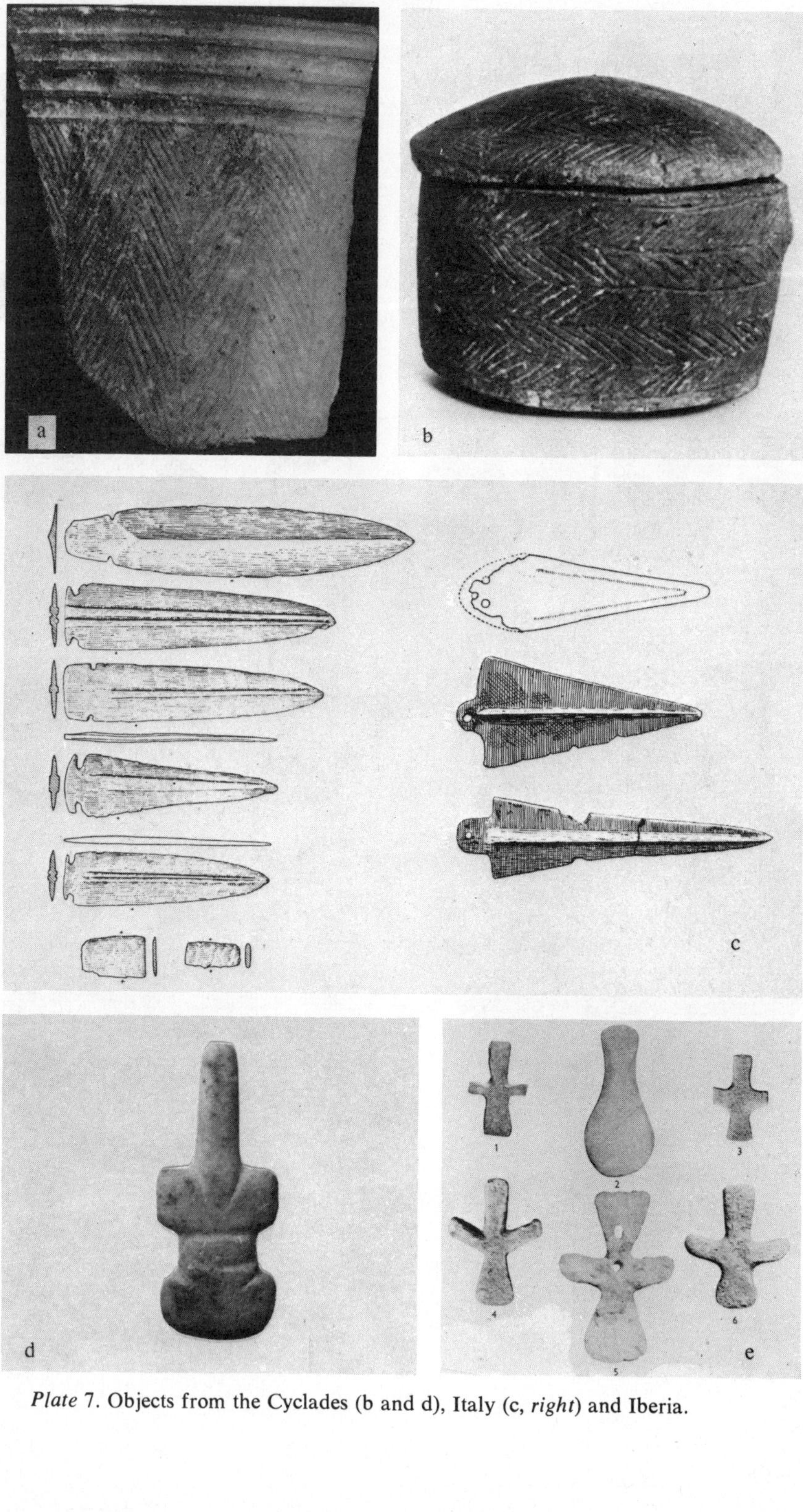

Plate 7. Objects from the Cyclades (b and d), Italy (c, *right*) and Iberia.

Plate 8. Pottery from Italy (c and e), Iberia (a) and the Aegean.

3) The Characterisation of Obsidian and its Application to the Mediterranean Region (with J. R. Cann)

In 1964 the techniques of trace-element analysis had not yet successfully been applied to the characterisation of archaeological materials. The problems of the British faience beads had been approached in this way, but without conclusive results, in a pioneering paper by Stone and Thomas (1956). Dr Cann and I were very lucky therefore, that obsidian proved so suitable a material for characterisation by trace-element methods. The underlying geochemical reasons for this have been reviewed by Dixon (1977).

The method used here, optical spectroscopy, has since been supplemented in research on Mediterranean obsidians by fission-track analysis (Durrani *et al.* 1971), and by neutron activation analysis (Aspinall *et al.* 1972 ; Hallam *et al.* 1976). Work of a more comprehensive nature has been carried out in the Aegean (Renfrew *et al.* 1965) and in the west Mediterranean (Hallam *et al.* 1976).

In general the results reported here hold up well, although it is now clear that two of the natural sources of obsidian provisionally indicated on fig. 1 do not exist: there is no source at H (Mt Hargitta in Romania—see Nandris 1974) nor at M (the Afyon area of Turkey—see Renfrew *et al.* 1966). Moreover Keller (1970) has shown that two of the Lipari obsidian outcrops were formed since prehistoric times.

Comparable work on obsidian has now been carried out in several parts of the world, and characterisation by trace-element analysis has become a standard archaeological research technique.

BIBLIOGRAPHY

Aspinall, A., Feather, S. W. and Renfrew, C. (1972) Neutron activation analysis of Aegean obsidians. *Nature, London* 237, 333–4.

Dixon, J. E. (1977) Obsidian in the Mediterranean and Near East, a geologically oriented review, in Taylor, R. E. (ed.) *Advances in Obsidian Glass Studies.* Park Ridge N.J. ; Noyes, 288–333.

Durrani, S. A., Khan, H. A., Taj, M. and Renfrew, C. (1971) Obsidian source identification by fission track analysis. *Nature, London* 233, 242–5.

Hallam, B. R., Warren, S. E. and Renfrew, C. (1976) Obsidian in the Western Mediterranean. *Proc. Prehist. Soc.* 42, 85–110.

Keller, J. (1970) Datierung der Obsidiane und Bimsstoffe von Lipari. *Neues Jb. Geol. Paläont. Mitt.* 2, 90–101.

Nandris, J. (1975) A re-consideration of the south-east European sources of archaeological obsidian. *Bull. Inst. Archaeol.* 12, 71–94.

Renfrew, C., Cann, J. R. and Dixon, J. E. (1965) Obsidian in the Aegean. *Annu. Brit. School Archaeol. Athens* 60, 225–47.

Renfrew, C., Dixon, J. E. and Cann, J. R. (1966) Obsidian and early cultural contact in the Near East. *Proc. Prehist. Soc.* 32, 30–72.

Stone, J. F. S. and Thomas, L. C. (1956) The use and distribution of faience in the Near East and prehistoric Europe. *Proc. Prehist. Soc.* 22, 37–84.

THE CHARACTERISATION OF OBSIDIAN AND ITS APPLICATION TO THE MEDITERRANEAN REGION

Evidence of contact between cultural groups is of great importance to the study of prehistory. Although the development of absolute dating methods has decreased our dependence on the discovery of such contacts for chronology, they are essential material when the origin and spread of culture is being studied. In the past, cultural contacts have generally been demonstrated by typological similarities of artefacts, but unfortunately many typological comparisons are open to discussion, and it can be exceedingly difficult to be certain of direct contact by this means alone.

The importance in this respect of the study of raw materials used in places far from their place of origin and presumably deliberately imported has long been realised. Recently more attention has been paid to the careful characterisation of such materials ; the detection, that is, of properties of the specimen under study which are characteristic of material from particular sources. By this means it is often possible to assign a source to a given specimen. The petrological identification of British neolithic stone axes is perhaps the most comprehensive archaeological characterisation study yet undertaken. Demonstrations of trading links made by such methods, if based on a sure identification and a comprehensive survey of possible sources, are not open to the criticism and doubt which may be directed at typological similarities. The variety of techniques now available for the analysis and identification of materials makes this field a promising one for the archaeologist.

Obsidian, a volcanic glass, fractures conchoidally in the same manner as flint, and was widely used in Neolithic and Early Bronze Age times for the making of tools. It is found in many, but not in all, regions of recent volcanic activity, so that there are, for example, about 25 sources in the Mediterranean area. There are, generally speaking, enough sources in the regions in which obsidian is found to make detailed characterisation worthwhile, for an extremely restricted origin would render further identification superfluous, as recognition of the material would be characterisation enough. On the other hand there are not so many sources as to make the task an impossible one, as would probably be the case with flint. The material thus seems a very suitable one for a characterisation study. Characterisation of the sources in a particular region makes it possible to assign a place of origin to an excavated artefact after the analysis of its properties, and thus enables the postulation of trading links.

The world has many sources of obsidian, in New Zealand, North America, Mexico, Japan and Iceland, for example, and most of them were used in prehistoric times. It was decided, however, to limit the area of study to the Mediterranean lands and those nearby areas such as Hungary, Persia and Abyssinia which might have supplied the Mediterranean cultures. The method described below should be applicable to other regions where obsidian is found, and it is hoped that the present article may suggest applications to such industries as those of Central and North America.

Obsidian

Obsidian is a volcanic glass formed when certain sorts of lava are cooled in circumstances preventing their crystallising properly. The lava must be very viscous, a condition which is only met when there is a large proportion of silica present. Thus not all lavas can form obsidian, and there are many volcanoes, such as Vesuvius or those of Hawaii, where the lavas have never been sufficiently rich in silica for its formation to take place.

Age also limits the availability of obsidian, for with exposure to weathering and to the hot ground water often present in volcanic regions, it first becomes hydrated, losing its property of conchoidal fracture, and later completely crystalline. Nearly all obsidians of pre-Tertiary date have by now lost their glassy properties, particularly that of conchoidal fracture, and most of those considered here date from the Quaternary. This restriction very conveniently limits the number of sources which have to be considered which would otherwise be very numerous. The hydration process is the basis of obsidian dating (Friedmann and Smith 1960), but is not relevant to the characterisation of the material.

The sources now known in the Mediterranean region are shown in fig. 1. The adequacy of cover depends entirely on the state of the geological know-

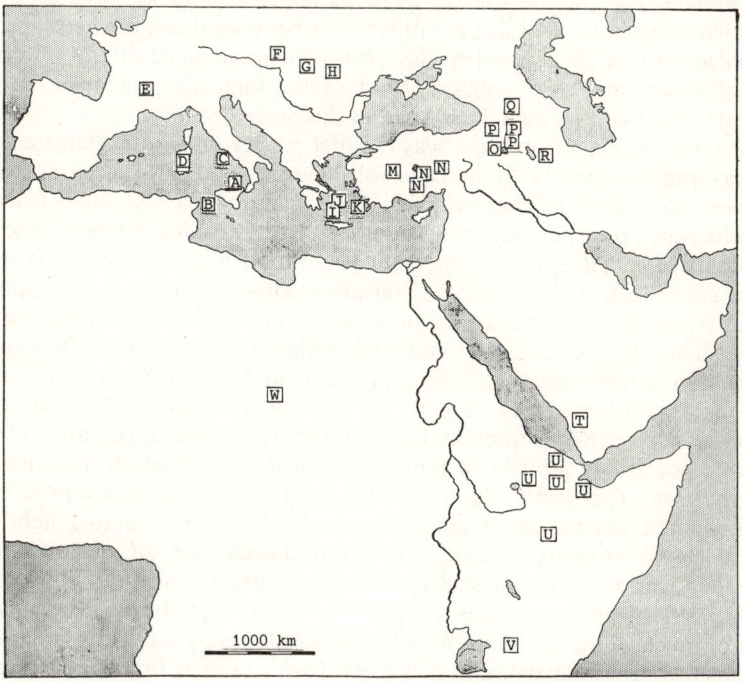

Figure 1. Obsidian sources in and near the Mediterranean region.
A Lipari; B Pantelleria; C Palmarola; D Sardinia; E Auvergne; F Slovakia; G Tokay region in Hungary; H Mt Hargitta in Rumania; I Melos; J Antiparos; K Giali; M Afyon; N South Anatolian sources; O Lake Van; P Armenian sources; Q Caucasus; R Lake Urmia; T Arabia; U Abyssinian sources; V Kenya; W Tibesti.

ledge of the particular regions. The map should be comprehensive for Europe, but several new sources have recently been reported in West Anatolia, and the extent of those in the south and in Armenia is not yet known. No sources are yet known from Iraq, Syria, the Lebanon, Jordan or Israel, but there are several volcanic districts in this region, such as the Jebel Druz, and the possibility of new sources being discovered cannot be ruled out. A source in Abyssinia was first mentioned by Pliny, and there are several more there as well as in Kenya and south-west Arabia, so that the map is rather schematic for those regions. The outline, however, does seem fairly clear and probably will not need major alteration. Obsidian tools are found with a much wider distribution than of the sources, and it is the problems so created that this paper sets out to investigate.

Method

The adequate characterisation of obsidian entails finding a property or set of properties of obsidian which are the same, or nearly so, for specimens from the same source and which differ between obsidians from different sources ; properties, that is, homogeneous within sources and heterogeneous between them. It is necessary therefore to test properties of obsidians extensively in a single source area to establish the likely range of properties, the homogeneity of the source, while as many sources as possible should be tried in order to establish the differences between them, the heterogeneity between sources. This problem has been recognised since the magnitude of the obsidian trade was realised. Most of the methods previously used to examine the material have been tried in the present study.

The appearance of obsidian was the first property to be investigated, and it was found possible to describe obsidians adequately in terms of six properties: colour in transmitted light, colour in reflected light, fracture, translucency, transparency with internal structure, and lustre. These are summarised in table II. In general it was found that appearance is not a good guide to the provenance of obsidian, although when it is supported by analyses of the kind later undertaken, meaningful statements can be made. Thus Evans (1921, 87 and 412) believed that the white spherulites present in a rare variety of obsidian found at Minoan Knossos indicated an origin in Lipari. This is certainly not so, as analyses 77 and 68 of material selected from finds at Knossos for its spotted appearance clearly show. They fall in group I of table II, while the specimens from Lipari lie in group 4a. The small island of Giali in the Dodecanese seems a more likely source. On the other hand, a green colour in transmitted light is a characteristic property, although not a necessary one, of obsidian from Pantelleria, Lake Van, Abyssinia, and other sources contributing to groups 4b, 4c and 4d of the division established below. Equally the pearly lustre seen in much of the obsidian from Melos is only rarely met elsewhere (as in specimen 8, from Lipari), and if it is used with caution in a specific region it can be of some use.

The examination of thin sections of obsidian with the petrological microscope is not satisfactory, for the better the obsidian, the fewer and smaller are the crystals it contains, and it is through their study alone that character can be ascribed. No systematic variation between areas was observed using this method. The refractive index and density were considered by Wainwright (1927) and Frankfort (1927, p. 190). They were determined for the first 55 obsidians studied here. Certainly there is some systematic variation between sources, the green obsidians of groups 4b, 4c, and 4d with, for example, a rather higher refractive index and density than the others, but overlap is considerable, and the method was not considered worth pursuing.

One of the standard methods for investigating rocks is the process of ordinary chemical analysis by which the proportions of the major constituents present in the rocks are determined. This method has been used by Georgiades (1956) for the Aegean sources of Melos, Antiparos and Giali, and for these a meaningful difference was found, although that between Melos and Giali was only slight. But the method is unlikely to achieve a high degree of differentiation when applied to a larger area, because the major element composition of obsidian falls within a very restricted field. It is, in addition, time consuming, and has the severe disadvantage of requiring several grams of material from each sample.

Cornaggia, Fussi and d'Agnolo (1962 and 1963) have tried several of these methods, finding most of them inconclusive. They decided finally to rely on analyses of the manganese and phosphorus contents, and drew a distinction between the obsidians of Palmarola, Lipari, Melos and Pantelleria in this way. They conclude, by application of this method, that the obsidian used in Malta was largely of Melian origin, but this is at variance with the results obtained in the present investigation.

The method found most satisfactory was that of spectrographic analysis. By means of the optical spectograph the amounts of trace elements (elements present in proportions between one part per million and about one per cent) are measured. Only a small fragment of sample, 60 milligrams in weight, is required for burning, which is naturally an advantage when artefacts have to be sampled. The method is essentially that used by Stone and Thomas (1956) for faience, and by various workers for the analysis of metal artefacts (Britton and Richards [1963], Aitken [1961, 160]). The instrument employed was the Hilger-Littrow E 478 spectograph belonging to the Department of Mineralogy and Petrology, in Cambridge. Details of the method used have been given by Nockolds and Allen (1953). All of the samples were run with a palladium internal standard to check consistency of burning, and, in order to eliminate systematic errors due to variation from plate to plate, the order of burning was rearranged so that samples from the same region were distributed on several plates. Calibration curves were determined using a range of standard trace elements mixed with a powder of standard intermediate rock composition. Measurements of the intensities of the spectral lines of particular elements were thus converted to parts per million of the elements in the specimen. Quantitative values for 16 elements were determined for each specimen, and the results are given in table II. Beryllium and scandium were sought, but detected in only a few specimens and in very small quantities. Several other elements were below the limit of sensitivity in all the samples tested. Some contamination was introduced in about half the specimens by crushing in a stellite mortar. Thus the values for chromium, nickel, cobalt and copper, actually present in very small quantities, were clearly incorrect and have been omitted.

Interpretation of Results

When the specimens from natural sources are listed (those specimens marked with an asterisk in table II) certain features are apparent. Comparison of the analyses for a given pair of sources may show little significant difference for some trace elements while for others there is a very marked distinction. Compare, for instance, the barium, zirconium and niobium contents of the obsidians from Melos, Lipari and Pantelleria. Barium and zirconium are the two elements showing the greatest differences in this way, and fig. 2 is a graph on a logarithmic scale of the content of barium against that of zirconium for all the specimens analysed.

These analyses suggest a division of the specimens into six major groups which are indicated in fig. 2. Other pairs of elements can be used to simplify the picture and corroborate it where necessary; thus iron and strontium have been used to separate the Sardinian obsidians forming group 2a from the Anatolian ones of group 2b. Niobium and yttrium are similarly used in fig. 3 for the subdivision of group 4, for while some separation in this group is achieved with barium and zirconium, it is not in itself very adequate.

The basis for these divisions is in the first instance an empirical one.

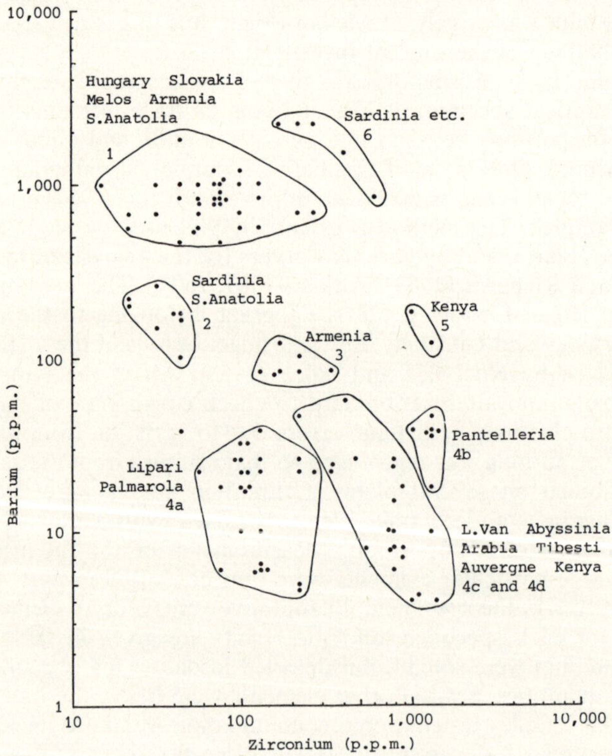

Figure 2. Graph showing the barium and zirconium content of all the specimens analysed, and the division into groups.

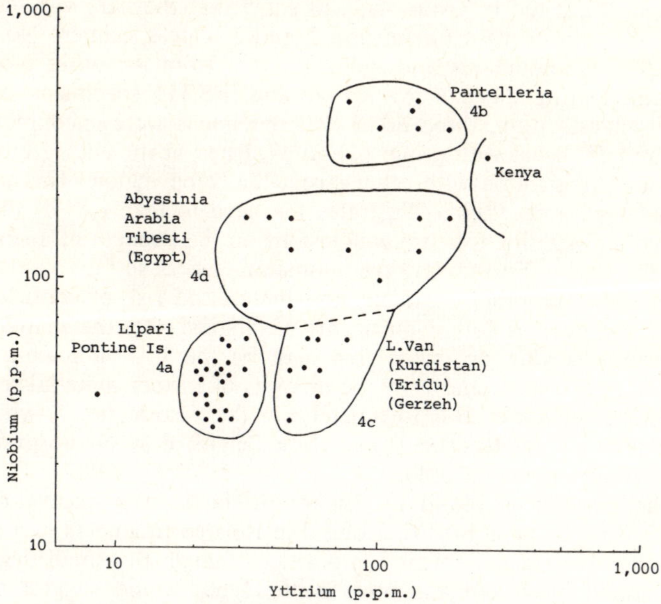

Figure 3. Graph showing the niobium and yttrium content of specimens in group 4 and the division into sub-groups.

Specimens from a single source have a restricted range of composition, while many different sources may be adequately distinguished. Clearly too wide a variation within a single source would make the method impracticable, and it is important that specimens of a single flow and from a single region should have similar composition (Burkitt, 1953, 26). It was decided to test this important point at the outset, and specimens collected from different locations in Lipari and Vulcano where obsidian occurs naturally were selected. These are shown in fig. 4. A comparison of analyses

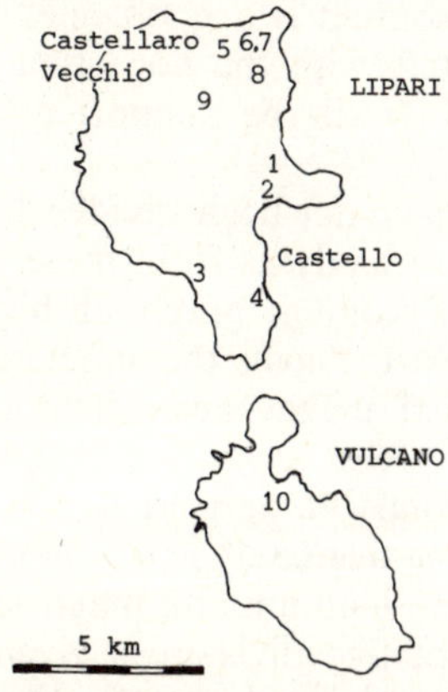

Figure 4. Sketch map showing the location of sources sampled in Lipari and Vulcano. Numbers 11 and 12 are artefacts from Castellaro Vecchio, number 13 from the Lipari Castello.

of numbers 1 to 10, listed in group 4a, will show that they are very consistent, which is again brought out in figs. 2 and 3. One specimen, No. 7, listed in group 6, is anomalous and quite different from the other pieces from the island. During the course of analysing the 115 specimens considered in this investigation, three other odd specimens were encountered (numbers 67 and 71, listed with group 6, and 87, listed at the end of group 4). They are not comparable with others from the same region. This proportion is not at all great, but it illustrates the need to take two or three specimens from a given site, for firm conclusions on the strength of a single analysis may be unwise. Fortunately the anomalous pieces so far found are different from all of the other obsidians and there is no risk of confusion. When an odd specimen is found on an archaeological site, the matter is obviously worth following up, since this may be the first indication of material from a new source, and only the analysis of further material from the site can make this clear. But fortunately, in the case of no. 7, which, like 6 and 8, is from the Rocche Rosse (Mte Pelato) flow on north-east Lipari this possibility does not hold.

Three further specimens found on Lipari, artefacts from excavations, were analysed. It might be argued that burial in isolated fragments in a wet soil might change the trace element composition, though the small degree of hydration found by Friedmann and Smith (1960) would suggest that this is not likely to be the case, but the results show that the artefacts fall well within the range of composition of the geological specimens.

Specimens from Sardinia fall into two separate groups, 2a and 6, and a similar effect is shown by specimens from Armenia, South Anatolia and Kenya, but this does not affect the clarity of the division into groups and sub-groups. In general the high degree of conformity for the Lipari area is supported by the results from other sources.

While the validity of the method depends largely on the consistency of analyses from each source, its value lies in the differences between those from different sources, which allow the sources to be distinguished. These criteria can then be used to ascribe the raw material of artefacts to specific sources. In most cases the separation between sources is a good one, and ten groups or sub-groups are at present suggested, with the hope that the additional very tentative subdivision of group 1 will be supported and clarified by further analyses.

So far the samples from the Pontine Islands have not been divided from those from Lipari because of the small number of analyses from these, but in fact they occupy a region on the barium/zirconium graph of higher zirconium and lower barium than those of Lipari. Again the inadequate representation of Abyssinia, Arabia and Tibesti makes any attempt to separate them unwise at present.

It should be noted that the separation of groups 4c and 4d is not yet entirely secure, and that although in group 1 some degree of separation can be achieved using the elements strontium, yttrium, niobium and magnesium this cannot be regarded as certain yet. The tentative division is given in tables I and II, and when more results become available the application of the statistical technique of discriminatory analysis should bring better definition.

Although the division into groups thus achieved is an empirical one, it is in basic agreement with petrological theory. The concept of petrographic provinces, the occurrence of rocks of the same general type in a particular area, is well established, and it has been often observed that trace elements show some consistency within a province. The high concentration of zirconium in group 4b from Pantelleria is not unexpected, corresponding to the known properties of pantelleritic obsidians (Carmichael 1962; Zies 1960) while that of groups 4c and 4d corresponds to obsidians of peralkaline type. Groups 2, 3 and 4a are obsidians of alkaline type, while group 1 is composed of calcalkaline obsidians. The method thus allows the separation of obsidians into several groups on the basis of their trace element composition, in a manner that could be to some extent anticipated by petrological theory. The interpretation of these groups, however, and their implication for prehistory is purely an archaeological matter.

Archaeological Interpretation

Many consequences follow from the division of obsidians into the groups and sub-groups listed in table II. In the ideal case, where each source is the single member of a distinct sub-group, the analysis of an artefact would allow an unequivocal decision on the origin of the raw material. In practice, as explained above, at least two or three artefacts should be analysed from a single site. At first sight the overlap between sub-groups that occur, for instance in group 1 or perhaps between 4c and 4d is a considerable obstacle. But sometimes chemically similar sources are geographically so far apart, or so remote, that confusion is unlikely. Thus even had it not been possible to distinguish sub-groups 2a and 2b, the interpretation would have been easy, since Sardinia is not a likely source for finds in the Near East, nor South Anatolia a plausible provenance for material in Sardinia.

The use of distribution maps is a help for some of the problems that arise, but until sufficient results are available to plot a period by period distribution, some features may be obscured. Moreover, on sites served by more than one obsidian source it is desirable to establish the proportions from each through the successive phases. Some of these points are brought out in the succeeding regional discussion. In some regions the various problems arising are best left until more analyses are available, but it is hoped that the examples given will illustrate the potentialities of the method.

WEST MEDITERRANEAN

The method has given particularly clear results in this area since all the sources relevant fall into different groups (see fig. 5). The source in the Auvergne probably does not have obsidian of quality suitable for artefacts. But those of Lipari and the Pontine Islands (cf. Buchner 1949), of Pantelleria, and of Sardinia (cf. Puxeddu 1955–7) were much used in prehistoric times. The important source in Melos is considered here for convenience (Bosanquet 1904). The origin of the obsidian used in the neolithic of Malta (the Temple Cultures and their predecessors) has long been a controversial matter. On the grounds of appearance two varieties would seem to be present, one with the greenish colour in transmitted light that has proved often to be a property of group 4b, 4c and 4d. The other is black and the recent work of Cornaggia, Fussi and d'Agnolo (1962 and 1963) suggested that it

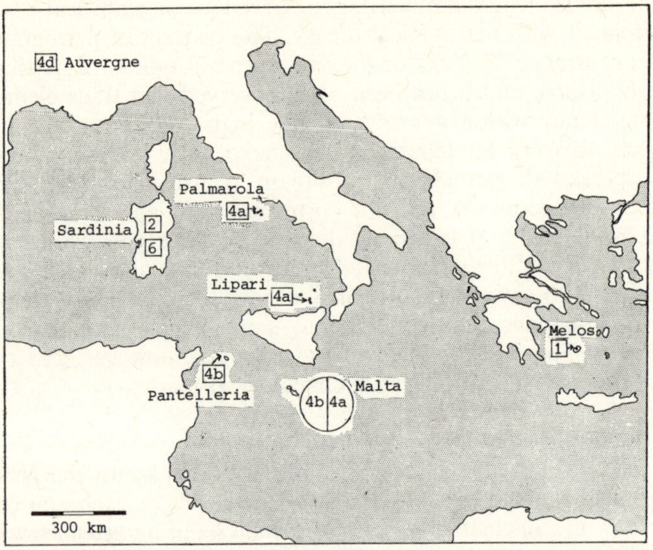

Figure 5. Maps of sources (indicated by squares) in the West Mediterranean. The numbers indicate the groups to which the obsidians belong.

is of Melian origin, although it does not show the pearly lustre often seen in Melian obsidian. The recent excavations at Skorba in Malta (Trump 1961) produced quantities of obsidian in a clear succession from the earliest Neolithic to the end of the Neolithic period and afforded the opportunity of making a period by period study of the Maltese obsidian. This is the ideal in any stratified site where more than one obsidian source is operating. Dr Trump kindly provided samples from several phases, of both apparent varieties, together with figures for the occurrence at the site of each. These are given in fig. 6. The analyses (see table II, groups 4a and 4b) demonstrate that at Skorba obsidian was used from both Pantelleria and Lipari from the Ghar Dalam phase (impressed ware Neolithic) onwards. The 100 per cent correlation in the analyses between origin and appearance suggests that appearance may safely be taken as an indication of origin for the specimens not analysed.

It is surprising to find Malta using two sources from this early date, probably near the beginning of the 4th millennium BC, and perhaps transport at that time was more efficient than has been thought. The use of Pantellerian obsidian in Neolithic times is also rather unexpected since no Neolithic remains are yet known from the island, although these must now be sought. It is interesting too that there is a sharp decline in the proportion of Pantellerian obsidian used in the Red Skorba phase which, in Dr Trump's words, 'although negative evidence, must be significant'. Such a drop might be related to the stronger links at this time, indicated by the similarity of the Red Skorba ware and the pottery of the Diana phase in Lipari, links which are less apparent in the pottery of the preceding Grey Skorba period. But the possibility of the re-use of obsidian makes it unwise to make over-precise chronological equations between utilisation and cultural contact.

GREY			GREEN					
No.found	No.tested	Result	No.found	No.tested	Result	Cultural Phase	Total Found	% Pantelleria
96	2	4a, 4a	21	2	4b, 4b	Ghar Dalam	117	17.9
29	2	4a, 4a	11	2	4b, 4b	Grey Skorba	40	27.5
63			1			Red Skorba	64	1.7
23	2	4a, 4a	3			Zebbuġ	26	11.5
2			0			Mġarr	2	-
33			4			Ġgantija	37	10.8
3			1			Saflieni	4	-
8	2	4a, 4a	0			Tarxien	8	-

Figure 6. Table showing the utilisations of obsidian at Skorba by periods. The grey obsidian is from Lipari, and the green from Pantelleria.

Other sites in the West Mediterranean may be expected to give an equally clear picture. The total absence of obsidian tools in Iberia is perhaps surprising, and none are yet reported from the coast of North Africa. But the presence of obsidian in West Greece, in Dalmatia, throughout Italy and in South France may give useful indications of cultural links.

EAST MEDITERRANEAN

The application of the method to the Aegean is rendered more complex by the difficulties involved in dividing group 1 as well as the uncertainties surrounding the west Anatolian sources. At present the indications are that early neolithic Knossos was importing obsidian from Melos in the 6th millennium BC. Melos is indeed the nearest source to Crete, but the conclusion has serious implications for the Cyclades since until recently no indications of Neolithic occupation had been found in the islands. The probability that the 'liparite' of Minoan Knossos is derived from the island of Giali has been mentioned above. It is certainly of group 1 and thus cannot derive from Lipari. The low percentage of calcium noticed by Georgiades (1956) for the obsidian of Giali is seen in the analyses of numbers 77 and 68, listed as group 1(a), in table II. The source in Antiparos is not an important one (and preliminary results of tests on samples from here shows that it belongs to group 4a). More analyses are to be conducted with the aim of giving statistical support to the sub-group divisions and to indicate the origin of obsidian in such contexts as pre-pottery Neolithic in Thessaly.

The Near Eastern sites for which samples have been analysed, together with the known sources are shown in fig. 7. Although samples are available from very few sources in Anatolia, the analysis of artefacts from the source regions serves considerably to amplify the picture. No sources are yet known between Anatolia and Arabia, west of the Zagros mountains. The nearest sources to Jericho are thus distant, and it was of some interest to investigate the origin of the blades and chips found there in the pre-pottery Neolithic 'A' levels (numbers 50, 51 and 76, listed with group 2b). They are all of group 2b and compare closely with specimens from Neolithic Mersin and from surface collection at Bor and Gazi in the volcanic region of Kayseri, north of Mersin, where sources are known to exist. Unless a natural source

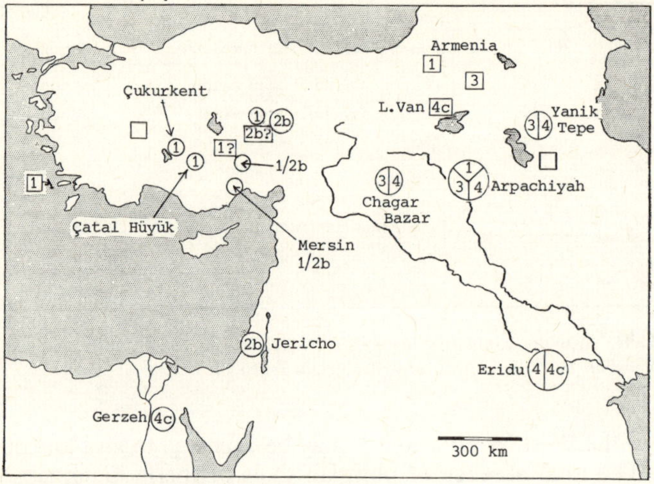

Figure 7. Map of the Near East showing the sources of obsidian (indicated by squares) and its utilisation. Circles indicate sites for which obsidian has been analysed. The numbers indicate the group or groups represented.

can be located much nearer at hand, the conclusion is inescapable that Jericho was importing obsidian from the Kayseri region of south Anatolia in the 7th millennium BC.

The obsidian of Lake Van was likewise exported over considerable distances, certainly in Halafian times and probably far earlier. It is found at Chagar Bazar, Arpachiyah and probably as far south at Eridu (numbers 69 and 70 listed in group 4c). The complexity of the situation is illustrated by Arpachiyah, which at this time was importing obsidian from Lake Van (group 4c), from the source in eastern Armenia also supplying Yanik Tepe (group 3), and possibly from a further unlocated source (number 79, listed at the end of group 1). Once again more work, particularly in the source areas, will be needed to fill in the picture in detail, but the outlines at least now seem clear.

EGYPT

The source of the Egyptian obsidian which is already found from predynastic times, was held by Lucas (1948) to be Abyssinia, while Wainwright (1927) advocated Lake Van, then the only source known in Anatolia. But the sources in south Anatolia supplying Mersin and indeed Jericho must also be taken into account.

Three of the five specimens here analysed fall in group 4d, one from Gerzeh is in group 4c, and there is one in group 6 which may be comparable with a specimen from Eritrea. Unfortunately the division between sub-groups 4c and 4d is not entirely satisfactory, so that it cannot be asserted that three specimens are from Abyssinia or Arabia and one from Lake Van. On the contrary, a supply from Lake Van is improbable on other grounds, for no group 4c material (which is characteristically green in colour) has yet been identified west of Chagar Bazar. Moreover one might expect material of groups 2 or 3 from the sources in south Anatolia to reach

Egypt together with that from further east. But of the twelve further pieces of Egyptian obsidian so far examined, although not yet analysed, none has the grey or colourless appearance in transmitted light which would suggest such an origin.

Thus a consideration in terms of distribution can be of value when the group division is not secure, and the analysis of further artefacts from the regions between Egypt and Lake Van can be expected to decide the matter one way or another. At present, however, Abyssinia or Arabia are the more likely sources even though they are in fact more distant from the lower Nile than is Lake Van.

Prospect

The principal concern in the present paper has been to illustrate the scope of the method. Some topics have not been touched on—such as the results from Hungary, Slovakia and Vinča. Indeed more analyses are certainly needed to solve many of the problems presented. Every attempt was made, however, to obtain as wide a range of specimens as possible, so that although the existing groups may be further subdivided later, it is not likely that many more will be added.

It is hoped that further research will finally solve the problem of the Egyptian obsidian. And when the Anatolian sources are better known, a very clear picture should emerge for the Near East and probably Iran, although a statistical treatment of results may be necessary. The Aegean is at present being studied in greater detail, and again suggests a surprising scale and scope of trade in Neolithic times. Indeed the most surprising result of the present work, apart from the early use of such sources as Pantelleria and Melos, has been the light it has thrown on the efficiency of early prehistoric transport. [1964]

ACKNOWLEDGEMENTS

Our first debt is to Dr S. R. Nockolds of the Department of Mineralogy and Petrology, Cambridge, for permission to use the Department's spectroscope, and to Mr R. Allen for much assistance in its use. We are grateful to all those who have supplied us with material for analysis, for one of the principal concerns has been to obtain suitable specimens. Many are acknowledged in table I, and we hope that others who have supplied material not yet analysed, and whose help will be specifically acknowledged when it is, will accept our present thanks. The specimens from the Museum of Archaeology and Ethnology, Cambridge, were supplied through the courtesy of Dr G. H. S. Bushnell and Miss M. Cra'ster ; those from the British Museum (Natural History) by the kindness of the Dr P. M. Game and Dr G. F. Claringbull, and those from the Petrie Collection, University College, London, through that of Dr A. J. Arkell.

BIBLIOGRAPHY

Aitken, M. J. (1961) *Physics and Archaeology*.

Bosanquet, R. C. (1904) The Obsidian Trade. *Excavations at Phylakopi in Melos* (Society for the Promotion of Hellenic Studies Supplementary Paper IV).

Britton, D. and Richards, E. E. (1963) Optical Emission Spectroscopy and the Study of Metallurgy in the European Bronze Age. Brothwell, D. and Higgs, E. (eds.) *Science in Archaeology*.

Buchner, G. (1949) Ricerche sui giacimenti e sulle industrie di ossidiana in Italia I. *Riv. Sci. Preist.* (Fasc. 1–2), 162.

Burkitt, M. C. (1953) Note in Garstang, J., *Prehistoric Mersin*, p. 26.

Carmichael, I. S. E. (1962) Pantelleritic liquids and their phenocrysts. *Miner. Mag.* 33, 109.

Cornaggia Castiglioni, O., Fussi, F. and d'Agnolo, M. (1962–3) Indagini sulla provenienza dell'ossidiana in uso nelle industrie italiane I and II. *Atti Soc. Ital. Sci. Nat.*

Evans, Sir A. (1921) *The Palace of Minos,* vol. I.

Frankfort, H. (1927) Studies in Early Pottery of the Near East, Part II: Europe and the Aegean and their Earliest Interrelations. *R. Anthrop. Inst. Occasional Paper* 8.

Friedmann, I. and Smith, R. L. (1960) The Method of Obsidian Dating. *Amer. Antiq.* 25, 476.

Geordiades, A. N. (1956) Recherches sur les obsidiennes de Grèce. *Prakt. Akad. Athinon* 31, 150.

Lucas, A. (1948) *Ancient Egyptian Materials and Industries.* 3rd ed., p. 473.

Nockolds, S. R. and Allen, R. (1953) The geochemistry of some igneous rock series, I. *Geochim. et Cosmochim. Acta* 4, 105.

Puxeddu, C. (1957) Giacimenti di ossidiana del Monte Arci in Sardegna e sua irradazione. *Studi Sardi* 14–15.

Stone, J. F. S. and Thomas, L. C. (1956) The use and distribution of Faience in the Near East and Prehistoric Europe. *PPS* 22, 37.

Trump, D. (1961) Skorba, Malta and the Mediterranean. *Antiq.* 35, 300.

Wainwright, G. A. (1927) Obsidian. *Ancient Egypt* (1927), Part III.

Zies, E. G. (1960) Chemical analyses of two pantellerites. *J. Petrology* 1, 304.

Figs. 1, 4, 5 and 7 supplement the information in the columns headed District and Site.)

Abbreviations: G.H.S.: Geological hand specimen; BM: British Museum (Natural History); MAAC: Museum of Archaeology and Ethnology, Cambridge; MP: Museum of Mineralogy and Petrology, Cambridge; U.C.: University College, London.

Group	No.	District	Site	Cultural context	Object	Collected by:	Received from:	Reference	No.
1(a)	19	Hungary	Tolcsva, Tokay region	(Source)	G.H.S.	Not known	BM	BM 67440	19
,,	58	,,	Mad, Tokay region	(Source)	G.H.S.	Not known	BM	BM 46034	58
,,	59	,,	Tolcsva, Tokay region	(Source)	G.H.S.	Not known	BM	BM 67439	59
,,	22	,,	Derekegyhaza Farm near Borsod	Bükk culture, Early Neolithic	Blade	Excavations of L. Clarke and S. Tompa, 1927	MAAC		22
,,	60	,,	Derekegyhaza Farm near Borsod	Bükk culture, Early Neolithic	Blade	Excavations of L. Clarke and S. Tompa, 1927	MAAC		60
,,	62	Jugoslavia	Vinča	8.7 metres, probably Starčevo culture	Blade	Excavations of M. M. Vasić	MAAC	38.467	62
,,	94	Hungary	Herpaly	Neolithic	Blade	L. Clarke	MAAC	28.267	94
,,	95	,,	Herpaly	Neolithic	Blade	L. Clarke	MAAC	28.267	95
1(b)	21	Slovakia	Hlinik, near Banska Stiavnica	(Source)	G.H.S.	Not known	MP, Schemnitz collection	Slide 88433	21
,,	61	,,	Hlinik, near Banska Stiavnica	(Source)	G.H.S.	Not known, 1892	MP		61
1(c)	25	Melos	West of Adhamas	(Source)	G.H.S.	Miss V. Seton-Williams, 1959	The same		25
,,	26	,,	West of Adhamas	Unstratified	Flake	Miss V. Seton-Williams, 1959	The same		26
,,	23	,,	Phylakopi	Unstratified	Core	Mrs K. Bolton, 1955	The same		23
,,	24	,,	Phylakopi	Unstratified	Flake	Miss V. Seton-Williams, 1959	The same		24
,,	27	Greece	Tiryns	Unstratified	Blade	Not known	BM	BM 1927, 1186	27
,,	63	,,	Paros	Unstratified	Flake	L. Whibley, 1906	Fitzwilliam Mus., Cambridge		63
,,	36	Crete	Knossos	Bottom of Early Neolithic I	Blade	Excavations of Professor J. D. Evans, 1960	The same	N 60 A 23	36
,,	37	,,	Knossos	Early Neolithic II	Flake	Excavations of Professor J. D. Evans, 1960	The same	N 60 XY6B	37
,,	38	,,	Knossos	Late Neolithic	Flake	Excavations of Professor J. D. Evans, 1957	The same	N 57 B 1	38
,,	64	,,	Knossos	Bottom of Early Neolithic I	Chip	Excavations of Professor J. D. Evans, 1960	The same	N 60 AC 25	64
,,	65	,,	Knossos	Bottom of Early Neolithic I	Flake	Excavations of Professor J. D. Evans, 1960	The same	N 60 AC 26	65

TABLE I continued.

Group	No.	District	Site	Cultural context	Object	Collected by:	Received from:	Reference	No.
1(d)	77	Crete	Knossos	Unstratified, probably late Middle Minoan or early Late Minoan	Bowl fragment	Excavations of Mr Sinclair Hood	The same		77
,,	68	,,	Pseira	Unstratified	Core	Mr M. C. Burkitt	MAAC	55.68c	68
1(e)	28	Armenia	Kars district	(Source)	G.H.S.	Not known	BM	BM 1925 (925)	28
,,	29	,,	North of Erivan	(Source)	G.H.S.	Not known	BM	BM 1942, 33	29
1(f)	39	S. Anatolia	Mersin	Neolithic	Blade	Excavations of J. Garstang	Mr M. C. Burkitt		39
,,	41	,,	Çatal Hüyük	Early Neolithic	Blade	Excavations of Mr James Mellaart	The same		41
,,	42	,,	Çatal Hüyük	Early Neolithic	Blade	Excavations of Mr James Mellaart	The same		42
,,	43	,,	Çatal Hüyük	Early Neolithic	Blade	Excavations of Mr James Mellaart	The same		43
,,	44	,,	Çukurkent	Unstratified	Blade	Miss V. Seton-Williams, 1959	The same		44
,,	99	,,	Bor, near Melendiz Dag	Unstratified	Flake	Mr Gavin Brown, 1962	The same		99
,,	100	,,	Bor, near Melendiz Dag	Unstratified	Flake	Mr Gavin Brown, 1962	The same		100
,,	101	,,	Ekrek, near Kayseri	Unstratified	Flake	Mr Gavin Brown, 1962	The same		101
,,	103	,,	Hazarşah, near Kayseri	Unstratified	Lump	Mr Gavin Brown, 1962	The same		103
1	79	N. Iraq	Arpachiyah	Tell Halaf or Ubaid period	Blade	Excavations of Professor M. E. L. Mallowan	The same		79
2a	91	Sardinia	Crabi (Villaperuccio)	Unstratified	Lump	Dr Enrico Atzeni	The same		91
,,	93	,,	Puisteris (Mogoro)	Unstratified	Flake	Dr Enrico Atzeni	The same		93
2b	50	Jordan	Jericho	Pre-pottery Neolithic 'A' (VT)	Chip	Excavations of Dr K. M. Kenyon	The same	IpE 209.36	50
,,	51	,,	Jericho	Pre-pottery Neolithic 'A'	Chip	Excavations of Dr K. M. Kenyon	The same	PPi	51
,,	76	,,	Jericho	Pre-pottery Neolithic 'A'	Flake	Excavations of Dr K. M. Kenyon	The same		76
,,	40	S. Anatolia	Mersin	Neolithic	Blade	Excavations of J. Garstang	Mr M. C. Burkitt		40
,,	98	,,	Bor, near Melendiz Dag	Unstratified	Flake	Mr Gavin Brown, 1962	The same		98
,,	102	,,	Gazi, near Melendiz Dag	Unstratified	Flake	Mr D. H. French, 1962	Mr Gavin Brown		102
3	30	Armenia	Bayezid	(Source)	G.H.S.	Not known	BM	BM 93035	30
,,	46	N. Iraq	Arpachiyah	Tell Halaf or Ubaid period	Blade	Excavations of Professor M. E. L. Mallowan	The same		46

Group	No.	District	Site	Cultural context	Object	Collected by:	Received from:	Reference	No.
3	45	N.W. Persia	Yanik Tepe, near Tabriz	Uppermost Chalcolithic building level	Flake	Excavations of Dr Charles Burney	The same	YT MC5 286	45
,,	86	,,	Yanik Tepe, near Tabriz	Late Chalcolithic	Flake	Excavations of Dr Charles Burney	The same	YT MC8 286	86
,,	85	N.E. Syria	Chagar Bazar	Tell Halaf peiord	Flake	British Museum excavations	MAAC	36.165	85
,,	55	Greece	Rhodes	(?Source)	Chip	Not known	BM	BM 1936, 1246	55
4a	1	Lipari	Forgia Vecchia	(Source)	G.H.S.	Tempest Anderson, before 1905	MP		1
,,	2	,,	West of Mte. Rosa	(Source)	G.H.S.	G. W. Buttler	MP		2
,,	3	,,	West side of Mte. Guardia	(Source)	G.H.S.	Not known	MP		3
,,	4	,,	La Forbica, on S.E. coast	(Source)	G.H.S.	G. W. Buttler	MP	Slide 88358A	4
,,	5	,,	N.W. corner of Mte. Pelato	(Source)	G.H.S.	T. G. Bonney, 1908	MP		5
,,	6	,,	Rocche Rosse	(Source)	G.H.S.	T. G. Bonney, 1908	MP		6
,,	8	,,	Rocche Rosse	(Source)	G.H.S.	T. G. Bonney, 1908	MP		8
,,	9	,,	Mte. Chirica	(Source)	G.H.S.	H. B. Guppy	MP		9
,,	10	Lipari Is.	Vulcano, flow at N. of island	(Source)	G.H.S.	G. W. Buttler	MP	Slide 2368	10
,,	11	Lipari	Castellaro Vecchio	Castellaro Vecchio period	Core tool	Not known	Mlle. M. Cavalier		11
,,	12	,,	Castellaro Vecchio	Castellaro Vecchio period	Flake	Not known	Mlle. M. Cavalier		12
,,	13	,,	Lipari Castello	Capo Graziano period	Flake	Not known	Mlle. M. Cavalier		13
,,	52	Malta	Not known	Unstratified	Chip	Not known	BM	BM 1927, 1187	52
,,	106	,,	Skorba	Ghar Dalam phase	Blade	Excavations of Dr David Trump	The same	SB 4	106
,,	107	,,	Skorba	Ghar Dalam phase	Chip	Excavations of Dr David Trump	The same	FB 6	107
,,	110	,,	Skorba	Grey Skorba phase	Chip	Excavations of Dr David Trump	The same	Sk.FB 2	110
,,	111	,,	Skorba	Grey Skorba phase	Chip	Excavations of Dr David Trump	The same	Sk.HC 2	111
,,	112	,,	Skorba	Zebbug phase	Blade	Excavations of Dr David Trump	The same	Sk. B5	112
,,	113	,,	Skorba	Zebbug phase	Chip	Excavations of Dr David Trump	The same	Sk.OB6	113
,,	114	,,	Skorba	Tarxien phase	Blade	Excavations of Dr David Trump	The same	Sk.N3	114

TABLE I continued.

Group	No.	District	Site	Cultural context	Object	Collected by:	Received from:	Reference	No.
4a	115	Malta	Skorba	Tarxien phase	Chip	Excavations of Dr David Trump	The same	Sk.F6	115
”	17	Pontine Is.	Palmarola, Punta Vardella	(Source)	G.H.S.	Dr Georgio Büchner	The same		17
”	56	”	Palmarola, Punta Vardella	(Source)	G.H.S.	Dr Georgio Büchner	The same		56
”	18	”	Ponza	Unstratified	Blade	Dr Georgio Büchner	The same		18
”	57	”	Ponza	Unstratified	Blade	Dr Georgio Büchner	The same		57
4b	14	Pantelleria	La Mantua, W. of Punta Pozzalana	(Source)	G.H.S.	G. W. Buttler	MP	Slide 2606	14
”	15	”	La Mantua	(Source)	G.H.S.	G. W. Buttler	MP	Slide 29745	15
”	16	”	Not known	Unstratified	Flake	Not known	Mrs Peggy Guido		16
”	104	Malta	Skorba	Ghar Dalam phase	Lump	Excavations of Dr David Trump	The same	SB 6	104
”	105	”	Skorba	Ghar Dalam phase	Blade	Excavations of Dr David Trump	The same	CB 6	105
”	108	”	Skorba	Grey Skorba phase	Chip	Excavations of Dr David Trump	The same	Sk.FB2	108
”	109	”	Skorba	Grey Skorba phase	109	Excavations of Dr David Trump	The same	Sk.AB3	109
4c	81	Lake Van	South rim of crater, Nemrut Dag	(Source)	G.H.S.	Not known	BM	BM 1917, 631, (16)	81
”	82	”	Within crater, Nemrut Dag	(Source)	G.H.S.	Not known	BM	BM 1917, 631 (9)	82
”	83	”	South rim of crater, Nemrut Dag	(Source)	G.H.S.	Not known	BM	BM 1917, 631 (18)	83
”	47	N. Iraq	Arpachiyah	Tell Halaf or Ubaid period	Blade	Excavations of Professor M. E. L. Mallowan	The same		47
”	78	”	Arpachiyah	Tell Halaf or Ubaid period	Flake	Excavations of Professor M. E. L. Mallowan	The same		78
”	84	N.E. Syria	Chagar Bazar	Chalcolithic period	Blade	British Museum excavations, 1936	MAAC	37.264B	84
”	69	S. Iraq	Eridu	Unstratified	Blade	Not known	MAAC	A.S.1919	69
”	70	”	Eridu	Unstratified	Blade	Not known	MAAC	A.S.1919	70
”	75	Egypt	Gerzeh	Tomb 185, Predynastic Sequence Date 43–70	Chip	Excavations of Sir Flinders Petrie	Petrie Collection, University College, London	Petrie etc., Labyrinth of Gerzeh, p. 24	75
4d	31	Abyssinia	Abasurin, on border of Abyssinia and British Somaliland, S. of Zeilah	(Source)	G.H.S.	H. M. O'Byrne	MP	Slide 30419	31
”	66	”	Medje	(Source)	G.H.S.	Not known	BM	BM 1929, 1829, (23)	66
[illegible]	[illegible]		North of Waldia	(Source)	Flake	David Matthews	MAAC	[illegible]	[illegible]

Group	No.	District	Site	Cultural context	Object	Collected by:	Received from:	Reference	No.
4d	96	S.W. Arabia	Huraidha in the Hadhramut	Temple Area VI B, probably 6th to 1st century B.C.	Core	Excavations of Miss G. Caton Thompson	MAAC (51.615B)	*Soc. Ant. Res. Mem.*, XIII, 1944, p. 134	96
,,	97	,,	Huraidha in the Hadramut	Tomb A 6	Blade	Excavations of Miss G. Caton Thompson	MAAC	*Soc. Ant. Res. Mem.*, XIII, 1944, p. 134	97
,,	35	Kenya	Elementeita, Karandusi river	'Closing stages of Kamasian pluvial'	Hand axe	Excavations of Dr L. S. B. Leakey	MAAC	31.506e	35
,,	72	Egypt	Naqada	Tomb 499, Predynastic	Bead	Excavations of Sir Flinders Petrie	Petrie Collection, U.C., London	Petrie, *Ancient Egypt*, p. 88	72
,,	73	,,	Abydos	Royal Tombs, W 38, Protodynastic	Vase fragment	Excavations of Sir Flinders Petrie	Petrie Collection, U.C., London	Petrie, *Ancient Egypt*, p. 88	73
,,	49	,,	Abydos	Tomb 1606, Pre- or protodynastic	Blade	Egypt Exploration Society excavations, 1925–6	MAAC (26.543)	*J. Egypt. Arch.*, XVI, 1930, p. 214	49
4e	33	Tibesti	Enneri Tabitiou	(Source)	G.H.S.	P. W. Johnston	MP	Slide 87671	33
,,	53	,,	Enneri Tabitiou	(Source)	G.H.S.	P. W. Johnston	MP	Slide 87695	53
4	89	Auvergne	Des Chazes, Cantal	(Source)	G.H.S.	Not known	MP		89
,,	48	S. Iraq	Eridu	Unstratified	Blade	Oscar Rappach	MAAC	32.335F	48
,,	87	N.W. Persia	Yanik Tepe, near Tabriz	Early Bronze Age II	Flake	Excavations of Dr Charles Burney	The same	YT L3A 286	87
5	34	Kenya	Harvey's Farm, Naivasha	(Source)	G.H.S.	S. H. Reynolds	MP	Slide 23037	34
,,	54	,,	S.W. shore of Lake Naivasha	(Source)	G.H.S.	Not known	BM	BM 85753(18)	54
6a	90	Sardinia	Roja Cannas (Mogoro)	Unstratified	Lump	Dr Enrico Atzeni	The same		90
,,	92	,,	Puisteris (Mogoro)	Unstratified	Flake	Dr Enrico Atzeni	The same		92
6	7	Lipari	Rocche Rosse	(Source)	G.H.S.	H. S. Washington	MP	*Am. J. Sc.*, 50, 1920, p. 462	7
,,	67	Eritrea	Arafali	(Source)	G.H.S.	Not known	BM	BM 1922, 240 (6)	67
,,	71	Egypt	Not known	New Kingdom	Statue fragment	Not known	Petrie Collection, U.C., London	Wainwright, *Ancient Egypt*, 1927, p. 91	71
–	20	Rumania	Técsö, Sighet	(Source)	G.H.S.	Not known	BM	BM 1906, 165	20
–	74	N. Iraq	Zarzi cave, Sulaimani	Upper palaeolithic, Zarzi B	Core scraper	Miss Dorothy Garrod	MAAC (30.16)	*Am. Sch. Pr. Res. Bull.*, 6, 1930, p. 16	74
–	88	Auvergne	Gergara near Clermont	(Source)	G.H.S.	Not known	MP		88

TABLE II. THE TRACE-ELEMENT COMPOSITION OF THE OBSIDIANS ANALYSED

Analyses in parts per million (p.p.m.) are given for 16 elements for each of the specimens analysed

Abbreviations:

An asterisk in the second column indicates that the sample is not from an artifact but comes from a natural source.

Ba: Barium; Sr: Strontium; Zr: Zirconium; Y: Yttrium; Nb: Niobium; La: Lanthanum; Rb: Rubidium; Li: Lithium; Mo: Molybdenum; Ga: Gallium; V: Vanadium; Pb: Lead; Sn: Tin; Ca: Calcium; Fe: Iron; Mg: Magnesium; Sc: Scandium.

For convenience the analyses of calcium and iron have been divided by 100.

The sign < signifies 'less than'.

The abbreviations used for the colour of the specimens in transmitted light are: R: Red; G: Grey or Smoky; B: Black; W: Clear (white); E: green or brown.

A cross in the column headed Suitability indicates that the fracture is irregular or pitchy. In other cases it is conchoidal.

The scale used in the Transparency/Translucency column signifies: 0: not transparent/opaque; 1: not transparent/almost opaque; 2: not transparent/fairly translucent; 3: fairly transparent/almost opaque; 4: fairly transparent/fairly translucent; 5: fairly transparent/translucent; 6: transparent/translucent.

Remarks are: P: pearly lustre; S: striations in transmitted light; V: white spots (vesicles), M: mottled in direct light; C: opaque clouds.

Serial No.	Nat. Source	Origin	Group	Ba	Sr	Zr	Y	Nb	La	Rb	Li	Mo	Ga	V	Pb	Sn	$\times 10^{-2}$ Ca	$\times 10^{-2}$ Fe	Mg	Colour (trans.)	Suit-ability	Transparency/ Translucency	Remarks
19	*	Hungary	1(a)	560	78	130	31	30	80	63	32	<3	12	<5	44	<10	78	79	240	R		1	M
58	*	,,	,,	1200	78	100	22	10	120	250	130	<3	12	8	38	<10	78	120	850	G		2	
59	*	,,	,,	1000	78	76	22	<10	120	160	56	<3	12	<5	44	<10	54	93	170	G		2	
22		Derekegyhaza	,,	680	87	22	22	30	<50	63	32	<3	8	<5	33	<10	46	45	110	W		6	S
60		,,	,,	560	78	22	18	10	<50	160	100	<3	8	<5	44	<10	54	65	210	W		6	
62		Vinča	,,	1000	95	15	22	<10	<50	125	56	<3	12	<5	38	<10	62	65	210	W		6	
94		Herpaly	,,	680	52	32	15	10	<50	160	75	<3	8	<5	44	<10	62	65	210	G		5	S
95		,,	,,	1000	95	22	15	15	100	63	32	<3	8	<5	44	<10	62	65	240	G		5	
21	*	Slovakia	1(b)	1000	370	76	11	30	63	160	3	<3	12	12	33	<10	72	65	850	G	X	1	
61	*	,,	,,	1200	210	76	10	15	120	160	10	<3	12	20	38	<10	93	120	1300	G	X	0	
25	*	Melos	1(c)	830	95	56	13	30	63	63	18	<3	5	7	25	<10	78	45	370	G		2	P
26	*	,,	,,	830	140	76	11	46	<50	80	32	<3	5	8	33	<10	72	45	300	G		2	S, P
23		Phylakopi	,,	460	95	76	15	30	<50	63	32	<3	12	10	25	<10	93	55	560	G		1	P
24		,,	,,	1000	170	100	15	30	63	63	32	<3	12	8	25	<10	93	55	560	G		1	P
27		Tiryns	,,	830	170	76	11	30	<50	40	24	<3	12	10	38	<10	78	65	560	G		1	P
63		Paros	,,	680	140	56	<10	<10	50	50	32	<3	12	12	29	<10	120	93	1000	G		1	
36		Knossos	,,	830	170	76	11	30	<50	80	32	<3	5	10	29	<10	72	55	460	G		1	S, P
37		,,	,,	830	170	76	11	30	<50	63	32	<3	12	15	25	<10	120	55	670	G		1	P
38		,,	,,	830	140	76	11	37	<50	63	24	<3	8	8	25	<10	78	55	460	G		1	P
64		,,	,,	560	95	56	11	<10	63	80	24	<3	8	15	25	<10	110	79	1000	G		4	
65		,,	,,	1000	170	56	10	10	<50	63	32	<3	8	12	29	<10	120	79	1300	G		2	P
77		Knossos	1(d)	1000	78	44	11	10	80	80	24	3	8	5	29	<10	46	55	300	G	X	6	V
68		Pseira	,,	1800	95	44	11	15	80	80	42	4	12	7	44	<10	62	93	850	G	X	6	V
28	*	Armenia	1(e)	680	170	100	22	46	63	80	32	<3	8	12	38	<10	72	55	560	R		1	M
29	*	,,	,,	830	210	130	15	60	63	63	32	<3	12	10	38	<10	72	45	460	G		2	
39		Mersin	1(f)	1000	170	130	15	46	63	80	24	3	12	8	38	<10	72	65	300	G		5	C
41		Çatal Hüyük	,,	680	78	220	22	30	63	160	42	<3	17	6	33	<10	46	79	300	R		1	M
42		,, ,,	,,	1000	140	76	13	37	100	130	32	<3	17	10	33	<10	72	55	240	G		4	S

Serial No.	Nat. Source	Origin	Group	Ba	Sr	Zr	Y	Nb	La	Rb	Li	Mo	Ga	V	Pb	Sn	$\times 10^{-2}$ Ca	$\times 10^{-2}$ Fe	Mg	Colour (trans.)	Suit-ability	Transparency/ Translucency	Remarks
44		Çukurkent	1(f)	830	170	56	15	37	63	80	24	3	8	7	38	<10	72	65	300	G		2	C
99		Bor	,,	830	95	44	13	15	100	100	13	3	8	6	29	<10	62	65	270	G		2	C
100		,,	,,	460	78	44	15	15	<50	100	42	<3	17	<5	38	<10	46	65	240	W		6	
101		Ekrek	,,	560	95	56	18	30	100	80	24	<3	12	<5	52	<10	54	65	210	G		2	C
103		Hazarşah	,,	560	110	100	18	30	80	80	24	3	12	<5	44	<10	54	120	300	G		5	
79		Arpachiyah	1	680	52	270	22	22	150	160	56	3	17	8	44	<10	54	140	670	E		0	
91		Sardinia	2a	180	35	44	22	60	80	125	32	<3	12	<5	38	<10	46	93	300	G		2	
93		,,	,,	150	35	32	18	46	<50	160	32	<3	17	<5	38	<10	41	79	240	G		5	S
50		Jericho	2b	100	8	44	15	30	63	63	13	<3	8	<5	29	<10	31	37	80	G		5	
51		,,	,,	220	8	22	15	46	120	100	32	<3	17	<5	38	<10	31	37	72	W		6	S
76		,,	,,	220	<10	22	13	15	63	125	32	<3	8	<5	33	<10	27	55	240	G		6	
40		Mersin	,,	180	<10	44	15	37	<50	63	10	<3	8	<5	29	<10	35	37	85	G		6	
98		Bor	,,	180	13	44	18	22	63	125	42	3	17	<5	38	<10	41	55	130	G		5	S
102		Gazi	,,	260	20	32	13	37	100	100	32	<3	12	<5	38	<10	41	65	170	G		5	C
30	*	Armenia	3	83	<10	340	18	30	150	80	24	7	8	<5	29	<10	35	65	240	G		0	
46		Arpachiyah	,,	100	29	220	22	37	<50	100	56	<3	17	5	38	<10	27	55	110	G		1	S
80		,,	,,	83	16	220	25	30	46	160	130	<3	17	<5	38	<10	41	120	210	G		5	
45		Yanik Tepe	,,	83	16	170	25	46	<50	100	42	<3	8	<5	33	<10	31	45	110	G		0	
86		,, ,,	,,	83	20	170	25	22	80	125	56	3	17	<5	52	<10	31	79	210	G		5	
85		Chagar Bazar	,,	120	43	170	31	30	80	160	75	<3	22	<5	44	<10	35	93	240	G		2	
55	?*	Rhodes	3	83	78	130	22	46	120	160	42	3	8	7	29	<10	62	79	460	G		2	
1	*	Lipari	4a	38	20	130	25	30	100	160	100	5	17	6	44	<10	46	93	170	G		4	S
2	*	,,	,,	18	16	100	31	46	100	200	42	4	17	5	38	<10	46	93	110	G		1	
3	*	,,	,,	6	<10	76	22	46	63	320	100	3	12	<5	33	<10	41	55	48	G	X	1	
4	*	,,	,,	6	8	130	22	30	100	200	56	5	7	<5	38	<10	46	79	110	R	X	1	M
5	*	,,	,,	10	16	130	22	46	150	160	42	4	12	<5	25	<10	46	65	72	G		4	
6	*	,,	,,	26	<10	220	22	37	100	200	42	5	17	5	38	<10	54	93	300	G		4	
8	*	,,	,,	6	8	130	22	46	100	250	56	4	17	<5	33	<10	46	65	72	G		1	P
9	*	,,	,,	6	<10	130	22	46	100	200	56	5	17	<5	33	<10	41	65	110	G		6	
10	*	,,	,,	26	35	130	25	46	100	200	42	5	8	7	44	<10	62	79	240	W	X	5	V
11		,,	,,	18	<10	100	25	46	100	160	42	3	17	7	38	<10	46	79	300	G	X	4	
12		,,	,,	10	<10	100	22	46	100	130	32	3	17	<5	33	<10	41	79	110	G		6	
13		,,	,,	6	8	130	22	46	100	200	56	4	17	<5	33	<10	46	55	72	G		4	V
52		Malta	,,	18	<10	76	25	46	100	250	100	5	17	5	33	<10	46	79	72	G		2	S
106		Skorba	,,	26	20	100	22	30	120	200	56	3	17	<5	38	<10	54	120	170	G		3	
107		,,	,,	22	20	100	25	30	150	200	75	4	22	<5	38	<10	62	120	130	G		4	V
110		,,	,,	22	20	100	25	30	120	200	56	6	17	5	38	<10	46	120	130	G		3	V
111		,,	,,	22	16	130	31	37	120	200	56	5	17	5	38	<10	54	93	130	G		4	
112		,,	,,	22	16	56	25	30	100	200	56	3	12	<5	38	<10	46	93	110	G		4	
113		,,	,,	32	24	100	31	60	150	200	42	4	17	<5	52	<10	54	140	170	G		4	
114		,,	,,	22	24	100	22	37	120	250	75	3	17	5	44	<10	54	93	170	G		3	S
115		,,	,,	26	20	100	25	37	150	160	42	5	8	<5	38	<10	54	93	130	G		4	
17	*	Palmarola	,,	5	<10	220	25	60	100	200	24	<3	17	<5	44	<10	31	65	72	G		2	
56	*	,,	,,	22	<10	270	25	46	150	500	180	4	22	<5	74	<10	46	200	850	G		2	S

TABLE II continued.

Serial No.	Nat. Source	Origin	Group	Ba	Sr	Zr	Y	Nb	La	Rb	Li	Mo	Ga	V	Pb	Sn	$\times 10^{-2}$ Ca	$\times 10^{-2}$ Fe	Mg	Colour (trans.)	Suit- ability	Transparency/ Translucency	Remarks
18		Ponza	4a	5	<10	220	25	60	100	400	32	3	17	<5	38	<10	35	79	85	G		2	
57		,,	,,	18	<10	100	22	37	150	400	75	<3	17	<5	44	<10	41	93	210	G		2	
14	*	Pantelleria	4b	38	<10	1300	76	290	220	80	8	10	22	<5	<20	<10	31	440	460	E	X	3	S
15	*	,,	,,	38	<10	1000	76	460	320	130	10	15	29	<5	<20	<10	31	370	460	E		4	
16		,,	,,	18	<10	1300	190	370	260	160	32	10	22	<5	<20	<10	21	370	72	E		4	S
104		Skorba	,,	38	<10	1300	140	460	320	200	75	10	47	<5	29	<10	41	630	85	E		4	
105		,,	,,	38	<10	1300	100	370	320	125	42	7	22	7	29	<10	31	630	85	E		5	
108		,,	,,	46	<10	1300	140	370	380	160	56	8	47	10	38	<10	31	630	110	E		3	
109		,,	,,	38	<10	1300	140	460	470	160	42	10	38	15	33	<10	27	630	110	E		4	
81	*	Lake Van	4c	10	<10	790	46	46	150	125	56	4	17	<5	38	<10	23	200	31	E		6	
82	*	,, ,,	,,	26	<10	470	59	60	180	160	75	3	22	<5	44	<10	27	170	48	G	X	2	
83	*	,, ,,	,,	22	<10	340	46	46	100	125	42	4	17	<5	38	<10	27	120	39	E		2	
47		Arpachiyah	,,	<5	<10	1000	59	60	120	200	56	5	22	<5	38	<10	15	140	21	E		6	
78		,,	,,	8	<10	790	76	60	220	160	42	5	22	6	44	<10	21	250	60	E		6	
84		Chagar Bazar	,,	7	<10	890	59	46	180	200	100	4	29	<5	44	<10	21	250	39	E		6	
69		Eridu	,,	8	<10	790	46	30	150	160	75	3	22	<5	38	<10	21	170	21	E		6	
70		,,	,,	10	<10	790	59	37	150	200	100	3	22	5	44	<10	21	250	27	E		6	
75		Gerzeh	,,	15	<10	790	46	37	180	125	42	4	22	<5	38	<10	54	200	85	E		5	
31	*	Abyssinia	4d	26	24	790	46	80	<50	200	56	<3	17	<5	33	<10	27	140	370	E	X	0	
66	*	,,	,,	26	<10	790	76	130	320	160	42	4	29	12	74	47	23	260	110	E		2	
32		,,	,,	10	<10	1300	140	130	120	160	32	5	22	<5	29	<10	17	170	21	E		6	
96		Hadhramut	,,	<5	<10	1300	190	170	120	320	100	6	38	<5	74	10	15	250	21	E		6	
97		,,	,,	8	<10	890	100	180	180	200	75	<3	29	6	44	<10	17	300	27	E		6	
35		Kenya	,,	<5	<10	1100	260	290	320	160	32	6	29	<5	25	<10	27	440	21	E	X	1	
72		Naqada	,,	56	<10	410	31	80	220	160	18	6	29	5	33	<10	31	300	170	E		2	
73		Abydos	,,	22	13	340	46	170	180	160	18	7	22	6	38	<10	31	370	60	E		2	
49		,,	,,	8	<10	540	38	170	150	80	10	3	17	<5	25	<10	31	200	31	E		4	
33	*	Tibesti	4e	6	<10	790	46	130	220	160	42	5	29	<5	20	<10	23	300	21	E	X	0	
53	*	,,	,,	18	<10	890	140	170	220	160	42	5	22	<5	33	<10	23	470	48	E		2	
89	*	Auvergne	4	46	20	220	31	170	120	400	6	5	22	5	33	<10	23	79	170	E	X	1	
48		Eridu	4	22	<10	220	22	30	100	400	320	<3	17	<5	44	<10	41	93	85	G		1	
87		Yanik Tepe	,,	38	20	44	<10	37	100	80	24	4	8	5	33	<10	41	55	2800	W		6	
34	*	Kenya	5	120	13	1300	400	800	320	160	32	7	38	<5	20	<10	35	440	85	E	X	1	
54	*	,,	,,	180	13	1000	260	460	320	160	32	6	29	<5	89	63	41	440	85	E		3	
90	*	Sardinia	6a	2200	170	170	15	37	150	160	18	<3	22	20	44	<10	72	140	1300	G		1	
92		,,	,,	2200	210	220	15	30	120	200	18	<3	17	15	38	<10	78	200	1700	G		2	
7	*	Lipari	6	830	170	620	59	60	100	25	10	<3	17	5	20	<10	110	170	210	G		1	
67	*	Eritrea	,,	2200	43	270	31	80	180	100	10	<3	12	6	33	<10	54	300	110	E	X	1	
71		Egypt	,,	1500	16	410	46	80	150	63	10	4	22	<5	33	<10	46	200	21	E		2	

4) Cycladic Metallurgy and the Aegean Early Bronze Age (with an Appendix by J. A. Charles)

The importance of the contribution made by Cycladic Islands to the original and flourishing early bronze age of the Aegean has been recognised since the last century. It is surprising, then, that by 1967 very little more had been published about the area than was available to Gordon Childe when he wrote the appropriate chapter in the first edition of *The Dawn* (Childe 1925, ch. III). The past decade, however, has seen a re-awakening of interest in the area (see, for instance, Renfrew 1972 ; Doumas 1977).

With the development of a coherent internal chronology it has proved possible to re-assess the supposed relations between the Cycladic Islands and other areas, notably the West Mediterranean and the Balkans (chapters 2, 5, 9 and 11). This work has considerably diminished the significance of the islands as a source of innovation for regions west and north of Greece, while at the same time emphasising the dynamic role of the Cyclades within the cultural development of the third millennium Aegean.

The significance of early Aegean metallurgy for the origin and development of civilisation in the area is now widely appreciated (Branigan 1974). Following the discussion of silver and lead in the present paper, Branigan (1968) wrote his valuable survey of their use in pre-palatial Crete. Grave D from Kapros in Amorgos, first published by Dümmler, has recently been reconsidered by Thimme (1977).

The accompanying paper by J. A. Charles has stimulated a good deal of further interest in the early production of arsenical bronzes (McKerrell and Tylecote 1972), and he has added the following note:

> Since this paper was written Dr E. A. Slater (1972), working with Dr Charles has determined the vapour pressure of arsenic over relevant molten copper arsenic alloys. The values obtained, of the order of $1–4 \times 10^{-3}$ atmospheres over alloy melts of between 5–10 wt % arsenic in copper, are lower than expected and reduce the significance of the argument concerning the ease of arsenic loss from alloys by volatilisation. Ready arsenic loss by oxidation at all stages of extraction and fabrication remains, however, a significant disadvantage to the use of the arsenical material.

BIBLIOGRAPHY

Branigan, K. (1968) Silver and lead in pre-palatial Crete. *Amer. J. Archaeol.* 72, 219–29.

Branigan, K. (1974) *Aegean Metalwork of the Early and Middle Bronze Age.* Oxford: Claredon Press.

Childe, V. G. (1925) *The Dawn of European Civilisation.* London: Kegan Paul.

Doumas, C. (1977) *Early Bronze Age Burial Habits in the Cyclades* (Studies in Mediterranean Archaeology 48). Göteburg.

McKerrell, H. and Tylecote, R. F. (1972) The working of copper-arsenic alloys in the early bronze age. *Proc. Prehist. Soc.* 38, 209–18.

Renfrew, C. (1972) *The Emergence of Civilisation, the Cyclades and the Aegean in the Third Millennium BC.* London: Methuen.

Slater, E. A. (1972) *Metallurgical Aspects of Bronze Age Technology*. Ph.D. Thesis, Cambridge.

Thimme, J. (1977) Grave D at Kapros on Amorgos, in Thimme, J., Getz-Preziosi, P. and Otto, B. (eds.) *Art and Culture of the Cyclades*. Karlsruhe: C. F. Muller 581–3.

CYCLADIC METALLURGY AND THE AEGEAN EARLY BRONZE AGE

The Aegean Early Bronze Age does not develop gradually and uniformly. On the contrary, the early phase in each cultural region is little more than an extension of the Neolithic, from which it is distinguished principally by a variation in ceramic styles. In the following phase there is a sudden expansion: Early Helladic II, Early Minoan II, Troy II and the Keros-Syros culture of the Cyclades are now more prosperous societies, on the very threshold of urbanisation. Their wealth is illustrated by rich finds, including gold and silver, such as those of Levkas and Zygouries in Greece, Mochlos and Lebena in Crete, Troy and Poliochni in the East Aegean and Syros and Amorgos in the Cyclades. The closing phase of the Early Bronze Age is in most regions less brilliant (Crete is apparently an exception): it is a period of consolidation already belonging to the Middle Bronze Age. There is no such burst of cultural activity again until the Late Bronze Age and the empires of the Minoans and Mycenaens.

The contrast between the remarkable cultural intensity of the Early Bronze 2 period and the preceding phases has not often been sufficiently appreciated, for there has been a tendency among scholars to see in the Aegean Early Bronze Age some essential overall unity, often an ethnic one, on very doubtful grounds. Not until this phase, in fact, are the signs found of extensive commercial intercourse, and not until then is there significant indication of metallurgy in the Aegean.

It is the purpose of the present article,[1] in presenting new evidence for the importance of metallurgy in the Cyclades at this time, to illustrate the extent to which trade and commerce, stimulated by the new technology, brought about an international spirit, new to the Aegean, with in its wake the first urban societies of Europe. In the first section the Cycladic culture sequence, hitherto not precisely defined, is briefly set in its Aegean context. The evidence for various aspects of Cycladic metallurgy is then examined—the important role of lead and silver as well as copper, the rich and aristocratic tomb finds of Amorgos and other islands, the Kythnos hoard, which documents the importance of tools as well as the weapons and luxury goods of other finds, and the remarkable series of daggers and spearheads from Amorgos. Analyses are now available for many of these. In the metallurgical appendix by Mr J. A. Charles, the important point is established that arsenic-bronze was deliberately produced at this time for reasons which are intelligible today.

This material leads to the conclusions presented in the last three sections. The speed of the spread in the knowledge and practice of metallurgy is the most surprising of these. The widespread, broadly based nature of the new prosperity is probably the most important. We are faced not with an empire based upon a single dominant region, but with a number of autonomous areas, each of which had something to contribute to the international spirit of the time.[2]

Early Cycladic Chronology

During the past fifteen years, the chronology of the Aegean Early Bronze Age has been much more precisely defined.[3] The Cincinnati excavations at Troy[4] have put the culture sequence of the Troad on a sound basis. The recent excavations at Lebena and Knossos in Crete[5] have at last given a stratigraphical substantiation for Evans' Early Minoan subdivisions, emphasising the importance of the Early Minoan II period. In southern Greece, the excavations at Lerna and Eutresis[6] have defined the Early Helladic cultures more clearly, emphasising the poverty of the Early Helladic I period, and the wealth of Early Helladic II.

In the Cyclades a systematic re-examination of the extensive material available,[7] and in particular of Duncan Mackenzie's unpublished Daybooks, a careful record of the excavations at the key site of Phylakopi,[8] has allowed the definition of three principal Early Bronze Age cultures and of their geographical and chronological extent.[9] The sequence, based on internal Cycladic evidence alone, is corroborated and supplied with an absolute chronology in terms of years, by comparison with the well-established sequence of Crete and south Greece, and to a lesser extent the Troad.[10] The earliest of the three groups, the Grotta-Pelos culture, includes much of the cemetery material classed by Aberg and Childe in their Pelos Group.[11] It has proved possible to equate this with the domestic material found stratified below the First City at Phylakopi and at Professor Kondoleon's important site at Grotta in Naxos.[12] Thus in addition to the funerary pottery, largely pyxides and footed jars, often decorated with herringbone incisions, there is a new range of ceramic forms, prominent among which is the open bowl with inturned, rolled rim, which has been justly linked with those of the Kum Tepe Ib culture of the Troad.[13] Schematic figurines, and marble vases of well-defined shape are also found. The Grotta-Pelos culture thus differs in important respects from what earlier writers have termed 'Early Cycladic I', and the Early Cycladic I, II, III terminology has been deliberately avoided as bringing in preconceptions and *a priori* assumptions of equivalence with Early Helladic I, II and III, and Early Minoan I, II and III, which seem undesirable.[14]

At this time, some contact between the cultures of the Aegean, seen in the import of objects, was beginning, where previously it is documented only by the transport of the raw material, obsidian, from Melos.[15] Interestingly, apart from the Kum Tepe Ib bowls, and certain signs of Anatolian influence in Crete, the objects which are found in foreign contexts are principally Cycladic—clay bottles in Crete and Thermi, marble rhyta in Samos and Iasos—and Early Minoan I or Early Helladic I finds are not made outside their homelands. Direct contacts in the Early Bronze 1 phase[16] are thus extremely rare, and are totally insignificant beside those of the Early Bronze 2 phase.

The Keros-Syros culture includes the 'Syros Group', with the rich finds from the cemetery of Chalandriani in Syros.[17] Dark-on-light painted ware, comparable with that of Early Helladic II, is now found for the first time in the Cyclades, and the folded-arm figurine of marble (pl. 3, 15 and 16) makes its appearance. Typical also are the footed jars and 'frying pans' with their incised and stamped decoration. They are accompanied by a new range of marble vessels. Sauceboats, often with 'Urfirnis' decoration are of fairly common occurrence, and the Anatolian *depas* cup is found in Syros. Copper, and sometimes bronze, objects are now found.

At Phylakopi, the Keros-Syros culture is represented only by a few sherds between the Grotta-Pelos levels and those of the Phylakopi I culture. Indeed it is nowhere convincingly stratified above deposits of the Grotta-Pelos culture. The distribution, however, overlaps extensively with that of its predecessor in a manner which demonstrates that they are not contemporary—there are important finds in Naxos, Siphnos and especially in Keros, at the important site of Dhaskalio, excavated recently by Mr C. Doumas. Scarcely anywhere are Grotta-Pelos and Keros-Syros finds made in the same grave, and a detailed consideration of the grave groups documents the homogeneity and distinctness of each.

The chronological position of the Keros-Syros culture is confirmed by the many links which are now seen with the other Early Bronze 2 cultures of the Aegean. Cycladic folded-arm figurines of marble are now found extensively in Crete, where they first occur in Early Minoan II contexts. They are found also on the Greek Mainland, where the most important links are provided by the pottery. 'Urfirnis' sauceboats and Early Helladic II patterned ware are common to both areas. There are links too with the East Aegean. By far the most important of these from the chronological standpoint are the finds of early Helladic II/Keros-Syros sauceboat fragments at Thermi, Poliochni and in late Troy I and Troy II.[18] Although the context of these Aegean imports has been doubted,[19] it would seem that they established an important chronological link between Early Helladic II, together with the Keros-Syros culture, (and hence Early Minoan II) and Troy II.

The extent of contact at this time is very striking (pl. 12) particularly since such contact in the preceding and succeeding periods was much less marked. The distribution of one-handled cups, for example (of which just a few are of Early Bronze 1 date) links all the regions of the Aegean at this time in a manner without precedent in the earlier record. Only Crete remains a little cut off from Anatolian or Helladic influence, having contacts principally with the Cyclades. This is the period too of the earliest fortified settlements or townships in the Cyclades and the Greek Mainland. Troy and Thermi were fortified in the preceding period, but it is now that the well-known wall with bastions at Chalandriani finds counterparts at Lerna and at Panermos in Naxos.

The Phylakopi I culture, seen at the type site in Melos, in Paros, Naxos, Thera and elsewhere, succeeds the Keros-Syros culture in these islands. The principal ceramic finds consist of incised pottery—duck vases and conical pyxides—and dark-on-light painted ware, including beaked jugs, inturned-rim bowls and the characteristic kernoi.[20] Phylakopi is now a considerable town, although still unfortified, and burial was in rock-cut tombs rather than in cist graves.

Finds of duck-vases on the Greek Mainland suggest that the Phylakopi I culture may overlap with the Middle Helladic. But in the Second City of Phylakopi Minyan ware and Middle Minoan I Kamares ware is found, so that the culture of the First City is still essentially Early Bronze Age.

There is evidence, however, that the Keros-Syros culture persisted into the time of the Phylakopi I culture both in Amorgos and south Naxos, in a late form which has been termed the Amorgos Group. Thus Phylakopi I vessels are sometimes found in cist graves with goods of Keros-Syros tradition,[21] together with daggers. These daggers, although originating in the Early Bronze 2 period, clearly were still made well into the Middle Bronze Age.

This account of the Cycladic culture sequence, although brief, will serve as a necessary background for the consideration of the metal finds. Other arguments are required to set up the absolute chronology, which is not strictly relevant here. The essential point is to establish the contemporaneity of the Keros-Syros culture with the other Early Bronze 2 cultures of the Aegean, whose duration was probably from c. 2500 BC to c. 2100 BC.

Early Working of Lead and Silver

Lead, because of its low melting point — 327° C, compared with 1083° C for copper—is one of the easiest metals to work.[22] In the Near East it makes its appearance as early as copper, being found at Çatal Hüyük in the seventh millennium BC.[23] It is found rather frequently in the Aegean Early Bronze Age, more so perhaps than is generally realised, on nearly as many sites as copper. A *frequent* use seems to have been the manufacture of rivets for the repair of broken pottery. Plate 2b shows a red slipped-and-burnished Early Helladic bowl from Aegina, repaired in this way.[24] Other Early Helladic sites where lead rivets were used for this purpose are Asea,[25] Asine,[26] Ay. Kosmas[27] and Zygouries,[28] where a lump weighing 1,200 grams, evidently held in reserve for such use, was found.

Similar finds have been made in the Cyclades at Phylakopi, Chalandriani and in Naxos.[29] At Phylakopi lead ingots in the form of discs were found [30] (pl. 2a) although the stratigraphical position was not clear. Tsountas at Chalandriani likewise found evidence for the actual working of lead on the site, with rivets, ingots and the use of a flat sheet of the metal, apparently to repair a broken pot. There is evidence of lead metallurgy from the important settlement of Ay. Irini in Kea.

Lead ores are of common occurrence in the Cyclades, being known from Melos, Kimolos, Antiparos, Thera, Anaphi, Seriphos, Mykonos, Kea and other islands.[31] Their ready availabilty led to their use at an early date. In 1964 I found a small fragment of cast lead on the surface at the Grotta-Pelos settlement site of Cheiromylos in Dhespotikon,[32] and this may be the earliest indication of metallurgy in the Cyclades. Significantly the site is only a couple of kilometres from Ay. Georgios in southwest Antiparos, where galena was mined into the present century.

Lead, despite its softness, was not used exclusively for minor domestic repairs. From Antiparos again comes the little lead figurine. (Cat. no. 1, pl. 1 and 2) which is of considerable interest in its own right. It was found by Bent, as were other objects of lead and silver (Cat. no. 2 to 6 ; pl. 2) in a grave in his 'richer cemetery' on that island.[33] The cemetery is probably to be equated with the Krassades of Tsountas.[34] These objects were first published by Edgar,[35] who erroneously described the figurine as of silver. It is flat and not well preserved, but the elbows show that the arms were either folded at the waist, like the folded-arm figurine, or meeting at the waist, like the Plastiras type,[36] or conceivably supporting the breasts, as in a small marble figurine from Ios, now in the Fitzwilliam Museum, Cambridge.[37] Another Early Cycladic figurine of lead was described by Wolters, who first doubted and then accepted its authenticity.[38] It was found on the island of Ios, and was given by Finlay to the National Museum in Athens,[39] where it cannot at present be located. Although the lead figurine from Troy is probably rather later,[40] and the origin of an example from Crete is not certain,[41] these Cycladic finds are sufficient to substantiate the existence of metal figurines in the Aegean Early Bronze Age. Their existence at this time in Central Anatolia has been magnificently documented by the finds at Horoztepe.[42]

No attempt will be made here systematically to collect all the instances of lead objects in the Aegean Early Bronze Age. In the East Aegean they are evidenced, for example, by the elegant bracelet or diadem from Thermi,[43] and in Crete by the double axes from Mochlos.[44] Further examples are listed in the Catalogue (v. infra). The remarkable ship models from Naxos, hitherto unpublished, are of great importance however, not only from a metallurgical standpoint but for the light they throw on Early Bronze Age shipping (Cat. no. 12–14, pl. 1 and 3).

That these ship models have not previously been published is perhaps at first sight surprising, since they have been in the possession of the Ashmolean Museum, Oxford, for nearly 30 years. It may be that the rather unexpected material of which they are made has led to doubts as to their authenticity. But the realisation that lead was, in fact, a popular material invalidates such an argument, and there seems little doubt that they are genuine.

No. 12 of the Catalogue was reputedly found in Naxos with the two marble figurines no. 15 and 16 (pl. 3). This sets it therefore in the Keros-Syros culture. The other boats may originally have been part of the same find, although this cannot now be established. What is particularly interesting is that these supply independent corroboration, in a totally unexpected way, for the incised representations of boats on the Syros 'frying pans',[45] as well as solving a long-standing problem as to which end of these was, in fact, the bow.

The boats are each made of three lengths of lead. The prow and keel is a rod of lead, flattened by hammering along two-thirds of its length to form a flat bottom for the boat, while the sides are formed of two similar flat strips. The prow rises steeply—this higher projection, contrary to the views of some scholars[46] is clearly the bow—while a part of the length towards the stern is canted at a more gentle angle, just as the Chalandriani incisions show.

These boats had no sails: the models and the incised 'frying pans' agree on this, and the supposed masts on the Orchomenos sherd[47] appear to be accidental incisions. Unlike the contemporary models from Palaikastro and Mochlos[48] they are long boats, and on the 'frying pans' they are frequently shown with about a dozen oars on each side. If this figure be accepted, they will have been capable of very impressive speeds. Until the last century there were pirate ships in the Islands, all of this type, and the tradition of shipbuilding and seafaring, whether by trader or pirate, thus extends back over four and a half millennia.

Silver occurs widely in association with lead ores, from which it is extracted by the process of cupellation. It is not surprising, therefore, that finds of Early Cycladic silver objects are common, although gold is scarcely ever found.[49] Silver can occur too in the native form, and this can usually be identified on analysis by the presence of various impurities. The diadem and dish from Amorgos[50] proved on analysis to contain 5% gold, and are probably of native silver. On the other hand Partington cites the great purity of silver found at Troy[51] as proof that cupellation was already known at the time.

In any case, silver was widely used in the Cyclades, and on the Greek Mainland—the tweezers at Manika are all of silver.[52] In Crete, on the other hand, despite the silver daggers from Koumasa,[53] gold is the more common.

The silver diadems of Amorgos and Syros are well known,[54] and bracelets are of common occurrence. Three forms of bracelet are known: the torque of twisted silver, as found by Bent on Antiparos (Cat. no. 2, pl. 2), the simple bangle of circular section (Cat. no. 10, pl. 2) which in one case is lengthened to form an arm spiral (Cat. no. 9, pl. 2) and the flat bracelet. This is concave in section, and may be undecorated like the example from Dokathismata in Amorgos[55] or another unpublished find, supposedly from Pholegandros, and now in the Fitzwilliam Museum, Cambridge.[56] On the other hand the terminals may be decorated with light incised lines (Cat. no. 8, pl. 1 and 2) as in a specimen from Amorgos in the National Museum in Copenhagen.[57]

Silver pins are found in the Cyclades, usually with vase heads (as in finds by Mr C. Doumas at the cemetery of Ay. Anargyroi in Naxos), or other embellishment.[58] Beads are also found. All the silver finds known from the Cyclades are to be set in the Keros-Syros culture[59] (although some in the Amorgos Group, which is of longer duration). Together they make impressive testimony to the wealth of the time.

Dummler's Grave Group 'D' from Kapros in Amorgos

(plate 4, with no. 17, plates 1 and 10)

In 1896 F. Dümmler published an account of a visit to Amorgos[60] with drawings which he made in Athens of objects said to derive from that island. The interest of this record is that the original associations of the finds are given. Frau F.-M. Fischer Bossert has already published another grave group[61] which is now divided between the Ashmolean Museum and the National Museum in Copenhagen, and from the association she has drawn important chronological conclusions. The contents of Grave D at Kapros, now in the Ashmolean Museum and here published in their entirety for the first time, are likewise of interest, particularly in their exotic nature.

The site of Kapros lies in a fertile valley, one and a half kms. northeast of the port of Katapola in west Amorgos. It is situated on the right side of the stream, dry in summer, which runs down from Mt Profitis Ilias to the sea at Katapola. The location of the settlement is not clear, but slabs from cist graves are now incorporated in the modern field wall. I was told there in 1964 that in recent years as many as 60 cist graves have been opened, some of them containing large figurines of marble. I was given the foot of one of these (now in the Katapola Museum), which will have been of the folded-arm form, and must have stood originally to a height of some 50 cm.

Most of the finds (Cat. no. 17–29, pl. 1, 4, 10) were illustrated by Dümmler, although he showed only 6 of the pendant beads of necklace Cat. no. 24, where 14 complete beads and several fragments are now preserved. He referred to four figurines, but it was Wolters who first illustrated these.[62] There is a discrepancy between the sizes given by Dümmler and those of the figurines illustrated by Wolters, moreover only two of the four in Oxford (Cat. no. 26 and 28, pl. 4) correspond to his illustrations, so that the association of the Ashmolean figurines with the remainder of the finds cannot be regarded as certain. One of the figurines figured by Wolters is now in the Antikensammlung in Munich,[63] and the form would seem to belong with the Grotta-Pelos culture.

A green-stone spoon, strengthened with silver, was also published by Wolters as belonging to this group[64]: it is now in Athens. The stone is the same as that of the handles, Cat. no. 20 and 21 (pl. 4), and similar finds have been made by Mr C. Doumas in the Keros-Syros culture cemetery at Ay. Anargyroi in Naxos.[65] This stone, termed 'natronagalmatolith' by Blinkenberg,[66] has been identified as anhydrite or calcite,[67] both common enough in the Cyclades. There are further examples of these handles in the National Museum in Copenhagen. The green beads of necklace Cat. no. 23 (pl. 4) seem also to be of this stone.

Shell figurines, like Cat. no. 26 and 27 (pl. 4), are unusual, but there are two similar examples from Paros in the Fitzwilliam Museum in Cambridge.[68] The 'ivory' fragment is a unique find in the Cyclades (Cat. no. 25, pl. 4) but bone with similar incised concentric circles is known from Second City and later contexts at Troy.[69] Incised or stamped concentric circles are so common upon the pottery of the Keros-Syros culture that there is nothing remarkable in finding a similar motif upon the ivory. The seal (Cat. no. 19, pl. 4) is likewise unique in the Cyclades, although the angle-filled cross device at the end is commonly found on Minoan seals, and in the East Aegean, as well as on pottery of the Keros-Syros culture.[70] There are related forms in the Lerna sealings[71] on the Greek mainland. Frankfort classed this seal as Jemdet Nasr on account of the square 'loop-bore' suspension, but this early date is disputed by Dr V. E. G. Kenna.[72] The form is certainly a new one to the Aegean: there is a similar form of seal only at Poliochni,[73] which is different again in material and decoration. Frankfort's very early date of 3000 BC can certainly be set aside, and a date at the very end of the Early Bronze Age, perhaps c. 1900 BC, would seem more appropriate.

The silver bowl (Cat. no. 17, pl. 1 and 10) is in some ways the most interesting object in the group, being the only metal vessel now preserved from the Cyclades. Dümmler illustrated a little footed cup of silver[74] from a grave at Notina in Amorgos, but its whereabouts are not now known. Rare as the find is, however, it is not without parallels. The famous gold bowls, supposedly from Euboia and now in the Benaki Museum,[75] and the silver bowl in the Metropolitan Museum in New York[76] (pl. 10e) belong to this period. The tombs at Mochlos in Crete produced a silver cup, and a silver bowl was found in the Second City at Troy.[77] Other metal vessels are also illustrated in pl. 10.

These finds establish amply that the ownership of vessels of precious metals was not limited to the rulers at Troy or Alaca or Horoztepe. Although Greece, Crete and the Cyclades cannot boast of treasures like those of the rich Anatolian sites, they were certainly not backwaters at this time. The relationship of some of these vessels to ceramic forms is discussed below.

Another indication of the wealth of Amorgos during this period is the size and quality of the numerous folded-arm figurines of marble that have been found there, and the number of spearheads and daggers from the cist graves. The very numerous finds from Chalandriani in Syros, Ay. Anargyroi in Naxos and Dhaskalio in Keros give a similar indication of prosperity.

The Kythnos Hoard and Other Tools

Hoards of tools are extremely rare in the Aegean Early Bronze Age. Indeed to the European prehistorian the relative scarcity of metal finds in general is surprising—there is certainly nothing to compare with the extensive finds of central and northern Europe. Perhaps the use of the sea as the principal means of communication is in part responsible. The well-known double axe is essentially a later form, and indeed one does not tend to regard the shaft-hole axe as an Aegean shape at all. The few finds that are now known, however, may serve to correct that impression. Of these the Kythnos hoard is the most important.

In 1866 the British Museum purchased from a Mr C. Merlin a hoard of tools of copper or bronze, which are described in the catalogue as 'from the Isle of Thermia', the Cycladic island today called Kythnos. Although some of the objects were illustrated at the time, and some again since,[78] it has never been published in full.

The hoard contained, as well as the four shaft-hole tools, three massive flat axes (Cat. no. 34–6, pl. 5 : 35 and pl. 6) and three narrow flat axes or chisels (Cat. no. 37–39, pl. 5 : 39 and pl. 6). The larger axes, each with a perforated heel for mounting, are classed by Deshayes in his monumental survey[79] as Type K4, which includes also examples from Naxos, the East Aegean island of Saria and various East Mediterranean sites. The distribution of Type K focuses on Syria rather than Anatolia or the Aegean, but the Syrian examples are chiefly later than the Cycladic ones.

The narrow flat tools from the Kythnos hoard are again perfectly at home in the Aegean. They fall in Deshayes' Type C4b, distinguished by the divergent sides, straight heel, long narrow blade and rounded cutting edge. Other finds of this form have been made in Amorgos, Naxos[80] and Levkas.

Flat axes and adzes are in fact fairly common in the Aegean, including the Cyclades, often as stray finds. Deshayes lists 59 from the Aegean, of which 18 are Cycladic. There are three unpublished Cycladic examples in the Museum of Archaeology and Ethnology, Cambridge,[81] and three more are published here (Cat. no. 43–5, pl. 9). The first from Amorgos, no. 43, falls in Deshayes' Type D2b, together with an adze of Early Helladic II date from Eutresis.[82] Another, from Paros, no. 44, broken at the cutting edge, compares most closely with an axe from the Eutresis hoard.[83] The third, no. 45, from Amorgos, falls apparently in Deshayes' Type B3a, resembling B3b examples from Eutresis and Amorgos in several respects.

The shaft-hole tools from the Kythnos hoard are in some ways more interesting. The axe-adze (Cat. no. 30, pl. 5–6) affords the best evidence for the date of the find. It compares closely with the axe-adze from the Early Helladic II hoard of Pit 5 at Eutresis.[84] With its flaring profile, corresponding to Deshayes' Type B1, it falls amongst a large series of axe-adzes from the Aegean which are distinguished by the absence of a collar from those of Iran and the Near East, and by a number of traits from those of the Balkans. The various parallels seem to place this and other tools of the Kythnos hoard in the Early Bronze 2 period of the Aegean, and hence within the span of the Keros-Syros culture.

The flaring line of this axe-adze form was replaced in the Aegean by a more straight-profiled variety, seen chiefly in Crete, and in the Late Minoan period by a form in which the adze is more sharply differentiated from the axe. The distribution of this later form is centered on Crete,[85] but there are two examples from Naxos (Cat. no. 41 and 42, pl. 9) and one from Athens.[86]

The first of the shaft-hole axes from the Kythnos hoard (Cat. no. 31, pl. 5–6) is of a notably simple form, again virtually restricted in its distribution to the Aegean, although there is a possible prototype from Iran. Other examples of similar shape are finds from Delphi, Gaudourophas and from a Middle Minoan 1 context at Palaikastro.[87] There is nothing here to contradict the Early Bronze 2 date suggested for the axe-adze.

The second shaft-hole axe from the hoard (Cat. no. 32, pl. 5–6) has a much less rounded butt. Indeed so long is the butt that the form suggests itself as a prototype for the symmetrical form, the familiar double axe. Rather similar tools are known from Chios[88] and in two unpublished specimens in Copenhagen. Deshayes suggests an Anatolian prototype, corresponding to Stronach's Type 2,[89] and an Early Bronze 2 date again seems appropriate.

The third shaft-hole axe from Kythnos (Cat. no. 33, pl. 5–6) with its curious button butt presents something of a problem, since there is nothing quite like it known, apart from a very similar object from Naxos, now in Copenhagen.[90] Deshayes puts them in a separate category, Type G2a.[91] Stronach compares the form with examples in his Type 1,[92] which would be chronologically acceptable, but the similarity does not seem a close one. So far the form is uniquely Cycladic.

Now the remarkable thing about the distributions of these four types, with shaft-holes, is that they are essentially Aegean. The axe-adze described is of a form restricted to the Aegean, the third of the shaft-hole axes with the knob on the butt is restricted to the Cyclades, while the other two are not notably well represented further east. The ultimate inspiration for these forms may well be an oriental one, but its expression in these precise forms is an Aegean contribution, and it would be wrong to see the Aegean smiths as following slavishly supposed eastern prototypes.

The three other tool hoards from the Aegean Early Bronze Age do not contradict this picture (cf. the map, pl. 11). That from Eutresis contains an axe-adze and flat tools from open moulds.[93] The Petralona hoard, on show in the Thessaloniki Museum, is to be published by Mrs A. Sakellariou. It contains, in addition to flat axes or chisels, several shaft-hole axes of a type familiar from Poliochni, where it occurred with several daggers in the deposit of Vano 829.[94] This deposit is probably to be set in the Early Bronze 2 period, on account of the Early Helladic II/Keros-Syros culture sauceboat fragments from levels of the same phase,[95] and the Poliochni axe is consequently older than several others of this form.[96] The Thebes hoard,[97] which is to be set in the Early Helladic II or III period, contained another example of this shaft-hole axe, together with flat axes, awls and chisels and an early occurrence of the double-axe. The shaft-hole axe of this type should certainly be included in the Aegean repertoire of the time, although it has not been found in the Cyclades, and it may be of Aegean origin.

Shaft-hole tools of two other types have been found in the Cyclades. The first, a shaft-hole axe of bronze (Cat. no. 40, pl. 9) is from Amorgos. The form is close to Maxwell-Hyslop's Type 3,[98] for the axe is considerably thicker at the shaft-hole than it is along the length of the blade. It compares also with two examples from Crete,[99] and may be of Early or Middle Bronze Age date.

Double axes have also been found in the Cyclades: some 16 are quoted by Deshayes, and among unpublished examples is one from Naxos in the Museum of Archaeology and Ethnology in Cambridge.[100] The form is essentially a Middle and Late Bronze Age one,[101] but there was one from a First City context at Phylakopi,[102] an example from Thebes has been cited above, and that from the Tlos hoard[103] may be of Early Bronze Age date. The miniature examples in lead from Mochlos[104] have already been mentioned. Number 32 from the Kythnos hoard is itself, although asymmetrical, not so far from a double axe in shape, and there seems to be no difficulty therefore in finding an Aegean prototype for this essentially Aegean, and especially Cretan, form.

These, however, add little to the picture presented by the Kythnos hoard, that in the Early Bronze 2 period, useful tools as well as weapons and ornaments were made in the Aegean, including the Cyclades. Many of them are local forms.

Cycladic Daggers and Spearheads (plate 7)

That the Cyclades formed an important centre in the distribution of Aegean dagger finds has long been realised. To the present time, however, no systematic survey of Aegean weapons of the Early Bronze Age has been undertaken, and although an exhaustive study would be beyond the scope of the present paper, it is important to establish the basic distinctions in order to set in their contexts the 26 daggers here published, most of them for the first time.

In what follows, no firm distinction is made between daggers and spearheads, since the difference is one of mounting. Probably the slotted examples were used as spearheads (although it is curious that they are not followed in the archaeological record by numerous socketed spearheads). The terms 'dagger' and 'spearhead' are used loosely for convenience. In the same way 'sword' merely implies a long dagger, of length greater than about

40 cm. Halberds (where the blade is mounted transversely to the shaft) have at times been claimed in the Aegean, but an asymmetrical blade cannot alone be a sufficient indication that such mounting was used.

The essential feature of the Aegean dagger series is that the separate tang, as an aid to hafting, was not much in favour. This is in marked contrast to the Anatolian series, where a tangless dagger or spearhead is an oddity. Not all Aegean examples are included in the rather pragmatic classification which follows, but it allows for all the daggers and spearheads known from the Cyclades (see pl. 7).

I. DAGGERS WITH RAT-TAIL TANG

Ia. *Without slots.* This is equivalent to Stronach's Anatolian spearhead Type 1,[105] and is common in Anatolia and Cyprus.[106] It is known in the Cyclades from a single find, in the Keros-Syros culture settlement of Panermos, excavated by Mr C. Doumas, and to be published by him. There are other examples in the Troad (pl. 7 : Ia).

Ib. *Slotted.* This is Stronach's Anatolian Type 2. In the Cyclades it is known from a single find at Dokathismata in Amorgos.[107] It occurs in the Troad and elsewhere in Anatolia, notably at Horoztepe (pl. 7 : Ib).

II. SLOTTED DAGGERS / SPEARHEADS (WITHOUT RAT-TAIL TANG)

IIa. *With well-defined tang and round shoulders.* Catalogue no. 47–50 (pl. 5, 7 : IIa, 9). This is essentially a Cycladic type, being known from Stavros in Amorgos,[108] the examples listed here, from Levkas and Troy, and an example in the National Museum in Copenhagen.[109] Probably the type is of Cycladic origin.

IIb. *Shoulders narrowing to the tang.* Catalogue no. 51 (pl. 7 : IIb). This is equivalent to Stronach's Anatolian spearhead Type 3a. The description includes many varieties of form, and indeed probably more than one type. It is known in the Cyclades from only two examples. The first is from Amorgos, now in the British Museum (Cat. no. 51). The other, considerably longer and made of tin-bronze, was found at Chalandriani in Syros by Frau E.-M. Fischer Bossert, and is to be published by her. The type is probably an Anatolian one.[110]

IIc. *Constricted and then broadening at the butt, to form a tang.* Catalogue no. 52 (pl. 7 : IIc and 9). This form is known from two examples, one from Arkesine in Amorgos,[111] and the other from the same island (Cat. no. 52). Typologically it might be placed midway between IIa and IIb.

IId. *Other slotted varieties.* Catalogue no. 53 (pl. 7 : IIb and 9). There are several types in this group. First, the form with four holes in the blade for hafting purposes. An example (Cat. no. 53) from Arkesine in Amorgos was described by Dümmler and has been most fully published by Frau Fischer Bossert.[112] With this may be set the other varieties of Stronach's spearheads Type 3b and 3c,[113] chiefly from Crete. The spearheads from Sesklo and Levkas[114] may also be set in Class IId.

III. SHORT DAGGERS

There are several classes of Aegean daggers which are both flat and short, generally less than 12 cm in length.

IIIa. *Tanged.* These are uncommon in the Aegean. Examples are known from Arkesine in Amorgos,[115] Chalandriani in Syros, and elsewhere (pl. 7 : IIIa).

IIIb. *Cretan type.* Very broad butted, often rather shield-like in shape, sometimes with a scalloped butt. These have been found exclusively in Crete, where they first occur in Early Minoan II contexts[116] (pl. 7 : IIIb).

IIIc. *Round heeled.* This form, very common in western Europe, is rare in the Aegean. The best known examples are those from Ay. Marina in Phokis (pl. 7 : IIIc)[117] and another was found by Frau E.-M. Fischer Bossert at Chalandriani.

IV. BROAD BUTT DAGGERS, GENERALLY WITH TWO OR FOUR RIVET-HOLES, SYMMETRICALLY PLACED

Often the dagger has a rhomboidal section resulting in a central rib. This rib has been used as an important classificatory criterion by some writers, but in most daggers it is no more than a low prominence formed by two of the faces which define the dagger's rhomboidal section. This is the most common Aegean form.

IVa. *Straight butt.* Cat. no. 54–62 (pl. 7 : IVa, 8 and 9). This form is very common in the Cyclades, being known from Ormos Apollona and Karvounolakkoi in Naxos,[118] Dokathismata in Amorgos[119] and numerous other finds from that island (Cat. no. 54–62, and two unpublished examples in the Fitzwilliam Museum, Cambridge: GR.14 and 14a.1901). One in the National Museum, Copenhagen, is apparently from Melos (ABa.955), and there are at least four unpublished specimens in the Apeiranthos Museum, Naxos. A remarkable find from Spedos in Naxos, now in the Naxos Museum, appears to be silver plated. It is 35 cm in length, decorated with incised grooves, and may well date from the Middle or Late Bronze Age.

The form is very common also in Crete, from such sites at Koumasa, Platanos, Pyrgos, Mallia, Palaikastro, Lebena and doubtless others.[120] It appears to be the commonest form in Mainland Greece also, being known from Zygouries, Lerna and Levkas.[121]

This is clearly the principal Aegean form: it is not found, apparently, in Anatolia. Occurring in Early Bronze 2 contexts in the Cyclades and on the Mainland, it is not yet attested with certainty as early Minoan II in Crete, where the short dagger of Class IIIb is at first the commonest form.

IVb. *Rounded butt.* Cat. no. 63 (pl. 7 : IVb and 8). This form, almost invariably with midrib, and sometimes rather long, shows typological development towards the swords of Class VII. There is an example from Amorgos (Cat. no. 63), and another in the Apeiranthos Museum. The form occurs in Middle Helladic Lerna, Athens,[122] and especially in Crete.

V. BROAD BUTT FLAT DAGGERS WITH A SINGLE ROW OF RIVETS

The rivets are usually flat headed and are often very prominent. Cat. no. 65 (pl. 5 and 7 : V).

This form is more easy to recognise than to characterise. It has both a tapering and tongue-shaped variety, the second being the later, continuing into Late Bronze Age contexts. Probably Class V is not earlier than the Middle Bronze Age. It is known from Kapsalon in Amorgos and other sites on the island, as well as from Levkas, Sesklo, Drachmani in Phokis,[123] and many Middle Minoan contexts in Crete. A short dagger from Ay.

Marina in Phokis might be a prototype.[124]

A badly corroded dagger from Amorgos, now in the Ashmolean Museum (Cat. no. 64; pl. 9), is probably of this type. According to the Museum records, it was found in a cist grave, together with a ribbed duck-vase[125] and a beaked jug[126] (both forms of the Phylakopi I culture) and a 'prochos' bottle,[127] a form particularly associated with the Amorgos Group. These finds suggest a date in the Phylakopi I culture, towards the end of the Early Bronze Age.

VI. NARROW BUTT DAGGERS WITH VARIOUS RIVET ARRANGEMENTS
(Cat. nos. 66 and 67, pl. 7:VI and 9)

In this form, the narrow butt is the equivalent of a tang. The type corresponds to Stronach's dagger Type 6. It is not common in the Cyclades, and is found more often in Anatolia and in Cyprus.[128]

VII. DAGGERS AND SWORDS WITH PROMINENT MIDRIB, USUALLY WITHOUT RIVETS
(Cat. nos. 68-72, pl. 5, 7:VII and 8)

A single example is known from a Cycladic grave,[129] but there are others in the Apeiranthos Museum, and Mrs A. Ozanne (née Furness) acquired others at Vroutsi north of Kastraki in Amorgos[130] (Cat. no. 70 and 71). Two more from the same island are in the Ashmolean Museum in Oxford (Cat. no. 68 and 69). There is an Early Bronze Age find from Levkas,[131] and they are common enough in Crete. This Class would in fact include the long swords of the Late Bronze Age of Karo's Type A—Cat. no. 71 has the tang which is one of Type A's defining features. Most of those here listed are probably earlier however, as well as shorter, and are prototypes for the fully developed Aegean sword.[132]

OTHER DAGGERS

Most Aegean spearheads and daggers can be fitted into the above categories, partly since these are not very closely defined. The tanged dagger from Manika[133] has however a definitely Anatolian look, and will not fall into any of them. Many other varieties of daggers are also found in the Troad and at Poliochni.

Two principal conclusions arise from this survey. First, the dagger appears simultaneously in the Cyclades, Crete and Mainland Greece in the Early Bronze 2 period. Furthermore the forms which subsequently are the most important, especially Classes IIa and IVa, are Aegean inventions, the former probably a Cycladic one.

There is admittedly some Anatolian influence in the Keros-Syros culture, indicated by daggers of Class Ia and IIb, and this is also suggested by the Manika dagger. The dagger develops in all four regions from this time, but finds are notably more abundant in Crete and the Cyclades (especially Amorgos) than in the Mainland of Greece or West Anatolia.

Classes I to IV, and VI, begin in the Early Bronze Age, but their duration has not been established, and unfortunately no clear stratigraphical evidence has yet been obtained for them in Crete. The type IV dagger, however, clearly contributed in the formation of the sword of Karo's Type A. In Amorgos these daggers last through the time of the development of the Phylakopi I culture, and despite the absence of Middle Cycladic associations, it is likely that their use continued well into the Middle Bronze Age.

Cycladic Technology

Several sites in the Aegean have yielded remains of metal working. The most important finds are those by Dr D. Theocares in Attica, but slag and moulds were also found in various levels at Poliochni.[134]

In the Cyclades there are several sites with such remains. Chalandriani in Syros, with its rich grave-goods as well as copper slag and schist moulds for flat axes and chisels,[135] is the most notable. Tsountas recovered copper slag at Avyssos in Paros.[136] Signs of metallurgy, with crucibles, were detected at Phylakopi in Melos.[137] The blue pigment contained in the little pots from the Louros grave[138] is probably azurite, a copper ore, and several of the islands have ore deposits.[139]

Bivalve moulds have not been found in the Aegean, but their existence may be assumed for the manufacture of some of the shaft-hole tools, such as Cat. no. 30–33. The clay mould at Poliochni[140] indicates also the use of the *cire perdue* method. Probably, however, open moulds like those of Chalandriani were most widely used, with forging and cold-hammering to produce the desired refinements in shape. Mr J. A. Charles, in his Appendix, has emphasised the beneficial effects of alloying copper with arsenic to facilitate cold-working and especially hot-working. It seems that archaeologists have insufficiently realised the results which may be achieved by working in this way. For instance, none of the daggers of Classes I to VI here described is likely to have been cast in a bivalve mould, even when there is a medial rib. The daggers of Italy (Remedello—Rinaldone) and Spain (Alcalà etc.) are likely to have been shaped by hammering-up also, rather than by any more complicated process of casting.

The Aegean tin problem still remains a central one for the Bronze Age, since no tin sources whatever are known in the area.[141] When tin-bronze is found, therefore, the tin must either have been brought in from some distant source such as Italy and Spain, or have been found in small and probably alluvial deposits, now worked out, of which no trace is to be found today.

Tin-bronze is indeed rare in the Aegean Early Bronze Age. Few of the objects which have been analysed for the present study are of tin-bronze. The two bronze axe-adzes from Naxos (Cat. no. 41 and 42) and the sickle from Amorgos[142] (Cat. no. 46) are of Late Bronze Age date. The three swords from Amorgos (Cat. no. 70–72), now in Athens, are likewise later than the Early Bronze Age, as may also be the shaft-hole axe (Cat. no. 40).

Only three Cycladic daggers are of tin-bronze: the example of Class V from Tomb 10 at Kapsalon in Amorgos,[143] a specimen of Class VI from the same island (Cat. no. 67), and the dagger of Class IIb from Chalandriani in Syros. To this list should be added the tin-bronze bracelet from Tomb 14 at Dokathismata in Amorgos.[144]

Regrettably few Early Bronze Age metal objects have yet been analysed from the Greek Mainland, and none yet published is of tin-bronze. Early and Middle Minoan objects in the Herakleion Museum have been analysed by the Arbeitsgemeinschaft für die Metallurgie des Altertums, Freiburg.

Of the several Early Minoan daggers, only one had a significant quantity of tin, and few even of Middle Minoan date were of tin-bronze.[145]

In the East Aegean, tin-bronze was more common at this time, in the Early Bronze 2 phase.[146] Of the 22 analyses of Troy II date materials given by Bittel, 15 are of tin-bronze, 4 are low in tin but with high arsenic (greater than 3%), and 3 have small quantities of tin and arsenic. Interestingly, 3 of the tin-bronzes have more than 5% lead.[147] So high a proportion of lead is not seen in any of the other Aegean analyses available, although Cat. no. 42 and 62 have more than 2% lead.

There is no known source for the Cycladic or Troadic tin in Anatolia,[148] and the import of the material to Kültepe in Cappadocia in the Middle Bronze Age confirms that there was no local supply in that part of Anatolia. Indeed no source is known in the East Mediterranean.

Sources in the West Mediterranean have been suggested. Iberia certainly has abundant tin, but this is located in the west. The absence of any tin from the objects which have been analysed from Los Millares or Vila Nova de São Pedro[149] is itself an argument against its export at that time. It is true that ingots of copper have been found in Sardinia, and these may well have been exported to the Aegean (they are unlikely to be from the Aegean) but they are later in date. There is indeed no evidence that tin was used in the area at all at so early a period. Even the supposed tin button from a Rinaldone context at Mte Bradone, quoted by Childe as evidence for the tin trade, is a disappointment, proving as it does to be of antimony.[150] There is thus no evidence for a tin trade with the West Mediterranean in the Early Bronze Age.

The apparent abundance of tin in the Early Bronze 2 Troad may indeed be the best clue to its origin. And the only object of pure tin from the Aegean Early Bronze Age is from the nearby site of Thermi.[151] As yet one can only hazard a guess, but the most likely source for the Early Bronze Aegean would seem to be some alluvial deposit of tin, in or near the Troad, which is now worked out. This would explain its early occurrence and frequency in the Troad, and seems a more probable explanation than some hypothetical and distant tin trade, for which there is no good evidence.

For the Cyclades, however, it is not the lack of tin but the response to it which is the more significant. It has been known for some time that Cycladic and other bronzes sometimes contain a high proportion of arsenic, rather than of tin. There has been disagreement, however, as to whether or not these arsenic-bronzes were the result of deliberate alloying rather than the chance selection of copper ores rich in arsenic.[152]

There are notable high percentages in the analyses here quoted. In four daggers and a sword (Cat. no. 54, 58, 59, 63, 69) the proportion of arsenic is greater than 4%. Significantly, perhaps, all four of the daggers are of Class IV. There is an appreciable amount of arsenic also in dagger no. 53, and in a chisel (no. 38).[153] A saw excavated by Stephanos at Aïla in Naxos[154] had 2.62% arsenic.

Mr J. A. Charles, in his Appendix, establishes clearly the beneficial consequences which the alloying with arsenic will have had upon the properties of the bronze, especially for objects to be further worked by forging, which most of the articles here, and certainly all the daggers, were.

He gives compelling reasons for accepting this arsenic-bronze as a deliberate alloy, the result of adding specially selected arsenic-rich minerals to the smelting mix. His technical arguments seem to settle the matter, and it now appears proven that deliberate alloying was carried out in the Cycladic Early Bronze Age.

The Origins of Aegean Metallurgy

There is no long ancestry for the metallurgy of the Early Bronze Age in the Aegean. In Anatolia, the use of native copper is attested as early as Early Neolithic Çatal Hüyük,[155] and the casting of copper is indicated both by slag at that site and by a macehead from Chalcolithic Can Hasan.[156] At Beycesultan too, in the Late Chalcolithic period, there was some expertise in the manufacture of copper tools.[157] But in the Aegean, use of metal in the Neolithic period is attested solely by the two copper axes, with a couple of gold pendants, from Late Neolithic levels at Sesklo in Thessaly,[158] and by a copper axe stratified below a Late Neolithic floor at Knossos in Crete.[159] Traces of copper from the surface at the Late Neolithic site of Kephala in Kea[160] may indicate some Cycladic use at this time also.

No single object of metal is known from the Early Helladic I culture of Mainland Greece, while the Louros necklace and possibly Bent's Antiparos finds, described above, are the only metal objects which might be ascribed to the Grotta-Pelos culture. There is no metal in Crete from stratigraphically authenticated Early Minoan I levels. Only in the East Aegean is metallurgy attested so early. At Poliochni, the first metal finds are in the blue phase, to be correlated with Troy I. The finds from the First City at Troy are not impressive—Dörpfeld[161] listed only a few trinkets of gold, a ring of tin-bronze and two knives, a ring and pins and needles of copper. The Cincinnati excavations there had similar finds.[162] At Thermi, however, there were more impressive finds: axes, daggers, and a bangle, probably of tin.

It thus seems likely that metallurgy came earlier to the Troad than to the remainder of the Aegean. But it should not be overlooked that Early Helladic II/Keros-Syros imports are found already at Thermi and Troy I. It may be, therefore, that the later part of Troy I phase is contemporary with Early Helladic II, the Keros-Syros culture and Early Minoan II, and should consequently be set in what has here rather loosely been termed the Early Bronze 2 period. The priority of northwest Anatolian metallurgy over that of the remainder of the Aegean is not yet established beyond question.

The notion conforms, however, to the belief that metallurgy came to the Aegean from the east. Whether its origins were in Mesopotamia or southern Anatolia, metal working was practiced in both areas well before its relatively sudden arrival in the Aegean. A number of metal types in the Aegean certainly seem to be imports from the Troad, showing Anatolian influence—the tanged dagger, the slotted dagger of Class IIb, and probably some of the awls and pins of Syros.[163]

What has to be emphasised, nonetheless, is the essential autonomy of the Aegean Early Bronze Age. After an initial impetus, which our ignorance of the Late Neolithic and Anatolian Late Chalcolithic makes it very difficult to document, it developed in its own way, with its own metal types. The most common Aegean dagger, Class IVa, is certainly of local origin (cf. the distribution, pl. 11). So too is the slotted spearhead of Class IIa, which probably originated in the Cyclades. The idea of the shaft-hole tool may be an eastern one, but some of the forms discussed above are purely Aegean. The range of metal types at the time is an impressive one, and such forms as diadems of sheet metal, and especially tweezers (distribution, pl. 11) are apparently local also.

The originality and independence of the industry correlates with the cultural autonomy which is evident from other finds. Despite the intensive trading which clearly took place in the Early Bronze 2 period, each local region had its own culture, which is best characterised today by the ceramic material. It is less clearly seen among the metal finds (contrast pl. 11 with pl. 12), but the concentration of Type IIIb daggers in Crete, for instance, shows that there was some regionalism even in metallurgy. The idea of metallurgy may have been brought to the Aegean from outside, but the manner of its adoption was very much a local affair. Its impact on the Aegean, and its influence in bringing together the disparate cultures of the various regions, is discussed in the next section.

The International Spirit of the Aegean Early Bronze 2 Period

Metallurgy developed rather suddenly in the Aegean, in several regions, in the Early Bronze 2 period. There are other and remarkable changes in the archaeological record at this time, and it is of interest to consider to what extent these events are related.

In the Late Neolithic of the Aegean, such homogeneity as there may have been in the earlier phases disappears completely. Very little contact of any kind can be documented between the different regions, although obsidian from Melos is still found in Crete and the Mainland.[164] The 'coal scuttle' of Sesklo is found again at Kephala in Kea,[165] and the Elateia rhyton has parallels as far away as Danilo,[166] but these are rare examples, which simply serve to underline the cultural isolation of the various regions. Only the distribution of the rolled-rim bowls at the end of the Neolithic[167] suggests some more prolonged influence.

At the outset of the Early Bronze Age, the same is true, and few if any direct imports into one region from another can be recognised during Early Bronze 1, although some of the new forms of Early Minoan I have Anatolian resemblances. The one-handled cup (distribution, pl. 12) is already found, however, at Thermi, Eutresis[168] on the Greek Mainland and at Lebena in Crete.[169]

It is against this background that the extensive contact which came about in the Early Bronze 2 period seems so astonishing an innovation. The *depas* cup, for instance, has an extensive distribution throughout Anatolia, and certainly originates there, but it is found in the Cyclades and the Greek Mainland (distribution in the Aegean, pl. 12). The 'sauceboat' is certainly a Helladic or Cycladic form, but it is found in the East Aegean. The marble folded-arm figurines are undoubtedly Cycladic in origin, yet exports or copies are numerous in Crete and the Greek Mainland (pl. 12). These distributions suggest something of a cultural continuum in the Early Bronze 2 period. This is not, however, a cultural unity, for each region retains its identity, which is seen in many other finds of more restricted distribution.

The widespread adoption of these forms indicates a very marked increase in trade and in contact: there is something of an international spirit at this time. It seems to have been the result, principally, of the impact of metallurgy.

Metal vessels are extremely rare in the Aegean Early Bronze Age, but those few that have survived bear a striking relation to the dominant ceramic forms, which must have been radically influenced by them. The Urfirnis 'sauceboat' of Early Helladic II and the Keros-Syros culture (pl. 10: b is from Chalandriani) has been recognised for some time[170] to be an imitation of the elegant drinking cup of gold, an example of which survives (pl. 10: a). The *depas* cup, with its prominent handles, seen at Orchomenos and Chalandriani[171] (pl. 10: d from Troy) as well as widely in west and central Anatolia, now has a prototype in silver[172] (pl. 10: c). The elegant cups of Syros and Siphnos[173] have a metal counterpart at Troy,[174] and there can be little doubt that the new fashion in the Aegean for thin-walled pottery, with an elegant flowing line, is a consequence of the imitation of metalwork.

Probably the Early Helladic II open bowl [175] is an imitation of a metal prototype which has not survived (compare however pl. 10: e and pl. 10: 17). Even the 'frying pans' of the Keros-Syros culture have plausible metal prototypes in the Alaca treasure[176] and in recent finds in the Troad,[177] where a wide range of metal vessels is now seen. In Crete, as elsewhere, the various handled jugs may indicate metal prototypes which have not survived,[178] and indeed the widespread appearance in the Aegean at this time of the 'hand-grip' handle may reflect the influence of metal forms. The Middle Minoan I footed bowl, with its twisted rim has a silver counterpart from Gournia,[179] which it undoubtedly imitates.

Metal forms were imitated even in marble: there are versions of the two-handled cup at Knossos[180] and in Lerna III.[181] A complete footed sauceboat in marble, from the Cyclades, is now in the National Museum in Athens.[182] It is interesting, indeed, to speculate whether the folded-arm figurine of marble may not itself derive from a metal prototype. Metal figurines are attested in the Cyclades, as discussed above, and one from Ios was apparently of the folded-arm form, perhaps not unlike the silver figurine from Horoztepe.[183] It cannot be excluded that the Cycladic marble workers, already skilled during the time of the Grotta-Pelos culture in the making of schematic figurines, copied a metal prototype when forming the new convention of the folded-arm representation.

The influence of metallurgy upon the cultures of the period is thus a profound one, influencing the forms of expression as well as the economy. It is difficult for us today to reconstruct the economy of those times, and easy to exaggerate the economic importance of prehistoric trade. Before trade can play an important economic role in society, there must both be a useful commodity to be traded, and a market for it. Now, contrary to the view of some writers, obsidian can never have been required in sufficient bulk to have had any major economic significance.[184] It is unlikely that essential foodstuffs were traded in great quantities in prehistoric times, since until organisation was rather more efficient and sophisticated, as in Classical times, a regular supply could not be assured. A society consequently had to be largely self-supporting in its diet and could hardly depend on irregular and uncertain supplies of food from outside.

The arrival of metallurgy must radically have changed the situation, hitherto unfavourable to extensive or systematic trade. For the first time there existed, in localised regions, a commodity universally desirable and with considerable economic and political significance. Its impact on crafts—as illustrated by the Kythnos hoard—and on warfare—as demonstrated by the Amorgos daggers—must have been immense. In the early stages, finished objects were probably traded, as documented by the Manika dagger and the spearheads of Class IIb. Later, with the dissemination of the essential technological 'know-how' whose spread is indicated by the slags of Askitario, Chalandriani and Avyssos, the raw material itself may well have been traded, or at least the local, Aegean-made products of the craft.

Fortunately we have, on the 'frying pans' and in the models (pl. 3), documentation for the very adequate shipping available, and the transport of the copper ore, or of ingots like those of the Middle and Late Bronze Age[185] must have been perfectly feasible. The systematic and well-organised metal trade of the Assyrian colony at Kültepe was undertaken only a little after this time,[186] and the Cape Gelidonya wreck[187] shows that, in the second millennium at least, both copper and tin formed important sea cargoes.

We do not, however, have to imagine so extensive or far-reaching a trade in the later third millennium. There is little evidence, for instance, that the Aegean was already in systematic trading contact with Italy or Sardinia, let alone Spain. Indeed it may be wrong to imagine a bulk trade in raw copper at so early a date; perhaps only the finished objects were traded. But some systematic and regular trade within the Aegean is certainly indicated.

Some of the consequences of this trade have already been discussed. The principal metal types have a wide and rapid distribution: double-spiral pins, awls in incised bone handles and tweezers, as well as tools, weapons and more precious objects, are widely found. One result of the numerous contacts which are implied by these distributions must have been the widespread exchange of information of various sorts. This, ultimately, was more important than the transport of the objects themselves. For any major increase in the amount of contact between human groups, in the information communicated between them, marks a significant increase in the complexity of society. Whereas the Aegean formerly comprised a number of separate and unconnected cultural regions, it became at this time, or began to become, a larger cultural organism. The regions probably remained autonomous politically—there is no evidence for an 'empire' until the Late Bronze Age—but economically and culturally the Aegean became something more than the simple juxtaposition of unrelated cultures which it was in the Late Neolithic.

Urbanisation is not easy to define, nor to recognise in the archaeological record. But while Dhimini was only a fortified village, Lerna and Phylakopi as well as Troy II and Poliochni may be regarded as towns. Specialisation of labour is as much a criterion as fortification or population-size, and it is certainly exemplified in the metallurgy, while the town-plan of Phylakopi and the sealings of Lerna suggest a fairly advanced social organisation.

In the third period of the Early Bronze Age many of these advances are consolidated, but the international spirit declines somewhat. The stimulating transition to a metal-using society has had its impact, and the metal vessels, for instance, have lost their novelty, and their shapes no longer pre-occupy the potter. The metal types remain widespread, and new ones are introduced, but the trade must in some way have changed in character, for in the archaeological record, signs of contact actually diminish. The painted wares of Lerna IV, for instance, do not have the widespread distribution of the Urfirnis and patterned ware of Early Helladic II.

The coming of metallurgy to the Aegean can thus be correlated with the increase in trade and specialisation and other signs which indicate the process of urbanisation. Of course the importance of the role of metallurgy in bringing about such changes could easily be exaggerated. Indeed metal only came to these regions rather belatedly, when their cultures were, in a sense, ready for the innovation, and ready to support the specialists which the craft demands.

There is still much to learn about the preceding Late Neolithic and Early Bronze 1 periods, and until this background is better understood, our comprehension of the remarkable economic expansion of the Aegean Early Bronze 2 period will remain an imperfect one. The impact of metallurgy, and the social contacts which resulted, are likely, however, to be the key to our understanding of the unifying features which appear in the archaeological record of the time. Some of these were retained throughout the Middle Bronze Age, and served as a basis for the subsequent development of Aegean civilisation. [1967]

Catalogue of Unpublished or Republished Objects

Objects with a BM serial number are in the British Museum. Numbers 70–72 are in the British School of Archaeology at Athens. The remainder are in the Department of Antiquities, the Ashmolean Museum, Oxford.

1. Lead figurine. BM 84,12–13,20. Head missing, left arm broken. Height 4·9 cm. Found by J. T. Bent [188] in a cist grave in Antiparos. Pl. 1 and 2.

2. Silver torque. BM 84,12–13,21. Diameter 11·3 cm., thickness c. 0·4 cm. Found by Bent in a cist grave in Antiparos.[188] Pl. 2.

3–6. Four small lead (?) bracelets. BM 84,12–13,22 to 25. Numbers 3 and 4 have a flat-ended section, numbers 5 and 6 have a circular section, thickness c. 0·4 cm. Present diameter c. 4 cm. Found by Bent in a cist grave in Antiparos.[188] Pl. 2.

7. Lead fragment. AE 243. Lower surface smooth, upper rough. Probably cast in an open mould. Length 8·6 cm., thickness 1·2 cm. From Amorgos, bought in Athens 1893. Pl. 2.

8. Silver bracelet. AE 253. Concave section. Terminals decorated with incisions. Present diameter 6·5 cm., thickness 0·1 cm. From a cist grave in Amorgos. Bought in Athens in 1896. Pl. 1 and 2.

9. Silver arm spiral. AE 255. Present length 4·0 cm., diameter 5·0 cm., thickness 0·3 cm. Provenance as no. 8. Pl. 2.

10. Silver bracelet. AE 260. Circular section. Present diameter 6·5 cm., thickness 0·3 cm. Provenance as no. 8. Pl. 2.

11. Lead (?) bracelet. AE 254. Circular section. Present diameter 6·9 cm., thickness 0·5 cm. Provenance as no. 8. Pl. 2.

12. Lead boat. 1929.26. Made from 3 strips of lead. Length 40·3 cm., width 3·3 cm. Found in a cist grave in Naxos with figurines, cat. no. 15 and 16. The find is said to have comprised four boats (possibly including cat. no. 13 and 14) and three figurines. Bought in Athens in 1917 by Professor R. M. Dawkins and presented by him to the Ashmolean Museum through Sir Arthur Evans. Pl. 1 and 3.

13. Lead boat. 1938.725. Originally the longest of the three boats. Preserved length 39·0 cm. From Naxos. Presented by Sir Arthur Evans. Pl. 3.

14. Lead boat. 1938.726. Preserved length 34·0 cm. Provenance as no. 13. Pl. 3.

15 and 16. Marble folded-arm figurines. 1929.28 and 27. Height 18·4 and 13·5 cm. respectively. Provenance as number 12. Pl. 3.

17. Silver bowl. AE 158. Max. diameter 9·2 cm., thickness 0·1 cm. From Dümmler's cist grave D[189] at Kapros in Amorgos. Pl. 1 and 10.

18. Needle of copper or bronze. AE 164. Square section. Length 4·9 cm., thickness 0·1 cm. Provenance as no. 17 (not illustrated).

19. Greenstone cylinder seal. AE 159. Suspension loop. The cylinder is carved at the side and the end. Height 4·6 cm., height of design 3·3 cm., diameter 1·9 cm. Provenance as no. 17. Pl. 4.

20. Greenstone handle. AE 160. Of calcite or anhydrite. Not wheelturned, not pierced at end. Length 6·7 cm., diameter 1·6 cm. Provenance as no. 17. Pl. 4.

21. Greenstone handle fragment. AE 161. Of calcite or anhydrite. Not wheelturned, pierced at end (possibly to take the needle, no. 18 above). Length 3·2 cm., diameter 1·7 cm. Provenance as no. 17. Pl. 4.

22. Three silver beads. AE 163. Flat silver foil, with oblique rippled decoration of straight lines, rolled to form beads. Length 4·3 cm., diameter 0·9 cm. Provenance as no. 17. Pl. 4.

23. Five stone beads. AE 162. Three green (cf. no. 20 and 21). Two, of the same material as the green ones, are pale brown. Tubular, swelling at the middle. Neatly pierced. Length from 3·8 to 2·4 cm., diameter 1·0 to 0·8 cm. Provenance as no. 17. Pl. 4.

24. Fourteen pendant beads, and four fragments. AE 166. White stone, probably limestone. Graded in size from 5·3 to 4·5 cm. Provenance as no. 17. Pl. 4.

25. Rectangular piece of ivory (?) with incised concentric circles at the edge. AE 165. Motif of circles, recurring five times, each with a central point and two concentric rings. Length 5·5 cm., width 1·6 cm., thickness 0·5 cm. Provenance as no. 17. Pl. 4.

26. Shell figurine. AE 156. Arms apparently folded, legs separated, head delineated with facial features. Back plain. Height 5·4 cm., thickness 0·7 cm. Probably from Dümmler's Grave D, with no. 17. Pl. 4.

27. Shell figurine. AE 157. Schematic 'violin figurine'. Long neck without separate head. Height 4·7 cm., thickness 0·5 cm. Possibly from Dümmler's Grave D, with no. 17. Pl. 4.

28. Marble figurine. AE 1551. Arm stumps, separate legs and head. Height 9·5 cm. Probably from Dümmler's Grave D, with no. 17. Pl. 4.

29. Marble figurine. AE 154. Folded arms. Height 16·8 cm. Possibly from Dümmler's Grave D, with no. 17. Pl. 4.

30. Axe-adze. BM 66,2–7,10. Circular shaft hole. Length 11·6 cm., length of axe blade 3·8 cm., length of adze blade 2·9 cm. Weight 250 grams. From the Kythnos hoard.[190] Pl. 5 and 6.

31. Shaft-hole axe. BM 66,2–7,7. Circular shaft hole. Length 15·8 cm., length of blade 7·7 cm. Weight 1,490 grams. Provenance as no. 30. Pl. 5 and 6.

32. Shaft-hole axe. BM 66,2–7,7. Circular shaft hole. Length 10·6 cm., length of blade 6·0 cm. Weight 950 grams. Provenance as no. 30. Pl. 5 and 6.

33. Shaft-hole axe. BM 66,2–7,8. Circular shaft hole. Length 15·6 cm., length of blade 6·8 cm. Weight 1,250 grams. Provenance as no. 30. Pl. 5 and 6.

34. Flat axe. BM 66,2–7,1. Square perforation. Edge bevelled at both faces. Length 19·8 cm., thickness 0·9 cm. Weight 940 grams. Provenance as no. 30. Pl. 6.

35. Flat axe. BM 66,2–7,2. Square perforation. Edge bevelled at both faces. Length 19·9 cm. thickness 0·7 cm. Weight 710 grams. Provenance as no. 30. Pl. 5 and 6.

36. Flat axe. BM 66,2–7,3. Square perforation. Edge bevelled at both faces. Length 17·1 cm., thickness 0·9 cm. Weight 710 grams. Provenance as no. 30. Pl. 6.

37. Flat axe (narrow). BM 66,2–7,4. Edge bevelled at both faces. Length 21·7 cm., thickness 0·4 cm. Weight 250 grams. Provenance as no. 30. Pl. 6.

38. Flat axe (chisel). BM 66,2–7,5. Bevelled at one face. Length 18·6 cm., thickness 0·5 cm. Weight 145 grams. Provenance as no. 30. Pl. 6.

39. Flat axe (chisel). BM 66,2–7,6. Edge bevelled at one face. Length 16·2 cm., thickness 0·5 cm. Weight 135 grams. Provenance as no. 30. Pl. 5 and 6.

40. Shaft-hole axe. 1927.2968. Oval shaft-hole. Length 14·5 cm. Length of blade 7·3 cm. From Amorgos, bought in Athens 1893. From the collection of Sir John Evans, presented by Sir Arthur Evans in 1927. Analysis infra. Pl. 9.

41. Axe-adze. AE 86. Oval shaft-hole. Length 14·0 cm. Length of axe blade 4·5 cm. Length of adze blade 4·1 cm. From Naxos, bought in Athens in 1895. Analysis infra. Pl. 9.

42. Axe-adze. AE 87. Oval shaft-hole. Length 17·9 cm. Length of axe blade 5·1 cm. Length of adze blade 4·7 cm. From Naxos, bought in Athens in 1895. Analysis infra. Pl. 9.

43. Flat axe (chisel). 1927.1357. Edge bevelled at one face. Length 15·9 cm., thickness 0·5 cm. From Amorgos, bought in Athens in 1883. Analysis infra. Pl. 9.

44. Flat axe. 1910.618. Edge damaged. Length 12·8 cm., thickness 0·4 cm. Bought in Paros. Analysis infra. Pl. 9.

45. Flat axe. AE 236. Edge bevelled at both faces. Length 6·2 cm., thickness 0·8 cm. From a cist grave in Amorgos, bought in Athens in 1893. Analysis infra. Pl. 9.

46. Sickle. 1927.1362. Broken at tip. Length 23.5 cm. From Amorgos,[191] bought in Athens in 1883. Analysis infra. Pl. 9.

47. Dagger (spearhead) Class IIa. AE 237 (1896.20). Medial ridge. Length

15·2 cm. From Amorgos, bought in Athens 1896. Analysis infra. Pl. 9.

48. Dagger (spearhead) Class IIa. 1927.1361. Medial ridge. Length 19·5 cm. From Amorgos, bought in Athens 1883. Analysis infra. Pl. 9.

49. Dagger (spearhead) Class IIa. BM 81,5–9,5. Medial ridge. Length 18·8 cm. Weight 110 grams. From Amorgos. Presented to the BM by A. W. Franks in 1881. Pl. 5.

50. Dagger (spearhead) Class IIa. BM 81,5–9,6. Flat section. Length 17·9 cm. Weight 100 grams. From Amorgos. Presented to the BM by A. W. Franks in 1881. Pl. 7 : IIa.

51. Dagger (spearhead) Class IIb. BM 81,5–9,7. No prominent medial ridge, but thickens at middle. Length 17·0 cm. Weight 85 grams. From Amorgos. Presented by A. W. Franks in 1881. Pl. 7 : IIb.

52. Dagger (spearhead) Class IIc. AE 233. No prominent medial ridge, but central thickening. Length 20·5 cm. From Amorgos, bought in Athens in 1893. Analysis infra. Pl. 7 : IIc and 9.

53. Dagger (spearhead) Class IId. AE 231. Broad thick blade, tapering at edge, pierced with four holes for mounting. Length 23·5 cm. From Arkesine in Amorgos.[192] Bought in Athens in 1893. Analysis infra. Pl. 7 : IId and 9.

54. Dagger Class IVa. AE 238. Prominent medial ridge. Four rivet holes. Length 17·1 cm. From Amorgos, bought in Athens. Analysis infra. Pl. 8.

55. Dagger Class IVa. AE 240 (1898.17). Medial ridge. Four rivet holes. Length 18·1 cm. From Amorgos, bought in Athens. Analysis infra. Pl. 8.

56. Dagger Class IVa. 1927.1360. Prominent medial ridge. Four rivet holes. Length 14·6 cm. From Amorgos, bought in Athens 1883. Analysis infra. Pl. 8.

57. Dagger Class IVa. AE 230 (1893.61). Slight medial ridge. Two rivets (length 0·6 cm). Length 17·1 cm. From Amorgos, bought in Athens. Analysis infra. Pl. 8.

58. Dagger Class IVa. AE 239. Slight medial ridge. Four rivet holes. Length 21·4 cm. From Amorgos, bought in Athens. Analysis infra. Pl. 8.

59. Dagger Class IVa. AE 252 (1893.60) Slight medial ridge. Five rivet holes, with three rivets (length 1·6 cm). Length 20·0 cm. From Amorgos, bought in Athens. Analysis infra. Pl. 8.

60. Dagger Class IVa. BM 81,5–9,8. Prominent medial ridge. Two rivet holes. Length 22·4 cm. Weight 100 grams. From Amorgos, presented to the BM by A. W. Franks in 1881. Pl. 7 : IVa.

61. Dagger Class IVa. AE 229. Flat section. Four rivet holes, with two square rivets (length 1·0 cm). Length 15·4 cm. From Amorgos, bought in Athens 1892. Pl. 9.

62. Dagger Class IVa. 1927.1358. Flat section, four rivet holes. Length 12·2 cm. From Amorgos, bought in Athens in 1883. Analysis infra. Pl. 9.

63. Dagger Class IVb. 1927.1359. Medial ridge. Originally four rivet holes. The rounding of the butt is not as pronounced as in some of this class. Length 15·9 cm. From Amorgos, bought in Athens in 1883. Analysis infra. Pl 7 : IVb and 9.

64. Dagger Class V. AE 267. Flat section. Three rivet holes in line. Fragmentary. The original shape, and hence the attribution to Class V, is uncertain. From Amorgos. Associated, according to the Museum Catalogue, with a duck-vase, a beaked jug and a 'prochos' bottle. Pl. 9.

65. Dagger Class v. BM 81.5–9,4. Flat section. Four rivet holes in line. Length 12·1 cm. Weight 35 grams. From Amorgos, presented to the BM by A. W. Franks in 1881. Pl. 5.

66. Dagger Class vi. AE 234 (1893.64) Flat section. Three rivet holes. Length 19·4 cm. From Amorgos, bought in Athens in 1893. Analysis infra. Pl. 7 : vi and 9.

67. Dagger Class vi. AE 235. Slight medial ridge. Two rivet holes. Length 16·6 cm. From Amorgos, bought in Athens in 1893. Analysis infra. Pl. 9.

68. Dagger Class vii. AE 241 (1896.22). Prominent midrib. Length 19·7 cm., from Amorgos. Analysis infra. Pl. 8.

69. Dagger (sword) Class vii. AE 242 (1896.21). Prominent midrib. One rivet preserved (length 0·9 cm). Length 33·2 cm. From Amorgos, bought in Athens in 1893. Analysis infra. Pl. 7 : vii and 8.

70. Dagger (sword) Class vii. British School at Athens B 181, B. Medial ridge. Two narrow decorative ribs run parallel to the central ridge on each side of it. Preserved length 36·0 cm. Bought in 1949 near Vroutsi in Amorgos by Miss Audrey Furness.[193] Analysis infra. Pl. 5 and 8.

71. Dagger (sword) Class vii. British School at Athens B 181, C. Medial ridge. A narrow decorative rib runs parallel to the central ridge on each side of it. The butt has a tang. Preserved length 25·6 cm. Provenance as no. 70. Analysis infra. Pl. 5 and 8.

72. Dagger Class vii. British School at Athens B 181, A. Medial ridge which is not as prominent as those of no. 68 and 69. This dagger might equally be classified with those of Class iva. Length 19·5 cm. Provenance as no. 70, above. Analysis infra. Pl. 8.

NOTES

[1] Acknowledgements. For these see original publication.

[2] The abbreviations used in the notes are those recommended in *AJA* 69 (1965) 199 ff, together with the following:

Bossert: Bossert, E. M. Zur Datierung der Gräber von Arkesine auf Amorgos *Festschrift für Peter Goessler* 23 f.

D–S: Τσοῦντας, Χ. Αἱ Προϊστορικαὶ Ἀκροπόλεις Διμινίου καὶ Σέσκλου.

Deshayes: Deshayes, J. (1960) *Les Outils de bronze de l'Indus au Danube*, Institut Français de Beyrouth Bibliothèque Archéologique et Historique, Tome LXXI.

Eutresis: Goldman, H. (1931) *Excavations at Eutresis in Boeotia.*

Levkas: Dörpfeld, W. (1927) *Alt-Ithaka.*

Mochlos: Seager, R. (1912) *Excavations in the Isle of Mochlos.*

Montelius: Montelius, O. (1924) *La Grèce préclassique* I.

Papathanasopoulos: Παπαθανασόπουλος, Γ. (1961–2) Κυκλαδικὰ Νάξου. *Arch. Delt.* 17 Α′.

Poliochni: Bernabò Brea, L. (1964) *Poliochni, città preistorica nell'isola di Lemnos* I.

Stephanos: Stephanos, C. (1905) Les Tombeaux prémycéniens de Naxos. *Comptes Rendus du Congrès Archéologique à Athènes*, 215 f.

Stronach: Stronach, D. B. (1957) The development and diffusion of early metal types in Early Bronze Age Anatolia. *Anat. St.* 7, 89 f.

Thermi: Lamb, W. (1936) *Excavations at Thermi in Lesbos.*

Troy: Blegen, C. W., Caskey, J. L., Rawson, M. and Sperling, J. (1950) *Troy* I.

Ts. 1898: Τσοῦντας, Χ. (1898) Κυκλαδικά, *Arch. Eph.* 137 f.

Ts. 1899: Τσοῦντας, Χ. (1899) Κυκλαδικὰ II *Arch. Eph.* 73 f.

[3] Caskey, J. L. (1964) Greece, Crete and the Aegean Island in the Early Bronze Age. *CAH* I, ch. XXVI; Weinberg, S. S. (1965) The Relative Chronology of the Aegean in the Stone and Early Bronze Ages, in Ehrich, R. W. (ed.) *Chronologies in Old World Archaeology.*

[4] Cf. *Troy.*

[5] Hood, M. S. F. (1963) Stratigraphical excavations at Knossos, 1957–61. Κρητικὰ Χρονικά; 'Αλεξίου, Σ. (1963) *Οἱ Πρωτομινωϊκοὶ Τάφοι τῆς Λεβῆνος καὶ ἡ 'Εξέλιξις τῶν Πρωτομινωικῶν Ρυθμῶν*. Κρητικὰ Χρονικὰ 88 f.

[6] Caskey, J. L. (1960) The Early Helladic Period in the Argolid. *Hesperia* 29, 285 f.; Caskey, J. L. and E. G. (1960) The Earliest Settlement at Eutresis. *Hesperia* 29, 126 f.

[7] Renfrew, Colin. *The Neolithic and Early Bronze Age Cultures of the Cyclades and their External Relations*, doctoral thesis at the University of Cambridge, submitted April 1965.

[8] Mackenzie, Duncan. *Daybooks of the Excavations at Phylakopi in Melos, 1896, 1897, 1898 and 1899*. Unpublished transcript by Colin Renfrew, 1963, available at the library of the British School of Archaeology at Athens, the Library of Classical Archaeology, Cambridge, and the Library of the University of Cincinnati.

[9] They differ in various significant respects from those outlined in the clear and useful summaries of Weinberg and Caskey, op. cit. (supra, n. 3).

[10] Renfrew, Colin. Crete and the Cyclades before Rhadamanthus. Κρητηκὰ Χρονικὰ 18,107.

[11] Åberg, N. (1933) *Bronzezeitliche und früheisenzeitliche Chronologie* IV, 60; Childe, V. G. (1957) *The Dawn of European Civilisation* (6th ed.) 51.

[12] Atkinson, T. D., Mackenzie, D. *et al.* (1904) *Excavations at Phylakopi in Melos* (Society for the Promotion of Hellenic Studies, Occasional Paper 4) 239; Κοντολέον, Ν. (1949) 'Ανασκαφαὶ ἐν Νάξῳ, *Praktika*.

[13] French, D. H. (1961) Late Chalcolithic pottery in north-west Turkey and the Aegean, *Anat. St.* 11, 99 f.

[14] This point, which is of great methodological importance, cannot be adequately treated here, cf. Renfrew op. cit. (supra, n. 7) 10 f.

[15] Renfrew, C., Cann, J. R. and Dixon, J. E. (1965) Obsidian in the Aegean. *BSA* 60, 225 f.

[16] The terms 'Early Bronze 1', 'Early Bronze 2', etc., which are not capable of precise definition, are throughout applied to the Aegean rather loosely, for the sake of convenience.

[17] *Ts. 1899.*

[18] *Thermi* 90, fig. 524; *Poliochni* pl. CXXIX c; *Troy* 40, 54, 222.

[19] Mellaart, J. (1957) Anatolian chronology in the Early and Middle Bronze Age, *Anat. St.* 7, 79; French, D. H. op. cit. (supra, n. 13) 117.

[20] Atkinson *et al.*, op. cit. (supra, n. 12) pls. IV, VII, IX.

[21] Dümmler, F. (1886) Mitteilungen von den griechischen Inseln. *AM* 11, 15 f.

[22] It is much easier to smelt also. The ore, galena, smelts below 800° C, and Tylecote, R. F. (1962) *Metallurgy in Archaeology* 76, has determined by experiment that it is possible to smelt lead in a hot camp fire, surrounded by a ring of dry stones. The cupellation of argentiferous lead, to obtain silver, requires a temperature of about 1100° C.

[23] Mellaart, James. Excavations at Çatal Hüyük 1963. *Anat. St.* 14, 111 and pl. XXV a.

[24] I am grateful to Professor E. Kunze for permission to illustrate this unpublished find from the excavations of Welter, cf. Welter, G. (1938) *Aegina*.

[25] Holmberg, E. J. (1944) *The Swedish Excavations at Asea in Arcadia* 131.

[26] Frödin, O. and Persson, A. W. (1938) *Asine* 257.

[27] Mylonas, G. (1959) *Aghios Kosmas* 138 and fig. 132.50.

[28] Blegen, C. W. (1928) *Zygouries* 184.

[29] Atkinson *et al.*, op. cit. (supra, n. 12), pl. XL, 21; *Ts. 1899* 126; *Stephanos* 224.

[30] Atkinson *et al.*, op. cit. (supra, n. 12) 92.

[31] Κορδελλᾶς, Α. (1902) 'Ο Μεταλλευτικὸς Πλοῦτος καὶ αἱ 'Αλυκαὶ τῆς 'Ελλάδος.

[32] Cf. *Ts. 1898* 176.

[33] Bent, J. T. (1884) Researches among the Cyclades, *JHS* 5, 53.

[34] *Ts. 1898* 140.

[35] Edgar, C. C. (1896–7) Prehistoric tombs at Pelos. *BSA* 2, 49 and fig. 18.

[36] Cf. Zervos, C. *L'Art des Cyclades* 110, fig. 112.

[37] Budde, L. and Nicholls, R. (1964) *A Catalogue of the Greek and Roman Sculpture in the Fitzwilliam Museum, Cambridge* pl. 2, 13.

[38] Wolters, P. (1898) Praehistorische Idole aus Blei. *AM* 23, 462, and (1890) *AM* 25, 339.

[39] Athens NM 7817, Μόλυβος 71.

[40] Schliemann, H. (1880) *Ilios* 337.

[41] Evans, A. J. *Cretan Pictographs and the Mycenaean Script* 132, fig. 137.

[42] Tezcan, B. (1960) New finds from Horoztepe. *Anatolia* 5, pl. XXIV.

[43] *Thermi* 206, fig. 61.

[44] *Mochlos* 36.

[45] *Ts. 1899* 90, figs. 16–22. Compare also the engravings on two stones from south-east Naxos, cf. Doumas, C. (1965) Korphi t'Aroniou, *Deltion* 20, 49, fig. 4 and pl. 35.

[46] Dussaud, Sovoronos and Koster, quoted by Marinatos, S. (1933) La Marine crétomycénienne. *BCH* 57, 182.

[47] Kunze, E. *Orchomenos* III, pl. XXIX, 3.

[48] *Mochlos* fig. 48, 31.

[49] There is a single gold bead from the cemetery of Phyrroghes in Naxos, see *Papathanasopoulos* 224 and pl. 71. The rich ores of Siphnos were presumably not discovered until the Iron Age.

[50] *Ts. 1898* 187 and pl. 8, 1 and 3.

[51] Partington, J. R. *The Origins and Development of Applied Chemistry* 347 f.

[52] *Παπαβασιλείου, Γ., Περὶ τῶν ἐν Εὐβοίᾳ 'Αρχαίων Τάφων* figs. 4 and 13, pl. H 3.

[53] Xanthoudides, S. *The Vaulted Tombs of the Messara* pl. XXIX, b, 212–14.

[54] *Ts. 1898* pl. 8, 1; *Ts. 1899* pl. 10, 1.

[55] *Ts. 1898* pl. 8, 2.

[56] Inv. no. GR.7.1901.

[57] Inv. no. 4675.

[58] Naxos Museum 4018 and 4019, cf. Ντοῦμας, Χ. (1961–2) 'Ανασκαφαὶ ἐν Νάξῳ. *Arch. Delt.* 17 B′, 272 f.

[59] The silver beads in the Louros grave, belonging to the developed Grotta-Pelos culture, are an exception: *Papathanasopoulos* pl. 67.

[60] Op. cit. (supra, n. 21).

[61] *Bossert* 23 f.

[62] Wolters, P. (1891) Marmorkopf aus Amorgos, *AM* 16, 48.

[63] Zervos, op. cit. (supra, n. 36) 77, fig. 48.

[64] Wolters, op. cit. (supra, n. 62) 50. Athens NM 4275 and 4276.

[65] Naxos Museum 4016, cf. Doumas op. cit. (supra, n. 58); also Copenhagen National Museum 3263.

[66] Blinkenberg, C. (1896) Antiquités prémycéniennes. *Mém. Soc. Roy. Ant. du Nord.*

[67] Kindly identified from examples in the Athens National Museum by Professors A. N. Georgiades and G. M. Paraskevopoulos.

[68] Budde and Nicholls, op. cit. (*supra*, n. 37) pl. I, 5–7.

[69] Blegen, C. W. (1963) *Troy and the Trojans* pl. 26. The material of this find from Amorgos has not been examined scientifically, and its identification as ivory is uncertain. Ivory was commonly used in Crete at this time, however, for seals.

[70] Matz, F. (1928) *Die frühkretischen Siegel* pl. II.7a, pl. III.10, pl.. IX, X etc.; *Poliochni* pl. CLXVIII, 9 and pl. CLXXV, 3–4; an impression from Syros is published by Bossert, E.-M. (1960) Die gestempelten Verzierungen auf frühbronzezeitlichen Gefässen der Ägäis, *JdI* 75, 1 f. Vessels in the Mykonos Museum bear similar stamped decoration.

[71] Heath, Martha C. Early Helladic Clay Sealings from the House of Tiles at Lerna *Hesperia* 27, pl. 21–22.

[72] Personal communication. Cf. Frankfort, H. (1939) *Cylinder Seals* 70 and 301; also Buchanan, Briggs (1960) *Ancient Near Eastern Cylinder Seals in the Ashmolean Museum. I. Cylinder Seals* no. 741.

[73] Bernabò Brea, L. (1957) Recenti scavi a Poliochni nell'isola di Lemnos, *Bd. A.* 42, 208, fig. 25.

[74] Dümmler, op. cit. (supra, n. 21) Beilage 1, 4. There is also a fragmentary silver dish from Dokathismata in Amorgos, *Ts. 1898* pl. 8, 3, which is now in the National Museum in Athens.

[75] Segall, B. *Katalog der Goldschmiede-Arbeiten, Benaki Museum* pl. 1–3 and 67–68. The silver bowl, pl. 69, has several similarities with the Kapros bowl.

[76] Accession no. 46.11.1 (purchased 1946, Joseph Pulitzer bequest), cf. Richter, G. M. (1935) *Handbook of the Greek Collections, Metropolitan Museum of Art* 16 and pl. 11, i. Another similar bowl, reputedly found with this one, is illustrated by von Bothmer, D. *Ancient Art from New York Private Collections* no. 96.

[77] *Mochlos* 52 and fig. 22 (v.1.8); *Troy* fig. 359; cf. also the Troy treasures, Schmidt, H. (1902) *Heinrich Schliemanns Sammlung trojanischer Altertümer* 225 f.

[78] Franks, A. W. (1867) Communication, *Proceedings of the Society of Antiquaries* 3, 435 and fig. p. 437; *Montelius* pl. IV, 1, 6 and 7; *British Museum Bronze Age Guide* (1920) 163, fig. 174

[79] *Deshayes* 75.

[80] *Papathanasopoulos* pl. 77.

[81] Foster Bequest, 128, 131 and 132.

[82] *Eutresis* fig. 286, 1.

[83] *Eutresis* fig. 287, 1.

[84] *Eutresis* fig. 287, 2.

[85] Cf. Hutchinson, R. W. (1950) Battle axes in the Aegean. *Proc. P. S.* 16, 52 f.

[86] *Montelius* fig. 488.

[87] *Deshayes* II, 79; *Montelius* pl. 4, 11.

[88] Ridgeway, W. (1901) *The Early Age of Greece* I, 51, fig. 27.

[89] *Stronach* 118.

[90] *Montelius* pl. 4, 8.

[91] *Deshayes* 193.

[92] *Stronach* 118, n. 202.

[93] *Eutresis* fig. 287.

[94] *Poliochni* pl. CLXXIII.

[95] *Poliochni* pl. CXXIX c.

[96] *Deshayes* 92; *Stronach* 120.

[97] Platon, N. and Stassinopoulou-Touloupa, E. Ivories and Linear B Tablets from Thebes. *ILN*, December 5, 1964, 89 and fig. 5.

[98] Maxwell-Hyslop, R. (1949) Western Asiatic shaft-hole axes. *Iraq* 11, 92.

[99] *Montelius* pl. 4, 4 and 9; *Deshayes* II, 105 f.

[100] Foster Bequest 129; also A.1904.525 from 'one of the Cyclades'.

[101] Bucholz, H.-G. *Zur Herkunft der Kretischen Doppelaxt*.

[102] Dawkins, R. M. and Droop, J. P. (1911) Excavations at Phylakopi in Melos. *BSA* 17, 22 and pl. XIV.59.

[103] Przeworski, S. *Die Metallindustrie Anatoliens* 40 and pl. IX, 10 (I am indebted to Mr David French for this reference).

[104] *Mochlos* 36.

[105] *Stronach* 104.

[106] Catling, H. W. (1964) *Cypriot Bronzework in the Mycenaean World* 56 and figs. 1 and 2.

[107] *Ts. 1898* pl. 12, 2. In Anatolia Stronach quotes Larisa, Troy, Alaca, Horoztepe, Til Barsib.

[108] *Ts. 1898* pl. 12, 5.

[109] *Levkas* pl. 63, 1 and 2; Schmidt, H. op. cit. (supra, n. 77) no. 5848; Copenhagen National Museum 3121.

[110] *Stronach* 111, Type 3a (Thermi, Troy, Larisa, Ahirköy).

[111] *Ts. 1898* pl. 12, 1.

[112] *Bossert* 23 f.

[113] *Stronach* 97 (Chrysolakkos, Marathokephalon, Chaimazi).

[114] *D–S* pl. 4, 10; *Levkas* pl. 73, 16.

[115] *Bossert* pl. 14, 1–2.

[116] E.g. *Mochlos* fig. 12 and 44; Xanthoudides, op. cit. (supra, n. 53) pl. XXIV, 1193–4, pl. XXXIX, 1432–3.

[117] Sotiriades, G. (1912) Fouilles préhistoriques en Phocide. *REG* 25, 276, fig. 15, right.

[118] *Papathanasopoulos* pl. 77; *Stephanos* 224.

[119] *Ts. 1898* pl. 12, 8.

[120] Early Cretan metalwork is the subject of a special study by Dr Keith Branigan (1968), *Copper and Bronze Working in Early Bronze Age Crete*. In view of his work, no attempt has been made here to survey the Cretan material in detail.

[121] Blegen, op. cit. (supra, n. 28) 182 and pl. XX, 25; Caskey, J. L. (1955) Excavations at Lerna, 1954. *Hesperia* 24, pl. 23, b; *Levkas* pl. 63 a, 3 and 4.

[122] Caskey, J. L. (1957) Excavations at Lerna, 1956, *Hesperia* 26, pl. 42, c; *Montelius* pl. 7, 9.

[123] *Ts. 1898* pl. 12, 3 and p. 190, fig. 11; *Levkas* pl. 73, 15; *D–S* pl. 4, 11 and pl. 5, 16; Σωτηριάδης, Γ. (1908) Προϊστορικὰ ἀγγεῖα Χαιρονείας καὶ Ἐλατείας. *Arch. Eph.* 93, fig. 16.

[124] Sotiriades, G. op. cit. (supra, n. 117) fig. 15, right.

[125] Museum no. AE 265; cf. Caskey, op. cit. (supra, n. 122) pl. 42, d.

[126] Mus. no. AE 264, cf. Atkinson *et al.*, op. cit. (supra, n. 12), pl. IX, 1.

[127] Mus. no. AE 262, cf. *Bossert* pl. 13, 6.

[128] Catling, op. cit. (supra, n. 106) 60, fig. 3, 7–11.

[129] *Ts. 1898* pl. 12, 6.

[130] Cook, J. M. (1951) Archaeology in Greece 1949–50. *JHS* 71, 251.

[131] *Levkas* pl. 62, 3.

[132] Sandars, N. K. (1961) The First Aegean Swords and their Ancestry. *AJA* 65, 17 f.

[133] Παπαβασιλείου, op. cit. (supra, n. 52) 11, fig. 13. (This observation was suggested by Mr David French.)

[134] Θεοχάρης, Δ. (1952) Ἀνασκαφὴ ἐν Ἀραφῆνι, *Pratika* 129 f; *Poliochni* 591, 658.

[135] *Ts. 1899* 124, figs. 35–7.

[136] *Ts. 1898* 176.

[137] Dawkins and Droop, op. cit. (supra, n. 102) pl. VII, lower; also Atkinson *et al.* (op. cit., supra, n. 12) 190.

[138] *Papathanasopoulos* 132.

[139] Κορδελλᾶς, op. cit. (supra, n. 31); Davies, O. (1935) *Roman Mines in Europe* 256 f.

[140] *Poliochni* pl. LXXXV, d.

[141] Davies, O. (1929) Two north Greek mining towns. *JHS* 49, 89, reviewed the evidence and suggested one source only at Itea (Kirrha) in Phokis. This site has been convincingly dismissed by Miss Sylvia Benton (1964) No tin from Kirrha in Phokis, *Antiquity* 38, 138.

[142] *Deshayes* 147, no. 2801, pl. XLVI, 19 and LXII, 8.

[143] *Ts. 1898* 190, pl. 12, 3 (12·85% tin).

[144] *Ts. 1898* 187 and pl. 8, 2 (13·52% tin).

[145] Cf. also Mosso, A. (1910) *The Dawn of Mediterranean Civilisation* 307.

[146] Schmidt, op. cit. (supra, n. 77) no. 5801, 5855, 5823; Schliemann, H. Ilios, *The Country and City of the Trojans* 477; Bittel, K. (1959) Beitrag zur Kenntnis anatolischer Metallgefässe des dritten Jahrtausend v. Chr *JdI* 74, 1.

[147] Bronze with a high proportion of lead appears to be a deliberate product in the Late Bronze Age of Britain, cf. Smith, M. and Blin-Stoyle, A. E. (1959) A sample analysis of British Middle and Late Bronze Age material using optical spectrometry. *Proc. P. S.* 25, 188 f.

[148] Forbes, P. J. (1964) *Studies in Ancient Technology* IX, 130.

[149] Junghans, S., Schröder, M. and Sangmeister, E. (1960) *Metallanalyse kupferzeitlicher und frühbronzezeitlicher Bodenfunde aus Europa* no. 297, 737 and 825.

[150] Childe, V. G. op. cit. (supra, n. 11) 241; Cambi, L. (1958–9) I metelli dei cimeli della grotta tombale di Monte Bradone. *Bulletino di Paletnologia Italiana*, NS XII, 67–8, 221 f.

[151] *Thermi* 215. The possibility that this also is of antimony cannot be ruled out, as Mr J. A. Charles has pointed out to me.

[152] Caley, E. R. (1949) On the prehistoric use of arsenical copper in the Aegean region. *Hesperia* Suppl. 8, 60 f; Przeworski, S., op. cit. (supra, n. 103) 107–8; Selimkhanov, I. R. (1962) Spectral analyses of metal articles from archaeological monuments, *Proc. P. S.* 28, 76 f; Selimkhanov, I. R. (1964) Was native copper used in Transcaucasia in Eneolithic times. *Proc. P. S.* 30, 69 f.

[153] The curiously high content of zinc in Cat. no. 47 has yet to be explained. The spearhead is, indeed, of brass, apparently the earliest object known of this alloy. Cf. Moorey, P. R. S. (1964) An interim report on some analyses of Luristan bronzes. *Archaeometry* 7, 79.

[154] *Stephanos* 224; *Papathanasopoulos* pl. 62, b.

[155] Mellaart, op. cit. (supra, n. 23) pl. XXXV a, slag p. 114.

[156] French, D. (1962) Excavations at Can Hasan. *Anat. St.* 12, 33.

[157] Lloyd, Seton and Mellaart, James (1962) *Beycesultan* I, 285.

[158] *D–S* 352. For the gold from Sesklo, ibid. 350, 291.

[159] Evans, A. J. *The Palace of Minos* IV, 14 and fig. 3, f.

[160] Cf. Caskey, J. L. (1964) Excavations in Kea, 1963. *Hesperia* 33, 314 f.

[161] Dörpfeld, W. *Troja und Ilion* 324.

[162] *Troy* 42.

[163] *Ts. 1899* pl. 10. The bird-headed pins of bone have bronze counterparts at Thermi (*Thermi* pl. XXV, 31.18 and 31.19). For the wider affinities of the spiral-headed pins, see Childe, V. G. (1936) The axes from Maikop and Caucasian metallurgy. *Liverpool Annals of Archaeology and Anthropology* 23, 113 f and pl. LII, c. Direct East Mediterranean influence must also be considered a possibility now, in view of the daggers from Byblos imported to Crete at least as early as the Middle Minoan I period, cf. Branigan, K. (1966) Byblite daggers in Cyprus and Crete, *AJA* 70, 123 f.

[164] Renfrew *et al.*, op. cit. (supra, n. 15) 225 f.

[165] *D–S* 116, 3 and pl. 21, 1; Caskey, op. cit. (supra, n. 160) pl. 46, e–f.

[166] Weinberg, S. (1962) Excavations at prehistoric Elateia, *Hesperia* 29, fig. 12; Korošec, J. (1964) *Danilo in Danilska Cultura* pl. 36.

[167] French, op. cit. (*supra*, n. 13).

[168] Caskey, J. L. and E. G., op. cit. (supra, n. 6) 141, fig. 7, 111.6.

[169] Renfrew, op. cit. (supra, n. 10).

[170] Childe, V. G. (1924) A gold vase of Early Helladic type. *JHS* 44, 163. Compare also the three-spouted vessel, Zervos, op. cit. (supra, n. 36) fig. 185–6, with the metal version from Troy, Schmidt, op. cit. (supra, n. 77) no. 5863.

[171] Kunze, op. cit. (supra, n. 47) pl. XXIII, 1; Caskey, J. L. (1964) Chalandriani in Syros. *Essays in Memory of Karl Lehmann* 63 f, fig. 8.

[172] Barnett, R. D. (1963–4) A review of acquisitions, 1955-62, of Western Asiatic antiquities. *BMQ* 27, no. 3–4, 79 and pl. XXIX, b.

[173] *Ts. 1899* pl. 8, 3–4.

[174] Schmidt, op. cit. (supra, n. 77) no. 5685, 5973.

[175] Caskey, J. L., op. cit. (supra, n. 6) 291, fig. 1, B, D and E. It is unlikely that the Late Neolithic thin-walled pottery vessels of the Greek mainland were based on metal prototypes as suggested by Schachermeyr, F. *Die älteste Kulturen Griechenlands* (1955) 126 f. So early a *Metallschock* is not supported by evidence of metal vessels, nor indeed by other metal finds.

[176] Mellink, M. (1956) The tomb at Alaca Hüyük and the Aegean world. *The Aegean and the Near East: Studies Presented to Hetty Goldman* pl. IV–VI.

[177] Bittel, op. cit. (supra, n. 146) Abb. 1–2.

[178] But cf. the gold jug from Horoztepe, Tezcan, B., op. cit. (supra, n. 42) pl. XV.

[179] Boyd Hawes, H. (1908) *Gournia* pl. C, 1.

[180] Åberg, op. cit. (supra, n. 11) p. 89, fig. 174; cf. Schmidt, op. cit. (supra, n. 77) no. 5873 in silver.

[181] Caskey, J. L. (1956) Excavations at Lerna, 1955. *Hesperia* 25, 164, fig. 4. This is the more squat form of *depas* cup, corresponding to Troy form A 44 rather than A 45.

[182] Athens, National Museum 6292.

[183] Tezcan, op. cit. (supra, n. 42) pl. XXIV, 1–2.

[184] Renfrew, Cann and Dixon, op. cit. (supra, n. 10) 241.

[185] Bucholz, H.-G. (1958) Der Kupferhandel des zweiten vorchristlichen Jahrtausends, *Minoica, Festschrift zum 80. Geburtstag von Johannes Sundwell* 92 f.

[186] Goetze, A. *Kleinasien* (Handbuch der Altertumswissenschaft III, 1.3.3.1) 67.

[187] Bass, G. F. (1961) The Cape Gelidonya Wreck, Preliminary Report. *AJA* 65, 267 f.

[188] Edgar, C. C., op. cit. (supra, n. 35).

[189] Dümmler, op. cit. (supra, n. 21).

[190] Franks, etc., op. cit. (supra, n. 78).

[191] Cf. supra, n. 142.

[192] Cf. supra, n. 112.

[193] Cf. supra, n. 130. The narrow ribs on each side of the central rib are a common feature on Minoan weapons, cf. Branigan, op. cit. (supra n. 163) 123.

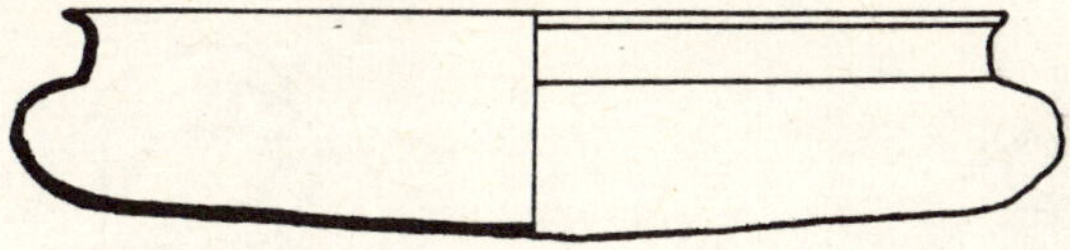

17

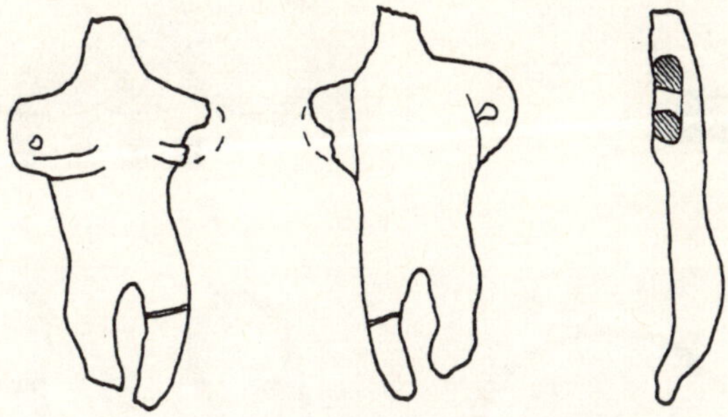

1

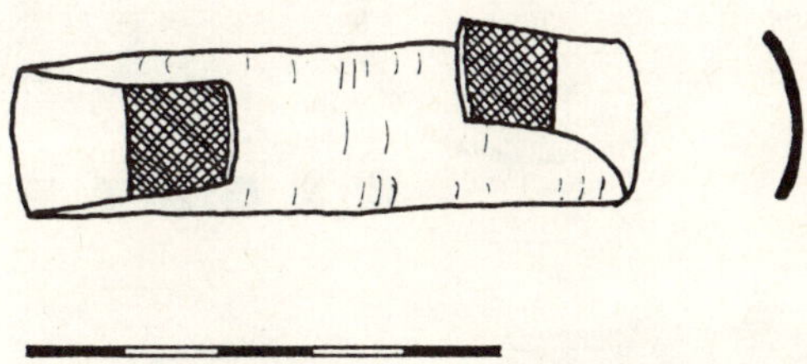

8

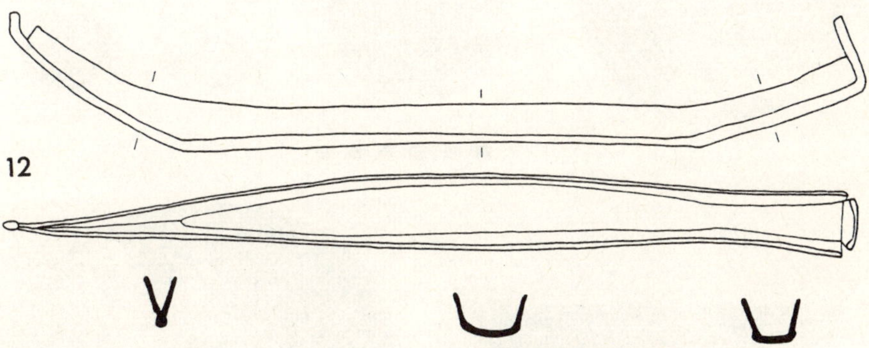

12

Plate 1. Silver bowl and bracelet from Amorgos, lead figurine from Antiparos, and lead boat from Naxos. See catalogue.

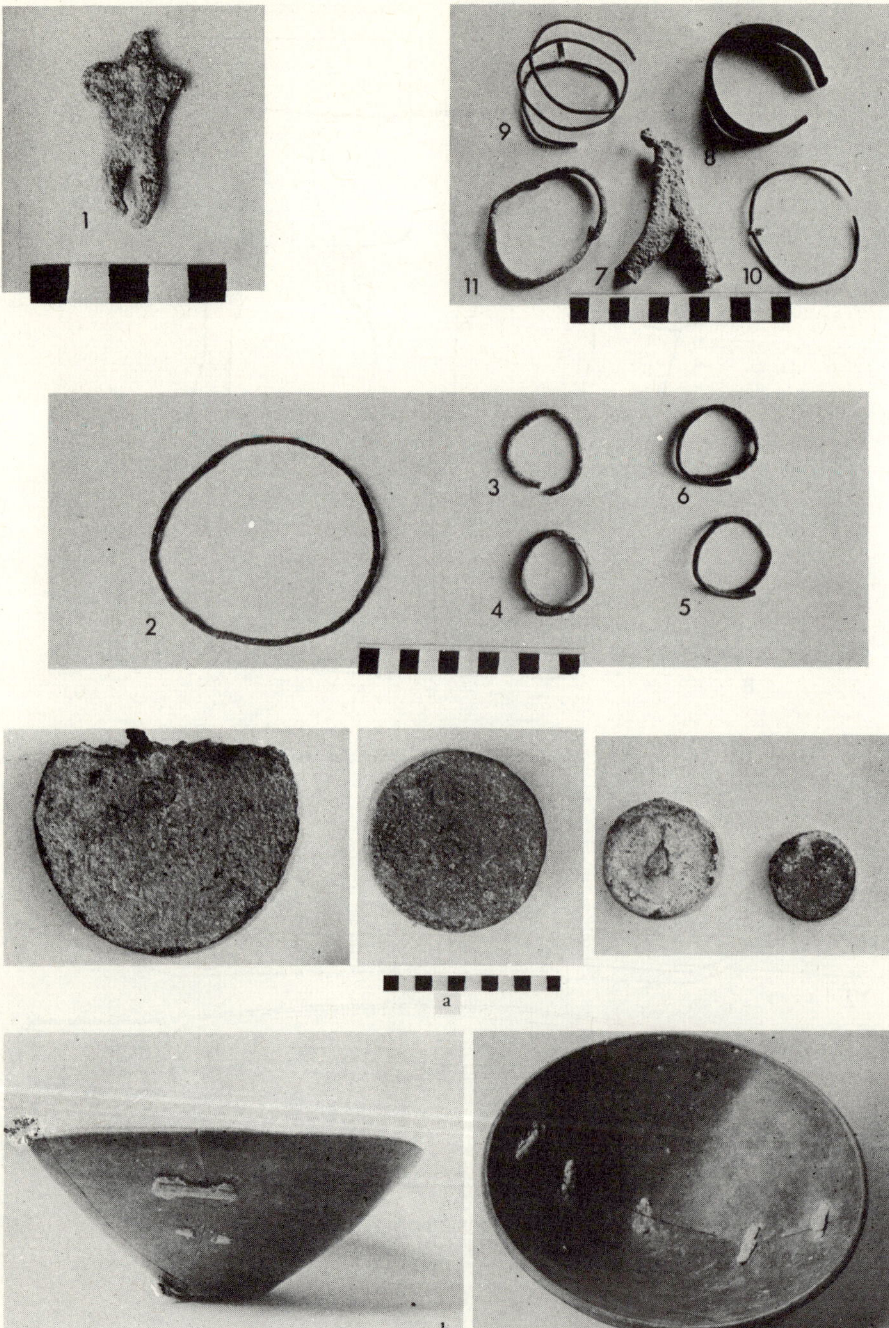

Plate 2. Lead and silver objects: 1-6 from Antiparos, 7-11 from Amorgos; (a) lead ingots from Phylokapi in Melos; (b) early Helladic bowl from Aegina repaired with lead rivets.

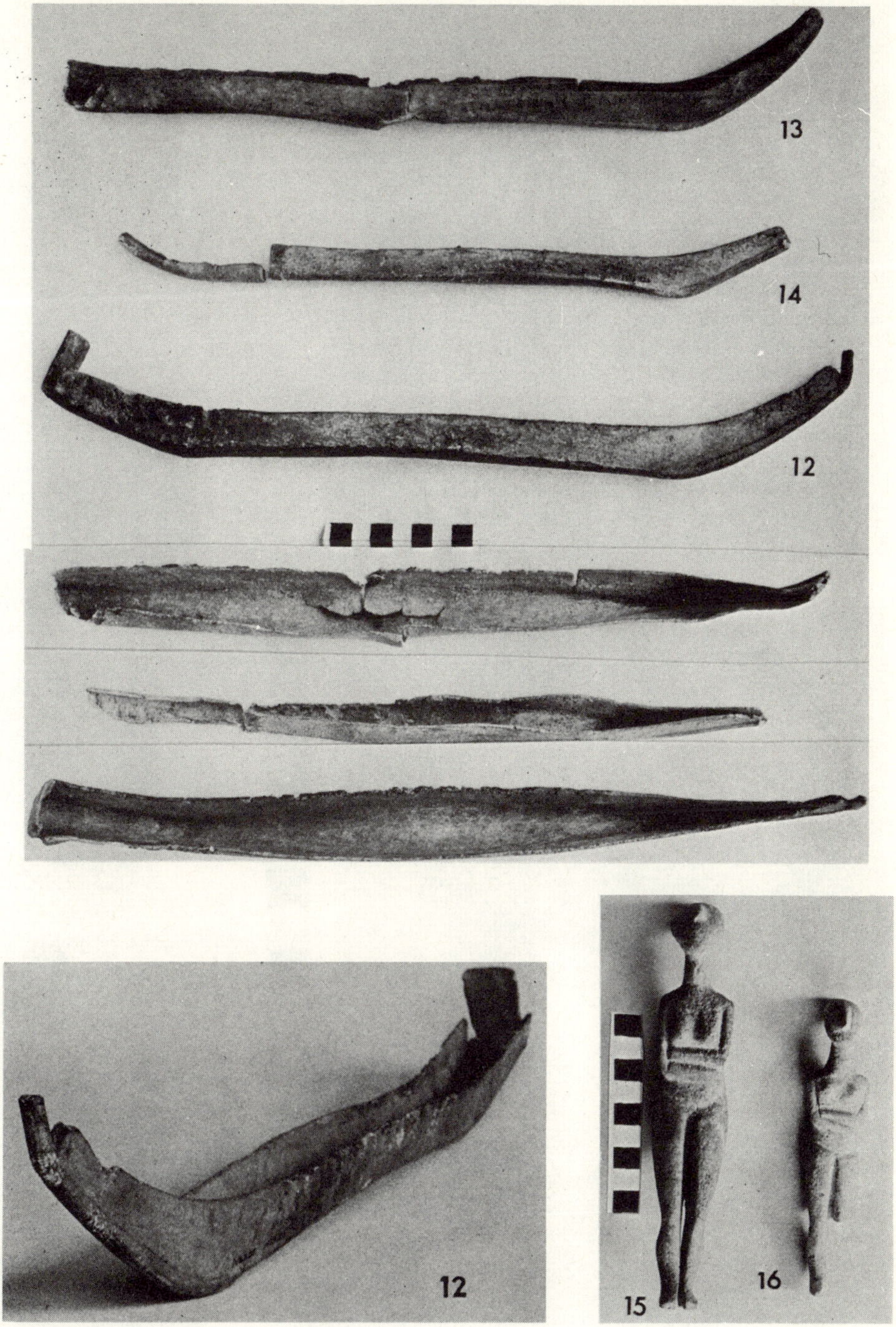

Plate 3. Lead boat models from Naxos, with associated marble figurines.

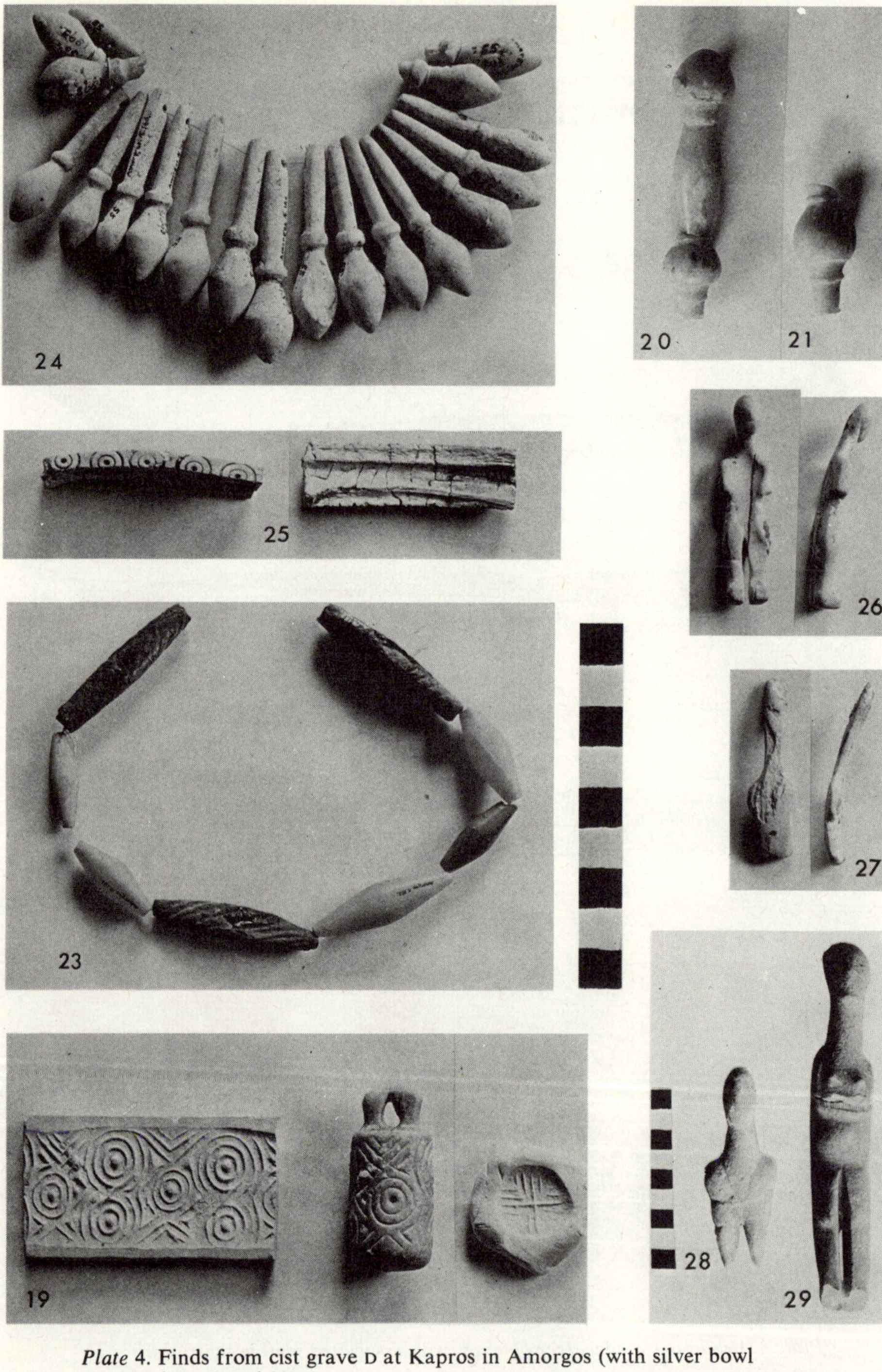

Plate 4. Finds from cist grave D at Kapros in Amorgos (with silver bowl no. 17, plates 1 and 10).

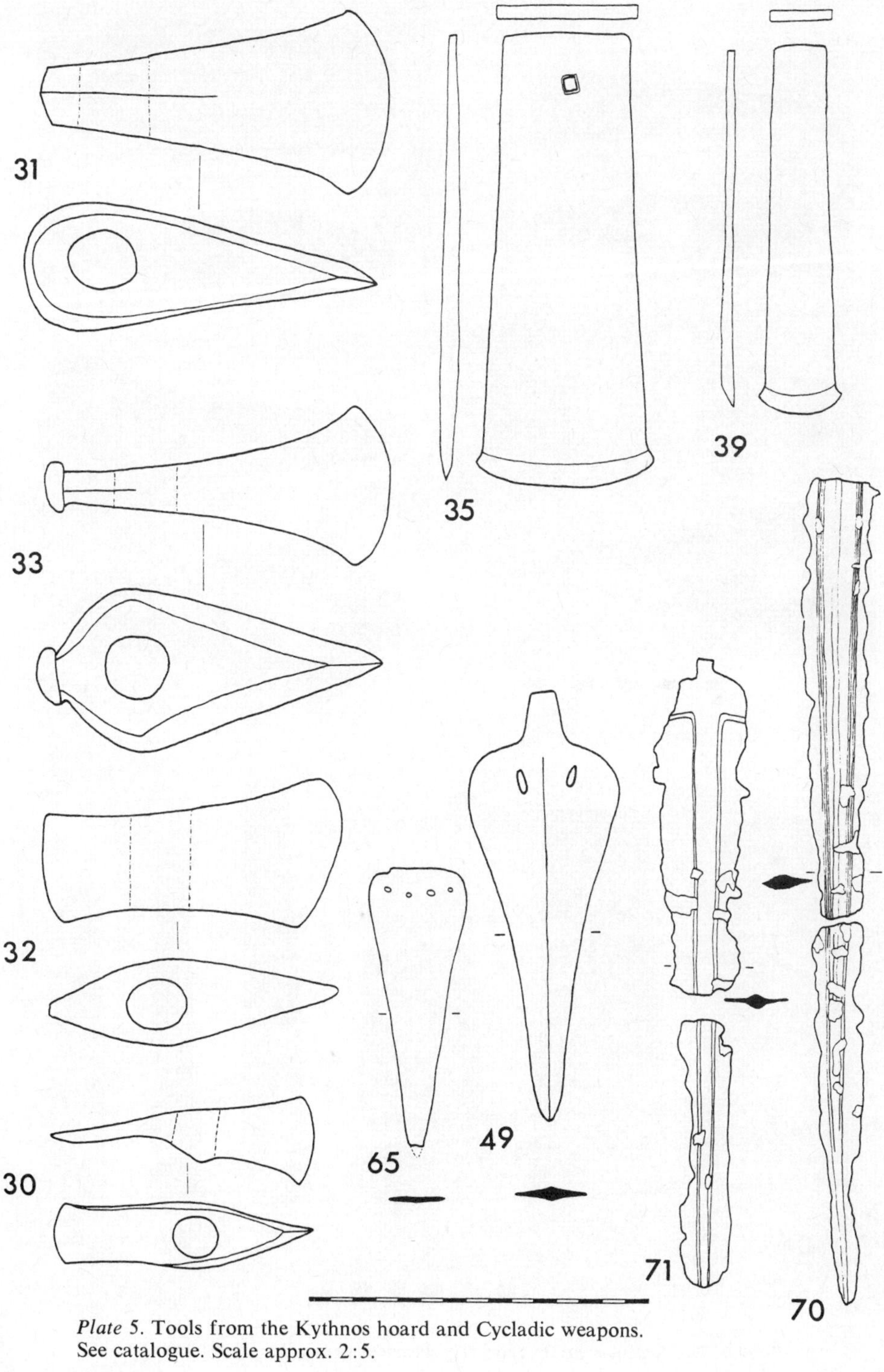

Plate 5. Tools from the Kythnos hoard and Cycladic weapons. See catalogue. Scale approx. 2:5.

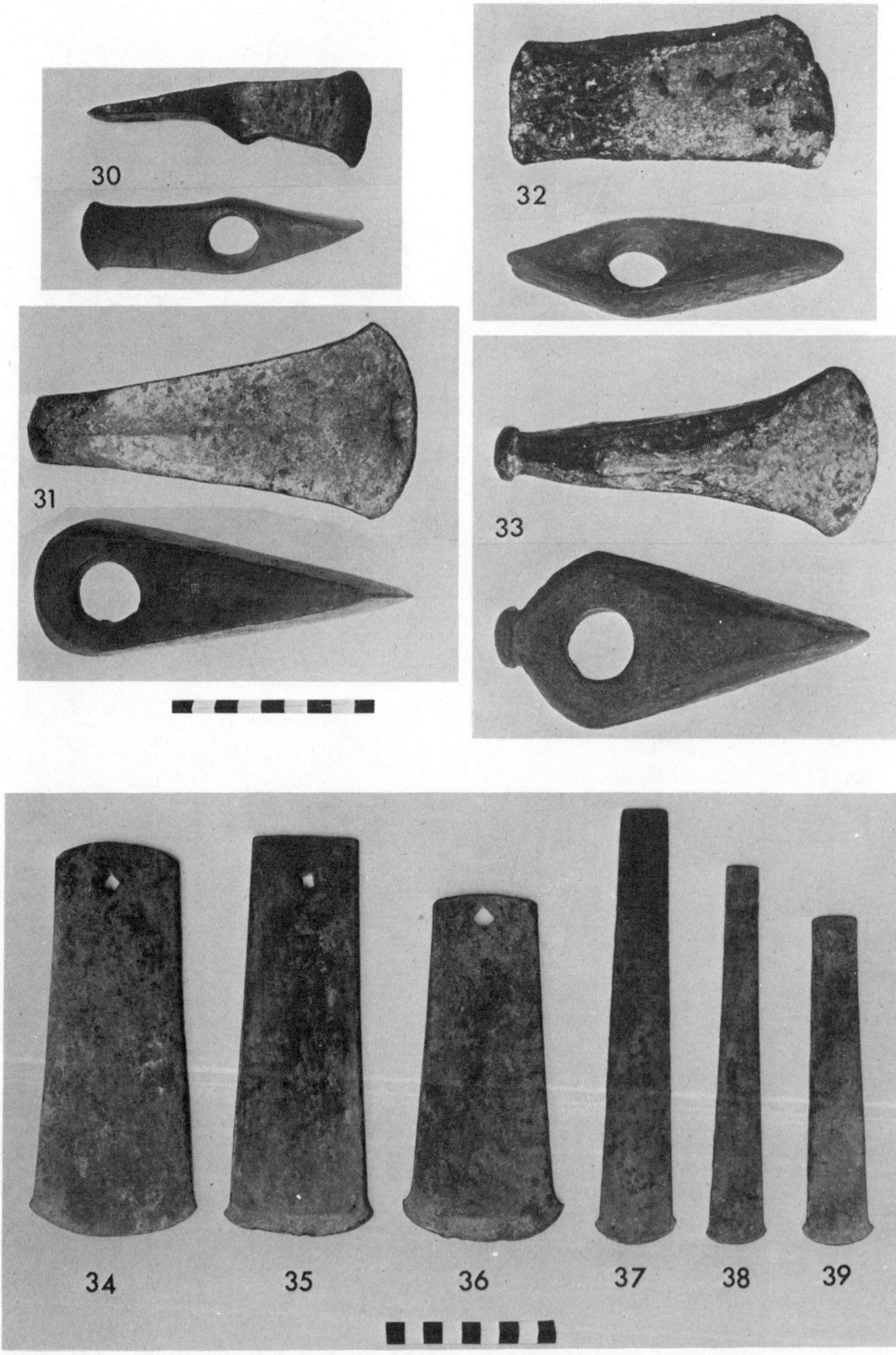

Plate 6. The Kythnos hoard (courtesy Trustees of the British Museum).

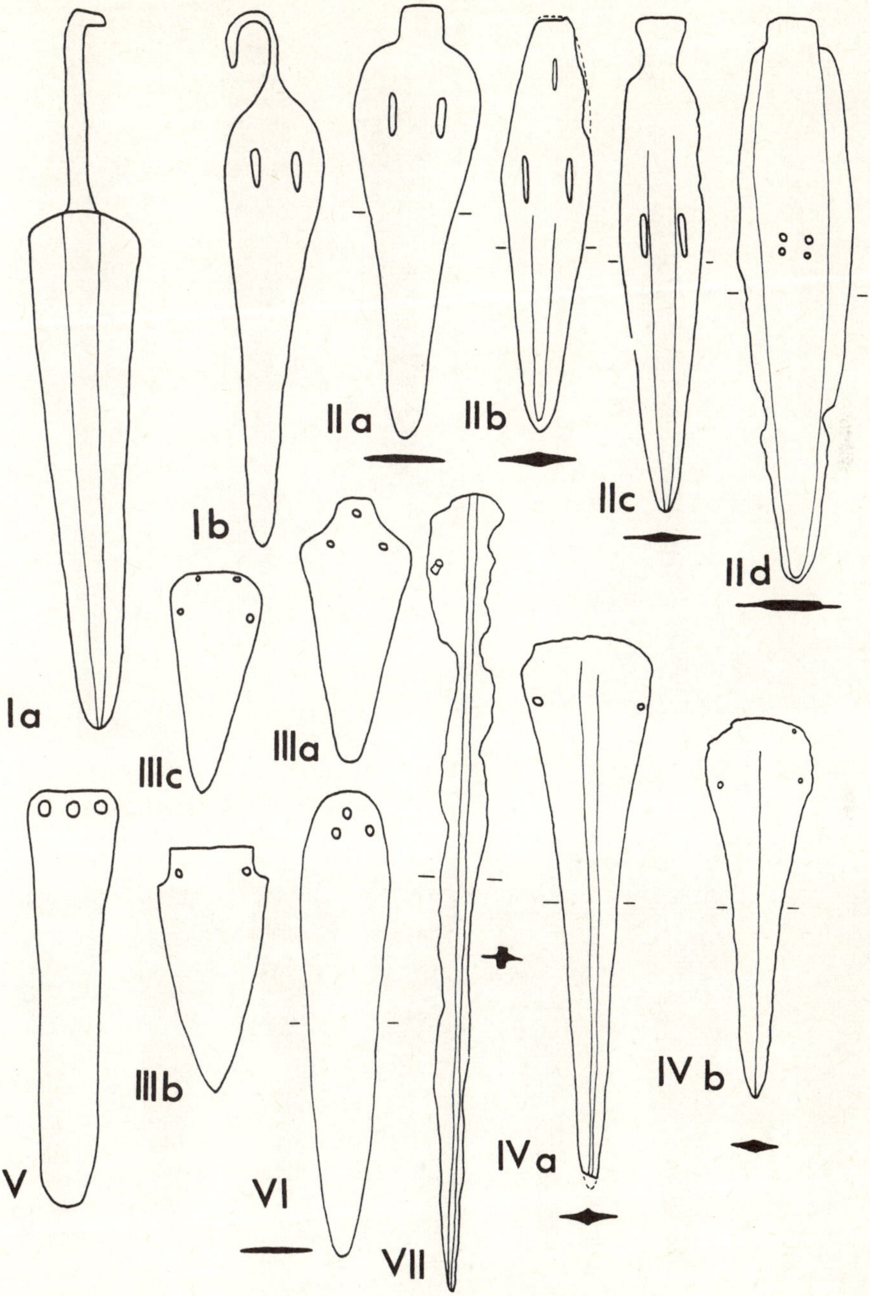

Plate 7. Classification of Aegean daggers. Ia (Cyprus); Ib (Dokathismata in Amorgos); IIa 50 (Amorgos); IIb 51 (Amorgos); IIc 52 (Amorgos); IId 53 (Arkesine in Amorgos); IIIa (Arkesine in Amorgos); IIIb (Crete); IIIc (Phokis); IVa 60 (Amorgos); IVb 63 (Amorgos); V (Sesklo); VI 66 (Amorgos); VII 69 (Amorgos). Scale approx. 1:3.

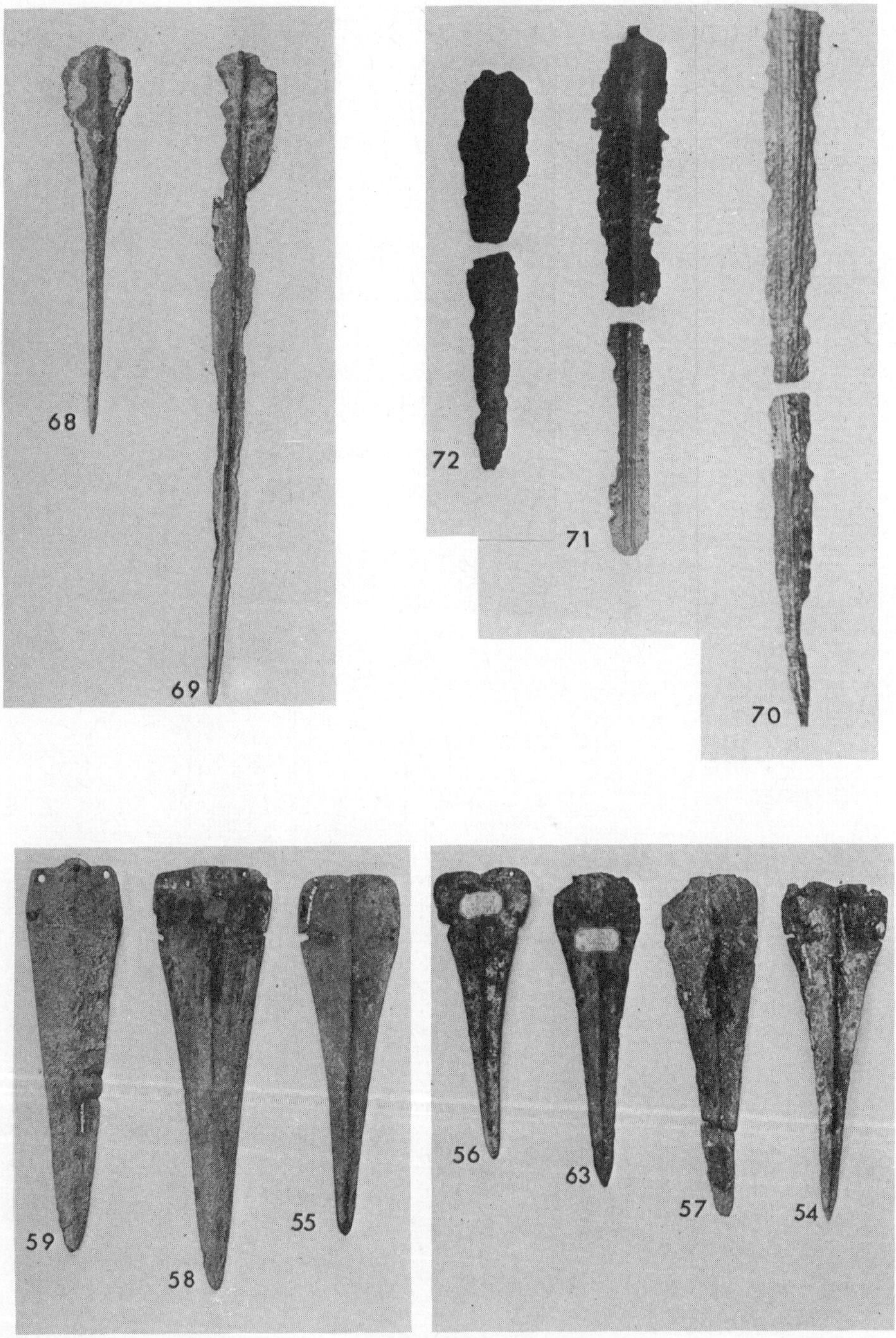

Plate 8. Daggers and swords (classes IV and VII) from Amorgos. Scale 1:4 approx.

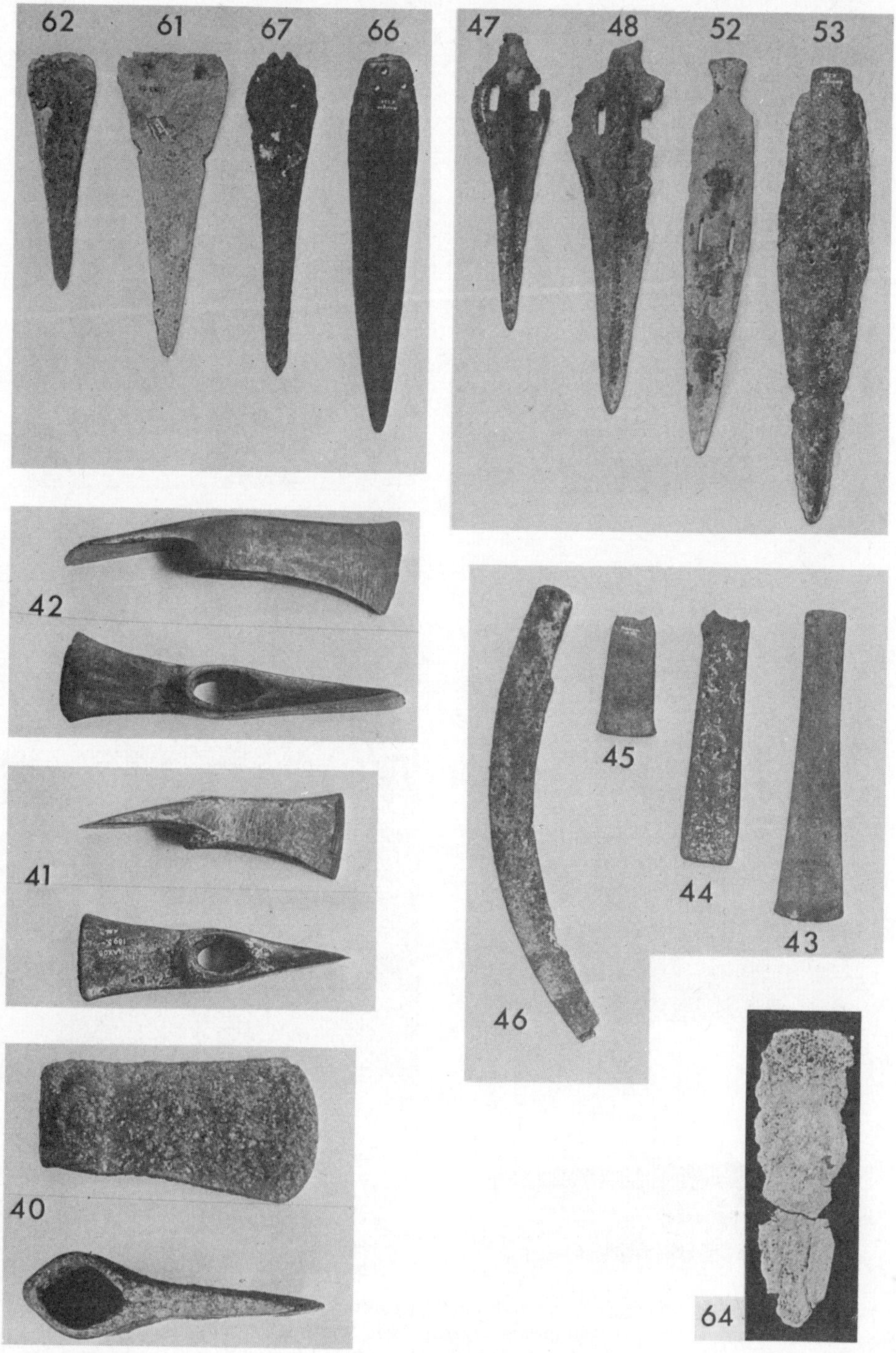

Plate 9. Cycladic tools and daggers. Scale 1 : 4 approx.

Plate 10. Early Aegean metal and pottery vessels. Sauceboats: (a) gold (Arcadia); (b) clay (Chalandriani). *Depas* cups: (c) silver (Troad); (d) clay (Troad, *cf.* Chalandriani. Bowls: (e) silver (? Euboia); (no. 17) silver (Kapros in Amorgos). (c and e courtesy Trustees of the British Museum and of The Metropolitan Museum of Art).

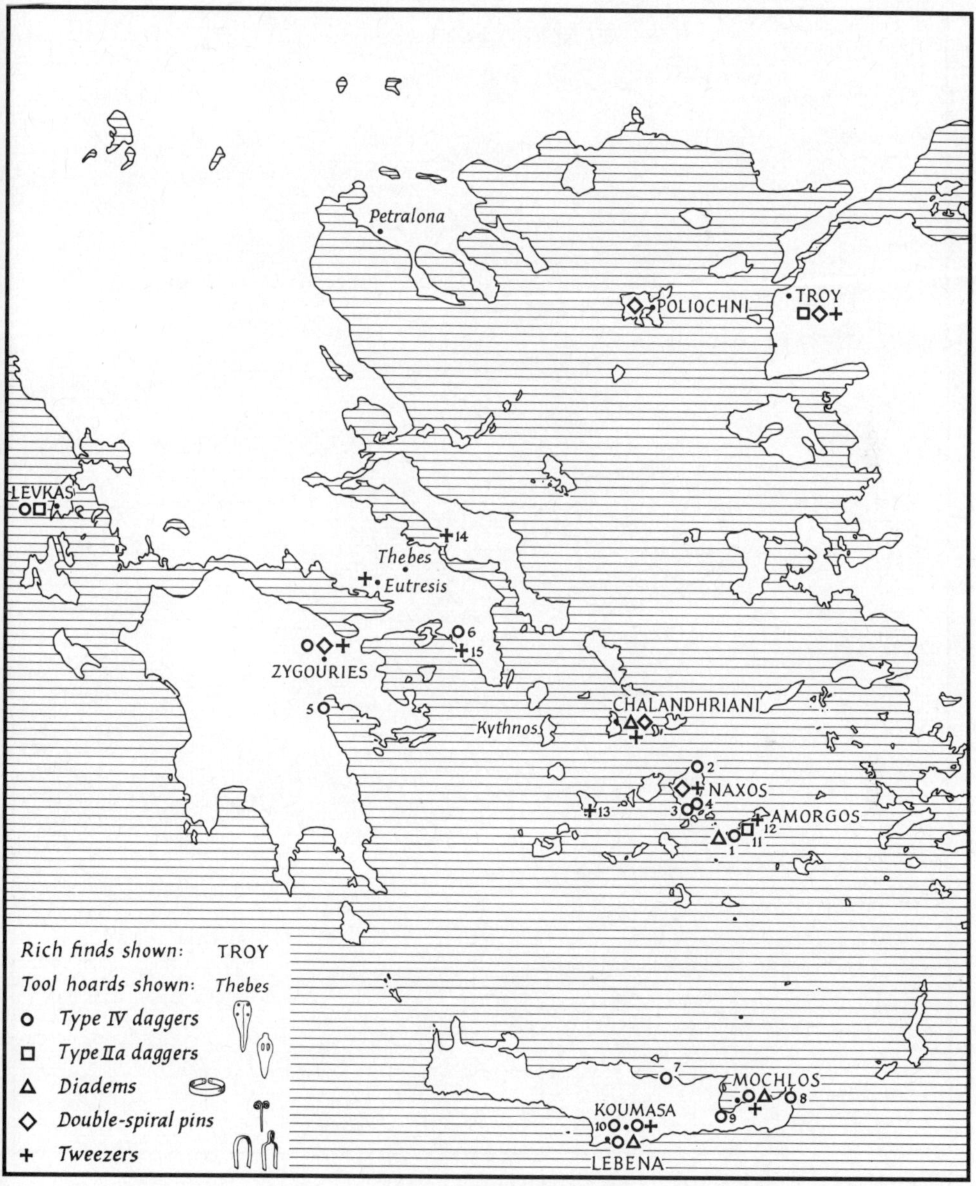

Plate 11. Important metal finds of Aegean Early Bronze Age.
1 Dokathismata (Amorgos); 2 Ormos Apollona (Naxos); 3 Spedos (Naxos); 4 Panermos (Naxos); 5 Lerna; 6 Athens; 7 Pyrgos (Crete); 8 Palaikastro (Crete); 9 Gournia (Crete); 10 Platanos (Crete); Stavros (Amorgos); 12 Kapsala (Amorgos); 13 Akrotiraki (Siphnos); 14 Manika; 15 Ay. Kosmas.
The list of Class IV daggers in Crete is not complete.

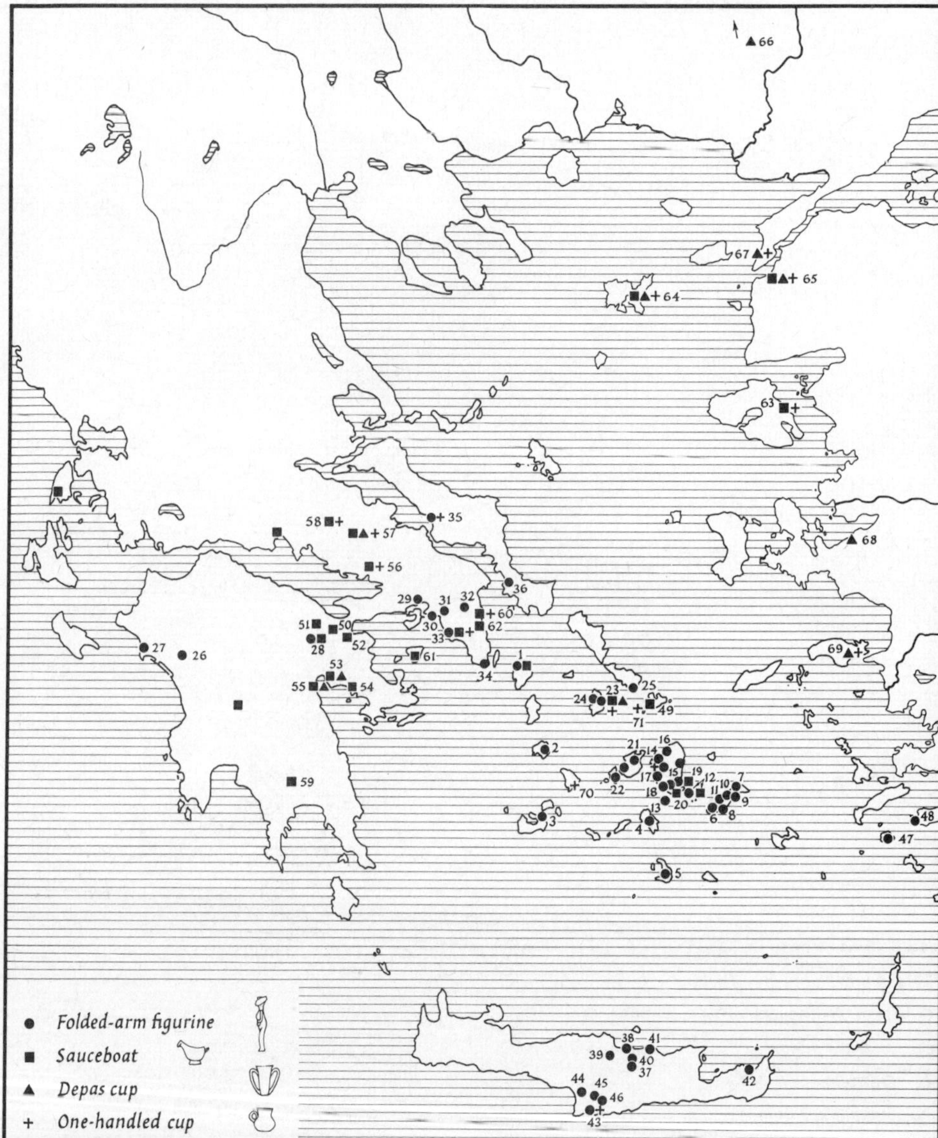

Plate 12. Local types and cultural continuum in E.B.2 Aegean.
1 Ay. Irini (Kea); 2 Seriphos; 3 Phylakopi (Melos); 4 Ios; 5 Thera; 6 Dokathismata (Amorgos); 7 Aigiali (Amorgos); 8 Stavros (Amorgos); 9 Kapsala (Amorgos); 10 Kapros (Amorgos); 11 Kato Akrotiri (Amorgos); 12 Keros; 13 Herakleia; 14 Trymalia (Naxos); 15 Ay. Anargyroi (Naxos); 16 Akrotiri (Naxos); 17 Kastraki (Naxos); 18 Karvounolakki (Naxos); 19 Panermos (Naxos); 20 Spedos (Naxos); 21 Paros; 22 Antiparos; 23 Chalandriani (Syros); 24 Pidima (Syros); 25 Tenos; 26 Neraida (Olympia); 27 Ay. Andreas (Messenia); 28 Zygouries; 29 Eleusis; 30 Piraeus; 31 Athens; 32 Brauron; 33 Ay. Kosmas; 34 Sounion; 35 Manika; 36 Styra; 37 Knossos; 38 Herakleion; 39 Tylissos; 40 Tekke; 41 Pyrgos; 42 Siteia; 43 Lebena; 44 Ay. Onouphrios; 45 Platanos; 46 Koumasa; 47 Nisyros; 48 Kap Krio; 49 Mykonos; 50 Corinth; 51 Korakou; 52 Gonia; 53 Tiryns; 54 Asine; 55 Lerna; 56 Eutresis; 57 Orchomenos; 58 Ay. Marina; 59 Amyklai; 60 Raphina; 61 Aegina; 62 Askitario; 63 Thermi; 64 Troy; 65 Poliochni; 66 Michailitch; 67 Protesilaos; 68 Bayrakli; 69 Heraion; 70 Akrotiraki (Siphnos); 71 Delos. Many further sites with finds of sauceboats are known from the Greek mainland. There are many southern and inland Anatolian sites with finds of *depas* cups.

METAL ANALYSES, by Mrs A. Millett, and others

Analyses 40–69, of objects in the Ashmolean Museum, Oxford, were conducted, principally by Mrs A. Millett, at the Oxford Research Laboratory for Archaeology and the History of Art, through the kindness of the Director, Dr E. T. Hall. Analyses 70–72, of objects in the British School of Archaeology at Athens, were supplied by Professor E. Sangmeister of the Arbeitsgemeinschaft für die Metallurgie des Altertums bei dem Römisch-Germanischen Zentralmuseum, Freiburg.

Cat. no.	Object	% Cu	Sn	Pb	As	Sb	Ni	Bi	Fe	Zn	Ag	Au	Co
40	Shaft-hole axe	88·0	8·8	0·59	—	0·14	0·12	<0·01	0·038	—	0·078	—	—
41	Axe-adze	91·5	7·3	0·26	0·79	—	0·026	<0·01	0·055	—	<0·005	—	—
42	Axe-adze	88·5	8·3	2·1	—	—	0·062	<0·01	0·084	—	0·011	—	—
43	Flat axe	99·3	<0·1	0·11	—	—	0·018	<0·01	0·034	0·16	0·32	—	—
44	Flat axe	95·2	—	0·25	3·4	—	0·66	0·32	—	—	0·018	—	—
45	Flat axe	95·8	0·85	0·13	1·1	—	0·11	0·080	1·9	—	0·088	—	—
46	Sickle	92·2	5·5	1·1	0·66	—	0·046	<0·01	0·028	—	<0·005	—	—
47	Dagger Class IIa	94·0	—	0·5	—	—	0·072	<0·01	—	5·1	0·037	—	—
48	Dagger Class IIa	99·8	—	0·45	—	—	0·18	<0·01	—	—	0·029	—	—
52	Dagger Class IIc	97·0	0·24	0·13	1·5	—	0·30	<0·01	0·56	—	0·051	—	—
53	Dagger Class IVa	95·5	—	0·1	3·5	—	0·012	<0·01	0·38	—	0·022	—	—
54	Dagger Class IVa	95·0	—	—	4·9	—	0·029	<0·01	0·11	—	0·064	—	—
55	Dagger Class IVa	99·1	—	0·54	—	—	0·15	<0·01	0·023	0·14	0·022	—	—
56	Dagger Class IVa	99·2	—	0·38	—	0·12	0·13	<0·01	0·018	—	0·18	—	—
57	Dagger Class IVa	99·9	—	—	—	—	0·032	<0·01	0·070	—	0·0054	—	—
58	Dagger Class IVa	90·0	—	0·054	9·5	0·18	0·23	0·04	—	—	0·03	—	—
59	Dagger Class IVa	90·2	—	0·19	9·5	—	0·045	0·011	—	—	0·032	—	—
62	Dagger Class IVa	96·5	0·27	2·6	—	—	0·0063	<0·01	0·50	—	0·057	—	—
63	Dagger Class IVb	90·7	—	0·19	8·7	—	0·024	<0·01	—	—	0·04	—	—
66	Dagger Class VI	99·2	0·18	0·17	—	—	0·058	<0·01	0·30	—	0·023	—	—
67	Dagger Class VI	95·0	4·4	0·93	—	—	0·036	<0·01	0·18	0·15	0·066	—	—
68	Dagger Class VII	98·0	—	1·2	—	—	0·067	<0·01	0·020	0·40	0·036	—	—
69	Dagger Class VII	91·5	—	0·024	7·7	—	<0·01	<0·01	—	—	0·073	—	—
70	Dagger Class VII	88·4	8·3	2·2	0·79	Sp	0·16	0·01	+	0	0·17	0	0
71	Dagger Class VII	92·1	6·1	0·64	1·0	0	0·12	Sp	+ +	0	0·02	0	0·09
72	Dagger Class VII	91·7	6·7	0·4	1·0	Sp	0·06	0	+	0	0·19	0	0

Appendix, by J. A. Charles: Early Arsenical Bronzes—A Metallurgical View

The extensive use of arsenical copper, frequently of high arsenic content, in the Cyclades during the E.B. 2 period is apparent from Dr Renfrew's study. The question arises as to whether such high arsenic alloys were made intentionally or whether they were merely the result of impure raw materials. Archaeologists have been led to support both views as to the significance of this particular material, and the idea of purposeful arsenic addition to copper to produce an alloy as the forerunner or the alternative to tin bronze is not an original one. [1-5] It is clear, however, that although the opinion has been expressed before, the metallurgical advantages which would arise from the use of such an alloy, and the various factors which have to be considered in deciding whether or not control was exercised in its manufacture, have not been defined.

After initial discussions, the receipt of analytical data from Dr Renfrew and some study of the literature, personal judgement has hardened strongly towards the view that the high arsenic content copper found extensively in the Early and Middle Bronze Age periods was an intentionally produced alloy. This short appendix presents the factors which have been considered in reaching this conclusion.

The Effect of Arsenic on the Castability of Copper

Arsenic is a useful deoxidising agent in copper. During melting in air, or during smelting and refining, when an oxidising environment is produced in the later stages, considerable quantities of oxygen can dissolve in molten copper. This oxygen is not released as a gas as a result of the marked fall in solubility on solidification, but separates as Cu_2O, which forms a lower melting point eutectic with copper at the grain boundaries of the solidifying metal (ill. 1a). This grain boundary eutectic makes the copper less ductile and has a serious effect on the cold-workability. Further, the contact of the solidified metal with hydrogen-containing gases during subsequent furnace reheating (e.g. prior to forging) results in reaction with the grain boundary eutectic oxide, resulting in blistering, cracking and surface embrittlement. Open-fire heating with charcoal would, however, be unlikely to give this effect.

When arsenic is added to copper containing appreciable quantities of oxygen in solution, arsenious oxide forms as a separate phase which is insoluble in the copper and which separates from the liquid, eventually as a sublimate. Arsenic will also reduce any copper oxide formed during the process of solidification to give discrete particles,[7] rather than the eutectic grain boundary network of copper oxide more harmful to ductility. Lowering the oxygen content of the copper will mean that castings will be more liable to porosity, due to the solution of hydrogen in the molten metal and its rejection from solution during solidification, since an equilibrium between the two gases in solution must exist, but such porosity would not affect the ductility or workability of the material and any flaws would weld up satisfactorily during forging. A sophisticated craftsman might therefore put value on the use of arsenical copper for forged articles but less on its presence in articles to be cast for purely decorative purpose and not worked. In this connection it should be noted that in tin bronzes the tin reduces the soluble copper oxide to give tin oxide, but this is both insoluble and heavy and remains entangled in the melt. Such bronze is mechanically weak and porous. In modern alloys either zinc or phosphorus are added as deoxidisers, if possible before the addition of tin forms stable tin oxides, and instead give oxides which separate freely to the surface of the molten metal. Arsenic would be similarly beneficial as an addition for tin bronze. Even relatively recently, Vaders[8] has stated that Cu-As alloys have superior casting and mechanical properties to tin bronzes.

The effects of arsenic in producing copper castings most suitable for subsequent forging is thus clearly established.

The Effect of Arsenic Additions on the Mechanical Properties and Workability of Copper

First, it should be noted that the maximum solid solubility of arsenic in copper is of the order of 8%, and that this solubility does not change markedly with temperature (ill. 1b). This is in contrast to the tin bronzes, where the solubility of tin falls markedly with temperature from a maximum of about 15% to a low figure at room temperature (ill. 1c).

In both cases the stable *a* phase is ductile and readily worked, although increasing in strength and hardness with alloy content. In the case of tin bronzes, however, repeated hot-working (i.e. slow cooling) and reheating over a temperature range where the *a* phase alone is no longer the only stable phase, and when the brittle δ or ϵ phases can separate (e.g. 600–200°C, depending on the tin content), could reduce the workability. Cast tin-bronze consisting of the *a* phase only at elevated temperatures will generally not separate δ or ϵ phases on normal fairly fast cooling as achieved in a mould, since the attainment of the equilibrium structures is dependent on diffusion which does not have a chance to take place. Thus the *a* solid solution can be retained in a metastable condition at room temperature and it can be cold worked, having appreciable ductility. Reheating and warm-working, however, can facilitate diffusion and the attainment of the equilibrium two-phase structure which would tend to be harder and less easily worked without cracking. Butts[9] makes the comment that tin bronzes generally have poor hot working characteristics but that alloys with up to 10% tin can be cold-worked. In the arsenical copper, however, a cast alloy containing up to 8% arsenic can be readily worked over a wide range of temperature without embrittlement due to the appearance of a second phase. Quite obviously, unless some tendency to cracking appeared as a result there would always be a desire to carry out the rough shaping of an object while the metal was hot since this would reduce the effort required to obtain the necessary initial heavy deformation in, for example, producing complexities of shape such as a ribbed dagger blade. Deformation carried out above the recrystallisation temperature does not result in hardening or strengthening of the metal and, similarly, annealing to this temperature, or a temperature near to it, will remove the hardening effects of cold work. In this context the use of arsenic is significant since it raises the recrystallisation tem-

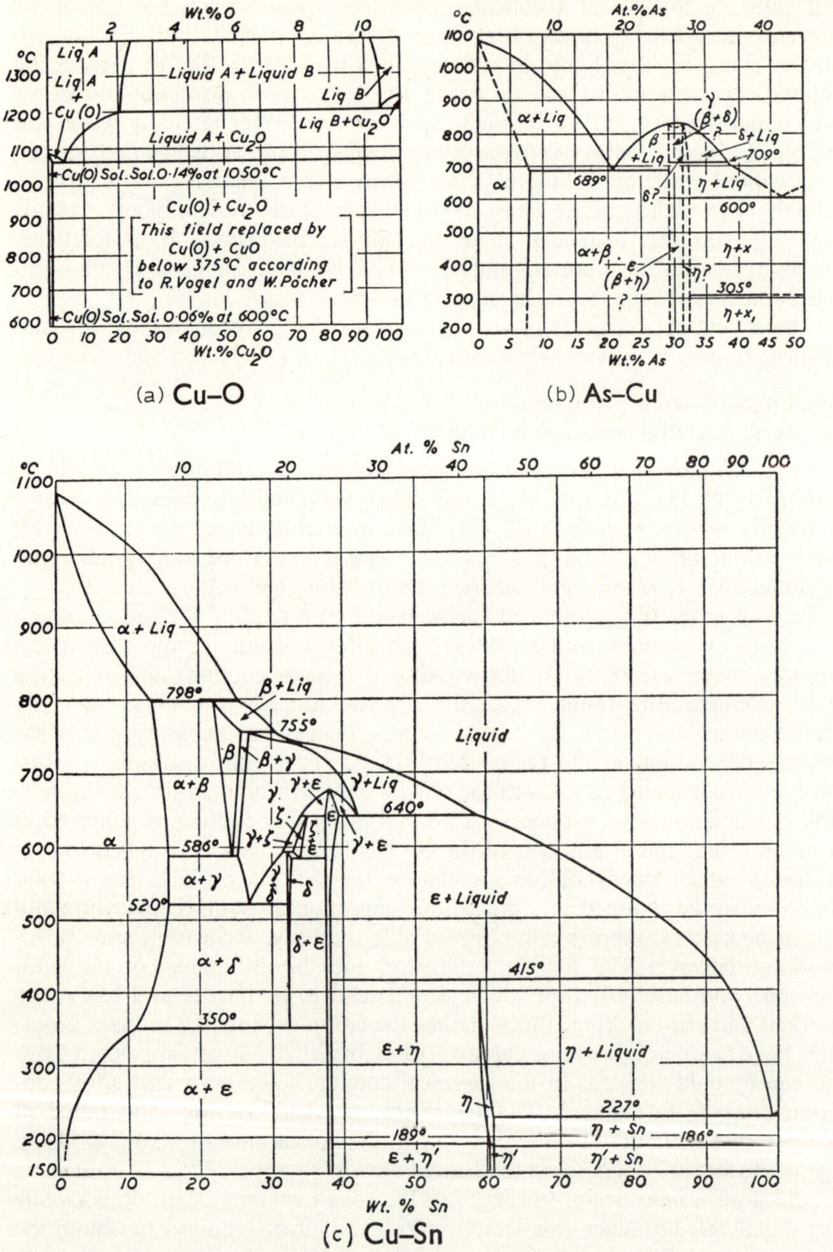

Illustration 1. Phase diagrams representing the constitution of alloys of (a) copper/oxygen; (b) copper/arsenic; (c) copper/tin, at various temperatures under equilibrium conditions. After Smithells (6).

perature of copper and therefore the temperature at which it retains strength obtained by cold work (which is one of the reasons for its main use in modern times, for components in steam boilers) and thus also the reheating temperature to which the material can be raised for further work without full softening.

These generally predictable properties of copper-arsenic alloys are in line with the results obtained by Hanson and Marryat,[7] in what is perhaps the most detailed account of the properties of the system available (it must be admitted that modern interest and data is sparse, mainly because arsenic has a disastrous effect on the electrical conductivity, and electrical uses of copper are among the most significant today). Although most of the quantitative data on properties given in their paper are confined to fairly low arsenic contents, they found that with even up to 7% arsenic the alloys possessed remarkable ductility and could be worked hot or cold to any extent by hammering without cracking. The effect of arsenic in promoting workability was most noticeable in copper of higher oxygen content, as might be produced under crude conditions.

Much more recently Maréchal[5] has carried out tests on work-hardened and annealed Cu-As alloys (up to 8% As) and tin-bronzes (up to 8% Sn) and has shown that in the cold worked state in particular the hardness of the two materials is very similar and that the arsenic-containing alloys soften rather less readily with reheating, re-emphasising the effect on the recrystallisation temperature.

It is thus clearly established that with even up to 8% As the alloys are readily worked, hot or cold, and can give strengths and hardness equivalent to tin bronze, and that the presence of arsenic is particularly beneficial in maintaining the workability of copper which would otherwise contain copper oxide.

Arsenical copper is also recognised as having superior corrosion and erosion resistance to other coppers, a further advantage in its use for steam boilers. In view of the relatively low rate of corrosion of copper under normal conditions, however, it is probably more doubtful that this property had significance in its historical use.

The Production of the Alloys from Available Minerals

Accepting the fact that arsenic in copper would have given beneficial effects in the arts of casting and working, can we be sure that control was knowingly exercised in the selection of raw materials? Or was the production of these arsenical copper artefacts the result of a purely chance selection of native metals and minerals, i.e. using copper ores or native copper containing substantial quantities of arsenic as an impurity? The arsenic content of native copper is always low and can be ruled out as a source of the alloying element. It is true that in many copper deposits the individual copper minerals Enargite Cu_3AsS_4 (19% As and 46% Cu) and Tennantite Cu_3AsS_3 (21% As and 53% Cu) are associated with sulphide copper minerals and that from analyses available the average arsenic content of randomly mined ores from these deposits can rise as high as 9% As, which, if all recovered, would lead to a much higher value in the smelted copper. Such very high concentrations of arsenic are, however, rare. Arsenopyrite (FeAsS) is also sometimes associated with copper sulphide ores and can lead to substantial arsenic contents.

There are two aspects of the problem, however, which have so far been overlooked, and which make the consideration by the statistical treatment of ore analyses relative to the final metal compositions largely irrelevant as far as arsenic is concerned.

First, sulphide minerals of copper, with which arsenic may be associated, must be converted to the oxide prior to reduction to the metal by carbon, or if separation from the earthly constituents of the ore is to be achieved by the more sophisticated method of producing a molten sulphide (matte), this must be subsequently converted to the metal by exposing to air or blowing with air. In both cases arsenious oxide is formed from arsenic present and this sublimes at a very low temperature (As_2O_3 melts at 313°C and sublimes at 457°C). Arsenic metal itself has a boiling point of only 616°C (as compared with the melting point of copper 1083°C) and would have a high vapour pressure over a solution in molten copper leading to losses, similar to those encountered with zinc from brass. All the world's sources of arsenic are indeed as a by-product oxide fume in the smelting of other metals and where arsenic is not required in the final metal the ease of formation and the volatility of the oxide are welcome aids to its separation. It would be equally true to say, however, that to prevent arsenic loss from high arsenic concentration, should it be desired, would be extremely difficult during the process of smelting an oxidised solid ore or of oxidising sulphur and iron from a molten matte.

The Swedish Boliden Mining Co., which is the world's largest arsenious oxide producer, substantially exceeding world demand (although doubtless not from choice), treats the highest arsenic copper ore at present utilised, containing approx. 2% copper, 29% sulphur and 9% of arsenic. By roasting (heating in air) the arsenic content of the raw material is brought down to 0.2% and the sulphur to 9% prior to smelting to form a matte in a reverberatory furnace. The next highest known arsenic content worked is at Butte, USA, where the ore *concentrate* (produced by crushing and a large degree of separation from the gangue) contains 1.6% As. This is reduced to a low figure in the smelted metal, 80% of the arsenic being driven off in roasting, with further loss in smelting and refining.

It is suggested therefore that because of the facility with which arsenic is lost and the general level of arsenic in most ores, *random* copper ore selection would be unlikely to yield arsenic contents of up to 8% in the final copper. Such high arsenic concentrations would only be obtained by selecting particularly arsenic-rich mineral pieces—such as contain enargite or tennantite or arsenopyrite mixed with copper sulphide—or by making heavy additions of non-cupriferous arsenic minerals such as orpiment (As_2S_3) or realgar (As_2S_2) to the smelting mix. It is even possible that native arsenic metal might have been added to the molten copper—the metal and its sulphides are found in volcanic areas as sublimate deposits although no definite information is yet forthcoming as to their occurrence in the Cyclades.

Second, the quantities smelted and the method of working from course-sized surface deposits would obviously mean that hand-sorting of valued minerals from worthless rock would be quickly established on the basis of the colour of the minerals, as a form of concentration. In this connection it is important to note that the colours of the more common copper minerals are as follows:

Chalcopyrite	$Cu_2S.Fe_2S_3$	gold to brass yellow
Bornite	$5Cu_2S.Fe_2S_3$	bronze-yellow to copper-red (bluish iridescent tarnish)
Chalcocite	Cu_2S	black-grey, parts frequently alter to malachite (green)
Malachite	$CuCO_3.Cu(OH)_2$	green
Azurite	$2CuCO_3.Cu(OH)_2$	blue
Chrysocolla	$CuO.SiO_2.2H_2O$	blue
Cuprite	Cu_2O	red
Chalcanthite	$CuSO_4.5H_2O$	blue

Enargite and tennantite are both blackish-grey with a metallic lustre and are very different in appearance from the copper minerals listed above (with the possible exception of chalcocite). Native arsenic is a silvery-white metal which oxidises to a grey powder quite rapidly on exposure to air. Orpiment and realgar are both very strongly coloured and were utilised as pigments in later civilisations, if not in the Early Bronze Age. It is impossible to believe that the same craftsmen that produced the workmanship of the forged blades, etc., were not sufficiently alert to control the use of raw materials to a substantial extent on this basis of hand sorting by colour.

From the argument presented, the use of high arsenic concentrations could also be expected to lead to difficulty in obtaining regular compositions in the alloys as compared, say, with the addition of tin, due to the heavy losses of arsenic. It is interesting to note that whereas there may well be some incidence of arsenical copper and arsenic minerals, as well as copper, in the Aegean generally, tin is not recorded. The chief mineral, tin oxide, is a heavy, dark black-brown mineral with a semi-metallic lustre or fracture. Metallic arsenic has an appearance somewhat similar to metallic tin and has a similar whitening effect on the colour of copper when alloyed. It is not difficult, therefore, to imagine that contact between the Cyclades and the Anatolian region, where it appears that tin bronze was already being purposefully made, would have led to a craft development in which a search for similar colour and weight minerals and metals would have developed to produce competitive materials.

It is also interesting to note that very rarely does the arsenic content of tin bronze from the period contain more than 0.5% As, a maximum figure which might be expected from the smelting of randomly selected ore without particular effort to remove or make additions of arsenic. Similarly arsenical coppers of high arsenic content do not contain tin. These observations support the view that high arsenic contents were intentional.

The Replacement of Arsenical Copper by Tin-Bronze

The natural question arises: if arsenic was so useful an addition to copper why did its use gradually give way to tin bronze, which does not appear to have any particularly superior properties, and why has it only restricted applications today? The answer as to the gradual cessation of its use in history clearly lies in the extreme toxicity of practically all arsenic salts, particularly the oxides, so readily formed during the processing of arsenic-containing minerals. Even in relatively modern plants, with fume-arresting equipment fitted to furnaces, considerable damage can be done to both plant and animal life in the immediate vicinity. Anyone smelting arsenical copper material and producing high arsenic content molten copper under crude conditions, without highly sophisticated ventilation control and extremely stringent personal hygiene, would run the strong risk of death by poisoning. Clearly, the persistent use of the material for 300 to 400 years must mean that some system of control was developed to minimise risk, but the use of a completely safe alloying material such as tin, producing a very similar material, but without the difficulty of fume losses, would have obvious advantage and would gain acceptance. In modern times the effect of the increased strength retention at moderate temperature in worked material has maintained a use for the alloy in boiler fireboxes, etc., but the main modern uses for copper are electrical, where As is extremely deleterious. If a copper base alloy is required in a hardened condition for, say, a chisel, even superior alloys such as Cu-Be or Cu-Al would be used.

Conclusion

From the study of the subject so far it is concluded that arsenical copper of high arsenic content can be regarded as an intentionally produced material, representing a definite phase of technological development in the Bronze Age. It is considered that its gradual replacement by tin bronze as the main form of strengthened copper was not because of any superior properties in the alloys but because of difficulties associated with the high volatility of arsenic and its compounds, leading to uncertain metal composition and the risk of poisoning.

BIBLIOGRAPHY

1. Caley, E. R. (1949) On the prehistoric use of arsenical copper in the Aegean region. *Hesperia* Suppl. 8, 60–3.
2. Moorey, P. R. S. (1964) An interim report on some analyses of Luristan bronzes. *Archaeometry* 7, 72–9.
3. Selimkhanov, I. R. (1962) Spectral analysis of metal articles from archaeological monuments of the Caucasus. *Proc. Prehist. Soc.* 38, 68–76.
4. Braidwood, R. J., Bruke, J. E. and Nachtrieb, N. H. (1951) Ancient Syrian coppers and bronzes. *J. Chem. Educ.* 28:2, 87–96.
5. Maréchal, J. R. (1958) A study of the mechanical properties of arsenical copper. *Metaux Corrosion Industries* 33:397, 377–83.
6. Smithells, C. J. (1962) *Metals Reference Book,* vol. I (3rd ed., London).
7. Hanson, D. and Marryat, C. B. (1927) An investigation of the effect of impurities in copper. *J. Inst. Met.* 37, 121–68.
8. Vaders, E. (1954) New copper alloys particularly suitable for the production of cast parts. *Zg. Metallk.* 45:97, 528–33.
9. Butts, A. (1954) *Copper, the metal and its alloys.* New York.

5) The Autonomy of the South-East European Copper Age (with Appendixes by J. A. Charles and J. Frierman)

The ideas set out here, involving the independent invention of copper metallurgy in the early Balkans, have provoked some lively controversy. In the first place the notion has seemed implausible to some scholars specialising in the early history of metallurgy (e.g. Wertime 1973). At the same time, however, discoveries continue to be made which emphasise the variety and vigour of this early metallurgical industry, most notably the golden treasures from the cemetery at Varna in Bulgaria (Gimbutas 1977 ; chapter 18, below) and the evidence for early copper mining at Rudna Glava in Jugoslavia (Jovanovic 1971) and at Aibunar in Bulgaria. The evidence thus confirms the level of technological competence documented by Dr Charles in Appendix I.

An important corrective to Appendix II has been published by Kingery and Frierman (1974). The Karanovo VI sherd in question, after careful re-examination, now proves to have been fired 'at a temperature less than 800° C and probably at about 700° C', rather than between 1,000° C and 1,050° C. The evidence from this sherd can therefore no longer be taken to indicate that ceramic technology had developed to a level where the melting point of copper was routinely being reached. (For further discussion of determination of temperature of firing see Tite [1969].) The Appendix still has value, however, as a pioneering investigation into Balkan pyrotechnology, and in stressing the possible relationship between the origins of metallurgy and ceramic technology.

A number of leading Balkan scholars, including Milojčic and Dumitrescu (1970) continue to argue the traditional Troy-Vinča equation rejected in this article, but most scholars in the West (with the notable exception of Hood [e.g. Hood 1973]) are now in agreement with the broad synchronisms outlined here (e.g. Tringham 1971). Unanimity is still far off : Makkay (1976, 263) has written of 'the absurd theory that in Renfrew's opinion the Bodrogkeresztúr culture is contemporaneous with the end of the Dimini period (Dimini IV). As will be demonstrated below, this theory is simply impossible.' On the other hand the views outlined here are maintained by Bulgarian scholars such as Georgiev (1970), whose work at Karanovo, described below, provided the original stratigraphic evidence to question the traditional view. It is confirmed by their important excavations at the Bulgarian early bronze age site of Ezero (Georgiev and Merpert 1973) which they identify as contemporary with Troy I–IV.

The evidence of radiocarbon dating is further considered in chapter 8.

BIBLIOGRAPHY

Dumitrescu, V. (1970) The chronological relation between the cultures of the eneolithic Lower Danube and Anatolia and the Near East. *Amer. J. Archaeol.* 74, 87–103.

Georgiev, G. I. (1970) Über die Stratigraphie und Chronologie des Neolithikums, Aneolithikums und der Frühebronzezeit in Südbulgarien, in Filip, J. (ed.) *Actes du* VII *Congrès International des Sciences Préhistoriques et Protohistoriques,* Prague : Institut d'Archéologie, 397–400.

Georgiev, G. I. and Merpert, N. I. (1973) Die Siedlung Ezero und ihre Stellung in der Frühebronzezeit Osteuropas, in *Symposium über die Entstehung und Chronologie der Badener Kultur*. Bratislava: Slovenska Akademie Vied, 215–58.

Gimbutas, M. (1977) Gold treasure at Varna. *Archaeol.* 30, 44–51.

Hood, M. S. F. (1973) The Baden culture in relation to the Aegean, in *Symposium über die Entstehung und Chronologie der Badener Kultur*. Bratislava: Slovenska Akademie Vied, 111–30.

Jovanovic, B. (1971) *Metalurgija Eneolitskog Perioda Jugoslavije*. Beograd: Archaeoloski Institut.

Kingery, W. D. and Frierman, J. D. (1974) The firing temperature of a Karanovo sherd and inferences about South-East European chalcolithic refractory technology. *Proc. Prehist. Soc.* 40, 204–5.

Makkay, J. (1975) Problems concerning copper age chronology in the Carpathian basin. *Acta Archaeol. Acad. Sci. Hungar.* 28, 251–300.

Sherratt, A. (1976) Resources, technology and trade: an essay in early European metallurgy, in Sieveking, G., Longworth, I. H. and Wilson, K. E. (eds.) *Problems in Economic and Social Prehistory*. London: Duckworth, 557–81.

Tite, M. S. (1969) Determination of the firing temperature of ancient ceramics by measurement of thermal expansion. *Archaeomet.* 11, 131–44.

Tringham, R. (1971) *Hunters, Fishers and Farmers of Eastern Europe*: 6000–3000 BC. London: Hutchinson.

Wertime, T. (1973) How metallurgy began, a study in diffusion and multiple invention, in Garašanin M., Benac, A. and Tasic, N. (eds.) *Actes du* VIII *Congrès International des Sciences Préhistoriques et Protohistoriques,* II. Beograd, 481–91.

THE AUTONOMY OF THE SOUTH-EAST EUROPEAN COPPER AGE

Ten years have now elapsed since the death of V. Gordon Childe, whose great achievement it was to relate the many disparate elements of European prehistory into a single coherent whole. These ten years have seen not only the sustained application of radiocarbon dating to the south-east European Neolithic (Quitta 1967 ; Kohl and Quitta 1966), but the publication of important stratigraphic sequences, especially that of the great tell at Karanovo in Bulgaria (Georgiev 1961). Both these advances put in question one of the essential elements in Childe's structure for the chronology of Europe: the chronological equation between Troy I and the Vinča culture of Jugoslavia (Childe 1929, 32 ; 1927 ; 1939).

This is the cornerstone for the Neolithic and Early Bronze Age of much of Europe, and to remove it would cause widespread changes both in chronology and culture history.

The crucial importance of this point has been well expressed by Professor Clark (1938): 'Thanks to the synchronisms established between Troy and Iberia and the western Mediterranean on the one hand, and central and northern Europe on the other, any important alterations in the absolute dating of the successive "cities" is bound to affect the dating of every culture in Europe of the period, much in the same way as fluctuations in the price of certain key commodities are felt in the exchanges of the whole world.' Today, of course, it is not so much the absolute dating of Troy which is in question, but the synchronisms with Europe: the effect, however, is the same.

Briefly, on the now conventional view, if Early Vinča (and hence the Late Neolithic of south-east Europe) is contemporary with Troy I and with the Early Bronze Age of the Aegean, the succeeding Copper Age (i.e. Chalcolithic) of south-east Europe must be later than these. This phase is in turn succeeded by the central and south-east European Early Bronze Age. By this means the beginning of the Unětice culture, for example, is conventionally set around 1700 BC (Childe 1957, 134).

It was James Mellaart who, in a brilliant paper (1960), first indicated how the evidence of radiocarbon appears at variance with this structure. He showed that C-14 dates put Early Vinča well before the beginnings of Troy I. But by putting back the beginning of Troy itself (which has not been directly dated by C-14) to around 3500 BC, he perpetuated the view that there was a west Anatolian influence from Kum Tepe or Troy, on the formation of the Gumelnitsa and Salcutsa cultures of the Balkan Chalcolithic. Even his partial acceptance of the implication of the radiocarbon dates produced some strong reactions (Garašanin, 1961) and many Balkan scholars continue to hold that the Vinca and related cultures are the product of Early Bronze Age Aegean or Near Eastern influences (Milojčic 1965 ; Popovic 1965 ; Srejovic 1963 ; Galovic 1967).

It is the purpose of the present article[1] to summarise the evidence—much of it from Bulgaria—which clearly indicates that Troy I and the Aegean Early Bronze Age are later than the Balkan Chalcolithic and have as their contemporaries the Early Bronze Age cultures of Bulgaria, Romania and Hungary (in the first instance the Cernavoda, Ezero and Baden cultures, which begin the Balkan Early Bronze Age). If this be accepted it follows that the preceding Neolithic and Chalcolithic cultures of the Balkans are contemporary with the Neolithic of Greece. Probably metallurgy must then have originated independently in the Balkans, where it certainly antedates the use of metal in the Aegean. It follows too that the Early Bronze Age of central and south-east Europe must be set several centuries earlier than hitherto, and there is now a strong case for arguing that the Unětice culture began comfortably before 2000 BC (Renfrew 1968*b*).

None of this would have surprised Gordon Childe: he foresaw it all, and indeed suggested much of it. He put the matter in a nutshell (1957, 123) when discussing the Hungarian Copper Age: 'In other words the Aegean and Asiatic parallels to Bodrogkeresztúr metal types might just as well give *termini ante* as *termini post quos*. Still, independent invention of casting is hard to admit.' The last point is, of course, one of the key issues which has to be argued in detail. Childe realised, and clearly stated, that the diffusion of metallurgy and other cultural traits from the Near East to Europe was an assumption, a *hypothesis,* rather than a conclusion substantiated by incontrovertible evidence. Of his book, *The Dawn of European Civilisation,* he wrote (1958, 70): 'The sole unifying theme was the irradiation of European barbarism by Oriental civilisation.' And in his still very useful article *The Orient and Europe* (1939, 10) he quoted the 'normative principle' used by Montelius: 'At a time when the peoples of Europe were, so to speak, without any civilisation whatsoever, the Orient, and particularly the Euphrates region and the Nile valley were already in enjoyment of a flourishing culture. The civilisation which gradually dawned on our Continent was for long only a pale reflection of Oriental culture.' This statement of Montelius was described by Childe as 'a hypothesis rather than a conclusion', and was resolved by him into 'five propositions treated as axioms'.

These are worth quoting today: '(1) Civilisation in the Orient is extremely ancient; (2) Civilisation can be diffused; (3) Elements of civilisation were in fact diffused from the Orient to Europe; (4) The diffusion of historically dated Oriental types provides a basis for bringing prehistoric Europe within the framework of historical chronology; (5) Prehistoric European cultures are poorer than contemporary Oriental cultures, i.e. civilisation is later in Europe than in the East.'

These five axioms, of which only the first can be accepted without hesitation today, are, as Childe indicated, the foundation on which the diffusionist view of European prehistory must rest. But the time has now come to work out European prehistory on other principles than these. John Nandris has recently stressed the European origin of many features in the European First Neolithic (Nandris 1968), and similar arguments hold for the foundations of civilisation in the Aegean (Renfrew 1964, 111; 1967*a*, 15) and for many other episodes in the prehistory of Europe (Clark 1966; Renfrew 1967*b*). And it is surely more fruitful to try to grasp the processes of culture change, the economic and social factors which result in technological innovation and cultural progress, than to ascribe such changes, without conclusive arguments, to influx from an area which is outside our specific field of investigation.

It must be stressed here that Childe knew what he was doing—and indeed he accepted the implied challenge of studying the innovations in their supposed home-territory in *The Most Ancient East.* He knew and stated clearly that elements in his reasoning were based on hypothesis, and, had he lived, he would long ago have seen and stated most of the arguments presented here, as well, perhaps, as demolishing some of them. What is at stake, however, is not only the chronological priority of the south-east European Chalcolithic over Troy I, nor simply the independent invention of metallurgy. European prehistory has for long had a preoccupation with *origins* and with the way in which ideas and cultural traits were transmitted. Today it seems more fruitful to consider *process* and the way in which such features were *invented.* A necessary preliminary is the reconsideration of the supposed relations between prehistoric Europe and the Orient.

The Chalcolithic of South-East Europe

The Later Neolithic (or Chalcolithic) of south-east Europe has been the subject of intensive investigation in recent years. And indeed probably more is known about the Gumelnitsa and Salcutsa cultures of Bulgaria and Romania than any other cultures of prehistoric Europe at any period (see map, fig. 1).

Four village settlements have been excavated virtually *in toto*: at Cascioarele on the Danube (Dumitrescu 1965), at Chotnica near Tirnovo (Angelov 1958) and at Tell Azmak (Georgiev 1965) and Iassa Tepe (Detev 1959) in the Maritsa valley of Bulgarian Thrace. The overall village plan has been revealed by these excavations—at Chotnica what may have been a shrine was documented by a hoard of golden ornaments from one structure (Venedikov 1965, pl. I–V). And the workshop of a craftsman producing bone figurines was found in another (Angelov 1961). The houses were built of *pisé,* unbaked mud set on a wooden framework (Georgiev 1961, pl. II

Figure 1. Map of important Chalcolithic sites in south east Europe, with their principal Aegean contemporaries.

and XVII–XIX). Each contained an oven, grain bins and querns. Agriculture was a major concern, documented by amazingly abundant finds of emmer, einkorn, six-row barley, and, in the Maritsa valley, lentils and vetch.[2] The livestock from some sites has been intensively studied (e.g. Detev 1954): at Bikovo bones of domestic cattle, sheep, goat, pig and dog were found, as well as *Bos primigenius*, bear and deer. There is evidence of fishing from various sites, including Russe on the Danube (Georgiev and Angelov 1957, 67). Metal objects are fairly common (cf. fig. 12): they include flat axes (Georgiev and Angelov 1957, 70), awls, double-spiral pins, fish-hooks and shaft-hole axes of the Vidra type (fig. 2, 5, 6, 4 and 3 ; Mikov 1939, 203). The most characteristic feature of the abundant and varied pottery is the graphite-painted decoration (pl. II) (see Appendix I). There is a wide range of figurines (Petkov 1950 ; pl. IV, c) as well as models of furniture (Detev 1950*a*, 15) and house models (Georgiev 1961, pl. XVI).

The chronological position of the Gumelnitsa culture complex is assured by stratigraphic excavations, notably at Karanovo (Georgiev 1961) and Hîrsova (Galbenu 1962). The centre of its distribution is the Danube valley (fig. 1), but it extends south across Bulgaria to Sitagroi-Photolivos, Dikilitash, and other sites in the Aegean region (French 1964) and westwards to Bubanj Hum near Niš (Garašanin 1958) pl. 8–10).

But this Gumelnitsa-Salcutsa complex is only one of a number of prosperous Balkan cultures of the time. They are summarised schematically, in 'chest-of-drawers' form, together with their predecessors and contemporaries, in the table on p. 144. And while there is controversy about the absolute date of these cultures and their relations with the Aegean, their relative chronology in the Balkans, as represented here, would be agreed by most scholars (cf. Berciu 1961*a* ; Ehrich 1965 ; Milojčic 1949*a*).

Gumelnitsa and Salcutsa are contemporary with the later, Pločnik, phase of the Vinča culture of Jugoslavia (Vinča C-D). Our knowledge of this culture has been greatly increased recently by the excavations of R. Galovic (1959) and J. Glišic (1964) near Pristina in southern Jugoslavia. Vinča house-plans have been revealed and well published at the site of Banitsa (Todorovic and Cermanovic 1961). The wealth and variety of the Chalcolithic Vinča culture, like that of Gumelnitsa, is reflected in the impressive finds of figurines, some very large (Galovic 1959, pl. 1), and in the numerous discoveries of metal objects, best exemplified by the Pločnik hoard (Grbic 1929, 15).

In Moldavia and the Ukraine, the Cucuteni Tripolje complex gives a similar picture of prosperity (Passek 1961 ; Gimbutas 1965*a*), and the practice of metallurgy is attested by several finds, notably the impressive Karbuna hoard (Sergeev 1963), where over 400 copper artefacts were found in a pot of the Precucuteni phase. The distribution of metal working cultures at this time includes Hungary and Transylvania, where the Tiszapolgar and Bodrogkeresztúr cultures were flourishing, recently discussed in English in considerable detail by Mme Bognar-Kutzian (1965).

In each of these regions the prosperous Chalcolithic cultures were terminated, perhaps abruptly, and succeeded by a very different group of cultures. In both Bulgaria and Romania we see a culture with unpainted pottery, the Cernavoda-Ezero culture, replace the rich Chalcolithic pots with their often elaborate painted decoration. The presence of cord-ornamented pottery (pl. III) at such sites as Cernavoda (Berciu 1961*a*, 482), Tell Dipsis—i.e. Ezero (Georgiev and Merpert 1965, 151) and Ezerovo on Lake Varna (Margos and Tontcheva 1962, 8) perhaps links the Cernavoda-Ezero culture with the Usatovo-Gorodsk culture, which succeeds Tripolje in the Ukraine. And in Hungary and beyond the Baden-Pécel culture, which succeeds and terminates Bodrogkeresztúr, shares some ceramic forms, notably the jars and some of the jugs, with the Cernavoda-Ezero culture (Banner 1956).

It is interesting to note that metal objects are found rarely at this time, the beginning of the Early Bronze Age.

Broadly speaking there are two theories to account for these widespread changes of culture at the end of the Chalcolithic. Both of them assume that the Baden and Cernavoda-Ezero cultures are related, and that they reflect a partial change of population. Both were foreseen (inevitably!) by Childe. The first sees the Baden culture as the product of strong influences from Anatolia (Kalicz 1963) ; Garašanin (1965 5) speaks of a 'complexe balkano-anatolien' in the Late Neolithic which would be followed by another such complex in the Early Bronze Age.

The second theory emphasises the resemblance between the Cernavoda-Ezero culture and the Kurgan cultures north of the Black Sea (Gimbutas 1965*b*, 21 ; cf. Merpert 1961). This theory would see the ochre graves of Baia-Hamangia and doubtless the splendid example recently excavated by Dr B. Nikolov near Vratsa in N. W. Bulgaria (personal communication) as further evidence for the spread of such 'Kurgan people' from the east. Much of the evidence in favour of both views is impressive: it is discussed further in the next section.

In any case, it is now clear that the full Bronze Age of south-east Europe developed from the Baden and related cultures (Gimbutas 1965*b*, 185 ff ; Berciu 1967, 67 f), although the extent of Aegean and Near Eastern influence at this time is in doubt.

All this would be agreed by scholars holding the migrationist diffusionist view as much as by those seeing independent invention and development as the more plausible hypothesis for the Copper Age. The crux lies in the question of Aegean relations. Broadly speaking the diffusionist, such as Professor V. Milojčic (1949*b*) would base the chronology of south-east Europe on synchronisms as indicated in the table, fig. 2a. Here early Troy is contemporary with early Vinča (Vinča-Tordos) and the south-east European Early Bronze Age with the Middle or Late Bronze Age of the Aegean. Support for this theory comes from the analogy between the darkfaced wares of Vinča and those of Troy I, from the presence of incised signs on pottery of the Vinča culture (Schmidt 1903, 457), and from the existence of metallurgy in the Balkan Copper Age, which the diffusionist sees as derived from the Aegean Early Bronze Age.

The alternative proposed here is seen in the table, fig. 2b. Troy I is now contemporary with the Cernavoda-Ezero-Baden horizon. Vinča and Gumelnitsa are contemporary with the Aegean Neolithic, and the Early Bronze Age of south-east Europe is equated with the Early Bronze Age, and perhaps also the Middle Bronze Age of the Aegean. The arguments in favour of this view, where the south-east European Copper Age is an autonomous and independent development, are set out below. The case rests on three arguments: the Bulgarian stratigraphy (with the Aegean parallels of Karanovo VII), the Radiocarbon chronology, and the elements of continuity in the cultural development from the First Neolithic to the end of the Chalcolithic.

(a)

	AEGEAN		BALKAN		
	Later Neolithic	E.B.A.	Later Neolithic	Chalcolithic	E.B.A.
EARLY	Late Sesklo Neolithic Urfirnis				
	Matt-painted ware Dhimini		Starčevo III–IV Körös		
LATE		Troy I–V Early Minoan I–III Early Helladic I–III		Vinča A–D Gumelnitsa Bodrogkeresztúr	↓

(b)

AEGEAN		BALKAN			
Later Neolithic	E.B.A.	Late Neolithic	Chalcolithic	E.B.A.	
Late Sesklo Neolithic Urfirnis		Vesselinovo Vinča A–B Tisza			EARLY
Matt-painted ware Dhimini			Vinča C–D Gumelnitsa Bodrogkeresztúr		
	Troy I–II Early Minoan I–II Early Helladic I–II			Cernavoda-Ezero Baden-Pécel	LATE

Figure 2. Relative chronology of the Balkans and the Aegean: (a) as conventionally represented; (b) as here proposed.

The Bulgarian Sequence

The 12 metre section at the tell of Karanovo provides a crucial framework for the prehistory of the region. Childe of course appreciated the importance of the Thracian Neolithic material, in this key area between Europe, the Aegean and Anatolia, and one of his earliest publications deals with the topic (Childe 1923; cf. Childe 1956). Progress was hampered, however, by a stratigraphical confusion whereby the position of the Vesselinovo culture below and before the Chalcolithic was not clear until very recently, and these plain-faced wares of what we now recognise as the period of Karanovo III (Georgiev 1961) were not distinguished from the later material of Karanovo VII.

Table. The Bulgarian neolithic sequence with contemporary sites in the Aegean and the Balkans

Karanovo level	Culture	Other Bulgarian sites	Contemporary sites in SE Europe
—	Full EBA	Junatsite Raskopanitse	Periam, Nagyrév, Glina III, Folteşti, Bubanj Hum II, Vučedol, Troy III–V
VII	Cernavoda– Ezero (Dipsis)	Ezerovo, Michailitch, Vesselinovo II, Sv. Kirilovo	Baden-Pecél, Hissar II, Bubanj Hum Ib, Troy I–II, Early Helladic I–II (Eutresis)
VI	Gumelnitsa– Kodjadermen	Russe, Razgrad, Iassa Tepe II, Chotnica II, Tell Azmak II, Krivodol	Gumelnitsa, Salcutsa, Vinča C–D, Bodrogkeresztúr, Tiszapolgar, Cucuteni A, Tripolje B, Dikilitash, Photolivos III, Bubanj Hum Ia, Dhimini, Saliagos, Aegean Later Neolithic, Early Emborio (VI and V together)
V	Maritsa	Maritsa, Sava, Chotnica I	
IV	Kalojanovetz	Kalojanovetz	E. Boian
III	Vesselinovo	Vesselinovo I, Iassa Tepe I	Vinča A–B, Paradimi I, Sesklo
II I	Karanovo	Tell Azmak I, Kremikovci, Kapitan Dimitrievo I, Slatina	Starčevo, Criş, Pre-Sesklo, Early Elateia

In brief, the First Neolithic of the Karanovo-Kremikovci culture, closely related to Starčevo, is succeeded by the Late Neolithic Vesselinovo culture, with its plain, undecorated pottery, knobbled handles of clay legs (fig. 3). The Vesselinovo culture is succeeded by the Gumelnitsa-Kodjadermen culture, the full Chalcolithic of Bulgaria (with its earlier Maritsa stage). Details of many Chalcolithic sites are given in English in the very valuable survey of J. H. Gaul (1948), which was, however, written before the crucial excavations at Karanovo.

The Gumelnitsa levels, as stated above, are followed at several sites, notably Karanovo and Ezero by materials of the Cernavoda-Ezero culture, corresponding to Karanovo VII. There is now rather more evidence for the developed Bulgarian Early Bronze Age than existed a few years ago. The transition to Middle Bronze Age is apparently documented at Junatsite (Mikov 1939*b*) and at Dr Detev's important site Raskopanitse, near Manole (Detev 1950*b*). There is no longer any reason to feel that the Bulgarian

Bronze Age is inadequately documented, or that a long chronology in the early phases will leave a gap later in the sequence.

(a) *Development of the Vesselinovo Culture.* One of the most interesting results of the excavations of the Karanovo culture levels at Tell Azmak (Georgiev 1695) and of the Vesselinovo levels at Iassa Tepe (Detev 1959) has been to demonstrate the continuity between the two cultures, a point well brought out by Dr Georgiev at the International Conference of Prehistoric and Protohistoric Sciences at Prague in 1966.

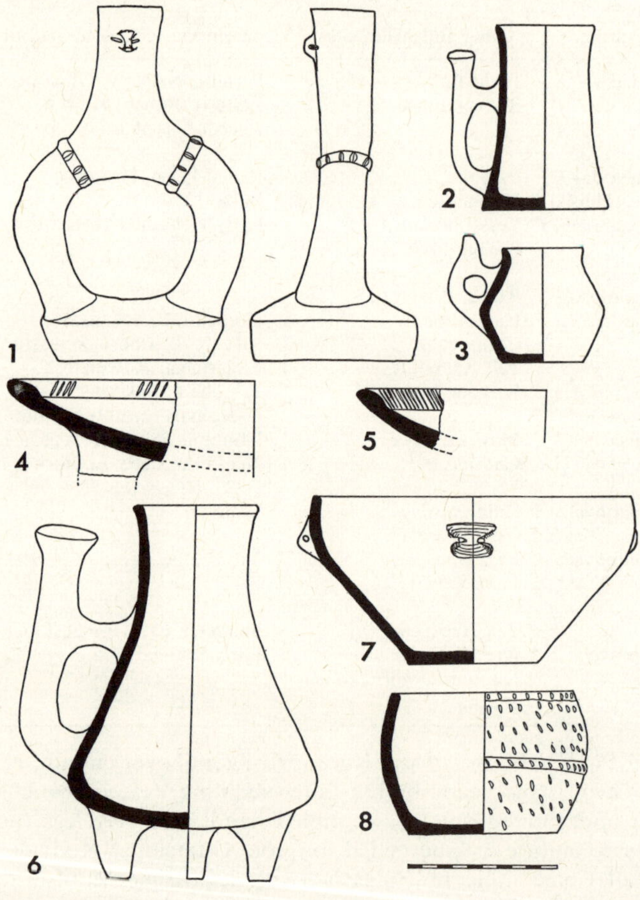

Figure 3. Typical shapes of the Vesselinovo culture (Karanovo III) from Iassa Tepe. Scale 1:5.

The point is most clearly made by the pottery. The principal shapes of the Vesselinovo culture are illustrated in fig. 3 from finds made at Iassa Tepe by Dr Detev, who kindly allowed me to draw them. Of particular note are the footed bowls (fig. 4, 1 ; fig. 3, 4 and 5) which have a thickened or 'rolled' rim. (This feature is clearly the ancestor of the Gumelnitsa form which Mellaart in his article (1960, fig. 2) tried to link with Troy I and Kum Tepe Ib shapes.) Another *Leitform* is the footed jug with prominent knob-

or horned-handle (fig. 3, 6) for which perhaps not altogether convincing parallels have been suggested at Büyük Güllücek and other sites in west Anatolia and the Aegean. The simple, carinated and well-burnished bowl (fig. 3, 7) resembles a series of bowls at Vinča and indeed the well-burnished, undecorated pottery of the two cultures gives a very similar impression.

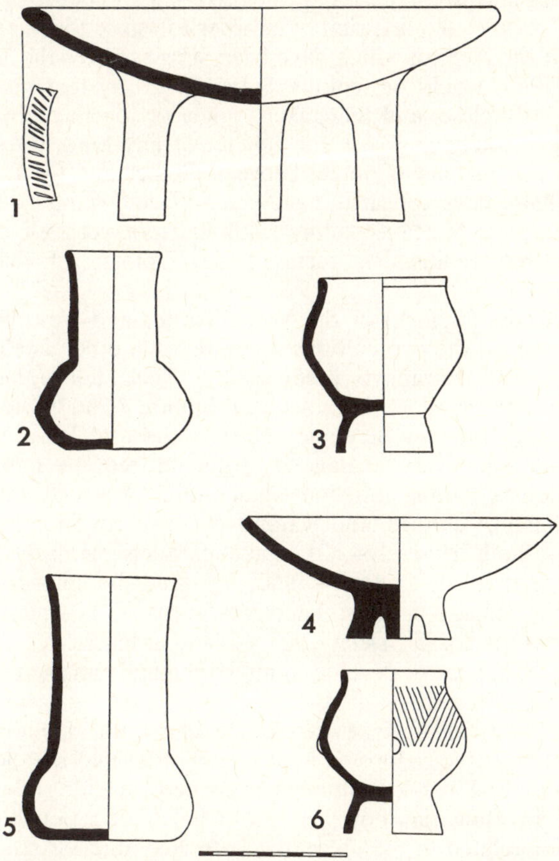

Figure 4. Pottery shapes of the Vesselinovo culture (nos. 1 to 3, from Iassa Tepe) and of the Karanovo culture (nos. 4 to 6, from Tell Azmak), indicating ceramic continuity. Scale 1:5.

Evident precursors for some of these shapes of the Vesselinovo culture (fig. 4, 1–3) were found in levels of the late Karanovo culture at Tell Azmak (fig. 4, 4–6), and Bulgarian scholars including Mikov, Georgiev and Detev, regard the Vesselinovo culture as a direct development from its predecessor. The distribution of sites is a similar one, and indeed at most sites of the Karanovo culture the early levels are overlain by deposits of the Vesselinovo culture. Many other features, including the clay 'altars' (Detev 1959, 31) and simple figurines (*id*., 33, 37) common in the Vesselinovo culture find prototypes in the Early Neolithic (Georgiev 1961, pl. VII and fold-out plate, lower right) and there seems no reason to suggest any outside influence.

A very similar process of development has been hinted for the Vinča culture (Grbic 1956) which has many elements of continuity with Starčevo. Of course the figurines of Vinča-Tordos (Vinča A-B) are more impressive—but there seems little good reason to derive them from the Cyclades, as Garašanin has sought to do (1961, 277 ; cf. Srejovic 1963, 9). Nor is there any very plausible Aegean prototype for the incised signs (Todorovic and Cermanovic 1961, pl. XXXIV). To list, simply in order to refute them, all the possible parallels with the Aegean which have been suggested for the Vinča culture (cf. Popovic 1965) would be tedious. Suffice it to say that none of them appears particularly close, and that taken, singly or together, they do not make an altogether convincing case for contact of any kind, direct or indirect, between the two regions. (Contact between Greece and the Danilo culture, on the other hand does appear to have taken place [Weinberg 1962, 190].) On the contrary, the Vinča economy (although not yet well documented) as well as the architecture, seems a development of that of Starčevo.

The analogies in the development of the Vinča-Tordos and Vesselinovo cultures are striking. Indeed the two cultures resemble each other as closely as did their Starčevo and Karanovo predecessors. Their tell-settlement economies may be broadly similar, the houses at Banitsa (Todorovic and Cermanovic 1961, 12 and 14) may be compared with those of Iassa Tepe, and the pottery shows some very analagous forms. Indeed the parallels between the two regions continue into the Chalcolithic. The clay 'altars' which began in the Starčevo culture (and Karanovo I) and continue in late Vinča (pl. I, 4 ; Garašanin 1951, 164, 31) have parallels similarly zoomorphic, at Iassa Tepe II (pl. I, 5 ; Detev 1960, 10). And the curious clay plaques with meander decoration from later Vinča (pl. I, 1) find close parallels at Iassa Tepe II (pl. I, 2–3 ; Detev 1965, 66) and at Russe.

In short, both cultures appear to develop uninterruptedly from the underlying First Neolithic foundation.

(b) *Development of the Bulgarian Chalcolithic.* The Late Neolithic of Servia (Vinča-Tordos) clearly develops without interruption into the closely similar Chalcolithic (Vinča-Pločnik), although even here outside influence has been suggested. In Bulgaria, however, the Chalcolithic Gumelnitsa culture is not so closely related to the preceding Late Neolithic Vesselinovo culture.

There are, of course, many elements of continuity: the shape of the dominant ceramic form, the bowl, is similar, although now it is often decorated with graphite paint (pl. II , 1). And the hole-necked jug (pl. II, 3) is a direct development from the Vesselinovo predecessor (pl. II, 4). The settlement pattern does not change: every tell where Vesselinovo levels have been excavated has material of the Karanovo V and VI cultures above.

But the lively curvilinear decoration of the pottery, the incisions, the encrustation with red and sometimes white colouring matter, and several new shapes, do indicate innovations and other influences. Fortunately these features of the Karanovo V (Maritsa) culture are very well documented north of the Stara Planina range at the sites of Sava near Dalgopol (Vajsová 1966, 22) and Chotnica I (id., 14). Clearly many features of the Gumelnitsa culture developed from the preceding Boian culture of Romania. The transition has been well studied in Romania, and evidently many of the features of the Bulgarian Gumelnitsa culture developed in the region of the Gumelnitsa type-site in the Danube valley (see the useful maps given by Comsa 1962).

There are, indeed, very few features in the Bulgarian Chalcolithic where an Aegean derivation is possible, let alone desirable (but see Nemejcová-Pavukóvá 1966). The existence of the askos shape in Early Neolithic Greece robs the feature of any chronological significance, and although some of the marble figurines of the Gumelnitsa culture (pl. III) (Petkov 1950; especially Georgiev 1962, 64, fig. 8) do have a superficial resemblance to the Folded-Arm figurines of the Cycladic Early Bronze Age (Renfrew 1969), the heads are very different. As Childe indicated, the metallurgy is the most interesting point, and it is discussed below. It would be pointless to list the other parallels that have been put forward simply in order to refute them.

(c) *The Bulgarian Early Bronze Age* (map, fig. 9). Two important excavations at Ezerovo and Ezero have recently provided rich material of the Bulgarian Early Bronze Age, a period hitherto best known from the finds at Michailitch (Mikov 1948) which through the kindness of Dr Mikov I am able to illustrate here.

The more northerly site is Ezerovo—not to be confused with Ezero—on (or rather in) the lake of Varna in north-east Bulgaria. Here Dr G. Toncheva has carried out rescue operations, recovering from the lake bed a large quantity of exceptionally well-preserved material. There are two locations, of which Ezerovo 1 (Margos and Toncheva, 1962) is apparently the earlier. Tentatively the Bulgarian Early Bronze Age may be divided into four phases, the Ezerovo 1 material representing the earliest.

Phase 1. In the Ezerovo 1 assemblage are simple jugs and askoi (op. cit., fig. 5) as well as hole-mouthed and broad-neck jars (id., fig. 6), some of which have analogies in shape (but not decoration) with Kurgan III and IV pottery illustrated by Dr Marija Gimbutas (1965*a*, 487, fig. 44). However only a single sherd of cord-impressed ware was found at Ezerovo 1, and the pottery is not usually decorated. In general it has similarities with that of the Early Bronze Age at Cernavoda in the Romanian Dobrogea (Berciu 1961*b*, 121).

Phase 2. The second locality, Ezerovo 2, has a much greater range of pottery, as yet unpublished, to which Dr Toncheva kindly allows me to refer. It has close analogies both with that from Michailitch and from Tell Dipsis (Ezero) levels V and VI.

Here the forms of Phase 1 continue, although the neck of the askos is now more closely defined, and the wide-mouthed jars now have finger-impressed decoration at the rim. The jugs also have more closely defined necks and sometimes the handles are knobbled (fig. 5, 1 and fig. 10). A single, three-legged cooking pot was found. There is a range of open bowls, some of which have a heavy tubular lug at the rim (pl. IV, 6 and 10). And, most significantly, there is a large series of cord-impressed dishes known as *Fischplatten*. This, apparently the only corded form at Ezerovo 2, is a small open bowl on a low foot or stand, often with a flattened rim. It is decorated both inside and outside with incisions and with cord-impressions (pl. III, upper). The flat stand base is sometimes polygonal.

Phase 3. A later, third phase is also represented at Ezero (Dipsis), levels I to IV. The finds correspond to those at Sv. Kirillovo, including jugs with high-flung handles (Georgiev and Merpert 1966, fig. 1, 7 and 15–16).

Phase 4. The jugs of Phase 3, and the Fischplatten are seen also in the lower levels at Junatsite (Mikov 1939*b*). In the higher levels there, as at Raskopanitse (Detev 1950*b*), come the curious handled cups with a pointed base which are seen also at Bubanj Hum II (Garašanin 1958, pl. 12, 5) and, according to Garašanin, in the later Baden-Pécel culture.

It is thus possible to suggest a provisional and very tentative schema for the Bulgarian Early Bronze Age:

Phase	*Dipsis* (Ezero)		*Other sites*	
4	—		Junatsite, Raskopanitse	Bubanj Hum II
3	I II III	Sv. Kirillovo, Karanovo VII		
2	IV V VI VII	Ezerovo 2	Michailitch	
1	VIII IX —	Ezerovo 1		
	X XI	(Chalcolithic)		

The place in this sequence of the Ochre Grave near Vratsa, excavated by Dr B. Nikolov, is not yet clear. The schema establishes the long duration of the Early Bronze Age, and by implication that of the Baden culture. At Ezero the Early Bronze Age levels are 4 metres deep.

(d) *Troy Parallels for the Bulgarian Early Bronze Age.* The materials of the Bulgarian Early Bronze Age present a number of striking parallels with Troy I and Troy II, and it seems that there can be little doubt of the chronological equation between Karanovo VII, or more precisely, Bulgarian Early Bronze 2 and Troy I and II.[3]

The most curious points of similarity are between the clay 'anchors' of Michailitch (pl. III and fig. 5, 5 ; Mikov 1948, fig. 10) and the clay 'anchors' of Poliochni (fig. 5, 11 ; Brea 1964, pl LXXXIII, a and b) the clay axe from Thermi (fig. 5, 8 ; Lamb 1936, pl. XXIV, 31, 24) finds parallels at Michailitch too (pl. III and fig. 5, 2a and b ; Mikov 1948, fig. 11).

More widespread, however, are the parallels between the bowls, notably the form with inturned rim and a high handle, and that with a horned tubular-lug handle. Both are seen at Michailitch and contemporary sites (fig. 5, 3 and 4) and are common in the Troy I culture (fig. 5, 9 and 10). The jugs are similar also: the frequent knobbled handles of the Ezero culture (fig. 5, 1) are seen also at Thermi (fig. 5, 7 ; Lamb 1936, 81).

A *depas* cup of typical Troy II–IV form was found at Badere near Michailitch (fig. 11, 1 ; Mikov 1948, fig. 12). It was not stratified, however, and does not come from the site of Michailitch itself as some have claimed. Fragments of others are known from the same region of south-east Bulgaria (Dimitrov 1943). Merpert has reported fragments of the same type from levels V and VI at Ezero (Merpert 1966, 25, and oral information), but these have not yet been illustrated. Georgiev and Merpert equate the Early Bronze Age levels at Ezero with Troy I to IV, and the evidence in favour of their claim seems very convincing.

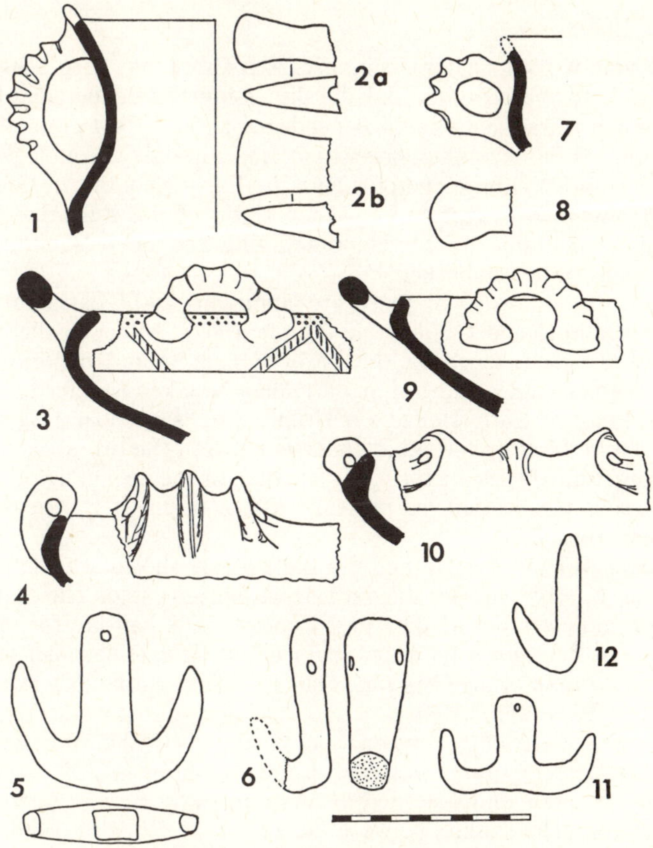

Figure 5. Ceramic forms from Michailitch (nos. 1 to 6) and from the Troy I culture (nos. 7 to 12). (Nos. 7-9 and 12 from Thermi in Lesbos, no. 10 from Troy, no. 11 from Poliochni in Lemnos). Scale 1 : 5.

Although the chronological position of the Cernavoda-Ezero culture seems perfectly clear, it is still difficult to suggest a sound historical explanation for the Bulgarian Early Bronze Age material. We do not even know for sure whether the Troy-Ezero similarities are due to influence from Anatolia, as most scholars would suppose, or to an influence from the Balkans upon Troy, as Mellaart suggested (1960, fig. 1) for a later period in the Early Bronze Age. In any case, there are few or no Trojan affinities in the earliest phase of the Cernavoda-Ezero culture, as seen at Ezerovo 1, i.e. in the tentative Bulgarian Early Bronze 1.

The Ochre Graves at Baia-Hamangia in the Dobrogea are apparently later than the first Cernavoda culture materials from the same district, and the chronological position of that near Vratsa is not yet known. Moreover there was only a single sherd of cord-impressed ware at Ezerovo 1.

Is there perhaps a possibility that the Gumelnitsa/Cernavoda-Ezero hiatus was neither directly caused by a Trojan irruption, nor by the arrival of Kurgan peoples?

Absolute Chronology

The Troy I–Karanovo VII synchronism, discussed above, has been achieved without reference to radiocarbon, and the discussion has deliberately been conducted in such a way as to avoid dependence upon a C-14 chronology. At the other end of the Neolithic, one would tend to relate chronologically the Starčevo-Karanovo culture complex with the Early Neolithic of Greece, again without reference to carbon-14. The position of the Bulgarian Late Neolithic and Chalcolithic as contemporary with the later Neolithic of Greece can therefore be established.

Turning now to radiocarbon, there are numerous C-14 dates for the Balkan, Late Neolithic and Chalcolithic (Quitta 1967). Although there are no dates for Troy itself, those for the Early Helladic I and II periods at Eutresis and Lerna (Kohler and Ralph 1961) may be taken to refer to Troy I and Troy II. Finds of Early Helladic II Urfinis ware 'sauceboat' fragments in Late Troy I and Troy II, and other contacts between the two areas make this reasonable (Renfrew 1964 ; 1967, 3). The date of the beginning of Troy I admittedly remains uncertain at present: it has been set by Blegen at 3000 BC (Blegen 1963, 174).

The C-14 dates for the Aegean and the Balkans are shown schematically in the table, fig. 6, each with its standard deviation indicated. The scale in the left margin indicates the BC date based on the 5568 half-life for radiocarbon. In the right margin is the supposed 'true' BC date, in calendar years, based on the calibration of the C-14 time scale by dendrochronology (Stuiver and Suess 1966 ; Suess 1967).

The table gives a striking confirmation of the view that the Balkan Copper Age is contemporary with the Later Neolithic of the Aegean (Dhimini, Saliagos, etc.), and preceded the Aegean Early Bronze Age by at least a millennium.[4] The conflict between fig. 2a and fig. 2b is resolved conclusively in favour of the latter.

Although there are no dates yet from Bulgarian sites of the Karanovo VII culture, dates from the related Cernavoda culture and the Hamangia ochre graves show that these must be recognised as broadly contemporary with Troy I and the earlier Aegean Early Bronze Age.

The contemporaneity of the fourth millennium Aegean and Balkan Late Neolithic (and Chalcolithic) sites is illustrated on the map, fig 1. Important Aegean and Balkan Early Bronze Age sites are shown on the map, fig. 9, and again they are broadly contemporary. However, some of these settlements, like Pecica and Schneckenburg, may be contemporary with the end rather than the beginning of the Aegean Early Bronze Age.

The C-14 dating is thus perfectly in accord with the stratigraphically based conclusions reached above. And indeed there seems no good evidence pointing in the other direction, with the possible exception of the much-discussed Tărtăria tablets. These small pieces of baked clay, with incised signs found at Tărtăria, ostensibly on levels of the Vinča-Tordos culture (Vlassa 1963) have been likened by the late A. Falkenstein (cf. Milojčic

1965) to tablets of the Protoliterate period of Sumer. Milojčic has used the supposed synchronism as evidence against the C-14 dates for south-east Europe. And Popovic has quoted them (1965) as further evidence for the Near Eastern origin of the Vinča culture.

E. Neustupny has questioned the stratigraphy at Tărtăria (1968a), pointing out that clay anchors, undoubtedly later than Vinča-Tordos, were found in the same deposit. But he avoids the possible corroboration of the Vinča-Tordos context given by the many signs already known from pottery of that culture (Schmidt 1903 ; Childe 1929, 33). The solution offered by Berciu (1967, 161) seems on balance more acceptable. He suggests that these signs are not to be considered as true 'writing', and that their resemblance to signs of Uruk IV is a fortuitous one. They would thus reflect a local development in the Vinča culture, unconnected with the development of writing which took place far away, and perhaps a millennium later. In any case, the Tărtăria tablets, doubtful as they are, seem insufficient to overthrow the entire system of C-14 dating, built up on a global basis by numerous scientists over the past 20 years.

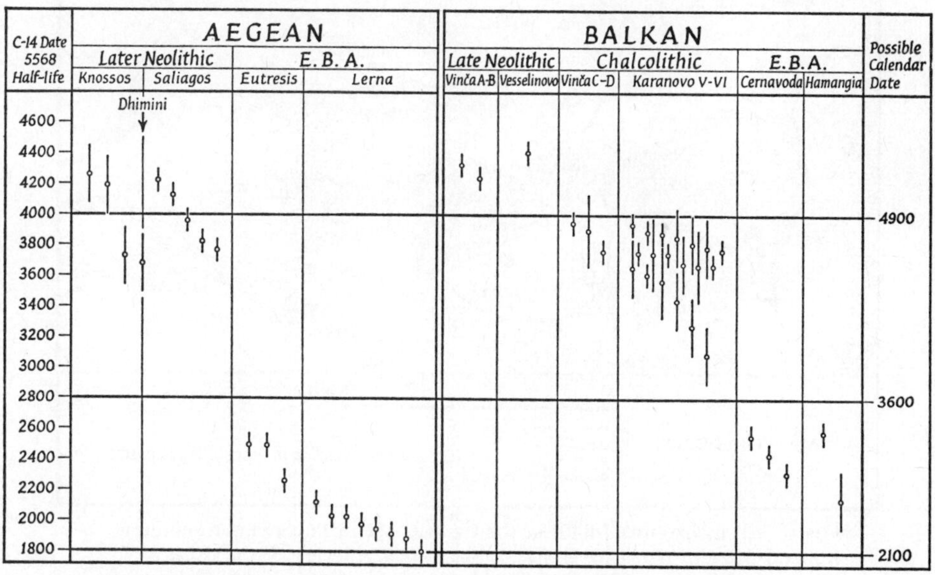

Figure 6. Radiocarbon dates for the Chalcolithic and Early Bronze Age of the Balkans, compared with radiocarbon dates for the Aegean Later Neolithic and Early Bronze Age.

The Independent Invention of Metallurgy

The most interesting problem of the Copper Age, as Childe saw, is the origin of its metallurgy. Although an independent origin was suggested a long time ago (Hillebrand 1929), most writers have felt that the appearance of metal objects in the Balkans was a clear sign of outside influence.

The problem cannot be solved by an attempt to emphasise the simplicity of the metal forms or the absence of any alloying of the copper to make bronze. Indeed the competence of the Balkan metal smiths should not be underestimated. It has sometimes been held that the copper shaft-hole axes—which are the most sophisticated product of the time—could have been made simply by hammering and annealing lumps of native copper, with the insertion of the shaft-hole through drilling (Deshayes 1960). Here I am greatly indebted to Mr J. A. Charles who has examined two shaft-hole axes of the Balkan Copper Age, made available by the Ashmolean Museum in Oxford, through the kindness of Mr Humphrey Case (Appendix 1).

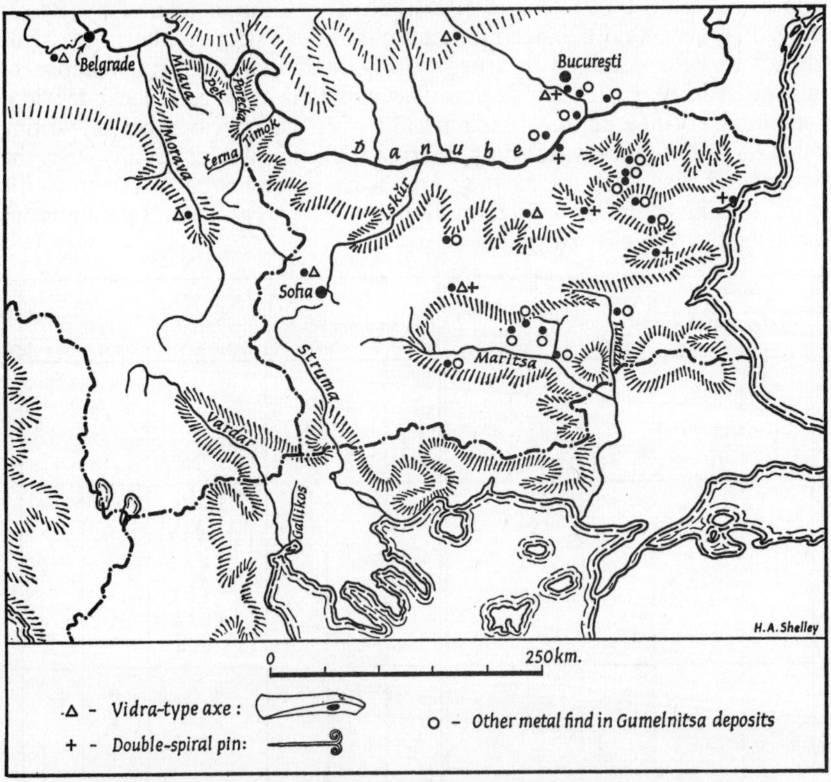

Figure 7. Principal metal finds of the Copper Age in Bulgaria and southern Romania. (Vidra-type axes from: Velika Crljeni, Pločnik, Teiu, Vidra, Slivenitsa, Gabarevo, Chotnica. Double-spiral pins from: Vidra, Gabarevo, Russe, Sultan, Zavet, Varna. Further stratified finds: Tangiru, Cascioarele, Glina, Gumelnitsa, Devetaki, Voina, Razgrad, Janka, Kodjadermen, Denev, Mečkur, Sv. Kirilovo, Karanovo, Bikovo, Deve Bargan, Rašev.)

Several problems arise in assessing the metallurgical competence of these very early craftsmen. Did they understand the basic technique of melting the metal and casting it? Or was their skill, as some have suggested, like that of the American Indians of Lake Superior, simply in hammering, perhaps with the use of heat (annealing)? And if the sophisticated shapes, notably the axe-adzes, were cast, was this in open or in bivalve moulds? Was the shaft-hole inserted subsequently by drilling? And, if casting was practised, was the smelting of ores to produce copper also understood?

Some of these questions have been definitely answered by previous work. In the first place it should be stressed that there is as yet no clear evidence of the alloying of copper (whether with tin or arsenic) at this early period. Bronze was first produced, it seems, during the succeeding Early Bronze Age.

That the shaft-hole tools were often cast was documented by H. Müller through metallographic examination (Pittioni 1957, 25, and fig. 17) and independently by Patay, Kimner, Szabo and Sinay (1963, 53), and again by Voce (Coghlan 1961). This point is corroborated by Mr Charles's study.

In many cases it appears that native copper was used. This is Mr Charles's tentative conclusion for the two specimens which he has analysed, and has been suggested by several other writers (see Bognár-Kutzián 1963, 563). In other cases it seems that the smelting of copper ores was also practised—among the analyses of Otto and Witter (1952), nos. 249 and 251, for example, have impurities greater than one would normally expect from native copper. Mr H. H. Coghlan considers that 'we must admit that smelting was known in the Balkan Copper Age' (personal communication). The conclusion must be that both native copper and copper smelted from its ores were used.

The two problems have hitherto not been resolved, although both were carefully considered by Coghlan (1961) in a valuable paper, with metallographic analyses by Dr E. Voce and Mr I. M. Allen. Was the bivalve mould used, and how was the shaft-hole produced?

Both are now elegantly elucidated in Mr Charles's study. He has taken sections from two tools:

(i) a shaft-hole axe of Vidra type (Ashmolean Museum 1927, 1521) from Sir Arthur Evans's collection, bought 'near Pressburg, Hungary' in 1876 (pl. v, 3);

(ii) an axe-adze of typical Copper-Age form (Ashmolean Museum 1927, 1541) from Sir Arthur Evans's collection, bought 'near Belgrade' in 1876 (pl. v, 1). This artefact had been previously examined by Voce (Coghlan 1961).

Both these objects can, on typological grounds, be ascribed to the Copper Age (Tiszapolgar-Bodrogkeresztúr Vinča C-D) without hesitation. Mr Charles refers also to a simple axe or chisel, Ashmolean Museum 1927, 1492, again from Sir Arthur Evans's collection, bought 'near Pressburg, Hungary' in 1876 (pl. v, 2).

In the first place, both the axes studied have a high copper oxide content on the upper surface, which decreases markedly towards the lower surface. This clearly indicated that both were cast in an open mould, the rather elaborate shape of the axe-adze being produced by subsequent forging. The metallographic examination does not conflict with previous studies, but it takes the matter considerably further, and it is now clear that in general these tools were produced without the use of bivalve moulds. This does not, of course, exclude the possibility that evidence may yet come to light to indicate the use of bivalve moulds in some cases during the Balkan Copper Age. But at present, its use, like that of tin to alloy copper, must be discounted.

Mr Charles's study also solves the problem of the shaft-holes. He has clearly shown that these were not produced by drilling but by casting round a core, probably of charcoal, which was set firmly in the mould before the molten copper was allowed to run in. After the forging process, to shape the tool, the shaft-hole was freed from partial obstruction by 'drifting'—the process of forcing an object of circular section, possibly the shaft itself, through it.

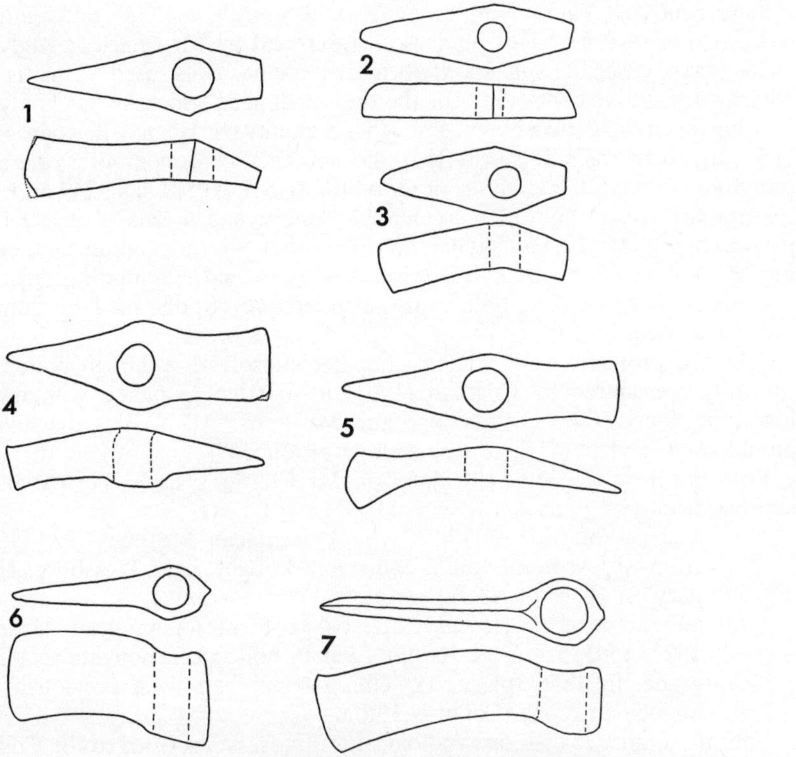

Figure 8. Shaft-hole tools of the Bulgarian Chalcolithic (nos. 1 to 5) and Early Bronze Age (nos. 6 and 7). Nos. 1, 4 and 5 of copper, 2 and 3 of stone, 6 and 7 of copper or bronze. Scale 1 : 5.
(1 from Slivenitsa near Sophia (after R.Popov). 2 dark grey sedimentary stone, Plovdiv region (Plovdiv NM 1473). 3 green-brown stone, from Teteven (Plovdiv NM 3108). 4 from Plovdiv (Plovdiv NM 443). 5 from Pamuecii near Stara Zagora (Plovdiv NM 1169). 6 from Plovdiv region (Plovdiv NM 780). 7 from Bratsigovo (Rhodope) (Plovdiv NM 3323).)

A very clear picture of the production process appears from this study, and one is impressed with the very effective use which the early metallurgists made of the limited technical means at their disposal. It is of note also that a possible evolutionary sequence can be seen in the metallurgical techniques used: casting in an open mould (for fig. 12, 1–2, and pl. v, 2), then casting with the use of a core for the shaft-hole (fig. 12, 3 and pl. v, 3),

Figure 9. Map of some important Early Bronze Age sites in south-east Europe, with notable Aegean contemporaries.

and finally of casting, with improved technique, and subsequent skilful forging, to produce the axe-adze (pl. v, 1).

We are thus in the face of true copper metallurgy, not just the hammering of native copper. And its invention, if a local one, was not a trivial matter.

The metal types of the Copper Age of Bulgaria and neighbouring lands fall into two classes (fig. 12). First there are the flat axes, awls and needles which are a feature of early metallurgy in most parts of the world, and which cannot be considered as evidence either of local or foreign origin.

The *double-spiral pins*, however (fig. 12, 6), whose distribution in Bulgaria is given in the map, fig. 7, have been the subject of comment, notably by Childe (1936). But the Aegean examples, which have been suggested as prototypes, all belong to the Early Bronze 2 period, after 2500 BC (Renfrew, 1967) and are consequently much later. Indeed the Bulgarian and Rumanian finds are easily the earliest known of this form.

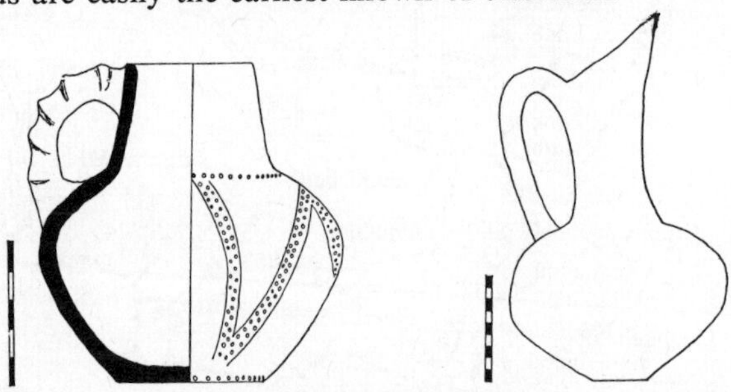

Figure 10. Jugs from the Bronze Age of Bulgaria, resembling Aegean forms. *Left*: from Michailitch, Early Bronze Age. *Right*: from Russe, later Bronze Age. Scales in centimetres.

The situation with the *shaft-hole axes* is similar. Both Driehaus (1952) and Vulpe (1964) agree that the earliest is the Vidra-type axe (fig. 8, 1 ; pl. v, 3) whose distribution is given in fig. 7. It has possible prototypes in stone (fig. 8, 2–3 ; Deshayes 1960). The distribution of this and other shaft-hole tools in Bulgaria has been discussed by Mikov (1961). The Gumelnitsa context for the Vidra type is undoubted, and has been further confirmed by the recent stratified find at Chotnica (Angelov 1958, 395).

The more developed axe-adzes, which also belong to the Copper Age, have the centre of their distribution in Hungary and Transylvania, but they are found too in Bulgaria (fig. 8, 4–5). Both the axes and axe-adzes must clearly be distinguished from the wide-bladed axe with sleeve shaft-hole (fig. 8, 6–7) which does not appear in south-east Europe until the Early Bronze Age. The earliest recorded finds of shaft-hole tools in the Aegean are of Early Bronze Age date (Renfrew 1967, 8).

These shaft-hole tools, skilfully forged after casting, where a core was used to produce the shaft-hole, and dating from the 4th millennium BC, are perhaps the earliest metal objects known in the world of such complexity. Although simple copper objects—beads and awls—have been found in very early contexts at Çatal Hüyük, Çayönu and Beycesultan in Anatolia (Mellaart 1964, 114, and pl. xxxv ; Lloyd and Mellaart 1962, 285), only at Can Hasan (French 1962, 33) has anything been found in a context earlier than the Early Bronze Age which would require more than simple hammering. And the mode of manufacture of the Can Hasan mace-head has not yet been established.

There is as yet nothing of comparable complexity from the Neolithic period of Iran, although of course there is a copper bead of very early date from Ali Kosh (Hole and Flannery 1967, 177). And in Mesopotamia, although metallurgy is documented in the Halaf culture at Arpachiyah, the first indication of possible shaft-hole tools is seen in the curious clay models of the Ubaid period (Childe 1954, 117). Not until the Protoliterate period are copper shaft-hole axes found. These are all, like their contemporaries at Maikop, of the wide-bladed form seen in the Early Bronze Age of the Aegean and the Balkans at about the same time, or a little later (cf. fig. 8, 6–7). They do not resemble those of the Chalcolithic Balkans. There thus seems no possibility of deriving the Balkan Chalcolithic shaft-hole axes and axe-adzes from the Orient.

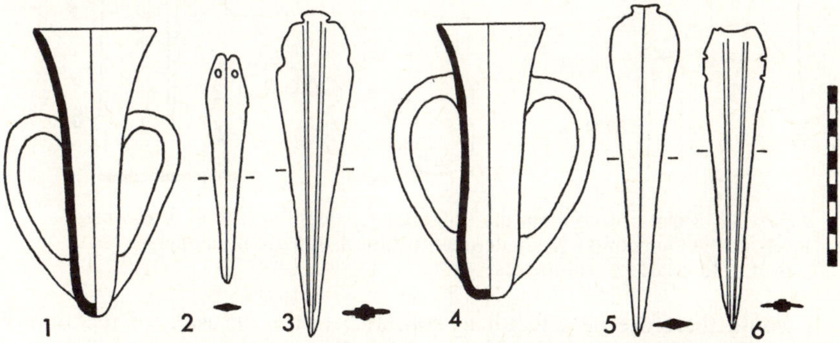

Figure 11. Two-handled ('depas') cup and daggers from the earlier Bronze Age of Bulgaria (nos. 1 to 3), with related forms from the Early Bronze Age of the Aegean. Scale in centimetres.
(1 from Badere near Michailitch, 2 from Archar, 3 from Bela Slatina, 4 from Troy II, 5 from Poliochni 'Red' phase, 6 from Koumasa, Crete.)

The third distinctive metal form of the time is the flat *pendant of gold* (fig. 12, 7), often with repoussé dots, common in Hungary and Transylvania (H. Dumitrescu 1961). Three examples have been found in Bulgaria, without including the Chotnica hoard. The gold pendant from Late Neolithic Sesklo in Greece (Tsountas, 1908, 350, fig. 291), which is often compared with these, is not in fact closely similar, and is in any case no earlier. Again the distribution is a Balkan one.

It is important also to stress the metallurgical isolation of the Balkans during the 4th millennium BC. To the north-east, north of the Black Sea, metal is not found until the period of the Karbuna hoard, and there is general agreement that the objects of the period are related to those of Hungary and Romania. It has not seriously been suggested that the Caucasus region was practising metallurgy at this early time, although the possibility of influence from this direction in the Balkan Early Bronze Age is, of course, a very real one. To the south, in the Aegean, the earliest well-dated metal find[5] is the Late Neolithic settlement and cemetery at Kephala in Kea, set at about 3000 BC. A copper axe from Late Neolithic Knossos (Evans 1935, 14, and fig. 3, f) and similar axes from Late Neolithic Sesklo (Tsountas 1908, 352) could be a little earlier, but these are isolated finds, and do not indicate any flourishing metallurgical practice before the full Early Bronze Age. In Anatolia the finds at Can Hasan and Beycesultan already cited indicate the use of copper, but apparently in a small way, and these and copper beads and awls from a number of very early sites constitute the sum of the evidence at present available.

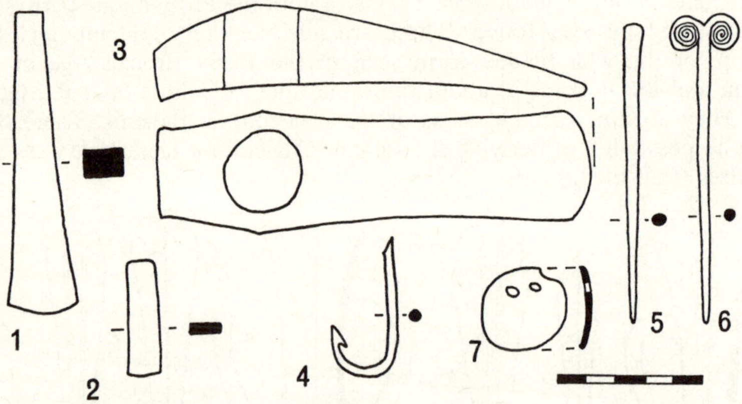

Figure 12. Metal objects from the Bulgarian Chalcolithic, found in stratified levels of the Gumelnitsa-Kodjadermen culture. 1 to 6 are of copper, 7 is of gold. Scale in centimetres.

It would therefore be difficult to substantiate the diffusion of metallurgy to the Balkans from the Orient, if the chronology argued above be accepted. Of course it could be argued that since copper beads are found at Çatal Hüyük and Ali Kosh in the 7th millennium BC, metal was used earlier at these sites than in the Balkans. This is demonstrably true. And it is always theoretically impossible to *disprove* the diffusion of a trait which occurs in two places. One can merely indicate that there are no sound arguments to support it.

At this point it should be recalled that metallurgy, like farming, was never a single invention, but a number of distinct and separate discoveries. In most areas the first stage may have been the use of native copper to make beads. The find of beads and simple objects of copper at Ali Kosh or Çayönü, possibly worked by hammering alone, is in fact less remarkable than finds of neatly perforated beads of stone at these sites.

Probably the next development was annealing—the hammering of heated metal to shape it—and this may have led to the melting of metal and the appreciation of its potentialities for casting. This stage seems to have been reached at Çatal Hüyük (Mellaart 1964, 114) but is not yet documented from any completely aceramic sites, and the melting and smelting of copper was probably a result of the development of kilns for firing pottery. It seems altogether possible that the beginnings of metallurgy at Çatal Hüyük were independent of developments at Çayönü, and both unrelated to metal working at Ali Kosh: there is no reason why these rather simple metallurgical discoveries need have occurred in a single region of the Near East.

When the casting of copper has been mastered—and it requires a temperature of about 1,100° C—it seems a natural step to add interesting looking stones (i.e. ores) to the crucible in the hope that they may behave in the same way as the stones (i.e. lumps of native metal) already used. Here it may be relevant that some ores, such as the lead ore galena, have a distinctly metallic appearance. In fact copper carbonate will smelt at a much lower temperature—about 700° C—than the melting point of copper, although a reducing atmosphere is needed. Once copper was cast, it is not surprising that it was smelted from its ores as well. The chronology of these stages in the Near East has been well presented by Wertime (1964). They took place very nearly as early in the Balkans.

In south-east Europe the important step of casting in a mould with core, to produce a shaft-hole, was also taken. But perhaps surprisingly there seems no evidence that the copper was ever alloyed with tin to give bronze, until the Early Bronze Age (Sangmeister in Bognár-Kutzián 1965, 563). This is a major step which the Balkan smiths failed to take, and the softness of their tools, all of pure copper (although hardened by cold-working), must have been a serious disadvantage.

That Balkan metallurgy evolved over a considerable period is documented by the occasional metal finds in contexts actually earlier than the full Copper Age, perhaps as early as the end of the 5th millennium BC. Copper bracelets occur in the Neolithic Tisza culture of Hungary (Bognár-Kutzián 1965, 333) which preceded the Tiszapolgár culture, and Nestor has referred to copper objects in Precucuteni Boian (Vidra phase) and Vinča A levels (Nestor 1955).

Metal ores are of course abundant in the Carpathians, and also in the Balkan peninsula south of the Danube (Gaul 1942). And evidence for local working during the Copper Age, which could in any case safely be assumed, has in fact been found (Georgiev and Angelov 1957, 126; Georgiev 1958, 381).

At this point it is necessary to set the practice of metallurgy in the Balkans in a wider technological and economic context.

Evidently the agricultural economy of the Maritsa and Lower Danube valleys was an efficient and successful one. The best evidence for this is in the tells themselves: the deposits at Karanovo attain a depth of 12 metres, and at Djadova near Novo Zagora there is a mound 18 metres high. At sites in Bulgaria the Gumelnitsa levels attain a depth of 7 to 8 metres.

There is, indeed, no evidence of shifting agriculture such as was practised by the Danubian farmers further north, and whether or not there was any system for leaving land fallow, it did not necessitate moving the village. Each village apparently supported 20 to 30 families, and settlements in the fertile Maritsa valley are spaced about 5 kilometres apart.

Trade is already attested by the widespread finds of bracelets of the shell called *Spondylus gaederopus,* and a workshop for their manufacture was found at Hîrsova (Galbenu 1962, 295). Their concentration in the Lower Danube valley, and relative scarcity in the Aegean,[6] suggests a possible Black Sea origin at least in some cases (although it has yet to be established that this bivalve was native to the Black Sea in the 4th millennium BC). The yellow flint of Madara was also traded (cf. Georgiev 1959), and obsidian from the Hungarian and Slovakian sources was traded across the Hungarian plain and south as far as Vinča (Cann and Renfrew 1964, 126) and to Lumea Noua (Alba Iulia) in Romania already in Early Neolithic times (Renfrew, Cann and Dixon 1965, 247). It did not, however, reach Bulgaria.

Shaft-hole tools of stone were manufactured, and some kind of drill was used to bore the holes. And it seems likely that this tool type of the Gumelnitsa period was inspired by the shaft-hole tools of antler which are common in earlier periods also.

The ovens seen already in the Karanovo I culture must certainly have been adapted for firing pottery by the Chalcolithic period. Through the kindness of Mr Jay Frierman of the University of California at Los Angeles, it has been possible to investigate this question further (Appendix II). A small sherd with graphite-painted decoration (pl. VII, lower) typical of the Karanovo VI culture, which I collected at Karanovo in 1966, was submitted to him for test. It transpires that the pot was fired to about 1,050° C, and in a deliberately controlled reducing atmosphere. If the atmosphere were not reducing, the graphite would burn away, and the body of the pot would be red and not black—an effect commonly seen on pots of the Karanovo VI culture found in houses which had been destroyed by fire.

Now the exciting thing about these conditions is that they are precisely those required for copper metallurgy. Copper melts at 1,083° C, and for successful smelting a reducing atmosphere is needed. It is clear therefore that refractory technology in the south-east European Chalcolithic had evolved sufficiently, in the firing of pottery, to provide the conditions required for the smelting and casting of copper.

We have seen then that Balkan metallurgy does seem to develop over a long period, from about 4000 BC. There are no indications of influence from Aegean or Anatolian metallurgy, and the principal metal types are local ones. Ceramic technology had already produced the necessary refractory know-how, and the impressive use to which this experience was put in the working of copper (but not bronze) is documented in Appendix I. There is no reason to postulate outside influence in this matter, and indeed, given the technological background of the Balkan Chalcolithic the development of such skilled craftsmanship is not particularly surprising.

Conclusion and Implications

It has been argued that the Late Neolithic and Chalcolithic cultures of south-east Europe developed, essentially independently of Oriental or Aegean influence, on the sound economic basis (farming and tell settlement) of the First Neolithic. The long chronology suggested both by stratigraphic evidence and by Radiocarbon has here been accepted. In consequence, the Balkan Chalcolithic sites are contemporary with the later Neolithic of the Aegean (map, fig. 1). And the chronological priority of the local metallurgy over that of the Aegean, as well as the numerous local and independent features, makes the case for independent invention of metallurgy a strong one.

The matter does not stop there, however. If we accept that Vinča, Gumelnitsa and their contemporaries are independent of Troy and the Aegean, the entire Neolithic development of central and northern Europe—after the inception of the Neolithic economy, which was at least Aegean if not Near Eastern in origin (Renfrew 1968a)—seems to be a local one. This produces a radical change in our thinking.

Moreover the early date for the Early Bronze Age of south-east Europe presents problems—even accepting that the Karanovo VII and Baden cultures may have been of long duration. This early date is reinforced by tree-ring calibration of C-14 dates (Suess 1967). It now appears that a C-14 date of 1700–1600 BC (on the 5,568 half-life) for the Unětice culture may correspond to a corrected date in calendar years of well before 2000 BC. Although this has implications for the Wessex culture (which must on this basis antedate the Mycenaean civilisation [Renfrew 1968*b*]), the interest here is again rather in south-eastern Europe. There are, as yet, no C-14 dates for the Pecica and Nagyrev cultures. But it seems very possible that these may soon be dated well before 2200 BC (in calendar years). If this comes about, all the supposed oriental imports at the beginning of the European Early Bronze Age—the ingot torques, 'Cypriote' knot headed pins and so forth (Childe 1929, 221 ; Childe 1957, 134 ; Gimbutas 1965*b*, 34)—will be earlier than their supposed prototypes at Byblos (Dunand 1937 ; Schaeffer 1949, 107) which are themselves fairly well dated by historical means, supported in some cases by C-14 dates.

This is not the place to argue in detail the status of the European Early Bronze Age, but in fact the local origin of these somewhat sacrosanct metal types need not cause any very great surprise, since their number is small, and they do, in fact, fit naturally into the Central European assemblage. This would leave prehistorians free to view the development of the European Early Bronze Age as something largely independent of Aegean or Anatolian influence until Mycenaean times. Of course some Early Bronze Age metal types (fig. 8, 6–7 ; fig. 11, 2–3) do have impressive Mediterranean parallels, but is it not time to abandon the notion of itinerant Oriental smiths in the European Early Bronze Age? I believe that the rich European Bronze Age—which is, after all, a uniquely European phenomenon—will prove also to be substantially free from Oriental influence.

In his Retrospect (1958, 74) Childe said that he had come to 'recognise how right Hawkes had been in 1940 when in his *The Prehistoric Foundations of Europe* he had insisted that by the Bronze Age, Europe had achieved a kind of culture distinctively its own'. If we can see this yet more clearly today, it is only because Childe and his colleagues so thoroughly laid the foundations for further research. [1969]

Plate I. Similar forms from the late Neolithic and Chalcolithic of Serbia and of Southern Bulgaria. Clay 'altars' and decorated plaques from Vinča (nos. 1 and 4) and from Iassa Tepe (nos. 2, 3 and 5, after Detev). Scale 2:5 approx.

Plate II. Ceramic continuity between the Vesselinovo and Gumelnitsa cultures. 1 to 3, graphite-painted ware of the Gumelnitsa culture from the Plovdiv region (no. 3 from Kapitan Dimitrievo); 4, jug of the Vesselinovo culture from Iassa Tepe. Scale 2:5 approx.

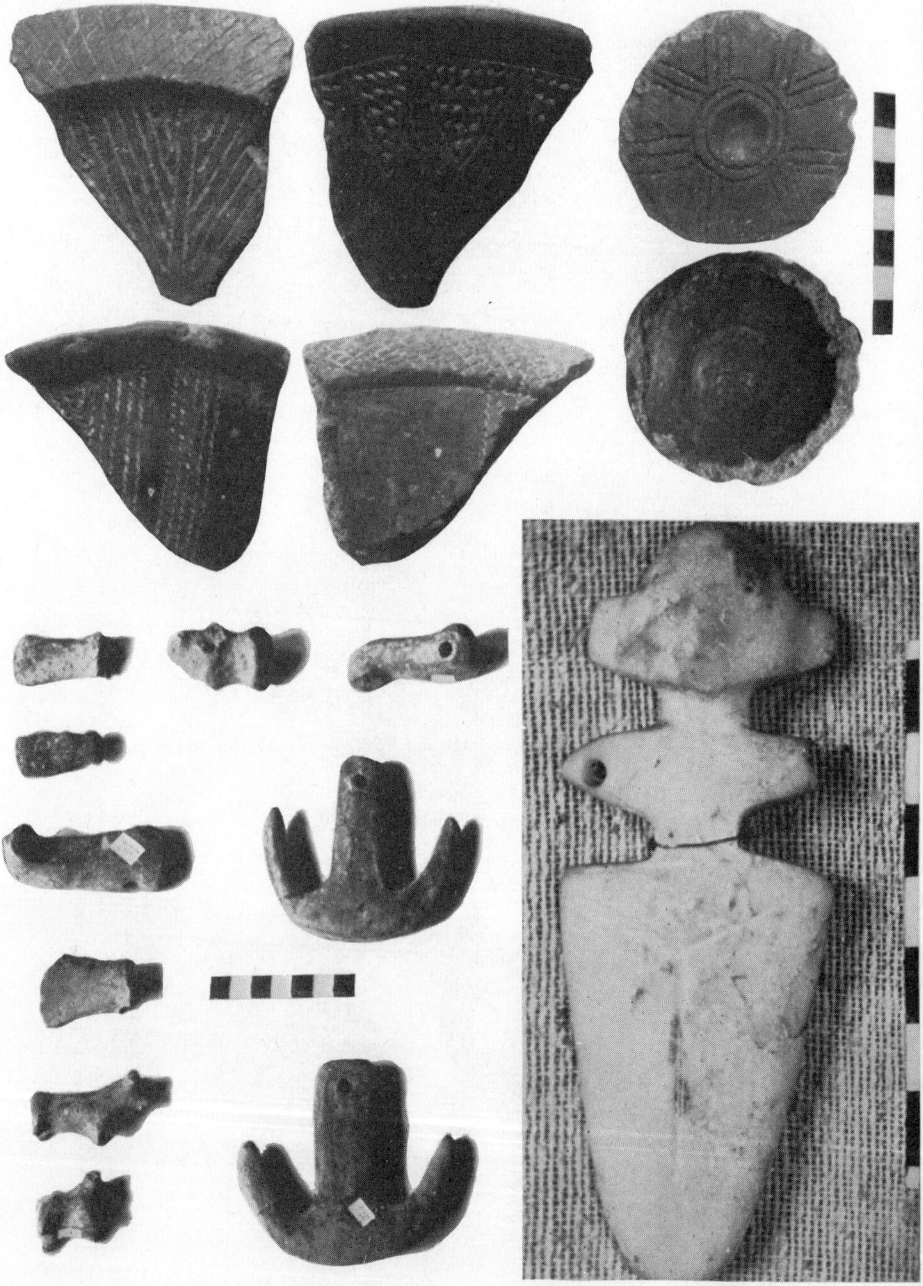

Plate III. Pottery of the Bulgarian Early Bronze Age from Michailitch. *Upper*: Corded ware. *Lower left*: Clay anchors, animals and axes of Troy I type. *Lower right*: Marble figurine of the Gumelnitsa-Kodadermen culture from Karanovo.

Plate IV. Pottery of the Bulgarian Early Bronze Age from Michailitch. *Upper*: Impression-decorated coarse ware. *Lower*: Bowls with tubular lugs of Troy I type.

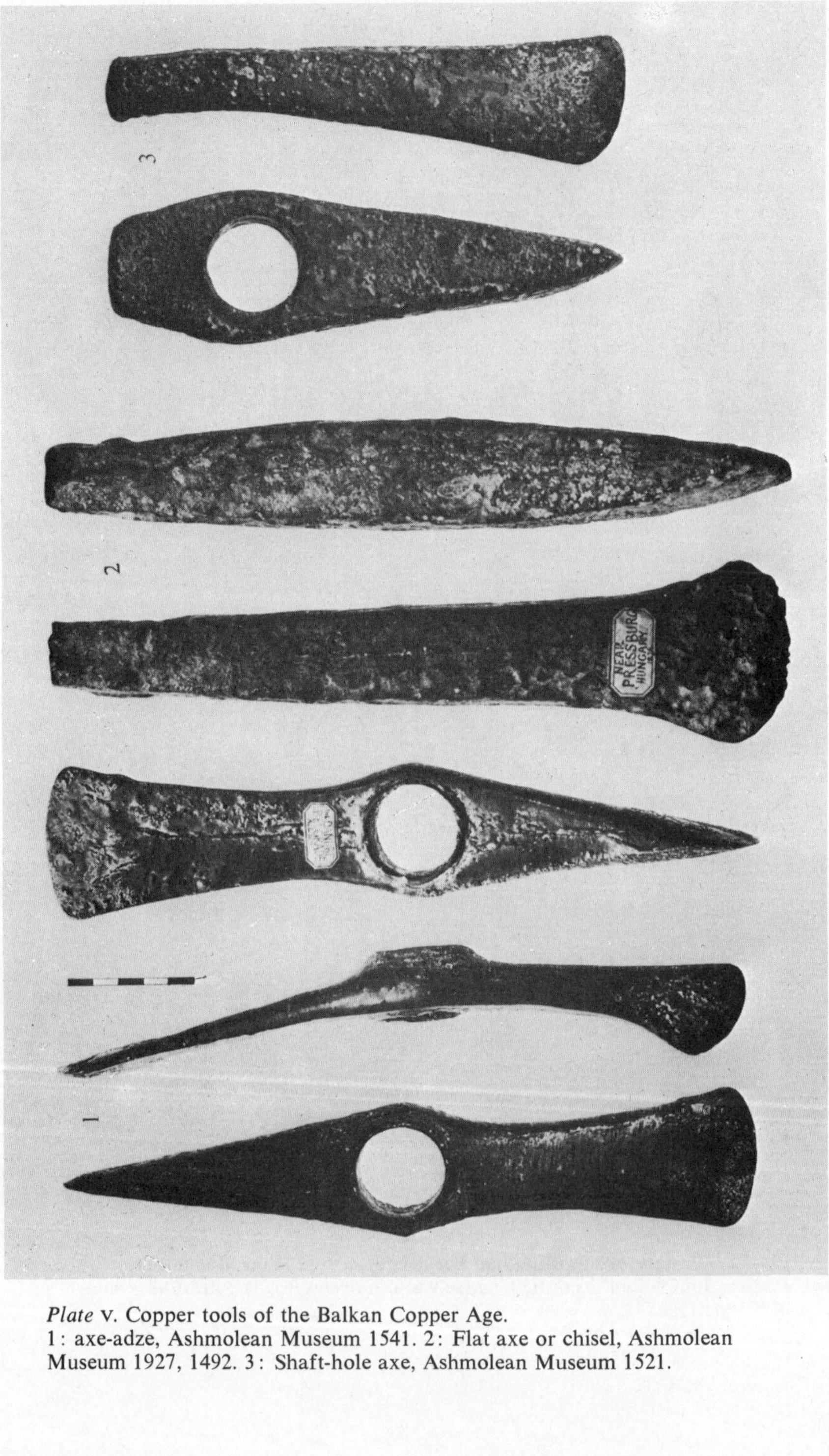

Plate v. Copper tools of the Balkan Copper Age.
1: axe-adze, Ashmolean Museum 1541. 2: Flat axe or chisel, Ashmolean Museum 1927, 1492. 3: Shaft-hole axe, Ashmolean Museum 1521.

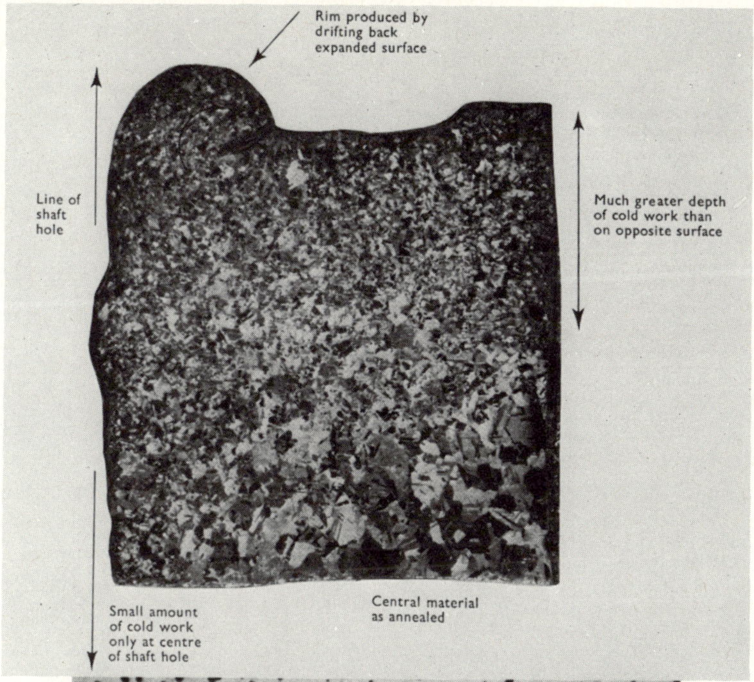

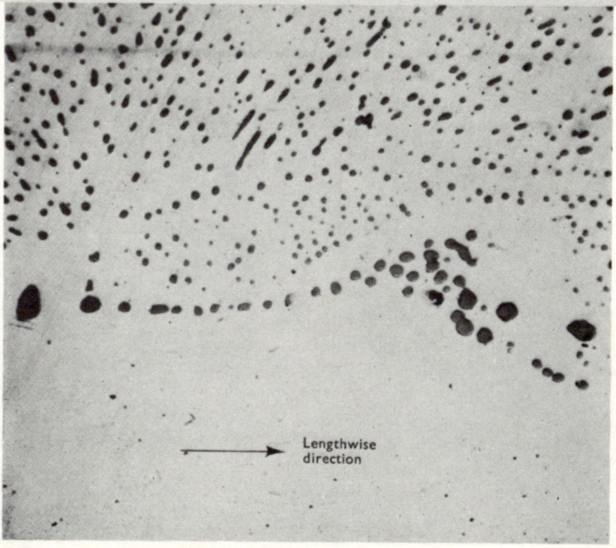

Plate VI. *Upper*: Axe-adze 1541. Microstructure of section to half thickness, from underside. Etched $FeCl_3$ in alcohol, × 6 approx.
Lower: Shaft-hole axe 1521. Junction between a primary copper dendrite and the copper-oxide eutectic. Oxide particles randomly distributed in relation to the length. Unetched, × 140.

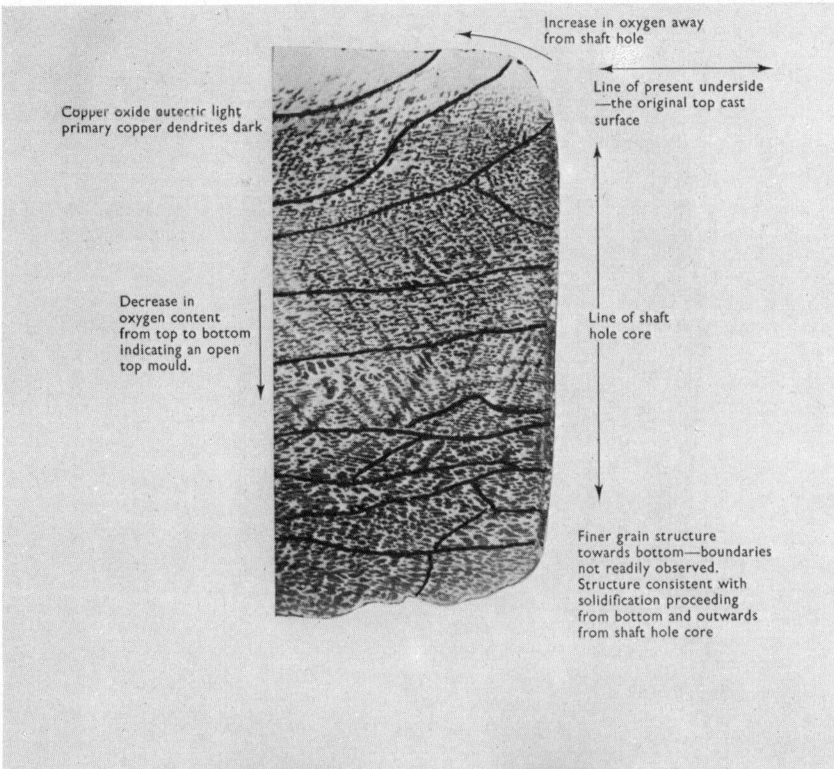

Plate VII. *Upper*: Shaft-hole axe 1521. Section of axe at shaft-hole indicating the use of an open mould and shaft-hole core. Unetched, oblique illumination, × 7.5.
Lower: Graphite-painted sherd of the Gumelnitsa culture from Karanovo (see Appendix II). Length *c.* 10 cm.

Appendix I, by J. A. Charles: A Metallurgical Examination of South-East European Copper Axes

Simple Shaft-Hole Axe

ASHMOLEAN MUSEUM 1929, 1521, FROM HUNGARY

Examination was by taking and preparing a metallographic specimen from the side of the shaft-hole towards and in line with the cutting edge, in a similar manner to those previously examined by others and as reported by H. H. Coghlan (1961). Sawings obtained in this operation were used for spectroscopic analysis. The results obtained indicated an extremely high grade copper, probably reflecting native copper as the starting material, although it is difficult to be dogmatic on this point.

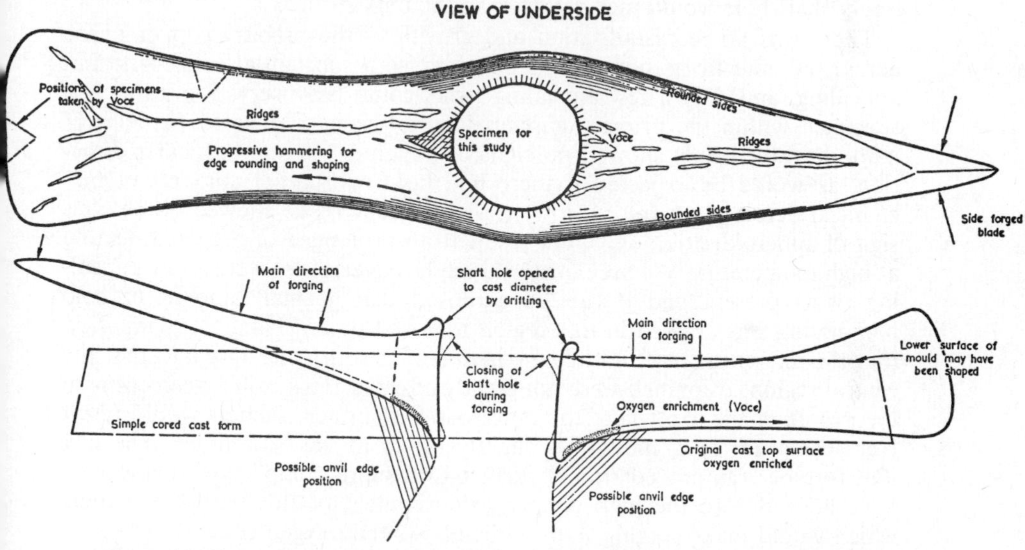

Figure 13. Sketch of axe-adze 1541, indicating suggested fabricating technique.

The metallographic structure was that of heavily oxidised copper with primary dendrites of copper in a copper-copper oxide eutectic matrix. The eutectic structure was everywhere consistent with an as-cast condition. The original very coarse macro-grain structure was just discernible in spite of the heavy oxide content and the observed position of the as-cast grain boundaries is indicated by lines drawn on the photograph of the dendritic structure as revealed by oblique illumination of the unetched specimen (pl. VII, upper). In this the primary copper dendrites of copper show dark. The directionality of these as-cast grains indicates a core material of relatively high conductivity, e.g. a dense charcoal stick, as opposed to a core of clay or stone. A charcoal stick would also have greater mechanical strength than clay.

It was clear that there had been no deformation of the material in the vicinity of the shaft-hole and that it was produced by casting round a core.

There was also a great increase in the oxygen content of the metal towards the upper flat surface, with approximately 0·4% oxygen at the upper surface decreasing from grain to grain to approximately 0·15% oxygen at the lower surface. There was no discontinuity in structure or oxygen content as would result from re-melting of the surface. Such re-melting has been proposed to explain surface concentrations of oxide, but if present it should be readily discernible metallographically, particularly as regards the effect on the morphology of the eutectic oxide phase in the underlying solid material near the interface. A most important feature was that the amount of oxygen enrichment at the surface decreases towards the shaft-hole rim, as would be expected with solidification developing from the upper part of the core (pl. VII, upper). This proves beyond doubt that the shaft-hole was cast in and not drilled out in any way. It also proves that such oxygen enrichment was not due to subsequent melting during annealing, when the edge of the now empty shaft-hole would melt rather than the bulk surface.

There was no recrystallisation and growth of the primary copper phase across the eutectic as might have occurred with substantial cold work and annealing, and only a few annealing twins could be observed in an etched specimen within the primary copper dendrite arms. Elongated particles of oxide in the eutectic showed no signs of alignment in any particular direction, as would be expected if there had been substantial amounts of mechanical deformation (pl. VI, lower). The eutectic oxide showed no obvious sign of spheroidisation as would result from prolonged or repeated heating at high temperature. As previously stated, however, there were a few annealing twins present and it can be surmised that a small amount of cold hammering was applied in this region followed by annealing. It is my view that the axe ends were finished by hammering with annealing and that the central regions examined were not greatly affected. This is in agreement with the profile of the axe where the otherwise flat surface, such as would result from using an 'open mould', is slightly raised at the extremities. The fact that forging was not continued further to a more complicated shape may have been due to the high copper oxide content of this particular article which would make forging more difficult. As the oxygen content of copper increases, the hydrogen content decreases, and consequently the metal has better casting qualities in respect of freedom from porosity in the casting due to the release of hydrogen on solidification. On the other hand, increase in oxygen reduces the ductility and toughness of the copper, making it more difficult to work without cracking. Alternatively, it may represent an earlier state of development before the prevention of gross oxidation during melting and casting had been achieved and before forging to complex shapes was possible.

Axe-Adze

ASHMOLEAN MUSEUM 1927, 1541, FROM BELGRADE

A section was cut from the shaft-hole on the opposite side to that previously investigated by Voce and reported by Coghlan. The sawings were analysed spectroscopically and again showed an extremely high purity. Metallographic examination indicated the copper oxide content to be much lower than with axe 1521, approximately 0·1%.

The metallographic observations were entirely in agreement with Voce. The original as-cast copper oxide network has been deformed in the lengthwise direction of the axe, consistent with major deformation between the top and bottom surfaces. Although less marked than in axe 1521, there is more oxide at the upper surface, again decreasing in extent at the surface towards the shaft-hole, as consistent with the use of a core in an open mould. The structure of the metal adjacent to the shaft-hole and particularly towards the two surfaces shows shattered grains and deformed annealing twins indicating that final drifting or enlargement of the ends of the shaft-hole was carried out without subsequent annealing (pl. VI, upper). Away from the shaft-hole and the surfaces in the centre, the copper crystals are very large in relation to the original eutectic network with mainly undeformed twins, suggesting that after heavy deformation for initial shaping an anneal followed to enable the final surface working and cutting-edge sharpening operations to be carried out. The deformation of grains at the surfaces is most severe on the underside, suggesting that this final working was mainly carried on this side to produce the curved shape.

Discussion of Observations

When first examining the whole group of axes from the Ashmolean Museum illustrated by Dr Renfrew's photographs (pl. V) the possibility arose of the simple form 1521 being an early stage in the process of fabrication of a more complex shape. After the detailed examination of this simple type and comparison of structure with the more complex shape 1541, this possibility has definite substance. Most probably the simple solid form 1492 (pl. V, 1), cast in an open mould and forged to the cutting blade, represents the first stage beyond simply shaping lumps of native copper without melting. Alternatively, of course, this may not be an axe at all, but a heavy chisel where a shaft-hole would not be required. Rather more elaborate shaping and the provision of a cored shaft-hole (1521) could represent the next stage of development and this form might then have been used with further development and skill to larger sizes as the basis shape for the complex form of the axe-adze 1541.

When this last was first examined visually, the ridge along the under surface tended to suggest a bivalve mould and comment was made to this effect to Dr Renfrew, although the split in the line towards the adze end was confusing and the absence of a matching flash line on the top surface was also difficult to explain. (Similarly, there is an observable line along one side of 1492.) I am now confident that this is not evidence of a split mould, but most probably stems from the combined effect of mechanical working and subsequent corrosion. In my view the stages in the manufacture of such an advanced design of axe using the information from the simpler type was as follows:

The rough cored shape would be cast in a clay mould with a central charcoal core, moulded into position in the mould floor. The mould itself was probably set in the base of the well of a draughted fire such that native copper melted in the fire would run down into the mould. The mould would be heated from the fire above and solidification would not proceed until the mould had been filled and the fire had died down or had been dispersed.

The difference in oxide content between 1521 and 1541 may either be chance at a similar stage of development, or reflect an advance of technique. Clearly, in the smaller artefact the metal remained molten for a long time (large grains and continuous oxygen gradient from top to bottom) and possibly an advance in technique is reflected in the Belgrade axe 1541 in that the oxygen content is much lower and enrichment is more localised. Some provision may have been made for displacing the mould position away from the main combustion zone of the fire, so that with a hot charcoal cover the oxygen pick-up would be reduced.

The cast rough shape would then be forged against an anvil, probably with a curved anvil edge resting against the rim of the shaft-hole (fig. 13). It is clear from both visual and metallographic evidence that forging was mainly from one side, working along to give the splay of the flat blade and the enlargement at the shaft-hole. Working from mainly the underside would enable the curve of the blade to be produced. After the main shaping operation the axe would be annealed and then the final surface finish and configuration obtained by further cold work on an anvil. It is suggested that the ridge along the centre line of the underside corresponds to a feature of the final forging operation, which was mainly on this surface. Either this ridge was produced purposely for decorative or functional ends, or it results from the fact that if final hammering was carried out towards the edges to give rounding, a central region would be left in a relatively unworked condition. This would then be cathodic to the nearby worked surface during subsequent corrosion and would not be attacked to the same extent. A similar feature of preferential corrosion at regions of high hardness developed by cold work has recently been observed during the examination of a Minoan dagger (Charles 1968).

Forging to expand the length and breadth of the axe and to achieve the final complex shape would cause surface layers to expand over the centre as-cast diameter of the shaft-hole. This would be corrected by drifting in a tapered shaft at each side, which would raise the copper into a flange, particularly on the underside where the forged surface is almost flat around the shaft-hole. On the top side the effect of forging of the material around the shaft-hole against the edge of the anvil would be to give a more gradual slope of the surface and the drifting has given a less abrupt change of section. In fact, the final shape around the shaft-hole on this side may well have been obtained by hammering against the drifting tool. The technique of drifting an as-cast shaft-hole has sometimes been questioned as being illogical, but it is clearly necessary to restore a true bore in a forged casting. It enables final cold forging operations around the hole to be achieved with the drifting tool in place and, in any event, the final drift may well have been the shaft itself.

Appendix II, by Jay Frierman: The Balkan Graphite Ware

Graphite wares have been known for many years but, unfortunately, these very interesting ceramics have never been fully described.[7] Dr Colin Renfrew kindly supplied me with a sherd which he had collected on the *tell* of Karanovo, Bulgaria, in the summer of 1966. It is a typical Karanovo v or vi graphite ware belonging to the Gumelnitza culture (pl. vii, lower).

The clay is of medium fine texture. The surface has been coated with slip of the same composition as the body, and when leather hard, it was burnished on all surfaces. Graphite was applied to the burnished surface of the exterior and the upper part of the interior.[8] The usual ornament of black lines was produced by subsequent burnishings. The surface, where not coated with graphite, is black-brown ; the interior, at a fresh break, is an even dark brown.

The firing temperature in an oxidising atmosphere was between 1,000° C, at which point it was not yet sintered, and 1,105° C where the sample was vitrified into a dark-brown stone ware with a hardness of 7·5 Moh's scale.[9] At 1,200° C there was a complete fusion to a brown, glassy glaze. The hardness of the sample is slightly harder than 3 Moh's scale. Since fusible clays have an arrow firing range, it would be reasonable to assume a firing temperature of no more than c. 1,050° C.

There is a further complication, our tests indicate that the graphite on our sample burns off at 725° C in an oxidising atmosphere, and the ware assumes a pinkish colour. Therefore, it seems probable that after reaching 500° or 600° the atmosphere for the remainder of the firing had to be strongly reducing.[10] The evenness and the colour of the interior (supra) would indicate a slow thorough firing under reducing conditions, there being no grey zone of unburnt organic material in the centre of these wares.

Chemical analysis[11]	
MgO	2·21
CaO	1·76
Na_2O	3·77
Fe_2O_3	8·53
Al_2O_3	30·80
SiO_2	52·50[12]
MnO	<10 p.p.m.
TiO_2	<100 p.p.m.
Loss on ignition	6·53
Total	106·10%

This clay contains 16·27% of fluxes (MgO, CaO, Na_2O, and Fe_2O_3). This abundance contributes to holding the graphite on the surface. The high content of Fe_2O_3 (8·53%) together with the carbon derived from the reduction firing produce the dark surface.

Reconstruction of the Method of Manufacture

The vessels were formed by hand. They were then coated with slip, and when leather hard they were burnished. The graphite was applied after the vessel had dried.[13] The lines were then produced by further burnishing.

It would appear to be necessary to have some type of kiln in order to produce the prolonged period of reduction necessary to prevent burning of the graphite and to thoroughly and evenly fire the ware. Beehive bread ovens are common on the sites of this period, and it is likely that equally sophisticated arrangements for firing pottery were in existence.

The pink and pink-buff sherds, often with white spots, found on these sites are the result of being refired at 725° C or higher in an oxidising atmosphere. This was accomplished by occasional house or village fires. Evidence for such fires is common on many of these sites with their dependence on combustible materials for house construction.

In conclusion, one must mention the high aesthetic qualities of these wares. Their thin, hard, satin surfaces, and pleasing shapes, and strong ornament make them one of the handsomest wares of the 4th millennium BC in Europe.

NOTES

Since this article was written, two seasons' excavations at Sitagroi-Photolivos in North Greece have given stratigraphic corroboration that the Gumelnitsa culture is considerably earlier than the Aegean Early Bronze Age and Troy I. This point has cogently been argued by E. Neustupny in his article: Absolute chronology of the neolithic and aeneolithic periods in central and south-eastern Europe, *Slov. Archeol.* 16 (1968), 19–56.

[1] Acknowledgements. See original publication.

[2] Information based on the research of Mrs J. M. Renfrew (personal communication).

[3] The excavations at Sitagroi-Photolivos in north Greece, undertaken after this paper was written, in the summers of 1968 and 1969, confirm this equation. Stratum III at Photolivos shows many links with Gumelnitsa, and Stratum V has affinities both with Michailitch and Troy. I.

[4] Similar conclusions have independently been reached by E. Neustupny in an article published after this paper was written (Neustupny 1968*b*). In it the Jugoslav culture sequence is very carefully considered, and an early date (2300 BC) effectively argued for the beginning of the central European Early Bronze Age.

[5] Copper objects have now been found in Stratum III at Sitagroi-Photolivos, but so far there is nothing so complicated as the Bulgarian shaft-hole axes.

[6] Numerous bracelets of *Spondylus* have now been found at Sitagroi-Photolivos and an Aegean source, at least for some of the Balkan finds, seems more likely.

[7] Gaul, J. H. (1948) The Neolithic Period in Bulgaria. *Bull. Amer. School Prehist. Res.* 16, pp. 98–100, 203, note 150.

[8] Cones of graphite have been found at Janka, Kodza Dermen, and Meckur. Gaul, 1948, p. 98.

V. J. Fewkes and Gaul seem to leave some confusion as to whether the wares were graphite or manganese painted. The graphite wares have only a trace of Mn. The determination on our sample was made with a Norelco Standard X-ray Defractometer, copper K alpha source, rate of scan 1° per minute. The standard for comparison was a pure graphite crystal from Ceylon (UCLA mineral specimen, MS 128). This determination was expertly and graciously carried out by D. L. Weide, Curator, Geology Museum, UCLA.

[9] The ASTM method was used to determine fusion point temperature. Norton F. H. (1949) *Refractories*, 3rd ed. pp. 352–3.

[10] Although graphite combines with O_2 at c. 700° C, in the absence of air it is stable to over 3,000° C. Searle, A. B. (1950) *Refractory Materials: Their Manufacture and Uses*, 3rd ed.

[11] This work was excellently carried out by T. L. Reed of the Chemical Analysis Facility, Engineering Dept., UCLA. A B & L dual graded optical emission spectroscope with a tin oxide internal standard was used. The dilution was with graphite.

[12] The SiO_2 determination was by the ACS method, and we presume the c. 6% error in the total occurs in this analysis.

[13] Graphite is found in the metamorphic rocks of the Rhodope and Balkan Mountains (cf. Gaul, 1948, p. 99).

ABBREVIATIONS

IAI: *Izvestiya Archeologicheskaya Institut* (Sofia).

GNAMP: *Godishnik Narodniya Archaologicheski Muzei Plovdiv.*

SCIV: ·*Studii si Cercetari de Istorie Veche.*

BIBLIOGRAPHY

Angelov, N. (1958) Die Siedelung bei Hotnica. *Studia in Honorem Acad. D. Dečev* 389.

——(1961) Atelier d'idoles plates en os dans le tell près du village Hotnica. *Archeologiya* 3, 34.

Banner, J. (1956) *Die Péceler Kultur.*

Berciu, D. (1961*a*) *Contributii la Problemele Neoliticului in Rominia in Lumine Noilor Cercetari.*

——(1961*b*) Chronologie relative du nèolithique du Bas Danube à la lumière des nouvelles fouilles faites en Roumanie, in Soudsky, B. and Plesova, E. (eds.) *L'Europe à la fin de l'âge de la pierre.*

——(1967) *Rominia.*

Blegen, C. W. *et al.* (1950) *Troy,* vol. 1.

Blegen, C. W. (1963) *Troy and the Trojans.*

Bognár-Kutzian, I. (1965) *The Copper Age Cemetery of Tiszapolgár-Basatanya.*

Brea, L. B. (1964) *Poliochni, città preistorica nell isola di Lemnos* 1.

Cann, J. R. and Renfrew, C. (1964) The characterisation of obsidian and its application to the Mediterranean region. *PPS* 30, 111.

Charles, J. M. (1968) The metallurgy of a Minoan dagger—the first Sheffield Plate. *Antiq.* 42, 278.

Childe, V. G. (1923) Some affiliations of Chalcolithic culture in Thrace. *Man* 23, 4.

——(1927) The Danube thoroughfare and the beginnings of civilisation in Europe. *Antiq.* 1, 79.

——(1929) *The Danube in Prehistory.*

——(1936) The axes from Maikop and Caucasian metallurgy. *Lpool Ann. Archaeol. and Anthrop.* 23, 113.

——(1939) The Orient and Europe. *Amer. J. Archaeol.* 43, 10.

——(1954) *New Light on the Most Ancient East.*

——(1956) Anatolia and Thrace. *Anatol. Stud.* 6, 45.

——(1957) *The Dawn of European Civilisation.*

——(1958) Retrospect. *Antiq.* 32, 69.

Clark, J. G. D. (1938) Current prehistory. *PPS* 4, 221.

——(1966) The invasion hypothesis in British prehistory. *Antiq.* 41, 172.

Coghlan, H. H. (1961) Some problems concerning the manufacture of copper shafthole axes. *Archaeol. Austri.* 29, 57.

Comsa, E. (1962) Otnositelnaya Chronologiya i Razvitie Neolitskaya Kultur. *Dacia* 6, 53.

Deshayes, J. (1960) Les Origines de la métallurgie danubienne. *Acta Archaeol. Hungar.* 12, 69.

Detev, P. (1950*a*) Le tell Baniata près de Kapitan Dimitrievo. *GNAMP* 2, 1.

——(1950*b*) Le Tell Raskopanitse près de Manole. *IAI* 17.

——(1954) Tell près du village de Bikovo. *Godishnik na Muzeite v Plovdivski. Okrug* 1, 151.

——(1959) Materiaux de la préhistoire de Plovdiv. *GNAMP* 111, 3.

——(1960) Vorgeschichtliche Gefässe mit menschen-und tierähnlichen Darstellungen in Bulgarien. *Archaol. Anz.* (1960) 1.

——(1965) Modèles de décoration de l'énéolithique. *Archaeol.* 7, 65.

Dimitrov, D. P. (1943) Zweihenkelige trojanische Tonbecher aus Südbulgarien. *Archäol. Anze.* 57, 13.

Driehaus, J. (1952) Zur Datierung und Herkunft donauländischer Axttypen der frühen Kupferzeit. *Archaeol. Geogr.* 3, 1.

Dumitrescu, H. (1961) Connections between the Cucuteni-Tripolie cultural complex and the neighbouring eneolithic cultures in the light of the utilisation of golden pendants. *Dacia* 5, 69.

Dumitrescu, V. (1965) Cascioarele. *Archaeol.* 18, 34.

Ehrich, R. W. (1965) *Chronologies in Old World Archaeology* 403.

Evans, A. J. (1935) *The Palace of Minos* 4.

French, D. (1962) Excavations at Can Hasan. *Anatol. Stud.* 12, 33.
——(1964) Prehistoric pottery from Macedonia and Thrace. *Prähist. Z.* 42, 30
Galbenu D. (1962) Asezarea neolitica de la Hirsova. *SCIV* 13, 285.
Galovic, R. (1959) *Predionica, Neolitsko Naselje Kod Pristina.*
——(1962) Zelenikovo. *Zborn. Narodn. Mus. Beogradu* 5, 127.
Garašanin, D. (1951) *Hronologija Vincanske Grupe.*
Garašanin, M. V. (1958) Neolithikum und Bronzezeit in Serbien und Makedonien. *Ber. den Römisch-Germanisch Kommission* 39, 1.
——(1961) The Neolithic in Anatolia and the Balkans. *Antiq.* 35, 276.
——(1965) Considérations sur les influences sudorientales dans les civilisations préhistoriques des Balkans. *Rev. Etud. sud-est Europ.* 1, 5.
Gaul, J. H. (1942) Possibility of prehistoric metallurgy in the east Balkan peninsula. *Amer. J. Archaeol.* 46, 400.
——(1948) *The Neolithic Period in Bulgaria* (Bull. Am. Sch. Preh. Res. 16).
Georgiev, G. I. (1958) Über einige Produktionswerkzeuge aus dem Neolithikum und Äneolithikum in Bulgarien. *Studia in Honorem Acad. D. Dečev* (Sofia) 369.
——(1959) Über die Datierung der prähistorischen Siedlung bei Madara, Kreis Kolarovgrad. *IAI* 22, 29.
——(1961) Kulturgruppen der Jungsteinzeit und Kupferzeit in der Ebene von Thrazien, in Soudsky, B. and Plesova, E. (eds.) *L'Europe à la fin de l'âge de la pierre,* 45.
——(1962) Azmashkata moghila krai Stara Zagora. *Archaeol.* 41, 64.
——(1965) The Azmak Mound in southern Bulgaria, *Antiq.* 6.
Georgiev, G. I. and Angelov, N. (1957) Ausgrabungen an dem Sidelungshügel bei Russe. *IAI* 21, 41.
Georgiev, G. I. and Merpert, N. I. (1965) Raskopki Mnogosloinogo Poselniya ... 1963. *IAI* 28, 129.
——and——(1966) The Ezero Mound in south-east Bulgaria. *Antiq.* 40, 33.
Gimbutas, M. (1965*a*) The relative chronology of Neolithic and Chalcolithic cultures of eastern Europe in Ehrich (1965) 459.
——(1965*b*) *Bronze Age Cultures in Central and Eastern Europe.*
Glisic, J. (1964) Stratigraphie der Vinča Gruppe Siedlung bei der Spinnerei in Pristina. *Gla. Muz. Kosova i Metohije* 7 8, 11.
Grbic, M. (1929) *Pločnik.*
——(1956) Retention der Starčevo Kultur. *Archaeol. Iugoslav.* 2, 1.
Hillebrand, J. (1929) Über die Bedeutung des altkupferzeitlichen Bodrogkeresztur Kulturkreises. *Wien. Prähist. Z.* 16, 8.
Hole, F. and Flannery, K. V. (1967) The prehistory of south-west Iran, a preliminary report. *PPS* 33, 147.
Kalicz, N. (1963) *Die Péceler (Badener) Kultur und Anatolien.*
Kohn, G. and Quitta, H. (1966) Berlin Radiocarbon Measurements II. *Radiocarbon* 8, 27.
Kohler, E. L. and Ralph, E. K. (1961) C-14 dates for sites in the Mediterranean area. *Amer. J. Arch.* 65, 359.
Lamb, W. (1936) *Excavations at Thermi in Lesbos.*
Lloyd, S. and Mellaart, J. (1962) *Beycesultan* 1.
Margos, A. and Toncheva, G. (1962) La Cité lacustre préhistorique au village d'Ezerovo arr. de Varna. *Izv. Varnen. Arcaeol. Druzh.* 13, 1.
Mellaart, J. (1960) Anatolia and the Balkans. *Antiq.* 34, 270.
——(1964) Excavations at Çatal Hüyük 1963. *Anatol. Stud.* 14.
Merpert, N. I. (1961) L'Enéolithique dans la zone steppique de la partie européenne de l'URSS, in Soudsky, B. and Plesova, E. (eds.) *L'Europe à la fin de l'âge de la pierre* 176.
——(1966) Rannii Bronzovii Vek Yozhnoi Bolgarii. *Communications de la Délégation Soviétique au Premier Congrès des Etudes Balkaniques, Sofia.*
Mikov, V. (1939*a*) Tell près du village de Veselinovo *IAI* 13, 195.
——(1939*b*) Les Fouilles du tell près du village de Yunatsite. *Annu. Bibli. Mus. Nat. de Plovdiv* (1937–9) 55.
——(1948) Fouilles du site préhistorique près de Michailitch. *Raskopi i Prouchvaniya* 1, 7.
——(1961) Hâches-pioches en Bulgarie. *Izsled. v Pamet na Karel Shkorpil* (Sofia) 369.

Miločić, V. (1949*a*) South-eastern elements in the prehistory of Serbia. *Annu. Brit. School of Archaeol. Athens* 44, 258.

——(1949*b*) *Chronologie der jüngeren Steinzeit Mittel- und Südosteuropas.*

——(1965) Die Tontafeln von Tartaria und die absolute Chronologie des mitteleuropäischen Neolithikums. *Germania* 43, 261.

Nandris, J. G. (1968) Lepenski Vir. *Sci. J.* (January 1968) 64.

Nemejcová-Pavúková, V. (1966) Zur relativen Chronologie des Äneolithikums in Mittel- und Südosteruropa. *Germania* 44, 234.

Nestor, I (1955) La Métallurgie du cuivre et de bronze en Roumanie. *Nouv. Etud. d'Hist.* 1955.

Neustupny, E. (1968*a*) The Tărtăria tablets. *Antiq.* 43, 32.

——(1968*b*) Absolute chronology of the Neolithic and Aeneolithic periods in central and south-eastern Europe. *Slov. Archeol.* 14, 19.

Otto, H. and Witter, W. (1952) *Handbuch der ältern vorgeschichtlichen Metallurgie in Mitteleuropa.*

Passek, T. S. (1961) Problèmes de l'énéolithique de sud-ouest de l'Europe occidentale, in Soudsky, B. and Plesova, E. (eds.) *L'Europe à la fin de l'age de la Pierre* 148.

Patay, P., Kimmer, Z., Szabo, Z. and Sinay, G. (1963) Spektrographische und metallographische Untersuchungen kupfer- und frühbronzezeitliche n Funde. *Acta Archaeol. Hungar.* 15, 37.

Petkov, N. (1950) Classification des idoles plates en os de la civilisation énéolithique balkano-danubienne. *GNAMP* 2, 25.

Pittioni, R. (1957) Urzeitlicher Bergbau auf Kupfererz und Spuren-analyse. *Archaeol. Aust.* Beiheft 1.

Popovic, V. (1965) Une Civilisation égéo-orientale sur le moyen Danube. *Rev. Archéol.*, juillet-septembre 1965, 1.

Quitta, H. (1967) The C-14 chronology of the central and south-east European Neolithic. *Antiq.* 41, 263.

Renfrew, C. (1964) Crete and the Cyclades before Rhadamanthus. *Kret. Chron.* 18, 107.

——(1967*a*) Cycladic metallurgy and the Aegean Early Bronze Age. *Amer. J. Archaeol.* 71, 1.

——(1967*b*) Colonialism and Megalithismus. *Antiq.* 41, 276.

——(1968*a*) Greek Neolithic—backward or precocious? *Curr. Archaeol.*, March 1968.

——(1968*b*) Wessex without Mycenae. *Annu. Brit. School Archaeol. Athens* 63.

——(1969) The chronology and classification of the Early Cycladic figurines. *Amer. J. Archaeol.* 73, 1.

Renfrew, C., Cann, J. R. and Dixon, J. E. Obsidian in the Aegean. *Annu. Brit. School Archaeol. Athens* 60, 225.

Schaeffer, C. F. A. (1949) *Ugaritica* 2 (Mission de Ras Shamra II).

Schmidt, H. (1903) Tordos. *Ze. für Ethnogr.* (1903) 438.

Schmidt, R. R. (1945) *Die Burg Vučedol.*

Sergeev, T. P. (1963) Early Tripolje hoard in the village of Karbuna. *Sovietsk. Archaeol.* I, 135.

Srejovic, D. (1963) Versuch einer historischen Wertung der Vinča-Gruppe. *Archaeol. Iugoslav.* 4, 5.

Stuiver, M. and Suess, H. E. (1966) On the relationship between Radiocarbon dates and true sample ages, *Radiocarbon* 8, 534.

Suess, H. E. (1967) Bristlecone Pine calibration of the Radiocarbon time scale from 4100 BC to 1500 BC. *Radioactive Dating and Methods of Low Level Counting* (International Atomic Energy Agency, Vienna) 143.

Todorovic, J. and Cermanovic, A. (1961) *Banitsa, Siedlung der Vinča Gruppe.*

Tsountas, C. (1908) *Ai Proistorikai Akropoleis Dhiminiou kai Sesklou.*

Vajsova, H. (1966) Stand der Jungsteinzeitforschung in Bulgarien ; *Slov. Archaeol.* 14, 5.

Venedikov, I. (1965) *Les Trésors d'art des Terres Bulgares.*

Vlassa, N. (1963) Chronology of the Neolithic in Transylvania in the light of the Tartaria settlement stratigraphy. *Dacia* 7, 1.

Vulpe, A. (1964) Sur la chronologie des haches doubles en cuivre à tranchets opposés. *SCIV* 15, 443.

Weinberg, S. S. (1962) Excavations at prehistoric Elateia 1959. *Hesperia* 31, 158.

Wertime, T. A. (1964) Man's first encounters with metallurgy. *Science* 146, 1257.

6) The Tărtăria Tablets

This short note was the first consideration in English of the Tărtăria tablets. As anticipated here they were soon used as an argument by those favouring a short chronology for the Balkans (e.g. Hood 1967) for whom the suggestion of contact with Proto-Dynastic or Early Dynastic Sumer proved powerful support. The case against such an equation is argued in chapters 5 and 8. Other evidence favouring this case has been published by Hood (1973).

On the other hand the signs occurring in the Vinča culture, including those on the Tărtăria tablets, have now been carefully considered by Winn (1973), with the conclusion that they are of local origin. Such is also the conclusion of Gimbutas (1974, 85–7). Their occurrence in the Balkans has been compared (Renfrew 1973, 182–6) with the independent inception of a coherent system of signs—i.e. 'writing'— in Easter Island, where the development likewise seems to have been an indigenous one.

The discussion continues. I accept the view of Winn that the tablets should be set in the context of the use of signs in the contemporary Balkans, and continue to consider them as entirely unrelated to the early development of writing in the Near East, which in fact seems to have taken place rather later.

BIBLIOGRAPHY

Gimbutas, M. (1974) *Gods and Goddesses of Old Europe*. London: Thames and Hudson.

Hood, M. S. F. (1967) The Tărtăria tablets. *Antiq.* 41, 99–113.

——(1973) An early oriental seal impression from Romania? *World Archaeol.* 5, 187–97.

Renfrew, C. (1973) *Before Civilisation, the Radiocarbon Revolution and Prehistoric Europe*. London: Jonathan Cape.

Winn, M. M. (1973) *The Signs of the Vinca Culture—an Internal Analysis; their Role, Chronology and Independence from Mesopotamia* (Ph.D. dissertation, University of California at Los Angeles). Ann Arbor: University Microfilms.

THE TĂRTĂRIA TABLETS

Three clay tablets with incised signs, from a Neolithic context in Rumania, seem likely to become the next *cause célèbre* in prehistoric archaeology. Their discovery was announced by N. Vlassa (*Dacia* 7 [1963] 485 f), the excavator of the site of Tărtăria. He reports that they were found in a level of the Tordos phase of the Vinča culture.

The exceptional importance of the tablets was at once realised by V. Milojčic. He obtained the opinion of the late A. Falkenstein (*Germania* 43 [1965] that the Tărtăria tablets are related to tablets of Protoliterate Sumeria, such as those of Warka IV, and not an independent product. The evidence for a direct Mesopotamian and Aegean connection has been summarised by V. Popovitch (*Revue archéologique* 1965 : 2, 1 f).

The authenticity of the tablets appears established by their discovery during properly conducted excavations, and is supported by the appearance of similar signs on objects and pottery of the Vinča and Körös cultures

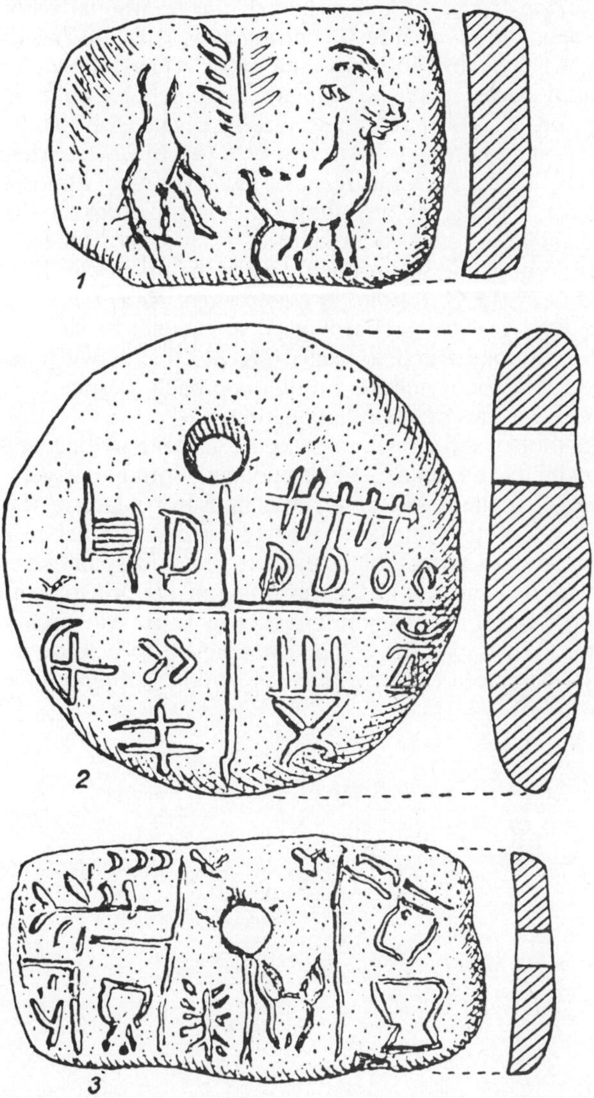

Figure 1. The incised signs on the Tărtăria tablets. Scale 1 : 1.

(Popovitch op. cit. 35 ; Childe, V. G. *The Danube in Prehistory* [1929], 33 ; Todorovic, J. and Cermanovic, A. *Banitsa* [1961], 42).

Many scholars would consequently date the Tărtăria tablets to around 3000 BC or a little later. This is broadly in conformity with the chronological views of such authorities on the Vinča culture as Milojčic, D. and M. Garašanin and V. Dumitrescu. Already this is a remarkable situation: writing in Rumania earlier than the sealings from the Early Helladic II town of Lerna III, and earlier than the first pottery marks at Phylakopi I, which have often been cited as the first evidence of Aegean writing.

But this dating of the Vinča culture is that of the traditional school of European prehistorians. It is in direct contradiction with the results of radiocarbon dating. All scholars (both pro- and anti-C-14) agree that Vinča-Tordos is considerably earlier than the Rumanian Gumelnitsa culture. The Gumelnitsa culture, on a C-14 chronology, clearly began early in the 4th millennium (Kohl, G. and Quitta, H. *Radiocarbon* 8 [1966] 27 ; cf. Mellaart, J. *Antiquity* 24 [1960] 270 f). No adjustment of half-lives or of atmospheric C-14 levels will make a radiocarbon dating for Vinča-Tordos in the 5th millennium BC equivalent to a calendar date of c. 3000 BC. Indeed such adjustments as have to be made will probably work the other way (Damon, P. E., Long, A. and Grey, D. C. *Journal of Geophysical Research* 71 [1966] 1055 f). There are very feasible archaeological arguments to support the longer radiocarbon chronology and it seems possible that it will one day supersede the more roundabout culture parallel approach, despite the considerable attraction of the Tărtăria-Warka equation.

If the signs on the tablets and elsewhere indeed constitute writing we shall have to face the possibility that on a C-14 chronology, writing emerged or at least began to emerge, perhaps independently, in Europe late in the 5th millennium BC. The alternative appears to be to reject radiocarbon completely as worthless, and to accept the presence, or at least influence, of Mesopotamian settlers in Rumania at the beginning of the 3rd millennium. Either conclusion will be of interest for Greek and European prehistory. But the first step must surely be for competent scholars to achieve a consensus that the signs are indeed to be regarded as writing. Is this certain?

[1966]

7) Neolithic Trade Routes Realigned by Oxygen Isotope Analyses (with N. Shackleton)

The continuing controversy over the chronological relationship between the copper age of the Balkans on the one hand, and the Aegean and Near East on the other, makes all the more interesting the undoubted exchange of the marine mollusc *Spondylus gaederopus* between the Aegean and the Balkans. It is in fact the only commodity for which such an exchange has been directly attested archaeologically at this early time. Aegean obsidian, for instance, has not been found in the Balkans, nor Carpathian obsidian in the Aegean (Renfrew, Cann and Dixon 1965).

Ultimately, however, the significance of the exchange must be seen in social terms: here the shell is a *primitive valuable* (Dalton 1977, 197) exchanged from the Aegean. As such it constitutes one of the few materials evidently functioning as a prestige good which was widely exchanged at so early a date. The exchange of amber from the Baltic to the Aegean in the 2nd millennium BC is another well-attested case although a later one. It has been suggested that the documentation of a prestige sphere of exchange may be relevant to the understanding of the origins of Balkan metallurgy (Renfrew 1978).

The technique of oxygen isotope analysis of marine shells recovered from archaeological deposits has been further applied by Shackleton to material from South Africa (1973) and from Nea Nikomedeia, in north Greece (1970). In these cases, however, the focus is on climatic and environmental questions rather than on the reconstruction of exchange patterns.

BIBLIOGRAPHY

Dalton, G. (1977) Aboriginal economies in stateless societies, in Earle, T. K. and Ericson, J. E. (eds.) *Exchange Systems in Prehistory*. New York: Academic Press, 191–2.

Renfrew, C. (1978) The anatomy of innovation, in Green, D. R., Haselgrove, C. C. and Spriggs, M. J. T. (eds.) *Social Organisation and Settlement* (British Archaeological Reports, Supplementary Series 47) 89–117.

Renfrew, C., Cann, J. R. and Dixon, J. E. (1965) Obsidian in the Aegean. *Annu. Brit. School of Archaeol. Athens* 60, 225–47.

Shackleton, N. (1970) Stable isotope study of the palaeoenvironment of the neolithic site of Nea Nikomedeia. *Nature, Land* 227, 943–44.

Shackleton, N. J. (1973) Oxygen isotope analysis as a means of determining season of occupation of prehistoric midden sites. *Archaeom.* 15, 133–42.

NEOLITHIC TRADE ROUTES RE-ALIGNED BY OXYGEN ISOTOPE ANALYSES

The distribution in the European neolithic objects, chiefly beads and bangles, made from the marine bivalve *Spondylus gaederopus* Linne gives a clear indication of a prehistoric trade in this attractive material. Clearly, either the ornaments or the unworked shells must have been transported by man from the sea where the animal lives. Recent work on other materials, supposedly traded from the Aegean region to the Balkans and central Europe, notably obsidian and faience, has suggested that prehistoric contacts between these areas were fewer than had been previously supposed. This finding seems to strengthen the possibility that the source for the *Spondylus* used in the Balkans and central Europe was not the Aegean but the Black Sea ; several authors have postulated its availability there in neolithic times. [1, 2] We report here preliminary investigations into the characterisation of the source of *Spondylus* shell through the analysis of the oxygen isotopic composition of the calcium carbonate of which it is constituted. Our results suggest the exclusion of the Black Sea as a source, and document the earliest known trading contacts between the Aegean and central Europe, in the fourth millennium BC.

The physical principle which we are utilizing in this study is that a mollusc deposits the calcium carbonate of its shell in isotopic equilibrium with the water it inhabits. That is to say, the proportion of oxygen-18 atoms to oxygen-16 atoms is governed by thermodynamical principles rather than by biological factors. In fact, the ratio of the two isotopes differs from that in the parent water by only a small amount, the extent varying slightly with temperature. From a geographical point of view this is of interest because it is sometimes possible to estimate palaeotemperatures through an analysis of the oxygen isotopic composition of a fossil shell.[3] From our point of view, it means that shells from two different sources may be differentiated clearly, either if the source regions have markedly different temperature regimes, or if they are characterised by watermasses of substantially different isotopic composition. Although we are not aware of any previous attempt to use the technique in this way, the idea was suggested some years ago by Keith *et al.*[4]

Isotopic Compositions of the Black Sea and the Mediterranean

In the initial stages of the project, we decided to restrict ourselves to differentiating between *Spondylus* from the Black Sea and from the Mediterranean. Here we are relying not on a climatic difference, but on a considerable difference in the isotopic composition of the waters.

The mechanism responsible for the fact that not all natural waters display the same $^{18}O/^{16}O$ ratio is a relatively simple one. Because water molecules containing ^{18}O are heavier than those containing ^{16}O, they have a slightly lower chance of evaporating into the atmosphere, so that water vapour in the air, and rain water, are slightly depleted in ^{18}O.[5] The differences are small, and are expressed as a deviation in parts per thousand from an arbitrary standard using the δ-notation :

$$\delta = 1{,}000 \left\{ \frac{R_{\text{sample}}}{R_{\text{standard}}} - 1 \right\}$$

where R is the ratio of ^{18}O to ^{16}O in sample and standard as indicated. All values quoted in this article are referred to the Pee Dee Belemmite standard.[6] In the oceans, the observed variations are very small except in regions where evaporation is high, leading to a high salinity and a positive o-value in the surface waters, and in regions where the admixture of fresh water reduces salinity and gives rise to a negative δ-value.[6] Several analyses have been published for Mediterranean water, which comes into the former category, in the range + 1·1 parts per thousand to + 1·3 parts per thousand,[6-8] these referring to water with a salinity of about 38·5 parts per thousand. (The values cited in references 7 and 8 have been converted from standard mean ocean water isotopic standard (SMOW) to PDB standard ; see ref. 9).

The Black Sea is largely isolated from the Mediterranean ; the water budget given by Sverdrup *et al.*[10] is: precipitation, 7,600 ; runoff, 10,400 ; inflow from Mediterranean, 6,100 ; evaporation, 11,500 ; outflow to Mediterranean, 12,600 (all figures in m^3/s). A comparison with the Caspian, where inflow is balanced by evaporation, suggests that the Black Sea would be expected to be isotopically slightly more negative ; Longinelli and Craig give a value of −2·4 parts per thousand for the Caspian[7] so that we might expect a value between −2·5 parts per thousand and −3 parts per thousand for the Black Sea. Very recently an even more negative value, —4·15 parts per thousand, has been published.[8] In any event there is clearly a substantial difference between its isotopic composition and that of the Mediterranean.

The second factor upon which the isotopic composition of shell carbonate depends is temperature, a factor whose importance was demonstrated by Urey.[11] The scale of the variation may be indicated by the fact that a seasonal change from 12° to 25° C would give rise to an isotopic variation through the shell of about 3 parts per thousand if growth continued throughout the year. Carbonate analyses are again expressed as δ-values in terms of the PDB standard. The generally used relationship between isotopic composition and temperature is[12]

$$T = 16{\cdot}5 - 4{\cdot}3\,(\delta_c - \delta_w) + 0{\cdot}14\,(\delta_c - \delta_w)^2$$

where δ_c and δ_w refer to carbonate and water respectively. The standard deviation among replicate analyses of carbonate is generally about 0·1 parts per thousand representing about ½° C.

Isotopic Analysis of Spondylus Shells from Neolithic Sites

The samples we have analysed are from settlement sites, datable between 4000 BC and 2500 BC in radiocarbon years. Tell Goljanio Delschevo[12] is in the Varna district, near the Black Sea coast of Bulgaria ; samples from this site (submitted by the excavator, Dr H. Vajsová Simeonová) were selected in view of the likelihood that they would, if the Black Sea were used at all as a source for the material, be from this source rather than from the much more distant Aegean. Sitagroi is a prehistoric settlement mound near Drama in Northern Greece, lying some 40 km from the Aegean sea coast (excavations here were jointly organised by C. R. and Professor Marija Gimbutas ; specimens from phase III occupation of site were selected and sampled by N. S. with permission from the Greek Archaeological Service). Gradeshnitsa in north-west Bulgaria and Vinča[15] near Belgrade in Jugoslavia are both more than 200 km from the sea (specimens from the surface of the Gradeshnitsa site were collected in 1966 with the collaboration of the excavator, Dr Bogdan Nikolov ; the Vinča specimens were selected from the collection in the University of Belgrade by permission of the curator, Mme Z. Letica). The results of the analyses are given in table 1.

Table 1. Carbonate analyses

Site and sample no.	δ ^{18}O (parts per thousand)	δ ^{13}C (parts per thousand)
Tell Goljanio Delschevo 3	−1·06	+0·21
Tell Goljanio Delschevo 5	+0·04	+1·14
Tell Goljanio Delschevo 6	−0·71	−0·29
Sitagroi 548	−0·27	+1·16
Sitagroi 817	−0·97	+0·50
Sitagroi 896	−0·55	+0·52
Sitagroi 1,446	−0·17	+0·87
Gradeshnitsa	−1·21	−0·04
Vinča	−0·91	+1·19

It is immediately clear that the analyses fall into a single group; the samples from the site near Varna on the Black Sea coast would be consistent with temperatures between about 24° to 19° C in water of isotopic composition +0·6 parts per thousand. A more positive water would imply a higher maximum temperature; the value chosen is a plausible summer value. If, on the other hand, our samples were by chance biased in favour of winter fragments, they would be consistent with temperatures between about 17° and 12° C in a water with isotopic composition −1 part per thousand. Thus even in the unlikely event of our having sampled fragments deposited in winter, the implied isotopic composition for the water is not nearly negative enough to be consistent with a Black Sea origin for the fragments found at Tell Goljanio Delschevo.

Analyses of Recent Shells

Because this conclusion was rather surprising, we carried out analyses of some recent shells from the Black Sea (specimens were supplied by Dr M. Demir, Marine Laboratory, Plymouth), which, in fact, confirmed our earlier findings. Three shells were analysed sequentially so as to obtain the maximum range of growth temperature (fig. 1). The overall range is satisfactorily large; if 24° C is used as a likely value for the maximum represented, the

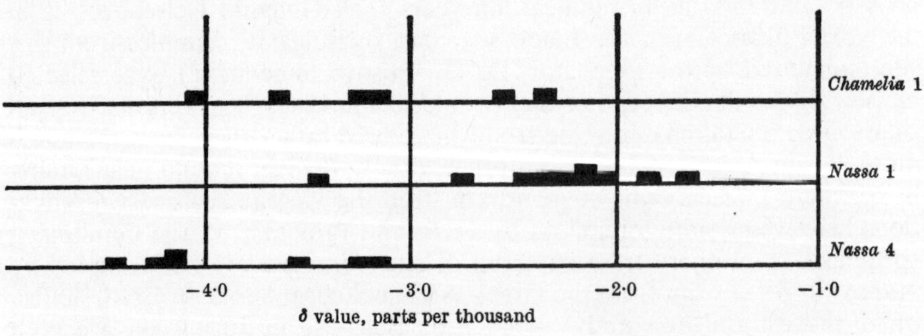

Figure 1. Oxygen-18 content of recent shells from the Black Sea. *Nassa* 1 and 4 are *Nassa* (*Hinea*) *reticulata* L., collected at a depth of 79 m at 41° 26′ 35″ N, 29° 09′ E. *Chamelia* 1 is *Chamelia gallina* (L.) collected at a depth of 33 m at 41° 17′ 15″ N, 28° 53′ E. Each analysis is of about 0.25 mg shell sampled with a fine file; samples were taken so as to cover as much of the growth season as possible.

minimum would be about 10° C and the water isotopic composition about −2·6 per thousand, in satisfactory agreement with the value estimated. There is not any overlap at all with the values in table 1. It is also of some significance that there is almost no overlap in carbon isotopic composition, the Black Sea samples giving δ-values for carbon of +0·28 parts per thousand to −3·77 parts per thousand (twenty-nine analyses). The factors governing carbon isotopic composition are complex,[3] but from the almost total separation it seems certain that the *Spondylus* from Tell Goljanio Delschevo are, indeed, of Aegean rather than Black Sea origin.

There are two further points which must be considered before our conclusion is finalised. First, it is necessary to know that the samples analysed do, in fact, represent original carbonate, rather than the product of a later recrystallisation. Carbonate undergoes isotopic exchange with groundwater if it does recrystallise ; this is fortunate in our case because it means that although marine shell might give the impression of having derived from the Black Sea if some exchange with isotopically light groundwater had taken place, the reverse is not possible.

Second, it is pertinent to ask whether the Black Sea could have had an isotopic composition closer to that of the Mediterranean a few thousand years ago. The answer is that, if anything, it would have been more negative, because up to about 8,000 years ago the Black Sea was largely filled with glacial meltwater and was isolated from the Mediterranean owing to the glacio-eustatic lowering of sea level.[13 14]

The extent to which our approach is capable of refinement is obviously complicated by the fact that the isotope ratio we measure depends on both the temperature and the isotopic composition of the water where the shells lived. Fortunately, however, only the first of these changes appreciably through the year (at least this is so away from river mouths). Although the objects analysed are often not large enough for many consecutive growth elements to be analysed, as the shells we chose from the modern Black Sea were, a number of small samples taken at random from several different shells is likely to represent a reasonable coverage of the growth season. Ideally, the analyses should cover a range wide enough to represent the maximum temperature range likely to have been experienced. If this were achieved, the isotopic composition of the water could be deduced within narrow limits ; this in turn should narrow down the number of likely sources. In the case of the samples from Tell Goljanio Delschevo, the three analyses represent a range of about 5 degrees C. Because it is unlikely that the shell grew below about 12° C or above 24° C, the water probably had an isotopic composition between −1·0 parts per thousand and +0·6 parts per thousand. This already suggests an Aegean source rather than, for instance, trade from a Cycladic Island. We are hopeful that, at least in some circumstances, we may be able to specify the likely sources of *Spondylus* from a critical site more precisely by analysing a greater number of samples.

Archaeological Implications

The conclusion that the *Spondylus* ornaments from Tell Goljanio Delschevo are of Aegean rather than Black Sea origin is at first a surprising one, because such ornaments are common in Bulgaria and Rumania from the time of the Hamangia culture[15] around 4000 BC in radiocarbon years to the end of the Copper Age Gumelnitsa culture around 2800 BC. We now plan to analyse samples from other sites near the Black Sea coast, in order to test the validity of the generalisation that all the Balkan *Spondylus* is of Aegean origin. The analyses from Gradeshnita and Vinča, supporting those of Tell Goljanio Delschevo, strongly suggest this to be the case.

Recent finds at Sitagroi, in the north Aegean region, have yielded, in levels of phase III, pottery which is unmistakably of Balkan Gumelnitsa type. It is precisely in these levels that 'bracelets' of *Spondylus* are most common, being rare in levels of the preceding phase II and absent in those of phase I. Finds of *Spondylus* are very common at this and other sites of the 4th millennium BC in the Plain of Drama, notably more so than at other sites in North Greece[16] or elsewhere in the Aegean,[17] where the animal itself is abundant. The Aegean coasts near the Plain of Drama now seem the most likely source for much of the Balkan *Spondylus*.

Ornaments of the shell are particularly numerous in graves of the 4th millennium Linearbandkeramik culture of central Europe.[18] We hope to investigate further the differentiations between the Aegean and the Adriatic as possible sources for this material. Already, however, an early, long-distance trade with the Aegean is documented in the Balkans by finds of surprising number.

Definitive elucidation of the trading mechanism must await further study. Yet already the demonstration of the Aegean origin of the material sets the whole question in a different light. Finds of *Spondylus* ornaments are numerous in eastern Bulgaria and Rumania, some of the sites actually lying very close to the shores of the Black Sea. The decreasing number of finds with distance from the source might have been interpreted as conforming very approximately to a straightforward down-the-line trading mechanism, of the kind which has been postulated for the obsidian trade in the Near East,[19] had the Black Sea been the source of the material. With the Aegean now recognised as the source the situation is transformed, for the quantities found do not decrease exponentially with distance from the Aegean coast as such a model would predict: finds are at least as common in Bulgaria and Rumania as in north Greece.

A different model, prestige chain exchange, is here proposed for the Balkan *Spondylus* trade. It has four defining characteristics: (1) the transfer of prestige goods takes place, often between persons of high status, on a basis of balanced reciprocity[20]; (2) the prestige goods are frequently handed on in subsequent exchanges; (3) such goods are not expended or utilised in daily life; (4) they appear in the archaeological record either as a result of deliberate burial (generally with the dead) or through loss or accidental breakage. A feature of such trade is that the traded goods are distributed over considerable distances, occurring in places remote from the source in quantities as great as at findspots nearer to it. Such now seems to be the situation in south-east Europe.

The best known exchange mechanism of this kind of recent times is the kula trade of the Trobriand islanders of the western Pacific,[21] a conventionalised gift exchange whose social significance far transcended the utilitarian or 'economic' value of the gifts.[22] As perhaps in prehistoric Europe, the most prized objects were bracelets of marine shell, and bead necklaces, many of them cut from shells of the genus *Spondylus*. [1970]

REFERENCES

1 Clark, J. G. D. (1952) *Prehistoric Europe: the Economic Basis*. London: Methuen, 241.

2 Rodden, R. J. (1970) *Acts of the Seventh International Congress of Prehistoric and Protohistoric Sciences* I, 411–13. Prague: Czechoslovak Academy of Sciences.

3 Bowen, R. (1966) *Palaeotemperature Analysis*. Amsterdam and New York: Elsevier.

4 Keith, M. L., Anderson, G. M. and Eichles, R. (1964) *Geochim. Cosmochim. Acta* 28, 1757.

5 Craig, H. and Gordon, L. I. (1965) Occ. Publs. Narragansett Mr. Lab. 3, 277.

6 Epstein, S. and Mayeda, T. (1953) *Geochim. Cosmochim. Acta* 4, 213.

7 Longinelli, A. and Craig, H. (1967) *Science* 156, 56.

8 Gat, J. R. and Carmi, I. (1970) *J. Geophys. Res.* 75, 3039.

9 Craig, H. (1970) in *Stable Isotopes in Oceanographic Studies*, 1. Pisa: Consiglio Nazionale della Richerche.

10 Sverdrup, H. U., Johnson, M. W. and Fleming, R. H. (1942) *The Oceans*. New York: Prentice Hall, 650.

11 Urey, H. C. (1947) *J. Chem. Soc.* 562.

12 Epstein, S., Buchsbaum, R., Lowenstam, H. A. and Urey, H. C. (1953) *Bull. Geol. Soc. Amer.* 64, 1315.

13 Vinogradov, A. P., Devirts, A. L., Dobkins, E. I. and Markova, N. G. (1966) *Radiocarbon* 8, 292 (sample Mo-287).

14 Zenkevitch, L. (1963) *Biology of the Seas of the USSR*. London: Allen and Unwin, 395.

15 Berciu, D. (1966) *Cultura Hamangia*. Romania, Bucharest: Academiei, R. S., 80.

16 Heurtley, W. A. (1939) *Prehistoric Macedonia*. Cambridge: University Press, 89.

17 Evans, J. D. and Renfrew, C. (1968) *Excavations at Saliagos near Antiparos*. London: British School of Archaeology at Athens, 65 and 127.

18 Vencl, S. (1959) *Archeol. Rozhl.* 11, 699.

19 Renfrew, C., Dixon, J. E. and Cann, J. R. (1968) *Proc. Prehistoric Soc.* 34, 328.

20 Sahlins, M. D. (1965) in Banton, M. (ed.) *The Relevance of Models for Social Anthropology*. (ASA Monograph 1). London: Tavistock Publications, 147.

21 Malinowski, B. (1950) *Argonauts of the Western Pacific*. London: Routledge Kegan-Paul.

22 Mauss, M. (1954) *The Gift*. London: Cohen and West, 22.

8) Sitagroi, Radiocarbon and the Prehistory of South-East Europe

The excavations at Sitagroi in north Greece were undertaken with the intention of resolving the controversy discussed in chapter 5 by means of well-stratified finds made within the Aegean basin. In this respect the most important finding was the documentation of a phase of occupation closely similar to the Gumelnitsa culture of Bulgaria and Romania (Sitagroi phase III). Preliminary reports of the excavation have been published (Renfrew 1970 ; 1973) and its significance is further assessed in chapter 17. The important site of Dikilitash, near Sitagroi has produced similar stratigraphic findings (Deshayes 1973).

The excavations also provided a well-stratified series of samples for radiocarbon dating, allowing a re-assessment in this paper of the absolute chronology of the Balkans. The application of radiocarbon dating to the Balkans was hotly opposed by Milojčic (1973) and is still rejected with equal vigour by Makkay (1976). It has however been adopted by Bognar-Kutzian (1972) and Gimbutas (1974), and further expounded with clarity by Neustupny (1973), an early advocate. It is now accepted in the West as a routine matter (e.g. Chapman 1977).

The question of the dendrochronological calibration of radiocarbon dates is considered more fully in chapters 15 and 17.

BIBLIOGRAPHY

Bognar-Kutzian, I. (1972) *The Early Copper Age Tiszapolgár Culture in the Carpathian Basin*. Budapest: Akadémiai Kiadó.

Chapman, J. C. (1977) *The Balkans in the Fifth and Fourth Millennia, BC with Special Reference to Social and Economic Aspects of the Vinča Culture*, unpublished Ph.D. dissertation. London: Institute of Archaeology.

Deshayes, J. (1973) La Séquence des cultures à Dikili Tash, in Garašanin, M., Benac, A. and Tasić, N. (eds.) *Actes VIII Congr. Internat. Sci. Préhist. et Protohist.* II, Beograd, 492–5.

Gimbutas, M. (1974) *Gods and Godesses of Old Europe*. London: Thames and Hudson.

Makkay, J. (1976) Problems concerning copper age chronology in the Carpathian basin. *Acta Archaeol. Acad. Sci. Hungar.* 28, 251–300.

Milojčic, V. (1973) Die C-14 Methode im Lichte der komparativ-stratigraphischen Befunde, in Garašanin, M., Benac, A. and Tasić, N. (eds.) *Actes VIII Congr. Internat. Sci. Préhist. et Protohist.* II, Beograd, 3–10.

Neustupny, E. (1973) Absolute chronology of the aeneolithic period, in Garašanin M., Benac, A. and Tasić, N. (eds) *Actes VIII Congr. Internat. Sci. Préhist. et Protohist.* II, Beograd, 243–7.

Renfrew, C. (1970) The Burnt House at Sitagroi. *Antiq.* 44, 131–4.

——(1973) The Aegean and the Balkans at the close of the neolithic period, the evidence of Sitagroi, in *Symposium über die Entstehung und Chronologie der Badener Kultur*, Bratislava: Slovenska Academie Vied, 427–40.

SITAGROI, RADIOCARBON AND THE PREHISTORY OF SOUTH-EAST EUROPE

The importance of the chronological relations between the Aegean and the Balkans for European prehistory as a whole was indicated in 1929 by Gordon Childe in *The Danube in Prehistory*, and in later works. He based his chronological structure of the contemporaneity of Vinča with early Troy, one of the basic foundations of the conventional chronology for Europe. Radiocarbon dates called this link into question (Mellaart 1960) although it has since been defended by some scholars (Garašanin 1961 ; Milojčic 1967). Excavations in Bulgaria supported the view that the Balkan Copper Age (Chalcolithic, Aeneolithic) preceeded the Aegean bronze age by a considerable span of time (Renfrew 1969), and this view has been confirmed by the 10-m stratigraphy at Sitagroi (Renfrew 1970).

The Sitagroi radiocarbon dates now allow of greater chronological precision. The evident relations of the site with the Balkans, and its location in the Aegean basin, give it a key position. For the first time it is becoming possible both to see the Balkan chronology through Aegean eyes, and to view the Aegean development from a Balkan standpoint. It now seems feasible to answer some of the questions posed by Mellaart in his 1960 article. The answers have a direct bearing upon our entire picture of the development of the early bronze age of Europe, from the Mediterranean to the North Sea.

The Sitagroi Dates and their Context

Excavations at Sitagroi were undertaken in 1968 and 1969, organised jointly by Professor Marija Gimbutas of the University of California at Los Angeles and the writer, and directed in the field by the latter. The project was supported by grant GS-1949 from the National Science Foundation, by the British School at Athens and the University of Sheffield, and owes much to Mrs C. Koukouli-Chrysanthaki, the local representative of the Greek Archaeological Service, which authorised the excavation. The excavation will be reported in full elsewhere: the intention here is simply to indicate the context of the radiocarbon samples.

In addition to several much larger areas, a sounding was excavated from the summit of the mound. This square, trench ZA, was of side 3 m, and revealed more than 10 m of stratified deposits. Quantitative study of the pottery permitted a division of the strata into five separate phases, of which the fifth and latest was subsequently subdivided. This stratigraphic sequence was confirmed by excavations on other parts of the site, so that the culture sequence does not rest on the evidence of ZA alone.

A brief synopsis of the sequence has already been published (Renfrew 1970). The pottery development may be summarised as follows:

Phase vb: Plain, unpainted pottery. One-handled cups common. At first sight there are resemblances to early bronze age Troy and the late Baden culture.

Phase va: The 'Burnt House' phase. Unpainted pottery, sometimes decorated with incisions somewhat reminiscent of the pottery of the Vučedol culture.

Phase IV: Plain dark wares, again with some Baden resemblances.

Phase III: The Dikilitash phase. Graphite-painted pottery and other features indicate contacts with the Maritsa-Gumelnitsa complex of Bulgaria and Rumania. Many other wares are entirely local.

Phase II: A variety of painted wares, showing slight resemblances to those of middle or late neolithic Thessaly.

Phase I: Dark faced wares. Some shapes resemble those of the Veselinovo (Karanovo III) culture of Bulgaria.

Many of the radiocarbon samples came from trench ZA itself. An approximate stratigraphic equation is possible for the adjacent square ZB, where a number of samples came from the wet-sieving operation conducted by Sebastian Payne. The samples from other areas are not linked directly with ZA by stratigrahpic means, but can be assigned a place in the ZA sequence on the basis of their associated finds.

In presenting these dates I should like to express our gratitude to the Radiocarbon Laboratories of the British Museum and of the Deutsche Akademie der Wissenschaften in East Berlin, as well as to Mr Richard Burleigh and Drs H. Quitta and G. Kohl for their cooperation and advice. The dates on the left are in precise stratigraphic order (table 1).

Of these dates only Bln 885 (6030 BC) fails to conform with the emerging pattern. Dr Kohl writes: 'Bln 885 is very uncertain since the quantity of carbon for analysis from this sample was very limited.' This sample is omitted from further discussion. (It should be noted that level ZB 112 was first assigned to the upper levels of phase III. The lower fill of a large pit, it contained at least one phase IV sherd. It is now regarded as very early phase IV. In addition, it is not at present clear whether the pottery in level ZA 16 should lead to its placing in late phase IV or early phase Va).

On two occasions the same sample was divided and determined by both laboratories: BM 650a and Bln ; BM 648 and Bln 779. In a further three examples the two laboratories ran different samples from the same stratigraphical horizon: QO 8, ZA 50, and PO 158 with 162. Each time the Berlin date was appreciably earlier than the British Museum date, and there is evidently the possibility of a systematic difference here between the determinations of the two laboratories. But even if this should be so (and no explanation can be found in terms of pre-treatment or analytical procedures), it does not result in major deviations from the stratigraphic order.

The dates, indeed, give a coherent sequence, and allow the time span in question to be divided into a number of periods, seen on the left in table 2. No date falls outside the period appropriate to its phase by more than one standard deviation, except for those dates in phase V, where there are special circumstances. It is at this time that there were, according to the calibration work of Professor Suess (1970), marked changes in the atmospheric concentration of radiocarbon. This implies that samples differing in true age by as much as 300 years could yield the same radiocarbon date of 1900 BC. The calibration curve (cf. Renfrew 1970, 284) suggests that if the transition from phase Va to Vb took place around 2300 BC in calendar years, samples from phase Va could yield radiocarbon dates falling before 2000 BC. In *radiocarbon* years there is an overlap between two periods which in reality were consecutive.

Table 1. Radiocarbon dates from Sitagroi in stratigraphic order

Phase	Level	Dates in precise stratigraphic order BC	other dates BC	Lab. no.	Material
vb	QO 8		1840±78	BM 653	Vetch
vb	QO 8		2135±150	Bln 781	Vetch
vb	PO 9	1920±100		Bln 780	Charcoal
vb	PO 23	2015±100		Bln 876	Charcoal
va	PO 158	2220±100		Bln 877	Charcoal
va	PO 162	1853±59		BM 652	Charcoal, from post-hole
IV/va	ZA 16	2360±100		Bln 782	Charcoal from beam
IV	ZA 29	2440±100		Bln 773	Acorns
IV	ZA 31	2600±100		Bln 879	Charcoal
IVc	ROc 59		2445±100	Bln 878	Charcoal
IV	ZB 108	2382±79		BM 651	Acorns, from flotation
IV	ZB 112	2413±56		BM 650a	Charcoal, from flotation
IV	ZB 112	2560±100		Bln 880	Charcoal, from flotation
III	ZA 41a	3150±120		Bln 774	Charcoal
III	ZB 125	3605±100		Bln 881	Charcoal, from flotation
III	ML 118		3417±85	BM 650b	Charcoal
III	MM 52		3845±100	Bln 882	Charcoal
III	MMb 69		3595±100	Bln 883	Einkorn, from flotation
II	ZA 50	3954±66		BM 649	Charcoal, from flotation
II	ZA 50	4290±100		Bln 884	Charcoal
II	ZA 52	3770±100		Bln 776	Charcoal
II	ZA 59	3970±120		Bln 777	Charcoal
(I)	ZA 63	(6030±150)		Bln 885	Charcoal
I	ZA 67	4315±75		BM 648	Charcoal
I	ZA 67	4675±170		Bln 779	Charcoal
I	ZA 70	4475±100		Bln 778	Charcoal

All dates are in radiocarbon years on the 5568 half-life. Two samples were divided, and half sent to each laboratory: BM 650a and Bln 880; and BM 648 and Bln 779.

Unfortunately no samples were available from the later levels of phase III (ZA levels 40 to 33). The material from these levels does show some development, however, so that this period, here termed 'Later Phase III' need not represent an interruption of occupation on the site.

The stratigraphic interpretation of *tell* sites such as Sitagroi does however still present some problems. For although there is a considerable continuity in the finds from successive phases, we cannot be certain whether the site was occupied continuously, or intermittently for short periods. As Professor Saul Weinberg has remarked in another context: 'Contiguity does not prove continuity.' Indeed on the model of short occupations separated by an abandonment of the site, it is possible to set the dates within a narrow minimum time range (table 2, centre). Once again, with the one special exception already discussed, no date falls outside its appropriate period by more than approximately one standard deviation. This exercise does not, of course, demonstrate that the site was in fact abandoned. These are, on the continuous occupation model, simply fortuitous bunchings of dates. Statistically they may be regarded as maximum confidence time spans, and we may be reasonably sure that the culture in question was in occupation of the mound during its maximum confidence span. They are seen in fig. 1, where they form a background to the presentation of dates from other relevant areas.

Table 2. Durations of the Sitagroi phases

Phase	Maximum duration of phase (radiocarbon years BC)	Minimum duration of phase (radiocarbon years BC)	Possible minimum duration of phase (calendar years BC)
vb	2000–1800	2000–1900	2250–2150
va	2300–1900	2150–1900	2600–2450
IV	2600–2300	2500–2400	3300–3100
Later III	?3100–?2600	Uncertain	
Earlier III	3800–3100	3750–3250	4700–4200
II	4300–3800	4200–3850	5200–4800
I	4700–4300	4500–4400	?5400–?5300

This kind of treatment, which is of great value in assessing the chronology of such a site, is only possible when we have a good series of dates whose stratigraphic order is precisely known. In this way it is possible to counteract to some extent the effect of random and other fluctuations upon the resulting chronology.

The Implications of the Sitagroi Dates

The Sitagroi dates are presented in stratigraphic order (fig. 1), together with selected dates from the Aegean and the Balkans. These dates are listed in table 4. Those for the Balkans and central Europe are from a number of recent publications (Kohl and Quitta 1966, 1967 ; Quitta and Kohl 1969 ; Neustupny 1968, 1969). A fuller discussion of the Aegean final neolithic and early bronze age chronology, with dates, will be found elsewhere (Renfrew 1972). These comparisons allow the clarification of a number of problems.

1. *The Aegean and the Balkans in the Neolithic Period.* The Sitagroi dates very strongly support the view that the Balkan chalcolithic (Vinča-Pločnik, Gumelnitsa, Karanovo V–VI) was contemporary with the later neolithic of the Aegean, long preceding the Aegean early bronze age or early Troy. The material of phase III at Sitagroi is undoubtedly very close to that of the Bulgarian chalcolithic, so that the stratigraphic and the radiocarbon evidence from the site speak in unison.

Excavation in the Balkans had already made clear that the Balkan late neolithic (Vinča-Tordos, Vesselinovo, Karanovo III) was still earlier. The material of Sitagroi phase I is again clearly related to it, and the radiocarbon dates agree with the stratigraphic findings.

We are now in a position to recover from the initial and understandable shock at the collapse of the old Vinča-Troy equation, and of so much that went with it. Indeed, seen through Balkan eyes the Aegean cultures of the time seem rather lacking in variety or invention. Only in Thessaly and the north, where the Dhimini culture and its contemporaries were under way, do we see the Balkan range of figurines, or the elaborately decorated pottery, or the early metallurgy. (The earliest copper in the Aegean is from the end of phase II at Sitagroi: copper is found too at Dhimini.) Indeed it would now be reasonable to regard Dhimini or Sitagroi III as chalcolithic in precisely the same sense as their Balkan contemporaries.

2. *The transition from Neolithic to Bronze Age in the Aegean.* The first impression of the phase V material at Sitagroi was that it resembled the finds of Troy I sufficiently closely for the two to be contemporary. Further study makes this resemblance less compelling, although there remains an evident general similarity between the pottery of Sitagroi IV and V and that of Kritsana or the Trojan early bronze age.

The radiocarbon dates for this material at first seemed rather late. So indeed did those for the entire Aegean early bronge age, before the application of the tree-ring calibration of radiocarbon. Dates of 1785 BC for Early Minoan II Myrtos, or of 2025 BC supposedly from late Troy I levels at Emborio did not make sense: they were far too late. The calibration brings them all into much better harmony with the existing historical chronology.

It seems likely now that Sitagroi phase IV—whose material has resemblances with Early Thessalian I—was in part contemporary with the Eutresis culture (Early Helladic I), although it may have begun a little earlier. Sitagroi Va and Vb may be very roughly contemporary with the Korakou culture (Early Helladic II) and the Tiryns culture (Early Helladic III) respectively. It does now seem likely that the Troy I culture began in later Early Helladic I times and extended into Early Helladic II (cf. Renfrew 1972, ch. 13), so that the Emborio date is no longer quite so shockingly late.

The big gap in radiocarbon years, and indeed in calendar years, between the late neolithic dates in the Aegean and those of the early bronze age is now very striking. I have suggested (loc. cit.) that we must think in terms of a final neolithic period, represented at Sitagroi by the later phase III material and early IV, in the Troad by Kum Tepe, in Crete by the 'subneolithic', and in south Greece by material which is now coming to light, for example, at the Franchthi Cave. The transition from neolithic to bronze age in the Aegean was a long one, of which we know as yet little. The long stratigraphic sequence at Sitagroi does give substance (as I believe will that of Emborio when it is published) to this hitherto unrecognised period which evidently lasted at least five centuries.

3. *The transition from Neolithic to Bronze Age in the Balkans.* A number of rather similar observations may be made in south-east Europe as a whole. All the published dates for the Cernavoda-Ezero culture levels at Ezero—which in Bulgarian terms represents the beginning of the early bronze age—may be set between 2600 BC and 2200 BC without statistical improbability. The dates for Karanovo V and VI and contemporary copper age levels at Tell Azmak may all be set before 3200 BC in radiocarbon years without statistical improbability. Between these two phases in Bulgaria and Romania is a transitional period, an 'Übergangszeit', which archaeologists are now beginning to discern (Morintz and Roman 1969). The sites of Cernavoda, Cotofeni and Foltesti have yielded relevant material, and the earlier finds from Ezerovo near Varna may belong here too.

Further north and west the gap between copper age and early bronze age is not so marked. In Hungary the early Baden culture, and notably the Boleraz group, can now be seen to fall in this period. Dr Evzen Neustupny (1968) has set out in convincing detail the arguments there for a long chronology.

Sitagroi, like these other sites, can be seen from the Balkan standpoint to participate in the long transition. The pottery of phases IV and V, and its Balkan relations, is at present the subject of special study by Mr Andrew Sherratt, and will be presented in detail by him in the final excavation report. Certainly the material of later phase III and of phase IV allows us to see the development at Sitagroi as a gradual local evolution. The long period which this development likewise occupied in the Balkans makes an explanation in local terms much more acceptable.

4. *The Aegean and the Balkans in the Early Bronze Age.* In the past it has been usual to see the Aegean and the Balkans as different culture areas (which in many senses they indeed are) and to discuss in isolation the development of the bronze age in each. For the first time, however, it is becoming possible to build up a chronological picture of the developments at this time in south-east Europe as a whole. Whether or not these were local, indigenous developments, a unified time perspective is useful.

The final neolithic of the Aegean was contemporary with the Romanian 'Übergangszeit' and with the early development of the Baden culture in central Europe. The view that the Baden culture derived from the Aegean early bronze age is no more acceptable than the previous arguments for the origins of Vinča. This final neolithic period falls between 3000 and 2600 BC in radiocarbon years, perhaps between 4000 and 3400 BC in calendar years.

Then, during the time of Sitagroi IV (2600–2300 BC in radiocarbon years), we see the development of the Eutresis culture (Early Helladic I) and perhaps already of early Troy I. This is the time of the Ezero culture in Bulgaria and of the developed Baden culture in Hungary and adjacent areas (Baden-Kostolac, etc.). It is the period indicated as 'Middle Aenolithic' in Neustupny's useful chronological table for central Europe (Neustupny 1968, 48–9). In calendar years it may last from 3400 to 2800 BC.

With Sitagroi V we are in the developed early bronze age of the Aegean (Early Helladic II and III), from 2300 to 1800 or 1700 BC in radiocarbon years. This is the time of late Troy I, Troy II and Troy III–VI. In central Europe this takes us through, and perhaps beyond Neustupny's 'Late Aenolithic', with Corded Ware, and then Bell Beakers. In west Hungary and also in Yugoslavia, the Vučedol culture occupies the earlier part of this phase, and has resemblances with the incised pottery of Sitagroi Va. Corded ware is seen at Sitagroi in small quantities in phase V.

It is likely that the fully bronze age cultures of Central Europe—including Nagyrév, Monteoru and Unetice (Aunjetitz)—were emerging in the later part of this period, which may extend from 2800 to 2100 BC in calendar years. East Hungary, and in particular Transylvania, seems to have been especially important, and although there are yet no relevant dates, we must expect radiocarbon determinations dating back to 1800 BC or 1900 BC for the Periam (Perjamos, Pecica) culture, corresponding to a beginning around 2300 BC in calendar years. The contemporary of Sitagroi Vb in Hungary may well be the Periam culture in Transylvania, and then the Early Nagyrév culture in eastern Hungary generally. It seems likely that the Monteoru culture in Romania and the Unetice culture in Czechoslovakia were developing shortly afterwards.

Certainly by the Aegean middle bronze age (i.e. beginning in 1800 or 1700 BC, radiocarbon years, c. 2100 BC, calendar years), when Sitagroi was abandoned, these cultures were in being. Before the end of the Aegean middle bronze age, around 1600 BC, the Nagyrév culture must have completed its evolution through the Hatvan stage to Otomani (Füzesabony), and the Tumulus culture have emerged to succeed Unetice in Czechoslovakia and Germany. Much of this is provisional at present, especially the absolute dates, but at least the outline is emerging. It is indicated, in geographically very compressed form, in table 3.

Table 3. Tentative chronological table for the neolithic-early bronze age transition in south-east Europe

Carbon-14 date BC (5,568 half-life)	Moravia	Hungary	Bulgaria and south Rumania	Sitagroi	South Greece	Troy	Date in calendar years BC
	Tumulus						
		Otomani	Monteoru	—	MBA	VI	
	Unetice	Nagyrév					
1800/1700							2100
		E. Nagyrév					
	?Unetice	Periam	?Monteoru	vb	EB 3	III-V	
1900/1800							2350
	Bell beaker	Bell beaker				II	
	+	+	?Mihailic	va	EB 2	+	
	Corded ware	Vučedol				Late I	
2300							2800
	Baden	Baden	Ezero	IV	EB 1	Early I	
2600							3400
	'TRB'	E. Baden	'Ubergangszeit'	(Later	Final	Kum	
		(Boleraz)		III)	Neolithic	Tepe	
3000		Bodrogkeresztur					4000
	Lengyel	Tiszapolgár	Karanovo	III	Late	?	
			V-VI		Neolithic		
3800							4700

At first sight this picture may seem somewhat complicated, but the broader outlines are beginning to emerge. Some de-Balkanisation of south-east European prehistory is now becoming possible. We can now look out from Britain, with our vested interest in Beakers and in the Unetice culture (by reason of Wessex) and discern the contemporary developments in Hungary, where Beakers may have originated, and where the bronze age began so early to flourish. The position of Sitagroi, looking Janus-like both to north and south, permits us to translate this into contemporary Aegean terms, where it comes out as early bronze age. Our own Beaker copper age comes long after the copper age of the Balkans and succeeds the Baden culture of that era. In Aegean terms it falls at the end of the early bronze age.

The development of our early bronze age (i.e. the Wessex culture and its contemporaries) was thus taking place at the time when the Nagyrév and

Unetice cultures were already well underway, in what in Aegean terms was the middle bronze age.

The emerging picture of this period is thus taking us beyond a simple denial of Vinča-Troy links, or of Wessex-Mycenae contacts. The developing pattern of radiocarbon dates is creating a new structure, in which the very slow formation of the central and east European early bronze age is becoming apparent. In calendar years we must now allow more than 1500 years from the evolution of Tiszapolgár to Nagyrév or Unetice, or from the time of Dhimini to that of Troy II, where until recently most archaeologists would have considered two centuries enough. The long stratigraphy at Sitagroi and the radiocarbon dates from it help, in the north Aegean, to give substance to this long development. [1971]

ACKNOWLEDGEMENT

In addition to thanking the two radiocarbon laboratories concerned—especially Dr H. Quitta and Mr Richard Burleigh—I should like to acknowledge the stimulus, more than ten years ago, of discussing the central European early bronze age with Dr John Coles. I am grateful to Mr Andrew Sherratt for information about the Ezero radiocarbon dates.

BIBLIOGRAPHY

Garašanin, M. V. (1961) The neolithic in Anatolia and the Balkans. *Antiq.* 35, 276–80.

Kohl, G. and Quitta, H. (1966) Berlin Radiocarbon measurements II. *Radiocarbon* 8, 27–45.

——(1970) Berlin Radiocarbon measurements IV. *Radiocarbon* 12, 400-20.

Mellaart, J. (1960) Anatolia and the Balkans. *Antiq.* 34, 270–8.

Milojčic, V. (1967) Die absolute Chronologie der Jungsteinzeit in Südosteuropa und die Ergebnisse der Radiocarbon (C 14) Methode. *Jb. des Römisch-Germanischen Zentralmuseums Mainz* 14, 9.

Morintz, S. and Roman, P. (1969) Über die Chronologie der Übergangszeit vom Äneolithikum zur Bronzezeit in Rumänien. *Dacia* 13, 61–71.

Neustupny, E. (1968) Absolute chronology of the neolithic and aeneolithic periods in central and south-eastern Europe. *Slov. Archeól.* 16, 19–60.

——(1969) Absolute chronology of the neolithic and aeneolithic periods in central and south-east Europe II. *Archeol. Rozhledy* 21, 783-810.

Quitta, H. and Kohl, G. (1969) Neue Radiokarbondaten zum Neolithikum und zur Frühebronzezeit Südosteuropas. *Z. Archäol.* 223–55.

Renfrew, C. (1969) The autonomy of the south-east European copper age. *Proc. Prehist. Soc.* 25, 12–47.

——(1970) The tree-ring calibration of radiocarbon: an archaeological evaluation, *Proc. Prehist. Soc.* 36, 280-311.

——(1972) *The Emergence of* civilisation *: the Cyclades and the Aeagean in the third millennium* BC. London.

Suess, H. E. (1970) Bristlecone pine calibration of the radiocarbon time-scale 5200 BC to the present, in Olsson, I. U. (ed.) *Radiocarbon variations and absolute chronology, Proceedings of the Twelfth Nobel Symposium.*

Table 4. List of dates used in fig. 1

Column	Site	Date BC	Lab. no.
Tiszapolgár*	Tiszapolgár-Csöszhalom	3990±100	Bln 513
,,	,,	3825±100	Bln 512
,,	,,	3925±100	Bln 510
,,	,,	3625±100	Bln 100
Bodrogkeresztur	Keszthely-Fenékpuszta	2940±80	Bln 501
,,	,,	2830±80	Bln 500
Baden-Kostolac	Oszentiván	2565±80	Bln 476
,,	Podolie	2505±80	Bln 556
,,	Hissar IIa	2220±120	Bln 351
,,	Pivnica	2160±160	KN-145
Hung.-Cz. EBA	Baracs (Nagyrév)	1785±80	Bln 340
,,	Prasklice (E. Unetice)	1895±80	Bln 475
Vinča A–B	Vinča A	4240±60	GrN-1546
,,	Predionica	4330±100	Bln 435
Vinča C–D	Vinča D	3895±160	GrN-1537
,,	Banjica	3760±90	GrN-1542
,,	Gornja Tuzla	3630±60	GrN-1974
Ochre Grave	Kétegyháza	2315±80	Bln 609
,,	Baja Hamangia	2140±160	Bln 29
,,	,,	2110±160	KN-38
Karanovo. *The dates for Karanova and Tell Azmak are as given by Kohl and Quitta (1966).*			
Cernavoda	Cernavoda	2555±100	Bln 61a
,,	,,	2435±100	Bln 61
,,	,,	2310±100	Bln 62
Ezero. *The dates for Ezero, Late Boian and Gumelnitsa A, are given by Quitta and Kohl (1969).*			
Sitagroi. *The dates are given above in Table 1.*			
Knossos	Knossos VI	4260±150	BM 273
,,	,, V	4190±150	BM 274
,,	,, IV	3730±150	BM 279
Saliagos	Saliagos	4222±74	P 1311
,,	,,	4124±79	P 1396
,,	,,	3959±87	P 1368
,,	,,	3825±84	P 1333
,,	,,	3766±85	P 1393
Dhimini	Dhimini	3680±150	H —
Kephala	Kephala (Kea)	2876±56	P 1280
Early Helladic I	Eutresis	2496±69	P 306
,,	,,	2492±57	P 307
Early Helladic II	Eutresis	2262±56	P 317
,,	Lerna	2120±65	P 318
,,	,,	2031±64	P 321a
,,	,,	2027±59	P 319
,,	,,	1946±58	P 321
,,	,,	1887±65	P 312
Early Helladic III	Lerna	1919±53	P 300
,,	,,	1803±93	P 299
Early Minoan II	Myrtos	2192±80	Q 953
,,	,,	1855±85	Q 950
,,	,,	1785±80	Q 951
Late Troy I	Emborio IV	2025±92	P 273

* Note that the dates for Tiszapolgár-Csöszhalom precede the full Tiszapolgár culture of the copper age.

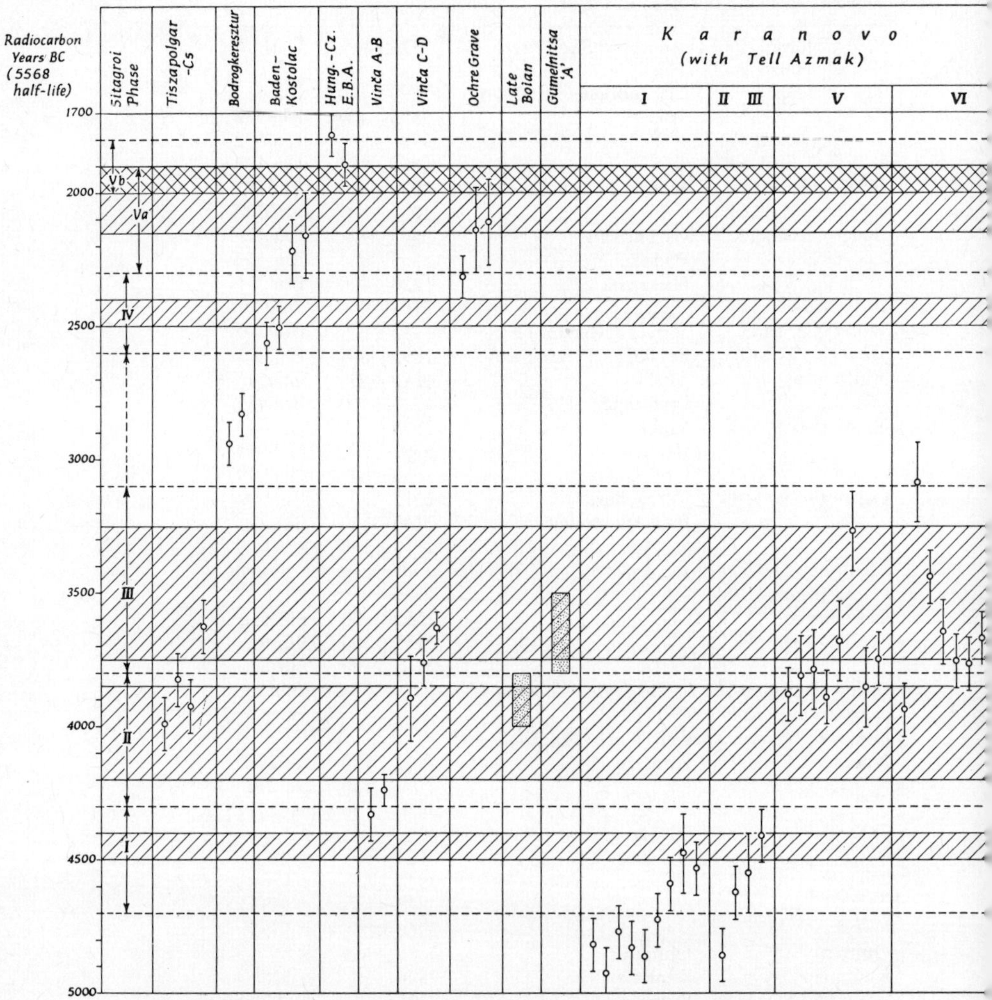

Figure 1. The radiocarbon dates for the successive phases at Sitagroi shown with other relevant dates from the Aegean and south-east Europe. Each date is shown with a range of one standard deviation. The shaded horizontal bands indicate the maximum confidence time-spans (see text) for the successive phases at Sitagroi.

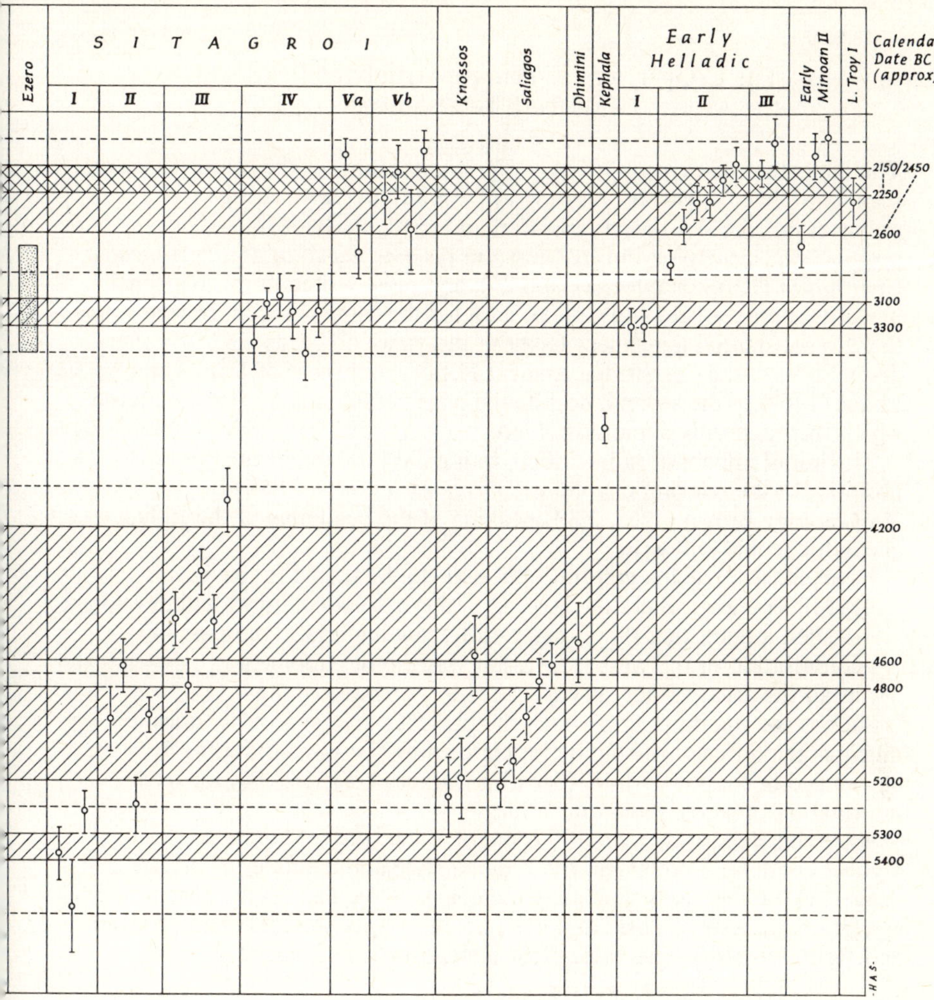
Ezero
SITAGROI
I
II
III
IV
Va
Vb
Knossos
Saliagos
Dhimini
Kephala
Early Helladic
I
II
III
Early Minoan II
L. Troy I
Calendar Date BC (approx)
2150/2450
2250
2600
3100
3300
4200
4600
4800
5200
5300
5400
-HAS-

9) The Copper Age of Peninsular Italy and the Aegean (with Ruth Whitehouse)

The important discoveries made in Crete at the turn of the century were seen by archaeologists at that time to have an obvious bearing on the prehistory of the West Mediterranean and particularly of Italy. The position was clearly set out by Mosso in his *The Dawn of Mediterranean Civilisation* (1910, chapters 21 and 25), and most writers from that time onwards (notably Peet and Childe) adopted the same position. Indeed there is substantial agreement between the views of Leeds (1924) in the first edition of the Cambridge Ancient History and those of Daniel and Evans (1967) in the second, despite the considerable mass of new material which they carefully summarise there.

The initial impact of radiocarbon dating did little to change this position. In the relevant chapter of *Chronologies in Old World Archaeology* Brown (1965, 330) speaking of the beginning of the Italian eneolithic, could still write:

> The cause of such a cultural upheaval can be traced to the eastern Mediterranean, where the Aegean and Anatolian cultures had developed to such a point that they sought trade, raw materials, and possibly colonisation in the west. The result was the development of new cultures in all the areas of our survey.

Such is the standard view which the present paper sets out to question, much as the diffusionist standpoint concerning the Balkans has been challenged in chapters 5 to 8. (See also Barker (1971, 189–90) for fresh information on early Italian metallurgy).

Since this paper was written the site of Tursi (prov. Matera) has yielded a grave containing pottery in the Laterza style and a copper or bronze dagger of Whitehouse's type B1 (Cremonesi 1976). The results of neutron-activation analysis of obsidian have now been published (Hallam, Warren and Renfrew 1976). The basic picture however is unchanged.

BIBLIOGRAPHY

Barker, G. (1971) The first metallurgy in Italy in the light of metal analyses from the Pigorini Museum. *Bull. Paletnol. Ital.* 80, 183–208.

Brown, D. F. (1975) The chronology of the northwestern Mediterranean, in Ehrich, R. W. (ed.) *Chronologies in Old World Archaeology*. Chicago: University Press, 321–42.

Cremonesi, G. (1976) Tomba della prima eta die metalli presso Tursi (Matera). *Riv. Sci. Preist.* 31, 109–34.

Daniel, G. E. and Evans, J. D. (1967) The Western Mediterranean, in *Cambridge Ancient History* II (2nd edition), ch. 36.

Hallam, B. R., Warren, S. E. and Renfrew, C. (1976) Obsidian in the Western Mediterranean. *Proc. Prehist. Soc.* 42, 85–110.

Leeds, E. T. (1924) The Western Mediterranean, in *Cambridge Ancient History* I (1st edition), ch. 21.

Mosso, A. (1910) *The Dawn of Mediterranean Civilisation*. London: Fisher Unwin.

Slater, E. (1971) Analyses of samples from the Pigorini Museum. *Bull. di Paletnol. Ital.* 80, 209–10.

THE COPPER AGE OF PENINSULAR ITALY AND THE AEGEAN

Italy, like several other areas of prehistoric Europe, enjoyed a flourishing 'Copper Age'—a period when objects of copper but not of bronze were in use, although not plentifully, and when various other changes in custom and material culture occurred, including transformations in the conventions of burial. These changes, like many in European prehistory, are often explained in terms of the 'diffusion' of 'cultural influences' from more advanced areas, notably the Aegean, or by the arrival of new groups of people from that region who would, it is sometimes thought, have set up 'colonies'.

The purpose of the present article is to examine the evidence for such explanations by comparing the Italian Copper Age finds with their contemporaries in Greece. This is made possible by the emerging radiocarbon chronology for both regions: the comparison may be made with equal effect by comparing dates either in radiocarbon years, or in calendar years as determined by the tree-ring calibration of radiocarbon. Only the direct comparison of radiocarbon dates (uncalibrated) with dates in calendar years has to be avoided.

After a short discussion of the diffusionist position, the Copper Age assemblages of Peninsular Italy are briefly reviewed. They are then compared with their contemporaries in the Aegean. It is concluded that there is no clear-cut evidence for 'colonies', the appreciable influx of population from the east, or the wholesale adoption of culture traits. Trade or exchange across the Adriatic no doubt took place, and it is possible that some metallurgical skills were learnt as a result of these contacts, but even this is highly doubtful.

The Diffusionist Position

In the early years of this century, the desire to date the prehistoric antiquities of Europe made it imperative to connect more distant regions to the historically dated civilisations of the Near East. Montelius, using his 'typological method', was able to do this in a series of steps, with the Aegean and Italy as important stages, extending ultimately to Scandinavia. His *Pre-Classical Chronology in Greece and Italy,* published in 1897, was a pioneering attempt in this sense. However, to relate the relative chronology of Italy to the absolute chronology which he had already obtained for the Aegean required the *assumption* that the Italian sequence followed, at least in part, that of Greece. Montelius made this assumption ; for to him 'it was natural that the civilisation coming from the east to Greece had a tendency to go further to the west . . . we find traces of an intercourse between Greece and Sicily already in the Mycenaean period'.

What was essentially the method of Montelius was used by Gordon Childe in the first edition of his *Dawn of European Civilisation* in 1925, and in later articles[2] he examined, and ultimately approved, this essentially diffusionist logic. For in order to date the European developments it was necessary to assume that they were later than their counterparts in the Near East, and indeed derived from them. So it was that Childe could write:[3]

> The Aegean inspiration of the copper age cultures of Sicily and Lower Italy seems at first glance obvious. In Sicily it was attested by the religious symbols, by bone ornaments of Troadic type, and by the hour-glass mugs. All this points to direct trade with the Aegean. On the mainland the inspiration may have partly been transmitted by Thessaly, but the pottery, the mace-heads, the punctured decoration of the metal plaques, all find an intelligible explanation to the east of the Adriatic. . . . Simultaneously with the introduction of the use of metals a change in the funeral rites denotes the influence of new ideas. . . . The rise of Aegean metallurgy was a perfectly intelligible and logical process. . . . Why then should not the collective tomb have originated in the Eastern Mediterranean too, and spread thence across Sicily to Iberia? That is the orthodox explanation and I believe it to be correct. Thus the Chalcolithic civilisation of the area we are studying reflects the spread of influences radiating from the Aegean just as might be expected. Those influences, mediated largely by maritime commerce, did not however stop short in Sicily, but reached Spain and France. . . .

This passage reflects the importance of Italy in Childe's scheme as a half-way house for the diffusion of influences to the west. For this reason the interpretation of the Italian Copper Age was crucial to that of western Europe as a whole, although in later editions of *The Dawn* the Danubian thoroughfare was credited with at least equal significance in 'the irradiation of European barbarism by Oriental civilisation'.

The development of Iberian studies followed a similar course, and in the last edition of *The Dawn*[4] actual colonies were identified in Italy, just as they were soon to be in Iberia[5]:

> After all, in historical times the first Greek colony in the West was planted at Cumae near Naples, not in Sicily nor the heel of Italy. A cemetery of pit-cave tombs at Paestum (Gaudo) near Salerno might represent a precursor a millennium earlier. . . . Trade from such a 'colony' might have promoted the rise in Central Italy of the Rinaldone culture . . . but while the tomb form and the metal gear may be of Aegean inspiration, other items in Rinaldone equipment are not. . . . Thus if southern and western influences travelled northward along the Tiber–Arno corridor, it provided a channel also for cultures adapted to the Temperate zone to spread south, and in the Apennine peninsula these proved the more viable.

Such views have formed the basis for the prevailing opinion concerning the Italian Copper Age. Radmilli[6] has written of: '. . . nuovi elementi e nuove genti, i protopastori, provenienti probabilmente dalle coste dell' Anatolia'. The two Tyrrhenian Copper Age groups, Rinaldone and Gaudo, are generally described as entirely intrusive, the other groups in the peninsula as hybrids with indigenous populations. The intruders are represented as mobile and warlike, probably practising a pastoralist economy and as responsible for the introduction of, *inter alia*, copper metallurgy, weapons such as daggers and battle axes, and the practice of collective burial in rock-cut tombs. This view has sometimes been challenged (e.g. by Trump),[7] but it remains the orthodox view among Italian scholars.[8] Our purpose is to examine the evidence upon which it is based.

Outline of the Peninsular Italian Copper Age

Our knowledge of the Copper Age is limited, as a high proportion of all finds come from tombs and very few from occupation sites: out of six well-defined groups in the peninsula, four are known almost exclusively from funerary material and the other two groups, though known mostly from domestic sites, both represent small and possibly specialised regional adaptions and so cast little light on any of the other Copper Age groups. The six groups are: Remedello in the Po valley; then on the west side of the peninsula, Rinaldone in central Italy and Gaudo in the south; on the east side, Conelle–Ortucchio in central Italy, Macchia a Mare in the Gargano Promontory and Laterza in the south (fig. 1). The following section consists of an outline account of these six groups, stressing in particular those fea-

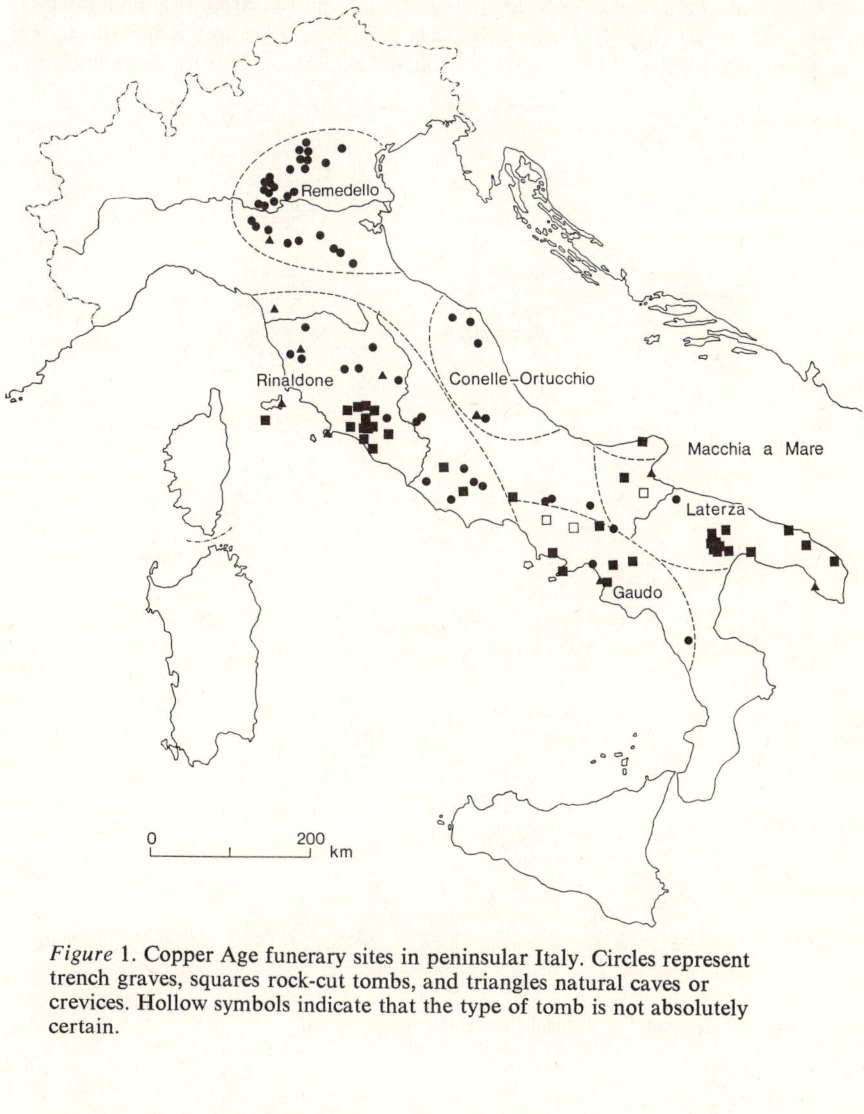

Figure 1. Copper Age funerary sites in peninsular Italy. Circles represent trench graves, squares rock-cut tombs, and triangles natural caves or crevices. Hollow symbols indicate that the type of tomb is not absolutely certain.

tures which have been used in the past to support an interpretation in terms of immigration or diffusion.

REMEDELLO (figs 1 and 2)

Distribution. The Po valley, both north and south of the river, and the adjoining Venetian plain.

Settlements. Open village sites and caves have yielded Remedello material, but in most cases the contexts seem to be mixed.

Burials. The normal burial rite was single inhumation in the contracted position, in oval or rectangular earth-cut graves; some slab-lined graves occur. In one case collective burial in a natural cave is recorded. Nearly thirty funerary sites of this culture are known (see Appendix II); most of these are single tombs or small groups of two or three, but large cemeteries do occur: Fontanella Mantovana had thirty-six tombs, Cumarola forty, and the type site at Remedello Sotto no less than one hundred and seventeen.

Grave Goods (fig. 2). *Pottery.* This is relatively rare and is usually found in women's tombs. The vessels normally have a dark burnished surface;

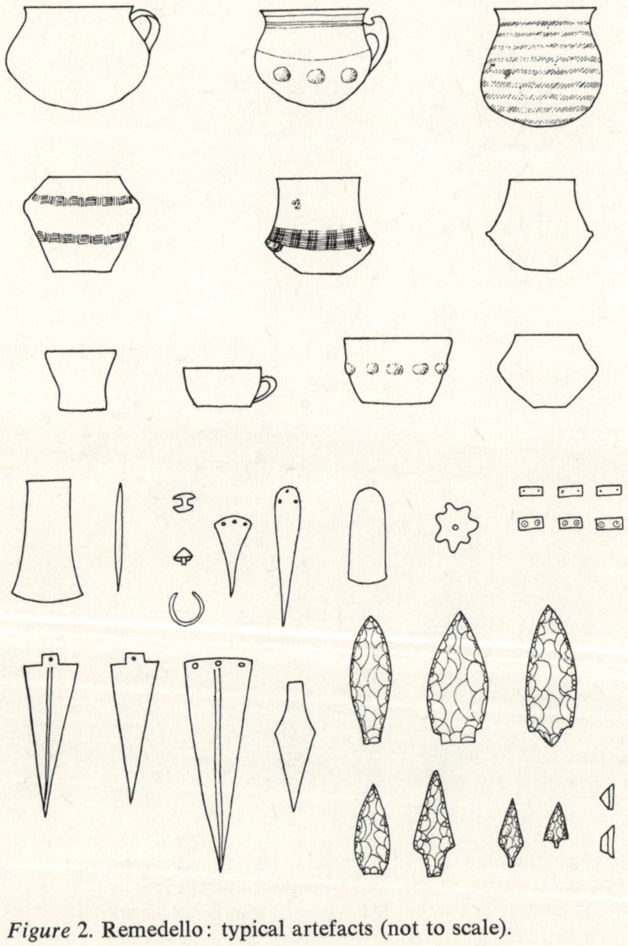

Figure 2. Remedello: typical artefacts (not to scale).

the forms include bulbous and carinated cups and jugs with single strap handles or lugs placed on the carination ; decoration is common, usually horizontal or vertical grooves, the two often placed in alternating zones. A small number of Beakers occur in separate burials which are near to or inside Remedello cemeteries.

Copper. This is fairly rare, occurring in only c. 10% of tombs, but quite a variety of forms appear: triangular daggers, with or without midribs and with or without tangs ; halberds ; flat axes ; awls ; and a few ornaments such as a cylinder of copper wire ; buttons and rivets with conical heads.

Silver. There are two exceptional ornaments of silver: a crutch-headed pin from Remedello itself and a pectoral from Villafranca Veronese (fig. 8*b*, *a*).

Flint. Flint weapons are the commonest grave goods. Tanged arrowheads and tanged or leaf-shaped daggers or spearheads occur in the majority of tombs. They are normally made on flakes and are bifacially worked. Occasional microliths are found.

Stone. Ground stone axes are found in a few tombs. Perforated tools do not occur, except on the single site of Cumarola, although a few axe-hammers have been found sporadically in marginal areas. Stone beads also occur.

Bone and shell. These were used for beads.

Other Finds. Sporadic finds of copper axes, a few copper daggers, and flint daggers and arrowheads occur throughout the Po valley and presumably belong to the Remedello culture.

References (see also Appendix II):

Acanfora *BPI* 65 (1956), with earlier references,

Malavolti, *Appunti* (1953),

Zorzi, *RSP* 15 (1960),

Cornaggia Castiglioni, *RSP* 18 (1963).

RINALDONE (figs 1 and 3)

Distribution. Tuscany and Lazio, in an area bounded on the west by the sea, on the east by the Apennines, on the north by the Arno, and on the south by the Tiber. A number of sites in Umbria and the Abruzzi, in the area of the Conelle–Ortucchio group and in Campania, in the Gaudo area, have strong affinities with this group.

Settlements. The Copper Age village on the site at Luni sul Mignone is assigned to the Rinaldone culture.[9] David Trump initially assigned the contemporary settlement at La Starza, Ariano Irpino, to this culture,[10] but later described it as Lagozza.[11] Rinaldone material also occurs in mixed contexts in caves and rock-shelters of this period, such as Riparo della Romita at Asciano[12] and Grotta dei Piccioni at Bolognano.[13]

Burials. Single burial in trench graves and single or collective burial in rock-cut tombs both occur, as well as occasional collective burials in natural caves or crevices. A recent study[14] has distinguished a coastal and sub-coastal zone in Lazio and Tuscany in which rock-cut tombs were most common, and a peripheral zone in the interior and to the north and south, in which single burials in earth graves was the predominant rite. More than thirty funerary sites are known in the Rinaldone area and several of the tombs in the Conelle–Ortucchio and Gaudo areas may belong to this group. The tombs occur singly or in small groups: the largest cemetery known is at Ponte S. Pietro and originally had at least fourteen tombs (see Appendix 2). The tombs used for collective burial do not contain many bodies ; the maximum recorded with any certainty is seven. With a single exception with two chambers, the rock-cut tombs are all of the single-chambered oven-shaped type, usually entered from a shaft.

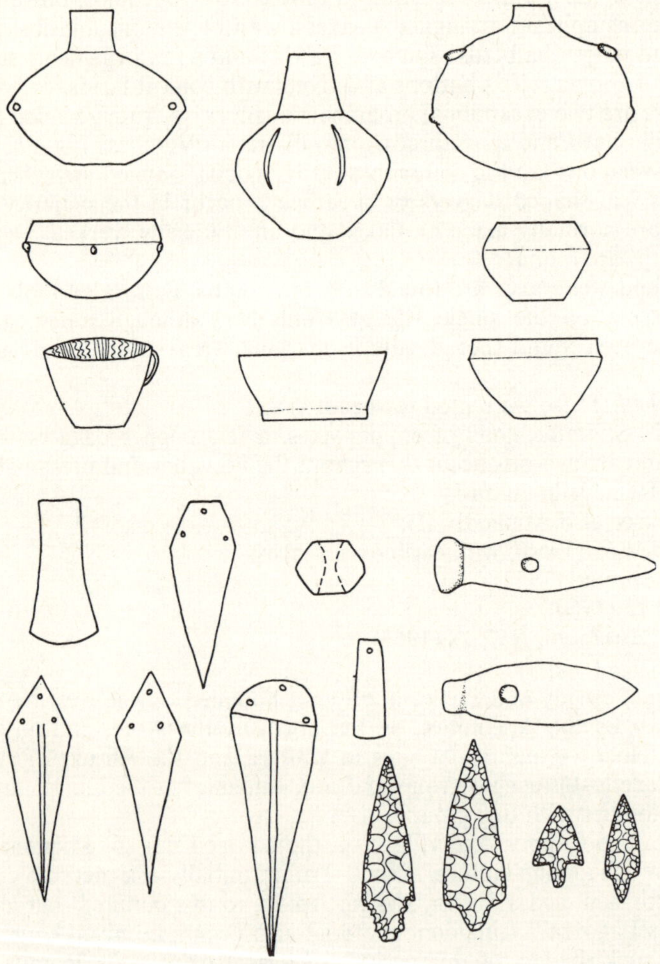

Figure 3. Rinaldone: typical artefacts (not to scale).

Grave Goods (fig. 3). The divergence in burial rite between the central and peripheral zones is accompanied by a difference in grave goods: both pottery and metal goods are more common in the rock-cut tombs than in the trench graves, and the forms vary also.

Pottery. This is medium to dark brown in colour, often with a high burnish ; it is usually undecorated, but is occasionally ornamented with applied cordons or studs, or pattern-burnished internally. The most common shape is a bottle, sometimes with horizontal or vertical tunnel handles, but cups and dishes also occur. In one tomb—Fosso Conicchio near Viterbo—Copper Age pottery not of Rinaldone type was associated with six Bell Beakers and four stone wristguards.

Copper. Copper weapons are very much more common in tombs of this group than anywhere else in Italy at this time and there is very little doubt that the copper ores of this zone, in the Colline Metallifere and perhaps on Monte Amiata, were being exploited. The forms include flat axes ; awls with square section ; flat daggers with rounded, triangular, trapezoidal heels and usually three rivets ; a few examples with midribs and one or two of the typical Remedello tanged forms ; at least one halberd blade is known, from Pomerance, and there are a few other halberd blades from surface sites in the area. Barfield [15] describes a shaft-hole halberd found in this area, which should probably be assigned to this culture.

Antimony. Three V-bored buttons of antimony were found with the Rinaldone burials in the cave at Monte Bradoni ; the metal is thought to come from a local source. Objects of antimony are recorded also from Ponte S. Pietro (fig. 8c).

Flint. Tanged arrowheads and triangular and leaf-shaped dagger–spear-heads, with or without tangs, are common finds in all tombs of this group. As in the Remedello area, they are normally made on flakes and are bi-facially worked, although some arrowheads are flaked on one surface only.

Stone. Perforated maceheads, axe-hammers, and battle-axes with knobbed ends are characteristic of this group ; the holes were made either by drilling or by percussion. Typical Beaker wristguards were found in association with the beakers themselves at Fosso Conicchio.

Bone and shell. These were not used by the Rinaldone people for grave goods.

Other Finds. Hoards of flat copper axes and isolated finds of axes and dagger blades occur throughout the zone and especially in the Monte Amiata area. They presumably belong to the Rinaldone culture. There are also many surface finds of flint weapons of this period.

References (see also Appendix II):
Barich *et al.*, *Origini* 2 (1968), with earlier references,
Radmilli, *RSP* 22 (1967), 24 (1969),
Rittatore Vonwiller, *RSP* 22 (1967), 23 (1968), 24 (1969),
Moretti, *RSP* 23 (1968).

GAUDO (figs 1 and 4)

Distribution. Limited to Campania, with a possible southward extension into Calabria. It could be regarded as a regional variant of the Rinaldone culture, to which it is closely related.

Settlements. There are open settlements of this period at La Starza, Ariano Irpino,[16] and Camposauro near Benevento,[17] but they have not yielded characteristic Gaudo pottery.

Burials. Collective burial in rock-cut tombs was the rule. Five cemeteries of rock-cut tombs are known and two isolated tombs of this group. There is also a trench grave possibly of this group at Roggiano Gravina in Calabria. An isolated trench grave at Toppo San Filippo and a cemetery of similar tombs at Gesualdo, both in the northern part of the area, are probably southerly examples of the Rinaldone group. Trench graves at Pontecagnano and burials in natural crevices at Paestum have yielded material of Laterza type. The largest cemetery of rock-cut tombs is the type site at Gaudo, near Paestum; at least twenty-six tombs have been excavated and the original number was certainly more. The tombs are of the oven-shaped type entered from a shaft; double-chambered examples are common. The numbers of bodies recorded from any one tomb varies from one to twenty-five.

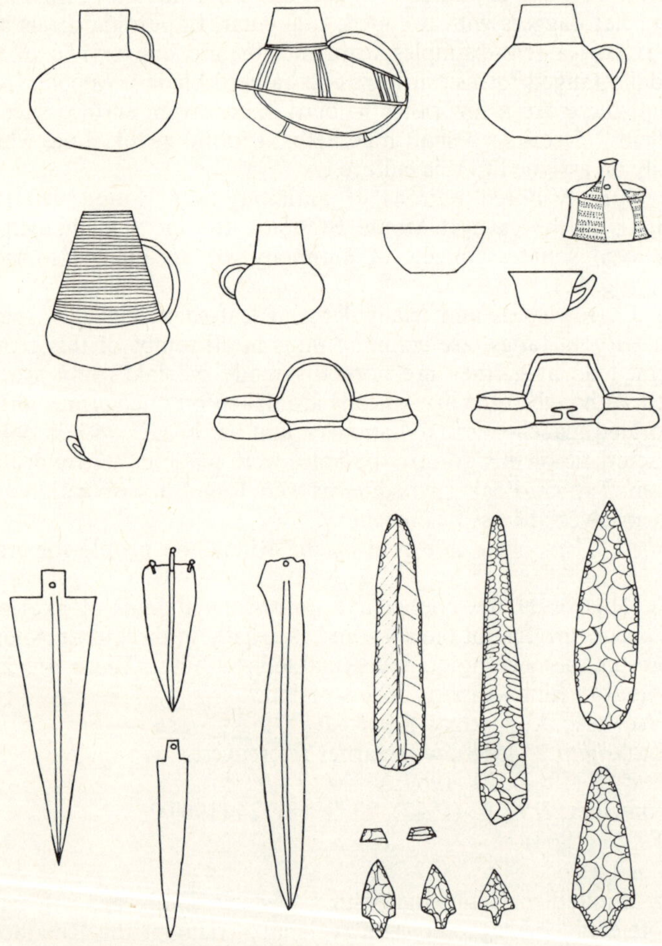

Figure 4. Gaudo: typical artefacts (not to scale).

Grave Goods (fig. 4). *Pottery.* This is medium to dark brown in colour with a high burnish. It is normally undecorated or with decoration limited to cordons in relief, but highly decorated lids occur, covered with incised and punctuated ornament, which foreshadows the characteristic decoration of the Apennine Bronze Age. The forms include high-handled cups and bottles, asymmetrical bottles described as 'askoi', double vessels, simple dishes, and bowls and conical lids.

Copper. This is less common than in the Rinaldone area (presumably due to the absence of copper ores in southern Italy). Axes are not found in the tombs and only daggers and awls are known. The awls are square in section. The daggers occur in a variety of forms: triangular forms with midribs and a straight or slightly rounded heel, long narrow and flat triangular forms with or without a tang, and a single example of the broad-heeled tanged Remedello form with midrib from Mirabella Eclano. A halberd blade was found at Roggiano Gravina in Calabria.

Silver. Two fragmentary cylindrical beads of silver wire were found in recent excavations at Gaudo, and a silver bracelet, 'che è rimasto in possesso dell'occasionale rinvenitore', allegedly turned up in the original excavations: nothing is known about its form.

Flint. Flint weapons are very common: as well as the usual bifacial tanged arrowheads and dagger–spearheads, there are so-called 'stiloid' daggers, made on long blades worked on one face only, and also geometric trapezes.

Stone. Ground stone tools and weapons do not occur as grave goods.

Bone and shell. A few ornaments are known, including two bone crutch-headed pins from Gaudo itself.

Other Finds. Isolated finds of flat copper axes, bifacial flint arrowheads and dagger–spearheads have been made in Campania and probably belong to this culture.

References (see also Appendix II):
Sestieri, *RSP* 1 (1946), 2 (1947),
Voza, *Atti della* VIII *e* IX *Riunione* (1964),
Buchner, *RSP* 5 (1950),
D'Agostino, *BPI* 73 (1970), *RSP* 23 (1968),
Ross Holloway, *AJA* 74 (1970), 75 (1971).

CONELLE–ORTUCCHIO (figs 1 and 5)

Distribution. Marche and Abruzzi.

Settlements. Unlike the previous groups, this culture is defined by material from settlement sites. Village sites in the open are known and at least one, Conelle itself, was surrounded by a ditch. Caves were also used for occupation.

Burials. A number of tombs in this zone have yielded typical Copper Age flint work, but lack diagnostic pottery types; although the evidence is lacking, they may well belong to the Conelle–Ortucchio group. The tombs are all trench graves with single or double contracted inhumations. They occur singly or in small groups.

Finds (fig. 5). *Pottery.* The typical pottery from the settlement sites is dark grey or black with a burnished surface; the most common forms are dishes, bowls, narrow-necked jugs with single handles, jugs with sloping mouths, and asymmetrical bottles ('askoi'). Although many vessels are undecorated, the most distinctive characteristic of this ware is its decoration of punctuated bands encrusted with white matter, so clearly anticipating that of the Apennine Bronze Age that some authorities have called this group 'Proto-Apennine'. The pots from the tombs at Recanati are all undecorated; they include single-handled jugs, simple dishes, and bipartite vessels with solid or perforated lug handles.

Copper. The tomb at Monsanvito yielded a flat copper axe, and a fragment of the same metal was found at Conelle.

Flint. Bifacially worked tanged arrowheads and dagger–spearheads of the usual kinds occur both as grave goods and on the settlement sites.

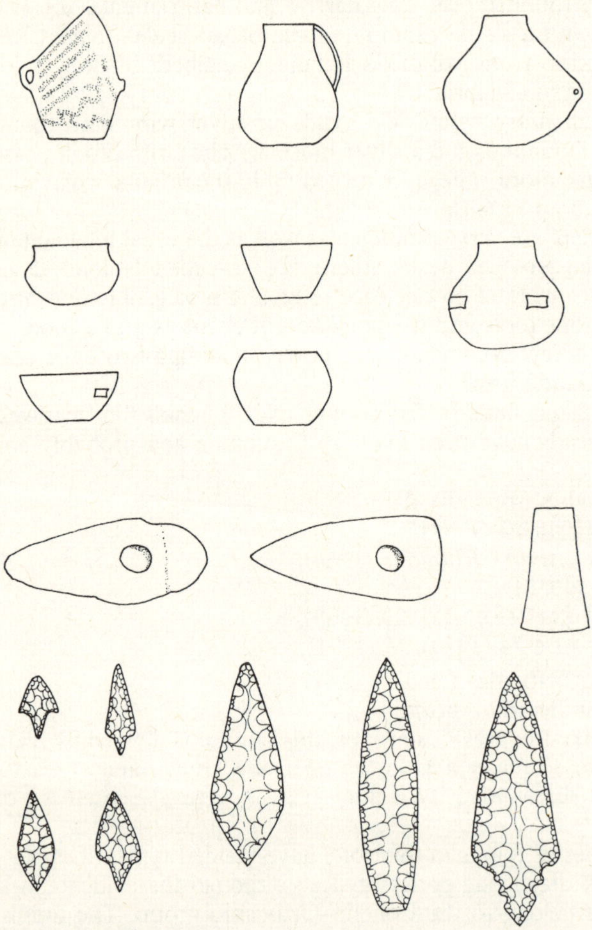

Figure 5. Conelle- Ortucchio: typical artefacts (not to scale).

Stone. Ground stone axes, perforated axe-hammers, and maceheads occur on the settlement sites and an axe-hammer was found in one of the tombs at Osimo. Stone ornaments occur.

Bone and shell. These were used for beads and other simple ornaments.

Other Finds. Sporadic finds of flint arrowheads and dagger–spearheads and occasional copper axes and daggers in the Marche and the Abruzzi probably belong to this culture.

Economy. Mixed economy with a notable emphasis on wild food products.

References (see also Appendix II):

Puglisi, *La civiltà appenninica* (1959),

Radmilli, *RSP* 14 (1959).

MACCHIA A MARE (figs 1 and 6)

Distribution. Along the coast of the Gargano Promontory.

Settlements. Open villages on coastal promontories or lake-sides ; clusters of circular huts with dry-stone footings. Caves were also occupied.

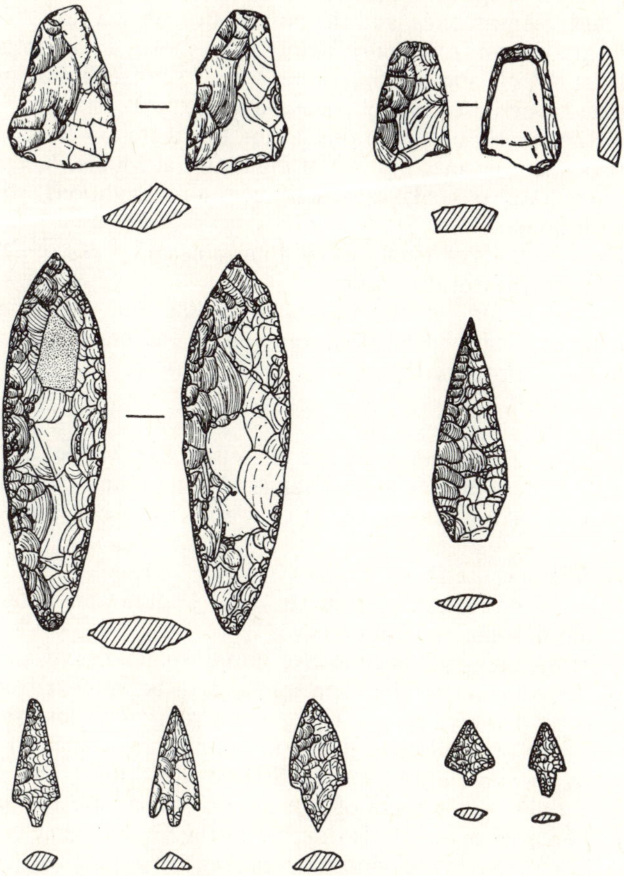

Figure 6. Macchia a Mare: typical flintwork. Scale 1 : 3.

Burials. Rock-cut tombs of the single-chambered type entered either directly from a cliff face or through a shaft ; bell-shaped examples entered through a hole in the roof also occur, but may not belong to this period. Most tombs have been robbed in Antiquity, but two at least have yielded typical Copper Age finds.

Finds. Pottery. This is characterised by a red fabric with many white calcareous inclusions. Unfortunately no forms are known, as the settlement sites invariably yield only very small and very worn sherds. Pottery of this type has been found, in fragments, in one rock-cut tomb at Monte Pucci.

Copper. The only evidence we have is two copper rings from a tomb at Monte Pucci ; their form is not known.

Flint (fig. 6). The best-known trait of this group is the so-called 'Campignian' flint industry, a macrolithic industry of crudely flaked tranchet axes, picks, chisels, etc., using local flint. This industry was certainly in existence during the Neolithic, but continued into the Copper Age, when it was associated also with typical Copper Age flintwork: bifacially pressure-flaked arrowheads and dagger–spearheads, and the pottery described above. 'Campignian' flint tools are known from many factory sites, mostly in the interior of the Gargano Promontory, and one flint mine. A very similar flint industry occurs in the Monte Lessini area in the Veneto, and in the Trentino.

Stone. Ground stone rarely occurs in this group, but there are occasional axes. A limestone pendant occurred in one of the tombs at Monte Pucci.

Bone. This is very rare, possibly caused by acid soil conditions, which would destroy much bone.

Other Finds. Sporadic finds of 'Campignian' flint tools and pressure-flaked arrowheads and dagger–spearheads occur.

Economy. Based on a combination of stock-breeding and gathering of seafood; there is no explicit evidence that agriculture was practised at all.

References (see also Appendix II):

Puglisi, *Atti Lincei* 8 (1950).

LATERZA (figs 1 and 7)

This group is sometimes named after the site of Cellino San Marco, but the site of Laterza near Matera, with a greater range of pottery and other artefact types, makes a better type site for what is in any case a rather diverse group.

Distribution. Apulia and the Materano.

Settlements. There is one possible open site near Matera and Laterza; material is also found in some occupation caves.

Burials. The most common rite is collective burial, sometimes of a large number of bodies, in rock-cut tombs. The tombs may be entered from a shaft or a *dromos,* or directly from a hole in the roof; two and three-chambered examples occur. Collective burial in natural caves and, on one occasion, in a trench grave are also recorded. Sixteen sites, either individual tombs or cemeteries (with a maximum of five certain tombs), are known in the main area, but Laterza material also occurs in the Gaudo cemetery at Mirabella Eclano, in some natural cavities with burials at Paestum itself, and in some simple earth graves at Pontecagnano and on the Aeolian Islands. Several of the sites listed belong to the 'Proto-Apennine' phase and were probably established at the end of the 3rd millennium BC (calendar years).

Grave Goods (fig. 7) *Pottery.* The Laterza group has a rich repertoire of pottery forms and decoration. The ware is usually dark and burnished. Open dishes and both open- and narrow-mouthed bowls predominate, but at a later stage (later on both typographical and stratigraphical grounds) single-handled cups also became common, especially a carinated form with a rounded lower part and a conical upper part. This form normally has an elbow handle on the carination; other forms have handles ending in knobs or studs or simple tongue handles. All these herald typical Apennine Bronze Age forms and indeed the development of Apennine pottery out of these 'Protoapennine' forms is documented on the stratified settlement site of Porto Perone at Leporano near Taranto.[18] Another characteristic of Laterza pottery is the raising of a section of the rim of shallow dishes to form a sort of elongated lug. Many vessels are decorated and a variety of techniques are employed: applied studs and ribs, impressions, soft incision, often in bands of lattice pattern, punctuated ornament, and shallow grooves on the inside and outside of open dishes.

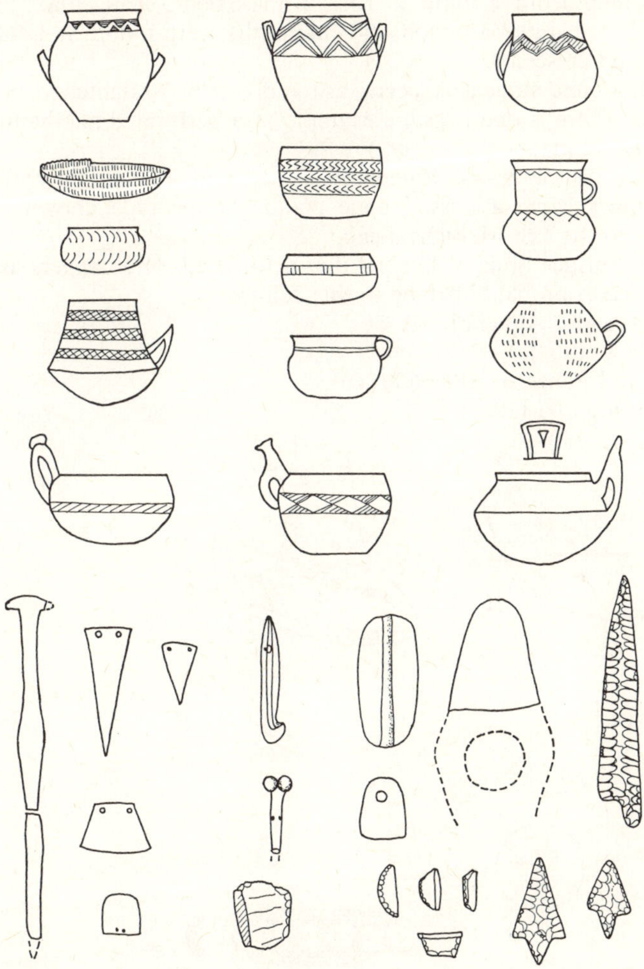

Figure 7. Laterza: typical artefacts (not to scale).

Copper. Copper is rare in this group, except at Laterza itself. Daggers and small knife-daggers occur, as do small blades with a transverse edge, which may have served as scrapers or perhaps as razors. A small ornamental piece was found at Gioia del Colle. Of particular interest are the two daggers from Tomb 3 at Laterza (type B5, fig. 10) with semicircular or crescentic hilts; there is another from Monte Bradoni in the Rinaldone zone, and another from Grotta Chiusazza in eastern Sicily, where it occurs in layer IV upper, in association with pottery of the Chiusazza and Malpasso styles, immediately underlying a layer of the Castelluccio culture.[19] All three contexts should be dated in the earlier part of the 3rd millennium BC (in calendar years).

Flint. Bifacial flintwork is rare in this group, in contrast to all the other groups in the peninsula. However, a few tanged arrowheads occur, and daggers occur as surface finds, as well as one exceptionally fine example, recorded as coming from 'a tomb' at Diso in the Salento Peninsula.[20] Flake and blade tools are quite common and microliths were found at Laterza, both trapezes and crescents.

Stone. Small ground stone axes occur, as too do arrow-straighteners of imported pumice. There is one possible example of a perforated axe-hammer. Stone beads and pendants also occur.

Bone. A bone fish-hook was found at Laterza, and from an exceptional tomb at Altamura came a bossed bone plaque of the type known from Sicily, Malta, and the east Mediterranean.

Other Finds. Surface finds of bifacial flint arrowheads and daggers and a few flat copper axes probably belong to this culture.

References (see also Appendix II):
Lo Porto, *NS* 8 (1963),
Biancofiore and Ponzetti, *BPI* 66 (1966),
Biancofiore, *Origini* 1 (1967).

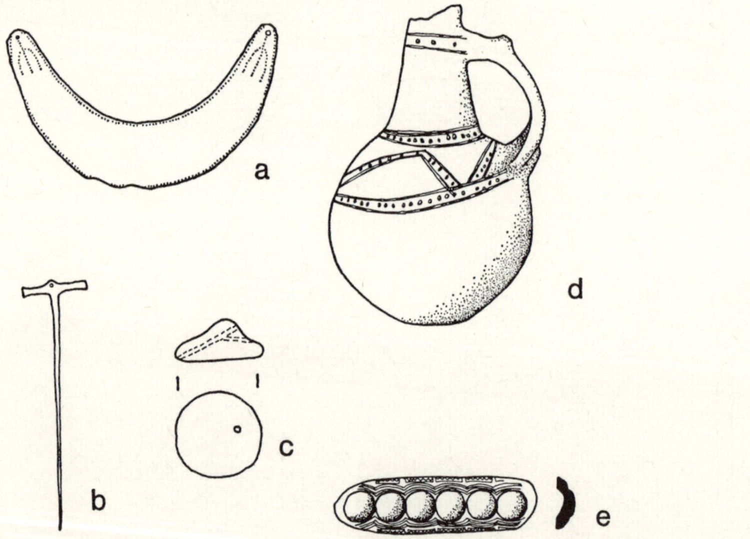

Figure 8. Exceptional objects of the Italian Copper Age (not to scale). (a) Silver pectoral from Villafranca Veronese; (b) Silver crutch-headed pin from Remedello Sotto; (c) Antimony button from Monte Bradoni; (d) Pottery jug from Gioia del Colle; (e) Bossed bone plaque from Altamura.

Chronology

The table (fig. 9) plots in schematic form the culture sequence in the various regions of Italy and the Aegean in the period c. 4000–1000 BC in C-14 years, c. 4800–1100 BC in calendar years. The list (Appendix I) contains all the relevant C-14 dates available for peninsular Italy and Lipari. These are also

Figure 9. Chronological chart showing schematically the culture sequence in various regions of the central Mediterranean and the Aegean in the period *c.* 4000-1000 b.c., C-14 years (*c.* 4800-1100 BC in calendar years). The vertical lines indicate individual C-14 dates, each shown with a single standard deviation. The dates are listed in appendix I.

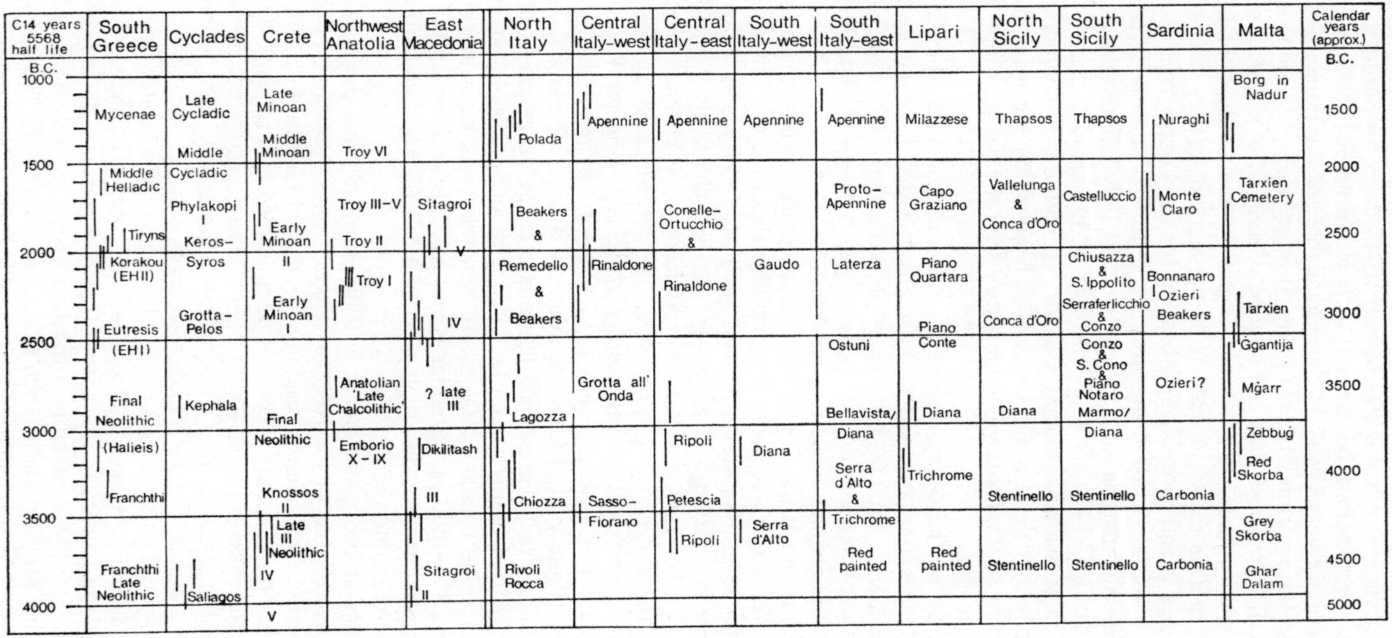

plotted in the table in the form of vertical lines, each representing the standard deviation of a single C-14 date. C-14 dates for Sardinia and Malta are plotted on the chart, but are not included in the list of dates.

There are very few C-14 dates available for the Italian Copper Age and these all come from settlement sites. It must be emphasised that the domestic material from these sites can only be correlated in a very general way with the funerary material which constitutes the main subject of this paper, and that therefore the C-14 dates from the settlement sites can only be used to provide a broad chronological bracket for the Copper Age in general.

With this reservation in mind, we note that several different groups of Copper Age material in north and central Italy fall into the period c. 2500–1800 BC in C-14 years (c. 3000–2200 BC in calendar years). There are no C-14 dates available for any Copper Age cultures in southern Italy, Lipari, or Sicily, but there is good reason to believe that the main groups in these areas are approximately contemporary with the dated groups in central and northern Italy.

We do not have any satisfactory *termini post quem* for the beginning of the Copper Age and it is at least possible that it began several centuries earlier than c. 2500 BC, C-14 years, in some areas. However, there are alternative explanations for the apparent gap between the end of the Neolithic and the beginning of the Copper Age.

For the end of the Copper Age we are equally without satisfactory *termini* as provided by C-14 dates, the available dates for the Bronze Age all being later by several centuries than c. 1800 BC, C-14 years, which is the latest date we have from a Copper Age site (see chart, fig. 9 and list of dates). However, for southern Italy we do have some chronological information about the end of the Copper Age. The lowest levels on the site of Porto Perone, Leporano[21] contain pottery of the type labelled 'Proto-Apenninnico B' by Lo Porto, in association with sherds of imported Middle Helladic pottery. Pottery of 'Proto-Apenninnico B' type developed out of Laterza ware and in fact represents a late phase in the development of this culture. The imported sherds cannot be dated with any precision, but should belong in the period c. 2000–1600 BC. In general terms we can perhaps see this period 2300–1600 BC (calendar years) as a phase in which the Copper Age Laterza culture was developing into the full Bronze Age (and truly bronze-using) Apennine Culture.

A similar procedure has been followed in plotting the radiocarbon dates from five regions of the Aegean. There are no radiocarbon dates as yet for this period from west Macedonia or central Greece, but a more complete sequence for Thessaly is soon to be published by Professor V. Milojčic. All available dates between 4000 BC and 1500 BC (in radiocarbon years) have been plotted. After this time dates obtained by conventional historical methods appear to offer a higher accuracy although they must not, of course, be compared with uncalibrated radiocarbon dates. Dates from Karatas and Beycesultan have been included in the column headed 'NW Anatolia' in view of the paucity of dates from that region itself: those from Karatas are assigned by the excavator to the late Troy I period and by other scholars including Mellaart and French to the time of Troy II. The appropriate levels at Beycesultan are regarded as 'Late Chalcolithic' in Anatolian terms.

In general the calibrated radiocarbon chronology for the Aegean, from 3000 BC onwards, agrees very well with the results of cross-dating with Egypt.[22] Before this time there are no Egyptian historical dates to support such a cross-dating.

The duration of the Aegean Early Bronze Age may be set from c. 2500 BC to c. 1800 BC in radiocarbon years: in calendar years from c. 3200 BC to c. 2100 or 2000 BC. Many of the most striking developments which we associate with the Early Bronze Age—the widespread use of bronze, rich finds of gold and silver, indications of intensive trade, stone fortifications, seal-stones and sealings, the construction of large buildings like those of Lerna or Vasiliki—are seen first in many regions in the Early Bronze 2 period. They have their precursors, of course, and stone fortifications are seen at Troy and Emborio in the Early Bronze 1 period, and perhaps earlier. In general terms the Early Bronze 2 period may be set between c. 2200 BC and c. 1900 BC in radiocarbon years ; in calendar years between c. 2700 BC and c. 2400 or 2300 BC.

One striking consequence of the new radiocarbon chronology for the Aegean, reinforced by the calibration, is the emergence of a period of nearly a millennium in radiocarbon years, from c. 3400 BC to c. 2500 BC (c. 4300 to c. 3200 BC in calendar years) which may be called Final Neolithic. Most of the material from Greece which has formerly been termed Late Neolithic can be set before this time. For instance the dates for the Late Neolithic of Knossos, for Saliagos, and for Dhimini in Thessaly (3680±150 BC) all fall before 3500 BC. This is the millennium in Greek prehistory of which we know least.

All of this makes possible a new view of the chronological relations between the cultures of Italy and the Aegean. The first and most important point is that the Italian Copper Age was the *precise contemporary* of the Aegean Early Bronze Age, and not its partial successor, as some have argued. Moreover the preceding period—3400 BC to 2500 BC in radiocarbon years—is much better represented in the west Mediterranean than in the Aegean, both by finds and by radiocarbon dates for them. The dates for the Diana culture of Lipari, the Ripoli culture of eastern Italy, and the Lagozza culture in the north span the period between the Red Skorba and Ggantija cultures in Malta, and set all these cultures contemporary with the little understood final Neolithic of the Aegean, as represented at the Franchthi and Kitsos caves on the mainland, the Attic-Kephala culture in the Cyclades, the pre-Bronze Age levels at Emborio in the eastern Aegean, later Phase III at Sitagroi in Macedonia, and perhaps the latest Neolithic at Phaistos in Crete.

The earliest dates for the Rinaldone culture suggest that its beginning may have been already in the Early Bronze 1 period of the Aegean, the earliest beakers in Italy falling at about the same time.

All of this therefore suggests that the Aegean was not so markedly 'in advance' of the west Mediterranean as has sometimes been assumed. We shall see, for instance, that cemeteries of rock-cut tombs make their appearance in Italy some time before they are seen in the Aegean.

This new framework allows us to look more carefully at the various contacts, real and imagined, between the west Mediterranean and the Aegean.

Direct Contacts between the Aegean and Peninsular Italy in Later Periods

In order to set the question of Copper Age contacts in a wider context, it is instructive to consider first the situation in later periods, when relations between the two regions seem to have been closer than during the 3rd millennium BC. Four phases may be recognised:

(*a*) Aegean Late Bronze Age, Apennine Bronze Age: from c. 1600 BC.

(*b*) Aegean Middle Bronze Age, Proto-Apennine culture of Italy, the Capo Graziano culture of Lipari, Castelluccio in Sicily, the Tarxien Cemetery culture in Malta: c. 2100–1600 BC (although beginning a little earlier in some west Mediterranean regions).

(*c*) Aegean Early Bronze Age, Copper Age cultures of Italy, Sicily, and Malta: c. 3200 to 2100 BC (in calendar years).

(*d*) Late and Final Neolithic of the Aegean, Neolithic of the west Mediterranean.

Mycenaean finds in south Italy and Sicily are well documented, especially pottery.[23] So numerous are the finds at some sites such as Scoglio del Tonno that Childe allowed Mycenaean influence and Mycenaean trade a decisive role in the development of the Italian Bronze Age. This view, although undoubtedly 'diffusionist', is supported by the evidence now available.[24] It seems perfectly possible that trading stations, which enjoyed special relations with ports in the Mycenaean world, and which may have supported a partly Mycenaean population, had an important innovating role. Seen from an Aegean standpoint also, this does look like a commercial trade, at least from the fourteenth century BC.[25] It is most clearly documented by pottery finds, but bronze ingot bars have also been found in the west Mediterranean,[26] and since these resemble the Minoan type, it seems likely that the Italian mineral resources were then being exploited by Aegean communities. From the middle of the 2nd millennium we find, therefore, a situation much like the one which some authorities have imagined for the Copper Age a millennium earlier. The evidence in Mycenaean times, whatever the defects in earlier periods, can certainly be used to support such a picture.

In the early second millennium (the Aegean Middle Bronze Age) signs of direct contact are much scarcer. Taylour identified sherds of Middle Helladic pottery from Filicudi and Lipari in the Aeolian Islands and from Monte Sallia in eastern Sicily.[27] Recently, however, Bernabò Brea[28] has demonstrated that the Monte Sallia vessel was a local product, resembling very closely numerous cups from a late Castelluccio site at Adrano, and he has cast doubt also on the identifications of the Aeolian Middle Helladic sherds. The only other site from which Middle Helladic sherds have been recorded is Porto Perone, Leporano in south-east Italy,[29] and this identification is accepted by Bernabò Brea. Thus a handful of sherds from a single site represent the only *certain* imports from the Aegean in the central Mediterranean before c. 1600 BC. Like the equivalent, if rather more numerous, finds of Middle Minoan pottery in the Levant, they need indicate nothing more than sporadic freelance commercial activity.[30] There is no need to see in them evidence either for highly organised commercial activity, whether or not in 'colonies', or for the movement from the Aegean of actual groups of people.

While incontrovertible evidence of this kind is rare—and no Italian imports to the Aegean have been recognised—there are further archaeological indications which must be considered. Bossed bone plaques from the Castelluccio culture of Sicily[31] have rightly been compared by Evans[32] with the specimen from the Tarxien cemetery in Malta.[33] The closest Aegean parallel is now the specimen from the Tiryns culture ('Early Helladic III') level at Lerna.[34] The similarities between these enigmatic objects are so great that a connection may reasonably be postulated. The Tiryns culture may be dated from c. 2300 to c. 2100 BC in calendar years and this early date accords well with the early radiocarbon date of 1930 BC from the Tarxien cemetery, equivalent to c. 2200 BC in calendar years.

The find from Altamura in south-east Italy[35] does not contradict this dating, since the later sites of the Laterza culture belong to a 'Proto-Apennine' phase, which should be dated to the few centuries on either side of 2000 BC in calendar years and is thus contemporary with the earlier part of the Tarxien Cemetery culture. The pottery from the Altamura tomb is rather atypical and has even been considered Iron Age by some authorities, but to us it seems to fit reasonably well into a 'Proto-Apennine' context. The Altamura plaque (fig. 8*e*) is shaped like the Castelluccio and Tarxien Cemetery examples, which are hollow, while the Aegean ones are solid. The decoration, on the other hand, is like those of the Aegean, where the ornament is on the background only with the bosses undecorated: the Castelluccio specimens have decorated bosses and a cross-hatched background.

Another possible indication of direct contact with the Aegean at the time of the Tarxien cemetery is afforded by the beads of faience found there in the cinerary urns. They are single pierced discs, only 3 mm in diameter, and are found in great quantities. It should be noted that they are not of the 'segmented' form found in Britain, and the single example that Stone[36] so described consisted of only one and a half segments, and was probably the result simply of the fusion of two disc beads.

At first sight these beads offer strong evidence for contact with the Aegean, but the case is in fact less clear. Faience beads are rare in the west Mediterranean, being known only from Fuente Alamo in Spain and Portella in Salina, one of the Aeolian islands, in the Middle Bronze Age.[37] These last may probably be accepted as Aegean in origin, but they are much later in date than the Maltese ones. The latter form a distinct local group, and it is quite possible that they were in fact manufactured in Malta. In the first place they are found with large quantities of similarly shaped beads of ostrich egg-shell, which they might well have imitated. There is direct evidence for bronze casting in the succeeding Borg in Nadur period, and the copper objects which make their appearance in Malta during the Tarxien cemetery period could well have been cast locally (although copper ores do not occur in Malta). It is possible, therefore, that the manufacture of faience in Malta was related to the growth of a local bronze technology, just as it has been suggested for early Bronze Age Britain.[38] Faience beads, kindly made available by the National Museum of Malta, have been submitted to Dr A. Aspinall and Dr S. Warren of the Postgraduate School of Physics at Bradford for neutron activation analysis. If the beads form a distinct group, in terms of their trace elements, different from those of other areas, local manufacture will become a distinct possibility. The beads would then no longer carry the implication of Aegeo-Melitensian relations. The ostrich egg-shell beads, on the other hand, were made of material presumably deriving from the north coast of Africa. More generalised similarities may be indicated between the pottery in some areas and that of the Aegean Middle Bronze Age. Evans has effectively made the case[39] for the Tarxien cemetery culture which, as he has shown, has similarities with the Capo Graziano culture of Lipari. Now that the Tiryns culture ('Early Helladic III') has been defined more closely as a result of Caskey's work at Lerna,[40] this can be seen as in many ways a more satisfactory point of comparison, but were it not for the actual import to the west Mediterranean of small quantities of Middle Helladic pottery, plus the evidence of the bone plaques, such ceramic analogies might not be altogether convincing.

THE OBSIDIAN TRADE

At this point it is essential to correct one misapprehension which has developed in the archaeological literature. In his excavations at Knossos, Sir Arthur Evans found considerable quantities of obsidian, most of it of plain black appearance, which was rightly thought to come from the Cycladic island of Melos. A second variety was found, white-spotted in appearance, which had been used principally for the manufacture of stone vases and other luxury objects. Following the advice of geologists, given solely on the basis of the similarity in appearance of this material to the obsidian found on Lipari, Evans[41] termed this variety 'liparite'. It was supposed that the Minoans, already in Middle Bronze Age times, and perhaps earlier, travelled west to Lipari to collect it. This has been used by several authors as a further indication of contact and trade between the Aegean and the west Mediterranean[42] and a whole case for contacts at the time of the Late Neolithic Diana culture of Lipari has been built up[43] based in part upon this evidence.

Unfortunately the suggestion that the white-spotted obsidian found at Knossos and other Minoan sites (including Mallia, Aghia Triadha, and Cycladic sites on Naxos and Kea) came from Lipari, was incorrect. A programme of trace-element analyses by means of optical spectroscopy[44] has shown that the 'liparite' of Knossos came in fact from the east Aegean island of Giali. The distinction between the Giali obsidian and that of other sources has been strengthened recently by neutron-activation analyses.[45] Indeed there is no good evidence to suggest that obsidian from any of the west Mediterranean sources reached the Aegean at any time during the prehistoric period.

The converse suggestion, that obsidian from Melos was reaching the west Mediterranean, was first put forward by Peet[46] and taken up by Evans,[47] and later by Cornaggia.[48] But again trace-element analysis has given no support for it, and all the west Mediterranean obsidians yet examined[49] are from west Mediterranean sources.

There are four source areas of importance in the west Mediterranean: Lipari, Pantelleria, the Pontine Islands, and Sardinia. The obsidian used in Malta, already from Early Neolithic times, came from the first two. Samples from Neolithic contexts on the Italian mainland have proved to come from the Lipari, Sardinia, and Palmarola (Pontine Island) sources, and a sample from the Trieste region comes also from Palmarola. The picture is therefore of a considerable traffic in obsidian already from Early Neolithic times *within* the west Mediterranean. There is so far no evidence for trade or traffic in obsidian between the west Mediterranean and the Aegean, or vice versa, at any time.

These remarks on obsidian refer to the Neolithic and Copper Age as well as to later periods. So far, for the Neolithic period, no actual imports from the Aegean have been identified in the west Mediterranean. A seated figurine, purchased in recent times in Malta,[50] is certainly very closely similar to those of the Greek Neolithic, but it may be a very recent import. There is no doubt, of course, that some of the essential components of the Neolithic way of life, notably the plant and animal domesticates themselves, derived ultimately from the east and were in some cases introduced to the west by settlers. But as Ammerman and Cavalli-Sforza have elegantly shown[51] this propagation is likely to have been the result of small local movements rather than long-distance migrations or contacts. Moreover, after the initial spread, the gradient in population density is never likely to have been so great again. There is thus little virtue in the argument that just because it happened once it could have happened again: to make this plausible some appropriate mechanism would have to be suggested.

The similarities between Italian Copper Age finds and their contemporaries in the Aegean will be discussed in the next section. But it is appropriate here to indicate that there is no evidence for direct contacts between the Aegean and different parts of the west Mediterranean at this time. The arguments against the arrival in Spain during the 3rd millennium of Aegean colonists have been set out elsewhere.[52] The calibrated chronology for Malta[53] makes impossible the Aegean origins sometimes claimed for a number of features, and Cycladic inspiration for the clay figurines found by Trump[54] now seems unlikely. The same view was tentatively expressed in 1965 for Sardinia,[55] and is strengthened by the recent discovery there by Dr Trump[56] of figurines in clay which could serve as prototypes for the marble statuettes found in Sardinia, some of which bear a suggestive resemblance to the Cycladic folded-arm figurines.

These comments certainly do not exclude the possibility of contacts between the Aegean and different parts of the west Mediterranean during the Copper Age. But if a sceptical position is adopted, it is striking how little hard incontrovertible evidence there is for such relations until the occurrence of Middle Helladic sherds in south-east Italy. We would argue that the evidence for contacts during the Copper Age has often been overvalued in the past, and that the rest of the west Mediterranean gives very little independent support to the case which can be made for peninsular Italy. This must now be examined more closely.

Innovations in the Italian Copper Age

The foregoing discussion has set a more critical context than is often presented for the discussion of Aegean influences upon the development of the Italian Copper Age. The principal innovations of the period will now be considered, leaving until last the inception of metallurgy, which was arguably the most important.

BURIAL CUSTOMS

The Italian Copper Age shows three different modes of inhumation. The first is burial in trench graves, cut into the earth or in rock. The burials are in the crouched position, sometimes with two in the same grave. This mode is almost universal in the Remedello group and in east central Italy, and occurs also on the periphery of the Rinaldone group and occasionally in the south. This manner of burial is, however, characteristic of almost all Neolithic groups in Italy, for example the Lagozza, Chiozza, and Ripoli cultures, as well as the southern Italian Neolithic. In contrast it was not the characteristic burial mode of any region of the Aegean during the Early Bronze Age. Crouched burial in earth graves within the settlement was the normal form of burial at Early Neolithic Nea Nikomedeia in North Greece, but in the later Neolithic burials of any kind are rarely found.

The second form of inhumation is collective burial in natural caves or crevices. This practice is seen in all areas of the peninsula, but is not typical of any group. This was not a normal Neolithic rite in Italy, but was practised on occasion by different Neolithic groups, e.g. the Sasso-Fiorano and Chiozza cultures and the southern Italian Neolithic. In the Aegean, burial in rock shelters and caves is common only in Crete, where it occurs in the Late Neolithic and Early Minoan periods. The Cretan instances are not necessarily earlier than the Italian ones, and there is certainly no reason to relate them.

The third form of burial, and the one to which an east Mediterranean origin is most often assigned, is the custom of single or collective inhumation in rock-cut tombs. Collective or occasionally single burial in this way is characteristic of the southern groups of the Italian Copper Age (Gaudo, Laterza, and Macchia a Mare), while rock-cut tombs were used for single or collective burial, although never for many individuals, in the central area of the Rinaldone groups.

In the Aegean this burial form became fairly common, and then only in two areas, during the later part of the Early Bronze Age. The earliest known example in the Aegean is a shaft with a single chamber at the bottom from the final Neolithic in the Athens Agora.[57] It can be dated to somewhere around 3000 BC in radiocarbon years, perhaps c. 3700 BC in calendar years. The form appears again in the Korakou culture (Early Helladic II) at Corinth,[58] but is first amply documented in the cemeteries at Manika in Euboia.[59] They are probably no earlier than 2000 BC in radiocarbon years, c. 2500 BC in calendar years. A little later a wide variety of rock-cut tombs is found at the site of Phylakopi in Melos, where they make their appearance during the time of the 'First City'.[60] Burial in rock-cut tombs was not in fact the dominant form in any major region of the Aegean at this time. In the Cyclades inhumation in cist graves was far more common, and this was one of the commonest forms in Mainland Greece also. In Crete, burial was collective, either in rectangular ossuaries, like those of Mochlos, or in the famous round tombs most common on the Mesara plain. They have at times been regarded as the starting-point for the whole custom of collective burial in built tombs, as seen in the west Mediterranean, and it is noteworthy that nothing similar is found in Italy.

Rock-cut tombs make their appearance in the West during the Neolithic period, and they are in fact known there very much earlier than in the Aegean. In Malta they occur in the Zebbug Culture around 3000 BC in radiocarbon years, c. 3700 BC in calendar years, and two southern Italian examples are earlier, and indeed Neolithic. Fonteviva on the Foggia plain[61] and the Pizzone site in Taranto must go back comfortably before 4000 BC in calendar years. A third Neolithic example at Serra d'Alto[62] should be approximately contemporary with the earliest Maltese examples. These Neolithic rock-cut tombs on the Italian mainland and some of the early Copper Age ones in Sicily were used for single or double burials ; collective burial, although found in natural caves at an earlier period, became associated with rock-cut tombs only rather later, possibly not till the 3rd millennium (calendar years). The Neolithic rock-cut tombs of Italy are the earliest known occurrences anywhere in the Mediterranean world, with the possible exception of Cyprus. It seems inescapable that the custom of burial in rock-cut tombs and indeed of collective burial as well, evolved in Italy quite independently.[63]

LITHIC INDUSTRY

One of the most striking components of the artefact assemblages of the Italian Copper Age is the flintwork, often with flat flaking (pressure flaking). This has sometimes been seen as an imported feature, but again the case merits further examination.

PRESSURE-FLAKED ARROWHEADS (figs 2-7)

Pressure-flaked flint arrowheads, usually bifacially worked, occur commonly in tombs of all groups, except Laterza, where they are found only rarely. The symmetrical tanged variety is by far the most common ; some have rudimentary barbs also, but well-developed barbs do not occur. Some shouldered, leaf-shaped, and hollow-based forms are found, but they are not common.

Pressure-flaked arrowheads or points are not, in fact, common in the Early Bronze Age of the Aegean. None has been found in Crete, or from the Early Cycladic cultures, and exceedingly few in Mainland Greece until the succeeding period, when they are almost invariably hollow-based.[64] Tanged forms are found at several sites in the Late Neolithic of the Cyclades, notably at Saliagos, Vouni, Mavrospilia, and Agrilia in the Cyclades[65] and at several Mainland sites, notably the Franchthi Cave. These contexts may be dated around 4000 BC in radiocarbon years. They are not found in Crete or western Anatolia. It seems possible that these tanged points of the Aegean Neolithic were used to tip fishing-spears rather than arrows. And certainly the form became very much less common during the 3rd millennium.

In Italy, by contrast, the Neolithic tradition in flint arrowheads continued uninterrupted into the Copper Age. They occur already in Middle Neolithic contexts in northern Italy (Chiozza culture) and in various later Neolithic groups (Lagozza, Ripoli, and Diana).

GEOMETRIC FLINTS (figs 2, 4 and 7)

Geometric flints, some microlithic, occur in Remedello, Gaudo, and Laterza contexts. Trapezes are most common, but triangles and crescents also occur. They are probably mounted as arrowheads and were perhaps used for hunting, while the bifacial ones were used in warfare.

They may represent an indigenous, ultimately Mesolithic, tradition of flint-working. Geometric flints are characteristic of some Neolithic groups in central and northern Italy, especially the Lagozza culture.

Geometric flints are not a significant feature of the Aegean Early Bronze Age, where blades were widely used, but without retouch. Geometric shapes have not been reported from the later Neolithic of the Aegean, and at Saliagos, where the industry has been studied in detail, they were not found.

DAGGERS (figs 2-7)

Flint daggers, like the arrowheads, are characteristic of all the Copper Age groups. They fall into two chief categories:

(*a*) The so-called 'stiloid' daggers made on long blades and worked on one face only. The working may consist of all-over pressure-flaking or a little marginal retouch only (fig. 4). These daggers never have a tang. They are limited in the main to the Gaudo region with a few strays in other areas.

(*b*) Bifacially pressure-flaked daggers. These occur in all groups and in a great variety of forms: leaf-shaped and shouldered types occur, but the majority are symmetrical with a central tang. The tang varies in shape and is sometimes flanked by lateral notches, which may imitate the rivet-holes of copper daggers.

Flint daggers, unlike the arrowheads, do not occur in Italy before the Copper Age, and it is generally held, probably rightly, that they were developed in response to the early use of metal daggers, while these were still rare and in short supply. Flint daggers simply do not occur in the Aegean. The nearest approach in flint to this form is seen there in the triangular flint 'spearheads' found at Late Neolithic Sesklo and Pyrgos in Thessaly.[66] They do not look like daggers, and there is no evidence that daggers were in use so early. The 'ovates' of Late Neolithic Saliagos[67] are the only other occurrence in the Aegean of pressure-flaked flint or obsidian larger than arrowheads. Indeed, apart from the very early industry at Çatal Hüyük and related sites in 7th- and 6th-millennium Anatolia, Egypt is the only other area where such flintwork is found.

The Italian flint daggers, especially those of the Remedello group, have been compared by Branigan[68] with Cretan copper daggers of the 'triangular type' (fig. 11, IIIb). One curious feature of some is the scalloped base, which is not seen on any Italian copper daggers, but is an Early Minoan feature. Certainly it does seem likely that the Italian flint daggers were inspired by prototypes in copper, and some of them do resemble local Italian forms. The possibility of Minoan prototypes in copper for some must seriously be considered. On the other hand, no Minoan copper daggers of this shape, with scalloped base, have been recognised in Italy, and this detail could simply be a local elaboration in flint of the simple dagger evolved locally. The resemblance in shape exists, but so far is only between flint forms in Italy and copper ones in Crete.

GROUND STONE (figs 2, 3, 5-7)

Simple ground stone axes occur in tombs of all groups except Gaudo. In addition, perforated stone tools occur in several of the groups: battle-axes in the Rinaldone group only, maceheads in the Conelle–Ortucchio and Rinaldone groups and axe-hammers in the same two groups, as well as in one cemetery in the Remedello area (Cumarola) and possibly also at Laterza (fig. 2, 3 and 5). Of these, only the true battle-axes are innovations in the Copper Age; axe-hammers and maceheads occur in several Neolithic groups in the peninsula, especially in the Ripoli culture.

Once again they are much more at home in Italy than in the Aegean, where perforated stone tools are not a common feature of the Early Bronze Age. They make their appearance in north Greece at the beginning of the period, in Phase v at Sitagroi and in Thessaly,[69] as well as at Troy and neighbouring sites. It seems likely that the idea was introduced to the north Aegean from the Balkans, where the bow drill was in use a millennium earlier in the Chalcolithic Gumelnitsa culture. It should be noted that the bow drill may have been in use at Neolithic Knossos, since perforated maceheads are found already in stratum VI,[70] but perforated stone tools are not common in Early Minoan Crete.

OTHER EVIDENCE

Several other classes of evidence, beyond that of metal objects, to be discussed in the next section, have been cited at different times, as indicating significant influence from the Aegean. These will also briefly be considered before the much more forceful and specific arguments relating to metallurgy are discussed.

POTTERY (figs 3 and 4)

A number of general forms in Italy have been compared with east Mediterranean shapes, notably single-handled cups (fig. 1, 2, 4) bottles (fig. 3, 5), and 'askoi' (fig. 4). Many of the resemblances are so general as to be altogether lacking in force. There are, for example, several forms of one-handled cup in the Early Bronze Age Aegean, one of them being of widespread distribution,[71] but this is not a common form in Italy. It has been suggested that the appearance of the handled cup in the Aegean, and of closed shapes suitable for containing liquids (such as the jug and 'duck vase') was related to the production of olive oil and wine which may have developed at this time. Analogous functional explanations could perhaps be propounded for the new range of handled shapes in the Italian Copper Age.

One jug, dark and burnished, from Gioia del Colle (fig. 8*d*) has been likened to pottery of the Early Bronze Age of Cyprus. It must be admitted that analogous forms are found in Cyprus,[72] where there is a wide range of jug shapes in Red Polished Ware.[73] Characterisation study of the clay and filler might determine whether this find is in fact an import: on present evidence the possibility cannot be excluded.

The same cannot, however, be said for some of the other ceramic finds which have been so described. The 'askoi' of the Gaudo culture, for instance, are not identical with those of the Korakou culture ('Early Helladic II') and do not at all resemble the 'duck vases' of the Cyclades. Multiple vessels in the Gaudo culture (fig. 4) do compare in form with Aegean products, and for this specific shape the possibility of eastern inspiration cannot be excluded.

In general a measure of continuity can be traced between the ceramic products of the Italian Copper Age and the preceding local Neolithic, for instance in the cup and bottle forms in the Ripoli and other painted ware groups. Dark burnished wares and simple bowl forms occur in the Lagozza culture, and impressed and studded decoration like those of the Copper Age

Laterza group occur in south-east Italian Neolithic wares. Continuity may in fact be greater than is at present apparent, since most of the Copper Age pottery known to us comes from funerary contexts, while that of the Neolithic is mainly domestic.

The Aegean resemblances of the pottery of Sicily and the Aeolian Islands were considered by Bernabò Brea,[74] who stressed the significance of the eastern Aegean. Cavalier[75] has studied the matter in detail. She comments on similar ceramic forms in the Diana culture of Lipari and in finds from Late Neolithic Greek sites, especially Orchomenos. The succeeding Piano Conte culture lacks such points of comparison, but she sees resemblances for its Sicilian contemporary, the Serraferlichio culture, in the Late Neolithic of Greece. Many of these similarities are very generalised, but it must be admitted that they are chronologically much more acceptable than the comparisons formerly suggested between the Diana culture and the Aegean Early Bronze Age—and they were made before radiocarbon dating established the revised chronology, with which they are in good accord.

It is not until the Piano Quartara culture of the Lipari Copper Age, and its Sicilian contemporaries, Conca d'Oro, Chiusazza, and Malpasso, that Cavalier discerns more numerous points of similarity, this time with the Early Bronze Age cultures of the eastern Aegean. Comparison is made with the bowls, lugged jars, and cups of Late Neolithic Tigani in Samos, and the one-handled cups and tunnel lugs of Poliochni. Some of the resemblances are suggestive, and in the presence of some indications of undoubted contact would well be taken as supporting evidence. But these direct indications are lacking and the ceramic similarities alone are not conclusive.

Again, in the succeeding Capo Graziano culture of the Lipari Early Bronze Age she discerns many points of similarity with Middle Helladic and the Tiryns culture ('Early Helladic III') of Greece—similarities shared with the Tarxien cemetery culture of Malta and to some extent with the Castelluccio culture of Sicily. Here analogies of shape and decoration are closer, and supported by the evidence of the bossed bone plaques, so that occasional contacts with the western Peloponnese—across the Ionian Sea—do seem indicated.

Judgement in all of this depends upon the personal and rather subjective assessment of similarities. We are inclined to accept the case for the Capo Graziano culture, at the end of the Aegean Early Bronze Age, while looking more sceptically at the supposed links with the eastern Aegean during the preceding Piano Quartera culture. No doubt there were occasional contacts across the Adriatic Sea from early Neolithic times, and they may occasionally have been reflected in ceramic innovations. Their influence was, however, very limited until the Capo Graziano, Castelluccio, and Tarxien cemetery cultures, and here the mechanism is hard to determine. It need have been nothing more than occasional and peaceful trade with the west Peloponnese, heralding the more systematic and commercial trading contacts of the later Bronze Age.

BONEWORK (fig. 8)

The bossed bone plaque from Altamura (fig. 8*e*) has already been discussed. It does indeed resemble other west Mediterranean and Aegean examples and may well date from a late phase of the Copper Age.

Two crutch-headed pins of bone from Gaudo have sometimes been suggested as imports. They are c. 10 cm long, and very similar in form to the silver one from Remedello (fig. 8*h*). They are decorated with grooves around the head and the upper part of the stem. Whatever the occurrences of the crutch-headed pin in central and eastern Europe, however, it is not seen in the Aegean Early Bronze Age. Nor is there any reason to see Aegean influence among the simple beads and pendants of bone and shell which occur in most Italian Copper Age groups, or in the bone fish-hook from Laterza (fig. 7).

OTHER INDICATIONS

In addition to the instances discussed above, the existence of bastioned settlements in the Sicilian Bronze Age has excited comment. There is an example from the Castelluccio culture at Mellili, and one of the Thapsos culture at Thapsos itself. The Thapsos culture, of course, is of a later period, when Mycenaean trading contacts are well documented by finds of Aegean pottery and metalwork. But even at this late time the site need not be regarded as a Mycenaean colony, and the existence of fortifications is to be interpreted in local terms. This argument applies with even greater force to the Castelluccio culture, in just the same manner as to the Copper Age of Iberia.[76]

Metallurgy

The most frequently quoted arguments for Aegean influences upon Italy have always related to metallurgy. Both the inception of metallurgy in Italy, and the origin of many of the forms are frequently traced back to the east Mediterranean. The case, however, is very far from conclusive, and it is perfectly possible that metallurgical skills reached Italy from the Balkans, where they were understood earlier than in the Aegean, or even developed locally and independently.

The principal arguments relate to the metallurgical techniques of smelting and casting copper, and to the daggers, of which Italy has a considerable variety. They of course raise general issues as to what precisely constitutes a 'parallel', and under what circumstances an implication of outside origin for innovations should be accepted. These questions have never satisfactorily been answered: the approach here is to prefer scepticism to ready acceptance, and to require cogent indications of contact.

Before discussing individual metal types, and then the origin of the technological processes themselves, it is necessary to consider the evidence put forward, most effectively by Branigan, for the presence in Early Minoan Crete of actual metal imports from Italy. This forms perhaps the most forcefully argued element in his case for Minoan influences on the west Mediterranean during the Aegean Early Bronze Age.[77] The others are similarities of the Italian flint daggers with those of Minoan Crete—discussed above—and similarities of the Italian copper daggers with those of Crete. The arguments for the last are not strong: as Branigan remarks[78]: 'Simple dagger types are so basic in design that we should not perhaps place too much emphasis on Aegean and Italian affinities in this field.' His conclusion[79] that 'there are no clear examples of Aegean daggers found in Italy' makes this suggestion of Italian daggers in Crete all the more central to the case for influential contacts between the two areas. It is, indeed, crucial to the view[80] that 'Crete was at this time acting, unconsciously, as a metallurgical intermediary between the eastern and western Mediterranean', and requires close examination.

This theory of Crete as intermediary between east and west was first adumbrated in an earlier article, resting in part on arguments about the use in Crete of obsidian from Lipari which were discussed above. He wrote[81]: 'It is thus clear that Crete was importing "Liparite" and that this stone was being used in the manufacture of bowls of Egyptian form. . . . With the island of Crete established as the intermediate stage, the transference of the pottery type in question becomes quite understandable.'

The demonstration, subsequent to the writing of that article, that the spotted obsidian in Crete came not from Lipari but from an Aegean source, weakened one of its central arguments, and the second, that ceramic influences from Egypt reached Lipari at the time of the Diana culture, conflicts with the calibrated radiocarbon dating evidence, presented above, which now puts the Diana culture of Lipari far earlier than the Fifth Dynasty of Egypt.

In the following year Branigan identified the three silver daggers from Koumasa in Crete as Italian imports, together with a very battered copper dagger from Agios Onouphrios, which was similar in form to two of the Koumasa silver ones and a triangular copper dagger from Mochlos tomb XIX.[82] One of the three Koumasa silver daggers (no. 214) is of a form widely known in Crete, with its rounded heel, concave edges, and four rivets, belonging to Branigan's Minoan Class III. In fact in his latest article on the subject[83] Branigan no longer includes this dagger in his list of Italian imports and the Mochlos triangular copper dagger receives no mention either. This leaves three daggers regarded as imports from Italy—two silver ones from Koumasa (no. 212 and 213) and the copper one from Agios Onouphrios—and these will be considered here. Branigan's arguments were originally based on both the typology of the daggers and the material used, but in his latest article only the typological arguments are employed.[84] Branigan claims that the three daggers have features alien to the Aegean tradition of metalworking in their proportions, riveting systems, and profiles and that in these respects they find parallels in a group of Italian daggers (see below, type A 2). In their proportions they are broader and shorter than Minoan daggers of the same general kind. They appear to have a four-square system of rivets, but Branigan argues convincingly that this arrangement was secondary and that the two Koumasa silver daggers originally had a straight line of four rivets at the base like the Italian examples and that rivets were added further down the blades when some of the original ones had broken. In their profiles they have low triangular midribs, like some of the Italian examples. These typological arguments carry some weight, but against them it can be argued that the Italian daggers do not provide *very* close parallels, and in any case daggers of this type are not very common in Italy: there are no more than six or seven known examples (and these include some daggers with only three rivets), compared to the three from Crete.

The argument about the material employed bears much less weight. There are no silver daggers from Italy and indeed very few silver objects of any kind. By contrast there are four silver daggers from Crete—the three from Koumasa and another found recently at Galana Kharakia 'of typical Minoan shape and proportions'[85]—and silver was quite widely used also for vessels and ornaments.[86] Of all these silver objects, Branigan now claims only two of the Koumasa daggers as imports from Italy.

An important element of the import theory was originally the assumption that silver was imported into Crete from the West because it was not thought to be available in the Aegean[87]:

> The Aegeans were interested in the metal deposits of the west Mediterranean. While only copper was needed Crete might have been able to supply its own needs and even those of the Cyclades as well. But it certainly could not supply tin or silver. The western Mediterranean could, and apparently did. . . . As well as providing us with the reason for Aegean contacts with the western Mediterranean, the use of silver and tin by Aegean metallurgists also provides us of course with the final proof that such contacts existed. The tin and silver deposits of Spain, Sardinia and Italy are the cause, and the Aegean influences on Italian metal-working the effect, of a process which seems to have developed towards the end of the 3rd millennium BC.

These arguments concerning silver are now open to question. For while silver is available in Spain and Italy, it was plentiful also in the Cycladic islands where lead ores are of frequent occurrence.[88] Indeed the small island of Kimolos near Melos was actually known as Argentière in Medieval times on account of these resources. There is ample evidence that these Cycladic sources were worked in the Early Bronze Age. Branigan in his recent and very useful article[89] 'Silver and Lead in Prepalatial Crete' now suggests the Minoans were obtaining their silver from the Cyclades, and advances the possibility that there were local sources of lead, and hence of silver, in Crete itself. In view of the well-documented availability of silver in the Aegean, the use of the material itself can any longer be taken as an indication of foreign origin.

The question of these silver daggers has been argued at some length, since they are, if their Italian origin is accepted, the last remaining categorical indication of direct contact between the two areas. Until the realisation was present that silver of local origin was being extensively used in the Aegean the argument by material carried some weight. It was this very feature which in the first place suggested a foreign origin since there are no exact parallels for these objects in Italy. Branigan himself has shown that one of the three is a Minoan form, and that the closest parallel in copper for the other two comes from Crete. And it is to him that we owe our knowledge of the fourth silver dagger recently discovered in Crete, which is accepted as of Cretan manufacture. The evidence which once sustained the theory of an Italian origin for them has disappeared. It has now become clear, as the Galania Kharakia find documents, that silver daggers *were* being made in Crete, although they are not known elsewhere in the Aegean or the west Mediterranean. Two of the four now known are of typically Minoan forms. The other two are different in detail from other Minoan daggers, with the exception of the Aghios Onouphrios example. It is perfectly possible that these minor differences arise through technological factors, since the hot- and cold-working properties of silver differ from those of copper and bronze. They are a further testimony to the skill of the Minoan smiths, who were at the same time making in silver both metal vessels and a considerable range of personal adornments.

If the silver daggers of Koumasa be set aside there still remain several points of similarity between the metal forms of Copper Age Italy and those of the east Mediterranean. These metal forms will now be considered.

Copper Forms

AXES (figs 2, 3, 5)

Tombs of the Remedello and Rinaldone groups and the tomb at Monsanvito in the Conelle–Ortucchio zone have yielded flat copper axes; similar axes occur as surface finds in southern Italy, but the Gaudo and Laterza people did not put them into tombs (stone axes are rare as grave goods in this area too). Most of the axes are simple and flat, but a few of the Rinaldone examples have hammered-up edges, heralding the low-flanged axes of the Early Bronze Age.

Flat axes of copper are a common feature of the early metallurgy of most areas of Europe. They are fairly common in the Cyclades, but astonishingly none at all are known from Early Minoan Crete, although there was a single find from the Late Neolithic level at Knossos. There is no reason to see Aegean influence in the Italian finds, and hammered-up edges are not seen in the Aegean Early Bronze Age.

DAGGERS AND HALBERD BLADES (fig. 10)

The variety of dagger and halberd blades in use in Italy during the Copper Age was quite considerable. For the purpose of this discussion they are divided into two series: blades with midribs and blades without midribs.

A. *Blades with Midribs*

A 1. Tanged Daggers: Barfield [90] type F. These usually have a broad base, concave or straight sides, a tang with a single rivet, and a pronounced midrib on both faces. They are characteristic of the Remedello group, but examples also occur in the caves at Vecchiano and Monte Bradoni in the Rinaldone area and as far south as Mirabella Eclano in the Gaudo area. Barfield believes that some of these may have been hafted as halberds.

The feature of a single narrow tang with a single rivet-hole is the most striking one of these Remedello daggers. It is not known in the Aegean. Branigan has pointed out [91] that possible prototypes for the form exist at Byblos on the Levant coast of Syria, but they are narrower and not so clearly triangular in shape. The possibility of contact, perhaps through Crete, as Branigan argues, must certainly be considered. But the similarities are very general.

A 2. Triangular blades with a straight or slightly curved heel with three or four rivets arranged in a straight line or a slight arc and a narrow midrib: Barfield [92] type E and a few of type C. The sides may be straight, slightly concave, or slightly convex. Some of these blades may have been mounted as halberds. There are examples from two or three Remedello sites, one in the Rinaldone area, and three in the Gaudo group.

Parallels are often quoted for these daggers in contexts of Early Minoan

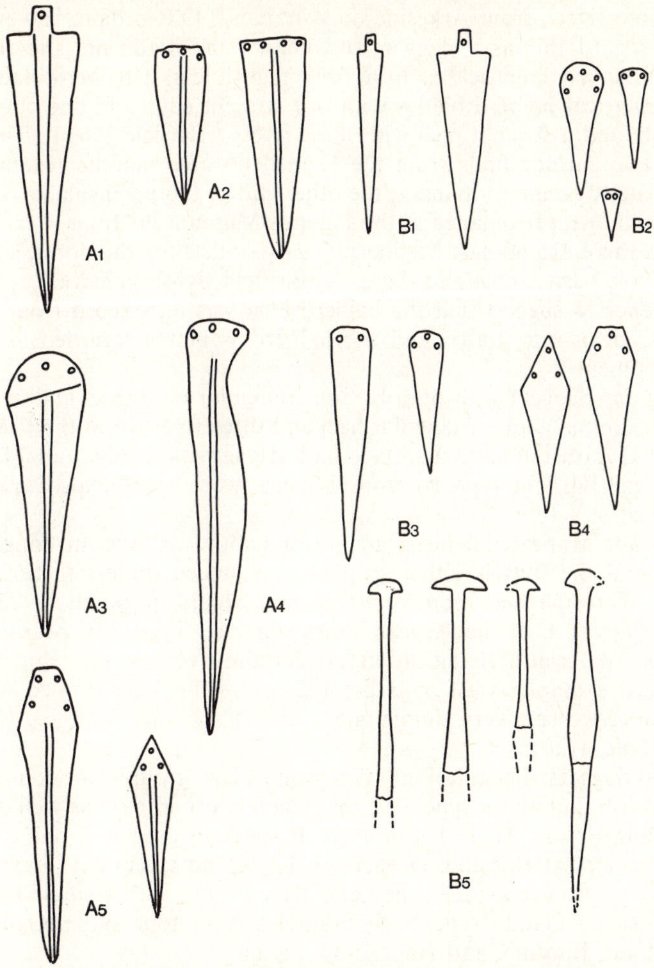

Figure 10. Italian Copper Age dagger types. Scale approx 1:6.

II, and the Keros–Syros and Korakou (E.H. II) cultures. The shape is very simple, and they do compare approximately with the Cycladic type IV (fig. 11). But the line of rivets along the base, sometimes three, but more often four, is an Italian feature. There is thus no real similarity at a detailed level.

A 3. Triangular blades with rounded heel, three large rivets, and a marked midrib. Barfield type C. This form, with its markedly rounded heel (in contrast to the slightly curving heel of some examples of type A 2), is an exclusively Rinaldone type. There are only two certain examples, one from Rinaldone tomb 3 and one from Pomarance; the Pomarance blade was almost certainly mounted as a halberd.

There are no good Aegean parallels for this form. Moreover the practice of mounting the dagger horizontally to form a halberd is not an Aegean practice. Only one dagger from the Aegean has been regarded as a halberd blade by some authorities, including Montelius and Childe.[93] It is a short blade with three rivets, from Arkesine on Amorgos.[94] O'Riordain, however, preferred to regard this as a dagger, and neither the blade nor the rivet arrangement is so asymmetrical as to make it plausible as a halberd blade.

A 4. Asymmetrical halberd blades with one straight edge and one curved one, a mid-rib, and a straight heel with three rivets: Barfield type G. There are possibly two surface finds from the Remedello area, another example from a tomb at Roggiano Gravina at the other end of the peninsula, and an example of unknown provenance in the Pigorini Museum in Rome.

Once again there are no east Mediterranean parallels for this form, since no halberds have been recognised there. As Barfield rightly remarks[95]: 'We have no evidence to suggest that the halberd idea was introduced from the East Mediterranean into Italy', and the halberd is better regarded as an Italian development.

A 5. Triangular daggers with midribs and triangular or trapezoidal heels. There is one example with a triangular heel and three rivets from the Rinaldone tomb of Guardistallo and a surface find of one with a trapezoidal heel and four rivets (Barfield type D) from Fojano near Arezzo, also in the Rinaldone area.

Triangular and trapezoidal heels are not a feature of Aegean daggers, where in general the butt is either straight or rounded, unless there is a distinct tang. Were the butt more rounded there would be points of comparison with type IV b of the Aegean series (fig. 11). Type 8 of Maxwell-Hyslop's Western Asiatic classification[96] is certainly very similar, but she does not record examples west of Babylonia before the Late Bronze Age. The form is in any case a very simple one.

B. *Blades without Midribs*

B 1. Tanged daggers. These fall into two groups. One group is the counterpart of the midrib daggers of type A 1; these have a broad base as well as a tang with a single rivet. There is one from Remedello itself and one from the Gaudo cemetery at Buccino. Daggers of the second group are long and slender with a very narrow base; they also have a tang with a single rivet. It is an exclusively Gaudo type, with examples from four sites: Gaudo, Mirabella Eclano, Buccino, and Roggiano Gravina.

The same remarks apply to this form as to form A 1, as concerns the possibility of east Mediterranean parallels. None in the Aegean are convincing, but a case could be made out for Syrian influences once again, where the narrow form is seen (Maxwell-Hyslop type 27).

There is also a single example of a typical 'West European' tanged dagger (fig. 2), found in association with beakers at Santa Cristina in the Remedello area.

The origin of the 'West European' or 'Beaker' dagger is linked with that of the Beakers themselves. As the designation 'West European' hints, an Iberian origin is often considered likely, but more recently east-central Europe has again seemed a more plausible place of origin, in Hungary or the Vučedol culture. A mould from the Baden culture site of Sarvas[97] produced daggers with a marked although narrow tang. Following the trail further south there is a find similar to the Beaker daggers, and possibly earlier, from Ezero in Bulgaria,[98] and in the Aegean the tanged form without rivet-holes occurs in Euboia.[99] The form is not at home in the Aegean, but is common

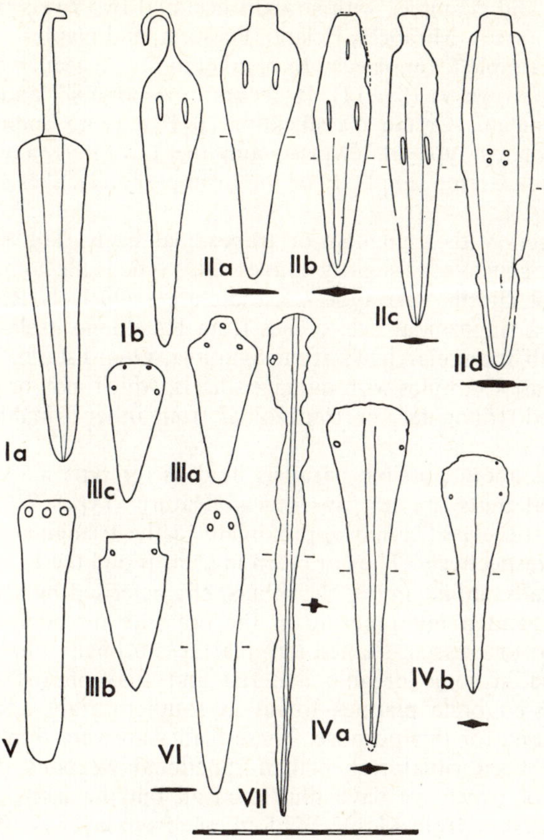

Figure 11. Aegean Early Bronze Age dagger types. Scale 1:5.

in Anatolia, forming type 2a of Stronach's classification.[100]

None of this elaborate chasing of parallels is necessary in discussing the Santa Cristina dagger: no doubt its ultimate ancestry is the same as that of the Beakers found with it.

B 2. Small triangular knife-daggers with concave sides, rounded heels, and two, three, or five rivets. Examples come mainly from the Rinaldone area, but there is one from Remedello itself and three from the Laterza area; there are also the well-known two from the Castelluccio culture cemetery at Monteracello in south-east Sicily. The last five examples all have two rivets.

Short, round-heeled daggers of this kind are seen in the Aegean, examples coming from Aghia Marina in mainland Greece and Chalandriani in Syros, as well as the example from Arkesine in Amorgos discussed in connection with type A 4. The Minoan short daggers, however, generally have flat, concave, or scalloped heels, and only Branigan's type V is convex, although not rounded. This is not a Near Eastern form.

B 3. Narrow triangular blades with straight sides. There are examples with slightly rounded heel and three rivets from Remedello and from Murgia

Timone (Laterza area) and examples with straight heel and two rivets from three sites in the Gaudo area: Mirabella Eclano, Paestum, and Naples.

This dagger, with its simple form, is easy to parallel in the Aegean, where its closest counterpart is type VI (fig. 11). It occurs in Amorgos[101] and resembles type I of Branigan's Cretan classification. It is a more common form in Anatolia (Stronach type 6), Cyprus, and the Levant (Maxwell-Hyslop type 22), but the extreme simplicity of the form perhaps makes such a derivation unnecessary.

B 4. Triangular daggers with triangular or trapezoidal heels. The sides may be straight, slightly concave, or slightly convex. This type is the counterpart of type A 5 without midrib. Like type A 5, these are exclusively Rinaldone forms. One with a trapezoidal heel comes from Rinaldone itself and there are examples with triangular heels from Sgurgola, Guardistallo, and Ponte S. Pietro. There are examples with damaged heels, which may originally have been rounded, triangular, or trapezoidal from other Rinaldone sites.

Analogous comments about possible parallels hold as for type A 5. Triangular and trapezoidal butts are not an Aegean feature. Types 21 and 23 of the Western Asiatic classification approximate to the triangular and trapezoidal butt-forms respectively. They are seen in Cyprus and the Levant.

B 5. This form is totally unlike any of the others, characterised by a very narrow tapering blade and a hilt tapering in the opposite direction and ending in a semicircular or crescent-shaped terminal. It is probably that the metal hilt was encased in some organic material and Biancofiore[102] has suggested that the bossed bone plaques found in southern Italy and in Sicily may have been used for this purpose. These blades are very thin and fragile and may have been ritual rather than functional weapons. Five examples are known (of which we have illustrated all but the last): two from Tomb 3 at Laterza, one from Monte Bradoni, one from layer IV upper of Grotto Chiusazza in eastern Sicily (in a Copper Age deposit immediately underlying a Castelluccio culture level), and a fifth in a private collection in Sicily.[103]

No daggers at all resembling these have been seen in the Aegean Early Bronze Age. But as Biancofiore points out,[104] the form resembles West Asiatic type 31 described by Maxwell-Hyslop.[105] In Anatolia there are no close parallels,[106] but flange-hilted daggers with crescent-shaped pommel do occur in the Levant from about 1800 BC.

Other Copper Forms

AWLS

These occur in the Remedello, Rinaldone, and Gaudo areas; they are always square in section. Quadrangular awls are common in the Early Bronze Age Aegean, as in many other areas of early metal-working.

RAZORS/SCRAPERS

The tombs at Laterza yielded fragments of ten sub-rectangular copper blades, each with two or three rivets along one edge and the other three sides all being probable cutting edges. Biancofiore[107] compared them to the 'women's knives' of Eskimo cultures. These blades are unique in Italy, although blades with transverse edges only are known from some of the

Castelluccio culture cemeteries in south-east Sicily, such as Monteracello and Mellili, where they are interpreted as razors. The Laterza tools might have been razors or alternatively kitchen tools such as scrapers. Razors are found in Crete,[108] but they do not resemble these objects, for the operative edges are not transverse.

ORNAMENTS

Copper ornaments are rare in all groups. A penannular ring and some buttons were found at Remedello ; two rings of unknown form in a Macchia a Mare tomb at Monte Pucci and a presumably ornamental fragment (fig. 7) from the Laterza tomb at Gioia del Colle. Unidentifiable copper fragments from other tombs may have come from ornaments. Naturally copper ornaments are found in the Aegean, especially pins, but they do not very strikingly resemble those of Italy.

SILVER (fig. 8a, b)

Despite the arguments discussed earlier in connection with the Koumasa silver daggers, silver objects are in fact rare in Italy. Two silver ornaments were found in tombs of the Remedello group and two silver beads at Gaudo ; a bracelet of the same metal was allegedly found in the original wartime excavations at Gaudo, but is now missing. No other silver objects are known from peninsular Italian Copper Age sites, although one or two pieces occur in the presumably contemporary Ozieri culture of Sardinia. Sources of silver (mostly from the lead ore galena) are available in Tuscany in the same area as the copper ores. Indeed one hill in this area, very near the Rinaldone site of Punta degli Stretti, is called Monte Argentario. No Rinaldone sites have yielded silver objects, but it is none the less possible that these sources of silver were exploited during the Copper Age. However, the Italian silver objects are sometimes thought to be of east Mediterranean origin. The Sardinian objects are probably of local silver (available in the south-west of the island).

The pectoral from Villafranca (fig. 8*a*) has been compared by Acanfora[109] with diadems from the El Argar culture of Spain. Branigan has made comparison with the gold metalwork of Crete and the two silver diadems from the Cyclades.[110] The only point of similarity, however, is the decoration with repoussé dots, which is nothing like the Syros silver diadem. The silver diadem from Dokathismata in Amorgos has openwork decoration.

The crutch-headed pin from Remedello (fig. 8*b*) has been compared by Acanfora[111] to pins in copper or bronze from the Bohemian Bronze Age. Whatever the validity of such comparisons, there is certainly nothing like it from the Aegean.

Two fragmentary cylindrical beads, made of silver wire, were reported from Gaudo. This is a simple type, yet despite this lacks Aegean parallels. In the Aegean the silver beads are chiefly of sheet metal.

ANTIMONY (fig. 8c)

Three V-bored conical buttons found in the funerary cave of Monte Bradoni in the Rinaldone area were originally thought to be made of tin, but on analysis proved to be of almost pure antimony.[112] Cambi also claims that some object or objects from the Ponte S. Pietro tombs, also of the Rinaldone group, are made of antimony, but he does not say what these are. Antimony is apparently available locally in the Rinaldone area. No objects of this metal are known from the Aegean, and it is exceedingly rare in the metallic state both in Egypt and the Near East.[113]

This summary survey of the principal metal types serves as a starting-point for a consideration of the status of early Italian metallurgy in general.

The Origins of Italian Metallurgy

One of the earliest indications of copper metallurgy in Italy is afforded by a find of copper slag from a level of the Diana culture on the Lipari acropolis.[114] The date in radiocarbon years is c. 3000 BC, equivalent to around 3700 BC in calendar years. Without specialist examination, however, it cannot be taken as proof of the smelting of copper from its ores ; the casting of native copper is a distinct possibility. Copper objects are found also on Neolithic sites in north and central Italy. A small fragment of copper was found already in levels of the Chiozza (Square Mouth Pottery) culture at Rivoli,[115] while three copper axes were found at Bocca Lorenza from levels of the same period.[116] These may be the earliest metal finds in Italy as a whole and it is perhaps significant that they lie north of the Po. Copper was almost certainly used in the north in the succeeding Lagozza period, to which may perhaps be ascribed a hoard of copper axes from Isolino,[117] and copper has been found in levels with Lagozza connections at Attigio near Ancona[118] and at Santa Maria in Selva.[119] The level in question at this site reputedly yielded a radiocarbon date (unfortunately not published by the laboratory) of c. 2600 BC, i.e. c. 3350 BC in calendar years, which is a little later that the Diana culture of Lipari. There are undated but very probable Neolithic finds also from Quinzano, Chiozza, Campegine, and Pescale,[120] from Grotta del Leone at Agnano,[121] and from sites in the valley of the Vibrata.[122]

All these finds are either certainly or probably prior to the Copper Age of Italy itself. Indeed it is clearly significant that there are at present at least as many copper finds from the later Neolithic of Italy as from the Aegean. The repertoire of finds prior to 3000 BC in calendar years is there equally scanty: an axe from Knossos, a pair of axes and a gold pendant from Late Neolithic Sesklo, a few pieces from Kephala in Kea, and a series of objects from Sitagroi in Macedonia—the earliest copper finds yet made in the Aegean.[123] There is consequently no very strong case to be made for an Aegean origin of the use of copper in Italy.

If the casting of copper was a technology which came to Italy from outside, the most likely source for it is the Balkans. For copper metallurgy was practised there at a much earlier date than in the Aegean.[124] The techniques of casting and perhaps smelting copper could have been learnt by the inhabitants of north Italy from their neighbours across the Adriatic Sea or north of the Alps. Two less likely places of origin could have been Iberia, where an early independent focus of metallurgy may be suspected although not yet demonstrated, and south-west Greece. No doubt there were contacts across the southern Adriatic, but there is little evidence that copper was cast or indeed worked at all in the western Peloponnese at this early time.

Finally, the possibility must be faced that the technique of casting copper (and perhaps even of smelting it) was independently invented in peninsular Italy. This can only be a suggestion, for there is no direct evidence to support it at present. But in view of the apparently independent invention of these techniques in the Balkans, such a possibility should not be excluded in a land so rich in ores (and very possibly in native copper) as Italy.

Whatever the explanation, copper was in use in Italy well before the inception of the 'Copper Age', so that any suggestion that it came about through east Mediterranean influences at that time cannot be accepted. The possibility remains, however, that its course of development during the Copper Age was substantially affected by such influences and contacts, and the technique of smelting could have been learnt from overseas.

Copper objects, some of them undoubtedly cast, have been found in tombs of all the culture groups of the period. They are most common in the Rinaldone area where burials have yielded more than sixty metal objects. Stray finds and hoards of copper objects are concentrated in the same region, where the principal copper ores of the peninsula occur, especially in the Monte Amiata and Colline Metallifere regions.

Remedello tombs have yielded more than thirty copper objects, and it is possible that some of the metal used in the north was imported from central Europe. The Gaudo tombs, of which fewer are known, have yielded twenty-one copper objects, and the Laterza group about fifteen, mostly from Laterza itself. The few known tombs in the Macchia a Mare and Conelle-Ortucchio areas have yielded only one or two objects in each.

Technologically the objects of the period are simple. Even the two-piece mould may not have been in use, for the midribs of the daggers could have been produced by hammering up. Nor is it certain the copper was yet smelted from its ores, rather than found in its native form and melted for casting. Metal analyses, moreover, show that tin was not used: there are no bronzes. This indeed is a telling argument against the supposed export of tin from Italy at this time to the Aegean. Had tin been systematically exploited in Italy for export it is hardly conceivable that it would not have been used for at least some local bronzes also. The same argument holds for Iberia, for despite some statements to the contrary there is no evidence for the use of tin there in pre-Beaker times. It is difficult to see how the theory of an early and flourishing tin trade between the Aegean and the west Mediterranean during the Italian and Iberian Copper Ages can be sustained in the face of such persuasive negative evidence. It has been argued elsewhere[125] that the puzzling question of the origin of the Aegean tin is likely to be solved in western Anatolia.

The early literature made much of the three buttons from Monte Bradoni which had been supposed to be of tin. This was taken as significant evidence for its exploitation and no doubt trade in it. The demonstration that they are of antimony[126] destroys this argument. Antimony is sometimes found in the native state, and it seems likely that these buttons were made of native antimony.

From the technological point of view the development of copper working during the Copper Age could have been an entirely local one. But this need not exclude the possibility that a number of innovations at the time had an overseas inspiration. This may be the case for the silver crutch-headed pin (perhaps an east-central European form).

The dagger was the most important new type, and its inspiration could have come from central Europe, from the Aegean, or even from the west if we think in terms of Beaker inspiration, which is perhaps unlikely. On the other hand, the broad, short daggers of the Remedello culture are a notable local feature which does not closely resemble those north of the Alps or in the Aegean. They are made, moreover, exclusively of copper, unlike the daggers from most other regions, where tin bronze is also found. (There are just a few arsenic bronzes in Italy at this time). Once again the possibility of a local invention should at least be contemplated.

Approximate Aegean parallels can, of course, be found for the tangless types with flat or rounded heels, forms A 2 and B 2. Levantine daggers, unlike those of the Aegean, generally have tangs or at least a fairly long and narrowing butt. Those of the Italian series which take such form, namely types A 1, A 5, B 1, and B 4, thus naturally resemble various individuals of the wide range of Levantine forms. But, supposing there were an entirely independent evolution of the dagger in the two regions, it is difficult to see how some such general analogies could be avoided. The same of course applies to type B 3, for which parallels can be found in both the Aegean and the Levant. But this simple, flat, narrow dagger, with short butt and two or three rivets, is so uncomplicated a form that such parallels entirely lack force. Only type B 5, with its crescentic pommel, stands apart from the rest of the Italian dagger series, and the Syrian parallels seem more promising, although they are rather late.

In general, however, the Italian copper daggers are varied, yet of the utmost simplicity. In such circumstances there certainly exist similarities with daggers in other regions, as we have seen. It is both possible and reasonable to see in such similarities corroboration for the view that the areas were in contact with each other. But it seems equally possible to dismiss all of them as fortuitous, and arising quite independently in the course of the evolution of metalworking in each area. The midribs and the various rivet arrangements must in any case be explained essentially in functional terms: they are not simply reflections of fashion, but solutions to the real problem of making blades strong and hafting them securely.

It is concluded, then, that a perfectly plausible case could be made for the independent invention of metallurgy in Italy—first hot working, then casting, then smelting—and its local evolution there to produce all the metal types seen in the Copper Age. Yet at the same time it is perfectly possible that the techniques of casting and smelting were learnt from neighbouring lands to the east and north. The dagger itself may first have been manufactured in Italy as a result of such contacts, and they may also have suggested to the local smiths some of the dagger forms which they produced. Between these two possibilities it is difficult to choose at the moment. On balance we prefer the first alternative. But in any case the metal industry of Copper Age Italy was something which evolved locally: it was not the work either of colonists or of immigrants.

Conclusions

A number of compelling arguments lead us to reject the widely held view that the development of the Italian Copper Age came about as a result of the arrival of immigrants or 'colonists' in Italy. In the first place there is no region in the Aegean, or indeed anywhere else, where the whole cultural complex of any of the Italian Copper Age groups can find a parallel. Many of the features of the Italian Copper Age, including all the tomb types, the practice of copper metallurgy, the flintwork, the ground stone, and many of the pottery forms are indeed seen in Neolithic contexts in the peninsula itself.

Many of the Copper Age features which do appear to be innovations—flat copper axes, stone battle-axes, and flint daggers for example—are unlikely to be of Aegean inspiration. And, as we have seen, there are no certain imports from the Aegean to the west Mediterranean before the Middle Helladic period around 2000 BC and very few before c. 1600 BC. All the objects of earlier date, considered by some to show Aegean influence, are probably of local manufacture. The craniometric evidence sometimes cited in support of migrationist views[127] must certainly be disregarded, in view of the notorious difficulty in interpreting such data and the small size of samples from both the Copper Age and the preceding Neolithic. Whatever conclusions we may reach about the degree of Aegean influence in Italy at this period, we must reject the notion that the Italian Copper Age was introduced lock, stock, and barrel by immigrants from the east.

It is in investigating the extent of peaceful contacts between Italy and the east Mediterranean, and assessing their influence, that difficulties of interpretation arise. On present evidence it would seem possible to deny that there was contact of any kind between Italy and the East before 2000 BC. Of course the first farmers in Italy used cereal crops and probably domestic animals which had an ultimately Near Eastern ancestry. But in this case the great increase in population density made possible by farming, and the consequent gradient of population density on the periphery of the expanding farming zone, offer a plausible mechanism. This is lacking for the 3rd millennium BC unless the notion of the western tin trade at that time be resuscitated.

On the other hand, some degree of localised contact and trade between regions should surely be envisaged, and no doubt the Straits of Otranto and perhaps the Ionian Sea were already occasionally being crossed. Some at least of the similarities observed—in the pottery perhaps, at least in the Capo Graziano culture, and in the bone plaques—could be explained in terms of casual and infrequent contacts of this kind.

None of this comes near to explaining *why* and *how* the cultures of the Italian Copper Age developed when and in the manner that they did. We believe that the answer to this question must be sought in local terms, and that the occasional contacts with the Aegean which no doubt took place were of no central importance to this process.

The answers will be found in terms of population, of developing farming practices and technology, and in the emerging social organisation and belief-systems which went with them. To attempt even an outline explanation for such processes in the Aegean in the 3rd millennium requires much space and a great deal more evidence than is yet available from prehistoric Italy.

Some elements which will one day figure in such an explanation are already apparent. Many of the characteristics of the Copper Age groups had already appeared during the Neolithic. These include all three chief burial types, many features of the technology of chipped and ground stone, and the use of copper itself. Moreover, the innovations of the Copper Age are very much what would be expected with a developing lithic and metal technology. Simple axe-, dagger-, and awl-forms could well have evolved locally, together with the working of silver and of native antimony. Flint daggers were the response of the flint-workers to the appearance of copper weapons.

The more significant social and economic developments—change in settlement pattern, an emphasis on warfare, and the incipient specialisation inherent in the practice of copper metallurgy—were not in any case such as would be transmitted by a process of 'diffusion' as a result of 'contact'. For while individual types—a dagger form, a pottery shape—can on occasion be so transmitted, the processes of growth in the developing culture system were not transferable by some such 'stimulus diffusion'. They can only be explained in terms of factors locally operating.

Several difficulties remain in constructing an alternative explanation. On the evidence available at present it is not possible to demonstrate the development of any specific Copper Age culture out of any given Neolithic one. Continuity of occupation is attested in some caves—e.g. Riparo la Romita at Asciano,[128] Grotta dei Piccioni at Bolognano,[129] Caverna dell'Erba at Avetrana,[130] and Grotta del Fico at Nardo[131]—and on a few open sites—e.g. Pescale di Modena[132] and La Starza, Ariano Irpino[133]—but it seems that these communities were the exception rather than the rule. The vast majority of Neolithic village sites were abandoned before the Copper Age. Those that remained in use were the home of peripheral and perhaps impoverished communities or, like La Starza, possessed of exceptionally good strategic positions.

It must be admitted that there is a lacuna in our knowledge of Italian prehistory between the latest dated Neolithic cultures and the Copper Age ones. In north and central Italy this falls between c. 2700 and 2300 BC (in radiocarbon years) and in the south between c. 2900 and 2300 BC. If the bristlecone pine calibration is employed this gap lengthens to a period of 500 years in the north and no less than 800 years in the south. Deposits belonging to the intermediate period no doubt exist, but the material has not yet been properly described or defined.

In Greece very much the same situation holds, and we know remarkably little of the recently defined final Neolithic.[134] Interestingly enough, much the same is true of the Balkans,[135] where the *Übergangszeit* between 3100 BC and 2600 BC (in radiocarbon years) is again conspicuously lacking in radiocarbon dates, or indeed at present in finds to be dated.

This situation should not be attributed to any irregularities in the radiocarbon calendar. There are dates from the Bodrogkeresztur culture of Hungary, as well as from Kephala in Kea, which fall within this period. In the British Isles dates are abundant over just this time range. Rather it reflects some more local cultural factor which remains altogether unclear. The beginning of the 3rd millennium BC (in radiocarbon years) is thus in our present state of knowledge something of a Dark Age in south Europe. We shall not fully understand the Copper Age of Italy, or the Early Bronze Age of the Aegean and the Balkans, until we know much more about it.

A first and positive step is to recognise our ignorance in this matter. Nothing is to be gained by inventing immediate solutions, either invading Indo-Europeans in south-east Europe, or Levantine or Aegean colonists and traders in Italy. Any theory needs at least a few supporting facts. The next step towards an understanding of the Italian Copper Age must be to look for them. [1974]

Appendix I: List of Radiocarbon Dates

A. ITALY

Laboratory and number	Culture or phase	Site	C-14 date BC 5,568 half-life
Birm 102	Rivoli Rocca	Rivoli Rocca	3720±130
Pi 4	Chiozza	Isola Virginia	3584±144
Pi 38	,,	,,	3376±180
Birm 103	,,	Rivoli Rocca	3270±120
Pi 28	Petescia	Petescia	3448±145
St 1344	Sasso-Fiorano	Luni sul Mignone	3445±80
R 349	Trichrome ware	Grotta Scaloria	3530±70
R 366	,,	Lipari Acropolis	3250±60
R 284	Serra d'Alto ware	Grotta del Santuario della Madonna	3605±70
R 283	Diana ware	,,	3160±70
R 180	,,	Lipari Acropolis	3050±200
R 182	,,	Contrada Diana	2935±55
R 104	Lagozza	Arene Candide	3125±45
Pi 34	,,	Lagozza	2844±90
R 78	,,	,, I	2785±50
R 78A	,,	,, Ia	2630±50
R 338	,,	,, Ib	3030±50
R 337	,,	,, II	2855±50
Pi 49	Ripoli	Grotta dei Piccioni III	2820±110
Pi unpub.	,,	Ripoli	3150±120
R 155	Beakers	Grotta del Pertusello III	2440±70
R 309	,,	Riparo Arma di Nasino VI	2270±55
R 311	,,	,,	1815±70
Pi 100	Rinaldone	Riparo la Romita, Asciano	2298±115
Pi 50	Rinaldone/Remedello	Grotta dei Piccioni IV	2356±105
St 2042	Rinaldone	Luni sul Mignone	2005±200
St 2043	,,	,,	2075±100
St 1343	,,	,,	1850±80
Pi 87	Polada	Barche di Solferino	1391±115
Pi 88	,,	Ledro	1187±105
R 294	,,	Polada	1380±65
R 295	,,	,,	1270±55
R 296	,,	,,	1295±55
R 275	Apennine	Arcevia	1315±55
R 117	,,	Porto Perone, Leporano	1150±60
St 1345	,,	Luni sul Mignone	1245±75
St 2045	,,	,,	1170±75
St 1147	,,	,,	1125±70

(For Malta, see Renfrew (1972), *Antiq*. 46.)

B. AEGEAN

Laboratory and number	Culture or phase	Site	C-14 date BC 5,568 half-life
P 1660	Final Neolithic	Franchthi	3311±64
P 1397	,,	Halieis	3152±72
P 1368	Saliagos	Saliagos	3959±87
P 1333	,,	,,	3825±84
P 1393	,,	,,	3766±85
BM 585	Cretan Late Neo.	Knossos II	3638±145
BM 579	,,	,,	3584±76
BM 571	,,	Knossos II/III	3686±94
BM 580	,,	Knossos III	3572±88
P 298	Anatolian Late Chalco.	Beycesultan XXXVI	3014±50
P 297	,, ,,	,, XXVIII	2740±54
BM 649	Sitagroi II	Sitagroi II	3954±66
Bln 883	Dikilitash	Sitagroi III	3595±100
Bln 882	,,	,,	3845±100
BM 650b	,,	,,	3417±85
Bln 881	,,	,,	3605±100
Bln 774	,,	,,	3150±120
P 306	Eutresis (EH I)	Eutresis	2496±69
P 307	,, (EH I)	,,	2492±57
P 317	Korakou (EH II)	,,	2262±56
P 318	,,	Lerna	2120±65
P 321A	,,	,,	2031±64
P 319	,,	,,	2027±59
P 321	,,	,,	1946±58
P 312	,,	,,	1887±65
P 320	Korakou/Tiryns	,,	1978±57
P 300	Tiryns (EH III)	,,	1919±53
P 299	,,	,,	1803±93
P 303A	Middle Helladic	,,	1798±108
P 303	,,	,,	1568±51
Q 953	Early Minoan II	Myrtos	2192±80
Q 950	,,	,,	1855±85
Q 951	,,	,,	1785±80
Pi 15	Middle Minoan	Phaistos	1525±120
St 1265	Middle Minoan III	Palaikastro	1500±75
P 273	Troy I	Emborio IV	2025±92
P 920	Late Troy I or Troy II	Karatas	2324±62
P 923	,,	,,	2278±62
P 917	,,	,,	2271±61
P 921	,,	,,	2188±62
P 918	Late Troy I	,,	2180±61
P 919	,,	,,	2176±60
Bln 880	Sitagroi IV	Sitagroi	2560±100
BM 650a	,,	,,	2413±56
BM 651	,,	,,	2382±79
Bln 878	,,	,,	2445±100
Bln 879	,,	,,	2600±100
Bln 773	,,	,,	2440±100
Bln 782	Sitagroi IV/Va	,,	2360±100
BM 652	Sitagroi Va	,,	1853±59
Bln 877	,,	,,	2220±100
Bln 876	Sitagroi Vb	,,	2015±100
Bln 780	,,	,,	1920±100
Bln 781	,,	,,	2135±150
BM 653	,,	,,	1840±78

Since this article went to press a series of C-14 dates from the rock-cut tombs at Buccino, prov. Salerno, has been published (Ross Holloway, R., *Buccino*, Rome, 1973). The dates, using the 5568 half-life, are listed here:

St 3627—2580±100 BC
St 3620—2370±120 BC
St 3633—1030±105 BC
St 3631—1970±360 BC
St 3628—2075±100 BC
St 3632—2155±120 BC
St 3634—2060±100 BC

The anomalous date—St 3633—was thought by the excavator to come from a sample contaminated by sewage. The remaining six dates form a reasonable group, covering the period c. 2600–2000 BC, equivalent to c. 3350–2500 BC in calendar years. These dates are consistent with the dates for Copper Age layers on central and north Italian sites, though St 3627 is earlier than any date previously obtained for this period.

The Buccino dates are of particular significance because they are the first Copper Age dates from southern Italy, the first Copper Age dates from funerary deposits anywhere in Italy, and because they are early and thus contribute towards closing the chronological gap between the latest dated Neolithic cultures and the earliest Copper Age ones, discussed on pp. 218 and 242.

Appendix II:
List of Copper Age Funerary Sites in Peninsular Italy

For the purpose of this section, the sites are listed under the headings 'Remedello area', 'Rinaldone area', etc. This cautious terminology is employed because not all the sites occurring within the areas in question are necessarily typical of the culture concerned. However, the different cultural groups do by and large cover distinct geographical areas, and it seems most convenient to divide the sites on a simple geographical basis. This list was compiled from a thorough, but not exhaustive, study of the literature. It includes all the sites referred to in the text.

REMEDELLO AREA

Prov. Brescia

Remedello Sotto. One hundred and seventeen trench graves. Colini 1898.
Roccolo Bresciani. One trench grave. Acanfora 1956, 343.
Santa Cristina. Two trench graves. Colini 1899, 28.
Ca di Marco. One trench grave. Colini 1898, 224–5.
Panesella a Volongo. Two trench graves. Colini 1898, 219 ; 1899, 31.

Prov. Mantova

Fontanella Mantovana. Thirty-six trench graves. Acanfora 1956.
Asola. Two trench graves. Colini 1898, 236.
Mosio. One trench grave. Colini 1898, 236.
Motta della Cappelletta. One trench grave. Colini 1898, 231.
Castel d'Ario. One trench grave. Colini 1898, 231.

Prov. Cremona

Calvatone. One trench grave. Cornaggia Castiglioni 1963.

Prov. Verona

Villafranca Veronese. One trench grave. Ghislanzoni, *BPI* 52 (1932) 9.

Quinzano. Number and type of burials unknown. Zorzi, F. *In memoria di F. Malavolti,* Modena, 1956, 139.

Fumane. Three trench graves. Ghislanzoni, *NdS* 1926, 358.

Casarole. Three trench graves. Battaglia, *Preistoria del Veneto e della Venezia Giulia,* Rome, 1958–9, 291–2.

Scalucce. Eight trench graves, Orsi, *BPI* 28 (1902) 172.

Carotta. One trench grave. Cipolla, *NdS* 1888, 217.

Soave. One trench grave. Battaglia, *Atti Soc. Natur. Matem. Modena,* 1919–20, 34.

Montecchio Maggiore. One trench grave. Battaglia, *Atti Soc. Natur. Matem. Modena,* 1919–20, 35.

Monte Loffa. Two trench graves. Zorzi 1960.

Prov. Parma

Castelguelfo. One trench grave. Malavolti 1953, 23.

Collecchio. Several trench graves. Malavolti 1953, 24.

Prov. Reggio Emilia

S. Ilario d'Enza. One trench grave. Malavolti 1953, 25.

Tana della Mussima. Natural cave with at least eighteen burials. Malavolti 1953, 24.

Chiozza di Scandiano. Eighteen trench graves. Zambotti, Laviosa, *Le più antiche culture agricole,* Milan, 1943, 75.

Prov. Modena

Cumarola. Forty trench graves. Malavolti 1953, 26.

Casinalbo. Probable tomb. Malavolti 1953, 25.

Prov. Bologna

Colunga. Two trench graves. Malavolti, *Emilia Preromana* 1 (1948), 56.

Bosco di Malta. Group of trench graves. Malavolti 1953, 27.

Prov. Ravenna

Borgo Rivola. Group of trench graves. Malavolti 1953, 27.

RINALDONE AREA

Prov. Pisa

Monte Bradoni. Natural cave ; several burials. Colini 1899, 301–6.

Guardistallo. One trench grave. Schiff Giorgini, *BPI* 41 (1915) 40–5.

Pomarance. Seven trench graves. Galli, *BPI* 38 (1912) 125–31.

Grotta di Castello, Vecchiano. Natural cave ; many burials. Colini 1898, 215.

Prov. Livorno

Pianosa. Rock-cut tombs, number unknown. Chierici, *BPI* 8 (1882) 1–21 ; 9 (1883) 48–60.

Elba, Grotta di S. Giuseppe. Natural cave ; many burials. Radmilli 1969.

Prov. Firenze

Battifolle di Cortona. One trench grave. Colini 1900, 139.

Montespertoli. Trench graves, number uncertain. Minto, *NdS* 1926, 272.

Prov. Siena

Belverde di Cetona. Natural caves. Calzoni, *Quad. Studi Etrusc.* 1 (1954) ; 2 (1962).

Pienza. Two trench graves. Becatti, *NdS* 1934, 42.

Camigliano. Four trench graves. Colini 1898, 233.

Prov. Grosseto

Punta degli Stretti. Natural crevices ; probably one burial. Minto, *BPI* 38 (1912) 132–5.

Corano. Many rock-cut tombs. Minto, *BPI* 40 (1914) 53–5 ; 41 (1915) 46–7 ; *BPI*, n.s. 2, 1938, 42.

Poggio Formica. Rock-cut tombs, number uncertain. Minto, *NdS* 1927, 279.

Botro del Pelagone. Rock-cut tombs, number uncertain. Minto, *BPI* n.s. 2, 1938, 41.

Garavicchio. Several rock-cut tombs. Cardini and Rittatore Vonwiller, *Quatenaria* 2 (1955) 312 ; 2 (1956) 261 ; 5 (1958–61) 336.

La Porcareccia. Seven rock-cut tombs. Rittatore Vonwiller, *RSP* 21 (1966) 428.

Prov. Perugia

Poggio Aquilone. One trench grave. Brizio, *NdS* 1899, 283, 9.

Prov. Terni

Stroncone. One trench grave. Colini, *BPI* 37 (1911) 63–71.

Narni. One trench grave. Colini 1898, 233.

Prov. L'Aquila

Camerata. One trench grave. Colini 1898, 212.

Prov. Viterbo

Rinaldone. Eight trench graves. Colini, *BPI* 29 (1903) 150–86 ; Pernier, *BPI* 31 (1905) 145–53.

Fontanelle. Four or more rock-cut tombs. Cardini and Rittatore Vonwiller, *RSP* 15 (1960) 235.

Ponte S. Pietro. Fourteen or more rock-cut tombs. Barich *et al.* 1968, 174, with full refs.

Chiusa di Ermini. Two rock-cut tombs. Rittatore Vonwiller, *RSP* 6 (1951) 8.

Tarquinia. One rock-cut tomb. Barich *et al.* 1968.

Palombaro. Eight or more rock-cut tombs. Rittatore Vonwiller 1968, 1969.

Naviglione. Eight or more rock-cut tombs. Rittatore Vonwiller 1969.

Fosso Conicchio. One rock-cut tomb. Finds include Bell Beakers. Moretti 1968 ; Ridgway 1972.

Prov. Roma

Cantalupo Mandela. Two or more rock-cut tombs. Colini 1898, 209–11.

Vigna Schiboni. One trench grave. Savignoni, *NdS* 1902, 114–15.

Prov. Frosinone

Alatri. One trench grave. Nicolucci, *BPI* 4 (1878) 163.

Sgurgola. One rock-cut tomb. Chierici, *BPI* 10 (1884) 141.

Casamari. Trench graves. Number uncertain. Barocelli, *BPI* 61 (1939) 26–31.

Valvisciolo. One trench grave and one natural cave. Barocelli, *BPI* 61 (1939) 31–36.

GAUDO AREA

Prov. Caserta

Contrada Cavone. One rock-cut tomb. Colini 1898, 235.

Caizzo. One tomb, type uncertain. Buchner 1950, 102.

Prov. Benevento

Toppo S. Filippo. One trench grave. Colini, *BPI* 31 (1905) 1–13.

Montesarchio. One tomb, type uncertain, D'Henry, *RSP* 26 (1971) 485.

Prov. Avellino

Gesualdo. Many trench graves. Colini 1898, 239–40.

Mirabella Eclano. Thirteen rock-cut tombs. Buchner 1950, 101.

Prov. Napoli

Contrada Materdei. Two rock-cut tombs. Buchner 1950, 102.

Carotto. One rock-cut tomb. Buchner 1950, 102.

Prov. Salerno

Gaudo. More than twenty-six rock-cut tombs. Sestieri 1946, 1947 ; Voza 1964.

Paestum, Temple of 'Ceres'. Two tombs in natural crevices. Voza 1962, 13–37.

Pontecagnano. Three or more trench graves. D'Agostino 1964.

Buccino. Six or more rock-cut tombs. Ross Holloway 1970, 145–7.

Eboli. Several rock-cut tombs. D'Agostino 1968.

Prov. Cosenza

Roggiano Gravina. One trench grave. De Franciscis, *BPI* 65 (1956) 213.

CONELLE–ORTUCCHIO AREA

Prov. Ancona

Monsanvito. One trench grave. Colini 1898, 216.

Osimo. Three trench graves. Annibaldi, *BPI* n.s. 8 (1951–2) 108–11.

Prov. Macerata

Recanati. Seven or more trench graves. Galli, *BPI* n.s. 5–6 (1941–2) 101–6 ; n.s. 8 (1947–50) 3–19.

Prov. L'Aquila

Assergi. Fifteen or more trench graves. Radmilli, *BPI* 66 (1957) 239–40.

Grotta a Male. Natural cave ; two burials. Peroni *BPI* 78 (1969) 155–7.

CENTRAL APENNINE AREA

Prov. Campobasso

Pozzilli. One trench grave. Colini 1898, 234.

Monteroduni. Two trench graves. Colini 1898, 235.

MACCHIA A MARE AREA

Prov. Foggia

Monte Pucci. Three or more rock-cut tombs. Rellini, *BPI* 50– (1930–1) 67–71 ; Battaglia, *RSP* 11 (1956) 1.

Grotta di Occhiopinto. Natural cave. Quagliati 1936, chapter 13.

LATERZA AREA

Prov. Foggia

Casone. One rock-cut tomb. V. Russi, pers. comm.

Belvedere. One tomb, type unknown. D'Agostino 1964, 104.

Prov. Bari

Andria. One trench grave. Jatta, *BPI* 31 (1905), 153–76.

Gioia del Colle. One rock-cut tomb. Gervasià, *I dolmen e la civiltà del bronzo nelle Puglie* (Trani, 1913).

Altamura. Three rock-cut tombs. Biancofiore and Ponzetti 1957.

Prov. Brindisi

Cellino San Marco. One rock-cut tomb. Lo Porto, *BPI* 71–2 (1962–3) 191–225.

San Vito dei Normanni. One rock-cut tomb. Lo Porto, *BPI* 73 (1964) 109–42.

Prov. Taranto

Laterza. Four or five rock-cut tombs. Biancofiore 1967.

Crispiano. One rock-cut tomb. Quagliati, *MA* 26 (1920) 433.

Prov. Lecce

Acquarica. One or more rock-cut tombs. Drago, *BPI* 64 (1954–5) 171.

Grotta del Fico. Natural cave used for burials. Palma di Cesnola and Minellono 1961.

Prov. Matera

Matera, Cappuccini. Two rock-cut tombs. Rellini, *Atti del Soc. Magna* Grecia, 1929, 137.

Matera, Serra Monsignore. Three or more rock-cut tombs, Rellini, op. cit. 1929, 138.

Matera, S. Francesco. One rock-cut tomb. Rellini, op. cit. 1929, 139.

Matera, S. Martino. Several rock-cut tombs. Rellini, op. cit. 1929, 139, 144.

Matera, Selva Venuso. One rock-cut tomb. Rellini, op. cit. 1929, 140.

NOTES

[1] In addition to the usual *BSA* abbreviations, the following are employed: *PPS*: *Proceedings of the Prehistoric Society*. *RSP*: *Rivista di Scienze Preistoriche*. More complete bibliographic details are given in the select bibliography below.

[2] Childe (1939) *AJA* 43, 10; id. (1958) *Antiq*. 32, 69.

[3] *Dawn* (1925) 96.

[4] *Dawn* (1957) ed. 6, 241.

[5] Blance *Antiq*. (1961).

[6] Radmilli (1963) *La preistoria d'Italia* 20.

[7] Trump (1966) *Central and South Italy before Rome* 84.

[8] Barich *et al*. (1968) *Origini* 2.

[9] Östenberg (1967) *Luni sul Mignone* 120–89.

[10] Trump (1963) *BSR* 31, 13.

[11] Trump op. cit., fn. 7, 68.

[12] Peroni (1962–3) *BPI* 71–2.

[13] Radmilli (1953) *RSP* 14.

[14] Barich *et al*., op. cit., fn. 8.

[15] Barfield (1969) *Origini* 3, 67–8.

[16] Trump (1963) *BSR* 31.

[17] Buchner (1950) *RSP* 5.

[18] Lo Porto, *NdS* ser. 8, 18, 280–380.

[19] Tinè (1965) *BPI* 74, 201–2.

[20] Jatta (1914) *La Puglia preistorica* 127–8.

[21] Lo Porto op. cit., fn. 18.

[22] Cf. Renfrew (1972) *Emergence of Civilisation* ch. 13.

[23] Taylour (1958) *Mycenaean Pottery in Italy and Adjacent Areas.*
[24] Whitehouse in Renfrew (ed.) (1973) *The Explanation of Culture Change.*
[25] Renfrew (1972) op. cit. fn. 22, 458–60, 470.
[26] Bucholz (1958) *JDAI* 74.
[27] Taylour (1958) op. cit. 13 16, 54.
[28] Bernabò Brea (1968–9) *Kokalos* 14–15, 56–7.
[29] Lo Porto (1963) op. cit. fn. 21, 329.
[30] Renfrew (1972) op. cit. 456, 458–9.
[31] Bernabò Brea (1957) *Sicily Before the Greeks*, pl. 41.
[32] Evans (1956) *Antiq.* 30.
[33] Evans (1971) *Prehistoric Antiquities of the Maltese Islands*, fig. 50.
[34] Caskey (1954) *Hesperia* 23, 22.
[35] Biancofiore (1967) *Origini* 1.
[36] Stone, in Evans (1971) op. cit. 235.
[37] Bernabò Brea (1957) op. cit. 126.
[38] Newton and Renfrew (1970) *Antiq.* 44.
[39] Evans (1965) *PPS* 23, 99.
[40] Caskey (1960) *Hesperia* 29.
[41] *PM* 1, 87 and 412.
[42] e.g. Taylour (1964) *The Mycenaeans* 149.
[43] Branigan (1965) *BPI* 16.
[44] Renfrew *et al.* (1965) *BSA* 60.
[45] Aspinall *et al.* (1972) *Nature, Lond.* 237.
[46] Peet (1909) *The Stone and Bronze Ages in Italy* 150.
[47] *PM* 1, 155.
[48] Cornaggia *et al.* (1962–3) *RSP* 18.
[49] Cann and Renfrew (1964) *PPS* 29.
[50] Evans, *A Pedro Bosch-Gimpera* (Festschrift, 1963).
[51] Ammerman and Cavalli-Sforza, in Renfrew (ed.) (1973) *The Explanation of Culture Change.*
[52] Renfrew (1967) *Antiq.* 41.
[53] Renfrew (1972) *Antiq.* 46.
[54] Trump (1966) *Skorba* pl. xxvi.
[55] Renfrew (1965) *Neolithic and Early Bronze Age Culture of the Cyclades and their External Relations.* Ph.D. dissertation, University of Cambridge 179.
[56] Personal communication.
[57] Shear (1936) *Hesperia* 5.
[58] Heermance and Lord (1897) *AJA* 1.
[59] Papavasileiou (1910) Peri tōn en Euboiā archaiōn taphōn.
[60] Renfrew (1972) *Antiq.* 46, 113.
[61] Personal communication, B. Jones.
[62] Drago (1947) *RSP* 2; Rellini 1925 *NdS.*
[65] Rellini 1925 *NdS*; Whitehouse, R. (1972) *Antiq.* 46.
[64] Bucholz (1972) *JDAI* 77.
[65] Belmont and Renfrew (1964) *AJA.*
[66] Tsountas (1908) *Ai archaiai Akropoleis Diminiou kai Sesklou*, pl. 42.
[67] Evans and Renfrew (1968) *Excavations at Saliagos*, fig. 61.
[68] Branigan (1966) *BPI* 75, 99–100.
[69] Tsountas (1908) op. cit. 324, fig. 251.
[70] Evans (1964) *BSA* 69, 156 and 231.
[71] Renfrew (1972) op. cit. 452–3.
[72] Gjerstad (1926) *Studies in Prehistoric Cyprus* 132, jug 1.
[73] Stewart (1962) *Swedish Cyprus Expedition* iv, part 1A, 107.
[74] Bernabò Brea (1957) op. cit. 62.
[75] Cavalier (1960) *BPI* 84.
[76] Renfrew (1967) *Antiq.* 41.
[77] Branigan (1966) op. cit. Id. (1971) *Origini* 5.
[78] Branigan (1966) op. cit. 97.
[79] Ibid. 107.
[80] Ibid. 102.

[81] Branigan (1965) *BPI* 16, 50.
[82] Id. (1966) op. cit. 103–7.
[83] Id. (1971) op. cit.
[84] Ibid. 48–51.
[85] Id. (1968) *Copper and Bronze Working in Early Bronze Age Crete* 53.
[86] Id. (1968) *AJA* 72.
[87] Id. (1966) op. cit. 107–8.
[88] Renfrew (1967) *AJA* 71, 4.
[89] Branigan (1968) *AJA* 72, 219–29.
[90] Barfield (1969) *Origini* 3.
[91] Branigan (1968) op. cit. = Bibliog. 1968*a*.
[92] Barfield (1969) op. cit.
[93] Childe (1957) op. cit. 53, fig. 26, 3.
[94] Bossert (1954) *Festschrift für Peter Goessler* 27 and pl. 14, 1–2.
[95] Barfield (1969) op. cit. 80.
[96] Maxwell-Hyslop (1946) *Iraq* 8, 12.
[97] Schmidt (1945) *Die Burg Vučedol* 143.
[98] Georgiev and Merpert (1966) *Antiq.* 40, 36.
[99] Papavasileiou (1910) op. cit. 12.
[100] Stronach (1957) *AS* 7.
[101] Renfrew (1967) op. cit. cat. no. 66 and 67.
[102] Biancofiore (1967) *Origini* 1, fig. 53.
[103] Tine (1965) *BPI* 201.
[104] Biancofiore (1967) op. cit. 218.
[105] (1946) op. cit. 33–6.
[106] Stronach (1957) op. cit. 102.
[107] Biancofiore (1967) op. cit. 216–17.
[108] Branigan (1968) op. cit. fig. 11.
[109] Acanfora (1956) *BPI* 65, 362.
[110] Branigan (1966) op. cit. 103.
[111] Acanfora (1956) op. cit. 372.
[112] Cambi (1958) *BPI* 67–8.
[113] Lucas (1962) *Ancient Egyptian Materials and Industries* 195.
[114] Bernabò Brea and Cavalier (1956) *BPI* 65, 35.
[115] Barfield (1971) *Northern Italy Before Rome* 49.
[116] Pellegrini (1910) *BPI* 36, fig. D; Barfield and Broglio (1966) *BPI* 75, 80–1.
[117] Barfield (1971) op. cit. 52.
[118] Lollini (1965) *Atti del VI Congr. Internaz.* 313.
[119] Personal communication, Dr G. Barker.
[120] Barfield (1966) *Memorie del Museo Civico di Storia Naturale, Verona* 14, 63
[121] Tongiorgi (1950) *RSP* 5.
[122] Colini (1900) *BPI* 27, 219.
[123] Renfrew (1972) op. cit. 308–13.
[124] Renfrew (1969) *PPS* 35.
[125] Renfrew (1967) op. cit. 13.
[126] Cambi (1958) op. cit.
[127] Baruch *et al.* (1968) *Origini* 2, 237.
[128] Peroni (1962–3) *BPI* 71–2.
[129] Radmilli (1959) *RSP* 14.
[130] Puglisi (1953) *RSP* 8.
[131] Palma di Cesnola and Minellono (1961) *RSP* 16.
[132] Malavolti (1953) *Appunti per una cronologia del neo-eneolitico emiliano* 26.
[133] Trump (1963) *BSR* 31.
[134] Renfrew (1972) op. cit. ch. 5.
[135] Renfrew (1971) *Antiq.* 45, 279.

BIBLIOGRAPHY

Acanfora, M. O. (1956) Fontanella Mantovana e la cultura di Remedello. *BPI* 65, 321–85.

Ammerman, A. J. and Cavalli-Sforza, L. L. (1973) A population model for the diffusion of early farming in Europe, in Renfrew, C. (ed.) *The Explanation of Culture Change : Models in Prehistory*. London: Duckworth.

Aspinall, A., Feather, S. and Renfrew, C. (1972) Neutron activation analysis of Aegean obsidians. *Nature, Lond.* 237, 333–4.

Barfield, L. H. (1966) Excavations on the Rocca di Rivoli (Verona) 1963. *Mem. Mus. Civ. Stor. Nat., Verona* 14, 1–100.

——(1969) Two Italian halberds and the question of the earliest European halberds. *Origini* 3, 67–83.

——(1971) *Northern Italy before Rome*. London: Thames & Hudson.

——and Broglio, A. (1966) Materiali per lo studio del neolitico del territorio Vicentino. *BPI* 75, 51–95.

Barich, B. E., Bonadonna, F. P., Borgognini, S. and Parenti, R. (1968) Trovamenti eneolitici presso Tarquinia. *Origini* 2, 173–246.

Belmont, J. S. and Renfrew, C. (1964) Two prehistoric sites on Mykonos. *AJA* 68, 395.

Bernabò Brea, L. (1957) *Sicily before the Greeks*. London: Thames & Hudson.

——(1968–9). Considerazioni sull'eneolitico e sulla prima età del bronzo della Sicilia e della Magna Grecia. *Kokalos* 14–15, 20–59.

——and Cavalier, M. (1956) Civiltà preistoriche delle Isole e del territorio di Milazzo. *BPI* 65, 7–99.

Biancofiore, F. (1967) La necropoli eneolitica di Laterza. *Origini* 1, 195–300.

——and Ponzetti, F. M. (1957) Tomba di tipo siculo con nuovo osso a globuli nel territorio d'Altamura (Bari). *BPI* 66, 153–88.

Blance, B. (1961) Early Bronze Age colonists in Iberia. *Antiq.* 35, 192–202.

Bossert, E.-M. (1954) Zur Datierung der Gräber von Arkesine auf Amorgos. *Festschrift für Peter Goessler* 23.

Branigan, K. (1965) A note on the chronology of the Diana culture. *BPI* 16, 46–52.

——(1966) Prehistoric relations between Italy and the Aegean. *BPI* 75, 97–109.

——(1968*a*) *Copper and Bronze Working in Early Bronze Age Crete* (*SMA* 19).

——(1968*b*) Silver and lead in prepalatial Crete. *AJA* 72, 219–29.

——(1971) Halberds, daggers and culture contact. *Origini* 5, 47–58.

Buchner, G. (1950) Appunti sulle collezioni preistoriche e protostoriche del Museo Nazionale di Napoli, in occasione del loro riordinamento. *RSP* 5, 97–107.

Bucholz, H. G. (1958) Der Kupferhandel des zweiten vorchristlichen Jahrhunderts. *JDIA* 74.

——(1962) Der Pfeilglätter aus dem VI. Schachtgrab von Mykene und die helladische Pfeilspitzen. *JDIA* 77.

Cambi, L. (1958) I metalli dei cimeli della grotta tombale di Monte Bradoni (Volterra). *BPI* 77–8, 137–45.

Cann, J. R. and Renfrew C. (1964) The characterisation of obsidian and its application to the Mediterranean region. *PPS* 29, 111–33.

Caskey, J. L. (1954) Excavations at Lerna 1952–3. *Hesperia* 23, 3.

——(1960) The Early Helladic period in the Argolid. *Hesperia* 29, 285–303.

Cavalier, M. (1960) Les cultures préhistoriques des Iles Eoliennes et leur rapport avec le monde égéen. *BCH* 84, 319–46.

Childe, V. G. (1925) *The Dawn of European Civilisation*. Ed. 1. London: Routledge & Kegan Paul.

——(1939) The Orient and Europe. *AJA* 43, 10.

——(1957) *The Dawn of European Civilisation*. Ed. 6. London: Routledge & Kegan Paul.

——(1958) Retrospect. *Antiq.* 32, 69.

Colini, G. A. (1898–1901) Il sepolcreto di Remedello Sotto nel Bresciano e il periodo eneolitico in Italia. *BPI* 24–8 (12 parts).

Cornaggia Castiglioni, O. (1963) Notiziario *RSP* 18, 320.

——Fussi, F. and D'Agnolo, M. (1962–3) Indagini sulla provenienza dell'ossidiana in uso nelle industrie italiane. *Atti Soc. Ital. Sci. Nat. Milano* 52, 310.

D'Agostino, B. (1964) Di alcuni rinvenimenti preistorici a Pontecagnano (Salerno). *BPI* 73, 89–108.

——(1968) Notiziario. *RSP* 23, 416–17.

Drago, C. (1947) Notiziario. *RSP* 2, 333.
Evans, J. D. (1956*a*) Bossed bone plaques of the second millennium. *Antiq.* 30, 80–93.
——(1956*b*) The 'dolmens' of Malta and the origins of the Tarxien Cemetery culture. *PPS* 23, 85.
——(1963) A marble statuette bought in Malta and its implications. *A Pedro Bosch-Gimpera en el Septuagésimo Aniversario de su Nacimento* (Mexico) 161.
——(1964) Excavations in the Neolithic Settlement of Knossos 1957–60. *BSA* 69, 132–40.
——(1971) *The Prehistoric Antiquities of the Maltese Islands.* London: Athlone.
——and Renfrew, C. (1968) *Excavations at Saliagos near Antiparos.*
Georgiev, G. I. and Merpert, N. J. (1966) The Ezero mound in south-eastern Bulgaria. *Antiq.* 40, 33–7.
Gjerstad, E. (1926) *Studies on Prehistoric Cyprus.*
Heermance, T. W. and Lord, G. D. (1897) Pre-Mycenaean graves at Corinth. *AJA* 1, 313.
Lollini, D. G. (1965) Il neolitico nelle Marche alla luce delle recenti scoperte. *Atti VI Cong. Internaz. Preist. e Protost.*, Roma, 1962 (1965).
Lo Porto, F. G. (1963) Leporano (Taranto). La stazione protostorica di Porto Perone. *NdS* ser. 8, 17, 280–380.
Lucas, A. (1962) *Ancient Egyptian Materials and Industries.*
Malavolti, F. (1953) *Appunti per una cronologia del neo-eneolitico emiliano.* Modena: Centro Emiliano di Studi Preistorici.
Maxwell-Hyslop, R. (1946) Daggers and swords in Western Asia. *Iraq* 8, 1–65.
Montelius, O. (1897) Pre-classical chronology in Greece and Italy. *JRAI* 26.
Moretti, M. (1968) Notiziario. *RSP* 23, 415.
Newton, R. G. and Renfrew, C. (1970) British faience beads reconsidered. *Antiq.* 44, 199–206.
Ostenberg, C. E. (1967) *Luni sul Mignone e problemi della preistoria d'Italia.* Lund.
Palma Di Cesnola, A. and Minellono, F. (1961) Gli scavi nella Grotta del Fico presso S. Maria al Bagno (Lecce). *RSP* 16, 57–83.
Papavasileiou, G. A. (1910) *Peri ton en Euboia Archaion Taphon.*
Peet, T. E. (1909) *The Stone and Bronze Ages in Italy.* Oxford.
Pellegrini, G. (1910) Stazione eneolitica della caverna Bocca Lorenza (Vicenza). *BPI* 36, 71.
Peroni, R. (1962–3) La Romita di Asciano (Pisa). Riparo sotto roccia utilizzato dall'età neolitica alla barbarica. *BPI* 71–2, 251–442.
Puglisi, S. M. (1950) Le culture dei capannicoli sul promontorio Gargano. *Atti dei Lincei, Mem.* ser. 8, 8, 3–57.
——(1953) Nota preliminare sugli scavi nella Caverna dell'Erba (Avetrana). *RSP* 8, 86.
——(1959) *La civiltà apenninica.* Firenze.
Quagliati, Q. (1936) *La Puglia preistorica.* Trani.
Radmilli, A. M. (1959) Notiziario. *RSP* 14, 320.
——(1963) *La preistoria d'Italia alla luce delle ultime scoperte.* Firenze.
——(1967) Notiziario. *RSP* 22, 443–4.
——(1969) Notiziario. *RSP* 24, 368.
Rellini, U. (1925) Scavi preistorici a Serra d'Alto. *NdS* ser. 6, 1, 257–95.
Renfrew, C. (1965) *Neolithic and Bronze Age Cultures of the Cyclades and their External Relations.* Unpublished doctoral dissertation, University of Cambridge.
——(1967*a*) Colonialism and Megalithismus. *Antiq.* 41, 276–88.
——(1967*b*) Cycladic metallurgy and the Aegean Early Bronze Age. *AJA* 71, 1–20.
——(1969) The autonomy of the south-east European Copper Age. *PPS* 35, 12–47.
——(1971) Sitagroi, radiocarbon and the prehistory of south-east Europe. *Antiq.* 45, 275–82.
——(1972*a*) *The Emergence of Civilisation: The Cyclades and the Third Millennium* BC. London: Methuen.
Ridgway, D. (1972) Beakers in central Italy. *Antiq.* 46, 52.
Rittatore Vonwiller, F. (1967) Notiziario. *RSP* 22, 444.
——(1968) Notiziario. *RSP* 23, 415–16.
——(1969) Notiziario. *RSP* 24, 370, 372.
Ross Holloway, R. (1970) Excavations at Buccino: 1969, *AJA* 74, 145–8.

——(1971) Archaeological news from south Italy. *AJA* 75, 75–8.
Schmidt, R. (1945) *Die Burg Vučedol*. Zagreb.
Sestieri, P. C. (1946) La necropoli preistorica di Paestum. *RSP* 1, 245–66.
——(1947) Nuovi risultati degli scavi nella necropoli di Paestum. *RSP* 2, 283–90.
Shear, T. L. (1936) The campaign of 1935. *Hesperia* 5, 20.
Stewart, J. R. (1962) The Early Bronze Age, in Dikaios, P. and Stewart, J. R. *The Stone Age and the Early Bronze Age in Cyprus* (*Swedish Cyprus Expedition* IV, part IA).
Stone, J. F. S. (1971) Faience beads from the Tarxien Cemetery in Evans 1971, 235–6.
Stronach, D. (1957) Metal types in Early Bronze Age Anatolia. *AS* 7, 89.
Taylour, W. (1958) *Mycenaean Pottery in Italy and Adjacent Areas*. Cambridge.
——(1964) *The Mycenaeans*. London: Thames & Hudson.
Tinè, S. (1965) Gli scavi nella Grotta di Chiusazza. *BPI* 74, 123–286.
Tongiorgi, E. (1950) Grotta di Agnano. *RSP* 5, 121.
Trump, D. H. (1963) Excavations at La Starza, Ariano Irpino. *PBSR* 31, 3–32.
——(1966*a*) *Central and Southern Italy before Rome*. London.
——(1966*b*) *Skorba: Excavations on behalf of the National Museum of Malta 1962–4. Research Report of the Society of Antiquaries of London.*
Tsountas, C. (1908) *Ai Proistorikai Akropoleis Dhiminiou kai Sesklou*. Athens.
Voza, G. (1962) *Mostra della Preistoria e della Protostoria nel Salernitano. Catalogo*. Naples.
——(1964) Ultimi scavi della necropoli del Gaudo. *Atti della VIII e IX Riunione Scientifica, Ist. Ital. Preist. Protoist.*, Florence. 265–74.
Whitehouse, R. D. (1973) The earliest towns in peninsular Italy in Renfrew, C. (ed.) *The Explanation of Culture Change: Models in Prehistory*. London: Duckworth.
——(1972) The rock-cut tombs of the central Mediterranean. *Antiq.* 46, 269–74.
Xanthoudides, S. A. (1924) *The Vaulted Tombs of the Mesara* (1924).
Zorzi, F. (1960) Notiziario. *RSP* 15, 228.

10) Malta and the Calibrated Radiocarbon Chronology (with an Appendix by Jane M. Renfrew)

The great stone monuments of Malta, and the finds that go with them, have long presented difficulties to the archaeologist. Gordon Childe took so pessimistic a view of these problems in the first edition of *The Dawn* that it is worth quoting in full all that he had there to say about Malta (Childe 1925, 101):

> It would take a whole book to give even the most cursory summary of the Maltese material. And then no progress would have been made. No significant parallels are at present known to the temples, the carving, the statuettes, or the pottery. Motives adorning the "neolithic" buildings and ossuaries have been derived by Sir Arthur Evans from the Middle minoan II decorative repertoire ; Professor Schuchardt has found in the same ornaments the prototypes of the Cretan. It is still quite impossible to say whether Malta played the role of master or disciple among her neighbours and fruitless speculations on this topic had best be omitted.

The situation was not significantly clarified until the systematic work of J. D. Evans (1953) who, relying partly on the Sicilian materials gathered by Brea (summarised in Brea 1959), was able to establish a clear culture sequence. This was modified by Trump as a result of his excavations at Skorba (Trump 1966), and remains the basis for our understanding.

Evans used arguments first outlined by Sir Arthur Evans to date the temples to the earlier part of the 2nd millennium BC. The radiocarbon dates from the samples which Trump recovered at Skorba suggested that an earlier dating was necessary. And of course the tree-ring calibration applied in this paper advocates a yet earlier chronology, and one that sets aside entirely the traditional links with the Aegean (see also chapter 2).

Recently it has been suggested that the development of the temples of Malta may be associated with the emergence of a chiefdom society (Renfrew 1974 ; discussed by Evans, 1977, 23–4) and the spatial data on which this argument in part rests has subsequently been subjected to further analysis (Renfrew and Level, 1979). Trump (1977) has recently considered the possible causes of the apparent hiatus at the end of the Tarxien period and the duration of the Tarxien Cemetery phase.

BIBLIOGRAPHY

Brea, L. D. (1957) *Sicily before the Greeks*. London: Thames and Hudson.

Childe, V. G. (1925) *The Dawn of European Civilisation*. London: Kegan Paul.

Evans, J. D. (1953) The prehistoric culture sequence of the Maltese archipelago. *Proc. Prehist. Soc.* 19, 41–94.

Evans, J. D. (1977) Island archaeology in the Mediterranean, problems and opportunities. *World Archaeol.* 9, 12–26.

Renfrew, C. (1974) Beyond a subsistence economy, in Moore, C. B. (ed.) *Reconstructing Complex Societies* (Supplement to the Bulletin of the American School of Prehistoric Research no. 20) 69–96.

Renfrew, C. and Level, E. V. (1979) Predicting centres from polities: the XTENT model, in Renfrew, C. and Cooke, K. (eds.) *Transformations : Mathematical Approaches to Culture Change*. New York: Academic Press.

Trump, D. H. (1966) *Skorba* (Research Reports of the Society of Antiquaries of London 22).

Trump, D. H. (1977) The collapse of the Maltese temples, in Sieveking, G., Longworth, I. and Wilson, K. E. (eds.) *Problems in Economic and Social Archaeology*. London: Duckworth, 605–10.

MALTA AND THE CALIBRATED RADIOCARBON CHRONOLOGY

Three new radiocarbon dates for Malta are now available, and serve to support the radiocarbon chronology established by Trump (1966, 48). In doing so they encourage the application to it of the tree-ring calibration of radiocarbon, with striking consequences. They harmonise well with the relative chronology for the Malta culture sequence as established by Evans and subsequently revised (Evans 1971, 207–28). All three samples have been dated at the British Museum Research Laboratory, to which grateful acknowledgment is made. The dates on the 5568 half-life for radiocarbon are given in the table 1.

Table 1. New radiocarbon dates for Malta (5,568 half-life)

Lab. no.	Site	Phase	Radiocarbon date BC	Material
BM 712	Skorba (GC 3)	Ggantija	2528 ± 56	Wood charcoal
BM 711	Tarxien	Tarxien cemetery	1404 ± 76	Carbonised seeds
BM 710	Tarxien	Tarxien cemetery	1336 ± 72	Carbonised seeds

The sample from Skorba, made available through the kindness of Mr Francis Mallia, Director of the National Museum of Malta, and of Dr David Trump, is from precisely the same context, in the Hut of the Querns, as a sample previously analysed, which gave a date of 3290 ± 150 BC (BM 142). That very early value has been questioned by Trump (1966, 48): 'from charcoal in the Ggantija phase Hut of the Querns, it is again too early compared with the two stratigraphically earlier Zebbug samples. The charcoal, spread across the whole hut floor, is certainly from a burnt roof, again quite possibly old heartwood from its timbers.' The new date presents no such problems, harmonising with the other available dates for Malta, and can be accepted as dating the Ggantija phase. The wood charcoal was examined microscopically by Mr David F. Cutler of the Jodrell Laboratory, Royal Botanical Gardens, Kew, and identified as belonging to the genus *Phillyrea*, among the *Oleaceae.*

Samples BM 711 and 710 were both from glass jars in the National Museum containing carbonised material and labelled 'Tarxien Cemetery'. It may be assumed that they were among the contents of cinerary urns excavated there by Sir Themistocles Zammit in 1915. The seeds are described by Dr J. M. Renfrew in a note following the present one. The dates obtained are later than BM 141, 1930 ± 150 BC, obtained some time ago for a sample of carbonised horsebeans from a similar context. The disparity may well be an indication of the duration of the Tarxien Cemetery culture. It should be noted that a sample of wood charcoal from the Tarxien Cemetery, BM 101, gave a date of 2535 ± 150 BC. This was quite reasonably described by Trump as 'impossibly high'. He suggested that the wood originally derived from a structure dating from the Tarxien phase at the site.

The radiocarbon dates now available for Malta are given in table 2 (cf. Trump 1966, 48, and Barker, Burleigh and Meeks 1969, 291). Beneath them are listed the three dates which fail to conform to the emerging pattern. They have been discussed by Trump, who has suggested the revised phase attribution given in parentheses.

Table 2. Malta radiocarbon dates (5,568 half-life)

Phase	Site	Lab. no.	Radiocarbon date BC
Tarxien cemetery	Tarxien	BM 710	1336±72
,, ,,	,,	BM 711	1404±76
,, ,,	,,	BM 141	1930±150
Tarxien	Skorba	BM 143	2430±150
Ggantija	,,	BM 712	2528±56
Zebbug	,,	BM 147	3050±150
,,	,,	BM 145	3190±150
Red Skorba	,,	BM 148	3225±150
Ghar Dalam	,,	BM 216	3810±200
,,	,,	BM 378	4190±160
Disputed dates:			
Tarxien cemetery (Tarxien)	Tarxien	BM 101	2535±150
Mgarr (probably Ggantija)	Mgarr	BM 100	2710±150
Ggantija (possibly Zebbug)	Skorba	BM 142	3290±100

Using the tree-ring calibration of radiocarbon (Suess 1970; Renfrew 1970), these dates may be given approximately in calendar years. Fig. 1 shows the values for the mean and the standard deviation expressed in *calendar years.* In some cases the kinks in the calibration curve give alternative dates for the calibrated mean date, and in such instances the range for the mean is indicated by a vertical bar. This, and the unequal length of the 'plus' and 'minus' components of the standard deviation, when expressed in calendar years, are products of the irregularities in the calibration curve. It should be noted that the calibration curve remains experimental and tentative at present (cf. Clark and Renfrew 1972), and the kinks in it have been questioned on statistical grounds. For heuristic purposes Suess's calibration curve has been followed closely in the compilation of fig. 1 and these wide ranges for the means and unequal 'plus' and 'minus' values for the standard deviation are a logical consequence. But further statistical work is likely to modify the shape of the curve, so that the dates in calendar years are not yet known as reliably or as accurately as the figure would suggest. It is itself experimental, and is open to modification in the light of further work. (The three dates questioned on archaeological grounds are indicated by open symbols, with broken lines for the standard deviation: very little weight should be attached to them.)

Stratified potsherds from Skorba and other Maltese sites were obtained and are now undergoing thermoluminescence analysis at the Research Laboratory for Archaeology at Oxford. The results, when available, should extend our knowledge of the Maltese chronology, for they will of course be

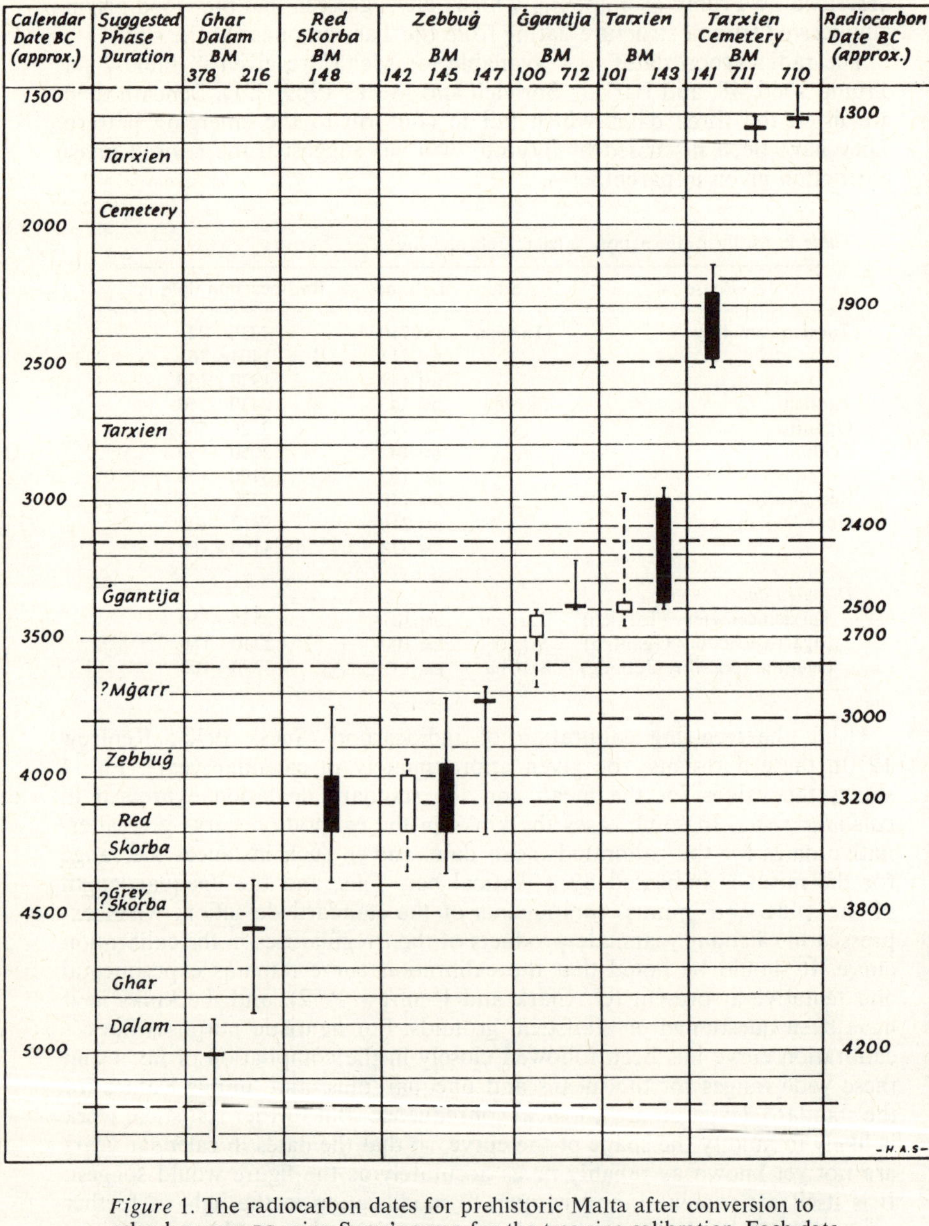

Figure 1. The radiocarbon dates for prehistoric Malta after conversion to calendar years BC using Suess's curve for the tree-ring calibration. Each date is shown with a range of one standard deviation, and the time range for the mean is indicated where applicable. (Three archaeologically uncertain dates are shown with open symbols and broken lines.) The inequalities in the deviations, and the time ranges for the means, arise from irregularities in the curve. It should be noted that the curve is at present tentative and experimental, so that the same applies to the calendar dates given here. Approximate time ranges for the successive phases are suggested in column 1.

expressed in calendar years, and quite independently of the radiocarbon time scale.

Fig. 1 shows how limited is the evidence at present on which to build a sound chronology for Malta. It is clear, however, that the dates for the temple period (for the Ggantija and Tarxien phases) cluster at present around 2600–2400 BC in radiocarbon years, or 3400–3000 BC in calendar years. Moreover the Tarxien Cemetery date of c. 1900 BC in radiocarbon years, or c. 2300 BC in calendar years, gives a *terminus ante quem* for the end of the temple cultures.

All of this directly contradicts the essentials of the traditional, pre-radiocarbon chronology. The most convincing piece of evidence for the traditional view was the similarity between the relief spirals in some of the temples and the spiral decoration in Middle Minoan II Crete (from c. 1900 BC at the earliest) and from Late Helladic I Greece (from c. 1650 BC). The arguments have recently been reiterated by Evans (1971, 219 and 224). Calibrated radiocarbon dates for the Tarxien phase falling much earlier than this disrupt the whole basis of the traditional, diffusionist system. Trump had already shown in 1966 how the uncalibrated radiocarbon dates conflicted with the traditional chronology. The discrepancy becomes inescapable after calibration.

Further dates for the early Tarxien Cemetery phase are still needed, however, in order to substantiate the early end of the Tarxien phase: at present too much weight has to be placed on the single determination, BM 141. Fortunately the beginning of the Tarxien phase, and the preceding Ggantija phase, are more securely documented.

Table 3. Approximate durations for the earlier Maltese culture periods

Phase	Suggested calibrated dates BC (1972)	Radiocarbon chronology BC (Trump 1966)	Traditional dates BC (pre-1960)
Tarxien cemetery	2500–1500	2000–1450	1450–1350
Tarxien	3300/3000–2500	2400–2000	1650–1450
Ggantija	3600–3300/3000	2850–2400	1800–1650
Mgarr	?3800–3600	2900–2850	culture sequence changed
Zebbug	4100–3800	3200–2900	
Red Skorba	4400–4100	3400–3200	
Grey Skorba	?4500–4400	3600–3400	
Ghar Dalam	5200–4500	3800–3600	2300–2100

No reliable chronology in calendar years can yet be put forward, but a first approximation is suggested in table 3 as a basis for discussion. For comparison, the uncalibrated radiocarbon chronology is given as set out by Trump (1966, 20), together with one version of the pre-1960, traditional chronology. (The Saflieni phase has been omitted for simplicity.)

Problems still remain—for instance a millennium seems a puzzlingly long time for the duration of the Tarxien Cemetery culture. But already the great antiquity of the temple cultures is evident. The temples themselves must, on this basis, rank as the earliest free-standing stone monuments in the world.

[1972]

ACKNOWLEDGEMENTS

I wish to thank Mr Richard Burleigh of the British Museum Research Laboratory for his cooperation, and Mr Francis Mallia, Director of the National Museum of Malta, with his assistant Mr Tancred Gouder, for their great kindness and generous assistance in Malta. Dr David Trump and Professor John D. Evans have willingly given their advice and help, and Messrs David Collison and Magnus Magnusson their lively and enthusiastic encouragement.

BIBLIOGRAPHY

Barker, H., Burleigh, P. and Meek, N. (1969) British Museum Natural Radiocarbon measurements IV. *Radiocarbon* 11, 278–84.

Clark, R. M. and Renfrew, C. (1972) A statistical approach to the calibration of floating tree-ring chronologies using radiocarbon dates. *Archaeom.* 14, Part 1, 5–19.

Evans, J. D. (1971) *The Prehistoric Antiquities of the Maltese Islands.* London.

Renfrew, C. (1970) New configurations in Old World archaeology. *World Archaeol.* 2, 199–211.

Suess, H. E. (1970) Bristlecone pine calibration of the radiocarbon time scale 5200 BC to the present, in (ed.), I. U. Olsson, *Radiocarbon variations and absolute chronology, Proceedings of the Twelfth Nobel Symposium.* London and New York.

Trump, D. H. (1966) *Skorba* (Reports of the Research Committee of the Society of Antiquaries of London, 22).

Appendix, by Jane M. Renfrew: Cultivated Plants from the Tarxien Cemetery, Malta

Two samples of carbonised seeds, obtained from the National Museum of Malta, have been examined prior to radiocarbon analysis (see preceding text). They derive from cinerary urns found in the Bronze Age cemetery at Tarxien.

The first sample, BM 711, consisted entirely of *Vicia faba* L., horsebeans. The following dimensions were obtained from twenty measured seeds: length 7·5–4·5, average 6·0 mm ; breadth 5·0–3·2, average 4·4 mm ; thickness 6·1–3·9, average 4·6 mm. These measurements agree closely with the dimensions obtained by Dr Hans Helbaek from a pure sample of *Vicia faba* v. *celtica* Heer, also from the Tarxien Cemetery (Helbaek 1971). He obtained the following measurements: length 7·95–3·48 mm ; breadth 5·86–2·75 mm ; thickness (90° to cotyledons) 5·12–2·56 mm.

The contents of the second sample, BM 710, include a wider range of species. The chief component was hulled six-row barley, *Hordeum vulgare* L., with the twisted lateral grains usually smaller than the symmetrical median grains. The following measurements were obtained from twenty grains: length 6·0–5·5, average 5·8 mm ; breadth 4·2–3·7, average 4·0 mm ; thickness 4·5–3·8, average 4·1 mm. The barley grains appear not well filled out. This suggests that they may have been harvested before maturity, or have been subjected to conditions of drought. Also present in this sample was a small number of seeds of *Vicia faba* L., five of which gave the following dimensions: length 6·0–5·5, average 5·8 mm ; breadth 4·2–3·7, average 4·0 mm ; thickness 3·8–4·5, average 4·1 mm. This fits well within the range of measurements for sample BM 711. Also present was a single lentil seed, *Lens esculenta* Moench. with a diameter of 2·9 mm.

The finds of hulled six-row barley and lentil are new for the Tarxien

Cemetery and expand our knowledge of the Early Bronze Age plant husbandry of Malta. Both barley and lentils have, however, been found in the Ghar Dalam phase of the early neolithic at Skorba. The Skorba barley was so distorted during carbonisation that it could not definitely be attributed to the two- or six-rowed forms, or determined whether it had been hulled or naked (Helbaek 1966). The lentils from Skorba were of the same small-seeded variety that is represented in the Tarxien Cemetery, with diameters from 3·25–2·60 mm. At Skorba the barley and lentils were associated with samples of wheat (*Triticum dicoccum* and *T. compactum*), but no wheat has yet been identified from the Tarxien Cemetery.

It appears then that there was a certain continuity between the Early Neolithic and Early Bronze Age agriculture in Malta, with horsebeans the only new crop introduced to the islands in the Early Bronze Age.

BIBLIOGRAPHY

Helbaek, H. (1966) Report on carbonised grain from AF 5, in Trump, D. H., *Skorba* (Reports of the Research Committee of the Society of Antiquaries of London 22), 53.

——(1971) Plant remains from the Tarxien Cemetery, in Evans, J. D., *Prehistoric Antiquities of the Maltese Islands,* 235.

11) Colonialism and Megalithismus

When this paper was published, the view that 'colonists' from the Aegean were responsible for early fortified townships in Iberia such as Los Millares and Vila Nova de São Pedro was almost universal. With them, it was argued (Blance 1961), they had brought the skills of copper metallurgy and indeed the practice of collective burial in built tombs, which in Iberia was translated into a megalithic architectural form. The position was authoritatively expressed in the monograph by Blance (1971).

The earlier idea of Bosch Gimpera, of Åberg (1921, 7) and of Leeds (1924, 590) that both megalith building and copper metallurgy developed autonomously in Spain and Portugal, was widely rejected in view of the colonialist argument, although the Leisners in their great study traced the origin in Portugal for the Iberian development of the megalithic tombs.

The sound archaeological basis for rejecting the colonialist view was set out in chapter 2. In the paper which follows radiocarbon dating is adduced to support that rejection (although the tree-ring calibration of radiocarbon had not yet been systematically applied). It now became possible to argue that copper metallurgy was indeed independently invented in Iberia, and there is a clear parallel here with the arguments developed in chapter 5 for autonomous metallurgical developments in the Balkans. Moreover the still earlier radiocarbon dates for megalithic tombs in Brittany supported the view that the collective monuments of western Europe could not all have an Iberian, still less an east Mediterranean origin.

The possibility thus clearly emerged (see Renfrew 1976) that we must imagine a number of separate areas in western Europe, in each of which a practice of collective burial in built stone tombs independently developed. The assumption of a single, unified origin for the megalithic phenomenon can now be stigmatised as 'Megalithismus'.

The reactions to these suggestions have been twofold. On the one hand, a number of scholars have accepted the implications, and looked more closely at the Iberian material to seek an understanding in social and economic terms of the development of proto-urban communities, copper metallurgy and collective burials (Chapman 1975 ; Gilman 1976). On the other, while carefully presenting the new radiocarbon and thermoluminescent dating evidence (Schubart 1965 ; Whittle and Arnaud 1975), many scholars have changed little, if at all, the 'Aegean influence' component of their views (e.g. Savory 1968 ; Schubart 1975). Many workers concerned with the origin of megalithic tombs in different parts of Europe utilise the very early Breton dates (e.g. Giot 1971), without necessarily accepting the implications presented here, often arguing that still earlier prototypes will emerge in Iberia when radiocarbon dating is more comprehensively applied there.

Systematic excavations at fortified, proto-urban sites such as Pedro do Ouro (Leisner and Schubart 1966) and Zambujal (Sangmeister and Schubart 1971 ; 1977) are providing important new data which will ultimately aid in resolving these problems. They still remain central to any more general understanding of European prehistory, and it is perhaps in some ways surprising that, other than in the works cited, they have not, over the past decade, been more energetically tackled.

BIBLIOGRAPHY

Aberg, N. (1921) *La Civilisation énéolithique dans la Péninsule Ibérique*. Uppsala.

Blance, B. (1961) Early bronze age colonists in Iberia. *Antiq*. 35, 192–202.

——(1971) *Die Anfänge der Metallurgie auf der iberischen Halbinsel* (Studien zu den Anfängen der Metallurgie 4). Berlin: Mann.

Chapman, R. W. (1975) *Economy and Society within Later Prehistoric Iberia, a New Framework*, unpublished Ph.D dissertation, University of Cambridge.

Gilman, A. (1976) Bronze Age dynamics in southeast Spain. *Dialectic. Anthrop*. 1, 307–19.

Giot, P. R. (1971) Radiocarbon dating and prehistoric chronology of Brittany. *Proc. Prehist. Soc*. 37 (2), 208–17.

Leisner, V. and Schubart, H. (1966) Die kupferzeitliche Befestigung von Pedro do Ouro, Portugal. *Madrider Mitt*. 7, 9–60.

Renfrew, C. (1976) Megaliths, territories and populations, in De Laet, S. J. (ed.) *Acculturation and Continuity in Atlantic Europe* (Dissertationes Archaeologicae Gandenses 16) 198–220.

Savory, H. N. (1968) *Spain and Portugal, the Prehistory of the Iberian Peninsula*. London: Thames and Hudson.

Sangmeister, E. and Schubart, H. (1971) Grabungen in der kupferzeitlichen Befestigung von Zambujal, Portugal, 1970. *Madrider Mitt*. 12, 11–45.

——(1977) Zambujal, eine befestigte Siedlung der Kupferzeit in Portugal. *Antike Welt* 8, no. 3, 23–34.

Schubart, H. (1965) Neue Radiokarbon-Daten zur Vor- und Frühgeschichte der iberischen Halbinsel. *Madrider Mitt*. 6, 11–19.

——(1975) *Die Kultur der Bronzezeit im Südwesten der iberischen Halbinsel* (Madrider Forschungen 9). Berlin: Gruyter.

Whittle, E. H. and Arnaud, J. M. (1975) Thermoluminescent dating of neolithic and chalcolithic pottery from sites in central Portugal. *Archaeom*. 17, 5–24.

COLONIALISM AND MEGALITHISMUS

Ideas and theories in prehistory often seem to have a life of their own, surviving and flourishing quite independently of the evidence upon which they might be supposed to rest. The biblical Lost Tribes, the Etruscan migrations of Herodotus, and the Phoenician merchants of Strabo, for example, served for centuries as a model for the explanation of Europe's remote past, unsupported in many cases by any evidence whatsoever.

It was perhaps natural then, when the brothers Henri and Louis Siret discovered in Almeria the first traces of the rich and exotic Chalcolithic culture of Spain (named now after its principal site at Los Millares), to see it as the work of Phoenician colonists. In this way they could explain the presence of such apparently 'civilised' features as built tombs of stone, female figurines, ivory combs, and axe and cuttlefish symbolism.[1] So they successfully launched the idea of colonists in Iberia, arrivals from the East Mediterranean and initiators of the Bronze Age in western Europe. The idea is still very widely accepted today.

While some later scholars completely rejected the notion of migration or influence from the east, preferring to see a purely local evolution, others, such as Wilke and Obermaier, modified it and strengthened it. They dropped the Phoenicians, and emphasised the Mycenaean similarities, especially of the Iberian corbelled burial chambers. These resemble the *tholos* tombs of Mycenae itself.

The view that any sophisticated features in Barbarian Europe (or indeed elsewhere) were of necessity derived from the Higher Civilisations, and in particular from Egypt, was taken over by Sir Grafton Elliot Smith and his 'heliolithic' adherents. European megaliths, especially Iberian megaliths, became the transformation of the Egyptian *mastaba*: 'When an important Egyptian colonist died abroad, his associates attempted to give him the rite of burial he would have had if he had died at home' [2]. He ingeniously overcame the lack of any evidence for an intervening stage between the Egyptian *mastaba* and the European megalith by inventing for himself an intermediate form, appropriate both in plan and section (fig. 1).

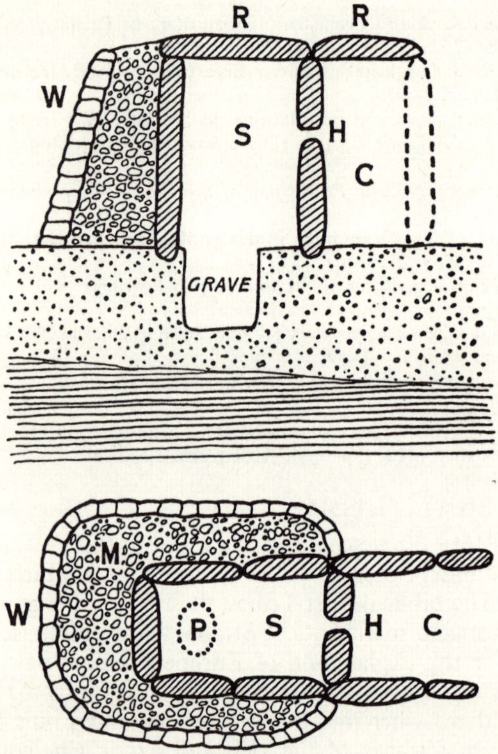

Figure 1. Support by Elliot Smith for his 'heliolithic' theory (from *Human History*, 1930). The caption read: 'Fig. 55. A hypothetical tomb, such as might be made for an Egyptian in a foreign land, without craftsmen sufficiently skilled to make a proper mastaba tomb as is shown in Fig. 54.'

This was an extreme case, and is today a discredited one, of what is now identified as a diffusionist kind of model,[2] with Egypt as the focal point. All inventions or cultural advances were explained as the result of cultural diffusion from there. Its magnificent absurdity was corrected in 1925 by Gordon Childe, who denied any direct Egyptian influence in western Europe. He saw too that the Spanish corbel-vaulted tombs must be earlier than the Mycenaean *tholoi.* One of his arguments [4] in correcting Nils Aberg's low chronology for the Neolithic of northern Europe, was that a more appropriate origin for the Spanish *tholoi* would be the Early Minoan tombs of southern Crete a millennium earlier.

Childe has been termed a moderate diffusionist: all his arguments were based on careful and informed cross-cultural comparison, and he discussed also the theoretical aspects of diffusion [5]. But it is important to realise that the whole of his chronology for Neolithic Europe rested upon two major *hypotheses*: that the east-central European Copper Age, and subsequently the Aunjetitz Bronze Age, were inspired by similar and *prior* developments in the Aegean and the Near East; and that the Chalcolithic/Early Bronze Age[3] cultures of Iberia, and at a further remove the entire megalithic movement in western Europe, were likewise preceded and inspired by developments in the Aegean world of the Early Bronze Age. Megalithic tombs in general, with collective burial, 'mother goddess' symbolism, spirals, metallurgy and other advanced features of Iberian and west European culture, owed their appearance in Europe to Aegean influence.

This hypothesis, as concerns Iberia, has recently been re-stated with great vigour and with a mass of careful documentation by Dr Beatrice Blance [6], and again in the recent important publication by Almagro and Arribas on Los Millares [7].

This notion of major Aegean influence on Chalcolithic Iberia has become one of the traditional cornerstones of European prehistory, so that much of the European development, including both metallurgy and collective burial, is derived from the east. It has proved remarkably durable. Although much of the original evidence for it has been refuted—such as the supposed Mycenaean origin of the *tholoi*, or of the temples and spirals of Malta—the old parallels are resuscitated instead in Early Minoan or Early Cycladic guise, and the basic conclusions are unchanged. There is now a tradition of acceptance for the hypothesis of Aegean influence. It depends on a diffusionist model, rarely explicitly stated, that developments—such as those of prehistoric Iberia—are less likely to have developed there than to have been imported from outside.

No one can question that cultural diffusion, whether by the agency of migration or of stimulus diffusion, is an important factor which works towards cultural change everywhere. It would be difficult to doubt, for instance, that the transition throughout Europe to a Neolithic way of life took place under influences diffused from the Near East. The purpose of this article, however, is to question whether in this case the evidence is good enough to suggest that diffusion from the Aegean—let alone actual colonists—was a major factor in the inception of the Iberian Chalcolithic, or in the development of megalithic tombs in western Europe.

There are three main tasks: to examine the diffusionist case, as admirably set out by Dr Blance, to understand how it is that the Iberian evidence can give rise to such conclusions, and to suggest an alternative view.

The 'Colonies'

The notion that there is no smoke without fire lends support to the colonist view: while individual parallels with the Aegean may not be impressive, in aggregate they often appear convincing. The dangers of this process, applied to the early American civilisations, have been succinctly illustrated by J. H. Rowe [8]. All traits of exotic appearance are selected, in a somewhat subjective manner, from their cultural contexts, and labelled as foreign or imported. The 'Import Ware' of Vila Nova de São Pedro, for instance [9], is in fact the defining ceramic characteristic of the Portuguese Chalcolithic culture of the Estremadura. Petrological examination has shown it to be of local manufacture. Pottery and other finds seem to be included in the colonist assemblage only if an Aegean parallel can be found for them, otherwise they are relegated as 'indigenous'. Richer sites (like Los Millares, Vila Nova de São Pedro or Almizaraque) are designated colonies, the remainder are native.[4]

In fact only a limited number of features link the different proposed 'colonies', each of which shows rich and striking local features. Three important features lie at the heart of the discussion.

1. *Fortified settlements, sometimes with semi-circular bastions.* Semicircular bastions are known from three Aegean Early Bronze Age sites: Chalandhriani in Syros, Panermos in Naxos, and Lerna.[5] There are a few further fortified sites of the period, notably at Troy, Thermi, Poliochni, Phylakopi and Askitario. In a valuable article, Arribas [11] lists no fewer than 24 fortified sites of the Iberian Bronze I (Chalcolithic), more than half of the total of settlement sites known. Some of these have not been excavated, and not all of these need in fact be as early as the Chalcolithic period. But it seems that there are more fortified sites known in Iberia than in the Aegean. Certainly the Iberian examples seem to amount to more than a few colonies. Surely the need for fortification requires a different explanation, in terms of the development of Iberian culture at the time and its growing complexity. The existence of bastions may likewise plausibly be explained functionally. Similar bastions have in fact been found at Buhen in XIIth dynasty Nubia. They are almost certainly independent of the Aegean examples. Their independent invention does not appear a particularly remarkable one.

2. *Copper metallurgy, and the use of the two-piece mould.* Metallurgy is an important feature of the period· but there seems little to link it with that of the Aegean. The midribs on the Alcalà daggers [13] could well be the result of annealing and hammering-up, and there is no good evidence for the use of the two-piece mould in Iberia at this time [14], so that this important piece of evidence disappears. The Alcalà dagger form is not closely similar to the Aegean ones, and the absence of such typically Aegean forms as double-spiral pins, spearheads and tweezers is more notable than the presence of such simple and functional objects as flat axes and awls, which are indeed ubiquitous in Europe. The early and sparing use of copper in the Vinča—Tordos and Boian cultures—before the development of metallurgy in the Aegean—and its early and sporadic occurrence throughout Anatolia and the Near East seem arguments for multiple independent discoveries of the use of copper, both by hammering and casting and its extraction from oxide and carbonate ores. Why not in Iberia?

3. *Collective burial in built tombs.* Collective burial in caves was already practised in Iberia in the Neolithic period [15]. Multiple burial in round tombs is seen in the Neolithic Almerian culture, and in the first Portuguese *antas* which may well be as early. These are very much earlier than the Mycenaean *tholos* burials (which were in any case not collective) and probably antedate the Early Minoan round tombs and graves of the Cycladic

Keros-Syros culture. They do find a better parallel in the recently discovered Neolithic cemetery at Kephala [16] in the Cycladic island of Kea (pl. 34*a*). There seem however no compelling reasons to link the simple form of the Kephala tombs with those of Almeria. To do so would necessitate a pre-colonist incursion from the Aegean in the Neolithic period. This necessity was not felt by Childe, although accepted by Siret and Blance.

It may be felt that these three important features of Chalcolithic Iberia, fortification, metallurgy and built tombs, are not surprising in a proto-urban culture, founded as it was on a very flourishing Neolithic, with which there is no apparent discontinuity.

The second objection to Aegean colonisation is the geographical and chronological dispersion, both in Iberia and in the Aegean, for the parallels cited, which themselves are not always impressive. The matter is made more difficult by the virtual absence of an absolute chronology (and disagreement over a relative one) for Iberia. So far the only fixed point is provided by a Carbon-14 date of 2345 ± 85 BC (H-204), apparently for the transition between Los Millares I and II, corroborated by the date of 2430 ± 120 BC (KN-72) for Almagro and Arribas's Tomb 19 at Los Millares, a round tomb with passage, and by a date of 2210 ± 110 BC for Praia das Maçâs in the Estremadura (west chamber) [17]. The early phase at Los Millares may thus well be earlier than the Aegean Early Bronze II period (that of Chalandhriani, Aghios Kosmas and Early Helladic II Lerna) where metallurgy and round bastions make their appearance. This objection applies equally to the painted ware of the Almeria district, which does not in any case resemble that of the Aegean.

Pattern-burnish ware was classed as 'colonist' by Blance on the basis of unstratified occurrence at Mesas de Asta and Carmona. It occurs also at Lapa do Fumo and Carambolo de Sevilla [18]. Its chronological position in Iberia is not clear, while the closest parallel in the Aegean is in the Late Neolithic at the end of the 4th millennium BC. But a far closer parrallel for the design has been indicated by Evans and illustrated by Bray [19] from the painted ware of the Italian Ripoli culture.

The schematic female figurines again are seen in the preceding Neolithic of Iberia. And examples of the 'Cycladic' violin form are rare. The very wide range of varieties includes a majority with well-delineated extended arms. These have clear parallels in the rock painting of the time and have plausible prototypes in the earlier 'Levantine' art.[7] There is no need to seek an eastern source for a 'mother goddess' if such a person be found desirable. The very wide range of Chalcolithic figurines—flat in Portugal, often round in the Badajoz and carved on phalanges in Almeria—do not have good parallels in the Aegean, unless the emphasis of the eyes is taken alone as a significant feature, nor is *Symbolkeramik* found there. On the contrary, when the complete ceramic assemblages of Iberia and the Aegean are compared, they are notably dissimilar.[8]

The use of rock-cut tombs by some of the original 'colonists' can hardly be an Aegean feature, since they do not appear in the Aegean until the end of the Early Bronze Age. Most of the Iberian ones are in the Portuguese Estremadura, where they are notably associated with Beaker burials. The tombs at Alcaide, quoted by Childe, had Argaric grave goods [23], but they do at least have a rather close parallel at Thapsos in Sicily (pl. 1b, 2a). But the context there is contemporary with the El Argar culture, and does not therefore bear on Chalcolithic Spain.

Other 'colonist' features cited by Miss Blance are the red monochrome and highly burnished grey wares, stone and bone containers, and herring-bone masonry. There is no way of refuting or substantiating such generalised traits. The site of Vila Nova de São Pedro does present a somewhat more specific parallel in the form of a bird-headed pin of bone, but the form is not identical with the examples from Syros and Thermi, and indeed neither this nor the 'vase-headed' pin is strikingly original. Vila Nova de São Pedro is indeed among the richest of the Iberian Chalcolithic settlements, but some of its features may be later ones, connected rather with Beaker developments.

The strength of the colonist theory is that it explains not only the possible origin of some of the 'exotic' traits, but why they are there. The ingenious suggestion that the colonists were metal prospectors is weakened however by the relative abundance of copper in the East Mediterranean, by the location of the tin ores of Iberia in the north-west (where 'colonist' features are rare), and by the total absence of tin in the local metal artefacts [24]. This would be strange if Los Millares were an intermediary in the tin trade from Galicia.

It fails, however, to account for numerous other exotic features including decorated phalanges, baetyls, pressure-flaked flint daggers, concave-based arrowheads, pinecones, sandals, mattocks, ostrich egg beads, amber, ivory combs, copper arrowheads (Palmella points), *Symbolkeramik*, schist croziers, and schist and clay plaques. Moreover it can point to no single undoubted import from the Aegean: obsidian, for instance, is never found, although materials from Africa are. Indeed the earliest certain imports to the west Mediterranean from the east are the faience beads from Fuente Alamo [25], and the Middle Helladic pottery of Monte Sallia in Sicily [26]. There is no indication of Iberian maritime mobility over great distances: the amber is probably Portuguese rather than north European, and the callais is as likely to derive from north-west Spain as from Brittany.[9]

Professor Evans has suggested how, in the Early Bronze Age, various cultural traits reached Iberia by the slow process of 'culture creep' [28], and, as we have seen, there is sound evidence for contact, at least with Italy and Sicily during the El Argar period and later. There is no reason why various Aegean cultural traits should not have reached Iberia by stimulus diffusion, although perhaps no conclusive evidence that they did. But this process can hardly have brought about the revolutionary cultural change, with the simultaneous acquisition of metallurgy, fortifications and megaliths, which the colonists are supposed to have wrought.

Iberian Development

It is interesting to enquire how such very different interpretations of the Iberian material are possible. The ambiguities appear to arise essentially from the complete absence of a reliable relative chronology. The consequent chronological freedom has allowed some scholars, such as Bosch Gimpera, to hold that the single polygonal chamber of inland Portugal was the ancestor of the Passage Graves, while others, such as Forde and Childe, saw them as late and crude imitations of the more sophisticated forms. So easily is the typology reversed.

Today there is broad agreement about the relation of the Chalcolithic to the Neolithic and to the Argaric Bronze Age. But within the period the position is chaotic. While the Almerian culture may be accepted as Neolithic, its subdivision by Siret, followed by the Leisners and by Blance, is entirely a typological one. Moreover it is not clear whether the divisions are of chronological significance (as broadly accepted by the Leisners) or of a cultural one (as suggested by Blance). Most writers today see the Portuguese simple chambers as Neolithic predecessors of the more elaborate Passage Graves, but their chronological relation to the Almerian graves is unknown.

At the other end of the Chalcolithic, the transition to the El Argar culture is equally vague. Clearly some Passage Graves (for example some of the Los Eriales group) were constructed, not merely re-used, in the Argar period. In the Tagus region there is mixing between Argaric and Chalcolithic materials, which are apparently not separated stratigraphically at Vila Nova de São Pedro. The copper or bronze Palmella points are sometimes found with Argaric materials, and occur in many megalithic tombs at Los Millares and elsewhere.

Within the Chalcolithic the chronological position of the Beakers is totally confused. They occur at nearly every 'colonist' site (fig. 2) and at not one of these are they convincingly separated from 'colonist' material. At only two sites is there a chronological subdivision within the Chalcolithic. Los Millares is divided on typological, not stratigraphical grounds. Although Beakers are generally placed in the later phase there [29], they are apparently found in Los Millares I also [30]. At Vila Nova de São Pedro they are not found in the earliest level, but it seems that they may occur in the next, which is contemporary with the construction of the defensive wall [31]. They are the principal ceramic feature of the Portuguese rock-cut tombs, and are mixed with 'colonist' material at Mesas de Asta, Carmona, Almizaraque and elsewhere. Among 'colonist' sites they are absent only at Alcala: they are absent too at Alcaide, but this is an Aegean site. The Iberian Beakers are closely associated with metal finds. Since sometimes they cannot be separated chronologically many 'colonist' traits may be due to Beaker influence, especially in Andalusia and the Estremadura.[10] Certainly one suspects that the V-perforated 'tortoise' buttons of Vila Nova de São Pedro and S Pedro de Estoril [33] would have been classed as colonist had they not first been identified as Beaker [34]. M. A. Smith has indeed emphasised the inconclusive nature of Beaker contexts in much of Iberia [35], and her objection to the identification 'Beaker folk', like mine to the notion of 'colonists', is essentially that it involves an arbitrary division of the material.

There is a great need for further stratigraphic excavation in settlements, following the lead given by do Paço at Vila Nova de São Pedro. Amidst the present lack of sound evidence, it is not unduly surprising that to sort the material into 'colonist' and 'indigenous' at first seems progressive. But a systematic division into cultural areas might be more productive—to speak of Iberia as a whole is excessively general.

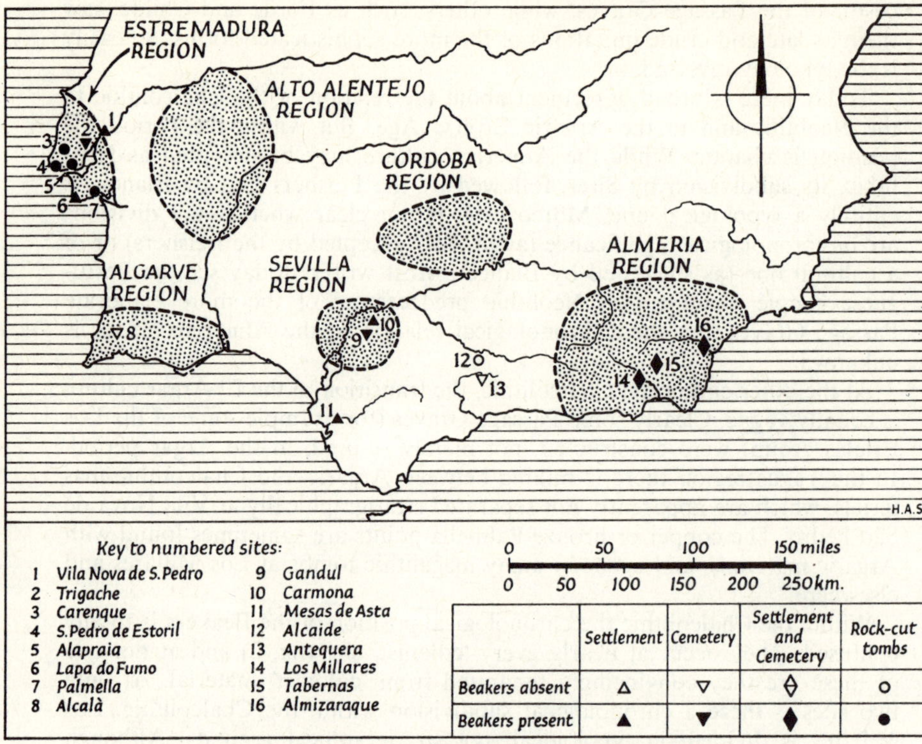

Figure 2. Cultural regions in the Chalcolithic of southern Iberia, indicating important 'colonist' sites and the presence of beakers at them.

On the basis, principally, of the excellent distribution maps of the Leisners,[11] at least six major regional groups may be distinguished in southern Iberia (fig. 2) on the distribution of graves, and the variation of grave goods :

A. Estremadura Group (Tagus estuary area). Corbelled tombs, rock-cut tombs, many concave-based arrows, tanged arrows, round limestone idols, Beakers, grooved and incised pottery ('Import Ware'), metal objects, Palmella points.

B. Alto Alentejo Group (Inland). Few concave-based or tanged arrows, schist plaques, croziers.

C. Algarve Group (Alcalà etc.). Corbelled tombs, concave-based arrows, no tanged arrows, baetyls, metal objects.

D. Sevilla Group. Cupola tombs with long passages, concave-based arrows, no tanged arrows, Beakers, some pattern-burnished ware (not in tombs).

E. Córdoba Group (Inland). Few concave-based or tanged arrows, paintings of schematic figures with arms defined (usually not in tombs).

F. Almeria Group (Los Millares, etc.) Corbelled tombs, concave-based and tanged arrows, many transverse arrows, *Symbolkeramik*, painted pottery, Beakers, stone figurines with arms defined, bone idols, phalanges, metal objects.

All of these share four additional features, as well as possessing Passage Graves: simple undecorated pottery, stone axes, flat-based triangular arrow-

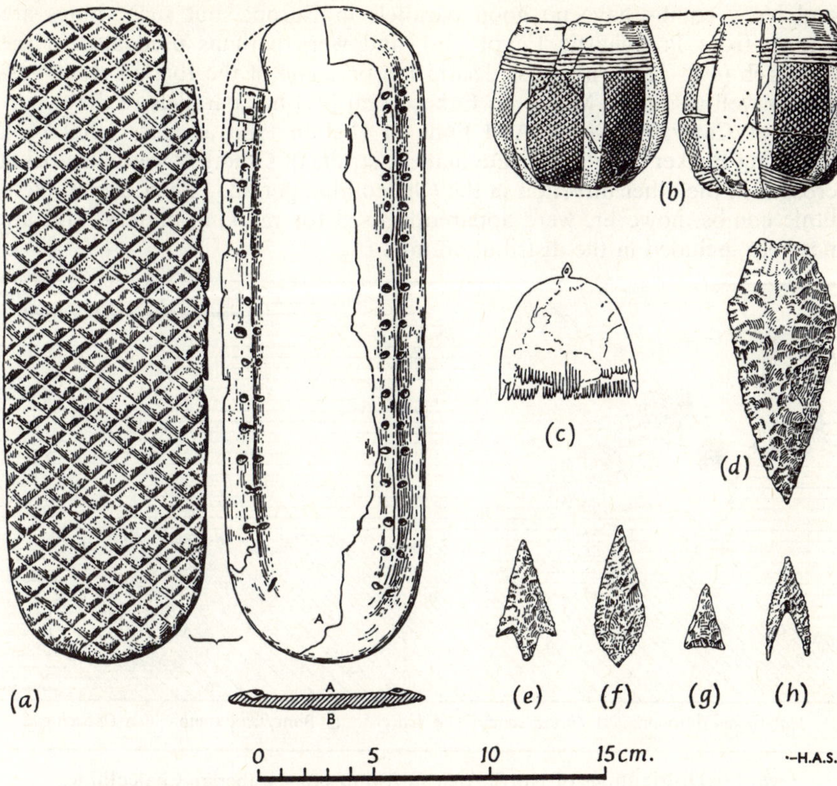

Figure 3. North African features of the Iberian Chalcolithic: (a) ivory sandal; (b) imitation ostrich egg; (c) ivory comb; (d-h) flat-flaked flint work (after Leisner, 1943).

heads with fine flat-flaked working, and schematic anthropomorphic figuration. There are seen already in the Neolithic Almerian culture and in the Portuguese Neolithic graves, although there is an evolution in the arrowhead. The rather schematic representation of the human form has a longer ancestry. The Chalcolithic cultures were certainly the inheritors of the preceding Neolithic.

Another contribution can be indicated. The Leisners and their predecessors already pointed out certain North African and Egyptian parallels in the Chalcolithic period [36], and Childe accepted the North African origin of the Almerian culture. It would be as extreme to derive the entire Iberian Chalcolithic from Africa as it is to do so from the Aegean. But at least there are some genuine African imports in Iberia (fig. 3 and 4), notably ostrich-egg beads (Grave 12 at Los Millares contained 800), and ivory, whether of hippopotamus or of elephant.[12] It seems likely that the magnificent flat-flaking of the daggers and arrowheads is of African inspiration, where there is a long tradition culminating in the Capsian Neolithic [37]. Flat-based, concave-based and tanged arrowheads are found there, and ostrich-egg shell beads are common [38]. The remarkable Iberian sandals and ivory combs have no good parallels in Europe, but such things are known from Predynastic Egypt [39], and were perhaps used also in the Maghreb [40]. The criss-cross decoration on some of the Iberian stone vessels as well as on the Monte do Cabeço seal [41] has parallels in the decoration of Capsian pottery. And finds of Iberian type at Gar Cahal [42], including Beaker sherds, indicate that the straits of Gibraltar were also being crossed in the other direction in the Chalcolithic period.[13] The Capsian Neolithic combs, however, were apparently used for marking pottery, and are not here included in the distribution map (fig. 4).

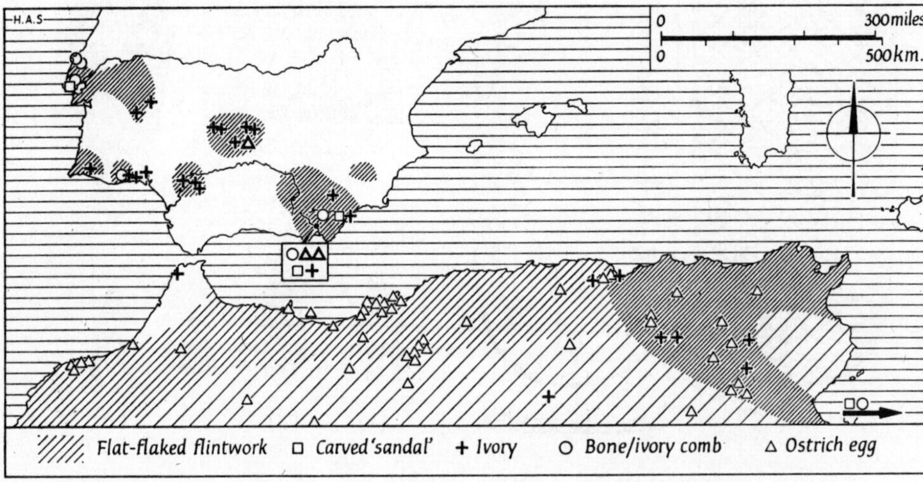

Figure 4. Distributions of North African features in the Iberian Chalcolithic.

The distinguishing features of the Iberian Chalcolithic may consequently be listed in a form which does not depend on massive cultural influence from outside, despite indications of contact with north Africa and within the west Mediterranean. They were at first limited to the coastal regions, for the Alto Alentejo and Córdoba regions retain a somewhat 'Neolithic' aspect until Argaric times. The following hypothetical processes may be suggested for the development from Neolithic to full Chalcolithic:

1. Full-scale passage graves developed from smaller local prototypes. The corbelled graves, of very limited distribution in Portugal, may have evolved in Almeria from the Almerian round tomb. From them developed in turn the Tagus rock-cut tombs and the magnificent graves with long passages of the Seville Group (Matarrubilla, Cueva de la Pastora) and of Antequera (Cueva del Romeral, pl. 2b).

2. Iconographic elaboration led to separated developments in the different regions: schist plaques in the Alto Alentejo, stone figurines and decorated phalanges in Almeria, schematic rock painting in Córdoba.

3. Ceramic elaboration, possibly with some influence from north Africa and Italy, led to painted ware and *Symbolkeramik* in Almeria, channelled ware in the Tagus, pattern-burnish ware in Seville. Beakers are particularly common in this region and in the Tagus district. The Leisners believe those of Almeria to be intrusive.

4. Copper metallurgy originated independently of outside influence and developed gradually in the metalliferous regions. Doubtless native copper was used in the first place. Its diffusion was aided by maritime contact between the coastal regions, and by the same processes which disseminated the Beakers. For the first time there was a valuable trading commodity, and the increasing prosperity and cultural contact stimulated an increase in the size of community and perhaps in degree of specialisation which is a first step towards urbanisation. The result was a flourishing proto-urban culture with notable achievements in architecture and in the crafts. A very similar process may be seen in the Aegean at about the same time, a little earlier in Sumer and in Egypt, and rather later in the Americas and in Africa. There is no convincing *a priori* reason why these processes in the different cultural regions of the world should be interconnected. In fact some were, others were not.

This view of a local development of culture and metallurgy in Iberia is, let it be admited, as much a hypothesis as the colonist view. But at least it avoids the early division of material into *a priori* 'colonist' and 'indigenous' categories. Ultimately, chronological evidence may be decisive against the colonist view, for C-14 dates towards the beginning of Early Helladic II (the proto-urban stage of the Aegean), of 2260 ± 56 BC (P-217), 2120 ± 65 BC (P-318), are not earlier than a developed stage of Los Millares. At present the Iberian chronology depends largely upon whichever of the current hypotheses for Beaker origins one accepts. If the Bell Beaker originated in Iberia, it must have done so before its appearance around 2200 BC in Holland. But there is at present no chronological evidence in Iberia to deny that some of the Beaker assemblage, such as the V-perforated buttons, may be much later. This may, of course, be part of a 'reflux' movement, but without better evidence from Iberia such a theory cannot receive very firm support.

The Iberian Chalcolithic may well have been underway by 2600 BC, comfortably before the inception of Aegean metallurgy [44]. But even if a shorter chronology be preferred, the Chalcolithic period must have lasted little less than a millennium. Within this period there is ample scope, geographical and chronological, for a gradual *process* of development, influenced by local factors in the various cultural regions and by their interrelation. This seems as likely as the overnight arrival of wisdom from the East.

Megaliths

As with Beakers or corded ware, the distribution of megalithic burial monuments has been and remains a central problem in European prehistory. There has been at times a tendency to lump all megaliths together as obviously related, the result of a single diffusionist movement, whether by colonisation or through the agency of megalithic missionaries. Sometimes the typological similarities have been emphasised at the expense of the cultural contexts, and it is this tendency which is here stigmatised by the German term 'Megalithismus'. (The Spanish 'megalithismo' does not have the same pejorative overtones.) Daniel, on the other hand, has recently called for a more cautious and critical approach, with fewer initial and implied assumptions [45]. The megaliths of Iberia have always been regarded by the colonialists as reflecting Aegean (or Egyptian) influences, which were then transmitted by the Atlantic route to the north-west. Other notable scholars have preferred a local evolution. And indeed the element in the colonialist theory that megaliths, especially corbelled Passage Graves, are derived from the east may well prove to be that theory's undoing.

Iberia has a wealth of varieties of megalithic collective tombs. But despite this range of types, the north European Gallery Grave, generally set in a long mound, is absent (except in Catalonia). A few striking tombs, such as the Cueva de Viera or the Cueva de Menga at Antequera, both in round mounds, cannot obscure this point. The standard form is the Passage Grave [46]. In France, both types are common, as in Ireland and north Britain, but in south Britain the Gallery Grave, whether Clyde-Carlingford or Severn-Cotswold in type, is more common. In Ireland the Passage Grave of the Boyne type is apparently later than the Gallery Grave. Indeed these arguments, the early C-14 dates for Wayland's Smithy and Monamore Cairn (3160 ± 110 BC, Q-675) and for 'unchambered' long barrows, and above all the discovery that these often covered some structure, albeit of wood, perhaps a prototype for the chambered barrow, has led to a general feeling that Gallery Graves, and megalithic collective burial in general, owe little to Iberian influence.

With Passage Graves, especially those of drystone construction with a corbelled vault, the position is different. Some of the finest Breton examples, such as Île Longue or Île Carn [47], show features, both in plan and construction, closely comparable with those of Iberia, notably the tombs of Los Millares, Seville and Alcalà [48], and again with the north-west, for example Corrimony, Maes Howe, Camster Round and tombs of the Boyne culture [49], so that there is a good prima facie case for some common origin or genetic relationship. It is of course supported by the fairly continuous distribution of megalithic tombs from Cadiz to the Shetland Isles, all broadly 'Neolithic' in date and with general similarities in grave goods (the so-called 'Western Neolithic' assemblage).

There are no megaliths in the Aegean. The orientalist approach has therefore been to regard the Iberian true megaliths (of orthostatic construction) as secondary to the *tholoi* or drystone corbelled tombs. These latter indeed have similarities in construction with those of the Mycenaean world, although the *dromos* is functionally conditioned by the necessity of an entrance passage into the mound. It became clear that the Iberian corbelled tombs were earlier than the Mycenaean *tholoi*, and Professor Piggott [50] neatly turned the tables by wondering whether the Mycenaean *tholoi* might not in fact be derived from Iberia, a suggestion that has not been warmly welcomed. *Nunquam ex Occidente lux!*

Of course some scholars derive the Mycenaean *tholoi* from the Minoan round tombs [51], although most of these seem never to have been vaulted. The Middle Minoan tomb at Kamilari (pl. 2c), for example, does not seem to have had a corbelled vault. Whether or not these tombs, which began in the Early Minoan I period, might possibly have served as effective prototypes for the impressive Iberian tombs, the little graves of Syros and Kephala (pl. 1a) are too small to carry much conviction, although they could conceivably have served as models for the Almerian round tombs.

The Early Minoan round tombs are not likely to be much earlier than about 2400 BC (on a C-14 chronology ; much earlier in calendar years).[14]

The radiocarbon dates for the Breton megaliths, including corbelled Passage Graves, provide something of a shock. Some are dated to about 3000 BC, notably Île Bono, 3245 ± 300 BC (Gsy-64) ; Kerléven, 2785 ± 125 BC (Gsy-111) ; Île Carn, 3030 ± 75 BC [53]. Here one must consider the validity of the French C-14 dates. That some material in megalithic tombs should be of much later date is not surprising, for it may well represent simply the continued use of a tomb of earlier construction, or the later construction of graves imitating earlier forms. This will be equally true in Iberia (cf. Anta dos Tassos, Portugal, 1370 ± 200 BC (Sa-199) and the corbelled chamber of Praia das Maçâs, 1700 ± 100 BC (17)). A C-14 date from a megalithic chamber should provide a *terminus ante quem* for its construction. But in the face of one or two extremely early dates in the 6th and 5th millennia BC (chiefly for cists within long mounds in Brittany) one is forced to fall back on the disappointing view that it is a *terminus post quem* for the death of the tree—the theory of bog oak. In such circumstances it might be argued that to accept any dates at all smacks of subjectivism. But it has to be emphasised that there now emerges a pattern for the Neolithic development of France and Britain [54] as indeed for the spread of farming throughout Europe. Neolithic pottery may be dated from about 3200 BC in Britain and earlier in France, and these dates are in broad conformity with C-14 dates for similar finds in the Breton Passage Graves set around 3000 BC. The acceptance by L'Helgouach, Giot and other scholars of these C-14 dates seems reasonable.

There remains then only the general problem of the overall validity and accuracy of the radiocarbon method. All dates in the present article have been quoted in radiocarbon years, based on the 5,568 half-life. It seems that any correction that has to be made to adjust these to calendar years will be on a world-wide basis, and will make them consistently several centuries older [55]. This may affect synchronisms with Egypt and the Near East, which have calendrical chronologies, but will apply equally to the Aegean as to the west European dates, on which the evidence here rests [56]. There seems little doubt that megaliths, including Passage Graves, were being constructed in north-west Europe by about 3000 BC (radiocarbon years) and hence perhaps by about 3700 BC (calendrical or true years).

The diffusionist is faced with a perplexing dilemma. The corbelled tombs of Spain resemble more closely the Breton Passage Graves than the Minoan round tombs. Either the Breton tombs derive from the Iberian ones, in which case the latter are 500 years earlier than the Aegean 'prototypes' ; or the Iberian are later than the Breton, from which they might then be derived. In either instance the argument deriving them from the east collapses. At present the beginning of the corbelled tombs of Iberia might be set as reasonably at 3400 BC as at 2400 BC. Only further excavation can resolve between these widely differing alternatives.

There is something very disappointing about all this confusion. After more than half a century of research, we simply do not know what was the origin of the European megaliths, or more precisely whether they had a single origin. We do not know whether the Iberian megaliths began earlier than the Breton ones. To assert that they did is at present little more than to state a personal preference between inadequately substantiated theories.

Much the same is true of the Iberian Chalcolithic development. The belief that it was instituted by colonists from the East Mediterranean has become one of those foundations upon which much of European prehistory has been built. But this belief may be totally wrong, and certainly it seems exceedingly difficult to substantiate at present with detailed and independent documentation. The alternative upheld here, that the Chalcolithic of Iberia developed locally, with the local invention of metallurgy and a minimum of outside influence, must equally be ranked a possibility. I believe that this theory does less violence to the existing evidence than does the colonialist view.

But in any case, more evidence is required. The real need in Iberia today is for further careful settlement excavation of the kind so ably executed recently by Almagro, Arribas, do Paço, Sangmeister, da Cunha Serrão and other of their Iberian colleagues. Settlements rather than tombs should one day provide the sound relative chronology which is at present lacking. Until this is forthcoming, it is difficult to see how further analysis of the available evidence can resolve with certainty the various possible explanatory hypotheses. And until such evidence is forthcoming we shall not understand properly the development of the Early Bronze Age in Iberia or the possible role of Mediterranean influences in the prehistory of western Europe. [1967]

NOTES

[1] The list illustrated by L. Siret [1] is: 1. cupola tombs; 2. funerary adzes; 3. axe symbol; 4. sign for water; 5. signs for rain or clouds; 6. sign for cuttlefish ('oculus motif'); 7. sign for the earth; 8. female statuettes; 9. worked flint; 10. hippopotamus ivory; 11. ostrich eggs; 12. alabaster vases.

[2] The value of examining the underlying principles for an archaeological theory, the model on which it is based, has been emphasised by Professor Stuart Piggott (3).

[3] The Los Millares culture and its contemporaries have been termed Eneolithic or Chalcolithic by some writers, or sometimes Early Bronze Age (= Bronze I). The term Chalcolithic is used here.

[4] Dr Blance started first with a careful and objective statistical analysis of the material, not published in her *Antiquity* article. What is in question here is the explanation adduced to account for it.

[5] The Aegean, and especially Cycladic, parallels are dealt with in greater detail in my Ph.D. thesis [10].

[6] The concept of functional association of cross-cultural traits has been accepted since the remarks of Tylor in 1889 [12]. It was central to Childe's concept of Urban Revolution that metallurgy and urbanisation were functionally related.

[7] See H. Breuil's work on Iberian rock art published in 1933 [20]. Not all of these are earlier than the marble figurines, but they have earlier prototypes. Egyptian prototypes for megalithic art and paintings are again argued by L. de Albuquerque e Castro [21].

[8] Childe, in more critical mood, actually dismissed this parallel, as well as those for the pottery and tombs, adding, 'Though much has been learnt about the Peninsula's prehistory and foreign relations in the past six years, reliable evidence for chronology based on an interchange of actual manufactures has not been achieved' [22].

[9] Amber sources in Europe, including Portugal, are mentioned by C. Beck *et al.* [27]. Siret suggested an Iberian source for callaïs (op. cit. [1] 39).

[10] It is not yet excluded completely that fortifications in Iberia may be a Beaker innovation. Apparently the fortified site (with circular bastions) at Lébous in the Hérault is of Beaker date (1930 ± 250 BC, Gif-156; compare 2010 ± 175 BC for La Grotte Murée, Montpezat, with Beakers, Gsy-116). Cf. [32].

[11] Students of Iberian prehistory will always be indebted to the Leisners for their admirable collection and presentation of so great a quantity of primary material.

[12] This is likely to be an import from Africa, although the possibility of fossil ivory cannot yet be excluded, cf. Leisner op. cit. 474.

[13] Other Beakers have been recorded in N. Africa [43].

[14] A radiocarbon date of 2400 BC (on the 5,568 half-life) may give a date in calendar years of around 3000 BC [52].

REFERENCES

1. Siret, L. (1913) *Questions de chronologie et d'ethnographie ibériques* 34, fig. 6.
2. Elliot Smith, G. (1930) *Human History* 364.
3. Piggott, S. (1959) *Approach to Archaeology* 3.
4. Childe, V. G. (1932) Chronology of prehistoric Europe: a review. *Antiq.* 211.
5. Childe, V. G. (1956) *Piecing together the Past* 135.
6. Blance, B. (1960) *The Origin and Development of the Early Bronze Age in the Iberian Peninsula,* unpublished Ph.D. thesis at the University of Edinburgh, partly summarised in her article, 'Early Bronze Age Colonists in Iberia'. *Antiq.* 192.
7. Almagro, M. and Arribas, A. (1963) *El poblado y la necrópolis megalitica de Los Millares.*
8. Rowe, J. H. (1966) Diffusion in archaeology. *Amer. Antiq.* 21, 334.
9. do Paço, A. and Sangmeister, E. (1956) Vila Nova de São Pedro, eine befestigte Siedlung der Kupferzeit in Portugal. *Germania* 34, 222. Illustrated by Miss Blance (op. cit. [6], pl. 25). (The broad grooving also seen on the pottery has no parallel in the Aegean Early Bronze Age.)
10. Renfrew, A. C. (1965) *The Neolithic and Early Bronze Age Cultures of the Cyclades and their External Relations* (unpublished, University of Cambridge).
11. Arribas, A. (1959) El urbanismo peninsular durante el bronce primitivo. *Zephyrus* 10.
12. Galton, B. B., *JRAI* 18, 270.
13. Leisner, V. and G. (1943) *Die Megalithgräber der iberischen Halbinsel, Der* Süden, pl. 79, 5–8 (Alcalà tomb 3) and pl. 14, 1 (Los Millares tomb 57).
14. This point, arising out of discussion with Mr J. A. Charles, is mentioned in Renfrew, C. (1967) Cycladic metallurgy and the Aegean Early Bronze Age. *Amer. J. Archaeol.* 71
15. del Castillo, A. in Pidal, R. M. (ed.) (1947) *Historia de España* 1, 506.
16. Caskey, J. L. (1964) Excavations in Keos 1963. *Hesperia* 23, 314, and pl. 45.
17. Almagro, M. and Arribas, A., op. cit. [7], 158, 263 and pl. 108 ; Leisner, V. and do Veiga Ferreira, O. (1963) *Revista de Guimaraes* 63, 360, 362.
18. Guerrevo, M. E. (1945) Excavationes de Asta Regia. *Acta Arqueol. Hispan.* 3, 39 and pl. 8 ; da Cunha Serrada, E. (1959) Ceramica com ornatos a cores de Lapa do Fumo. *Actas e Memorias do I. Congresso Nacional de Arqueologia.* Lisbon, 337 ; Bonsor, E. (1899) Les Colonies agricoles pré-romaines. *Rev. Archéol.* 35, fig. 83, 84, 86, 87.
19. Evans, J. D. (1956) Two phases of prehistoric settlement in the west Mediterranean. *Inst. Archaeol. Annu. Rep.* 13, 60 ; Bray, W. M. (1966) Neolithic painted ware in the Adriatic. *Antiq.* 102 and fig. 3.
20. Breuil, H. (1933) *Les Peintures rupestres schématiques de la Péninsule Ibérique* 2, fig. 27 and 37 ; (1933) 3, pl. 33, 37, fig. 38 ; (1935) 4, pl. 27, 35, etc.
21. de Albuquerque e Castro, L. (1959) A arte megalithica e as escritas ideograficas. *Actas e Memorias do I Congresso Nacional de Arqueologia,* Lisbon, 251.
22. Childe, V. G. (1953) The Middle Bronze Age. *Archivo Prehist. Levantina* 4, 167.
23. Gimenez Reyna, S. (1946) Necropolis de Alcaide. *Informes y Memorias* 12, 52. The Thapsos parallel was indicated by J. D. Evans, loc. cit.
24. Junghans, S., Schröder, M. and Sangmeister, E. (1960) *Metallanalysen kupferzeitlicher und frübronzezeitlicher Bodenfunde aus Europa,* analyses 297, 737, 825 ; do Paço, A. and Costa Arthur, M. L. (1952) *Zephyrus* 3, 31 ; do Paço, A. (1955) *Zephyrus* 6, 27.
25. Childe, V. G. (1957) *Dawn of European Civilisation* 6th edn., 284.
26. Taylour, W. D. (1958) *Mycenaean Pottery in Italy,* 54.
27. Beck, C. *et al.* (1965) *Archaeom.* 8, 97.

Plate 1. (a) Late Neolithic grave at Kephala in Kea, Cyclades.
(b) Rock-cut tomb at Alcaide, Spain.

Plate 2. (a) Rock-cut tomb at Thapsos, Sicily. (b) Corbelled burial chamber, Cueva del Romeral, Antequera. (c) Middle Minoan round tomb at Kamilari, Crete.

a

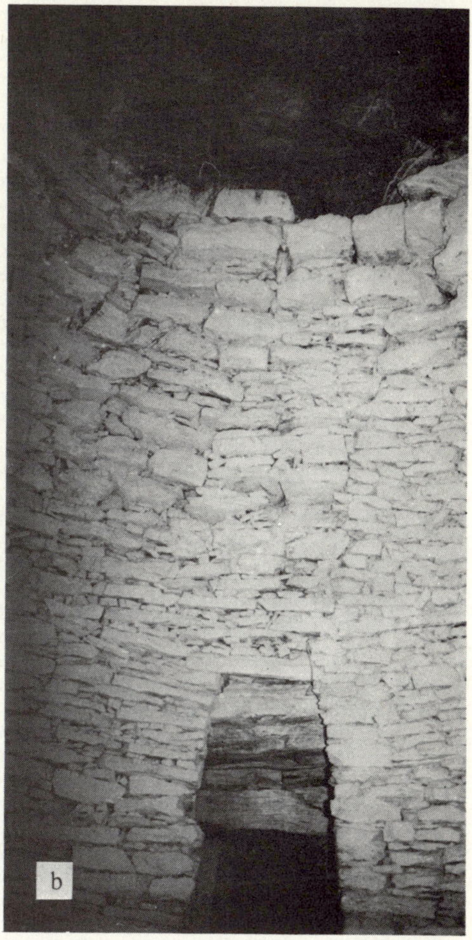

b

c

28. Evans, J. D., op. cit. [19], 67.
29. Almagro and Arribas [7], 236.
30. Leisner, op. cit. [13], 459, 566, 568, 590–1.
31. do Paço and Sangmeister, op. cit. [9], 222.
32. Arnal, J., Martin Granel, H. and Sangmeister, E. (1964) Lébous. *Antiq.* 191.
33. Leisner, V., do Paço, A. and Ribeiro, L. (1963) *Grutas artificialis de São Pedro do Estoril,* pl. 14.
34. Bray, W. M. (1964) Sardinian Beakers. *PPS* 30, 85, fig. 8.
35. Smith, M. A. (1953) Iberian Beakers. *PPS* 19, 106.
36. Leisner, V. and G., op. cit. [13], 558, 588.
37. McBurney, C. B. M. (1960) *The Stone Age of North Africa,* 247.
38. Forde-Johnstone, J. L. (1959) *Neolithic Cultures of North Africa,* 33 ; Camps-Fabrer (1966) *Matière et art mobilier dans la préhistoire nord-africaine et saharienne,* 295.
39. Childe, V. G. (1958) *New Light on the Most Ancient East,* 59.
40. Vaufrey, R. (1956) *Préhistoire de l'Afrique I, Le Maghreb* 411, and Camps-Fabrer, op. cit. [38].
41. Leisner, V. and G. (1959) *Die Megalithgräber der iberischen Halbinsel, Der Westen* I, 2, pl. 16, 1, 1.
42. Tarradell Mateu, M. (1955) Die Ausgrabung von der Gar Cahal, Schwarze Hohle, in Spanish Marokko. *Germania* 23, 13 and pl. 2.
43. McBurney, C. B. M., op. cit. [37], 255 (Beaker at Dar-es-Soltan) ; Camps-Fabrer, op. cit. [38], 494.
44. Renfrew, C., op. cit. [14], and see [52] and [56] below.
45. Daniel, G. E. (1970) Carbon 14 dates and the Chronology of European Megaliths. *Actes du VIIme Congr. Internat. Sci. Préhist. et Protohist.* I, 536–9.
46. Daniel, G. E. (1941) The Dual Nature of the Megalithic Colonisation of Prehistoric Europe. *PPS* 7, 1.
47. L'Helgouach, J. (1965) *Les Sépultures mégalithiques en Armorique* 22 (Île Longue) ; 37 (Île Carn) and Barnenez G.
48. Leisner, op. cit. [13], pl. 19 (Los Millares 47) ; pl. 60 (Cueva del Vaquero) ; pl. 61 (La Cañada Honda B), and pl. 77 f (Alcalà cemetery).
49. Henshall, A. (1963) *The Chambered Tombs of Scotland, I,* fig. 39, 114, 142 ; Piggott, S. (1954) *Neolithic Cultures of the British Isles,* 193.
50. Piggott, S. (1953) The Tholos Tombs of Iberia. *Antiq.* 137.
51. Hood, M. S. F. (1960) Tholos Tombs of the Aegean. *Antiq.* 166, discusses this question fully.
52. Cf. Stuiver, M. and Suess, H. E. (1966) On the Relationship between Radiocarbon Dates and True Sample Dates. *Radiocarbon* 8, 539.
53. *Antiq.* (1960) 147 n. 1.
54. Clark, J. G. D. and Godwin, H. (1962) The Neolithic in the Cambridgeshire Fens. *Antiq.* 10 ; Clark, J. G. D. (1965) Radiocarbon Dates and the Expansion of Farming Culture from the Near East over Europe. *PPS* 31, 58.
55. Damon, P. E., Long, A. and Grey, D. C. (1966) Fluctuations of Atmospheric C-14 during the Last Six Millennia. *J. Geophys. Res.* 71, 1055.
56. Many Aegean dates are given by Kohler, E. L. and Ralph, E. K. (1961) C-14 dates for sites in the Mediterranean area. *AJA* 61, 357. The adjustment proposed by Stuiver and Suess will result in a 'long' Aegean chronology, and may bring Aegean dates into better adjustment with the calendrical dates of Egypt.

12) Wessex without Mycenae

The real significance of 'Wessex without Mycenae' lies not so much in its early application of the tree-ring calibration of radiocarbon to European prehistory (see also Neustupny 1968 ; Bakker, Vogel and Wislanski 1969) but in its implications for the development of the European bronze age as a whole. It had for several decades been generally accepted that the early bronze age of central and north Europe, including the Unetice culture and its more northerly contemporary in south Britain, owed many of its metal forms, and indeed the whole inception of its metal industry, to the influence and activities of the Mycenaeans of south Greece.

Gordon Childe had expressed this view eloquently ten years earlier (Childe 1958, 124):

> While a distinctive bronze industry was being established around the Aegean, a neolithic economy still persisted north of the Balkans, the Alps and the Pyrenees. The Early Aegean Age corresponds in time to parts at least of Middle or Late Neolithic in Temporate Europe. But at least during the latter period, ripples generated by the Urban Revolution were already disturbing the self-sufficiency of the peasant communities. At the same time 'political events'—migrations and conquests—were preparing the sociological foundations for a Bronze Age economy.

On such a view the development of a flourishing bronze industry in central Europe was due to the activities of Mycenaean traders or metal prospectors in central and north Europe, who succeeded in setting up a trade in raw materials—copper and tin—which they arranged that their Mycenaean homeland should receive, in return for finished luxury goods.

Already before 1968 it was perfectly possible to question such a view: the evidence for direct contact in central and northern Europe was exiguous, and in the Aegean consisted solely of the Baltic amber found in Mycenaean burials. But it took the added support and encouragement offered by the calibration to aid in the explicit formulation of the arguments for the effective independence of the two areas.

Perhaps the only very persuasive indicator in Britain of Mediterranean contact at this time was offered by the faience beads found in early bronze age graves. They are the subject of chapter 13.

The controversy which these suggestions provoked is reviewed in chapter 14 (see also Snodgrass 1975). Here it is necessary only to refer to the more recent publication of much of the relevant data by Gerloff (1975) and to the chronological question. It should first be conceded (see chapter 14) that the few additional radiocarbon dates which have become available to supplement the very few from Wessex itself cited in this paper, have proved to be later than I suggested. The outcome, following the generally available calibration curves, is still to set the origins of the Wessex culture prior to the Mycenaean late bronze age, but does now allow a considerable overlap between them. McKerrell (1972) has, however, suggested an alternative calibration procedure, and hence argued that the Wessex culture is contemporary with Mycenae, thus opening the way again to all the traditional arguments about contacts between Britain and the Mediterranean.

His views concerning the calibration are reviewed in chapter 16. Here it should be sufficient to say that I do not accept them, and that, even if his calibration curve were a valid one, it would certainly not of itself re-establish that once plausible notion of a European early bronze age, dependent upon the Mycenaean world for its metallurgical skills, its metal forms, its system of social ranking and its economic development.

BIBLIOGRAPHY

Bakker, J. A., Vogel, J. C. and Wislanski, T. (1969) TRB and other C-14 dates from Poland. *Helinium* 9, 3.

Childe, V. G. (1958) *The Prehistory of European Society*. Harmondsworth: Penguin.

Gerloff, S. (1975) *The Early Bronze Age Daggers in Great Britain and a Reconsideration of the Wessex Culture* (Prähistorische Bronzefunde VI, 2). München: Beck.

McKerrell, H. (1972) On the origins of British faience beads and some aspects of the Wessex-Mycenae relationship. *Proc. Prehist. Soc.* 38, 286–301.

Neustupny, E. (1968) Absolute chronology of the neolithic and aeneolithic periods of central and south-eastern Europe. *Slov. Archaeol.* 16, 19–56.

Snodgrass, A. (1975) Mycenae, northern Europe and radiocarbon dates. *Archaeol. Atlant.* 1, 33–48.

WESSEX WITHOUT MYCENAE

The absolute chronology for the Early Bronze Age of Central and Northern Europe, including that for the Wessex culture of southern Britain, is not yet reliably established. This point was emphasised by V. Gordon Childe in his *Retrospect*,[1] and the following words were indeed the very last which he wrote. Speaking of 'the urgency of establishing a reliable chronology', he stated: 'A great deal of the argument depends on a precise date for the beginning of Unetice, that is at best very slightly the most probable out of perfectly possible guesses ranging over five centuries.'

At that time the basis for the absolute chronology of the Early Bronze Age was, as it largely remains today, a framework of synchronous links built up across Europe to the Mycenaean world of the Aegean Late Bronze Age. The assumption was made—and Childe stressed that it was an assumption— that European development and chronology were to be viewed in terms of 'the irradation of European barbarism by Oriental civilisation'.[2] Possible links for the European Early Bronze Age with Mycenae and indeed the Near East were eagerly sought in an attempt to build up a coherent chronology founded on this assumption.

The chronological correlations in the north—between Wessex, the later Unetice culture, and indeed the later Beakers of Britain and Northern Europe— are clear enough in outline, and they are not questioned here. What is in question is the validity of the supposed synchronisms which have been used to date Wessex and Reinecke's Period A2 to the time of the Mycenaeans. These synchronisms can be, and have been, doubted without reference to radiocarbon. But the point of the present article is to indicate that recent radiocarbon work puts C-14 dates for Wessex and its admittedly contemporary neighbours several centuries earlier than the beginning of the Aegean Late Bronze Age. The time has come to ask if we have not been building the chronology of the European Early Bronze Age upon a false premise.

Wessex and its Contemporaries

The Wessex culture was first defined in a classic paper by Professor Stuart Piggott,[3] a paper which remains basic today. Here he listed and discussed in detail the principal features of the culture, stressing the use of copper, gold, and amber, and indicating some of the possible links with the Mycenaean world, links which have been much discussed since. He stated that 'the imported pins show that the Wessex culture must broadly speaking run parallel with that of Aunjetitz, on conventional dating from 1800–1500 BC'. The presence of faience beads, then dated to 1400 BC indicated, he felt, a continuation until after that time. The pins in question are of crutch-headed type (four examples) and the type with perforated bulbous hollow head (from Camerton). Another significant indication of contact with the Unetice (Aunjetitz) culture was the presence there, for instance in the Dieskau hoard, of halberds and axes of English type.

In 1954 ApSimon discussed in detail the daggers of the Wessex culture,[4] distinguishing the triangular, six-rivet form, the Bush Barrow type, as characteristic of Wessex I, and the ogival, three-rivet, Camerton–Snowshill type, as typical of Wessex II. This division of the Wessex culture into two phases has been followed by most later writers.

The chronological position of Wessex *vis-à-vis* the Unetice culture was well summarised by Childe,[5] who put Wessex contemporary with Unetice, although not with its earliest phase. Setting aside the Mycenaean links, for the moment, most writers would agree that the Wessex culture began in the later part of Reinecke's phase A1, and flourished during Reinecke's A2, with the possibility of its survival into the earlier part of the Tumulus Bronze Age (Reinecke B1).

Conventional dates (based partly on Mycenaean links, of course) for Wessex I are: 1550–1500 (ApSimon), 1650/1600–1550/1500 (Hawkes), 1600–1550 BC (Atkinson) ; for Wessex II, 1500–1370 BC (ApSimon), 1550/1500–c. 1400 BC (Hawkes), 1550–1400 BC (Atkinson).

Although there are as yet no C-14 dates for the Wessex culture itself, we now have a few dates for late Beakers and for the Unetice culture, which give a fairly coherent pattern. The dates, as expected, show an overlap between late Beakers and early Unetice, and it seems reasonable to expect Wessex to date from about the same period. It will be convenient first to quote them on the standard 5,568 half-life for C-14, thus giving a date in conventional 'radiocarbon years'. In the next section an attempt is made to consider them in true calendar years.

First is the date of 1663 ± 160 BC (Bln-248) for the 'princely burial' of Helmsdorf,[6] datable to Reinecke's phase A2.[7] Beside this can be set the date of 1775 ± 80 BC (GrN-2996), which gives a *terminus ante quem* for a Unetice copper ornament from a grave at St Walrick in the Netherlands.[8]

The few dates as yet available from Brittany tend to place the Armorican Early Bronze Age at about the same time, as one would expect, following the chronological equation between Wessex and the Breton Dagger Graves, indicated by Piggott.

From the central grave at Kervingar, Finistère, in a barrow of the second stage of the Armorican Early Bronze Age, comes a date of 1600 ± 50 BC

(GrN-1670) ; and from a tumulus of the 'Old Bronze' period at Tuchenn Cruguel, Guidel, Morbihan, a date of 1320 ± 200 BC, (Gif-235) with the excavators' comment, 'rather too young'.

Four dates are available for the succeeding Breton Middle Bronze Age. From the barrow at Kervellerin, Cléguer, Morbihan, are dates of 1285 ± 110 BC and 1385 ± 110 BC (GsY-86) ; and from Lezommy, Cléder, Finistère, 1650 ± 200 BC (Gif-188) from the west grave, and 1200 ± 200 BC (Gif-189) from the south-east grave. These seem to confirm the dating of the preceeding Early Bronze Age. There are also fairly early dates for the Early Bronze Age material from Anlo in the Netherlands, 1670 ± 65 BC (GrN-852) and 1645 ± 85 BC (GrN-1977). All these dates serve to establish a broad time-range in radiocarbon years for the Early Bronze Age.

These dates are corroborated by those for Beakers in Britain and the Netherlands. Professor Piggott is so far the only writer to discuss in some detail the chronological relation between the later British Beakers and the Wessex culture, although D. L. Clarke by implication supports the overlap of the later Beakers and Wessex in placing[9] the beginning of the Wessex culture 'at the height of the Developed/Late Southern beaker expansion c. 1550 BC'. Piggott has stated[10]: 'the whole of the later phase of the Beaker cultures in Britain, and a *fortiori* that of the Long-Necked Beakers and the Dagger and Battle-Axe Graves, must also belong to the Reinecke A phase, and largely to the second part of it'. Dates for the later Beaker period in Britain should thus be approximately contemporary with Reinecke A2 and with at least the earlier phase of the Wessex culture. We have a couple of Beaker dates from Britain: 1800 ± 150 BC (BM-60) for 'B' Beaker pottery from Antofts Windypits, and 1850 ± 150 BC (BM-133) for 'Necked Beaker' pottery from Fifty Farm, Suffolk.

For Wessex itself there is none, although the Stonehouse dates are set out in the next section. However, a date of 1810 ± 90 BC (NPL-69) for the timber circle at a barrow at Bleasdale, Lancashire, may antedate the cremation urn of 'Pennine' type found there, and could possibly be contemporary with Wessex.

There are none the less several dates for British Middle Bronze Age material which should certainly be later than the Wessex culture. Even if we set aside those from the barrow at Amesbury—2010 ± 110 BC (NPL-77) ; 1640 ± 90 BC (NPL-75)—as possibly from a Chalcolithic context, we are left with several others which form a coherent pattern. At City Farm, Oxfordshire, a ring-ditch urn-cremation cemetery provided dates of 1510 ± 65 BC (GrN-1685) and 1490 ± 60 BC (GrN-1686), and a burial above Middle Bronze Age pottery at Codicote, Hertfordshire, gave a date of 1405 ± 160 BC (NPL-18). The pattern is filled out by the overhanging-rim urn burial at Swarkestone, Derbyshire, dated 1395 ± 160 BC (NPL-17) and dates from Penmaenmawr stone circle 278: 1405 ± 155 BC (NPL-10) and 1520 ± 145 BC (NPL-11). Other dates which further document this picture have been given by Mr Geoffrey Lewis in a recent paper.[11] The British Middle Bronze Age clearly begins, in radiocarbon years, c. 1500–1400 BC.

All this therefore serves to establish the relative chronology of the Wessex culture with respect to its north European neighbours. Some of these have been dated by means of radiocarbon determinations and the translation of these dates into calendar years becomes a crucial problem. It will be seen that they then conflict with the Mycenaean synchronisms, by means of which the Wessex culture has generally been dated.

Dendrochronology and Radiocarbon

Perhaps the most significant advance in radiocarbon dating, since its invention twenty years ago, has been the calibration of C-14 dates on an absolute time scale, provided by tree-ring dates. This effectively bypasses the discussion about the half-life of radiocarbon, and the possible errors caused in C-14 dates by fluctuations in the production of radioactive carbon (whether or not caused by variations in the earth's magnetic field) or its distribution in the ocean reservoir and in the atmosphere. By taking C-14 samples from reliably dated tree-rings, the date in 'radiocarbon years' for a sample of known true age—i.e. in calendar years—can be established, and a calibration chart built up which will automatically take into account the factors mentioned, and convert from 'radiocarbon years' to calendar years.

The first results using Californian bristlecone pine were reported by Damon, Long, and Grey,[12] and their reliability on a world-wide basis is supported by independent work in Japan.[13] Dr W. C. Ferguson of the University of Arizona at Tucson has now taken the bristlecone pine tree-ring sequence back to before 4000 BC, and the resultant calibration of radiocarbon years in terms of calendar years will have an important effect on European chronology. Just how important is indicated by fig. 1, which is taken from a recent paper by Suess.[14]

For example, a radiocarbon date of 2300 ± 50 BC (5,568 half-life) gives a date in calendar years of c. 2900 ± 80 BC. The several kinks in the curve indicate, of course, that a single C-14 date may not have a single equivalent in calendar years, and it is important always to consider the standard deviation of the dates. But the over-all message is clear: all C-14 dates over this time range become very much earlier when translated into calendar years.

In particular the mean date for the Helmsdorf barrow of 1663 BC now becomes c. 1900 BC; the mean date for St Walrick of 1775 BC becomes 2000 BC with the possibility that it may fall as early as 2300 BC. The mean date for the Armorican Early Bronze Age burial at Kervingar—and note that it belongs to the second phase of the Breton Early Bronze Age—becomes c. 1850 BC. Those from Early Bronze Age Anlo in the Netherlands become c. 1930 BC and c. 1900 BC respectively.

If these dates stood alone they could perhaps be dismissed. But C-14 dates from Rumania between 2600 BC and 2100 BC for the beginning of the Early Bronze Age[15] now fall between 3300 BC and 2500 BC in calendar years. And a coherent pattern begins to appear for the beginning of the Early Bronze Age in East-Central Europe as well as further north. In northern Europe there are, as yet, few radiocarbon dates for the Early Bronze Age itself, but the series of Beaker dates can be utilised here to set the upper limit. For instance an early Bell Beaker date for Vlardingen of 1940 BC[16] gives a date in calendar years of c. 2400 BC. And Sangmeister has stated that his Beaker *Rückstrom* movement took place during Reinecke's phase A1. All-over Corded Beakers, classed by Sangmeister as belonging to his 'Reflux' have been dated by C-14 to between 2200 BC and 1900 BC (radiocarbon years)—hence between c. 2800 BC and 2200 BC in calendar years, on the basis of the tree-ring calibration. It does seem, therefore, that the radiocarbon dates can be applied without endangering the relative chronology of the Chalcolithic and Early Bronze Age of Central and Northern Europe.

The British Beaker dates from Windypits and Fifty Farm conform well with this picture, being set, after calibration, c. 2250 ± 200 BC. And at the other end of the Wessex culture, the beginning of the Middle Bronze Age, set about 1500–1400 BC in radiocarbon years, becomes c. 1800–1700 in calendar years.

The dramatic nature of the change in British chronology which results from the dendrochronological calibration of the C-14 dates can most clearly be illustrated by means of the series of dates from Stonehenge. Both the radiocarbon date and their calibrated equivalent are set out in the following table.

Radiocarbon dates for Stonehenge, given both on the 5,568 half-life, and in 'true' calendar years after dendrochronological calibration.

Context	Period	Date (5,568 half-life) BC	Lab. no.	Approx. date in calendar years (using Suess calibration) BC
Primary silt of ditch	I	2180±105	I-2238	c. 2930–2550
Aubrey hole 32	late I	1848±275	C-602	c. 2500–1900
Bottom of incomplete R-hole	II	1620±110	I-2384	c. 2100–1700
Erection ramp of stone 56 (trilithon)	IIIa	1720±150	BM-46	c. 2450–1800
Bottom of Y-hole 30	IIIb/IIIc	1240±105	I-2445	c. 1700–1400

Professor Atkinson recently wrote[17] that the Stonehenge II/IIIa transition (which is generally linked with the Wessex culture) can be set in the seventeenth century BC, in radiocarbon years. This means that, in true years, on the basis of the bristlecone pine calibration, Stonehenge III—the sarsen structure with its trilithons—was constructed before 1800 BC and probably before 2000 BC.

Of course, all these early dates seem rather startling. Naturally we shall want to see corroboration, both by more C-14 dates for the European Early Bronze Age, and by more work of the kind undertaken by Suess and his colleagues. But it is worth following the implication of the new dating through to their final conclusions.

It begins to look as if Reinecke's A1 phase could be set from about 2400 BC to 2100 BC in calendar years. His A2 phase would begin about 2100 BC. There is no way of fixing its end at present, since the earliest fixed point in the European Bronze Age established through undoubted Mycenaean contacts is the link of early Urnfield (Reinecke D) with Late Helladic IIIB pottery at Scoglio del Tonno in southern Italy. Tentatively one could suggest the end of Reinecke's phase A2 at about 1800 BC. This will give a longer Middle Bronze Age than hitherto suggested in Europe, but the wealth of finds makes this not implausible.

With characteristic flexibility and intuition, Childe saw that the various 'Asiatic' parallels in East-Central Europe, notably in the Perjamos culture,

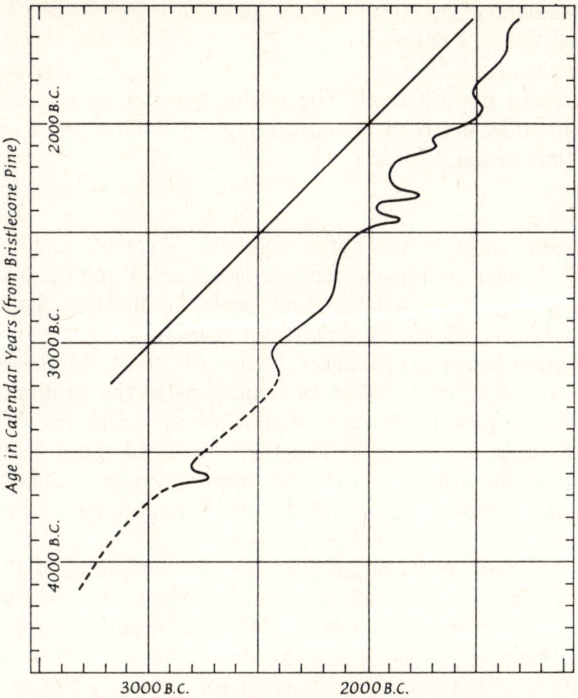

Figure 1. The relation between radiocarbon years and 'true' calendar years (dendrochronologically determined dates from bristlecone pine) from 4000 BC to 1500 BC (after Suess 1967).

which 'dated' the European Early Bronze Age, could be reinterpreted. The ingot torques, 'Cypriot' pins and so forth which are supposed to come to Europe from the Near East might in fact be earlier in Europe than at Byblos[18]: 'In that case their advent a century before or after 2000 BC would be a *terminus ante quem* for the beginning of Danubian IV.'

The beginning of the European Early Bronze Age has always—since 1929—been dated on the very questionable assumption that these types are imports into Europe. With the possible exception of the 'Cypriot' rat-tailed tanged daggers, which have no reliable associations in Europe anyway, all these types could very well be indigenous to Europe, and totally unrelated to the supposed parallels in the Levant.

All this discussion, of course, bears closely on the dating of the Wessex culture, which is closely bound up with that of the Unetice culture. If we accept that Wessex is broadly contemporary with Reinecke A2 (although beginning a little earlier) and that it continued perhaps into the early Tumulus culture (where the Camerton pin may belong), we may ascribe tentative dates on the new chronology to it.

If Wessex I — Reinecke period A2,
Wessex II — Later Reinecke A2 and early B1;

we may then suggest (in calendar years):

Wessex I = c. 2100 BC – c. 1900 BC,

Wessex II = c. 1900 BC – c. 1700 BC.

These figures are at present hypothetical. The essential point is not their precise value but the shift they imply in the chronology of Britain and Central Europe *relative* to that of the Aegean.

Mycenae and Radiocarbon

Unlike that for the Wessex culture, the chronology for Mycenae and the Late Bronze Age of the Aegean is not markedly lengthened by the dendrochronological adjustment of the radiocarbon time scale. In the first place, the Aegean Late Bronze Age is generally dated by Egyptian synchronisms, on the basis of the Egyptian historical calendar.[19] Secondly the C-14 chronology for the Aegean (on the 5,568 half-life, of course, as in the examples above and indeed on the 5,730 half-life) is too short when compared with that from the Egyptian cross-dating, as indeed are the C-14 dates from Egypt. The new calibration therefore brings the two approaches into a better equivalence, and does not produce the conflict with conventional dating which is seen further north.

For instance, a date of 1568 ± 51 BC (P-303) for the beginning of the Middle Bronze Age at Lerna now lies, after calibration, between 1940 BC and 1680 BC where the conventional date is c. 1900 BC. Again, a sample from the First Palace at Phaistos produced a radiocarbon date of 1525 ± 86 BC (Pi-15), considered by the excavators as 300 years too young.[20] The suggested calibration will put it between 1920 BC and 1700 BC in calendar years.

Professor Piggott has kindly pointed out that the same is true for the C-14 dates now available for the Royal Graves at Ur. In radiocarbon years they are much too young, but after calibration they are set around 2600–2400 in calendar years, which conforms much better with the historical dating for the Early Dynastic III period. Naturally it would be foolish to claim, on the basis of so few dates, that the calibrated C-14 chronology in the Aegean is in perfect agreement with the historical one. One problem is that the calibration has not so far been conducted in comparable detail for the period between 1500 BC and 0 BC (calendar years). But it can fairly be said that while in Northern Europe the Early Bronze Age dates are all set, after calibration, very much earlier than was previously estimated, the Aegean dates do not appear significantly changed.

Since we are now proposing to date the Wessex culture from 2100 BC to 1700 BC, while Late Helladic I, the first phase of the Mycenaean culture, begins about 1600 BC, the whole framework of supposed synchronisms for the Northern European Early Bronze Age, stretching across Europe to Mycenae, collapses. One has the simple choice either of retaining it and rejecting the C-14 calibration *in toto*, or of accepting the C-14 dates, at least tentatively, and following the consequences through.

Probably no one will be unduly dismayed if the old Periam–Byblos links[21] are scrapped. The other chronological links generally argued are those between Wessex and Mycenae, hence the title of this paper. These must now briefly be considered.

Wessex and Mycenae

Of the numerous supposed chronological links between Wessex and the Mycenaean world, the faience beads have always been the most uncertain. Childe himself reported them from Vinča and pointed out that they were common in the Eastern Mediterranean from about 3000 BC onwards.[22] They occur in what seem early contexts in the Periam culture and in Czechoslovakia. The study by Stone and Thomas,[23] although it failed to reveal by analysis any single source of the beads, demonstrated clearly their very wide chronological range. They occur, for instance, at Alaca Hüyük by about 2500 BC, and whether or not they were all made in the Mediterranean—which I do not believe—they have little chronological value.

Although the Baltic source of the Mycenaean amber has been called into question by recent work,[24] it seems possible that much of it will yet prove to have come from the Baltic. This would then establish contact with the north in Mycenaean times. And nobody can doubt the similarity between some of the Mycenaean amber objects, chiefly the perforated spacer-plates, and those from Europe. But if they originated in the north—whether in Wessex or in Denmark—the Mycenaean finds give *termini ante quos* for the date of manufacture in Northern Europe, not *termini post quos*. Amber spacer-plates continued in use after the Reinecke B2 phase in southern Germany,[25] and this may well be contemporary with the Early Mycenaean period. But neither these, nor the gold-bound amber disc from Isopata in Crete, can establish more than that Wessex is to be dated *earlier* than these Aegean contacts.

The goldwork of Wessex, especially such finds as the Rillaton cup, is often linked with the wealth of the Mycenaean Shaft-Graves. But it is difficult to see why. Both have gold, of course, but beyond that there is little resemblance: the neat incised linear patterns on the Wessex goldwork are not paralleled at Mycenae, where the decoration is predominantly curvilinear. And metal vessels were manufactured in the Aegean nearly a millennium before the Shaft-Graves.[26] Once again, if an Aegean prototype is desired—and it is difficult to see why it should be—we are not obliged to wait until Mycenaean times to supply one.

Professor Piggott has pointed out that the bone mounts of the Bush Barrow mace can be paralleled in very closely similar bone objects from Grave Circle B at Mycenae.[27] This circle can be set earlier than Circle A, perhaps beginning c. 1650 BC. But this is probably not early enough for Wessex, and in any case Dr David Clarke has recently suggested that Beaker decoration may provide a suitable prototype for the Bush Barrow mountings.

The other supposed links between Wessex and Mycenae are less impressive. There is no reason to suppose that Mycenaean influence had anything to do with the origins of metallurgy in northern Europe, where Beaker metallurgy was well under way much earlier. The Pelynt dagger is without association, as are the Falmouth ingot and the British double-axes, and the supposed Mycenaean dagger carved at Stonehenge,[28] if it really is Mycenaean in form, has no more chronological significance than the signature of Byron on one of the marble columns of the Temple of Poseidon at Sounion.

The links for Wessex with Brittany and with the Unetice culture of Central and Northern Europe seem far more reliable, and the culture can be most plausibly dated by them.

Early Metal Age Florescence in Europe

The dating here proposed can at present be regarded only as a suggestion. We have no C-14 dates for actual Wessex material, and it would be wrong to claim that the chronology is yet clear. But if the suggestion proves acceptable, the link between Wessex and Mycenae is thoroughly severed, since even the new Shaft-Graves there are not generally dated before 1650 BC.

It is therefore worth seeking a new explanation for the wealth of Wessex, if it can no longer be seen as a product of 'the irradiation of European barbarism by Oriental civilisation'. In the first place, it is worth noting that the Wessex culture, or what we know of it, was not so much a way of life as a way of death. All our documentation is from burials, and the true innovation is therefore princely burial, together with metallurgical and other technical advances.

We see somewhat analogous developments in other areas at just the time when metallurgy really gets under way—in Chalcolithic Iberia, in the Copper Age of south-east Europe, and the Early Bronze Age of Brittany. And in all these regions Mycenaean influence has sometimes been suggested. In reality, however, these are not contemporary: the Copper Age in south-east Europe precedes the Beaker period, while Wessex and the Breton Early Bronze Age are later. In Iberia, Beakers probably appear later than the Chalcolithic metallurgical development. And all of these advances precede the appearance of the Shaft-Graves at Mycenae by many centuries. There are none the less apparent similarities and analogies between the developments in each of these regions, and indeed with the development of metallurgy in the Aegean Early Bronze Age. Exotic goods appear, increased wealth is documented by finds of gold and precious metals, and daggers are found, as well as the ubiquitous flat axes.

In reality a similar *culture process* is at work in each area at these different times. The development of metallurgy was clearly accompanied by an increase in wealth as well as an improvement in weapons.[29] In some areas, for instance in the Aegean Early Bronze Age and in the Wessex culture, an accompanying social differentiation is documented by a number of very rich burials. Just as the arrival and development of agriculture produced similar changes at different times and in quite unrelated parts of Europe, so the discovery and development of metallurgy had consequences which were sometimes analogous in different and unrelated areas.

Here human societies are reacting in analogous ways not to a widespread climatic or ecological alteration, but to a purely human development: the enlargement of the human 'environment' brought about by the invention of metallurgy. Prehistoric archaeology has not yet developed suitable concepts or an appropriate vocabulary to deal with cultural advances taking place in communities which can no longer be described as 'subsistence economies', where food production is no longer the sole or decisive factor producing culture change. In these circumstances it is perhaps not surprising that a diffusionist explanation for culture change has so often been found acceptable.

Our understanding of the Wessex culture is thus more likely to be furthered by a consideration of the technical, economic, and social processes at work in Wessex[30] than by reference to the Aegean or to Mycenae. In comparison with the need to understand the dynamics of culture change at this important stage in the development of prehistoric Britain, the precise absolute dating of the Wessex culture[31] appears a secondary question indeed.

[1968]

NOTES

[1] Childe, V. G. (1958) Retrospect. *Antiq.* 23, 74.

[2] Childe, V. G. (1950) *Prehistoric Migrations in Europe* 6; id. (1939) The Orient and Europe *Amer. J. Archaeol.* 43, 10.

[3] Piggott, Stuart (1938) The Early Bronze Age in Wessex *PPS* 4, 52; and a detailed and more recent account of Mycenaean contact in Mycenae and barbarian Europe, *Sbor. Nar. Muz. v Praza* 20 (1966) 117. A more precise definition of the 'Wessex Culture' is now needed, with more clearly defined chronological subdivisions. The forthcoming study by Miss Sabine Gerloff will be very welcome.

[4] ApSimon, A. M. (1954) Dagger Graves in the Wessex Bronze Age. *Inst. Archaeol. Ann. Rep.* 10, 37.

[5] Childe, V. G. (1957) *The Dawn of European Civilization* 339.

[6] Kohl, G. and Quitta, H. (1966) Berlin radiocarbon measurements II. *Radiocarbon* 8, 29.

[7] von Brünn, W. A. (1959) *Die Hortfunde der früheren Bronzezeit aus Sachsen-Anhalt, Sachsen und Thüringen* 25.

[8] Butler, J. J. and van der Waals, J. D. Bell Beakers and early metal working, *Palaeohist.* 12, 54.

[9] Clarke, D. L. (1966) Reclassification of British Beaker pottery. *Palaeohist.* 12, 196.

[10] Piggott, S. Abercromby and after: the Beaker cultures of Britain re-examined, in Foster, I. L. and Alcock, L. (eds.) (1963) *Culture and Environment* 90.

[11] Lewis, G. D. (1966) Some radiocarbon dates from the Peak District. *Derbysh. Archaeol. J.* 86, 115.

[12] Damon, P. E., Long, A. and Grey, D. C. (1966) Fluctuations of atmospheric C-14 during the last six millennia. *J. Geophys. Res.* 71, 1055; cf. also Stuiver, M. and Suess, H. E. (1966) On the relationship between Radiocarbon dates and true sample age. *Radiocarbon* 8, 534.

[13] Kigoshi, K. and Kobayashi, H. (1966) Gakushin radiocarbon measurement. *Radiocarbon* 8, 55.

[14] Suess, H. E. (1967) Bristlecone pine calibration of the radiocarbob time scale from 4100 BC to 1500 BC, in *Radioactive Dating and Methods of Low Level Counting* (International Atomic Energy Agency, Vienna) 143. See also Ralph, E. K. and Michael, H. N. (1967) Problems of the radiocarbon calendar. *Archaeom.* 10, 3; and Bucher, V. and Neustupny, E. (1967) Changes in the Earth's magnetic field and radiocarbon dating. *Pamatky archeol.* 599.

[15] Ochre Grave, Baia-Hamangia: Bln-29, GrN-1995; Cernavoda-Ezero culture: Bln-61a, 61, 62. See also Neustupny, E. (1968) Absolute chronology of the Neolithic and Aeneolithic periods in central and south-eastern Europe. *Slov. Archeol.* 16, 19.

[16] Butler and van der Waals, op. cit. (n. 8), 47.

[17] Atkinson, R. J. C. (1967) Further radiocarbon dates for Stonehenge. *Antiq.* 41, 63.

[18] Childe, op. cit. (n. 5) 135.

[19] Hayes, W. C., Rowton, M. B. and Stubbings, F. H. (1962) Chronology: Egypt, Western Asia, Aegean Bronze Age. *Cambridge Ancient History* 1, ch. vi.

[20] Ferrara, G., Reinharz, M. and Tongiorgi, E. (1959) C-14 dating in Pisa. *Radiocarbon* 1, 107.

[21] Childe, V. G. (1929) *The Danube in Prehistory* 239; id. (1957) *The Dawn of European Civilization* 134; Gimbutas, M. (1965) *Bronze Age Cultures in Central and Eastern Europe* 34.

[22] Childe, V. G. (1956) *Prehistoric Communities of the British Isles* 145.

[23] Stone, I. F. S. and Thomas, L. C. (1956) The use and distribution of faience beads in the Near East and prehistoric Eurne. *PPS* 22, 37; Newton, R. G. and Renfrew, C. The Origin of the British Faience Beads reconsidered. *PPS* 35.

[24] Beck, C. W., Wilbur, E., Meret, S., Kossovo, M. and Kermani, K. (1965) The infra-red spectra of amber and the identification of Baltic amber. *Archaeom.* 8, 96.

[25] Sandars, N. K. (1959) Amber spacer-beads again. *Antiq.* 33, 292.

[26] Renfrew, C. (1967) Cycladic metallurgy and the Aegean Early Bronze Age. *Amer. J. Archaeol.* 71, pl. 10.

[27] Athens National Museum 8623, exhibited in April 1968 with material from Grave ×.

[28] Mr Grinsell points out that the Badbury carvings do, on the other hand, have some stratigraphic context.

[29] Renfrew, C. (1969) Trade and culture process in European Prehistory *Curr. Anthrop.* 10, April.

[30] For example the valuable paper by Britton, D. (1963) Traditions of metal-working in the Later Neolithic and Early Bronze Age of Britain *PPS* 29, 258

[31] For helpful and constructive criticism I am very grateful to Mr Andrew Fleming, Mr L. V. Grinsell, Mr Geoffrey Lewis, and Professor Stuart Piggott. The diagram, FIG. 1, was very kindly drawn by Mr H. A. Shelley.

Additional Note

Dr H. E. Suess of the University of California, San Diego, has kindly written recently to say that the period from 1500 BC to 0 BC has now been calibrated accurately. Moreover, since the first preliminary calibration curve (FIG. 1 above) was published, some 300 additional precision measurements have been carried out on bristlecone pine wood. As a result, some modifications have to be made to the published curve, which while only an approximation at the detailed level remains correct in general outline. It should be noted that while the kinks in the curve inevitably imply a greater time range for individual dates, they offer at the same time the possibility of very much more accurate dating of logs of wood which themselves contain a large number of tree rings.

Clearly it may be some time before the prehistoric chronology of Europe can be worked out precisely in calendar years. But already it is clear that significant changes in the conventional chronological picture will result.

13) British Faience Beads Reconsidered (with R. G. Newton)

In the light of the re-evaluation of the central and north European links with the Mediterranean world, reported in chapter 12, the small blue faience beads of the British early bronze age took on a new significance. Since the days of the early Cretan discoveries of Evans, it has been realised that these beads resembled those of the East Mediterranean world, and had probably an Egyptian origin (Evans 1909). This then constituted a crucial link between Britain and the Mediterranean world.

Stone and Thomas (1956) in a pioneering study had used the technique of trace-element analysis by optical spectroscopy in an attempt to ascribe the British examples to their place of manufacture. The attempt was not successful. But they had published their data, which were later re-examined by Dr Newton using the statistical technique of Element Analysis. The results, reported in this paper, showed that the British beads could be distinguished statistically from those Mediterranean examples which had been analysed, and might well be of local manufacture.

This interesting result led to a reconsideration of the material by McKerrell (1972) using the technique of x-ray fluorescence. His conclusion on the basis of the new analyses (which themselves remain at present unpublished) is that the British faience beads have a foreign, probably eastern origin. At the same time, however, trace-element analyses by the technique of nutron-activation (Aspinall *et al.* 1972) served to confirm the conclusions to which Newton's statistical work had led, contrasting the compositions of the Mediterranean and the British beads, and suggesting a different and perhaps local source of origin for the latter. The original analytical data published by Stone and Thomas have also been re-examined by Doran and Hodson (1975, 251–7) using the technique of cluster analysis, yielding geographical consistency within clusters, and thus supporting the case made in this chapter for independent origins.

This position has also been strengthened significantly by analagous neutron-activation work on early bronze age faience beads from Czechoslovakia and Hungary (Harding and Warren 1973). For this area at least it is now clear that the faience beads were locally made. In this context, the unsolved problem of the few faience beads of early bronze age Iberia should also be noticed (Harrison *et al.* 1974 ; Schubart 1976, 340).

The matter is not yet settled, as far as the British beads go, and further work is at present under way. I predict with some confidence, however, that the star- and quoit-shaped beads will prove to have been manufactured within Britain or Ireland, and I suspect that this is also true for most, perhaps all, of the segmented beads. If this be so, it will have demolished the strongest single argument for direct contacts between Britain and the Mediterranean at this early time.

BIBLIOGRAPHY

Aspinall, A., Warren, S. E., Crummett, J. G. and Newton, R. G. (1972) Neutron activation analysis of faience beads. *Archaeom.* 14, 27–40.

Doran, J. E. and Hodson, F. R. (1975) *Mathematics and Computers in Archaeology*. Edinburgh: University Press.

Evans, A. J. (1909) Criticisms on the paper of Dr Montelius. *Proc. Soc. Antiq. London* 22, 121–8.

Harding, A. and Warren, S. E. (1973) Early bronze age faience beads from Central Europe. *Antiq.* 47, 64–6.

Harrison, R. J., Martí-Jusmet, F. and Giró, P. (1974) Faience beads and Atlantic bronzes in Catalonia. *Madrider Mitt.* 15, 95–107.

Schubart, H. (1976) Relaciones mediterraneas de la cultura de El Argar. *Zephyrus* 26/27, 331–42.

Stone, J. F. S. and Thomas, L. C. (1965) The use and distribution of faience in the ancient East and prehistoric Europe. *Proc. Prehist. Soc.* 22, 37–84.

BRITISH FAIENCE BEADS RECONSIDERED

The 'faience' beads of the British Bronze Age have since the last century been appreciated as the product of a somewhat sophisticated technology. Although the possibility of local manufacture was seriously considered by earlier antiquaries, especially for the Scottish beads, in more recent years—since the writings of Childe and Piggott—a Mycenaean or Egyptian origin has been widely assumed for them.

The theory of import from the Mediterranean, which is very plausibly based on the close similarity of the European 'segmented' beads to those of Egypt and other East Mediterranean manufacturing centres, has not been subjected to any very searching criticism. It has indeed been assumed for the east and central European beads as well as those of the north-west, and this assumption created a climate of opinion favourable to the acceptance of other evidence for Aegean contact (amber beads, gold cups) which could then be used to date the Wessex culture and the developed Early Bronze Age cultures of central Europe.

When Stone and Thomas considered the subject in great detail in their important and valuable paper 'it was confidently expected, in view of earlier work, that clear trends in the composition of faience beads would be found which could be correlated with both source and date of manufacture' (1956, 75). The hope was that spectrographic analyses of the British beads would allow a division into groups correlating with analysis of Egyptian and Mycenaean beads. In this way both a source and a date of manufacture might be ascribed to the British finds. This hope was not fulfilled and they were 'therefore, somewhat reluctantly forced to the conclusion that the spectographic technique does not confirm the promise of earlier investigations'.

The invasionist/diffusionist hypothesis in European prehistory, so eloquently discussed by Childe, has been questioned recently by several authors (Clark 1966; Renfrew 1969*a*). And indeed the Mycenaean origin of the central European beads has been dismissed by Dr Gimbutas (1965, 46) on chronological grounds, although without necessarily assuming their local manufacture. Moreover the conventional dating of the Wessex culture of Britain is called into question by recent work on radiocarbon dates (Renfrew 1968), which suggests that the Wessex culture had perhaps ended by 1700 BC. All these shifts in opinion make the theory of import of the beads from the Mediterranean very questionable, and the time is ripe for a re-examination of the whole problem.

Fortunately Mr Thomas's analyses of both British and continental faience beads were published in the original paper. It should be emphasised that his analyses and the studies of the late H. C. Beck and the late J. F. S. Stone form the starting point for the present study, which would not have been possible without their meticulous and pioneering researches. Thomas's spectrographic analyses have been studied by a new statistical technique (Newton and Spurrell 1967*a* ; 1969) which showed that most of the variation in the figures for the various geographical groupings of beads can validly be expressed in terms of a few elements. On the basis of figures for three elements the beads analysed by Thomas have been divided into groups. Beads from Scotland and England can be distinguished, and separated from those of the Aegean and Egypt, by means of the analyses. In the first part of this article the division into groups is established.

The Analyses Reconsidered

The spectrographic data in Stone and Thomas's paper are of two kinds which they call 'quantitative' (their table II) and 'qualitative' (their table IV). We have made use of both sets and it may be helpful to give a brief description of the differences in technique used to obtain the two sets of data.

The data in table II were obtained by focusing an image of the arc on to the collimating lens of the spectrometer. This means that the light from the whole 'burn' is integrated by the spectrometer but the level of intensity is relatively low. Consequently the elements detected are represented in their proper proportions but the low sensitivity means that some elements (such as silver) may be missed altogether if they are present in low concentrations. Their results were graded on the scale '–, 5, 4, 3, 2, 1', each of the decreasing numbers representing a tenfold increase in concentration. For the convenience of our computer approach, and for comparison with the data from table IV, we transformed their scale to read '0, 1, 2, 3, 4, 5', and these transformed data are used hereafter.

The data in table IV were obtained by focusing the light from the arc on to the spectrometer *slit*. This means that more light is available (and consequently the sensitivity of detection may be five to ten times higher) but the arc tends to wander and hence (because the elements 'burn off' at different rates) the relative proportions of the elements may become distorted. The results were graded on the scale 0 to 10, each of the increasing numbers representing a twofold increase in line density (but not necessarily the same increase in concentration), and this scale was used on the computer without alteration.

A preliminary study of the data in both tables showed that the results were highly correlated, most of the elements having a statistically significant correlation with four or more (and sometimes eleven) of the others. This means that the data are difficult to handle by classical statistical procedures, and it is easy to see why Stone and Thomas despaired of drawing satisfactory conclusions ; nevertheless, it is interesting to see how near they came to solving the problem.

The new statistical technique (Newton and Spurrell 1967*a* ; 1967*b* ; 1969) had been specially devised to assist statisticians to analyse data where the variables are highly correlated. Earlier attempts to provide such assistance involved the construction of new uncorrelated variables by combining the existing ones, thereby causing some loss of their identity. The new approach retains the variables in their original form and uses the effects of their inter-correlations to indicate the ways in which they should be introduced into the prediction equation. In particular the technique indicates which variable must be retained to improve the prediction of the dependent variable. Thus, in our case its use showed that a good discrimination between the beads from the different geographical areas can be achieved only by using at least three chemical elements, i.e. tin and aluminium, and either magnesium or calcium.

This is not the place to go into a detailed statistical discussion of the way that the technique was used in re-examining the data, although the lines of approach can be indicated. The results for the concentrations of chemical elements in table II were regarded as the regressor variables, and all were used in the statistical study with the exception of silicon (which did not vary), and lithium, silver and cobalt (for which there were only a few entries). The real problem concerned the choice of the dependent variable, representing the geographical (or morphological) groupings in which the archaeologist may be interested. Here it is usually a matter of trial and error but our first guess was a particularly lucky one. The geographical groupings were coded: 1 = Syria ; 2 = 2nd millennium Egypt ; 3 = Knossos ; 4 = rest of the Egyptian beads ; 5 = Isles of Scilly ; 6 = Malta ; 7 = Bohemia and Moravia ; 8 = Wessex ; 9 = Scotland, and the computer print-out indicated that a 75 per cent success in discriminating between the areas could be achieved by using the data for tin, magnesium and aluminium.

This hastily-conceived use of nine groupings of the dependent variable would certainly not be recommended again and it was successful in this instance for two reasons only. First, most of the faience beads fell in groups 4, 8 and 9 (25 from Egypt, 9 from Southern England and 11 from Scotland) and, secondly, the Scottish beads contained greater quantities of the elements examined than did the Wessex beads, and those contained more than did the Egyptian beads. Thus, in effect, only three groupings were used, and they happened to be in ascending order. It would generally be much safer to be less ambitious and to start with only two groupings, or three if care is taken to adopt a suitably logical sequence. Other groupings could then be added as and when the 'key' to the situation emerged.

Another statistical study was carried out on the data from table IV after deleting silicon, vanadium and cobalt, and a 56% success in discrimination was achieved by using the data for tin, calcium and aluminium. The data for calcium and magnesium are highly correlated and thus the results from the two tables can be regarded as essentially equivalent.

In order to illustrate the conclusions from the data in Thomas's table II, a diagram needs to be drawn in three dimensions, but a convenient arbitrary way of using two dimensions is to plot the ratio of two of the elements against the third. Here we are mainly concerned with the differences between the Scottish and the Wessex beads, and all of these contain some tin (except Wessex bead no. 7 which does however contain tin in table IV) and it is convenient to plot the Mg/Sn ratio against Al, as is shown in fig. 1. All the Scottish beads have a Mg/Sn ratio of 1·0 or more, whereas the beads

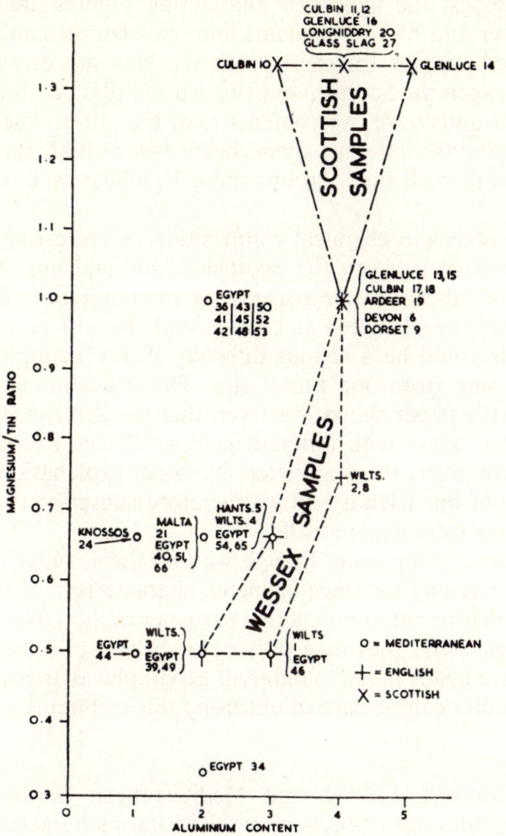

Figure 1. Plot of magnesium/tin ratio against aluminium content for all faience beads containing tin in Stone and Thomas (table ii, using the transformed data). Place of origin and sample numbers shown.

found in England generally have ratios of less than 1·0, and the beads from the two geographical groups thus fall into two areas on the diagram which meet at the point Mg/Sn = 1·0 ; Al = 4. Many of the Mediterranean beads contain no tin and they have therefore been ignored in this visual presentation ; only five of the Egyptian beads fall in either of these two areas of the diagram, and there is thus clear initial support for an hypothesis that the British beads did not come from Mediterranean sources. It is even easier to discriminate between the Scottish beads and any Mediterranean ones by adding the values (after transposition to our scale) for Mg + Al + Sn + Ti, because none of the twelve Scottish samples (ii faience and i slag) has a value less than 10 (average = 12.7) and none of the 40 samples from any other region (except England) has a value larger than 9 (average = 6·8). The hypothesis thus gains support when titanium is added to the picture.

An essentially similar diagram can be prepared to illustrate the conclusions from the data in Thomas's table iv, but in this case the calcium/tin ratio would be plotted against the figure for aluminium. Figures are also available here for the silver and barium contents and use of these can provide a third and improved support for the hypothesis. Now we can even achieve discrimination between the Scottish and English samples, the former tending to have higher Ba and lower Ag contents than the latter. The tin-containing Egyptian samples are different again, being low in both Ba and Ag, and our conclusion is that all three groups differ significantly in composition.

If we accept these differences in chemical composition as indicating statistically significant differences between the Scottish beads and any other group, we need to consider other possible reasons for the differences. Such a reason might be ion-exchange between the beads and the soil in which they were buried, and this could be a serious difficulty if, for example, all the Scottish beads had come from one burial site. The distribution map given in Stone and Thomas's paper shows, however, that the Scottish beads were found in at least four areas with different geological characteristics, and we therefore confidently reject this suggestion. No other explanation has yet occurred to us or any of our friends and we therefore subscribe to the hypothesis that the artefacts were made locally.

The spectrographic analyses, important though we find them, suffer from some insensitivity when searching for trace elements characteristic of those raw materials which may be present in only a few parts per million. Neutron activation analyses (Aitken 1961, 166) may provide a sharper tool for discriminating between faience beads made in different geographical areas, and it is hoped that further studies can be carried out using this technique.

Archaeological Implications

This separation of the Scottish, English and Mediterranean beads into groups, established above, does not of itself prove the local manufacture of the beads. But while the theory that all the beads were imported from the Mediterranean could still be upheld, it would require some very special pleading. Such pleading might be possible were there abundant evidence of Mycenaean or Egyptian influence on Bronze Age Britain, or even of evidence that beads with these compositions are to be found in the Mediterranean area.

In a recent paper (Renfrew 1968) it was argued that the Wessex culture of Britain was at an end before the emergence of Mycenaean civilisation. The dendrochronological calibration of radiocarbon dates would probably, for instance, set the construction of Stonehenge before 2000 BC. The faience beads of Britain would then comfortably antedate those of Mycenae. It has been authoritatively suggested that the faience beads of the early Unetice and Pecica cultures are likewise pre-Mycenaean (Gimbutas 1965, 46). Of course the manufacture of faience beads in the Mediterranean was already well under way: they are found in the Royal Tombs at Alaca Hüyük, for instance, as well as in Early Bronze Age Macedonia (Stone and Thomas 1956, 45 ; Heurtley 1939, 202, fig. 66j ; for the Indus finds, cf. Stone 1949, 201). But to suppose that the beads were imported to Britain in substantial numbers may well imply some pre-Mycenaean contact between Britain and the Mediterranean.

However, there is no good evidence for such contact: the western-most indication of sure and direct East Mediterranean contact in the West Mediterranean before Mycenaean times is the Middle Helladic pottery found in the Lipari Islands and in Sicily (cf. Renfrew 1967, 280). Faience beads are rare in France (Daniel 1960, 200, fig. 74) and only one has been found in Iberia.

The situation is equally difficult if one seeks an overland rather than a maritime route. If the ingot torques and knot-headed pins of the Pecica/Perjamos culture be discounted as evidence of Mediterranean contact (Renfrew 1969*b*) there is little left to establish relations at this time between the Aegean and central Europe. And indeed, with the exception of the finds at Arbon Bleiche in Switzerland and Odoorn in Holland, no faience beads have been found between Austria and Britain to make a link in the distribution in the two areas. It can be seen therefore that, far from conforming to a well-established trading pattern, the direct import of faience beads to Britain from the Mediterranean would be a rather precocious development—although not necessarily an inconceivable one.

Turning now to the British beads, the basic lists published by Beck and Stone (Beck and Stone 1935) and supplemented by Stone (Stone and Thomas 1956) suggest grave difficulties for the import theory. The commonest bead form in England, the segmented bead, does have close parallels in Europe and the Mediterranean, but the star and quoit beads present a very considerable problem. Fifteen quoit beads have been found in Britain, but only a single quoit bead is known from continental Europe, from Arbon Bleiche. So if this form was imported from the East Mediterranean, the oriental merchants dealt exclusively with Britain ; they left none behind at the place of manufacture ; and the chemical composition was unusual for the area.

Another type with a highly localised distribution in Europe is the star bead, a small cross bead with four arms (the 'four-rayed star'). In Europe it comes essentially from Hungary and the middle Danube. No prototype for this form has been suggested in the East Mediterranean, and it is difficult to see how import can be claimed.

The Scottish star beads are quite different from these small Hungarian beads, being larger, and with from five to nine points. Sixteen such star beads are reported from Scotland, three from Ireland, two from England and one from the Isles of Scilly. The distribution is thus preponderantly a Scottish one, and contrasts strongly with that for the segmented type, as Stone observed (Stone and Thomas 1956, 60). Of such star beads, only one has been found in continental Europe, significantly again at Arbon Bleiche on Lake Constance in Switzerland. Beck and Stone could find no prototype for this form in the East Mediterranean, and it is thus once again extremely difficult to view these beads as imports from Egypt or Greece. On the contrary, it seems very much more reasonable to view this remarkable find of a quoit bead and a star bead at Arbon Bleiche (the sole occurrence of either form in continental Europe) as imports from the British Isles. The same combination of star and quoit occurred again in a barrow west of Dorchester.

The distribution of these beads suggests their manufacture in Scotland, a view well stated by Ludovic Mann in 1906 (Mann 1905–6) but discounted, after careful consideration, by Stone and Thomas. Finds of faience beads in

Scotland have been most prolific in two areas. The Culbin Sands on the south side of the Moray Firth have yielded at least 15. And to the south west, the sands on the coasts of Ayrshire (Stevenston) and Wigtownshire (Glenluce) have produced about 20. Glass slag was also found at Culbin Sands, and although it has not been reliably dated (fission track dating might prove conclusive) the composition is essentially similar to that of the Scottish faience beads.

At this point the actual technique of manufacture of faience beads must be considered (cf. Lucas 1962, 156 ; Beck and Stone 1935, 207–11). The core of the bead is basically finely ground quartz (e.g. sand) cemented probably by an alkali and given the segmented shape before heating up to a temperature probably about 900° C. Then a low-temperature glaze was added in powdered form and fused on to the core by heating to around 700° C. This glaze, whose chief constituent was again silica, was coloured by the addition of copper or copper salts. Probably it was prepared separately and then powdered in order to be applied to the core of the bead. No stage in this process is technically a difficult one, since the temperatures required were less than those needed for the casting of copper which was already practised. And the possibility of using copper salts to colour glazes was probably clear enough to the early smiths. The use of two firings would not be unusual for early glassmakers although recent research into present day faience manufacture in Iran (Wulff, Wulff and Koch 1968) shows that one firing may sometimes be sufficient for faience.

The traditional Iranian method makes it unnecessary to prepare a glaze or frit separately, by means of a preliminary firing, and then to apply to the quartz core of the bead, before the final firing can be carried out. Instead, the core of the bead is packed, along with many others, into a glazing powder consisting of plant ash, copper oxide and other ingredients, and fired in a kiln. The entire surface of the object can be given a fine glaze coating in this way. The plant from which the ash is prepared, usually *Salsola kali* (the prickly saltwort), was widely known in ancient times, and indeed the modern word 'alkali' actually derives from the Arabic term for its ash, as does the modern Latin specific name for the plant. It is common on salt marshes throughout Europe, and may well have been available near the Culbin and Glenluce sands where undoubtedly other suitable plants, such as kelp, could be found. Thus it is possible that some or all of the faience beads were prepared, as they are in Iran today, by one firing instead of two. Recent work on the methods of faience production used by the ancient Egyptians (Noble 1969) suggests indeed that all Egyptian faience was produced by a self-glazing process, in a single step operation. The method proposed depends upon the capillary action ('wicking out') as the 'natron mixture', used to cement together the quartz core, dries out, and is brought to the surface. This method, unlike the Iranian one, does not require that the objects to be glazed be fired inside an enclosed container. Such a method, as used by the Egyptians, would seem the simplest way of producing faience, and it may well have been used in Britain also. But in any case the process of manufacture was a rather sophisticated one, involving considerable skill.

This is not by any means an isolated case of the achievement of striking results through technical ingenuity in the Early Bronze Age, despite very limited technical means. The manufacture of faience beads can have presented no serious difficulty to a craftsman skilled in the smelting and founding of copper and bronze. The likelihood is here reiterated that the Scottish beads were manufactured locally, at Culbin and probably Glenluce, and perhaps at other localities.

All that has been said so far in this section has been designed to show that the local manufacture of faience beads in Early Bronze Age Europe should not seem unduly surprising. The statistical analysis of the trace-element results, given above, turns the possibility into a very strong probability indeed. It is, of course, quite independent of the typological argument just outlined. All of the Scottish beads analysed–five segmented, four star and two quoit beads–fall within a homogeneous group, separable on the basis of the content of tin, magnesium and aluminium, from the other British beads and from the Egyptian and Aegean beads analysed (fig. 1).

An analogous case is provided by the two beads from Czechoslovakia, nos. 55 and 56, which are again unlike any of the other beads analysed.

It is of course possible that further analyses of Egyptian beads might reveal a few with similar tin and magnesium contents. But the separation and homogeneity of the Scottish group is noteworthy. Whether it springs from the precise technique of manufacture used, or from the ingredients, it argues in favour of local manufacture.

The case for local production is further corroborated by the analysis of the Culbin glass slag fragment (no. 27) which no one has ever regarded as other than local, although it may be a later product. It has a composition closely similar to the Scottish beads. This can hardly be coincidental: and if the slag is a local product (even if made at a much later date) it is difficult to see the beads, with their closely similar composition, as imports.

The Scottish segmented beads are separated by analysis from the other segmented beads and classed with the other Scottish forms. It seems likely then that segmented beads were made in Scotland as well as the star and quoit beads. The analyses suggest an analogous conclusion for the English segmented beads. These again form a homogeneous group distinguishable from those of other regions, as shown above, especially when the data for titanium, barium and silver are included. If the Scottish beads were made in Scotland, the same arguments hold that the English ones were made in England. The same can also be demonstrated for the glass beads from the Isles of Scilly which again form a separate group and can at present be presumed to be of local manufacture. The British beads seem therefore, on the basis of these arguments, to be essentially local products.

By way of corroboration, the rather similar case of the glass beads of the Austrian Urnfield culture may be cited (Neuninger and Pittioni 1958). Like the British faience beads, these had generally been regarded as imports from the Mediterranean. Trace-element analysis shows that they have an impurity pattern similar to that of the local Alpine copper objects and copper ores. This has been explained as the result of using local copper to colour the beads, and therefore seems to establish their local manufacture.

The only obvious alternative to local manufacture is the theory of separate consignments, already suggested by Stone to explain the dual distribution of the British beads: 'Surely this must mean two sea-borne expeditions at least to the islands with normal segmented beads alone during the primary establishment and floruit of the culture.' But with the need to explain the three British analysis-groups as well as the typological variation, the theory—formerly plausible—now becomes unnecessarily complicated. And neither the analyses nor the shapes of the Scottish beads can be matched in the Mediterranean. It seems that the existence of local centres of production is the most probable explanation.

The conclusion that the beads were locally made does not solve the problem of their innovation. The popularity of faience in Egypt and the frequency of the segmented shape in the East Mediterranean makes an independent invention in Britain of both the technique and the segmented form questionable. Of course it can be argued that the segmented form is known also in bone, gold and tin (Beck and Stone 1935, 213), and it is not a particularly elaborate one. Bone beads may well have been prototypes for faience ones both in Britain and in Egypt. It is perhaps significant that the appearance of the faience beads in central and north-west Europe is broadly contemporary with the development of bronze technology—in England as in Hungary, Czechoslovakia and Austria. The new technical competence which alloying, and perhaps the use of sulphide ores, implies might well result in such inventions as faience. But while the beads now seem to have been locally manufactured, a local origin for the form and for the process is uncertain. That problem remains an open one at present, and the analyses contribute little to it.

The notion of Mediterranean influence, and the import of beads, has often been accepted by central European scholars (Moucha 1958, 46) just as by British ones. But if we view the British faience beads as local products, the same conclusion may well hold for those of Poland, Czechoslovakia, Hungary and Russia, and the chief evidence for Aegean influence in central Europe at this period disappears. The time has now come to ask whether there was any *direct* contact between central Europe (or Britain) and the Mediterranean until well into the 1st millennium BC. [1970]

BIBLIOGRAPHY

Aitken, M. (1961) *Physics and Archaeology*.

Beck, H. C. and Stone, J. F. S. (1935) Faience beads of the British Bronze Age. *Archaeol.* 85, 203–52.

Clark, J. G. D. (1966) The invasion hypothesis in British archaeology. *Antiq.* 40, 172–89.

Daniel, G. E. (1960) *The Prehistoric Chamber Tombs of France*.

Gimbutas, M. (1965) *Bronze Age Cultures in Central and Eastern Europe*.

Heurtley, W. A. (1939) *Prehistoric Macedonia*.

Lucas, A. (1962) *Ancient Egyptian Materials and Industries*.

Mann, L. McL. (1905–6) Prehistoric beads of coarse vitreous paste. *Proc. Soc. Ant. Scot.* 40, 396–402.

Moucha, V. (1958) Faience and glassy faience in the Unetice culture in Bohemia. *Epitymbion Roman Haken* (Prague), 44–9.

Neuninger, H. and Pittioni, R. (1959) Woher stammen die blauen Glasperlen der Urnenfelderkultur? *Archaeol. Austr.* 26, 52–66.

Newton, R. G. and Spurrell, D. J. (1967*a*) A development of multiple regression for the analysis of routine data. *Appl. Statist.* 16, 51–64.

——(1967*b*) Examples of the use of elements for clarifying regression analyses. *Appl. Statist.* 16, 165–72.

——(1969) Element Analysis—the anatomy of multiple regression. *The Statistician,* 19, no. 1, 143–51.

Noble, J. V. (1969) The technique of Egyptian faience. *Am. J. Arch.* 73, 435–7.

Renfrew, C. (1967) Colonialism and Megalithismus. *Antiq.* 41, 276–88.

——(1968) Wessex without Mycenae. *Ann. Brit. Sch. Arch. Athens* 63, 277–85.

——(1969*a*) Trade and culture process in European prehistory. *Curr. Anthrop.* 10, 151–69.

——(1969*b*) The autonomy of the south-east European Copper Age. *PPS* 35, 12–47.

Stone, J. F. S. (1949) A second fixed point in the chronology of the Harappa culture. *Antiq.* 23, 201–5.

Stone, J. F. S. and Thomas, L. C. (1956). The use and distribution of faience in the ancient East and prehistoric Europe. *PPS* 22, 37–84.

Wulff, H. S., Wulff, H. E. and Koch, L. (1968) Egyptian faience, a possible survival in Iran. *Archaeol.* 21, 98–0.

14) Wessex as a Social Question

Ultimately the importance for European prehistory as a whole of this question of the 'Wessex culture' is not simply chronological, or a matter of contacts between two distant areas of Europe. These aspects of the problem were considered in the two preceding chapters. The issues which really matter are social and economic: what were the underlying causes of the changes in society at this time which are documented in the rich graves of the so-called 'Wessex culture'?

In recent years European scholars have increasingly come to realise the possibility of creating a social archaeology (Renfrew 1973*a*). Indeed it may be possible to see in them an early bronze age successor to the chiefdom society which has been proposed for the south-British late neolithic (Renfrew 1973*b*). Hierarchy and centralisation are reflected in different ways in the two classes of material, leading to speculations about 'group oriented' (for the late neolithic) and 'individualising' (for the early bronze age) chiefdoms (Renfrew 1974).

The time is now ripe for a systematic re-examination of the mortuary remains of the period, using the grave goods to reveal information about social structure rather than in an attempt to define notional 'cultures', the supposed equivalent of prehistoric ethnic groups.

In the words of David Clarke (1968, 233):

> The products of segments or classes of societies have often been elevated to full cultural status, so that a hundred rich graves, distinguished entirely by a small set of rank and prestige weapons, trinkets and gewgaws has given us a Wessex Culture whose domestic pottery and other cultural equipment belongs within the British Collared Urn culture.

BIBLIOGRAPHY

Chapman, R. W. (1977) Burial practices, an area of mutual interest, in Spriggs, M. (ed.) *Archaeology and Anthropology* (British Archaeological Reports, Supplementary Series 19) 19–33.

Clarke, D. L. (1968) *Analytical Archaeology*. London: Methuen.

Fleming, A. (1973) Models for the development of the Wessex culture, in Renfrew, C. (ed.) *The Explanation of Culture Change, Models in Prehistory*. London: Duckworth, 571–88.

Renfrew, C. (1973*a*) *Social Archaeology* (Inaugural Lecture). Southampton: University.

——(1973*b*) Monuments, mobilisation and social organisation in neolithic Wessex, in Renfrew, C. (ed.) *The Explanation of Culture Change, Models in Prehistory*. London: Duckworth, 539–58.

——(1974) Beyond a subsistence economy, the evolution of social organisation in prehistoric Europe, in Moore, C. B. (ed.) *Reconstructing Complex Societies* (Supplement to the Bulletin of the American Schools of Oriental Research no. 20) 69–95.

Shennan, S. (1975) The social organisation at Branč. *Antiq*. 49, 279–88.

WESSEX AS A SOCIAL QUESTION

The rich graves of the early 2nd millennium BC in south Britain, termed the Wessex culture by Stuart Piggott (1938), are still the subject of controversy. The real nature of the material as a closely related assemblage is still in question as also its date and whether or not those who used it were in contact with the Aegean world.

At the same time several points of agreement are emerging. In the first place it is clear that the sarsen structure of Stonehenge (IIIa) was built rather early. Christopher Hawkes has rightly stressed that there are no very strong arguments to link this phase of the monument with the Wessex culture, and that it could belong to the preceding 'Beaker period'. On the other hand, as R. J. C. Atkinson indicated at the recent conference on Wessex held in Newcastle, if the Wessex graves did begin as early as some have suggested, they and Stonehenge IIIa could still be contemporary. There is now, in any case, no argument for linking the major construction of Stonehenge with Mycenae, either in date or origin. At the same time, however, the radiocarbon date of 1240 ± 105 bc (I–2445) for Stonehenge IIIb/IIIc, calibrated to c. 1500 BC, compares with radiocarbon dates now available for later Wessex. So Stonehenge was still in use, and undergoing alterations, during the late Wessex period, and in this sense, at least, was 'contemporary with the Golden Age of Mycenae' (Selkirk 1972, 225).

The second, more fundamental point is that, whether or not exports from Mycenae or Egypt were reaching Britain, there is no evidence that such contact had any discernible influence upon the development of British society or its technology. At the Newcastle conference Keith Branigan reiterated the case for Aegean exports to Europe in the early bronze age (cf. Branigan 1970), but the opposing view was clearly presented by Anthony Harding. The only unequivocal evidence for Wessex-Mycenae contacts which he recognised was in the Mycenaean world, not in Wessex, and in the form of Baltic amber. My own view inclines to that of Harding, although Branigan can justly reply that the private collectors of Aegean artefacts in Britain, France and Germany in the eighteenth and nineteenth centuries AD must then have been exceptionally and singularly careless to lose all those artefacts, unfortunately without secure archaeological contexts, which go to make up his distribution maps.

The fascinating case of the faience beads is also relevant here. Their Mycenaean or Mediterranean origin has been called into question (Newton and Renfrew 1970; Aspinall *et al.* 1972), but defended by McKerrell (1972). The matter is still undecided, principally because analyses show them consistently to contain more tin than the majority of those from any other region. Stanley Warren pointed out to the Newcastle conference the very strong grounds for doubting a Mycenaean or Egyptian origin, and stressed that clearly some special recipe was being used to prepare the colouring agent for the beads. Until we really understand how this was prepared, a conclusive demonstration of their origin may elude us, and McKerrell may yet prove to be right. But it is now becoming generally accepted, following the work of Harding, Warren and Aspinall (cf. Harding 1971; Harding and Warren 1973), that the 'faience' beads of central Europe were locally made with local ingredients. If there, why not here? My personal indication is still towards a British manufacture, but in the face of McKerrell's reasoned arguments this is as yet far from established.

No one today, however, would claim that a Mycenaean or Egyptian origin for these beads, if accepted, has any very weighty bearing upon

Wessex origins. For this reason the problem of chronology is less important for its impact upon possible Mycenaean links than for its relevance to our understanding of the internal development of the British early bronze age and its relations with its north European neighbours.

Until about a year ago the calibrated radiocarbon dates for north European graves, with daggers and other objects related to those of Wessex, coupled with the assumption that the Wessex culture could not have lasted more than a few centuries, suggested dates for it between c. 2100 and 1700 BC (Renfrew 1968). Coles and Taylor, using the latter's close study of the goldwork, proposed a 'minimal view', a 'relatively short period' (Coles and Taylor 1971, 13), 'which in radiocarbon years is likely to be in or around the 17th century bc, and in calendar years the 20th century BC' (ibid., 8). There are now three sites with radiocarbon dates for graves with Camerton-Snowshill daggers, which may lead us to modify this picture. These are Hove (date 1239 ± 46 bc—BM 682), Earls Barton (1219 ± 51 bc—BM 680; 1264 ± 64 bc—BM 681), and Edmondsham (1119 ± 45 bc—BM 708). After calibration they suggest that such graves were being constructed until after 1500 BC in calendar years. We are therefore left with a dilemma, if we accept that these British dates may be taken at their face value. Assuming that the calibration has at least an approximate validity—and McKerrell's rather special use of the Egyptian dates to set up a new 'calibration' for the period (1972) was strongly questioned on statistical grounds by Malcolm Clark at Newcastle (cf. Clark and Renfrew 1973)—we have two choices. Either the continental relations of early Wessex must be sacrificed, so that Wessex could begin as late as may seem desirable and the minimal view upheld; or the Wessex graves *did* begin early, probably before 2000 BC, and the minimal view, while possibly applying to the goldwork, as Taylor argues, must be discarded for the Wessex series taken as a whole. My own preference is for the latter view, which would imply a Wessex duration of five centuries, from c. 2000 BC to c. 1500 BC. And this question of *duration* now now seems of greater interest for the understanding of the nature and origins of Wessex than that of *absolute date*. Further progress can only come from new radiocarbon dates, and from the long-awaited publication of Sabine Gerloff's important corpus and analysis of Wessex graves.

But what, in fact, is 'Wessex'? This is a question which much of the discussion of chronology or of beads and contacts manages to avoid. Ian Longworth showed at Newcastle, in a masterly analysis, how disparate are the ceramic associations among graves which are termed 'Wessex' on the basis of an appropriate dagger, or gold, or faience or amber among the grave goods. His phrase, 'a brief spell of conspicuous sepulchral deposition', comes to the heart of the matter, although the brevity, as we have seen, is still in question. The Wessex 'culture' consists solely and entirely of a number of individual burials beneath round barrows, singled out especially in Wiltshire, Dorset and Hampshire from many more, for the apparent wealth of their grave goods.

In attempting to explain the phenomenon, we are dealing in the first place with this custom of individual burial beneath barrows, a custom associated at an earlier date with beakers, alongside which gold objects occasionally occur. The size of some of the barrows, and the rather exotic assemblage (although the actual weight of gold is always small), are what create for us the 'Wessex problem'.

An important component of any explanation is likely to be found in the preceding late neolithic, where the size and distribution of the major henge monuments, in precisely the same areas where the rich Wessex graves later occur, indicate the emergence of larger social groups, possibly with some hierarchical structure, which might be termed chiefdoms (Renfrew 1973). I have shown elsewhere (1974) that these late neolithic chiefdoms, like those of neolithic Malta or even parts of Polynesia (e.g. Tongatapu) may be thought of as *group-oriented*—which implies that the community works are more prominent in the archaeological record than any striking display by individuals or any conspicuous consumption of personal wealth.

In the succeeding early bronze age in north Europe as a whole there is again evidence of what may still be termed chiefdoms, in the rich burials of north Germany, Brittany, Wessex and elsewhere. But we see them now as something different—these are *individualising* chiefdoms, where the personal wealth of the chief and its prominent display assume as much importance to the community as did formerly the great tribal meeting places and monumental works. The growth of hierarchically organised societies, with emphasis on the personal wealth of the 'chief' is yet more clearly seen in the Aegean early bronze age a few centuries earlier (Renfrew 1972, ch. 18).

Both there and in north Europe this social feature occurs together with the first regular use of bronze, not only for tools (mainly axes) and ornaments (e.g. pins) but above all for weapons—daggers. In all these cases attractive materials for personal adornment, including gold, are regularly used for the first time. In each the regular placing of rich grave goods beside individual burials makes its appearance.

The outline of an explanation is now beginning to take shape, and it is primarily a social one. The inception of bronze manufacture introduced into society a new form of wealth. The scope for potential peaceful competition within society which this offered was supplemented by the development of a totally new weapon for hand-to-hand combat, the dagger. (Its only rival, the battle axe, had been introduced only a little earlier, and was still in fashion.) My suggestion is that the powerful impact of the new technology, with all it implied for wealth, for display and for armed competition, is reflected in the shift in south Britain from group-oriented to individualising chiefdom society. The old solidarity of the late neolithic, seen in the great henges and culminating perhaps in Silbury Hill and Stonehenge IIIa, developed with the impact of the new technology into a materialistic, acquisitive, aggrandising society. Personal wealth and display became the recognised means by which leaders communicated their eminence and their power to those in the group inferior to them in status, hence enabling the group to retain some solidarity about the person of the chief.

A further factor of possible relevance here is the effect of a hypothetical population increase, with consequent pressure upon natural resources (cf. Sherratt 1972). This too may have contributed to a competitive situation, where the emergence of charismatic leaders, well-armed and skilled in war, could have been of adaptive value to the group. The appeal to a social explanation does not, therefore, imply a rejection of the environmental approach, for the two are closely interrelated. Indeed the subsequent development of the bronze age, with the emergence of a trade in raw materials and of local specialist industries is very much the story of the changes in the technological field (or subsystem) of society brought about in response to the demands set up in the social subsystem.

We are, of course, largely ignorant of whatever form wealth and display may have taken in the neolithic period. Who knows what perishable objects in Britain may have fulfilled the same function as the wooden prestige artefacts of the Polynesian chiefdoms? Yet it does seem striking that amber beads and ornaments are not in fact seen in Britain until the early bronze age, although the material was already known and available from palaeolithic times. Nor was gold, although used in beaker times, prominent until the Wessex graves, as a form of display accompanying the burial.

This little word-picture is only a first step towards an explanation for the Wessex graves. But already there are more detailed arguments supporting it—for instance the presence of the densest concentrations of Wessex barrows in precisely the areas where the late neolithic chiefdoms had their great centres (Renfrew 1973, cf. Fleming 1971). And the argument does have the merit of focusing upon the Wessex graves themselves, and keeping well clear of Mycenae. I am hopeful that more systematic work along these lines will justify the final conclusion of an earlier (1968) article, 'Wessex without Mycenae':

> Our understanding of the Wessex culture is thus more likely to be furthered by a consideration of the technical, economic and social processes at work in Wessex than by reference to the Aegean or to Mycenae. In comparison with the need to understand the dynamics of culture change at this important stage in the development of prehistoric Britain, the precise absolute dating of the Wessex culture appears a secondary question indeed.

[1973]

BIBLIOGRAPHY

Aspinall, A., Warren, S. E., Crummett, J. G. and Newton, R. G. (1972) Neutron activation analysis of faience beads. *Archaeom.* 14, 27–40.

Branigan, K. (1972) Wessex and Mycenae: some evidence reviewed. *Wilt. Archaeol. Nat. Hist. Mag.* 65, 89–107.

Clark, R. M. and Renfrew, C. (1973) The tree-ring calibration of radiocarbon and the chronology of Ancient Egypt. *Nature* (1 June) 266–70).

Coles, J. M. and Taylor, J. (1971) The Wessex culture ; a minimal view. *Antiq.* 45, 6–14.

Fleming, A. (1971) Territorial patterns in bronze age Wessex. *PPS* 37, 138–66.

Harding, A. (1971) The earliest glass in Europe. *Archeol. Rozh.* 23, 188–200.

Harding, A. and Warren, S. E. (1973) Early bronze age faience beads from Central Europe. *Antiq.* 47, 64–6.

McKerrell, H. (1972) On the origins of British faience beads and some aspects of the Wessex-Mycenae relationship. *PPS* 38, 286–301.

Newton, R. G. and Renfrew, C. (1970) British faience beads reconsidered. *Antiq.* 44, 199–206.

Piggott, S. (1938) The early bronze age in Wessex. *PPS* 4, 52–106.

Renfrew, C. (1968) Wessex without Mycenae. *Ann. Brit. School Archaeol. Athens* 63, 277–85.

——(1972) *The emergence of civilisation: the Cyclades and the Aegean in the third millennium BC*. London.

——(1973) Monuments, mobilisation and social organisation in neolithic Wessex, in Renfrew, C. (ed.). *The explanation of culture change: models in prehistory*. London.

——(1974) Beyond a subsistence economy: the evolution of social organisation in prehistoric Europe, in Moore, C. (ed.) *Reconstructing Complex Societies* (Supplement to the *Bull. Am. Schools Oriental Res.* 20) 69–96.

Selkirk, A. (1972) Wessex *with* Mycenae. *Curr. Archaeol.* 32, 225.

Sherratt, A. (1972) Socio-economic and demographic models for the neolithic and bronze ages of Europe, in Clarke, D. L. (ed.). *Models in archaeology*. London 477–542.

15) Problems of the Radiocarbon Calendar and its Calibration (with R. M. Clark)

The appropriate use of radiocarbon determination is no easy matter. It is complicated first by the margin of error through background radiation from which the laboratory measurements of the activity of samples cannot escape. Secular variation in the atmospheric concentration of radiocarbon necessitates the further correction or calibration of such measurements, with the aid of radiocarbon determinations for samples from dated tree-rings of the bristlecone pine, *Pinus aristata*.

The first such calibration curve was published by Suess in 1967, with a revised version three years later (Suess 1967 ; 1970). It was immediately clear that this would have a significant impact upon European prehistoric chronology, so that inferences based upon the simple compilation of uncalibrated radiocarbon dates (e.g. Thomas 1967) could be seriously in error. Preliminary assessments of the archaeological implications (Neustupny 1969 ; Renfrew 1970 ; 1971) suggested rather wide-ranging changes, reviewed in chapter 17.

Evidently the precise form, and the reliability, of the calibration curve to be used is a matter of some importance. Nearly all the published curves, such as those of Suess, Michael and Ralph, Wendland and Donley, and Switsur, reviewed in this paper, agree on the general magnitude of the correction. Despite misgivings among some archaeologists (e.g. Mackie *et al*. 1971) there is general agreement also about its general reliability (but see the introduction to the next chapter). What is less clear is the extent to which the longer-term deviations are accompanied by short-term kinks in the curve, as Suess has argued (Suess 1976 ; 1977).

The underlying statistical questions (see Clark 1977) which must govern a decision on these points, are reviewed in this paper. A revised calibration curve has been prepared by R. M. Clark (1975), taking into account the statistical problems reviewed here. It supersedes all previous work. All those who wish to calibrate radiocarbon dates in the most reliable manner now available are urged to use it.

BIBLIOGRAPHY

Clark, R. M. (1975) A calibration curve for radiocarbon dates. *Antiq*. 49, 251–66.

——(1977) Non-parametric estimation of a smooth regression function. *J. Roy. Statist. Soc. Series B* 39, 107–13.

MacKie, E., Collis, J., Ewer, D. W., Smith, A., Suess, H. and Renfrew, C. (1971) Thoughts on radiocarbon dating, *Antiq*. 45, 197–204.

Neustupny, E. (1969) Absolute chronology of the neolithic and aeneolithic periods of central and south-eastern Europe. *Archeo. Rozh*. 21, 783.

Renfrew, C. (1970) New configurations in Old World archaeology. *World Archaeol*. 2, 199–211.

——(1971) Carbon 14 and the prehistory of Europe. *Sci. Amer*. 225, 199–211.

Suess, H. E. (1967) Bristlecone pine calibration of the radiocarbon time scale from 4100 BC to 1500 BC. *Proceedings of the Symposium on Radioactive Dating and Methods of Low-Level Counting*. Monaco, March 1967, Vienna, I.A.E.A.

——(1970) Bristlecone pine calibration of the radiocarbon time scale from 5400 BC to the present, in Olsson, I. U. (ed.) *Radiocarbon Variations and Absoulte Dating* (Proc. Twelfth Nobel Symposium, Uppsala, 1969). New York: Wiley.

——(1976) A calibration curve for radiocarbon dates (reply to Clark). *Antiq.* 50, 61–2.
——(1977) The carbon-14 level during the fourth and second half of the fifth millennium BC and the carbon-14 calibration curve. *Proc. 9th Internat. Con. on Radiocarbon Dating, UCLA and UCSD* (in press).
Thomas, H. L. (1967) *Near Eastern, Mediterranean and European Chronology* (Stud. Mediterr. Archaeol. 17). Lund.

PROBLEMS OF THE RADIOCARBON CALENDAR AND ITS CALIBRATION

Since the development of the radiocarbon dating method in 1949, the question of the accuracy and reliability of radiocarbon dates has been much discussed. The more recent realisation that the concentration of radiocarbon in the atmosphere has not been constant through time, and that the extent of variation may be investigated, and dates corrected, by means of dendrochronology, has led to further discussion and created uncertainties in the minds of archaeologists as to the validity of the method as a whole and of its tree-ring calibration

Already in the early days it was rightly stressed that radiocarbon determinations were subject to irreducible experimental error, and that radiocarbon 'dates' required the application of statistical concepts in their interpretation. The attempts to produce and apply a calibration curve in order to obtain 'corrected dates' bring out this essential point: the interpretation and particularly the calibration of radiocarbon dates is a statistical problem demanding a proper consideration of the sources and magnitude of errors, both random and systematic. For instance the current dispute among physicists about the reality of the kinks in the Suess calibration curve (Suess 1970*a*; Barker 1971), although ultimately concerned with fluctuations in the concentration of atmospheric radiocarbon, can be reduced to the question of how the data (in this case radiocarbon determinations of dendrochronologically dated wood) should be manipulated. It is a *statistical* problem where the magnitude of the random error associated with the determinations assumes a central importance. It is because these problems have not been tackled systematically that there is as yet no acceptable calibration curve in existence to allow the reliable use of the numerous analyses of dated bristlecone pine samples conducted by the radiocarbon laboratories at La Jolla, Philadelphia and Tucson. This need not prevent the very approximate conversion of radiocarbon determinations to calendar years, accurate only to within a couple of centuries, but the use of the calibration data to give the more accurate calendar dates which they make possible requires much more careful treatment. The purpose of the present article is to review this problem, indicate some of the real difficulties and pitfalls (which some workers have unfortunately not been able to avoid) and show some of the features which a successful treatment of the problem must embody. Radiocarbon determinations of dendrochronologically dated samples cannot simply be applied directly and without further thought to yield 'calibrated dates'. Between the data and the conclusions lies a whole series of assumptions and procedures which require investigation.

The Physical Background

The radiocarbon dating method, as devised by Libby, rested upon six assumptions:

1. The secular constancy of atmospheric radiocarbon, i.e. that the concentration of radiocarbon in the atmosphere at any given location is constant through time.
2. The 'principle of simultaneity', that at any given time the atmospheric concentration of radiocarbon at any two points on the earth's surface is the same.
3. That the rate of decay of carbon-14, expressed by the half-life, is accurately known.
4. The atmospheric origin of the carbon in living organisms.
5. The absence of fractionation effects in living organisms, so that the isotopic composition of their carbon is in equilibrium with the composition of atmospheric carbon dioxide.
6. The isotopic integrity of the sample to be dated, its constituent carbon not being supplemented by extraneous material.

Each of these assumptions has been subjected to critical examination in recent years, and it is the first which proves the least warranted. The half-life of radiocarbon is a matter for measurement, and indeed recent work suggests that a value of 5,730 ± 40 yr is a more accurate estimate than the original Libby value of 5,570 ± 30 yr (although to avoid confusion dates are still published using the Libby value). The atmospheric origin of the carbon in plants and animals is well established, with a few exceptions (Shotton 1972), although there are problems in the case of marine and especially terrestrial molluscs, which are therefore not generally used as material for dating. Fractionation effects are small, although not negligible, but can be corrected conveniently through the determination of the stable carbon isotope ratios by means of the mass spectrometer. The isotopic integrity of the sample dated is a question relating to the specific sample in hand and remains a problem, but one which is routinely tackled in various ways. The principle of simultaneity has been investigated with care recently (Lerman *et al.* 1970), and it turns out that there is a small difference between the northern and the southern hemisphere in the atmospheric concentration of radiocarbon. But at locations of the same latitude the principle remains valid.

It is of course the first assumption which is not correct. In the first place there is the diluting effect of the large-scale burning of fossil fuels, particularly over the last century, which increases carbon-12 in the atmosphere without adding carbon-14. On the other hand, testing of nuclear weapons has increased the atmospheric carbon-14 concentration above the natural level. But as de Vries showed (de Vries 1958) there were significant fluctuations before that time.

In practice the only way of investigating the secular variations of atmospheric radiocarbon directly is to measure the radiocarbon content of samples whose date is very accurately known by independent means. Baxter and Walton (1971), for example, have very accurately measured variations in recent years using vintage whiskies whose organic content derives from cereal grains harvested in a known year. For earlier periods the annual growth of trees offers a comparable possibility, and several long-lived species have been used in this way, notably *Sequoia* (Willis *et al.* 1960) and the bristlecone pine, *Pinus aristata* or *Pinus longaevia* (Ferguson 1968; 1969). Varve sequences and lake deposits have also been used.

The result of these investigations, which no one now doubts, is that there have been considerable fluctuations in the atmospheric concentration of radiocarbon. Between about 5000 BC (the approximate chronological limit of the investigations so far published) and 1000 BC, the atmospheric concentration was greater than at present, so that uncorrected radiocarbon 'dates' are systematically too young. The statistical problems arise when more precise statements about the variations are desired.

The causes of the fluctuations must fall into two classes: changes in the rate of production of radiocarbon in the atmosphere by cosmic or solar radiation, or changes in the internal organisation of the earth's reservoir of radiocarbon—in the proportion of the total stored in the oceans, the atmosphere, the biosphere, etc. At present it seems likely that the major, long-term changes are related to changes in the intensity of the earth's magnetic field (Bucha 1970) with consequent effects of the cosmic ray flux. It has been suggested that shorter-term variations are related to changes in solar activity.

The Calibration Problem

The supposed physical reasons for the calibration are from the archaeologist's viewpoint secondary to the central problem, which is to extract or construct some simple, usable pattern from the data. These data consist of a series of paired values. The first value of each pair is the tree-ring date of the wood sample, which, in all cases older than about 2,000 years, at present implies a sample of bristlecone pine. The second value is the radiocarbon determination for that wood sample.

Both values of the pair may of course be subject to error. The tree-ring work on the bristlecone pine has been carried out by Professor C. W. Ferguson and his colleagues at the Laboratory for Tree-Ring Research at the University of Arizona. In matching a ring sequence in wood of an unknown date with the master tree-ring sequence, the process implies determining a unique fit. Errors in the tree-ring date assigned can thus only arise from gross errors of matching, or other errors in the master sequence. These in turn could arise only from gross errors, or from the undetected presence of additional growth rings or from missing rings. Ferguson has stated that missing and additional rings are not a major problem, and that he believes his tree-ring dates to be accurate to within considerably less than ten years. We are aware of no unfavourable or critical evaluation of his work, which has itself been widely accepted, and propose to accept that errors in the tree-ring date are of this order.

Secondly, the radiocarbon determinations are subject to error. (At this point we are considering errors in the precise estimation of the concentration of radiocarbon present in the specific sample in question. The separate question as to whether the radiocarbon content of the bristlecone pine wood accurately reflects that of the atmosphere at the time of growth is considered later: it is not in this sense a measurement error.) It is well known that the background radiation, affecting even a very well-shielded counter, sets irreducible limits upon the accuracy of individual determinations, although the random error involved may be reduced by counting over a very long period. This error is expressed by the 'plus or minus' figure quoted with each determination. Some laboratories increase this figure to include an estimate of error from other experimental sources as well as that arising from the background radiation, although a criticism to be levelled against many laboratories is that they are not explicit about just how this 'plus or minus' figure is calculated. The question is a crucial one, for it is the magnitude of this figure as much as the quoted value for the radiocarbon determination which determines the pattern which will emerge from a systematic consideration of the data taken together.

When an individual laboratory undertakes replicate determinations on each of a series of samples, it is possible to calculate an independent estimate of the standard error for the series and compare this with the standard error as quoted by the laboratory. For example, Clark and Renfrew (1972) used the differences between duplicate radiocarbon determinations by the La Jolla laboratory on 12 wood samples from Auvernier, Switzerland (Suess 1970*b*) to obtain an independent estimate of 48 yr for the standard error due to counting fluctuations at the La Jolla laboratory. This figure is in excellent agreement with the average standard error of 45 yr given by Houtermans (1971, p. 9).

It is clear that the counting fluctuations represent only part of the overall possible measurement errors of any radiocarbon date, and hence any quoted standard error, based on 'counting errors' only, should be regarded only as the minimum value of the real standard deviation associated with the radiocarbon date. Many radiocarbon laboratories suggest that any non-counting errors are negligible, but few have published any statistical evidence to support this assertion. In fact, a recent analysis by Clark and Renfrew (1973) of the differences in radiocarbon dates (Berger 1970, Edwards 1970) of 25 samples divided and analysed by two laboratories, BM and UCLA, throws considerable doubt upon it. The analysis showed that although there was no systematic difference between these laboratories with this series of samples, the true standard errors of the radiocarbon dates were possibly 40% greater than the quoted standard errors.

The archaeological requirement is that some continuous function (calibration curve) be constructed from the data to permit the conversion of radiocarbon dates to dates in calendar years.

The Calibration Function

The radiocarbon age of a sample is calculated from its measured radiocarbon content, utilising all six of Libby's assumptions. If the radiocarbon age y and corresponding calendar age x were plotted on a graph for a very large number of samples, the points (x,y) would lie exactly on the straight line $y = x$, *if* all measurements were without error, and *if* all six assumptions were correct. However, if assumption (1) only is incorrect, these ideal errorless measurements would lie on some smooth curve, expressible mathematically as

$$y = F(x) \tag{1}$$

The function F may be termed the 'calibration function'; its departure from linearity is directly related to any past secular variations in radiocarbon concentration. The physical background and the assumptions imply that there is only one radiocarbon age y corresponding to any given calendar age x, although several x's may give the same value of y.

On the other hand, given a sample whose radiocarbon age has been measured as $y \pm s$ years, the archaeologist wants to estimate the corresponding calendar age x. This implies that there is an 'inverse calibration function' allowing the determination of x from y of the form

$$x = G(y) \tag{2}$$

However, if there were several possible x's corresponding to the same y, G would not be a function in the usual mathematical sense (since a function can only have one value at any point).

Although, in practice, both the radiocarbon age y and the calendar age x are subject to measurement errors, it seems reasonable to ignore any errors in the calendar (tree-ring) ages, since these errors are small in both absolute and relative terms. Consequently the relationship between the observed radiocarbon age y and the calendar age x may be expressed either as

$$y - \epsilon = F(x) \quad \text{i.e.} \quad y = F(x) + \epsilon \tag{3}$$

or

$$x = G(y - \epsilon) \tag{4}$$

where ϵ denotes the unknown total error of measurement of the radiocarbon age of the sample in question. Since the quantity ϵ varies from sample to sample in a random fashion, a statistical analysis is obligatory.

The calibration function F and the inverse 'function' G are of course unknown, and some statistical procedure must be used to find suitable functions f and g as estimates of F and G respectively, using the available data. At first sight the choice between approximating F and approximating G appears quite arbitrary. The latter choice has the advantage of giving a direct answer to the archaeologist's question, but there are three compelling reasons why the former choice should be made.

First, if one seeks a relationship of the form (4), any approximating function g obtained by statistical methods will necessarily be a single-valued function. According to the fitted inverse function $x = g(y)$, there would necessarily be only *one* calendar date corresponding to each radiocarbon date. Furthermore, the model $x = g(y)$ does not rule out the possibility of there being several radiocarbon dates corresponding to the same calendar date. On the other hand, estimation of the 'direct' calibration function F by some approximating function f will necessarily produce a fitted curve with the correct characteristics (see fig. 1 and 2).

Secondly, any curve fitted to the data is of little value unless its precision can be assessed in relation to the known average magnitude of the measurement errors in the data on which it is based. Appropriate and valid statistical techniques are available for such an assessment only if F rather than G is estimated from the data.

Thirdly, if least-squares methods are used to fit model (4) to the data, the 'standard error of estimate' or root-mean-square of the residuals from the fitted curve $x = g(y)$ is meaningless. Computation of such a 'standard error', say s, suggests that, for example, the 95% confidence interval for the calendar date corresponding to radiocarbon date y is simply $g(y) \pm 1{\cdot}96s$, but this assertion is false. For a start, even if the measurement errors ϵ are exactly normally distributed, the residuals from the fitted curve $x = g(y)$ will not be distributed normally, and so the appropriate multiplier for 95% confidence limits will not necessarily be $\pm$ 1·96. Further, the precision of the calibrated radiocarbon date $g(y)$ depends on the shape of the curve near y, and so will depend on the radiocarbon date y. Such misinterpretation of the 'standard error of estimate' is less likely if the regression curve $y = f(x)$ is fitted instead.

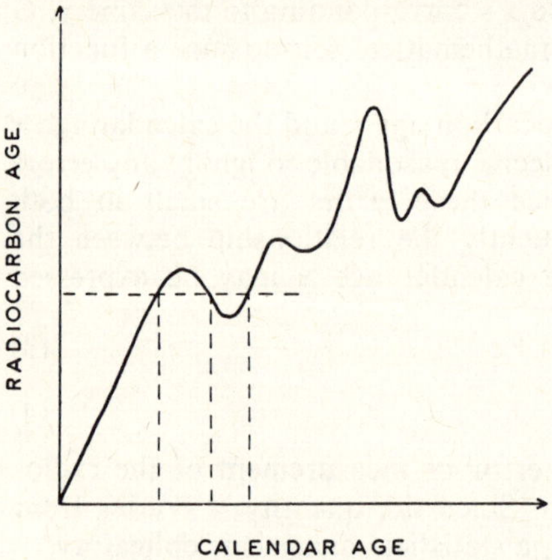

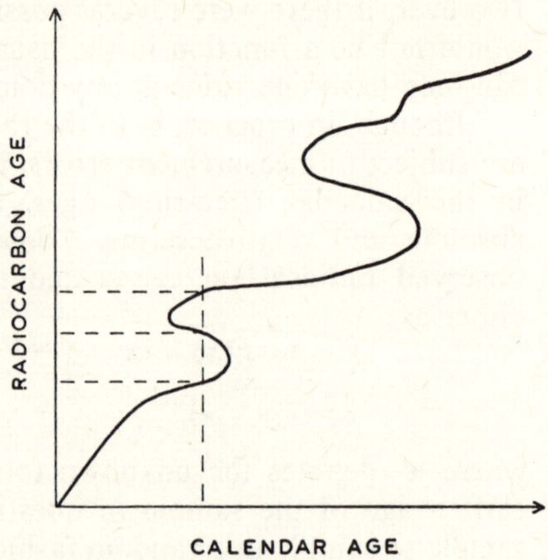

Figure 1 (*left*). General form of the calibration curve, according to the assumptions concerning the physical background to the problem. Only one radiocarbon age corresponds to any given calendar age, but there may be several calendar ages corresponding to a given radiocarbon age.
Figure 2 (*right*). Fitting the inverse function *g* could result in a fitted calibration curve like this. Only one calendar age corresponds to any radiocarbon age, but there may be several radiocarbon ages corresponding to the same calendar age.

Since at the present time the form of the true calibration curve F is unknown, an arbitrary choice must be made for the form of the approximating or smoothing function f. This choice will depend on the purpose of the calibration curve, that is, whether it is to be used for actual calibration of points or floating chronologies, for prediction of values outside the range of values covered, or to investigate the form of the relationship between the variables.

This distinction is important, and has been overlooked. For the archaeologist, the purpose of the calibration is the conversion of radiocarbon determinations to dates in calendar years, whereas the physicist may use the curve to explain past variations in the concentration of atmospheric radiocarbon. Calibration of radiocarbon dates requires only the existence of some smooth curve, which is simply a good fit to the data and need not necessarily have any geophysical interpretation. Elsewhere (Clark and Renfrew 1973), five of the desirable properties of such a calibration curve have been listed.

Possibly the most widely-used calibration curve is that published by Suess (1970*a*), which was obtained subjectively by simply drawing a freehand curve through the plotted data points. Clearly this curve should only be used as a rough guidline, since it fails to satisfy at least three of those five desirable properties. Its main disadvantage is that its precision cannot be reliably assessed, since it has not been obtained by an explicitly repeatable procedure.

Wendland and Donley (1971) have produced from 500 pairs of observations a single third-degree polynominal function allegedly defining the calibration relationship for the last 7,000 yr. However, their curve is obtained by estimating the *inverse* calibration relationship (4), a procedure shown above to be invalid, so that their results are of restricted value.

Their paper is misleading also in three other ways. First, the publication of a single figure of 120 yr for the 'standard error of the estimate' suggests that this is the standard error of *any* calibrated radiocarbon date calibrated by their curve. We explain below why this is incorrect. Secondly, the spectacular decrease in the standard error from the first- to the third-degree polynominal is in fact a reduction of only about 30%, not about 90% as their graph suggests. Finally, when comparing calibration curves for different laboratories, the authors do not use any of the existing exact small-sample statistical tests which would enable them to draw conclusions from the limited amount of data.

Various other forms of calibration curve have been used. Houtermans (1971) used a combination of periodic functions to obtain a relationship between ΔC^{14} values and calendar age. Clark and Renfrew (1973) fitted a continuous piecewise linear curve over a restricted time-range, that is, a series of straight line segments constrained to be continuous at their join-points. In addition, successive polynominal functions were fitted in the correct form, $y = f(x)$ in the notation of this paper. Recently, Clark and Sowray (1973) fitted a smoothing function comprising segments of different polynominal functions constrained to be continuous at their join-points.

Damon *et al.* (1972) have produced a table for the correction of radiocarbon dates, using polynominal curve-fitting and simple moving-averages. Although their results are based on nearly 600 radiocarbon dates, including some very recent determinations, their methods are inadequate from a statistical viewpoint. First, they use a criterion due to Chauvenet (1863) to reject outlying observations, although this criterion is known to be most unsatisfactory (Anscombe 1960). In any case, the number of observations rejected by this criterion is significantly greater than it should be, suggesting that the real calibration curve is not as smooth as claimed. Secondly, it is not clear whether higher-degree polynominals were fitted, or whether the chosen third-degree polynominal is in fact a good fit to the data. Thirdly, the formula (in table 2) for the standard error of a corrected radiocarbon date is fundamentally incorrect, as noted below.

Michael and Ralph (1972) and Switsur (1973) have used similar moving-average methods to obtain a smooth trend curve. These three papers have *assumed* implicitly that the calibration curve is very smooth. In consequence, the curves and tables in these papers must be regarded only as first-order approximations to the true calibration curve.

All the fitted calibration curves so far mentioned were determined, for mathematical and computational convenience, by a relatively small number of parameters, which are estimated from the data usually by some least-squares method. It may, however, turn out that the true calibration function F is not of parametric form, and can best be approximated by some non-parametric function-fitting technique, such as those proposed by Nadaraya (1970), Priestley and Chao (1972).

In general, a fitted calibration curve has to strike a balance between the two conflicting requirements that it should be both smooth and that it be a good fit to the data. At one extreme, any curve, however 'kinky', which joins up all the data points, will be an exact fit, whereas the smoothest possible curve, namely a straight line, could be a very poor fit. Work is at present in progress by R. M. Clark on a statistical method which allows some deliberate choice between these two extremes.

Inverse Calibration using the Direct Calibration Function

We have given some compelling reasons why estimation of the calibration relationship should proceed via the 'direct' calibration function F rather than the 'inverse' calibration function G. We now indicate how the fitted calibration function f can and should be used to solve accurately the archaeologist's problem: given a sample whose radiocarbon age has been measured as $y \pm s$ yr, what is the corresponding calendar age, X of the sample?

The observed radiocarbon age y may be regarded as an imperfect measurement of some quantity Y, which may be considered as the true radiocarbon age, in that y and Y would be equal if there were no measurement errors. In such a situation, if the calibration function F were known exactly as well, the corresponding calendar age X may be read directly and with no error from the graph of F. If F has kinks, there may be, of course, several X's corresponding to the same Y.

In practice, the true radiocarbon age Y is estimated by the observed radiocarbon age y with its associated standard error s, which enables one to construct, say, a 95% confidence interval for Y. Rather than knowing Y exactly, we must be content with the statement that we can be 95% sure that Y lies within the constructed confidence interval. If the calibration function F were known exactly, it would be then a simple matter to construct a corresponding 95% confidence region for the calendar age (see fig. 3).

It is clear from figure 3 that the width of the corresponding confidence region for the calibrated radiocarbon date depends critically on the shape of the calibration function. The confidence region is generally not symmetric about the calendar age(s) corresponding exactly to the observed radiocarbon date y, and may even comprise several distinct intervals. In principle, a calibrated radiocarbon date can be *more precise* than the corresponding uncorrected date, if the calibration curve is sufficiently steep.

This may be seen by comparing the lengths of intervals *A* and *a* in fig. 3. An example of this phenomenon is given by Vogel (in Olsson 1970, p. 125). The calibrated radiocarbon date of his sample 1 has an uncertainty of only ± 20 yr, whereas the uncertainty of the original radiocarbon date was ± 35 yr.

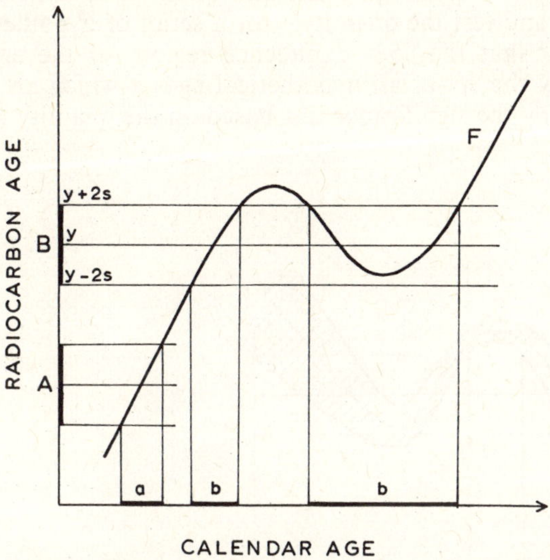

Figure 3. Radiocarbon calibration if the calibration function *F* were known exactly but the radiocarbon age *y* was measured with standard error *s*. The 95% confidence limits *A* and *B* for the true radiocarbon age correspond to 95% confidence regions *a* and *b* (respectively for the calendar age of the sample.

In practice, the true calibration function *F* is unknown and must be estimated from the data by some approximating function *f*. Since the data contain 'random' measurement errors, the fitted function *f* will necessarily have its own associated standard error, which in general will vary from point to point along the curve. This standard error enables one to construct a confidence band for the calibration curve, as in fig. 4. In general, this confidence band is narrowest in the middle of the time-period considered, and becomes wider at the extremes of the time-period. It seems reasonable to construct a confidence region *U* for the calendar age of the sample by considering the intersection of the confidence interval *A* for *Y* with the confidence band for the curve, as in fig. 4. Although this procedure is geometrically appealing, it does not produce an exact confidence region. If the confidence interval for *Y* and the confidence band for the curve are both 95% intervals, one can conclude that we are *at least* 95% sure that the calendar age of the sample lies in the constructed region *U*.

Fortunately, there is a simple statistical procedure for the construction of an *exact* confidence region for the calendar age of *X* of the archaeologist's sample. The method is based on the quantity

$$z = y - f(x)$$

which is the difference between the radiocarbon age for a suggested calendar age x as predicted by the fitted calibration curve $f(x)$ and the observed radiocarbon age y. If the postulated age x is correct, this discrepancy z should not be too different from zero, as judged by its standard error, which is easily obtained as a root-mean-square combination of the standard errors of the radiocarbon age y and the fitted curve f. In principle, one may compute and test the quantity z for a series of hypothetical ages x, and it turns out that the 95% confidence region for the actual calendar age X is simply the set of all hypothetical ages x which are *not rejected* at the 5% level by the significance test based on the quantity z.

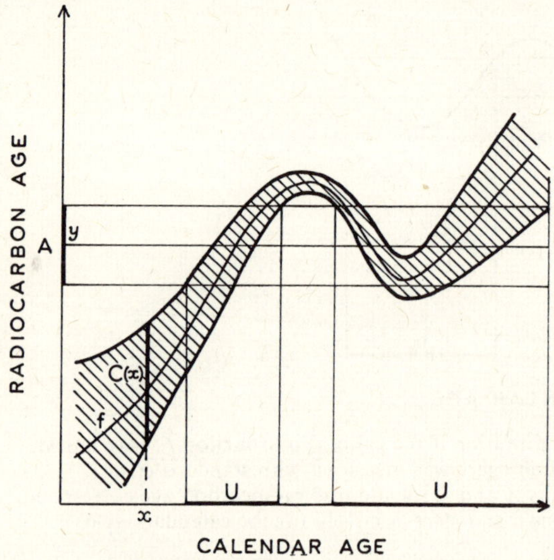

Figure 4. The shaded region represents a typical confidence band for the calibration function based on the fitted function f, to be interpreted in the sense that $C(x)$ represents a confidence interval for the position of the curve at the typical calendar age x. The region U is a possible but inexact confidence region for the calendar age of a sample whose observed radiocarbon age is y.

In practice, the boundaries of the resulting confidence region are given by an equation (see, for example, Brownlee [1960, p. 284], for the special case where f is linear), and so it is not necessary to compute and test the value of z for a large series of x values. This method is similar to that illustrated in figure 4, in that it involves all three factors affecting the precision of calibrated radiocarbon dates, namely (i) the standard error of the observed radiocarbon age, (ii) the standard error associated with the fitted calibration curve and (iii) the shape of this curve. However, in nearly all cases the confidence region U is actually wider than the exact 95% confidence region based on the statistic z.

The formula given by Damon *et al.* (1972) (and repeated by Switsur 1973) for the standard deviation of a calibrated radiocarbon date is incorrect, because it implies that any calibrated radiocarbon date is *always less* precise than the original radiocarbon date, and the corresponding confidence region is always a single symmetric interval. Fig. 3 and 4 make clear why this is not so.

Reliability of the Calibration

The calibration curve obtained, by a procedure as indicated above, is only as accurate as the bristlecone pine dendrochronology and the radiocarbon determinations themselves allow. The question of errors in radiocarbon determinations has been discussed at length, and there is no reason whatever to suspect gross errors in the methods of determination. The possibility of gross errors in the tree-ring chronology was touched on: there is no reason at present to suspect them. But this will not effectively be demonstrated until a chronology of comparable length can be built up using a different species in a region where the local climatic fluctuations are largely independent of those of the White Mountains of California.

At the same time there is the possibility of comparing the tree-ring chronology obtained for the bristlecone pine in the AD period with that from *Sequoia*, from *Cryptomeria japonica* in Japan, and from *Quercus* in Europe. In each case there is a range of radiocarbon determinations for wood samples of known age, and work is now underway to test their compatability in that time range. A rough and preliminary assessment suggests that the tree-ring counts agree well over the past 2000 yr BP. The likelihood of a major gross error in the count over the preceding five millennia was discounted earlier.

But even if the errors in measurement are understood, there are other possible sources of difficulty:

1. At the time of formation, does the concentration of radiocarbon in the bristlecone pine accurately reflect that in the atmosphere?
2. Is and was the atmospheric concentration of radiocarbon in the White Mountains of California the same as that in other parts of the world?
3. Is the isotopic integrity of the bristlecone pine assured?

Each of these must be taken in turn.

1. It has been suggested by some workers (cf. Berger 1970, p. 35) that the high altitude of the bristlecone pine may result in anomalies, by some mechanism such as the creation of the radiocarbon actually in the tree by the direct action of neutrons derived from cosmic radiation. This is an effect which can be checked back to 2000 BP by comparison with radiocarbon determinations on other tree species.
2. Problem 2 is simply a special consideration of the simultaneity principle. It can be tested directly today, and once again comparison back to 2000 BP is possible with different wood species growing in other localities in other continents.

   Such an analysis need not be restricted to a comparison of radiocarbon dates from wood samples from different species and localities but of the *same* calendar age. It is possible, using statistical methods, to test the validity of the simultaneity principle throughout any chosen time period, even if the tree-ring dates of the available relevant wood samples are all different. This is achieved first by fitting separate calibration curves using only the measurements on samples from each locality or species in turn, and then fitting a single calibration curve to the combined data. If the single curve fits the data just as well as the separate curves, as judged by an appropriate significance test, then there is no reason to doubt the principle of simultaneity on the basis of the available data.

Recently, Clark and Sowray (1973) have developed a method for testing the principle of simultaneity using only floating tree-ring chronologies, which thereby avoids the need for a master dendrochronology linking the sequence to the present.

3. The isotopic integrity of the bristlecone pine is a further serious question. It has been suggested that the very old rings in the heartwood of trees may conceivably pick up carbon from the living sap of the tree, thereby enriching their own concentration of radiocarbon. Rainer Berger has conducted experiments to investigate this effect (1970, p. 34).

   It would, however, be quite possible to test for this effect using data already published, if the full tree-ring information were also made available. For if it were the case that the heartwood of trees was becoming enriched in this way, a tree which began its growth in, say, 3000 BC, and died in 1000 BC, would display a year-ring for 3000 BC with marked radiocarbon enrichment. Yet a tree which began its growth in, say 4500 BC and died a little after 3000 BC would possess a year-ring for 3000 BC, which had been only very little exposed to the enrichment process.

   To test this effect, therefore, it is necessary only to consider a number of the matchings of the Ferguson sequence, and to analyse in each case the year-ring at the end of one tree's life span and the *same* year-ring (i.e. the ring for the same calendar year) at the beginning of the life span of the matching tree. In each case the latter should show a notably higher radiocarbon content. If such an effect is not seen, there is a clear indication that isotopic integrity is indeed preserved.

These are the only possible objections to the basic principles of the calibration which have occurred to us. They are all susceptible of testing, and at present there is no reason to suggest that they invalidate it. So far the only independent test of the calibration is the historical chronology for Ancient Egypt. Statistical tests have indicated (Clark and Renfrew 1973) that there is no incompatibility between this and the calibrated radiocarbon chronology, and that earlier suggestions to the contrary (e.g. McKerrell 1971 ; 1972) were not based on a complete analysis of the data.

Prospect

Given the large body of data now available, there is an urgent need for a calibration function, obtained by objective and repeatable procedures, whose associated errors may be expressed quantitatively with precision. It is clear to us that there will be no one calibration function which is right while all others are wrong, for different functions can legitimately be obtained using different procedures. The differences between them may now, however, be very great in practice. Work is now in hand to produce such a function using all the available tree-ring data.

At the same time it is clear that some of the radiocarbon laboratories concerned can markedly improve the usefulness of their future work by considering its statistical implications more carefully. In the first place they could state more precisely just how their published estimates of error, associated with each sample, are obtained. Secondly they could take care to run replicate samples regularly and to publish the results frankly, without blushing when they are widely different. For only in this way shall we have a valid measure of what the errors are in practice.

Thirdly, the laboratories concerned should run a series of replicated samples—for instance 20 samples could be divided each into five parts, and each of five laboratories run the complete series of 20 parts quite independently. This would give a valid measure of inter-laboratory errors, something not yet available from the tests on replicate samples which have been made. There are several indications of systematic errors between laboratories which have not yet been investigated. It would indeed be desirable that the samples be distributed from a single centre, and the results submitted, in secret, to that centre, to overcome the risk of determinations being revised. (We do not wish to imply any suspicion of incomplete candour by radiocarbon laboratories. But one problem which has arisen in connection with the Egyptian dates is the occurrence of occasional gross errors, through the occasional mistake or misunderstanding. It would be a rare paragon who would not correct such an oversight or blunder when it became obvious. Yet the whole value of the experiment would be to test for the frequency of such blunders as well as of other less gross errors.)

Fourthly, the excavator who has arranged with two or three laboratories to date four or five samples each from his excavation will get the best value if he takes five good samples of adequate size and divides each by three, sending one portion to each laboratory, than if he sends five different samples to each. This may be counter to expectation, but is clearly the way that accurate dates will be obtained. It is important that laboratories see and accept the necessity for this, and do not feel that they are being checked on in an unfriendly manner. The problem of inter-laboratory variation is too serious a matter to be avoided through fear of unfavourable comparisons. In this field all comparisons are useful and hence favourable.

And fifthly, the excavator stands to gain when the samples he submits are internally related chronologically. In the simplest case they will simply be in chronological sequence as determined by a stratigraphy (which of course implies the risk of reused wood, etc.). A series of dates in strict stratigraphic sequence, and from a single site, where the internal relationships allow a measure of control over the radiocarbon determinations, offers the possibility of a firm chronology (cf. Renfrew 1971 ; Olsson 1970, p. 125).

Of even greater value, however, is a series of samples whose interrelations are known in years. In practice this is only possible by means of floating tree-ring chronologies, such as those for Auvernier and Burgäschisee (Ferguson *et al.* 1966 ; Suess 1970*b*). These offer enormous scope for sound statistical interpretations (Clark and Renfrew 1972) and it is possible to obtain a calibrated date with a standard error of no more than 70 yr. The moral, therefore, is that tree-ring work should be undertaken on any site where there is hope of building up a floating sequence of a century or so.

Our general conclusion, therefore, is optimistic. At present there is no reason to doubt the validity of the general principles on which the calibration is based. Each step in the logic of the calibration can be tested. As yet, however, there is no adequate and detailed calibration curve in existence.

The accuracy of the calibration will depend ultimately upon the accuracy of the data. It is our central conclusion that progress here will come through a more careful programme of analyses with specific attention to determining the magnitude of errors objectively, by means of replicate samples. In the long run this will be more productive of an accurate calibration than simply an increase in the number of radiocarbon-dated tree-ring samples available. The calibration is here to stay, and its magnitude is now clear. The need now is to set it up with precision and on a sound objective basis, with a proper statistical appreciation of the errors involved. [1974]

BIBLIOGRAPHY

Anscombe, F. J. (1960) Rejection of outliers. *Technometrics* 2, 123–47.

Barker, H. (1971) Review of Olsson, I. U., in *Nature, Lond.* 231, 270.

Baxter, M. S. and Walton, A. (1971) Fluctuation of atmospheric carbon-14 during the past century. *Proc. Roy. Soc. London, Series A*, 321, 105–27.

Berger, R. (1970) Ancient Egyptian radiocarbon chronology. *Phil. Trans. Roy. Soc. London, Series A*, 269, 23–36.

Brownlee, K. A. (1960) *Statistical theory and methodology in science and engineering.* New York: John Wiley.

Bucha, V. (1970) Influence of the earth's magnetic field on radiocarbon dating, in Olsson, I. U. (1970) 501–12.

Chauvenet, W. (1863) Appendix: Method of least-squares, in *A manual of spherical and practical astronomy*. Philadelphia: J. B. Lippincott. (Appendix reprinted in 1868 as *A treatise on the method of least-squares.*)

Clark, R. M. and Renfrew, C. (1972) A statistical approach to the calibration of floating tree-ring chronologies using radiocarbon dates. *Archaeom.* 14, 5–19.

Clark, R. M. and Renfrew, C. (1973) The tree-ring calibration of radiocarbon and the chronology of ancient Egypt. *Nature, Lond.* 243, 266–70.

Clark, R. M. and Sowray, A. (1973) Further statistical methods for the calibration of floating tree-ring chronologies. *Archaeom.* 15 (2), 255–66.

Damon, P. E., Long, A. and Wallick, E. I. (1972) Dendrochronological calibration of the carbon-14 time scale. *Proc. 8th Internat. Conf. on Radiocarbon Dating, Lower Hutt City* 1, 45–59.

De Vries, H. (1958) Variations in concentration of radiocarbon with time and location on earth. *Koninkl. Nederl. Akademie van Wetenschappen, Amsterdam, Proc. Series B* 61, 94–102.

Edwards, I. E. S. (1970) Absolute dating from Egyptian records and comparisons with carbon-14 dating. *Phil. Trans. Roy. Soc., London, Series A* 269, 11–18.

Ferguson, C. W. (1968) Bristlecone pine, science and esthetics. *Science* 159, 839–46.

——(1969) A 7104-year annual tree-ring chronology for bristlecone pine, *Pinus aristata,* from the White Mountains, California. *Tree-Ring Bulletin* 29, 3–29.

——Huber, B. and Suess, H. E. (1966) Determination of the age of Swiss lake dwellings as an example of dendrochronologically-calibrated radiocarbon dating. *Z. Naturf.* 21A, 1173–7.

Houtermans, J. C. (1971) Geophysical interpretations of bristlecone pine radiocarbon measurements using a method of fourier analysis for unequally-spaced data, Ph.D. thesis, University of Berne.

Lerman, J. C., Mook, W. G. and Vogel, J. C. (1970) C^{14} in tree rings from different localities, in Olsson, I. U. (1970) 275–302.

McKerrell, H. (1971) Some aspects of the accuracy of C^{14} dating. *Scot. Archaeol. Forum* 3, 73–84.

——(1972) On the origins of British faience beads and some aspects of the Wessex-Mycenae relationship. *Proc. Prehist. Soc.* 38, 286–301.

Michael, H. N. and Ralph, E. K. (1972) Discussion of radiocarbon dates obtained from precisely dated Sequoia and Bristlecone Pine samples. *Proc. 8th Internat. Conf. on Radiocarbon Dating, Lower Hutt City* 1, 28–43.

Nadaraya, E. A. (1970) Remarks on non-parametric estimates for density functions and regression curves. *Theory of Probability and its Applications* 15, 134–6.

Olsson, I. U. (ed.) (1970) *Radiocarbon variations and absolute chronology* (Proc. Twelfth Nobel Symposium, Uppsala 1969) New York: John Wiley.

Priestley, M. B. and Chao, M. T. (1972) Non-parametric function fitting. *J. Roy. Statist. Soc. Series B* 34, 385–92.

Renfrew, C. (1971) Sitagroi, radiocarbon and the prehistory of south-east Europe. *Antiq.* 45, 275–82.

Shotton, F. W. (1972) An example of hard-water error in radiocarbon dating of vegetable matter. *Nature, Lond.* 240, 460–1.

Suess, H. E. (1970*a*) Bristlecone pine calibration of the radiocarbon time-scale 5400 BC to the present, in Olsson, I. U. (1970) 303–12.

Suess, H. E. (1970*b*) Calibrated radiocarbon dates, in Suess, H. E. and Strahm, C., The neolithic of Auvernier, Switzerland. *Antiq.* 44, 91–9.

Switsur, V. R. (1973) The radiocarbon calendar recalibrated. *Antiq.* 47, 131–7.

Wendland, W. M. and Donley, D. S. (1971) Radiocarbon—calendar age relationship, *Earth Planet. Sci. Lett.* 11, 135–9.

Willis, E. H., Tauber, H. and Münnich, K. O. (1960) Variations in the atmospheric radiocarbon concentration over the past 1300 years. *Radiocarbon* 5, 1–4.

16) Tree-ring calibration of Radiocarbon Dates and the Chronology of Ancient Egypt (with R. M. Clark)

When Willard Libby first developed the radiocarbon dating method, his principal test of its efficacity was to use it to determine the age of specimens already historically dated. For this he used organic materials derived from well-dated archaeological contexts in ancient Egypt (Libby 1955). At a first approximation the correlation between the two methods was a good one.

As the accuracy of laboratory measurement improved, however, and further suitable samples became available from Egypt, a discrepancy emerged (Libby 1963):

> The radiocarbon dates for Egypt for the period 4,000 to 5,000 years ago may be consistently too recent relative to the historical dates, but . . . the two sets of dates agree back to 4,000 years ago.

The realisation of the necessity of calibrating radiocarbon dates, which came some four years later as a result of tree-ring work, explained and rectified that discrepancy. The possibility now emerged, therefore, of comparing dendrochronologically calibrated radiocarbon dates for samples from early Egyptian contexts with their known historical dates. This would thus offer a test of the reliability of the calibration itself. Such is the purpose of the present paper.

The Egyptian radiocarbon determinations of historically dated samples had already been used by McKerrell, in two papers discussed in this chapter, to criticise the existing calibration and to propose his own alternative calibration curve for the period between 2000 and 500 BC. His arguments have since been set out at greater length (McKerrell 1975), and have influenced the views of Snodgrass (1975). In our understanding, his reasoning is based on an approach to calibration which is not statistically sound. The data have recently been re-examined with care by Clark (1978) who finds their conclusions statistically unjustified and the attempt to construct an alternative calibration curve based on the Egyptian historical calendar to be ill-founded.

The provisional conclusion must be that while the accuracy ascribed to radiocarbon determinations should not be exaggerated (see Clark 1975), no sound reason has yet been given to doubt the validity of the tree-ring calibration of radiocarbon.

BIBLIOGRAPHY

Clark, R. M. (1975) A calibration curve for radiocarbon dates. *Antiq.* 49, 251–66.

——(1978) Bristlecone pine and ancient Egypt—a reappraisal. *Archaeom.* 20, 5–18.

Libby, W. F. (1955) *Radiocarbon Dating*. Chicago: University Press.

——(1963) The accuracy of radiocarbon dates. *Science* 140, 278–80.

McKerrell, H. (1975) Correction procedures for C-14 dates, in Watkins, T. (ed.) *Radiocarbon Calibration and Prehistory*. Edinburgh: University Press, 47–100.

Snodgrass, A. M. (1975) An outsider's view of C-14 calibration, in Watkins, T. (ed.) *Radiocarbon Calibration and Prehistory*. Edinburgh: University Press, 39–46.

TREE-RING CALIBRATION OF RADIOCARBON DATES AND THE CHRONOLOGY OF ANCIENT EGYPT

Three radiocarbon laboratories, at La Jolla, Philadelphia and Tucson, [1-3] have obtained radiocarbon dates over the past decade for specimens of bristlecone pine already dated dendrochronologically,[4] thereby allowing the 'correction' of the radiocarbon scale. The calibration curve produced by Suess[5] is now widely used for this purpose. Its precise form has been questioned by some workers,[6] especially the validity of the 'kinks' or short-term fluctuations in the curve, and the nature of these short-term fluctuations in the atmospheric concentration of radiocarbon remains a problem.[7] In some quarters doubt has been expressed over the reality and magnitude of the first order deviation itself.[8]

The historical calendar of Ancient Egypt has been used several times for checking the value of the radiocarbon method[9] although more recently the divergence between the radiocarbon dates and the historical chronology has given grounds for disquiet. [10, 11] The discrepancies are reduced by applying the bristlecone pine calibration to the Egyptian radiocarbon dates, [12-15] but some scholars have suggested that this now makes these Egyptian dates systematically too old instead of too recent. One worker has indeed advocated the calibration of radiocarbon dates from archaeological samples by reference to the Egyptian dates alone and without regard to the bristlecone pine.[8,16]

Sufficient data are available to permit a statistical investigation of both problems, taking into account the experimental errors in the radiocarbon determinations. The time range selected covers the period from the beginning of the Egyptian historical chronology (about 3100 BC) to the first secure and astronomically verifiable Egyptian historical date (1872 BC).

Calibration Function

Any calibration curve based on tree rings is derived ultimately from the analysis of a series of tree-ring-dated wood samples, where each sample has both a tree-ring date (generally assumed to establish a date in calendar years with a probable error of less than two or three years), and a radiocarbon date with its attendant standard error arising chiefly from counting problems. Similarly, the historical data used for any check on the dendrochronological calibration arise from a series of samples each having, as well as a radiocarbon date (with standard errors), a date in calendar years assigned on the basis of its observed archaeological context and the appropriate historical calender.

Here we investigate the proposition that the calibration relationship connecting radiocarbon dates and their corresponding 'true' dates is the same in both sets of data. If this proposition is correct, it would lend support to the use of bristlecone pine radiocarbon dates to calibrate radiocarbon dates relevant to prehistoric material in general.

Our method assumes that the calibration relationship is of the form $y = f(x) + \epsilon$ where y denotes the radiocarbon date of a sample, x its corresponding 'true' date (as determined dendrochronologically or archaeologically), ϵ the random measurement error in the radiocarbon date, and f the unknown 'calibration function'. This function is approximated by fitting a suitable smoothing function *g*, using a weighted least-squares procedure. The hypothesis is then tested by standard statistical methods, especially by comparing the goodness-of-fit of a single smoothing function *g* fitted to the whole data, with that of two smoothing functions of the same type fitted separately to the two sets of data. If a common curve fits as well as two separate curves, one may conclude that there is only one calibration curve for both the Egyptian and bristlecone pine data. As the choice of type of smoothing function may be crucial, this method has the important advantage of enabling several possible such functions to be easily compared.

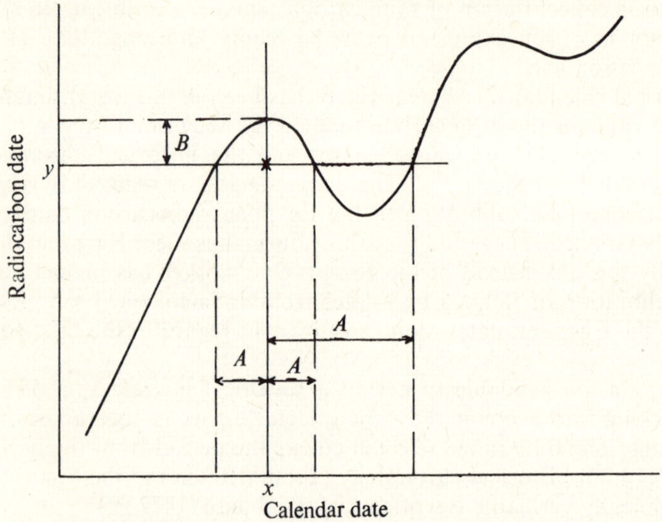

Figure 1. Methods (a) and (b) of matching a typical Egyptian sample against a fitted calibration curve. Method (a) considers the discrepancies *A* between the estimated and known calendar dates; method (b) considers the discrepancy *B* between the observed and predicted radiocarbon date. The cross represents a plotted point corresponding to the Egyptian sample, and the wavy line is the calibration curve.

Earlier workers have approached this problem by fitting a smoothing function *g* to the bristlecone pine data alone, and then matching the observations from individual Egyptian samples against that curve. This can be done in two ways: (a) by comparing, for each Egyptian radiocarbon date, the corresponding calendar date(s) as calibrated against *g* with the assigned historical date for that sample ; (b) by comparing, for each Egyptian historical date, the corresponding radiocarbon date as predicted by *g* with the date actually observed (see fig. 1). In both cases it must be remembered that the smoothing function *g* is only an estimate of the calibration function *f*, and therefore has its own associated standard error.

In such a procedure method (b) is preferable to (a) for two reasons. (i) It avoids the possibility of several calendar dates corresponding to a single radiocarbon date if there are 'kinks' in the calibration curve (see fig. 1). (ii) The comparison of predicted and observed radiocarbon dates is preferable to the comparison of predicted and observed calendar dates, for it is the radiocarbon dates which are subject to random errors of known magnitude. The errors associated with the tree-ring dates themselves are thought to be small,[4] whereas those involved in assigning precise historical contexts of samples of Egyptian material are difficult to quantify or treat statistically.

Recent workers[12,14] using method (a) have not correctly allowed for the standard error of a calibrated radiocarbon date. Such a standard error depends not only on that of the radiocarbon date itself, but also on the nature and precision of the smoothing function near the point of calibration. An important disadvantage of Suess's calibration curve[5] is that, as it is not determined by explicit reproducible methods its precision cannot be reliably assessed.

A crucial problem is the choice of type of smoothing function g. Among those already applied to radiocarbon determinations for samples of known age are linear functions,[17] periodic functions,[18] polynominals,[19] and the visual fitting of a subjectively-drawn curve.[5] There is no universally valid criterion for preferring a particular approach, and indeed it is relevant to consider some of the general criteria which might be thought desirable in a smoothing function.

(1) It should be derived by a reproducible and non-arbitrary method.

(2) There should be an objective method of testing whether the curve is an adequate fit to the data.

(3) The fitted smoothing function should in fact be an adequate fit to the data.

(4) There should be an objective estimate of the error in the fitted smoothing function.

(5) The smoothing function need not, however, possess the same general properties (such as continuity, smoothness) as the calibration function, although they may be desirable.

The choice of smoothing function will naturally depend on the purpose of the smoothing. In the case presented here, the smoothing is intended to facilitate the comparison of the Egyptian and bristlecone pine dates. We are not claiming to have produced a universal all-purpose calibration curve relevant to this time period. The production of a suitable calibration curve for use by archaeologists is a related problem at present under investigation. The physical background may well require that the calibration function f should have a bounded continuous first derivative, while the smoothing function g need not necessarily be constrained to have this property. For the present purpose, a discontinuous function, such as a series of unconnected straight lines, may be statistically convenient and quite valid, even if it would not be satisfactory as a calibration curve.

Evaluation of the Data

The data for our analysis consisted of the assigned historical dates, and the corresponding radiocarbon dates with their associated standard errors, for fifty-two Egyptian samples relevant to the time period 3100–1800 BC (calendar years), comprising fifty-one radiocarbon dates given by Berger[20] and Edwards,[21] with the subsequent corrections[22] noted, and one extra sample

(BM 236) found to be paired with UCLA 1208 (ref. 22). We also used the tree-ring date and radiocarbon date corresponding to each of fifty-seven specimens of bristlecone pine relevant to this time period, obtained from the list set out by Houtermans.[18] These specimens were dendrochronologically dated by the Laboratory of Tree-Ring Research, University of Arizona, and their radiocarbon dates determined by Suess at the La Jolla laboratory. Concerning the standard errors of these radiocarbon measurements, Houtermans[18] states only that they range from 4 to 7 per mil, and so we decided, in the absence of more specific information, to assign to these radiocarbon dates a common standard error of 5·5 per mil or 45·5 yr, the midpoint of the range.

In constructing a calibration curve, or comparing one proposed curve against another, the magnitude of the errors of measurement is of course important, as this determines how well a given smoothing function g approximates the unknown calibration function f. So, before fitting any smoothing function, it is essential to verify the quoted measurement errors whenever possible.

The standard error of 45·5 yr assigned to the La Jolla radiocarbon dates is at least partially verified by the estimated error variance, namely 2,263 on eleven degrees of freedom, obtained by Clark and Renfrew[17] by considering the differences[23] between replicate radiocarbon determinations carried out by the La Jolla laboratory on samples of wood from Auvernier, Switzerland. These Auvernier samples, however, were not of wood of the bristlecone pine, and so the quoted variance may not necessarily represent the precision of the La Jolla laboratory with bristlecone pine samples.

As many of the Egyptian samples were divided and analysed by both the BM and UCLA laboratories, the comparison allows the evaluation of interlaboratory variations, and hence of the published standard errors which the laboratories associate with their determinations.

Examination of the twenty-five paired differences so obtained showed that there was no systematic difference between these laboratories, but that the paired differences showed significantly greater variation than that expected due to measurement errors, the corresponding χ^2 value being significant at the 0·2% level. This implies that either the real measurement errors are greater than believed, or that there were some gross (non-counting) errors in some of the dates, or both. The standard errors of measurement would have to be 20% to 40% greater than the quoted standard errors in order to explain the full observed discrepancy.

McKerrell[8] has also concluded that there is no evidence of a systematic difference between these laboratories, but failed to note the excessive variation in the paired differences. The inclusion of two pairs omitted by McKerrell and the use of a more sensitive test does, however, document the excessive variability in the paired differences.

Some impression may be gained of the reliability of the ascription to the samples of a historical context by the Egyptologists concerned, together with the variation in the age of the samples when buried, by comparing the measured radiocarbon dates of samples from different archaelogical contexts reported as approximately contemporary. Several analyses are available from different contexts assigned archaeologically to the same period.

If these archaeological assignations are correct, the differences in the radiocarbon dates for them should be no greater than would arise from the laboratory measurement errors alone. The question here is not simply the major one of the validity of the Egyptian historical calender[11, 21, 24] but the more practical one of the precision with which these historical dates may be assigned, assuming for the moment their correctness, to the specific samples in question, on the basis of their stratigraphic contexts.

Ten groups of dates were considered, where all the samples within each group were supposedly of the same historical date, and their radiocarbon dates determined by the same laboratory. In three of these groups, the range of the corresponding radiocarbon dates was significantly greater than could be explained by measurement errors. Table 1 summarises the results of the ten significance tests performed using table 22 of Pearson and Hartley.[25]

Table 1. Significance of range of radiocarbon dates of supposedly contemporaneous Egyptian samples

Historical date	BM	UCLA
3025 BC	* (4)	—
3000 BC	—	ns (2)
2950 BC	ns	—
2650 BC	† (4)	ns (2)
2600 BC	ns (3)	—
2335 BC	ns (2)	ns (2)
2000 BC	ns (5)	‡ (4)

—, No dates available; ns, not significant at 5% level; *, significant at 5% level; †, significant at 0·1% level; ‡, significant well beyond the 0·1% level (about 0·001%). Number in parentheses is number of samples in each group.

These results imply (i) that some of the measurement errors are greater than indicated by the laboratories, or (ii) that certain groups of samples are not in fact contemporaneous (which was assumed in these tests), or (iii) there are gross errors in some of the radiocarbon dates. If the measurement errors were increased by 40%, as suggested previously, the two most significant groups would still show significantly large ranges. The observed discrepancies cannot be explained simply by increasing the standard error of measurement to the extent suggested by the interlaboratory comparison. But the four samples given an historical date of 2650 BC and the five corresponding to 2000 BC were of different materials (such as wood, linen, reed), and these samples might not be of identical age, even when they were buried.

It is concluded that some of the information concerning the fifty-two Egyptian samples is grossly in error; either some 'true' dates, or some radiocarbon dates, or their associated standard errors. This has not previously been demonstrated by a systematic statistical analysis, although Michael and Ralph[26] and Säve-Söderbergh and Olsson[27] have used qualitative comparisons to draw similar conclusions, the latter pointing to uncertainties in some cases about the archaeological date. There does not seem to be any independent objective method of deciding, on the basis of existing data, which pieces of information are wrong and by how much. We suspect that in some cases difficulties in stratigraphic interpretation have led to error. Admittedly, the assigned Egyptian historical dates are not claimed to be exact, but there seems to be no objective way of quantifying their lack of precision.

These results alone show clearly that the attempt to use the Egyptian historical dates as the basis for a 'calibration' of the radiocarbon chronology, quite independent of the bristlecone pine dendrochronology,[16] is not well founded.

These discrepancies make the Egyptian data less suitable for a check on the bristlecone pine calibration than might be hoped. Both Berger[20] and McKerrell,[16] however, have based comments on the calibration upon an examination of these Egyptian data, and it is important to consider such claims. In what follows analyses are therefore conducted on the provisional assumption that the assigned historical dates for the Egyptian samples are without error, and that the discrepancies observed are simply the result of high measurement errors of their radiocarbon dates. Although, as already noted, this assumption is not strictly warranted, it should not affect the conclusions unless the historical dates are very seriously in error, as the F-values in table 2 are not near the critical values.

Statistical Analysis

The problem of testing the hypothesis of a common calibration curve for the bristlecone pine and Egyptian data can be recognised as a special case of testing a sub-hypothesis in a general linear model, for which standard statistical techniques are available.[28] In order to apply these techniques, it was necessary to assume, at least provisionally, that the calendar dates assigned to all Egyptian and bristlecone pine samples were without error, and that the errors of measurement of the radiocarbon dates were normally distributed. It was also assumed that the standard errors of all radiocarbon dates used were equal to k times the corresponding reported standard errors. The factor k, initially unspecified but later estimated from the data, allows for possible underestimation by all three laboratories of their overall measurement error. As had been noted elsewhere,[29,30] the reported standard error refers only to 'counting error', which is only part of the overall measurement error. The preceding analysis of paired differences indicates that such underestimation of the real measurement errors could be substantial.

Two types of smoothing functions g were fitted to the data over the range 3100–1800 BC, using the method of weighted least-squares to allow for the differing precision of the radio carbon measurements. As the weights used in this procedure depend only on the relative magnitude of the standard errors of the radiocarbon dates, the weights can be chosen without knowing the actual value of the factor k. First, a single mth degree polynominal was chosen, giving in fact fourteen curves corresponding to the various values of m up to a maximum of 14 imposed by the limits of computer accuracy. Second, g was assumed to comprise seven straight lines constrained to be continuous as the six corresponding join-points (see fig. 2). The number of

Table 2. Comparison of goodness-of-fit of various smoothing functions applied to Egyptian, bristlecone pine and the combined data

Type of curve	Bristlecone pine data		Egyptian data		Combined data			Degrees
	Residual s.s.	m.s.e.	Residual s.s.	m.s.e.	Residual s.s.	m.s.e.	*F*-value	of freedom
Linear	310,319·72	75·11	337,186·78	82·12	661,938·08	78·65	1·08	2,34
Quadratic	291,545·86	73·47	333,640·54	82·51	657,691·58	78·76	1·63	3,34
Cubic	266,432·82	70·90	333,599·58	83·37	627,952·14	77·33	1·05	4,34
Quartic	266,371·64	71·57	320,793·39	82·62	625,044·44	77·52	1·14	5,34
Eighth degree polynomial	214,232·53	66·80	298,367·62	83·30	602,018·40	77·58	1·49	9,34
Fourteenth degree polynomial	167,840·19	63·21	270,739·99	85·54	543,762·94	76·05	1·05	15,34
Seven connected lines	151,717·62	55·64	300,483·77	82·64	539,256·58	73·07	1·64	8,34

Residual s.s., weighted residual sum of squares; m.s.e., mean-square-error. *F*-value is the value of the standard *F*-statistic for testing the hypothesis of a common calibration curve of the given type. Items *a*, *b* and *c* of Table 3 are given in the first, third and fifth columns respectively.

line-segments was restricted to seven because of computer capacity and the location of the resulting six join-points was estimated statistically without reference to Suess's curve.

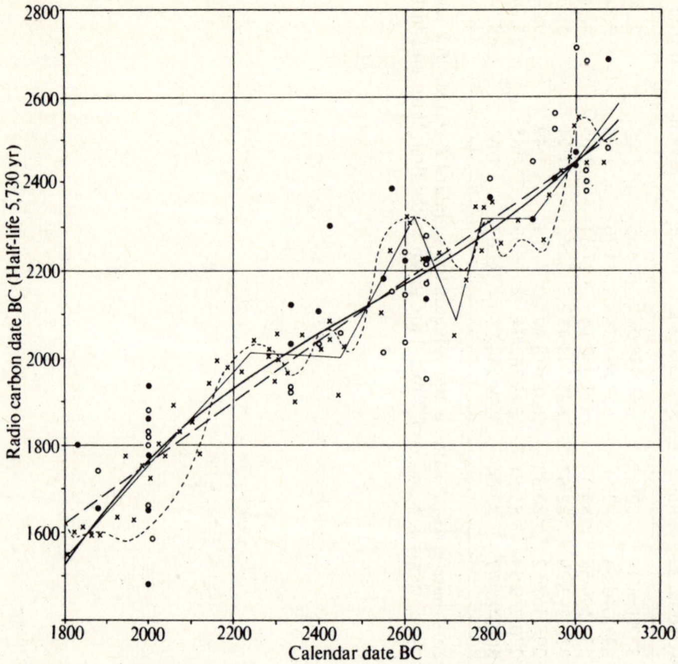

Figure 2. Relationship between radiocarbon dates and calendar dates, showing the curve published by Suess (short dashes) and three of the smoothing functions fitted by weighted least-squares: straight line (long dashes), fourth-degree polynomial (heavy line), and piecewise linear curve (light line). Crosses represent bristlecone pine data (LJ), open circles Egyptian data (BM), and solid circles Egyptian data (UCLA).

Amongst the Egyptian data, in most cases there was more than one radiocarbon date corresponding to each of the eighteen distinct historical dates. For the purpose of curve-fitting, each group of radiocarbon dates corresponding to each historical date could be replaced by a weighted mean radiocarbon date. The residual variation after fitting any smoothing function g to these data can therefore be partitioned into two components. The first component involves the deviations of the weighted groups-means from the fitted function, whereas the second component represents the within-groups variation for these radiocarbon determinations of supposedly contemporary Egyptian samples. Being the same for all fitted functions, this second component measures the intrinsic variable of the Egyptian data, which no amount of curve-fitting can reduce.

The corresponding analysis of variance is given in table 3 for the case where the function g is simply a straight line. The weighted least-squares procedure is exactly equivalent to transforming the data so that the transformed radiocarbon dates have a common error variance and then performing a standard least-squares analysis of the transformed data. In this particular case, the weights were chosen so that this common error variance was equal to $(45{\cdot}5k)^2$. Item *e* in table 3 is an unbiased estimate of this variance, even if the fitted straight line is not an adequate fit to the data and even if our hypothesis is incorrect. It follows then that the factor *k* must be at least 1·5 and possibly 1·8, implying that the true standard errors of the radiocarbon dates must be at least 50% and possibly 80% greater than the quoted standard errors. This reinforces the doubts expressed earlier concerning the validity of the Egyptian data.

Table 3. Analysis of variance due to fitting linear smoothing functions

Source of variation	Degrees of freedom	Sum of squares	Mean-square
Deviation of weighted group means from Egyptian line	16	111,724·76	6,983 *d*
Within-groups (Egyptian)	34	225,462·02	6,631 *e*
Total residuals from Egyptian line	50	337,186·78 *b*	6,744
Residuals from bristlecone pine line	55	310,319·72 *a*	5,642 *f*
Difference between lines	2	14,431·58	7,216 *g*
Residuals from common line	107	661,938·08 *c*	
Regression due to common line	1	5,895,145·74	
Total	108	6,557,083·82	

In table 3, comparison of items *d* and *f* with *e*, using the appropriate *F*-tests, shows that a straight line is in fact an adequate fit over the time range to both the Egyptian and bristlecone pine data separately. Moreover, comparison of items *g* and *e*, yielding the low *F*-value of 1·08, indicates that a single straight line fits the combined data just as well as these two separate lines. In other words, the hypothesis of a common calibration curve (in this case, a straight line) is well supported.

Similar tables of analysis of variance may be constructed for each fitted smoothing function, simply by substituting the value of items *a, b* and *c* given in table 2, and using the well-known structure of analysis-of-variance tables. The resulting *F*-values for testing the hypothesis of a common calibration function are listed in table 2. In all the cases considered, this hypothesis was supported, as testified by the low *F*-values. Table 2 also gives a comparison of the goodness-of-fit of the various smoothing functions when fitted to the combined data or to either the bristlecone pine or Egyptian data separately.

If the assigned historical dates of the Egyptian samples were not correct, then the various *F*-statistics would have only an approximate *F*-distribution, rather than the exact *F*-distribution assumed in the preceding significance tests. But, provided these dates are not very seriously in error, our conclusions remain the same, because the computed *F*-values are comparatively distant from the critical values. As there is no objective measure of the precision of these estimated dates, no completely objective statistical test of the hypothesis is possible, using the given data. Method (a) seems to overcome the problem by calibrating the Egyptian radiocarbon dates using a calibration curve based on bristlecone pine observations only, but there is then no objective way of comparing those calibrated dates with the assigned historical dates. Some assumption concerning the precision of these dates is thus necessary for any analysis, and our assumption facilitates the comparison of several smoothing functions. The remaining assumptions are likely to be at least approximately correct and, in any case, the analysis would be only marginally affected by small departures from them.

Validity of the Time Scales

Detailed analysis of the Egyptian data shows that, if major experimental errors be discounted, either the standard errors associated with the radiocarbon dates have been grossly underestimated, or some of the calendar dates assigned to samples on stratigraphic evidence are seriously in error, or both. It would therefore be ill-advised to use the Egyptian data to construct a calibration curve independent of the bristlecone pine chronology, although this has been suggested by McKerrell.

These deficiencies in the Egyptian data unfortunately preclude any completely objective statistical analysis, or any exact comparison of the two time scales. We claim, however, that our analysis is the most precise comparison possible in the circumstances. A more exacting test of the comparability of the two data sets could only be obtained with better data, and in particular better Egyptian data.

Nonetheless, although the comparison is not as precise as is desirable, the available information indicates that the hypothesis of a common calibration curve for the bristlecone pine and Egyptian data over the time period 3100 to 1800 BC is not contradicted, and suggestions to the contrary are not well founded. The conjunction of the bristlecone-pine-calibrated Egyptian radiocarbon dates and the historical dates for Ancient Egypt from 3100 to 1800 BC carries with it the implication that, within the error limits discussed, both chronological systems are correct. It seems unlikely that the Egyptian historical calendar, as reconstructed by Egyptologists today, and the bristlecone pine calibration of radiocarbon dates should be in error in precisely the same way over this range, so as to yield closely comparable yet erroneous calibration functions.

Our analysis thus lends support to the general validity of both the radiocarbon calibration and the Egyptian historical chronology. Further accurate work on Egyptian material is still required to reduce the level of error and thus to make the comparison more sensitive. But the present harmony gives some grounds for optimism concerning the validity of the bristlecone pine calibration as applied to prehistoric studies in general. [1973]

REFERENCES

1. Suess, H. E. (1967) *Proc. Symp. on Radioactive Dating and Methods of Low-Level Counting, Monaco, 1967*, 143. Vienna: IAEA.

2. Damon, P. E., Long, A. and Grey, D. C. (1970) in Olsson, I. U. (ed.) *Radiocarbon Variations and Absolute Chronology* 615. New York: John Wiley.

3. Ralph, E. K. and Michael, H. N. (1970) in Olsson, I. U. (ed.) *Radiocarbon Variations and Absolute Chronology* 619. New York: John Wiley.

4. Ferguson, C. W. (1969) *Tree-Ring Bulletin* 29, 3.

5. Suess, H. E. (1970) in Olsson, I. U. (ed.) *Radiocarbon Variations and Absolute Chronology* Plate I. New York: John Wiley.
6. Barker, H. (1971) *Nature* 231, 270.
7. Baxter, M. S. and Walton, A. (1971) *Proc. Roy. Soc. London, A* 321, 105.
8. McKerrell, H. (1971) *Scot. Archaeol. Forum* 3, 73.
9. Libby, W. F. (1949) *Radiocarbon Dating* 10, fig. 1. Chicago University Press.
10. Libby, W. F. (1963) *Science* 140, 278.
11. Smith, H. S. (1964) *Antiq.* 38, 32.
12. Suess, H. E. (1967) *Z. Phys.* 202, 1.
13. Renfrew, C. (1970) *World Archaeol.* 2, 199.
14. Vogel, J. C. (1969) *Helinium* 9, 19.
15. Derricourt, R. (1971) *J. Near Eastern Studies* 30, 271.
16. McKerrell, H. (1972) *Proc. Prehist. Soc.* 38, 286.
17. Clark, R. M. and Renfrew, C. (1972) *Archaeom.* 14, 5.
18. Houtermans, J. C. (1971) thesis, Univ. Berne.
19. Wendland, W. M. and Donley, D. L. (1971) *Earth Planet, Sci. Lett.* 11, 135.
20. Berger, R. (1970) *Phil. Trans. Roy. Soc. A* 69, 23.
21. Edwards, I. E. S. (1970) *Phil. Trans. Roy. Soc. A* 69, 11.
22. Barker, H., Burleigh, R. and Meeks, N. (1969) *Radiocarbon* 11, 281.
23. Suess, H. E. (1970) *Antiq.* 44, 91.
24. Hayes, W. C., Rowton, M. B. and Stubbings, F. H. (1962) *Cambridge Ancient History* 1, ch. 6.
25. Pearson, E. S. and Hartley, H. O. (1958) *Biometrika Tables for Statisticians* (second ed.) 1.
26. Michael, H. N. and Ralph, E. K. (1970) in Olsson, I. U. (ed.) *Radiocarbon Variations and Absolute Chronology* 109. New York: Wiley.
27. Säve-Söderbergh, T. and Olsson, I. U. (1970) in Olsson, I. U. (ed.) *Radiocarbon Variations and Absolute Chronology* 35. New York: Wiley.
28. Searle, S. R. (1971) *Linear Models*. New York: Wiley.
29. Neustupny, E. (1970) in Olssen, I. U. (ed.) *Radiocarbon Variations and Absolute Chronology* 23. New York: Wiley.
30. Hultin, E. (1972) *Etnologiska Studier* 32, 185.

17) The Tree-ring Calibration of Radiocarbon: An Archaeological Evaluation

By 1970 a clear and consistent pattern had emerged from the calibrated radiocarbon determination from prehistoric Europe and the Near East. Whereas dates from the east Mediterranean agreed adequately, after calibration, with the traditional historical chronology for the area (see chapter 16), those from Europe north and west of the Aegean did not. As this paper shows, a coherent explanation for this pattern can be formulated which accepts the calibrated radiocarbon datings, but calls into question assumptions about prehistoric Europe which had generally been little doubted in recent decades.

Certainly there are those who question these conclusions, either through doubts about some aspects of the calibration (e.g. McKerrell 1972), or indeed by a rejection of radiocarbon dating as a whole (e.g. Makkay 1976). It is difficult now to see what further arguments can be put forward in favour of the calibrated radiocarbon time scale beyond its harmony with other aspects of the physical sciences, the internal consistency of the dates (when due allowance is given for a statistical treatment of errors), and their general accordance with the historical chronologies of Egypt and Sumer. I have tried to show here how the stratigraphy at the site of Sitagroi in northern Greece, like that of Karanovo in Bulgaria (see chapter 5), works in the same sense.

It is time, therefore, to consider the wider implications of the calibration (cf. Fleming 1975). The first, undoubtedly, is that in giving us an objective method for establishing the absolute chronology of prehistoric Europe, it is no longer necessary to make the construction of a chronological framework the main object of archaeological research. That framework is now emerging, and we are no longer dependent upon a documentation of contact with historically dated areas in order to escape from our temporal ignorance. We can echo with renewed emphasis the words of Sir Mortimer Wheeler (1954, 215): 'We have been preparing timetables: let us now have some trains.'

This possibility of a reasonably secure and objective chronology now enables us to move beyond chronological questions and instead to formulate explanations—not simply to describe what happened in the past but to understand why. It is possible instead to think about the dynamics of culture change in the areas and periods under study.

For prehistoric Europe at least three major problems have emerged, with which some progress has already been made. The first is the development of proto-urban or small urban societies in different areas between 3000 BC and 0 BC. Their development in the Aegean is briefly considered in chapter 4, and in Iberia in chapters 2 and 11 (see Evans 1977). In the European iron age a similar process may be discerned, culminating in the 'oppida' whose urban nature impressed Julius Caesar (cf. Cunliffe and Rowley 1976). The beginnings of an explanation in social and economic terms, touched upon in question one has been further developed for the early Aegean (Renfrew 1972). The approach, using a division of the culture system into subsystems and a consideration of the interactions among these subsystems, has already been outlined for Iberia with very promising results by Chapman (1975). An outlook in some ways broadly analagous has been brought to the oppida of the iron age, for instance by Collis (1971 ; 1975) Cunliffe (1971), Haselgrove (1976) and Nash (1976). These are all early, indeed pioneering attempts and they contrast agreeably with the tendency so widespread in European archaeology until very recently to ascribe all change to external causes.

A second area where a picture different from the traditional one can now be seen to emerge is in the old problem of the megalithic collective tombs, discussed in the Introduction and in chapter 11. The possibility of multiple origins has now firmly to be faced, and again it can be set in a wider context, namely the construction of major monuments in segmentary societies, wherever their location (Renfrew 1976). Once a framework has been developed for the systematic comparison of analagous developments in the world, without *a priori* limitations of time and place, the very rich data available for prehistoric Europe will be found to have a much more general application and an interest wider than is at present realised.

The third field of enquiry where a substantial reorganisation of our ideas is now due is in the origins of metallurgy. In the paper which follows, the chronological evidence available is used very provisionally to suggest (see fig. 10) the existence of at least three foci for early copper metallurgy in early Europe and the Near East – in Iberia (see also ch. 11), in the Balkans (see ch. 5), and in the area embracing Mesopotamia, Iran and east-central Anatolia. In chapter 9 the possibility was tentatively suggested of a fourth such focus in Italy.

Against such proposals must be set the views of such a specialist in the early development of metallurgy as Wertime (1973, 876):

> My main difference of interpretation . . . lies in my belief that extractive-casting metallurgy was probably discovered in only one center, south-western Asia, and that secondary centers developed over thousands of miles through the search for minerals.

It is here that we return again to the very general problems of invention and contact, discussed in the introductory chapter, which preoccupied such early anthropologists as Tylor.

Once again the early European experience is likely to prove of great relevance in confronting a problem world-wide in its significance. Are we to believe that the discoveries of the metal-smiths of central and south America (see Bray 1971), or the early metal working (by annealing, however, not by casting) of the Old Copper Culture of north America (Griffin 1961), are ultimately the product of that same centre in southwestern Asia? And what of the precocious metallurgy of Thailand, whose bronze industry at present makes claims for the earliest deliberate metal alloys in the world (Solheim 1968 ; Gorman and Charoenwongsa 1976 ; Wheeler and Maddin 1976)? And if they are not all ultimately the outcome of a single sequence of discovery, but reflect instead indigenous and independent metallurgical developments, why not also in Iberia and the Balkans?

These are questions which demand a closer consideration of the nature and circumstances of innovation (cf. Renfrew 1978), both in social and economic terms, than they have yet received. They are important questions, where the evidence of European prehistory will have much to contribute that is of general relevance. It is thanks, at least in part, to radiocarbon dating and to its tree-ring calibration that we are now in a position to face them at all.

BIBLIOGRAPHY

Bray, W. (1972) Ancient American metal-smiths. *Proc. Roy. Anthrop. Inst. of Great Britain and Ireland for 1971*, 25–43.

Chapman, R. W. (1975) *Economy and Society within later Prehistoric Iberia, a New Framework,* unpublished Ph.D. dissertation, University of Cambridge.

Collis, J. R. (1971) Markets and money, in Jesson, M. and Hill, D. (eds.) *The Iron Age and its Hill-Forts.* Southampton: SUAS, 97–104.

——(1975) *Defended Sites of the Late La Tène in Central and Western Europe* (British Archaeological Reports, Supplementary Series, no. 2).

Cunliffe, B. W. (1971) Some aspects of hill-forts and their cultural environment, in Jesson, M. and Hill, D. (eds.) *The Iron Age and its Hill Forts.* Southampton: SUAS, 53–69.

Cunliffe, B. and Rowley, T. (eds.) 1976, *Oppida in Barbarian Europe* (British Archaeological Reports, Supplementary Series 11), Oxford.

Evans, J. D. (1977) Village, town and city in the Aegean and Italy, in Sieveking, G., Longworth, I. N. and Wilson, K. E. (eds.) *Problems in Economic and Social Archaeology.* London: Duckworth, 501–12.

Gorman, C. and Charoenwongsa, P. (1976) Ban Chiang, a mosaic of impressions from the first two years. *Expedition* 18 (4), 14–26.

Griffin, J. B. (ed.) (1961) *Lake Superior Copper and the Indians* (Museum of Anthropology, University of Michigan Anthropological Papers 17). Ann Arbor.

Haselgrove, C. (1976) External trade as a stimulus to urbanisation, in Cunliffe and Rowley (eds.) 25–50.

Makkay, J. (1976) Problems concerning copper age chronology in the Carpathian basin. *Acta Archaeol. Acad. Sci. Hungar.* 28, 251–300.

McKerrell, H. (1972) On the origin of British faience beads and some aspects of the Wessex-Mycenae relationship. *Proc. Prehist. Soc.* 38, 286–301.

Nash, D. (1976) The growth of urban society in France, in Cunliffe and Rowley (eds.) 95–134.

Renfrew, C. (1972) *The Emergence of Civilisation, the Cyclades and the Aegean in the Third Millennium BC.* London: Methuen.

——(1978) The anatomy of innovation, in Green, D. R., Haselgrove, C. C. and Spriggs, M. J. T. (eds.) *Social Organisation and Settlement* (British Archaeological Reports, Supplementary Series 47), 89–117.

Solheim, W. G. (1968) Early bronze in northeastern Thailand. *Curr. Anthrop.* 9, 59–62.

Wertime, T. A. (1973) The beginnings of metallurgy, a new look. *Science* 182, 875–86.

Wheeler, R. E. M. (1954) *Archaeology from the Earth.* Oxford: Clarendon.

Wheeler, T. S. and Maddin, R. (1976) The techniques of the early Thai metalsmith. *Expedition* 18 (4), 38–47.

THE TREE-RING CALIBRATION OF RADIOCARBON: AN ARCHAEOLOGICAL EVALUATION

It is now nearly twenty years since the first radiocarbon dates for the neolithic cultures of Europe astonished and perplexed prehistoric archaeologists by falling a millennium earlier than the existing chronologies had suggested. Since that time most (but not all) archaeologists have become reconciled to radiocarbon dating, and to a chronology for Europe based, at least for the neolithic period, on the radiocarbon dates which have become so widely accepted as now to be conventional.

But a second radiocarbon revolution is now taking place. The calibration of radiocarbon by tree-ring dating indicates that the now conventional radiocarbon dates are not early enough. Dates for the neolithic, and this time for the early bronze age also, will have to be set earlier by several centuries. The consequences of this second revolution for the picture we have of prehistoric Europe are in many ways more radical than those of the first. For this reason, perhaps, there has been a marked reluctance among some archaeologists to face the consequences of the new calibration, although an emerging consensus of opinion among botanists and physicists seems to favour it. The present article sets out to identify the three principal points of difference between the conventional chronology and that suggested by the tree-ring calibration of radiocarbon. It is argued that on independent archaeological evidence the new, calibrated, chronology can be seen to yield a plausible and coherent general picture. While many problems have yet to be clarified, there seems no reason why the new dating should not be welcomed as offering a stimulatingly fresh view of the prehistory of Europe.

The Basis for the Conventional Chronology

What may have been the first application of the natural sciences, in this case physics and mathematics, to archaeology and to chronology, came already in 1690, although it was not published until 1728. It was, appropriately, our greatest scientist and mathematician, Sir Isaac Newton (1728) who first brought the precision of modern astronomy to bear on the problems of early chronology.

He began his book *The Chronology of Antient Kingdoms Amended* with a perceptive comment:

'All Nations, before they began to keep exact account of time, have been prone to raise their Antiquities; and this humour has been promoted, by the Contentions between Nations about their Originals.'

First he made a critical study of the historical sources: 'The *Egyptians* anciently boasted of a very great empire under their kings . . . reaching eastward to the *Indies*, and westward to the *Atlantic Ocean*; and out of vanity have made this monarchy some thousands of years older than the world: let us now try to rectify the Chronology of *Egypt* by comparing the affairs of Egypt with the synchronising affairs of the *Greeks* and *Hebrews*.'

He established first what we would today call a relative chronology, a sequence of events and persons, using the sources then available to him, which were essentially the classical authors in Greek and Latin, together with the Bible. Then, by a stroke of great originality he calibrated this sequence, putting it on an absolute calendrical basis. This he did by establishing from the texts that the cardinal points of the equinoxes and solstices were in alignment, at the time of the Voyage of the Argonauts, with stars identifiable today. And by comparing this situation with that in 1690, and knowing the rate of precession of the equinoxes, he was able to calculate that:

> the Cardinal Points in the time between the Expedition and the end of the year 1689 have gone back from those *Colures*, one Sign, 6 degrees and 29 Minutes; which after the rate of 72 years to a degree answers to

2,627 years. Counting those years backwards from the end of the year 1689, or beginning of the year 1690, and the reckoning will place the *Argonautic* Expedition about 43 years after the death of Solomon (i.e. in 937 BC).

The records available to Newton would not be considered of great chronological value today. And the Egyptian records, upon which the historical chronology of the Old World now rests, had not been deciphered. But it is of interest that the earliest fixed date yet established for the historical chronology of Egypt, a date of around 1872 BC for the seventh year of the reign of the pharaoh Sesostris III (Hayes, Rowton and Stubbings 1962) is established by what is essentially the method pioneered by Newton. Once again the historical records document a precise astronomical event, in this case a heliacal rising of the star Sirius, and astronomical calculation permits the precise determination of this date in calendar years BC. In this way the essentially relative chronology offered by the records is converted into an absolute chronology, expressed in calendar years before the present era. Newton's method, as applied to the Egyptian records, is the basis for the early historical chronology of Egypt and the Near East, and hence ultimately of Europe. Before this first astronomical fix the dates become progressively less certain.

The traditional method for dating European prehistory, in the days before radiocarbon, was to try to relate events and developments in prehistoric Europe with supposedly contemporary ones in the Mediterranean, and ultimately with the Egyptian calendar. By 1878, Worsaae (1878, 126) had prepared an outline chronology for northern Europe, beginning the neolithic period about 2000 BC and the bronze age around 1000 BC.

Oscar Montelius, the great master of the 'typological method', set the whole procedure on a new and systematic basis (Montelius 1903). His procedure was first to establish, for a given region, the typological development of a specific artefact type—for example the copper and bronze daggers of Italy (Montelius 1903, 33). The next stage was to compare broadly similar types in different regions in order to build up an analogous development sequence by means of which different regions might be related. For example, the axe-adzes of the Hungarian copper age and of Sardinia were compared in this way with those of Troy (Montelius 1903, 22). The method was felt to be particularly satisfactory when the typological development with one area was seen to be closely similar to that in another: in such a case the sequences were said to be 'parallel'. Montelius operated on the assumption that most innovations originated in the Mediterranean and the Near East, and his thinking on this point was analysed into five axioms by Gordon Childe (Childe 1939, 10). On this assumption, and knowing the Near Eastern chronology, that of Europe was built up. In some cases the chronology was a long one, and it is interesting to note, as Professor Hawkes has pointed out, that the now conventional 'short' chronology for Europe was preceded in the time of Montelius and Sir Arthur Evans by a longer chronology with which the radiocarbon dates are in better agreement.

Sir Flinders Petrie was acutely aware of these chronological problems, and he was perhaps the first to use cross-dating, based on the actual exchange of goods between two areas, documented by finds in each recognised as imports. In this way the chronology of Minoan Crete was firmly linked to that of Egypt. He was also the first to use a statistical method, which today is termed seriation, to put into chronological order the abundant finds from the Egyptian Predynastic cemeteries. This gave, in the first place, a relative chronology, which he expressed in the form of arbitrary sequence dates (Petrie 1899). It is interesting to note that today, when radiocarbon dates require calibration to put them into calendar years, the entire radiocarbon chronology, expressed in C-14 years, is a relative chronology analagous in some ways to the sequence dates of Petrie.

The next great advance was brought about by Gordon Childe, who first systematically applied the German concept of 'culture' to the whole of European prehistory, creating the basic structural framework for the neolithic period which remains fundamental today. In the third edition of his great work *The Dawn of European Civilisation* in 1939 he published chronological tables for prehistoric Europe, which remained substantially unaltered in the 1957 edition. The early bronze age of the Aegean was seen as well under way by 2700 or 2600 BC and at this time the early neolithic cultures of central Europe were seen to be ending, the copper age cultures of the Balkans (notably the Vinča and Gumelnitsa cultures) just beginning, and the neolithic of northern Europe and the British Isles newly underway.

Then came radiocarbon dating, with its revolutionary impact upon the chronology of the neolithic everywhere. In general the radiocarbon dates did not greatly affect the Aegean dates, nor those of the European bronze age, from around 1800 BC. But they did set the neolithic period throughout Europe so very much earlier than had previously been thought, that the whole matter became the subject of controversy. And indeed radiocarbon dating is still not accepted by several scholars, including Professor Milojčic (1967). The impact of radiocarbon upon neolithic chronology was succinctly summarised in a clear diagram by Professor Grahame Clark (1965, 64, fig. 1).

In general the radiocarbon chronology was made to harmonise well with the historical chronology of the Near East, and with that for bronze age Europe. It is this chronological system, which has been widely accepted for the past ten years or so which is here termed the 'conventional chronology'.

Already, however, there were one or two problems. James Mellaart (1960) pointed out that the C-14 dates set in doubt the traditional chronological equation between the Vinča culture and the First City at Troy, a cornerstone of earlier chronologies. He tried to overcome this problem by setting Troy (which had not directly been dated by radiocarbon) back to a very early date.

Moreover, although the radiocarbon dates harmonised very well with the historical dates for Egypt as far back as about 2000 BC, before that time the historical dates were systematically older than the radiocarbon ones (cf. Smith 1964). At first it was suspected that the historical dates might be in error: now, on the other hand, it is the radiocarbon dates which are seen to need rectification.

The Tree-Ring Calibration of Radiocarbon

A new era in the understanding of prehistoric chronology began in 1960 with the publication of a paper reporting radiocarbon determinations made on wood from tree rings of the giant *Sequoia* going back as far as AD 600 (Willis, Münnich and Tauber, 1960). The counting of the rings allowed the date of the samples in calendar years to be known accurately. The radiocarbon dates correspond broadly, but not precisely, to the tree-ring dates. The discrepancies, which were of the order of 1·5%, were attributed to variations in the concentration of radiocarbon in the earth's atmosphere.

Meanwhile, at the Laboratory for Tree Ring Research at Tucson, Arizona, Schulman and then Ferguson (1968) were working on the tree-ring sequence of the fantastically long-lived bristlecone pine, *Pinus aristata*. This sequence has now been taken back to 5100 BC, and radiocarbon determinations of wood of known age have been made at Tucson, Philadelphia and La Jolla. This work has allowed the construction of a calibration chart (fig. 1), based on Suess (1967).

Although the chart is a provisional one, at a detailed level, and the precise nature of the kinks in it requires documentation by more analyses, there is widespread agreement that the accurate calibration chart which will be available in a few years time will look something like this. The divergence of several centuries between the radiocarbon and calendrical dates seems assured, and the curve will probably have kinks of this kind.

The purpose of the present article is to assess the calibration archaeologically ; further discussion of the calibration itself and its reliability, will be found elsewhere (cf. Suess 1967 ; Renfrew 1970*a*). The following are some of the points which have to be considered in any consideration of the calibration itself:

(1) Similar results have been obtained for different species of tree, back to the 1st millennium BC.

(2) Similar results are obtained in different regions, notably in Japan and the USA, and the fluctuations in the atmospheric concentration of radiocarbon are believed to be world-wide.

(3) The reasons for these fluctuations are not finally understood: it is possible that they are related to changes in the magnetic field intensity of the earth (Bucha 1967).

(4) The kinks in the calibration curve reduce, at certain periods, the precision with which a given carbon sample can be dated in calendar years.

(5) When a sufficiently long 'floating' tree-ring chronology is available, of the order of 300 years, radiocarbon dating samples spaced a given time apart (say separated by 20 years) allows the production of a date of great precision, accurate perhaps to within 40 years (Ferguson, Huber and Suess 1966). This has been used to good effect at the Michelsberg settlements of Burgäschisee-Süd and Thayngen Weier, and at Auvernier. This does not rely on the assumption that the tree-rings of California behave like those of central Europe, but simply that fluctuations in the atmospheric concentration of radiocarbon occur on a world-wide scale. The precision of this work highlights the value of establishing floating sequences of this kind for prehistoric Europe. The log coffins of Britain and Denmark, for instance,

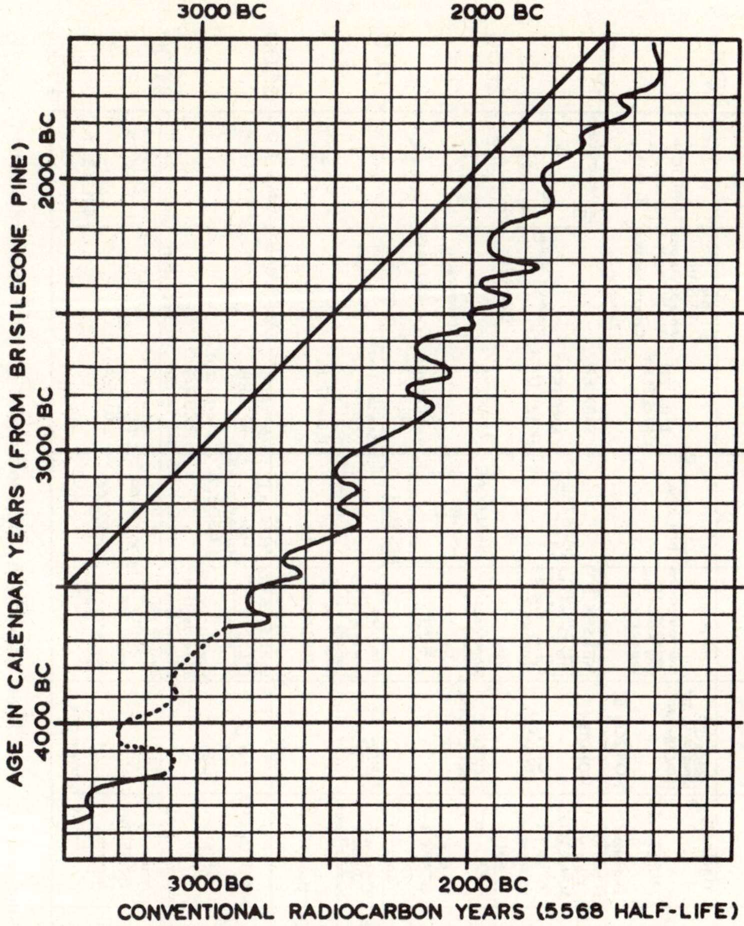

Figure 1. Provisional calibration chart, based essentially on the work of Suess (1967), showing the relationship between radiocarbon dates (5568 half-life) and dates in calendar years obtained from tree-ring counts of *Pinus aristata.* Note the ambiguities that may arise in converting C-14 dates to dates in calendar years. It is likely that further work will modify details of this calibration.

would be ideal for such work, and the associated finds could be dated in this way with great accuracy.

(6) The radiocarbon dates for Egypt in the 3rd millennium BC agree much better after calibration with the historical calendar (Neustupny 1968; Bakker, Vogel and Wislanski 1969; Renfrew 1970*a*).

(7) The thermoluminescent dating of pottery offers an entirely independent method for obtaining absolute dates for the period in question. At the Symposium on Archaeometry held at Oxford in March 1970, Dr D. W. Zimmerman reported results of a study of pottery of the Danubian I culture. The thermoluminescence dates harmonised well with the calibrated radiocarbon dates (cf. Neustupny 1970, 42).

CALIBRATED DATE B.C. (approx.)	EGYPT	SUMER	AEGEAN	SOUTH-EAST EUROPE	CENTRAL EUROPE	NORTH EUROPE	BRITAIN	ITALY	MALTA	IBERIA	FRANCE	CALIBRATED DATE B.C. (approx.)
	DYN. XVIII		MYCENAE									
1500	2 INTERMED. XIII XII 1 INTERMED.	HAMMURABI OF BABYLON	SHAFT GRAVES M.B.A. Phaistos (P 158) Palaikastro (St. 1265) M.M.I.	FÜZESABONY	TUMULUS L. AUNJETITZ Helmsdorf	BRONZE HORIZON III (HACHMANN) HORIZON II	M B A Swarkeston (NPL-17) Codicote (NPL-18) City Farm (GrN-1685) WESSEX II	Barche di Solferino POLADA	TARXIEN CEMETERY	EL ARGAR Anta dos Tassos Peñha Verde Cabezo Redondo Zambujal	BRETON Kervingar E.B.A.	1500
2000	VI V IV PYRA-	SARGON OF AGADE E.D.III Ur	Lerna IV (P 299) E.H.III	PERIAM + NAGYREV	St. Walrick EARLY AUNJETITZ VELUWE Vlaardingen Brabant	HORIZON I CIST GRAVES	Stonehenge III (BM 46) WESSEX I Antofts Windypits Fifty Farm (BM 133) Stonehenge I (C 602) (Aubrey Hole) 32 BEAKER Silbury Hill	(CASTEL-LUCCIO)	TARXIEN CEMETERY Tarxien (TxC) (BM 141)	Mallorca Beaker BEAKER	Les Mournouards II Lébous BEAKER Grotte Murée	2000
2500	MIDS III II	Royal Cem E.D.II E.D.I	Lerna III (P 318-321) E.H.II Chios (P-273) Sitagroi Vb TROY I Karataş	VUČEDOL CLASSICAL BADEN	Anlo AOC EARLY BEAKER Anlo 51	MIDDLE NEOLITHIC + P.G.	Stonehenge I (ditch) (C 602) Tara P.G. (D 43)	RINALDONE Asciano + Grotta Piccioni 4 REMEDELLO	TARXIEN SAFLIENI	Almizaraque LOS MILLARES Los Millares	+ Kermené S.O.M. Roucadour C	2500
3000	DYN. I	PROTO-LITERATE LATE URUK	E.H.I Eutresis (P 306-7) Sitagroi IV (BLN 773) KUM TEPE I	Cernavoda (Bln 62) CERNAVODA – EZERO Cernavoda (Bln 61a) EARLY BADEN EZEROVO	CORDED WARE Dölauer Heide Odoorn	Tustrup Ferslev T R B 'C' Mulbjerg	Arminghall (BM 129) New Grange P.G. (GrN 5462) Windmill Hill (enclosure) (BM 74) NEOLITHIC Ebbsfleet (BM 113)	Grotta Della	Skorba (Tx) (BM 143) ĠGANTIJA		Fort Harrouard Les Matignons CHASSEY +	3000
3500	GERZEAN	EARLY URUK Grai Resh (P 468-9)	Kephala (P 1280) FINAL NEOLITHIC Sitagroi III (BLN 774)	TRIPOLYE C	MICHELSBERG Thayngen Weier Burgaschisee	T R B 'A' Heidmoor	South St. L.B. (BM 356-7) Waylands Smithy Nutbane L.B. (BM 49) Willerby Wold LB Ehenside Tarn (C 462) Knockiveagh (D 37)	Madonna IV Lagozza Grotta Piccioni III LAGOZZA Arene Candide III	Mgarr (?Gg) (BM 100) MGARR Skorba (Zb) (BM 147) ŻEBBUĠ Skorba (Zb)	ALMERIAN Cabeço upper	LATE P.G. Kerleven P.G. Roucadour B	3500
4000	AMRATIAN	LATE UBAID Warka 17/18 EARLY UBAID	LATE NEOLITHIC Dhimini	Tell Azmak Varaşti L. GUMELNITSA	Elsloo RÖSSEN Dummer	ERTEBØLLE	Windmill Hill L.B. (BM 180) EARLY NEOLITHIC Newferry (D 36) Dalkey Island (D 38)	Arene Candide IV CHIOZZA	Skorba (R Sk) (BM 148) RED SKORBA	EARLY ALMERIAN	Sept Îles P.G. Île Carn P.G. EARLY CHASSEY	4000
4500												4500

Figure 2. Experimental chronology for Europe and the Near East, based on the bristlecone pine calibration of radiocarbon dates. The shaded area indicates the regions and periods where dates are based on a fairly reliable historical chronology. Names in capitals, (and + signs), refer to cultures, names in lower case to sites yielding dates on which particular reliance has been set (after Renfrew, 1970a).

These matters will not be further considered here, however. Instead the attempt will be made to produce a provisional and approximate chronology for prehistoric Europe between 4500 BC and 1500 BC, using the calibration curve given above. The discrepancies between the new, calibrated, chronology and the conventional chronology discussed above can then be located and considered.

Towards a New Chronology

The task of building up a coherent chronology for prehistoric Europe, based on calibrated radiocarbon dates, is a daunting one. One problem is that for certain regions and periods the requisite dates are not yet available. In forming the experimental table given here (fig. 2) I have tried to consider all the available dates, seeking first for a *pattern* of dates to establish a sequence within each region. An attempt has been made to fit the regions together so as to obtain a coherent picture for the whole area under consideration. Undoubtedly different approaches by different workers would yield a picture very different in detail. The broad outline is, however, clearly and unequivocally determined by the calibrated dates.

The following limitations should be noted: the table is experimental; the regions have been conflated to fit into a single page (the east, west, central and north Aegean in one column: Bulgaria, Rumania, Hungary and Jugoslavia in another); the table is selective; it has all the limitations of a rigid chest-of-drawers presentation.

In the case of Egypt there are historical dates from the time of the 1st Dynasty. The historical dates become reliable only in the time of the 18th Dynasty. For Sumer the historical dates are thought to be reliable from the time of Hammurabi or even Sargon of Agade: before this time there are a few radiocarbon dates. In the Aegean the historical dates are used from the middle bronze age, around 1900 BC. Before this time the radiocarbon dates are used: it should be noted however that there are no dates yet from Troy or Kum Tepe.

There are abundant dates for the neolithic period in south-east, central and northern Europe. From about 2500 BC, however, we are dependent on those for central Europe, and the bronze age cultures to the north and south-east have been dated by comparison with the central European early bronze age.

Britain has yielded abundant radiocarbon dates for the neolithic period. There are as yet, however, none for the Wessex culture. The dating for Wessex is achieved using a conventional view of the 'Wessex culture' based on those of Piggott and ApSimon. This allows the earlier Wessex culture to be equated with Reinecke's A2 phase in Germany, and later Wessex with the later part of that phase and with Reinecke's B1 phase. As Professor Hawkes has pointed out, the Wessex culture is not at present sufficiently clearly defined, and the forthcoming monograph by Dr Sabine Gerloff will be most useful here. Following these assumptions, however, the dates for Helmsdorf and St Walrick may be used to date Wessex I. And to those may be added that for another princely grave of Reinecke's A2 period, at Leki Male, which has yielded a radiocarbon date of 1655 ± 40 BC. (GrN 5037; Bakker, Vogel and Wislanski 1969). On calibration this may yield a date between 2100 and 1900 BC. These arguments suggest a date of perhaps 2100 BC for the beginning of the Wessex culture, although Professor Hawkes would prefer a date a century or so later.

The end of the Wessex culture (following the rather unsatisfactory criteria available) may be broadly contemporary with the secondary series collared urn from Barbrook II, the 'middle age' pottery from Codicote, the ring-ditch cremation cemetery at City Farm, Oxfordshire, and the Hilversum urn from Toterfout 74a (GrN-1828). These yield radiocarbon dates between 1510 and 1400 BC suggesting dates in calendar years of 1800 to 1700 BC and a possible end to the Wessex culture at about 1700 BC.

The picture given by the Italian dates is not yet a clear one: there are none for the Castelluccio culture of Sicily. In compiling the Malta dates the pattern established by Trump (1966) has been followed (cf. Renfrew 1970*a*). The Iberian sequence is unfortunately not very clear through the dearth of stratified sites, so that the Almerian culture and the beginning of the Los Millares culture cannot yet be accurately fixed. There are abundant dates for France.

Much of this is hypothetical, but the outline in general seems clear. The calibration of the chronology for south-east Europe has been independently and systematically undertaken by Dr E. Neustupny (1968 ; 1969). His careful compilation and analysis of the radiocarbon dates for that area yields results with which those presented here compare fairly well. His arguments have been attacked, but not I think seriously shaken, in a forceful article by Milojčic (1967) which defends the earlier chronologies and does not accept the validity of radiocarbon dates, still less of their dendrochronological calibration.

The chronology here built up now permits the fulfilment of our main purpose, the critical comparison of the calibrated and conventional chronologies.

The Discrepancies Examined

The main points of difference between the two chronological systems can most effectively be brought out by analysing more closely the logical structure of the conventional chronology. The period which most closely interests us here is not the early neolithic period, for which there are in any case no reliable historical dates. It is rather that period for which the Egyptian calendrical dates can plausibly be extended to the Aegean, from 3000 BC onwards, so that the conventional chronology stands on a reasonable historical basis.

The Montelian chronological system, modified and improved by Childe, is based on a long chain of successive typological and chronological links between adjacent regions. This is indicated diagrammatically in fig. 3. The basic source for the absolute historical dating is Egypt (with Mesopotamia): no other region has independent historical dates. By cross-dating, the chronology is carried to Crete, and less reliably to central Anatolia. By means of contact with the latter (and not directly Egypt), Troy and the rest of the Aegean are dated. And it is by contact with these last that the chronology is carried forward to south-east Europe, Iberia and so forth.

To date Britain, therefore, it is necessary to link first with France and

Germany, and at a second remove Iberia, Italy and south-east Europe and so on, by means of five stages, to Egypt.

Turning again to fig. 2, the shaded area indicates those places and periods which are reliably, or fairly reliably, dated by historical means. The calibrated radiocarbon dates support these datings. And outside the shaded area, if the actual dates in years be momentarily ignored, the relative chronologies of the regions, compared one with another, do not differ very much from those long ago established by Childe. The discrepancies occur in crossing from the unshaded to the shaded regions of the table. In other words the radiocarbon calibration has left certain areas of the chart untouched, and moved back chronologically, together and en bloc, the remaining cultures.

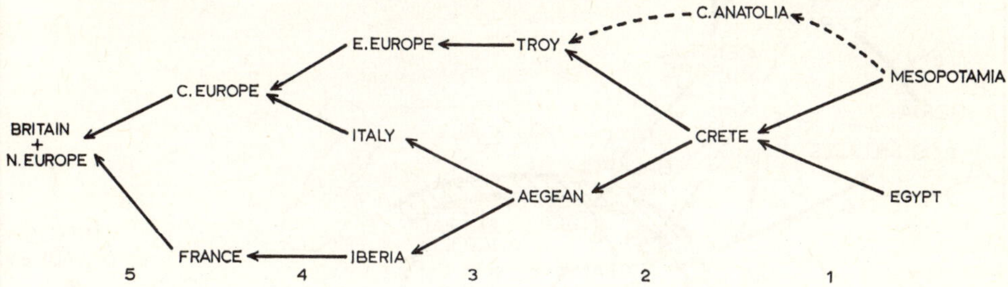

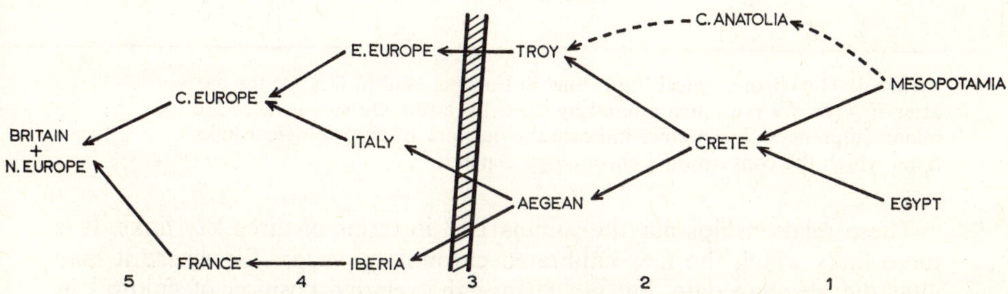

Figure 3a (*upper*). Logical structure of the conventional dating for European prehistory. All dates depend ultimately on the historical chronologies for Egypt and Mesopotamia, and are linked to these by a complicated network of links stretching across Europe.
Figure 3b (*lower*). The chronological 'fault line' that the dendrochronological calibration of radiocarbon dates produces. To the right of this line the conventional and calibrated dates (after about 3000 BC) are not significantly different. To the left of the line, the calibration sets all dates several centuries earlier.

This point is indicated by the fault line shown in figs. 3b and 4. This cuts across link 3 of the various chronological chains. The same point is made on the map, fig. 4, where the chronological 'fault line' is seen to run in an arc north and west of the Aegean. Within this line the dates back to 3000 BC are not significantly altered by the calibration, since they were in any case based on the historical calendar. On the other side of this line, to north and west, the cultures again hang together much as before, although the actual date in years is certainly changed. The fundamental changes occur, however, in making correlations and equations *across this chronological fault line*. It is across this line that the relative chronological relationships (indicated by the arrows) are so fundamentally altered

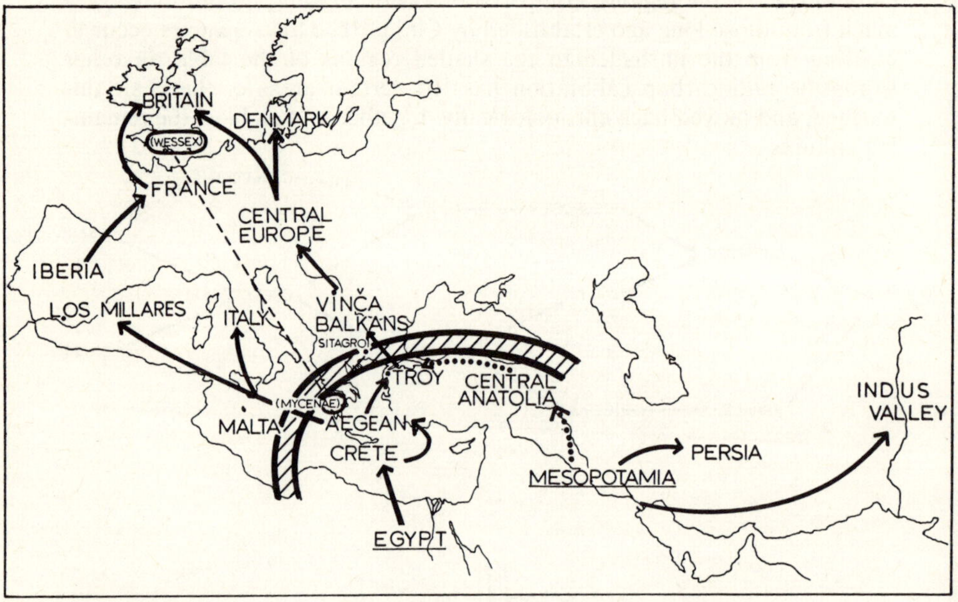

Figure 4. The chronological 'fault line' in Europe. Within this arc the dates after 3000 BC are not much altered by the calibration. Outside it there are major differences. The arrows indicate the network of chronological links upon which the conventional chronology depends.

These relationships may be summarised in terms of three key links. It is these links which the new calibrated chronology snaps. Elsewhere it may alter the absolute date, but not change the relative position of cultures in adjacent lands. These links are:

(1) The link between the Aegean early bronze age and the cultures of the west Mediterranean, especially the Almerian and Los Millares cultures of Iberia.

(2) The rather later link between the Mycenaean civilisation and the Wessex culture, and with the other early bronze age cultures in central Europe.

(3) The link between the Aegean, especially Troy, and the copper age cultures of south-eastern Europe, notably the Vinča and Gumelnitsa cultures.

It is on these links, and on these links alone, that the archaeological validity of the new calibration may be judged, since only here are the chronological relationships between adjacent regions fundamentally altered. In other cases the change is merely one of date, and not of relationship.

Put in these terms, the weaknesses of the conventional chronology can be seen to derive from a single, unsatisfactory procedural principle. It is simply that there has been too great a readiness to see in resemblances between artefacts of Europe and of the Aegean, indications of contact (and hence of contemporaneity) rather than merely indications of functional similarity emerging simply through similar adaptions in the light of rather similar problems.

This is, of course, simply the old diffusionist problem once again. And it is useful to remember that although Childe has been termed a 'moderate diffusionist', he specifically formulated 'the useful heuristic hypothesis that every invention has been made but once' (Childe 1956, 154). He explicitly set out to depict European prehistory in terms of 'the irradiation of European barbarism by Oriental civilisation' (Childe 1958, 70). Professor Hawkes has suggested, and there is support for the view in Childe's *Retrospect,* that Childe took up this position in some ways in reaction to the nationalistic theories of Gustav Kossinna (1905), or at least the nationalistic use to which they were put. He suggests that Childe deeply resented this misuse of prehistoric archaeology in the 1930's to lend spurious support to a nationalistic ideology, and that for this reason he strongly favoured and supported the Orientalist position of Montelius.

Once again it was the framework model adopted, rather than the basic data, which determined the ultimate form of the theory. And the central principle was the one explicitly formulated with exemplary clarity by Montelius in 1903 (Montelius 1903, 19). He used parallel developments in various regions as indicators of contact and hence of chronological information.

The simple moral which we can draw today is that a general parallel development in different regions does *not* necessarily imply any contact between them.

The foregoing lines are written on the assumption that the new and calibrated chronology is in fact preferable to the conventional one. But whether or not this is so, the basic difference between the two, which is manifest especially at these three crucial points, lies in the use of a diffusionist model for the conventional chronology (cf. Renfrew 1969*b*).

The three points of discrepancy must now briefly be considered.

1. IBERIA AND THE WEST MEDITERRANEAN

Since the time of the Siret brothers it has widely been assumed that the developments occurring in Iberia towards the end of the neolithic period—the new figurines and burial practices of the Almerian culture, the dolmens, passage graves and other megalithic tombs, the metallurgy and fortified settlements of the Los Millares culture—were the result of east Mediterranean influences, and could thus be used to date Iberian developments at the earliest to the time of Early Dynastic Egypt and of the Aegean early bronze age. This was stoutly maintained by Childe, who was indeed obliged to defend the synchronism between the early Los Millares culture and the later part of the Aegean early bronze age against Aberg's attempt to set up a still *shorter* chronology for prehistoric Europe in his *Bronzezeitliche und früheisenzeitliche Chronologie.* Childe's review of this work (1932) is especially instructive, since on the one hand he is arguing against Aberg's very short chronology, and on the other against the then traditional long chronology 'which placed the beginning of the New Stone Age in northern Europe seven or eight thousand years ago'. Today the latter position seems more reasonable than it did to Childe.

In the same volume of *Antiquity* as this review, was published the comprehensive *Chronological table of Prehistory* (Burkitt and Childe 1932) in which the implicit underlying assumption that the Iberian megaliths derived from the Early Minoan 'tholos' tombs, and the European megaliths from Iberia, is clearly apparent.

Childe's later writings emphasised this point rather less, although the Aegean/Iberian link remained one of the fundamental bases for his chronology. And yet he realised that this rested upon a rather dangerous diffusionist hypothesis, and expressed this awareness in his *Retrospect* (1958, 70): 'The sea-voyagers who diffused culture to Britain and Denmark in the first chapters in the first *Dawn* (1925)—and they were relegated to a secondary position in the second edition of *The Dawn* (1927)—though they do not hail from Egypt, yet wear recognisably the emblems of the Children of the Sun.'

The calibrated radiocarbon chronology destroys this dependence of the western Mediterranean upon the Aegean. The Almerian culture, with its supposedly Aegean schematic figurines and its collective burial in round tombs in some ways analogous to those of the Mesara, must have begun around 4000 BC, a millennium before the Early Minoan period. And the dates for Iberia (which are at present all too few) make possible the suggestion that the fortified settlement of Los Millares was constructed earlier than its supposed prototypes in the Cycladic islands and Mainland Greece.

These suggestions are supported by the new calibration, but they do not arise solely from it. Indeed a critical study of the Aegean and especially Cycladic early bronze age cultures, written before the new calibration was established (Renfrew 1965, 187), concluded that the chalcolithic there 'should be seen not as the result of direct colonisation but of local ingenuity . . . it would seem wiser to hold in doubt the question of Aegean influence on the Iberian neolithic and chalcolithic. Although such influence seems possible and even plausible, there is no reason why the Iberians should not have produced themselves most or all of the forms in use in chalcolithic times.'

The case against the view that the Iberian developments were the result of cultural influences diffused from the east Mediterranean has been argued in detail elsewhere (Renfrew 1967) and need not be reiterated here. The alternative was preferred that 'the chalcolithic of Iberia developed locally, with the local invention of metallurgy and a minimum of outside influence'.

Unfortunately the archaeological evidence alone is hardly conclusive: depending upon the framework model employed it can be used to support either the diffusionist view or the culture process view that the developments depended on the operation of local factors.

But in analysing the discrepancy between the conventional chronology and the calibrated radiocarbon chronology it can at least be said that there are independent archaeological arguments favouring the latter which were evolved before the calibration was effected. The same is true for the cultures of Malta, Sicily, Sardinia and Italy.

The first key link of the old chronology, that between the Aegean and the west, can thus be severed without doing violence to the archaeological findings. But, in fairness, we cannot yet say that the archaeology of Iberia indicates that it *must* be severed, only that it could be.

2. WESSEX

The second link, which relates Transalpine Europe directly to the Aegean world, is the chronological equation established between the Wessex culture of Britain and Mycenae. The possibility of such a connection was suggested by Piggott in his original study of the early bronze age in Wessex (1938, 95): 'the existence of such trade contacts between Mycenae and the north in the years around 1600 BC renders less startling the fact that the gold *pointillé* technique of the Breton and English dagger-hafts occurs not infrequently on the hilts of daggers both at Mycenae and elsewhere in Greece, that the Rillaton cup ... finds its best parallel in the two gold cups from Shaft-Grave IV, that gold-plated cones form a constant feature of Mycenaean grave furniture, ... while the practice of capping a stone bead with gold is essentially Mycenaean. Such resemblances may be individually fortuitous, but in their cumulative effect are too remarkable to dismiss.'

This suggestion was followed up by further work by other writers, so that the Mycenaean contacts were used to propose a shorter chronology than that put forward by Piggott, generally from about 1600 to 1400 BC.

In recent years Piggott (1966) and others have been more critical of these supposed links. But that the calibrated chronology, placing the Wessex culture perhaps between 2100 and 1700 BC, should set all of them in question, comes as something of a shock. It is possible, however, to question all the supposed links on purely archaeological grounds (cf. Renfrew 1968). And indeed some of them—the Rillaton gold cup, the Pelynt dagger, the carvings in Stonehenge—have never been very persuasive. There can be little doubt that the amber spacer plates of the Mycenaean world do in some way relate to those of central and northern Europe and of Wessex. But Wessex is at the earlier end of this chronological chain, and already in 1957 Miss Sandars (1957, 11) showed that von Merhart's reasoning could be extended to push the Reinecke B2 phase back into the sixteenth century BC using the evidence of the amber finds—a date close to that indicated by the calibrated radiocarbon dates. The final piece of evidence for the Mycenaean link was supposedly furnished by the faience beads, which were seen as imports to Britain from the Mycenaean world. But a re-interpretation of the trace-element analyses of Stone and Thomas has called this view into question (Newton and Renfrew 1970), and it now seems possible that the beads found in Britain were in fact made in Britain.

It seems, then, that the Wessex–Mycenae links can be broken without doing violence to the archaeological evidence. Deeper understanding must come from the further work now underway on the nature of the Wessex culture itself. Admittedly it seems unlikely that the Wessex–Mycenae links would have been rejected *in toto* had the calibration of radiocarbon not made this seem desirable. But, as in the case of Iberia, there is at least no difficulty in harmonising the archaeological material with the implications of the calibration. The supposed Mycenaean links with central Europe (cf. Gimbutas 1965, 32–69) seem equally vulnerable. These two crucial links fail, indeed, to speak conclusively either for or against the tree-ring calibration of radiocarbon.

3. SOUTH-EAST EUROPE

The third link, in the Balkans, furnishes a more decisive test, and indeed radiocarbon dating, still uncalibrated, already sets in doubt here the conventional relationships (Mellaart 1960). Recent excavations at Sitagroi in north Greece give direct stratigraphic support to the radiocarbon evidence and are in harmony with the calibration. Here, it seems, is positive archaeological evidence serving to upset the third fundamental tenet of the conventional chronology.

The Evidence of Sitagroi

The third basic chronological link, which the tree-ring calibration of radiocarbon sets in doubt, is the fundamental chronological equation between the early bronze age cultures of the Aegean, particularly of Troy, and the copper age cultures of the Balkans, notably Vinča and Gumelnitsa. This link was the chief of the two supports for Childe's chronology of Europe (the second being the Iberian one), and was described by him in detail in *The Danube in Prehistory.* Essentially the same case was reiterated, with a wealth of detail, by Professor Vladimir Milojčic (1949). The metallurgy of the Balkan copper age and many of the features of these very rich cultures are seen as the result of (and as evidence for) contact with the cultures of the Aegean early bronze age.

Radiocarbon dating, and more emphatically the calibration of the radiocarbon dates, directly contradicts this entire position. Indeed the earlier Vinča and Gumelnitsa cultures, on the calibrated chronology, are too early even to find a place on the table, fig. 2. There is a discrepancy between the two chronological systems of no less than two millennia at this point.

In a recent article in these Proceedings (Renfrew 1969*a*), an attempt was made to survey the evidence as it stood early in 1968. It was concluded that 'the late neolithic and chalcolithic cultures of south-east Europe developed, essentially independently of Oriental or Aegean influence, on the sound economic basis of the first neolithic'. The invention and development of metallurgy there was seen as a series of events independent of Aegean or Anatolian influence. The arguments for this view came chiefly from the Bulgarian evidence, notably at Karanovo, and from a consideration of the technology involved, based upon specialist studies by Mr J. A. Charles and Mr Jay Frierman.

The conclusions arising from the calibration of radiocarbon dates have been considered in considerable detail by Neustupny (1968 ; 1969), and the picture which he presents, like that summarised in fig. 2, flatly contradicts the old, conventional view, supporting instead the notion of independent origins for these cultures.

Here then is a test case where the two chronologies are at variance, and the archaeological data are not sufficiently plastic to be accommodated to both chronologies at the same time. The key area for investigation lies, of course, in the region of the chronological fault line indicated in fig. 4. To the south of it are the Aegean cultures whose synchronism with Egypt and Mesopotamia are not in doubt. And to the north are the cultures of south-east and central Europe, whose mutual relationships within that area are again not the subject of serious controversy. Ignoring the actual absolute dates, for the moment, the culture sequences for the regions within the Balkans and central Europe as produced by Milojčic, on the one hand, and as seen in fig. 2 on the other, can easily be reconciled. The discontinuity comes at this fault line, and here one system must be right, and the other wrong.

The possibility of resolving the controversy in favour of one or other view led me in 1965, and again in 1966, to undertake a site survey in precisely this 'fault-line' region, in the north Aegean lands of Macedonia and Thrace. Already French (1964) had reported potsherds from settlement mounds in this region with graphite-painted ware like that of the Gumelnitsa culture of Bulgaria, and other pottery resembling that of the Troy I culture. It therefore seemed possible that material both of Troy type and relatable to the Balkan copper age might be found stratified in the various levels at a single site. If they were found stratified together in the same stratum, this would strongly support the conventional chronology of Childe and Milojčic and throw doubt on the calibrated radiocarbon chronology. But if material related to the Balkan copper age were found well below material of the Trojan early bronze age in the stratigraphic sequence, this would substantiate the calibrated radiocarbon chronology and undermine the conventional picture.

During the summers of 1968 and 1969, excavations were conducted at Sitagroi in the Plain of Drama in east Macedonia. This is a large tell mound, more than 10 metres high, first reported by French and named by him 'Photolivos' (it has also been cited by other writers as 'Toumba Alistratiou'). The excavations were organised jointly by Professor Marija Gimbutas of the University of California at Los Angeles and the present writer, and directed in the field by the latter. They were supported by UCLA and the University of Sheffield, sponsored by the British School of Archaeology at Athens and authorised by the Greek Archaelogical Service whose representative in east Macedonia was Mrs C. Koukouli-Chrysanthaki. The excavations were supported by grant GS-1949 from the National Science Foundation, by the British Academy and by the sponsoring bodies.

The most challenging aspect of the project was the research undertaken into the ecological environment and farming economy of the settlement through the successive phases of its occupation. But neither this nor the well preserved structures recovered (cf. Renfrew 1970*b*) are relevant to the present problem. Here only the stratigraphic sequence is considered.

A central sounding, from the summit of the mound, revealed a stratigraphic sequence of more than 10 metres of deposit, all of it attributable to the later neolithic and early bronze age of the region. The stratigraphic sequence obtained was checked and documented by a series of stratigraphic trenches on other parts of the site. It was thereby established that the sequence revealed in the deep sounding ZA was of general validity for the site. This statement cannot of course be documented in detail here, but will be supported by appropriate evidence in the final excavation report.

On the basis of a quantitative analysis of the ceramic finds, undertaken with the collaboration of Miss Jenifer Marriott, the sequence at Sitagroi was divided into five major phases, of which the fifth has now been sub-

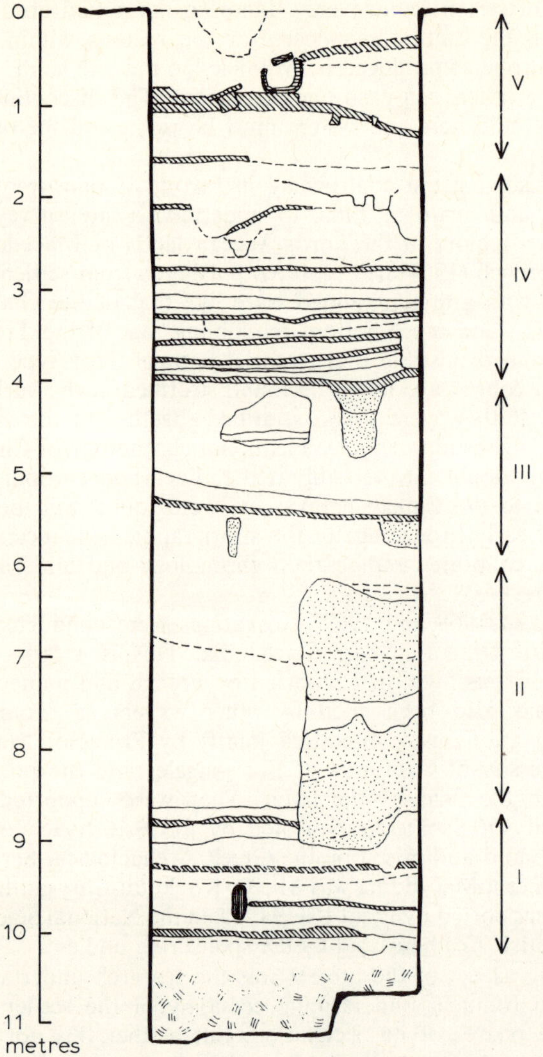

Figure 5. Schematic sketch section for the south face of trench ZA at Sitagroi, indicating the division of strata into phases.
(Drawn by Mr R. J. C. Wakeham.)

divided. The division is shown schematically in fig. 5, which is a sketch diagram of the south face of ZA: the detailed section of this and other areas will be presented in the final report.

The outcome was conclusive. The graphite-painted ware, and other finds obviously closely related to the copper age cultures of the Balkans, were restricted to levels of phase III. And the material relatable to the early bronze age cultures of Troy was essentially in levels of phase V. A glance at fig. 5 shows at once how strikingly at variance are these findings to the

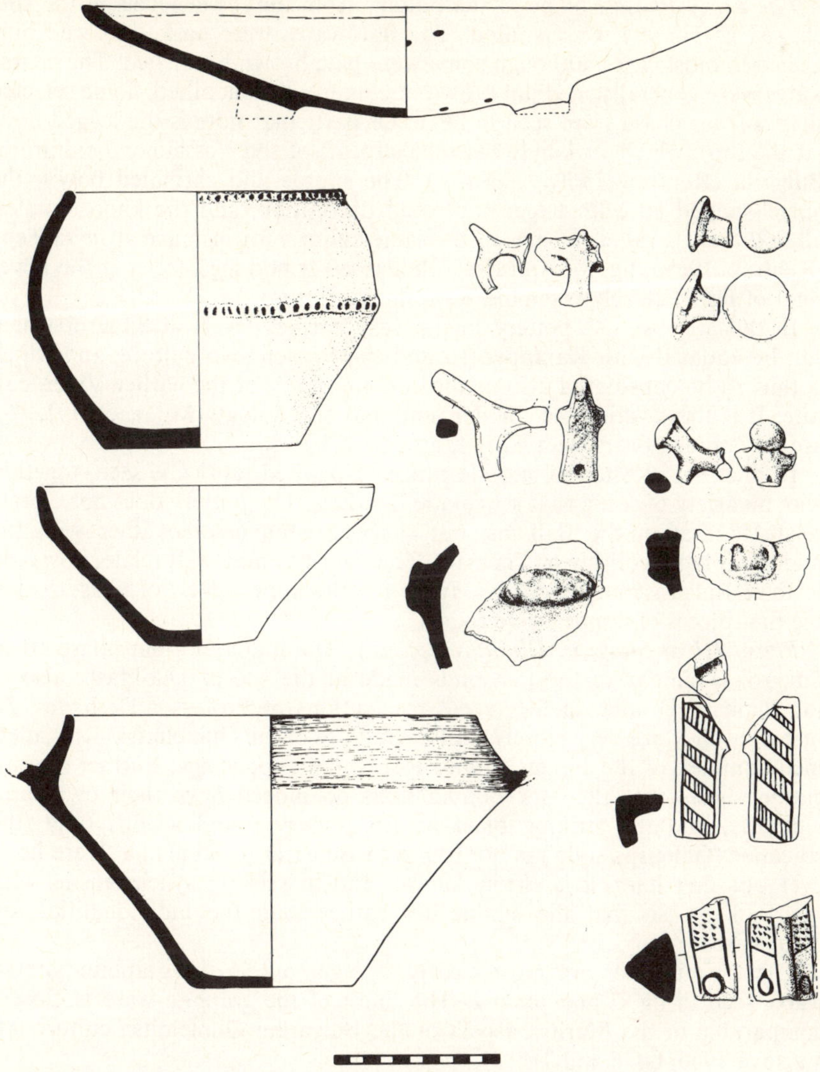

Figure 6. Pottery shapes from levels of phase I at Sitagroi. Most of the pottery is plain dark burnished, and resembles finds of the Vinča and Vesselinovo cultures. (Drawn by Miss Gayle Wever.)

conventional chronology, and how well they fit with the pattern of the calibrated chronology seen in fig. 2.

In view of the importance of this result, some of the material is illustrated here, and the following paragraphs of this section set out to document this statement. The general arguments, accepting the implications of the Sitagroi stratigraphy as discriminating between the conventional and calibrated radiocarbon chronologies in favour of the latter, is taken up again in the next section.

The Early Phases. None of the pottery from the lower levels of the site, classed as phase I, was painted. The fine wares were dark, and well burnished in most cases, although some were pale brown burnished. The coarse wares were generally medium brown in colour, and smoothed. Some selected shapes from phase I are seen in fig. 6. Of particular note is the legged bowl (at the top), which strikingly resembles forms of the Vesselinovo culture of Bulgaria (Renfrew 1969*a*, fig. 4, 1). The simple and carinated bowls, the barrel-shaped jar with finger-impressed decoration, and the knob handles, all find their parallels at sites of the same culture, for instance at Iassa Tepe (Renfrew 1969*a*, fig. 3). And the little incised tripod legs, (seen at the lower right of fig. 6) closely resemble Vesselinovo forms.

In this way we see pottery in the very earliest levels at Sitagroi which can be equated with Karanovo III and the Vesselinovo culture, and which is thus to be considered also as the contemporary of the earlier Vinča culture. It is these which, on the conventional chronology (Milojčic 1967, 16), are set contemporary with Troy I, around 2700 BC.

In phase II at Sitagroi, a wide range of painted fabrics is seen, together with a variety of somewhat schematic figurines. The pottery does not closely relate to that of the Balkans, but suggests comparisons rather with the middle to late neolithic of Thessaly. The figurines may well relate, however, to their Balkan contemporaries. It was in the upper levels of phase II that the first pieces of copper were found.

Phase III at Sitagroi (*Dikilitash phase*). The material from phase III at Sitagroi is similar to the rich finds made at the site of Dikilitash, also in the Plain of Drama, in the recent excavations of Professor Deshayes. At first sight they are very closely similar to those of the Gumelnitsa–Kodjadermen complex of the Bulgarian and Rumanian copper age. Further investigation shows that the Macedonian finds do indeed have their own individuality, and the striking black-on-red pottery found at this time (the so-called 'Galepsos style') is not found in Bulgaria or Rumania. Here however our first interest is chronological, and in seeking synchronisms with the Balkans, so that the similarities rather than the individualities are emphasised.

These similarities are most clearly brought out in the graphite-painted ware, seen in fig. 7 and pl. 1–2. The finest of the graphite ware is closely comparable to the Maritsa aspect of the Bulgarian Gumelnitsa culture (cf. Vajsová 1966, fig. 6 and 7).

Unfortunately the developmental sequence of the long-lived Gumelnitsa culture has never been clearly established in a satisfactory manner, with a sub-division into phases adequately defined. Vajsová has indeed outlined a sequence for Bulgaria in which the 'Maritsa culture' precedes the 'Gumelnitsa culture' proper for southern Bulgaria. This may well be the case, but we shall wish to see these stages based on the ample publication of the rich finds from the relevant excavations in southern Bulgaria before relying too heavily upon them.

Some of the finest of the Sitagroi graphite-painted ware, much of which comes from the lower part of the phase III levels, certainly resembles finds of the Maritsa culture, as defined by Vajsová. But in the upper levels of the phase III deposits are several finds relating to her later 'Gumelnitsa

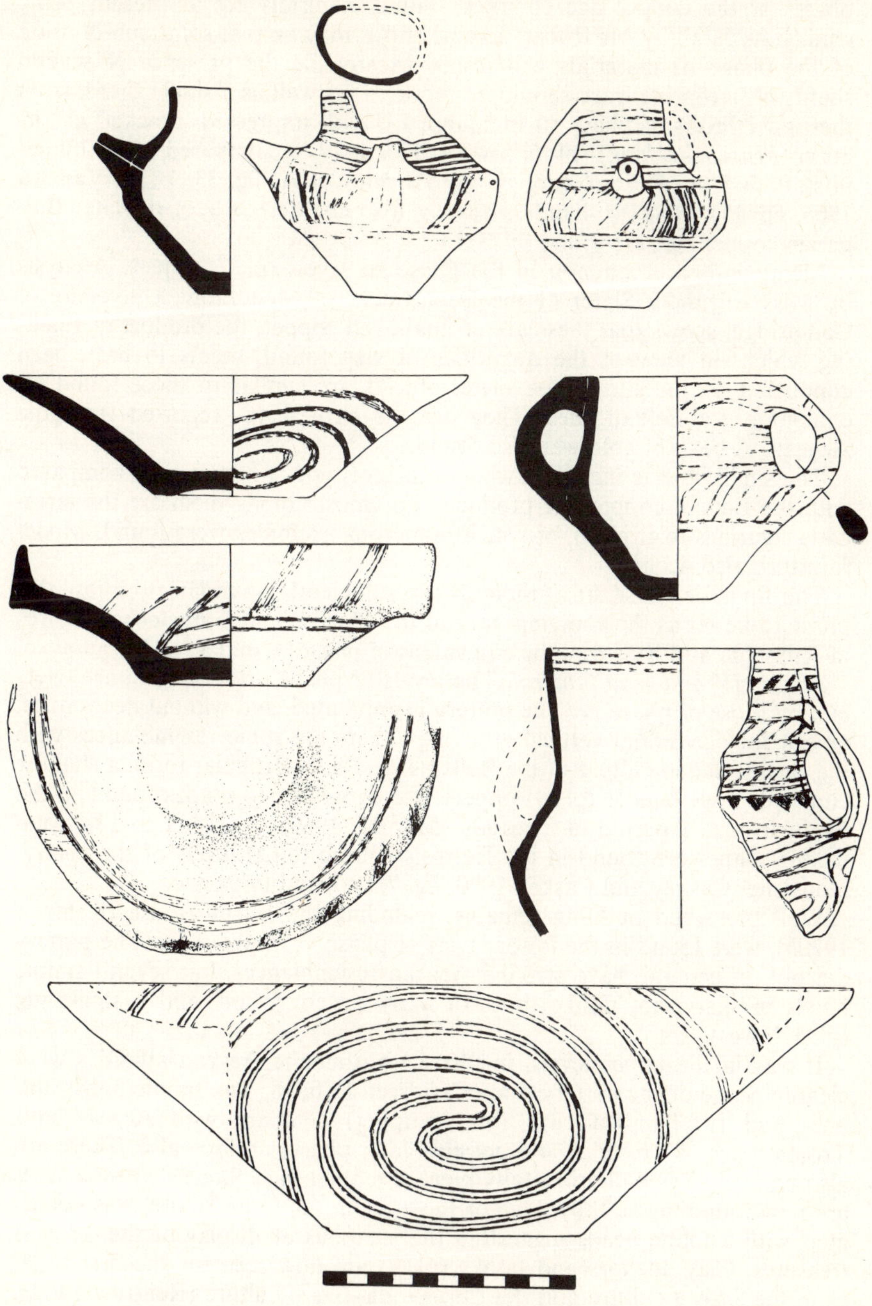

Figure 7. Selected pottery shapes of graphite-painted ware from different levels of phase III at Sitagroi. Many of these relate closely to the Maritsa and Gumelnitsa-Kodjadermen cultures of Bulgaria. (Drawn by Miss Gayle Wever.)

phase' of the copper age complex. These materials are at present being studied in detail by Mr Robert Evans, and it may be that some sub-division of the phase III materials will result. Meanwhile the presence of several sherds of barbotine ware should be reported, as well as a single sherd, from the upper levels of phase III in square ZA, with impressed 'bracket' decoration (*Muscheltechnik*) (pl. 6, lower). This may be compared with Gumelnitsa finds from Ruse (Georgiev and Angelov 1957, fig. 33, 1 ; cf. Vajsová 1966, fig. 17). And two-handled vessels, also characteristic of the later Bulgarian copper age, are found (pl. 3).

Metal finds are common in the phase III levels (pl. 7, upper). Analysis by Miss Elizabeth Slater of the Department of Metallurgy, University of Cambridge, shows that these are of unalloyed copper, the product of smelting which, in view of the quantities of slag found, seems to have been conducted on the site. These metal objects are similar to those found on contemporary Balkan sites. They are the earliest yet reported from the Aegean. A bead of gold was also found.

The small objects include a whole range of types which can be compared with the Balkan copper age products. Foremost among them are the terracotta figurines (e.g. pl. 4), of which numerous examples were found. Model furniture also occurs.

The finds of phase III at Sitagroi are sufficiently abundant to allow this phase to be set as the contemporary of the Maritsa and Gumelnitsa cultures of Rumania and Bulgaria, the equivalent of phases V and VI at Karanovo.

Phases IV and V at Sitagroi. The levels of phase III at Sitagroi are overlain by those of phase IV. The pottery is unpainted, and without decoration, except for occasional vertical grooving. There are some resemblances with the earlier Baden culture of the Balkans, and one particular form, a shallow cup with high handle (pl. 5, upper) is comparable to shapes found in the Early Bronze 1 period of Thessaly (Milojčic 1959, fig. 21, 11 to 13). Analogous shapes are found in the Eutresis culture (EH I) levels of the eponymous site (Caskey and Caskey 1960, fig. 7, IV 8 and IV 9).

Well preserved building remains, including the Burnt House (Renfrew 1970*b*), were found in the lower levels of phase V, in phase Va. The pottery did not, in general, have striking Aegean resemblances, but several simple bowls in shape not unlike those of Troy I were found, and a single jug (pl. 5, lower).

It was in the upper levels, in phase Vb, that the Aegean affinities were clearer. Some of the pottery shapes are seen in fig. 8. The simple bowls and one- and two-handled cups (pl. 6, upper) compare with Aegean and Trojan types of Troy I, II and possibly later phases at Troy also. There are also typically Trojan horizontally pierced tubular lugs. Stone shaft-hole axes are now found, as at Troy. One of these, from the Long House, was decorated with a feline head, suggesting the weapons of display of the Troy II treasures. Clay anchors and hooks (pl. 7) are now seen for the first time, as in the Troy I culture and the Cernavoda–Ezero culture (Renfrew 1969*a*, fig. 5 and pl. III). This material is at present being studied in detail, with special reference to its European parallels, by Mr Andrew Sherratt.

Subject to the results of this detailed study we may suggest the chronological equation of Sitagroi phase V with the Trojan early bronze age, prob-

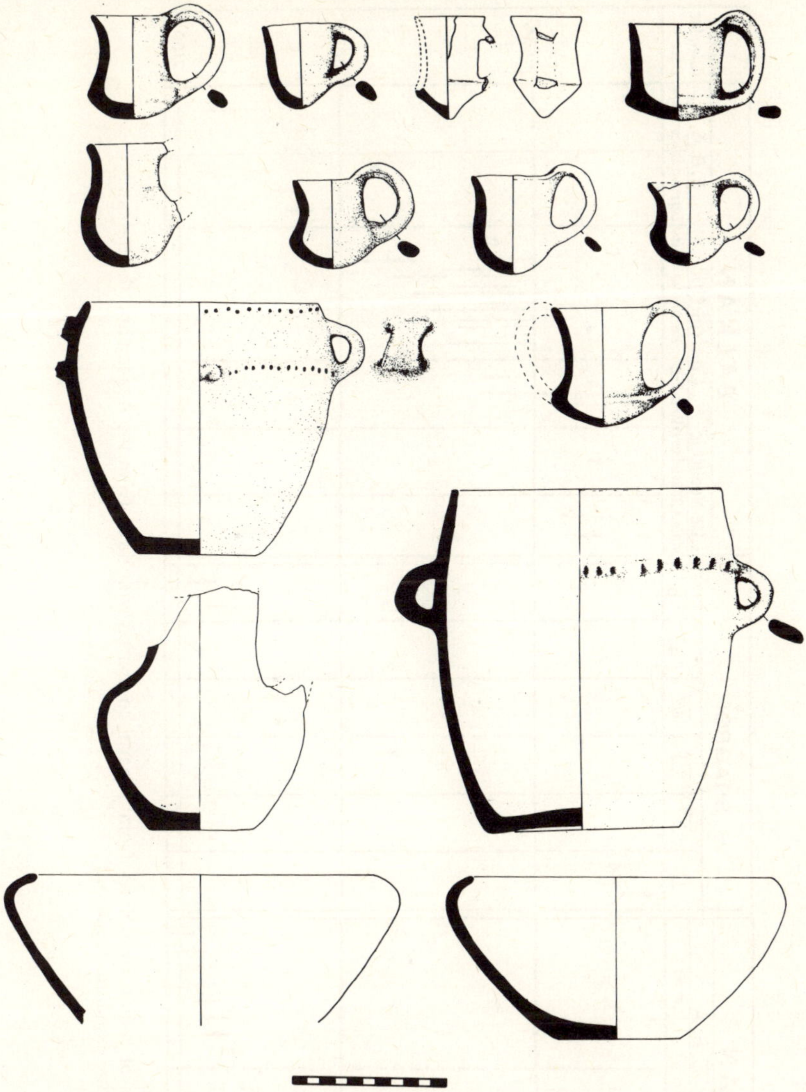

Figure 8. Selected pottery shapes from levels of phase Vb at Sitagroi. Most of the vessels are of dark burnished ware. The material from phase Vb shows similarities with finds from the earlier levels of the Early Bronze Age at Troy. (Drawn by Miss Gayle Wever.)

ably with cities I and II at Troy. There are also resemblances with the Baden culture, apparently with the classical and late phases.

The Radiocarbon Dates from Sitagroi. An initial series of 9 radiocarbon datings has been carried out by the radiocarbon laboratory of the German Academy of Sciences in Berlin, through the kindness of Dr Quitta. They are as follows:

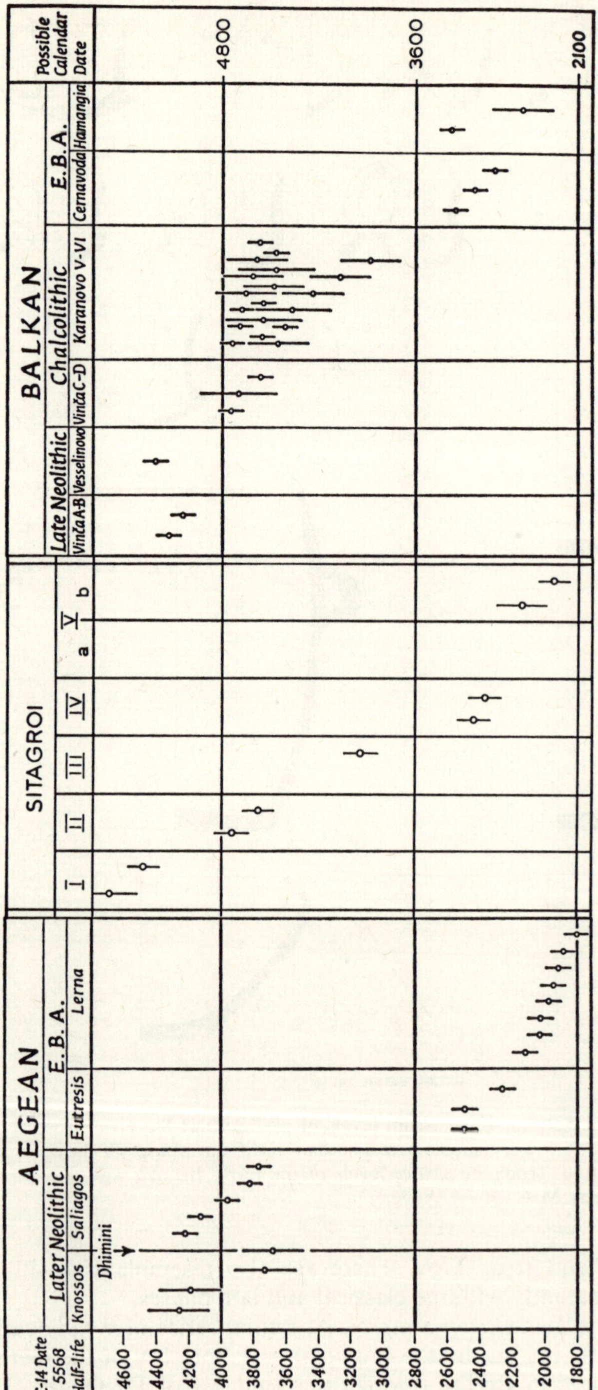

Figure 9. The first series of radiocarbon dates from Sitagroi compared with those from the Aegean and the Balkans (shown with a range of one standard deviation).

Phase v: 1920 BC ± 100 (Bln 780), and 2135 BC ± 150 (Bln 781)
Phase IV: 2360 BC ± 100 (Bln 782), and 2440 BC ± 100 (Bln 773)
Phase III: 3150 BC ± 120 (Bln 774)
Phase II: 3700 BC ± 100 (Bln 776), and 3970 BC ± 120 (Bln 777)
Phase I: 4675 BC ± 170 (Bln 779), and 4475 BC ± 100 (Bln 778)

These dates are calculated on the 5568 half-life. They have been plotted on fig. 9, showing them in comparison with the dates for the Aegean and the Balkans (cf. Renfrew 1969*a*, fig. 6).

The phase I dates coincide, as expected, with those for Vinča. The dates for phases II and III correspond to those of the Balkan chalcolithic, although more dates are needed for phase III. And the dates for phase IV and V correlate well with those for the Aegean early bronze age and that of the Balkans.

Clearly more dates are needed, and further samples have been submitted to Berlin and to the Research Laboratory of the British Museum. Thermoluminescence determinations are also being conducted by Dr D. W. Zimmerman and Miss J. Huxtable at the Research Laboratory for Archaeology at Oxford: it is hoped that these will give an independent check on the validity of the radiocarbon calibration. It is already clear, however, that the radiocarbon dates from Sitagroi support the observations and synchronisms based upon the stratigraphy.

The Sitagroi data thus constitute an important test case, coming from a region where the two chronologies are in conflict. They cast doubt on the validity of the conventional chronology, and hence tend to support the adoption of the new calibrated chronology.

Some Implications

The comparison of the conventional and calibrated chronologies has suggested that they come into basic conflict at three points: in the west Mediterranean, in Wessex, and in south-east Europe. In the first two of these there are arguments to favour both chronological systems, although the present writer finds more persuasive those favouring the calibrated radiocarbon chronology. In the third area, the Bulgarian finds, and now especially those at Sitagroi, favour the calibrated chronology rather than the conventional one.

It is clear, then, that there is a good case for exploring further the implications of the new chronology and for disregarding the old in doing so, while admitting that there remain arguments in favour of each.

Undoubtedly a whole series of studies will now be necessary for each area of Europe, in order to assess the significance of the new relationships which the calibrated chronology will dictate. For example, we see now the earliest passage graves in Europe around 4000 BC in France. Those of Denmark and Britain begin around 3000 BC, and it may be that those of Iberia commence also about this date. All of these are comfortably earlier than any built graves in the Aegean. It cannot now be doubted that the passage grave tradition is an independent European phenomenon. And a major problem now awaits investigation: do we now see the passage graves of Iberia, France, Britain and Scandinavia as entirely separate and independent developments, or are all to some extent, and however indirectly, inspired by Breton prototypes?

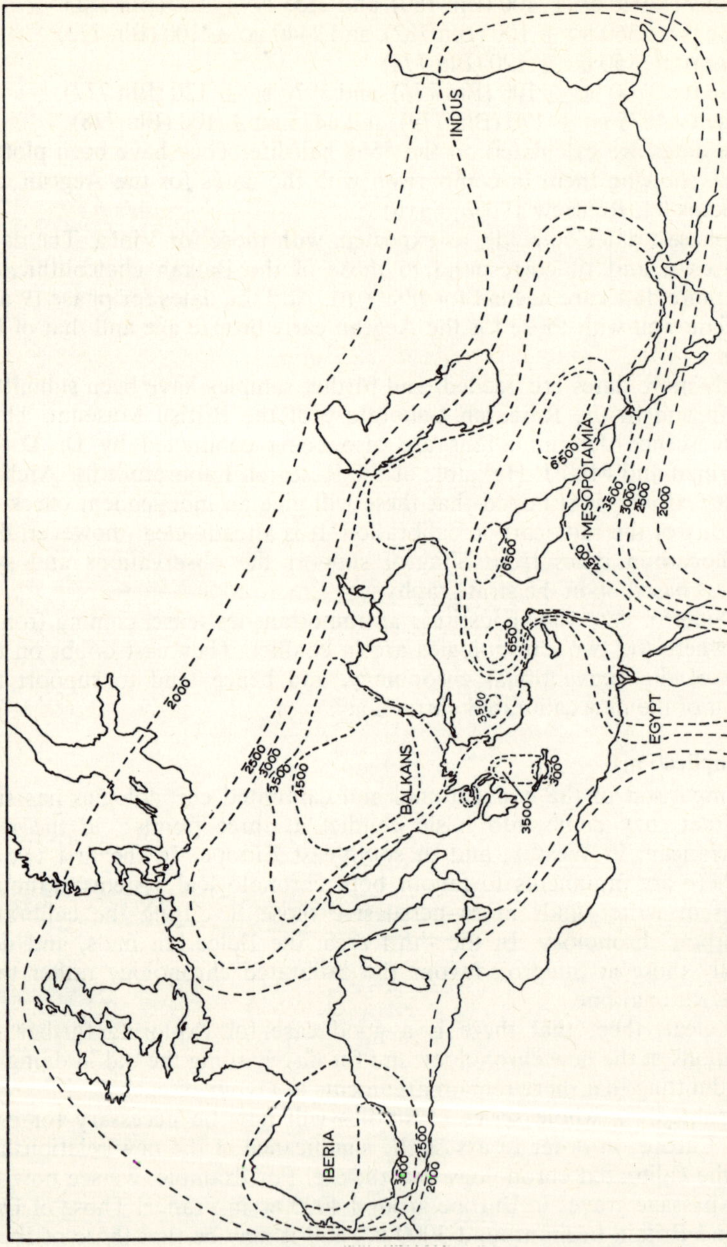

Figure 10. Preliminary isochronic map for the origin and development of copper and bronze metallurgy in Europe and the Near East. The isochrons, in calendar years BC, enclose areas where metallurgy was practised by the date in question. Note the three potentially independent regions of early metallurgy.

The astonishing originality of Malta is likewise brought out by these dates. The temples and rock-cut tombs there precede any known elsewhere in the world (cf. Renfrew 1970*a*). A whole series of new explanations is needed here.

Moreover the development of Old World metallurgy can now be seen in a new light. Obviously it has now to be considered without prior conceptions as to where it *should* have originated, and without a diffusionist framework model. In fig. 10 I try to outline the new configuration. The concept of the isochron, borrowed from Gordon Childe, is a particularly convenient one. The isochrons show the extent to which copper or bronze metallurgy (including the smelting of copper from its ores) was practised, in so far as present knowledge indicates, by the time in question.

Already by about 6000 BC in radiocarbon years copper objects are found at three sites in the Near East. The calibration does not yet go back so early, but at a guess these sites may well be dated before 6500 BC in calendar years. The first of these is Catal Hüyük, where the copper was already smelted (Neuninger, Pittioni and Siegl 1964). It is possible that the Ali Kosh bead was made from hammered native copper (Smith 1969, 427), in which case we cannot really speak of metallurgy in this sense, and the Çayönü and Suberde copper finds are not yet analysed. This first metallurgy isochron is thus based on the assumption that, as at Çatal Hüyük, the exploitation of native copper was soon followed by the discovery of smelting.

By the time of the second isochron at 4500 BC, metallurgy was established in at least two metallurgical provinces. The first includes the distribution of the Halaf culture, which was ending at about this time. Copper artefacts have been found at many sites throughout the Halaf cultural province, including Arpachiyah and Mersin. We may also assume that the knowledge of smelting was not lost in central Anatolia. In addition there are smelting crucibles from Tal-i-Iblis in Iran, radiocarbon dated to 4080 and 4090 BC (P 926A and P 929), so that metallurgy was practised there before 4500 BC in calendar years. And copper metallurgy was probably practised by this date in the Ghassulian culture of Palestine.

There is no evidence for metallurgy yet in the Aegean or north-west Anatolia, but what certainly appears to be a second and separate metallurgical province is seen in the Balkans. Here, well before 4500 BC, metallurgy is well underway, with casting and the production of the world's first shaft-hole tools of metal.

By 3500 BC the Near Eastern metallurgical province includes Egypt, where metal was smelted from the Gerzean period, although copper was cold worked already in the Badarian before 4500 BC. The Balkan province now includes the north Aegean, with sites such as Sitagroi and Dikilitash. There are finds of copper also by about this date in the Aegean, from Sesklo, Kephala in Kea and Knossos, and the smelting of metal was certainly understood in several places. But it cannot yet be said that metallurgy was widespread in the Aegean.

The isochron for 3000 BC now links the Balkans and the Near East, since there is now metallurgy at Troy and other sites in north-west Anatolia (although it may yet transpire that Troy I was not founded until sometime after this date). On the other hand metallurgy was not widespread elsewhere in the Aegean, being absent in the Eutresis culture (EHI) so far as present indications go, and rare in the Grotta-Pelos culture of the Cyclades and in Early Minoan I.

On the other hand it seems reasonably sure that metallurgy was by now underway in Iberia. Indeed I suspect that metallurgy had been invented in Almeria by 3500 BC. Siret (1913, 38) reported evidence of copper working from Almizaraque and indeed copper artefacts are found at several sites of the Los Millares culture, and in Portugal.

By 2500 BC metallurgy was well underway in Italy, where it may already have been practised by 3000 BC. Malta and France were not, however, so well advanced, nor probably was Britain. On the other hand metallurgy was widespread throughout central Europe. By this time metal was probably worked also in the Indus valley.

By 2000 BC metallurgy was practised in virtually the whole of Europe.

This sketch of European metallurgical origins is undoubtedly inaccurate in many places, since radiocarbon dates are frequently not available, and many finds pertaining to early metallurgy have yet to be made. In a year or two it will be superseded, one hopes, by a more amply documented outline. But already it suggests how the emerging pattern of radiocarbon dates can be used to build up a picture very different from that of a diffusion process creating 'ever widening circles' (Childe 1936, 170) round the single innovating area in the Near East. The radiocarbon dates certainly support the notion of several independent inventions of the different processes which constitute copper metallurgy.

Similar observations can certainly be made for other techniques and customs. Indeed the 'warrior aristocracy' seen in some areas of Europe in the early bronze age need show no influence from the Aegean or Mycenaean world. Again and again similar culture processes at work produce analagous or 'parallel' developments in different regions, without any significant contacts or 'diffusion' between them. We can now begin to see how the invention of metallurgy, and the adoption of the dagger, which took place in many areas of Europe around 2500 BC, favoured the creation of 'wealth', since for the first time there were precious objects of copper and gold, and of warfare. Naturally the archaeological record reflects this wealth, with new finds of gold, with dagger graves, and with exotic goods. It is this constellation of functionally related traits which has been wrongly signalled as a sign of 'irradiation' from the Aegean. Supposed morphological similarities among the artefacts are not always a good guide to inter-cultural contact, still less to chronology. The moral—and the opportunity—which the calibration offers is that we should and can now use artefacts not for chronological purposes, but rather as the starting point for studies of culture process, of how a culture develops and changes within a region through the operation of local factors.

Conclusion

The conclusion which may be drawn from the foregoing evaluation is that the calibration of radiocarbon by dendrochronology does make coherent archaeological sense, and that the new dates form a new but perfectly intelligible pattern. Of course this calibration is dependent upon the work of physicists and botanists, and if they were to change their minds once again the archaeologists would no doubt have to follow. But at the moment there seems to be a consensus among them, as emerged from the Uppsala conference (Neustupny 1970), that the new calibration is basically and in outline correct.

Equally it is clear that even if the outline seems to be acceptable, and probably reliable, the details are not yet certain, and the various kinks in the calibration curve (fig. 1) have yet to be supported by more dates. This means that we cannot yet finally and reliably calibrate our radiocarbon dates, which are best expressed still in radiocarbon years, on the 5,568 half-life, and followed, if we wish, by a suggestion as to what the approximate date in calendar years may be. Nothing will be more vexatious than to have quoted dates that are supposed to be 'calibrated', without our knowing by whom or how. One day, perhaps in a decade or more, a definite calibration will be accepted by international convention. Until then the basic data will be the C-14 dates, quoted on the 5,568 half-life and accompanied by their laboratory number.

But what we can do, and must do now, is to work out in outline how the calibration will affect our chronologies, not just in terms of years but in terms of relationships between different regions. We can establish, for instance, that the megaliths of western Europe were built, nearly all of them, before the pyramids of Egypt; that the Vinča culture and the first European metallurgy flourished some two millennia before the First City of Troy; and that Stonehenge was complete, and the Wessex culture well underway, if not ended, before the first Shaft Grave burials at Mycenae, and the beginnings of Mycenaean civilisation.

The chronological table given here (fig. 2) is therefore to be regarded as experimental, as a hypothesis, a basis for discussion. Doubtless it is wrong in places, it may be several centuries in error at various times. And ultimately it depends on the tree-ring calibration, which like all other products of the sciences, is corrigible and open to further interpretation in the light of further discovery. What can now be asserted, however, is that the new configuration of dates does make archaeological sense, and that the new dates need not introduce confusion into the prehistoric sequence, but rather serve to remove it.

Finally it should be admitted that the uncertainties remaining, which at present amount to at least a century or two in either direction, leave plenty of room for manoeuvre. No doubt our chronologies will for years to come, still, to some extent, show what we want them to, in the same way as Kossinna's.

Let us conclude then, as Sir Isaac Newton did (1728), in philosophical vein, that our chronologies are themselves artefacts, reflecting something of the beliefs and prejudices of their makers: 'We need not wonder, that the *Egyptians* have made their Kings in the first dynasty of their Monarchy, that which was seated at *Thebes* . . . to be very ancient and so long lived; since the *Persians* have done the like to their Kings . . . ; and the Syrians of *Damascus* have done the like to their Kings . . ., *worshipping them as Gods, and boasting their antiquity, and not knowing,* saith Josephus, *that they were but modern.*

'And whilst all these nations have magnified their *Antiquities* so exceedingly, we need not wonder that the *Greeks* and *Latines* have made their first kings a little older than the truth.' [1970]

ACKNOWLEDGEMENTS

At various stages in the preparation of this article I have greatly benefited from the advice or comments of Mr Arthur ApSimon, Mr Humphrey Case, Mr Andrew Fleming and Dr H. E. Suess. The pottery drawings are the work of Miss Gayle Wever, and the diagrams of Mr H. Walkland. The photographs were taken and processed by Mr P. R. Morley. I am very grateful to all these colleagues for their collaboration and advice.

REFERENCES

Bagger, J. A., Vogel, J. C. and Wislanski, T. (1969) TRB and other C-14 dates from Poland. *Helinium* 9, 3.

Bucha, V. (1967) Intensity of the Earth's magnetic field during archaeological times in Czechoslovakia. *Archaeom.* 10, 12–22.

Burkitt, M. and Childe, V. G. (1932) A chronological table of Prehistory. *Antiq.* 6, 185.

Caskey, J. L. and Caskey, E. G. (1960) The earliest settlements at Eutresis. *Hesperia* 29, 126.

Childe, V. G. (1932) Chronology of prehistoric Europe: a review. *Antiq.* 6, 206.

——(1936) *Man Makes Himself.*

——(1939) The Orient and Europe. *Amer. J. Archaeol.* 43, 10.

——(1956) *Piecing Together the Past.*

——(1958) Retrospect. *Antiq.* 32, 69.

Clark, J. G. D. (1965) Radiocarbon dating and the expansion of farming culture from the Near East over Europe. *PPS* 31, 58.

Ferguson, C. W. (1968) Bristlecone pine: science and esthetics. *Science* 159, 839–46.

Ferguson, C. W., Huber, B. and Suess, H. E. (1966) Determination of the age of Swiss lake-dwellings as an example of dendrochronologically çalibrated radiocarbon dating. *Z. Naturf.* 21 A, 1173–7.

French, D. H. (1964) Prehistoric pottery from Macedonia and Thrace. *Prähist. Z.* 42, 30.

Georgiev, G. I. and Angelov, N. (1957) Ausgrabungen an dem Siedlungshügel bei Ruse. *Izv. Archeol. Inst.* 21, 41.

Gimbutas, M. (1965) *Bronze Age Cultures of Central and Eastern Europe.*

Hayes, W. C., Rowton, M. B. and Stubbings, F. H. (1962) Chronology. *Cambridge Ancient History* I, Ch. VI.

Kossinna, G. (1905) *Die deutsche Vorgeschichte, eine hervorragend nationale Wissenschaft.*

Mellaart, J. (1960) Anatolia and the Balkans. *Antiq.* 34, 270.

Milojčic, V. (1949) *Chronologie der jüngeren Steinzeit Mittel- und Südosteuropas.*

——(1959) Ergebnisse der deutschen Ausgrabungen in Thessalien, 1953–8. *Jb. röm. german. Zentralmus. Mainz* 6, 1.

——(1967) Die absolute Chronologie der Jungsteinzeit in Südosteuropa und die Ergebnisse der Radiocarbon- (C14-) Methode. *Jb. röm.-german. Zentralmus. Mainz* 14, 9.

Montelius, O. (1903) *Die älteren Kulturperioden im Orient und in Europa,* I. *Die Methode.*

Neuninger, H., Pittioni, R. and Siegl, W. (1964) Frükeramikzeitliche Kupfergewinnung in Anatolien. *Archaeol. Austr.* 35, 98.

Neustupny, E. (1968) Absolute chronology of the neolithic and aeneolithic periods of central and south-eastern Europe. *Slov. Archaeol.* 16, 19–56.

——(1969) Absolute chronology of the neolithic and aeneolithic periods of central and south-eastern Europe II. *Arch. Rozh.* 21, 783.

——(1970) A new epoch in radiocarbon dating. *Antiq.* 44, 38.

Newton, Sir Isaac, 1728. *The Chronology of Antient Kingdoms Amended.* Dublin.

Newton, R. G. and Renfrew, C. (1970) British faience beads reconsidered. *Antiq.* 44, 199.

Petrie, W. M. F. (1899) Sequences in prehistoric remains. *J. Anthrop. Inst.* 29, 295.

Piggott, S. (1938) The early bronze age in Wessex. *PPS* 4, 52.

——(1966) Mycenae and barbarian Europe. *Sborn. Nar. Muz. v Praza* 20, 117.

Renfrew, C. (1965) *The Neolithic and Early Bronze Age Cultures of the Cyclades and their External Relations,* unpublished doctoral dissertation, University of Cambridge.

——(1967) Colonialism and Megalithismus. *Antiq.* 41, 276.

——(1968) Wessex without Mycenae. *Annu. Brit. School Archaeol. at Athens* 63, 277.

——(1969*a*) The autonomy of the south-east European copper age. *PPS* 25, 12.

——(1969*b*) Trade and culture process in European prehistory. *Curr. Anthrop.* 10, 151.

——(1970*a*) New configurations in Old World archaeology. *World Archaeol.* 2, 199.

——(1970*b*) The Burnt House at Sitagroi. *Antiq.* 44, 131.

Sandars, N. K. (1957) *Bronze Age Cultures in France.*

Siret, L. (1913) *Questions de chronologie et d'ethnographie ibériques.*

Smith, C. S. (1969) Analysis of the copper bead from Ali Kosh, in Hole, F., Flannery, K. V. and Neely, J. A. *Prehistory and Human Ecology of the Deh Luran Plain.*

Smith, H. S. (1964) Egypt and C-14 dating. *Antiq.* 38, 32.

Suess, H. E. (1967) Bristlecone pine calibration of the radiocarbon time scale from 4100 BC to 1500 BC, in *Radioactive Dating and Methods of Low Level Counting.* Vienna: International Atomic Energy Agency.

Trump, D. H. (1966) *Skorba.*

Vajsová, H. (1966) Stand der Jungsteinzeitforschung in Bulgarien. *Slov. Archaeol.* 14, 5.

Willis, E. H., Tauber, H. and Münnich, K. O. (1960) Variations in the atmospheric radiocarbon concentration over the past 1300 years. *Radiocarbon* 2, 1.

Worsaae, J. J. A. (1878) *Die Vorgeschichte des Nordens nach gleichzeitigen Denkmälern.*

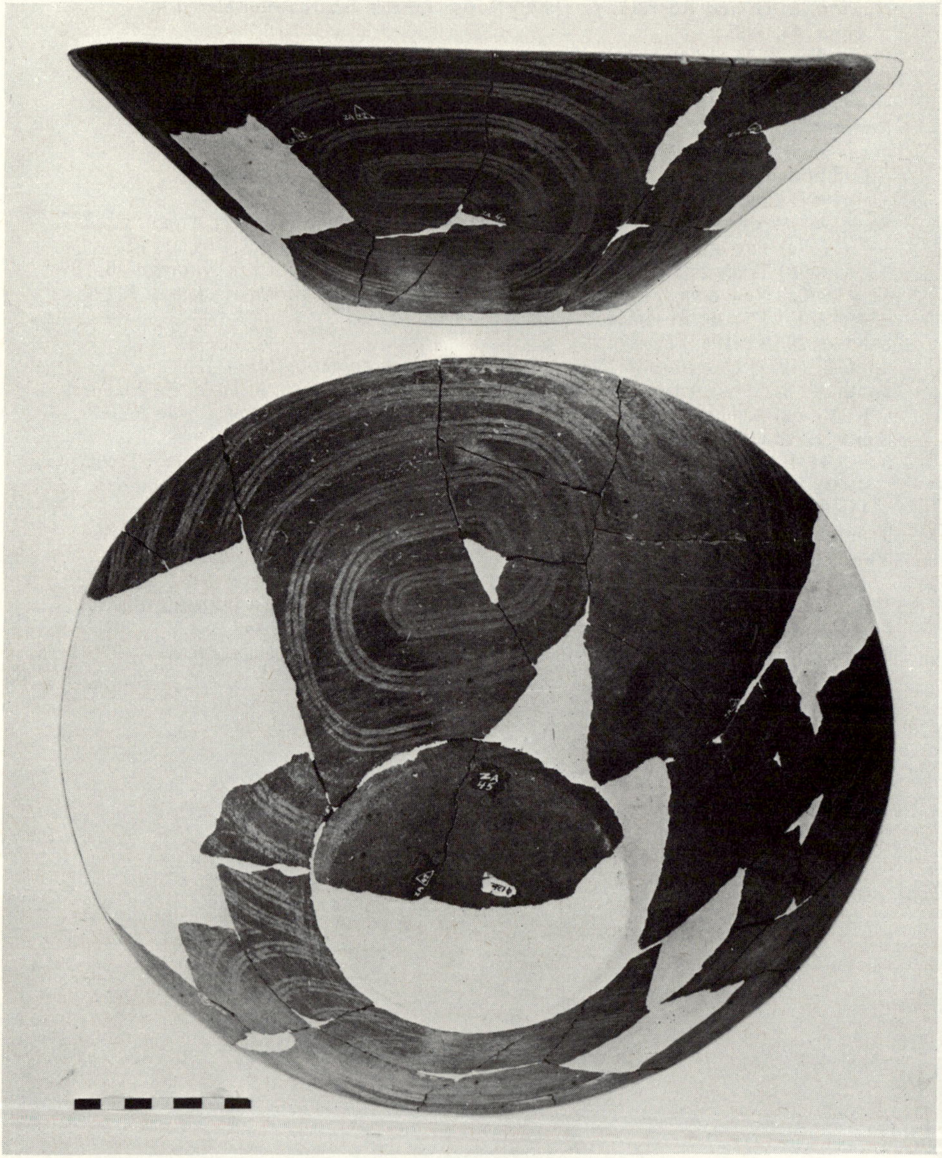

Plate 1. Ceramic bowl, decorated in graphite paint, from levels of phase III at Sitagroi. Scale in centimetres.

Plate 2. Ceramic vessels, decorated in graphite paint, from levels of phase III at Sitagroi. Scale in centimetres.

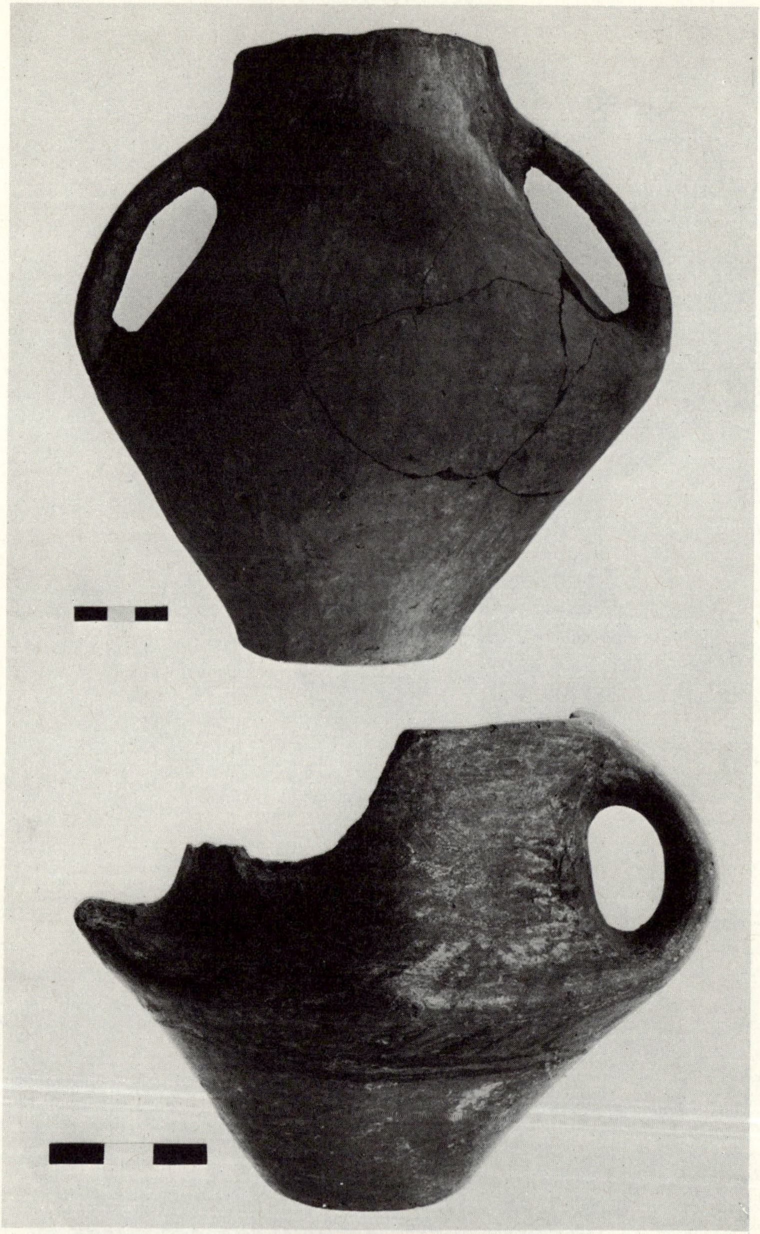

Plate 3. *Upper*: Two-handled pot of fine brown fabric from the upper levels of phase III at Sitagroi, resembling finds from the later Gumelnitsa and Salcutsa cultures of Bulgaria and Rumania.
Lower: Graphite-decorated pot from the upper levels of phase III at Sitagroi. It resembles those of the later Gumelnitsa culture.
Scales in centimetres.

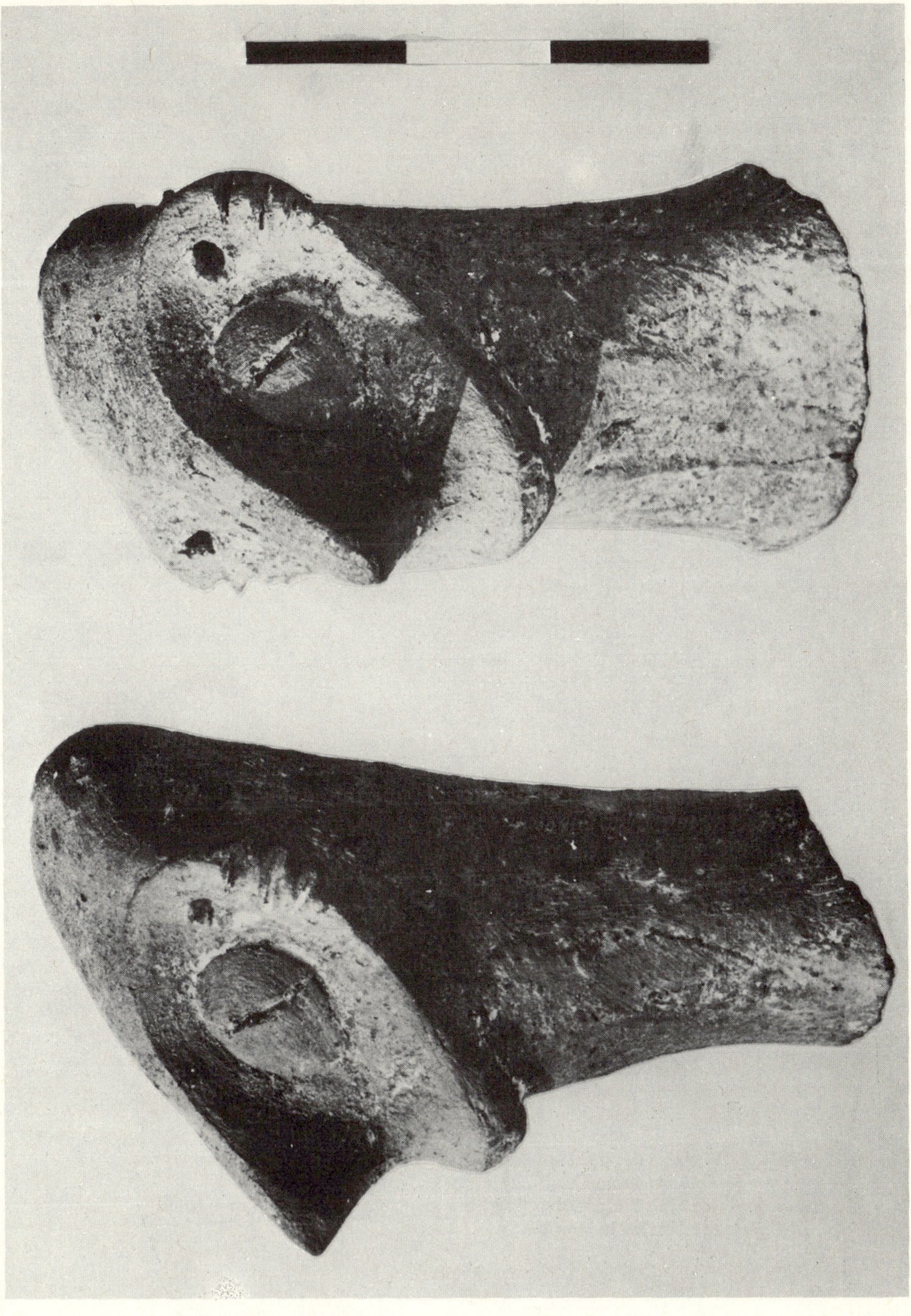

Plate 4. Terracotta head, one of many figurines from phase III at Sitagroi. Scale in centimetres.

Plate 5. Upper: One-handled dish, a typical form of phase IV at Sitagroi.
Lower left: Bowl from the Burnt House of phase Va at Sitagroi.
Lower right: Jug from phase Va at Sitagroi, the earliest instance found of this shape. Scales in centimetres.

Plate 6. *Upper*: One-handled cup from phase vb at Sitagroi. Similar finds are seen in Troy I and II, and in the Baden culture. × 1 approx.
Lower: Sherd with impressed decoration from the upper levels of phase III at Sitagroi, closely resembling finds from the later Gumelnitsa culture of Bulgaria and Romania. × 2 approx.

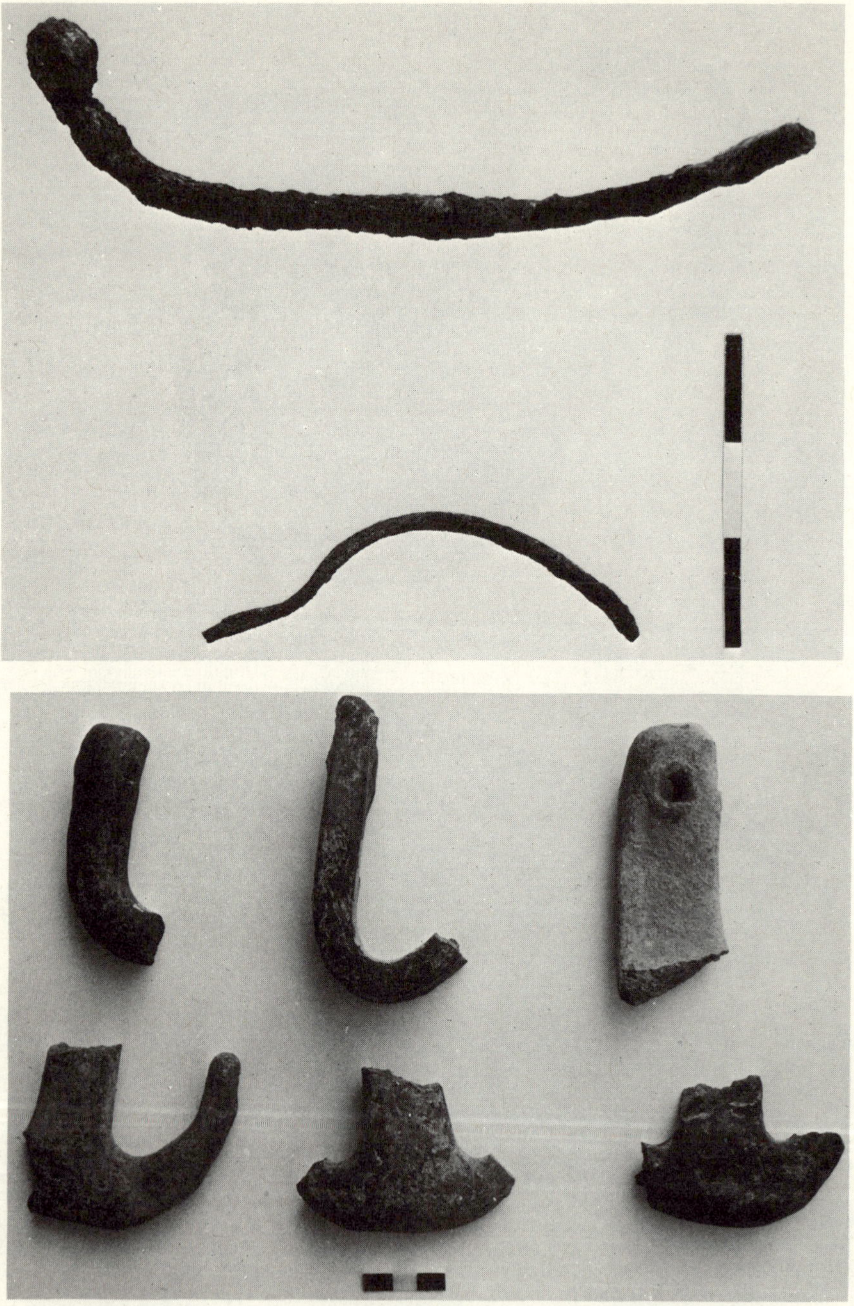

Plate 7. *Upper*: Typical copper finds from levels of phase III at Sitagroi. *Lower*: Clay anchors and hooks from phase Vb at Sitagroi. This form makes its appearance elsewhere in the Aegean in the Troy I culture. Scales in centimetres.

18) Varna and the Social Context of Early Metallurgy

This comment on the significance of the remarkable discoveries at Varna was written some years after the other papers in this volume. It reinforces them in the striking way which only the finding of entirely new material can do: an independent 'test' of the hypotheses advanced in them, which a decade ago were regarded in some quarters with scepticism.

If the Varna cemetery had been unearthed fifteen years ago, it would undoubtedly have been hailed as a striking instance of Aegean, or Anatolian, or even Sumerian influence upon the Balkans. Since goldwork comparable in size and accomplishment is not seen in those lands until the Early Dynastic III period, the time of the Royal Graves at Ur (Woolley 1934), and of the treasures of Troy II and Alaca, which cannot much antedate 2500 BC, such a date (or a later one) would inevitably have been assigned to the Varna finds. Indeed it would rather surprise me if those few stalwart scholars who still uphold the traditional view, such as Makkay, were to argue differently today. But of course many elements of the position set out in chapters 5, 8 and 17 were long ago argued by the Bulgarian scholar G. I. Georgiev, following his work at Karanovo. The case for the autonomous origin of metallurgy in the Balkans has been accepted by him and his colleagues, and indeed set out with clarity, using fresh supporting evidence by others such as Cernykh.

The extraordinary metallurgical originality of the Varna finds is at once obvious. The great third-millennium 'treasure horizon' (embracing Ur, Tepe Hissar, Alaca Hüyük, Horoztepe, Troy, Poliochni and even Levkas) is anticipated here by nearly two millennia. Only in the remarkable 'Treasure of the Cave' at Nahal Mishmar, in the Ghassulian culture of Palestine (Bar-Adon 1963; 1971) is there so striking an assemblage of metal at such an early period, although Nahal Mishmar is rich in copper and copper-arsenic rather than in gold. Both must comfortably antedate the earliest metal treasure yet found in Mesopotamia, Tomb 109 at Tepe Gawra (Maxwell-Hyslop 1971, 1), although I predict that comparable finds will yet be made in Mesopotamia at the same early date in the later 'Ubaid and early Uruk phases.

Less instantly obvious, perhaps, is the remarkable precocity of this emergence of a ranked society. Evidence of salient ranking has not been found at this early time in Mesopotamia (although the example of large predynastic religious structures such as the White Temple at Warka and the Eye Temple at Tell Brak may well imply that such evidence is yet to be discovered). Nor do the Egyptian predynastic graves of the period reflect such an impressive concentration of prestige goods, even accepting that these would not, in the Egypt of the time, necessarily be of metal.

Already, of course, from the earliest neolithic at Jericho there is a preoccupation with modelling of the head, brought to mind by the clay facial effigies in the Varna cemetery (plate 3b), their features emphasised by the addition of golden jewellery. And the great quantities of *Dentalium* shell perhaps echo for us the emphasis upon shell beads in the Natufian culture of Palestine, and indeed in some burials of the Upper Palaeolithic period. The inclusion of shaft-hole axes in the burials as weapons of display similarly recalls the finely worked obsidian daggers accompanying the interments at Çatal Hüyük.

None of these discoveries in earlier contexts, however, prepares us for the splendid 'sceptres' of Varna (plate 2a), held in the right hand, the stem sheathed in gold and surmounted by a finely worked shaft-hole axe of stone. Moreover the gold discs so widely distributed about some of the richer graves (plates 1b, 4a) clearly embellished a cloak or other fine item of apparel, a magnificent substitution for the bone or shell plaques with which such costumes may have been decorated at other times and places. The splendid gold pectoral plate and heavy gold armlets (plates 2b, 3a) find no equal in the early Old World.

Detailed analysis must inevitably await the full publication by Ivanov of the contents of each grave in the cemetery. Meanwhile the Varna graves offer for us what may be the earliest preserved evidence from any site in the world (using clear indication of 'personal' possessions, inferred from well-documented association with single burials) of a prominently ranked society. The chronological priority, however, is likely to be reversed at any time by Near Eastern finds. The broader significance of these finds lies rather in the recognition, argued in chapter 5 for the Balkans, in chapter 11 for Iberia and chapter 12 for south Britain, that formative processes were at work in these societies, processes which must be studied in their own terms, without preconceptions derived from other culture areas.

Finds like those of Varna not only confirm such an outlook, but offer the opportunity of studying the social structure of an early ranked society in much fuller detail than hitherto. To propose the inclusion of that society within the broad 'chiefdom' category, as suggested in the paper which follows, may be a legitimate first step towards a definition of its nature. But categorisation of such a kind is only a very preliminary form of analysis. It is the task of archaeology to make more subtle and illuminating statements about social structure, on the basis of the material evidence.

BIBLIOGRAPHY

Bar-Adon, P. (1963)The cave of the treasure. *Archaeology* 16, 251–9.

Bar-Adon, P. (1971) *The Cave of the Treasure. The Finds from the Caves in Nahal Mishmar.* Jerusalem.

Maxwell-Hyslop, K. R. (1971) *Western Asiatic Jewellery c. 3000–612 B.C.* London, Methuen.

Woolley, C. L. (1934) *Ur Excavations: The Royal Cemetery II.* London, British Museum.

VARNA AND THE SOCIAL CONTEXT OF EARLY METALLURGY

The discovery of what is demonstrably, on the basis of present knowledge, the earliest major assemblage of gold artifacts to be unearthed anywhere in the world is an event of some note, comparable in significance with Schliemann's find of the Great Treasure at Troy more than a century ago. The finds at Varna must be at least 1,500 years older than those of Troy II, yet apart from the original announcement by their excavator (Ivanov, 1975), and useful, although brief, descriptions by Gimbutas (1977*a* and *b*), the Varna cemetery has so far excited little archaeological comment. The publication by Ivanov (1978) of the first well-illustrated account of the cemetery allows an assessment of its importance. Its status as the oldest substantial find of gold emphasizes the position of south-east Europe as an early and independent centre of metallurgical innovation. But the gold is only one of several materials indicative of high status in the cemetery: what had hitherto seemed a moderately egalitarian society now displays clear evidence of salient ranking. This in turn has major implications for our understanding of the social context in which early metalworking in Europe developed and prospered.

The copper-age cemetery near the Lake of Varna, close to the Black Sea coast in north-east Bulgaria, was discovered accidentally in 1972. Since then excavations directed by Mr Ivan S. Ivanov of the Varna Museum, under the general oversight of Professor G. I. Georgiev and Dr M. Lazarov, have revealed a series of inhumations with remarkable grave-goods. In addition to pottery characteristic of the copper age Gumelnitsa culture, together with flints and stone tools, there are numerous copper tools, and a considerable quantity of goldwork: discs, pendants, beads, large armlets, pectoral plates, and mountings for the handles of weapons of display. A small selection of these objects was seen in the recent exhibition 'Thracian Treasures from Bulgaria' at the British Museum, but it is the great quantity of gold from the cemetery—Grave 43 alone contains 1·5 kilograms of bracelets, beads and other objects—and the early date which are of crucial interest.

At the time of writing some 130 graves have been excavated, and the cemetery is believed to contain many more. In several of the graves the deceased was buried in a contracted position, in others fully extended, a convention restricted in Bulgaria during the chalcolithic period to the north-east of the country. In 35 cases no skeleton was found in the grave: these are designated 'cenotaphs' or 'symbolic graves' by the excavator. That the absence of human remains from them is not simply a product of differential preservation is indicated by a clay mask which in three cases occupies the position in the grave where the head would have been. The 'mask' is embellished in each case with golden jewellery (plate 3b): earrings and diadems. In just a few of these symbolic graves, small quantities of disarticulated human bone were found, and it may be that excarnation prior to burial was practised, applied perhaps to some but not all members of the society. Certainly the extreme rarity of cemeteries in the Bulgarian copper age—none has been found associated with the great tells of the Maritsa valley—suggests that direct inhumation was by no means a standard practice for the disposal of the dead. Seen from this point of view the Varna symbolic graves need not present acute problems of interpretation.

Further description of the finds can be found in Ivanov's book (1978), although their full significance will emerge only with complete publication and the itemization of the contents of each grave in turn, allowing of quantitative cemetery analysis. Here it may be sufficient to draw attention to three important points.

Early Goldworking

The cultural context of the finds is clearly fixed by the graphite-painted pottery and other artifacts, placing it in the later chalcolithic of Bulgaria, equivalent to the Karanovo VI phase of Georgiev's fundamental sequence for the Maritsa valley (Georgiev, 1961). Radiocarbon dates for this period in south-east Europe (summarized in Renfrew, 1971) centre on the centuries between 3800 bc and 3400 bc in radiocarbon years, equivalent in calendar years to approximately 4600 to 4200 BC, using Clark's calibration curve (1975). The hoard of golden pendants from the settlement site at Chotnitsa (Angelov, 1959) are of comparable date. So (despite the arguments of Makkay, 1976, cf. Dumitrescu, 1961) are the other small gold pendants found sporadically in copper-age contexts in south-eastern and Carpathian Europe, including probably the pendant from a late neolithic context at Sesklo in Thessaly (Tsountas, 1908, 350).

That the gold at Varna is of Balkan origin need not be doubted when one recalls the wealth of later prehistoric gold finds from the same general area: the golden sword and daggers from Piersinari and the Ostrovul Mare treasure (Popescu, 1955), both in Romania, the golden dagger of the Vučedol culture from Mala Gruda in Jugoslavia (Parovic-Pešikan and Trbuhovic, 1971), and the great treasure of Vulchitran in Bulgaria (Mikov, 1958). Contrary to the opinion of Makkay (1976, 271) there is nothing in these finds which need indicate Aegean influence: indeed gold weapon blades are not known from the Aegean bronze age. The Balkan bronze age, like the copper age which preceded it, was very familiar with the use of gold. It should, however, be stressed that at Varna the gold was worked by hammering and there is no clear evidence there for the casting of gold.

This precocious use of the material may be contrasted with the situation in the Near East, where, in the words of Muhly (1977, 76):

> There is very little gold before 3000 BC, just as there is little or no tin bronze. After 3000 BC both gold and tin bronze appear together at a number of sites over a wide geographical area, from the Aegean to southern Mesopotamia.

Dr Joan Oates kindly points out to me that the earliest gold so far found in the Near East is a fragment of gold wire, dated by Woolley (1931, 344) to 'Ubaid levels at Ur, and that the earliest gold found in quantity in the area comes from levels X-IX, of the Uruk period, at Tepe Gawra (Tobler, 1950). It should be stressed here that the calibrated radiocarbon chronology for later prehistoric Mesopotamia is only now being established (Oates, 1972), and that many contexts will become earlier than the traditional chronology would suggest. The 'Ubaid context at Ur may yet go back as far as 5000 BC, which would be at least as early as the Varna finds, but the Uruk material at Tepe Gawra will not be so old. Gold in Egypt is not found till the Nakada II (Gerzean) period (Baumgartel, 1960, 3), which is likely to be later. So that, although comparably rich finds of gold as early as those of Varna may well yet be made in the Near East, where gold working began extremely early, it is at present the case that nothing so impressive, so sophisticated or so abundant as the gold of Varna has yet been found elsewhere at this early date.

Early Metallurgy in South-East Europe

The autonomy of Balkan copper metallurgy was argued some years ago (Renfrew, 1969) on the basis of the unbroken cultural evolution from neolithic to chalcolithic in the area and of radiocarbon datings. It is further supported by the tree-ring calibration of radiocarbon, although the prior development in the Near East of most of the relevant metallurgical techniques must be held clearly in view. The case for autonomy (but not necessarily for priority) is strongly supported by the Varna finds, which can be interpreted only within the context of the Gumelnitsa culture. Many of the gold forms may be related to those already current in other materials: pendants and bracelets may have ornaments of the shell *Spondylus gaederopus* as a prototype. Pendants of *Spondylus* occur already in the neolithic of the area (Karanovo II), and bracelets of large size have been found in important graves of the Karanovo V period near Varna by Mr Ivanov (pers. comm.). The shell in question was undoubtedly traded from the Aegean (Shackleton and Renfrew, 1970), probably up the Black Sea coast: the copper age was evidently a period of developed exchange networks. But at this time, as the finds at Sitagroi confirm, the Balkans not the Aegean had the initiative in metallurgical matters.

The scale and level of sophistication of the Balkan copper industry has been revealed by the excavation of copper mines of the Vinča period at Rudna Glava in Jugoslavia (Iovanovic and Ottaway, 1976) and now by those of Aibunar near Stara Zagora in Bulgaria, excavated by a joint Bulgarian-Russian project directed in the field by Chernykh (1975; 1976). The copper workings at Aibunar are an impressive sight, having the appearance of narrow fissures in the rock two or three metres wide, today cleared to a depth of four or five metres. Excavations have revealed that the ore veins have been dug out to a depth in places in excess of ten metres, and there are numerous finds of pottery of the Karanovo VI period, as well as two shaft-hole tools of copper. Chernykh has rightly argued that many of the copper tools of the Balkan chalcolithic are of copper smelted from ores such as those of Aibunar, although the extensive use of native copper also in the early stages of the development of metal-working in the Balkans should not be too hastily dismissed. Moreover, the existence of other copper mines in the Stara Zagora area has now been recognized (pers. comm., Prof. G. I. Georgiev), and comparable discoveries are perhaps to be expected from other areas, so that the attribution of copper artifacts from a very wide region specifically to Aibunar on the rather uncertain basis of trace-element analysis (cf. Muhly, 1977, 78) must be treated with caution.

The copper mines at Aibunar and Rudna Glava are at the moment the earliest known in the world. This in no way implies that comparable and perhaps earlier mines will not be found in due course in the Near East. But it does emphasize for us, as does the Varna material, that metallurgy developed rapidly in the Balkans into a considerable industry already in the fifth millennium BC.

The Social Context

The main importance of the Varna cemetery, I think, will prove to be as much social as metallurgical. Hitherto the prosperous Balkan copper age, as exemplified by the Gumelnitsa culture, has not given clear evidence of social differentiation. Certainly the stability of settlement, as reflected by the distribution of tell mounds, the variety of the artifacts, the range of figurines, the presence of signs interpreted by some as 'Proto-writing', and the development of craft specialization (Evans, 1973), give abundant evidence of a thriving society. But excavations of tell settlements have not documented prominent differences in status among houses or between their owners—unless the Chotnitsa gold find be interpreted in that light.

The Varna cemetery undoubtedly does now give striking evidence of such differentiation. There are poor graves as well as rich graves, and the richest contain a variety and a quantity of grave goods surpassing anything found, for instance, in the Wessex culture of the British bronze age, and rivalling the richest finds of the North German early bronze age such as Leubingen. This assessment need not depend upon any *a priori* judgement that gold was a commodity of particularly high value—clearly we are not justified in assuming it to be more esteemed than *Spondylus* or than copper. However, even a preliminary analysis of the contexts of the gold in the richer graves shows it occurring regularly in positions of particular significance. The diadems, earrings and beads adorning the head in the richest graves (as defined by range of goods, not by their material) are of gold. In several cases where weapons of display were carried in the right hand, for example in Grave 4, the shafts were embellished with gold (plate 2a).

Some of the richest graves were among the symbolic 'cenotaphs' (for example Grave 3), but there are sufficient finds with skeletons to allow some social analysis to proceed. Grave 43, for instance, with its great wealth of grave goods (plate 4a), was that of a man aged over 40. But there are very few child burials, unfortunately, so that the position of inherited versus ascribed status may be difficult to evaluate. Undoubtedly, however, the cemetery does give evidence for very salient ranking, and the wealth of grave goods is greater than one could anticipate for a cemetery serving simply a neighbourhood locality. The settlement associated with the cemetery has not been discovered, if indeed there is a single such settlement, but it must in any case be assumed, on the basis of the grave goods, that the cemetery holds the élite of a larger region than of just the few square kilometres which frequently constitute the territory surrounding chalcolithic tells.

These observations lead Ivanov (1978, 62) to consider the possibility of a state level of organization:

> The existence of property stratification, private property in large amounts and of great value, of crafts and commerce, suggest a form of social organization higher than the primitive communal system. And the next step is the state. Has there been already a state on our territory as early as the IVth millennium BC?

This same problem has been faced in other areas, using comparable evidence, and the concept of 'chiefdom' has been found useful in cases where there is pronounced ranking and a measure of centralized organization (Renfrew, 1973; Peebles and Kus, 1977). Using the criteria now becoming accepted by archaeologists, it seems permissible provisionally to regard the social structure at Varna as falling within the chiefdom category. The use of this concept avoids the term 'state', which for various reasons seems inappropriate to the Balkan copper age just as much as for Stonehenge or for the Wessex culture of Britain. Likewise it emphasizes the distinction between the new impression which the Varna finds give us of the social structure, and the markedly egalitarian organization previously postulated for the Balkan copper age.

All this has a very considerable bearing on the origins of metallurgy in the area. For it is clear that the main technical elements employed in the metal industry of the Karanovo VI period were available already in Karanovo V, if not earlier. The problem in explaining the rise of metallurgy is thus not simply a technical one, in elucidating the discovery or acquisition of the relevant metallurgical techniques, but a social one in defining the conditions favouring the wider adoption of the initial invention. It is this adoption rather than the technical invention itself which marks the effective innovation (Renfrew, 1978).

Metal objects were not initially very useful: they were less durable than their counterparts of stone. I believe, therefore, that it was the use of metal to manufacture ornaments and objects of adornment and display which was crucial to the early development of production, and through increased production to the improvement of technology. It is no coincidence, then, that the richest find of metalwork from the Balkan copper age should excel in gold rather than in copper. And probably it is no coincidence either that the first useful tool of copper, the shaft-hole axe of Vidra type, should closely imitate the stone shaft-hole axes which are found, with gold-mounted shafts, as weapons of display in the Varna cemetery.

The conditions necessary for the production of such conspicuous objects of metal were clearly more readily met in a ranked society than in an egalitarian one. The precocious development of copper metallurgy in what has hitherto appeared so egalitarian a context as the Balkan copper age was thus somewhat paradoxical. Varna removes that paradox, and the evidence of the cemetery strongly supports this social view of the origins of metallurgy: copper (and gold) in Europe was first produced not for utilitarian objectives, but to fulfil the social function of conspicuous display. [1978]

ACKNOWLEDGEMENT

I am very grateful to my friend Professor G. I. Georgiev for interesting discussions at Aibunar, Stara Zagora (Malka Vereya) and Varna; to Mr Mincho Dimitrov for showing me the finds in his museum store at Malka Vereya; and to Mr Ivan Ivanov for allowing me to study his discoveries in Varna and for useful information. I am indebted to Mr Dominic Flessati for his encouragement, and to Dr Joan Oates for information on early finds of goldwork in Mesopotamia.

BIBLIOGRAPHY

Angelov, N. (1959) Le trésor en or de Hotnica, *Archaeologiya*, 1, 38–46 (Sofia).

Baumgartel, E. J. (1960) *The cultures of prehistoric Egypt, II* (Oxford, Griffith Institute).

Chernykh, E. N. (1975) Aibunar: a Balkan copper mine of the fourth millennium BC, *Sovietskäya Archaeologija*, 4, 132–53.

——(1976) Metallurgiscshe Bereiche des 4.–2. Jahrtausend v. Chr. in der UDSSR, Paper presented to the IX Congress of Prehistory and Protohistory, Nice.

Clark, R. M. (1975) A calibration curve for radiocarbon dates, *Antiquity*, 39, 251–66.

Dumitrescu, H. (1961) Connections between the Cucuteni-Tripolje cultural complex and the neighbouring cultures in the light of the utilisation of gold pendants, *Dacia*, 5, 69–93.

Evans, R. K. (1973) *Craft specialisation in the chalcolithic period of the Eastern portion of the Balkan Peninsula* (Ph.D. dissertation, University of California at Los Angeles).

Georgiev, G. I. (1961) Kulturgruppen der Jungstein- und der Kupferzeit in der Ebene von Thrazien (Südbulgarien), in (eds.), J. Bohm and S. J. De Laet, *L'Europe à la fin de l'âge de la pierre* (Prague), 45–100.

Gimbutas, M. (1977*a*) Gold treasure at Varna, *Archaeology*, 30, 44–51.

——(1977*b*) Varna: a sensationally rich cemetery of the Karanovo civilization, *Expedition*, 19 (4), 39–47.

Iovanovic, B. and Ottaway, B. S. (1976) Copper mining and metallurgy in the Vinča group, *Antiquity*, 50, 104–13.

Ivanov, I. S. (1975) Raskopki na Varnenskija eneoliten nekropol prez 1972 g., *Izvestija na Narodnija Muzeji Varna* (Bulletin du Musée National de Varna), 11, 1–16.

——(1978) *Sukrovishtata na Varnenskiya Chalkoliten Nekropol* (Treasures of the Varna chalcolithic necropolis), Sofia, 'September'. (Text in Bulgarian with translation into Russian, English and German.)

Makkay, J. (1976) Problems concerning Copper Age chronology in the Carpathian basin, *Acta Archaeologica Academiae Scientiarum Hungaricae*, 28, 251–300.

Mikov, V. (1958) *Zlatnoto Sukrovishte ot Vulchitran* (Le trésor d'or de Valcitran), Sophia, Académie des Sciences.

Muhly, J. D. (1977) The copper ox-hide ingots and the bronze age metals trade, *Iraq*, 39, 73–82.

Oates, J. (1972) A radiocarbon date from Choga Mami, *Iraq*, 34, 49–53.

Parovic-Pešikán, M. and Trbuhovic, V. (1971) Iskopavania tumula ranog bronzanog doba u Tivatskom poliu, *Starinar*, 22, 129–41.

Peebles, C. S. and Kus, S. M. (1977) Some archaeological correlates of ranked societies, *American Antiquity*, 42, 421–48.

Popescu, D. and Popescu, V. (1955) Asupra tezearului de aur de la Ostrovul Mare, *Studii si Cercetări de Istorie Veche*, 4, 865–80.

Renfrew, C. (1969) The autonomy of the south-east European copper age, *Proc. Prehist. Soc.*, 35, 12–47.

——(1971) Sitagroi, radiocarbon and the prehistory of south-east Europe, *Antiquity*, 45, 275–82.

——(1973) Monuments, mobilisation and social organisation in neolithic Wessex, in (ed.), C. Renfrew, *The explanation of culture change* (London), 539–58.

——(1978) The anatomy of innovation, in (eds.), D. Green, C. C. Haselgrove and M. J. T. Spriggs, *Social organisation and settlement* (British Archaeological Reports, International Series 47), 89–117.

Shackleton, N. and Renfrew, C. (1970) Neolithic trade routes realigned by oxygen isotope analyses, *Nature*, 228, 1062–5.

Tobler, A. J. (1950) *Excavations at Tepe Gawra, II* (Philadelphia).

Tsountas, C. (1908) *Ai Proistorikai Akropoleis Dhiminiou kai Sesklou* (Athens).

Woolley, C. L. (1931) Excavations at Ur, 1930–1, *Antiq. J.*, 11, 343–81.

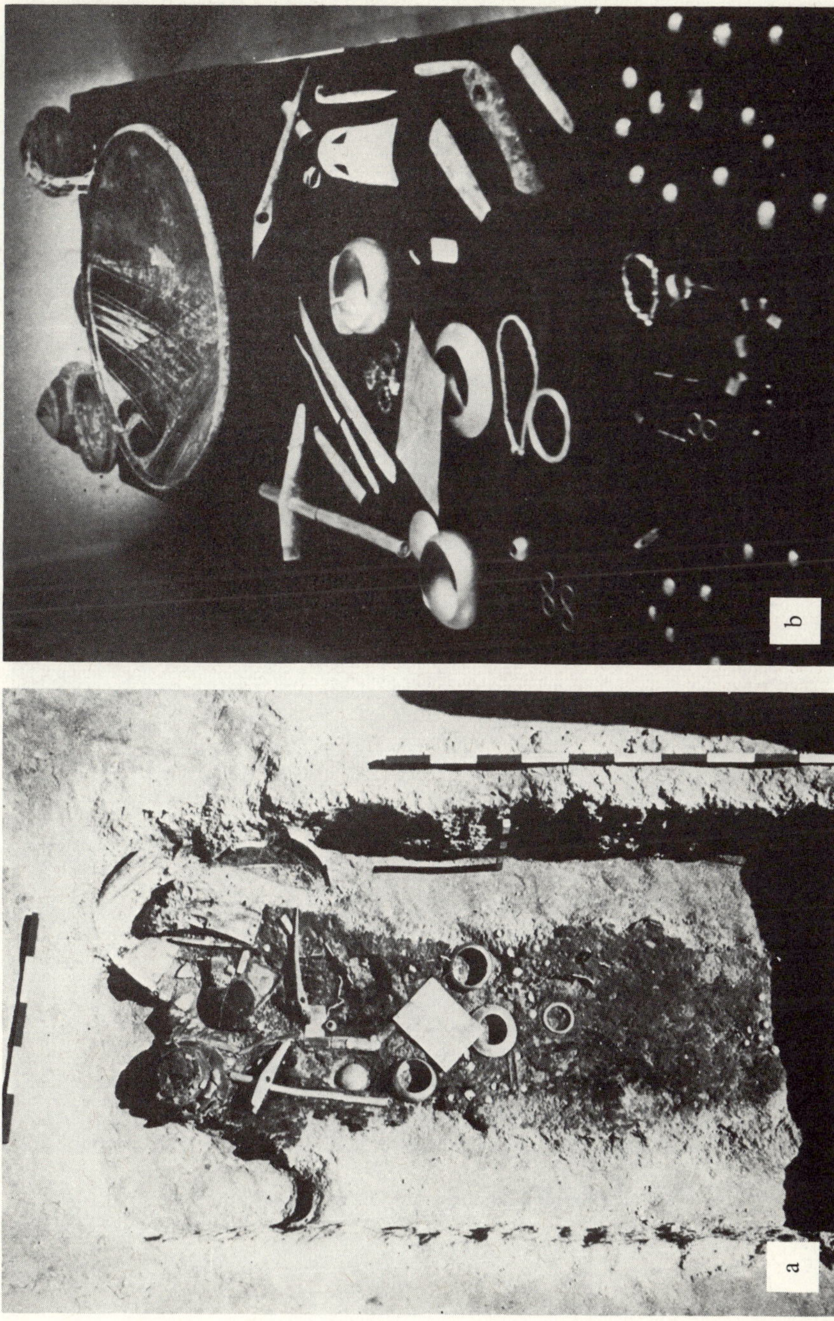

Plate 1. (a) Grave 4 during excavation (photo Ivan Ivanov).
(b) The contents of Grave 4.

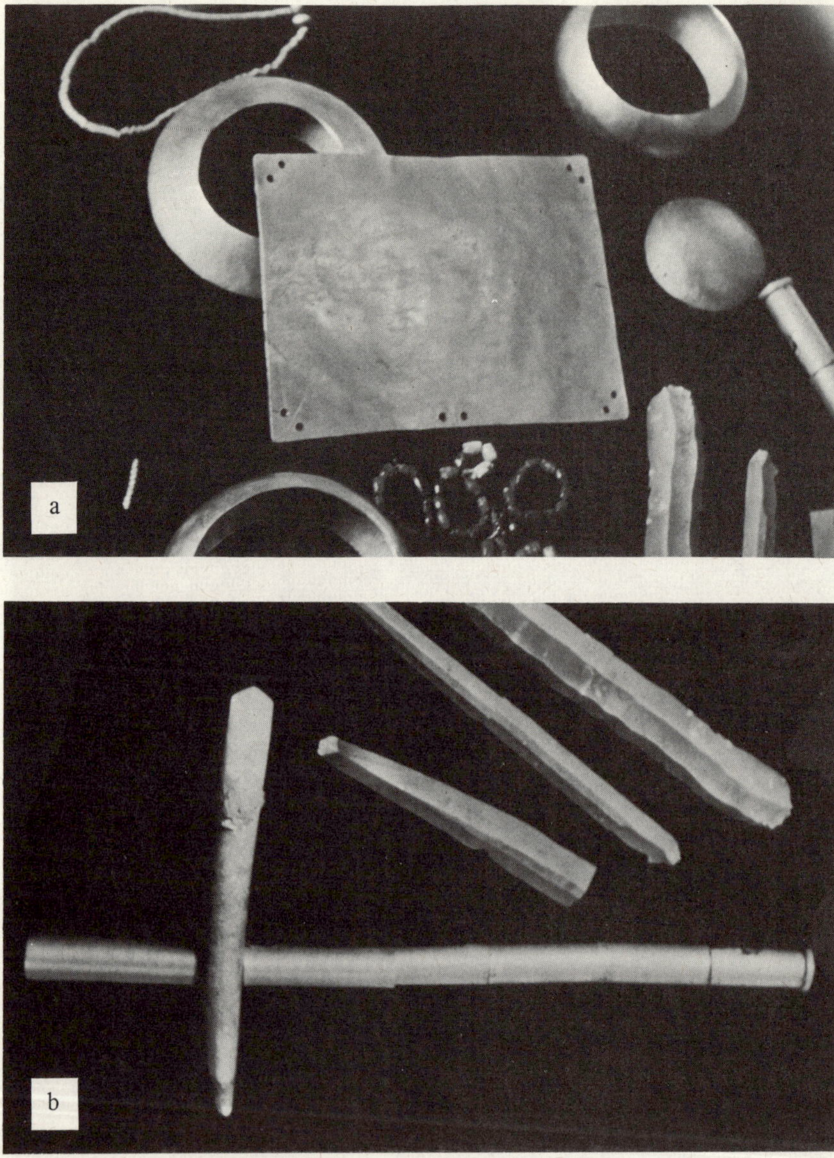

Plate 2. (a) The gold-mounted sceptre from Grave 4 (with flint blades).
(b) Gold pectoral plate.

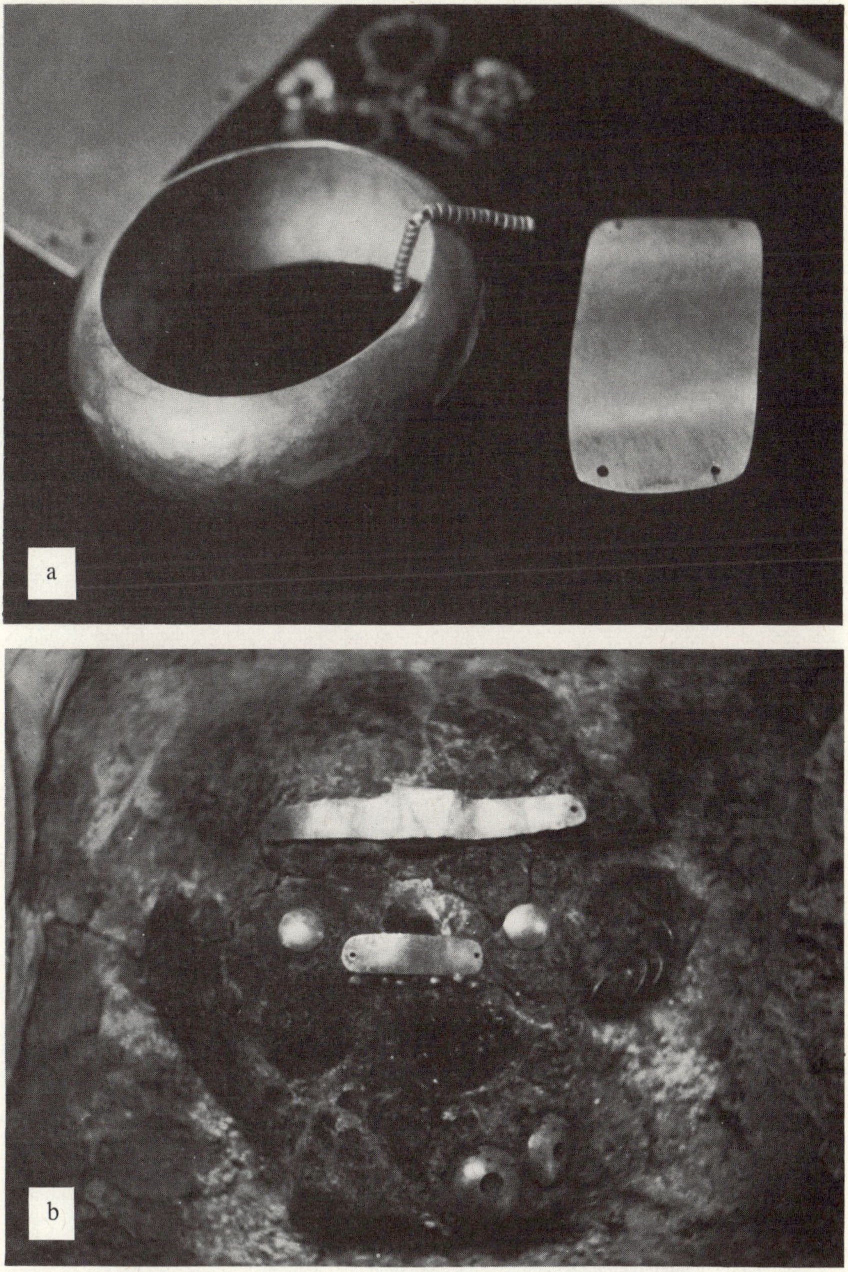

Plate 3. (a) Massive gold armlet. (b) Modelled clay face decorated with gold jewellery, from Grave 2.

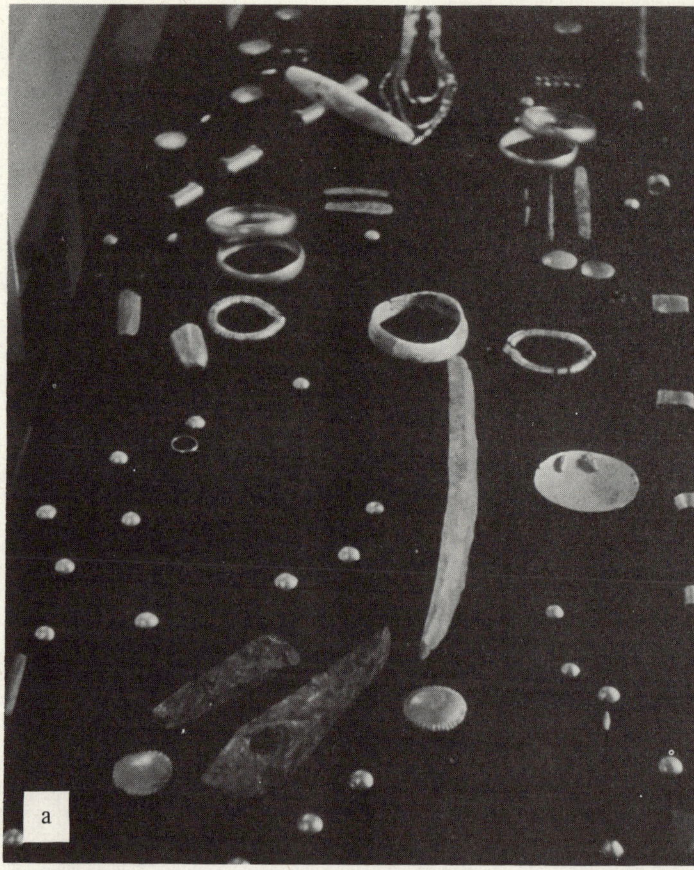

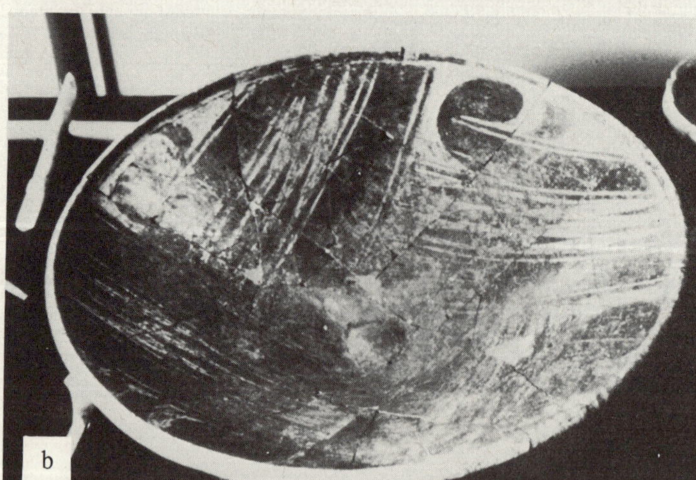

Plate 4. (a) Contents of Grave 43: note the long flint blade.
(b) Bowl decorated with gold, from Grave 4.

INDEX

Åberg, N., 89, 112, 262, 263, 264, 351-2
Abyssinia, obsidian from, 66, 68, 72, 76, 77
Acanfora, M.O., 237, 251
Adams, R.M., 22, 40
Aegean: burial conventions, *see* burial conventions, Aegean
 chronology: *see* chronology, Aegean
 daggers, 52, 97-101, 109-11, 123, 232-6, 239-40
 Early Bronze Age: autonomy of the regions, 89, 103-4; Cycladic metallurgy and, 87-136; duration of, 219; international spirit of, 88, 89, 104-7; local forms, 96, 97, 100, 103-4, 128; phases of, 88-9, 107; social organisation, 307; specialisation, 106-7; trade and commerce, 28, 88, 104, 105-6, 219
 Early Bronze 1 period, 88, 89, 104
 Early Bronze 2 period: contacts in, 89, 90, 91, 96, 100, 104-7, 219; cultural continuum, 105-7, 128; international spirit of, 104-7; prosperity of, 88, 106-7, 219; urbanisation in, 27, 37-8
 figurines, 45, 49, 56, 58, 61, 352
 fortifications, 51, 53-4, 56, 62, 90, 219, 229, 266, 352
 Iberia and: burial conventions, 9, 24, 25, 44, 45, 51-2, 53, 54, 262, 263, 265, 266-7, 273-4, 352; chronology, 49, 52-3, 54, 216-19, 244, 245, 262, 267, 273, 275, 350, 351-3; colonisation theory, 9, 10, 25, 39, 43, 44, 45, 51-4, 262, 263, 265-8, 276; colonies, case against, 52-4; colonies, case for, 51-2; fortifications, 9, 51, 53-4, 62, 262, 266, 351; metallurgy, 9, 24, 26, 51, 52, 53, 262, 265, 266, 339, 351; tin trade question, 106, 239, 241; urbanisation, 39, 273, 338
 Italy and: bonework, 228-9; burial conventions, 224-5; chronology, 49, 216-19, 244, 245, 350, 351-3; colonial theory, 43, 203-4, 240, 241; daggers, 50, 232-6, 239-40; direct contact in later period, 220-3, 241; flint, 225-6; lithic industries, 225-7; metallurgy, 229-39; non-metallic artefacts, 223-9; pottery, 50, 64, 227-8; tin trade question, 239
 Jugoslavia and, 43, 45, 47-8
 Late Bronze Age: civilisations, 36; contacts, 220
 Malta and, 43, 44, 48-50, 56, 61, 223, 255, 259
 metallurgy: *see* metallurgy, Aegean
 Middle Bronze Age, 220, 221
 nautical feasibility of contact, 45-7, 50, 51
 Neolithic, 35, 36, 104, 139, 143, 152, 153, 194-5, 219, 220, 242, 244
 obsidian used in, 35-6, 69, 75-6, 77, 183, 184
 Sardinia and, 44, 45, 50, 106
 Sicily and, 44, 45, 49-50, 203-4, 220
 South-East Europe and: *see* South-East Europe
Aegean – *contd*
 urbanisation, 27, 34-9, 106-7, 338
 West Mediterranean and, 43-64, 350, 351-3
 see also Cycladic, Helladic, Minoan, Mycenaean
 agriculture: efficiency in, and civilisation, 36-7, 38
 Italian, 241
 Malta, 260-1
 South East European, 142, 161, 162
Aitken, M.J., 40, 69, 77, 298, 302
Alcalà: daggers, 52, 266
 tombs, 274
Almagro, M., 52, 54
 and Arribas, A., 265, 277
Almerian culture, 51, 53, 266, 267, 271, 272, 348, 350, 351, 352
altars, clay, 147, 148, 164
amber: beads, 294, 308; characterisation study of, 28-9
 Iberian, 268
 Mycenaean, 24, 281, 289, 305, 353
 of Wessex culture, 283, 289, 294, 306, 308
 significance of, 23, 28-9
 source of, 23, 28
 spacer-plates, 289, 353
 trade with Baltic, 24, 28-9, 183, 281, 289 305
Ammerman, A.J., and Cavalli-Sforza, L.L., 223, 252
Amorgos: daggers and spearheads, 88, 95, 98-101, 106, 109-11, 121, 123, 124, 125, 235, 236
 finds, 88, 91, 108, 120, 127
 Grave D from Kapros, 89, 93-5, 108, 120
 Group, 91, 93
 lead and silver objects from, 93, 94, 107-8, 117, 118
 silver diadem, 93, 237
 tombs of, 88
 tools from, 95-6
Anatolia(n): chronology, 218, 244, 348, 354
 daggers, 98, 100, 103, 234-5, 236
 depas cups, 37, 38, 45, 90, 104
 influence in Crete, 89, 104
 metallurgy, 103, 106, 266, 339, 354, 365
 obsidian sources in, 32, 33, 68, 70, 75-6,77
 possible source of tin in, 239
 South-East Europe and, 139, 143, 151, 162
'anchors', clay, 150, 151, 153, 166, 360, 376
Angelov, N., 140, 158, 177, 380, 383
anthropologists, 19th C., 3-5, 9-10, 18-19
antimony, Italian artefacts in, 209, 216, 237-8, 239, 242
Antiparos, 91, 93, 103, 107, 117, 118
Apennine culture, 218, 220, 243
armlets, gold, 378, 379, 387
arm spiral, silver, 93, 107, 118
Armorican Early Bronze Age, 283-4, 285, 290
arrowheads: Balkan tanged, 47, 48
 Cycladic flint, 51, 225
 Iberian copper, 268, 269, 270

arrowheads – *contd*
Iberian flint, 53, 270, 271
Italian flint, 207, 209, 211, 212, 214, 216, 225
arsenical bronze: a metallurgical view, 130-6
Charles's paper on, 87, 88, 101, 130-6
deliberate alloying of, 88, 102-3, 130, 136
effect of arsenic on castability of copper, 130-1
effect of arsenic addition, 131-3
Italian, 240
production of alloys from available minerals, 133-5
replacement by tin bronze, 130, 135-6
askoi, 149, 210, 211, 227
Aspinall, A., *et al.*, 65, 252, 293, 305, 308
Atkinson, R.J.C., 305
Atkinson, T.D., *et al.*, 45-6, 54, 112
awls, 142, 158, 160, 207, 209, 211, 236, 242, 266
axes: Aegean: clay, 150,151,166; double, 9,96, 97; early copper or bronze, 103,160,238; flat metal, 95-6, 97, 109, 121, 122, 232; lead double, 92; narrow flat metal, 95, 109, 121; shaft-hole metal, 96, 97, 104, 109, 121, 122, 125; shaft-hole stone, 360
Breton/British jade, 29
British: double, 289; Neolithic, characterisation studies on, 66
Cycladic: metal, 95-7, 109, 125, 232; stone, 51
Iberian: flat copper, 266; stone, 51, 270
Italian: axe-hammers, 226-7; flat copper, 207, 209, 212, 232, 241, 242; stone, 207, 212, 216, 226
South-East European: clay, 150, 151, 166; flat metal, 142, 158, 168; shaft-hole metal, 142, 154, 155-6, 158, 159, 160, 168, 169, 170, 171-2, 378, 383; stone, 378, 383
Swedish bronze, 13
axe-adzes: Aegean metal, 96, 97, 101, 109, 121, 122, 125
chronology and, 342
South-East European, 154, 155-6, 157, 158, 160, 168, 169, 172-3, 342
Ay. Anargyroi, 93, 94, 95
Ay. Kosmas, 91, 127

B

Baden culture, 139, 143, 150, 163, 191, 192, 196, 197, 234, 360, 361
Bakker, J.A., *et al.*, 281, 282, 345, 347, 368
Balkans: absolute chronology, 190
Cycladic relations with, 45, 47-8, 87
in Early Bronze Age, 196-8
obsidian, 183
spirals, 48, 56, 59
transition from Neolithic to Bronze Age, 195-6
see also Bulgaria, Jugoslavia, Rumania, South-East Europe
Banner, J., 143, 177
Barfield, L.H., 232, 234, 252
Barker, H., 311, 324, 337
et al., 257, 260
Bastian, A., 4
battle-axes, 226-7, 241, 307
beads: amber, 294, 308
bone, 207, 302
copper, 158, 159, 160
faience, 31, 65, 69, 221, 268, 289-306, 353
glass, 301
gold, 113, 360, 379, 382
pendant, 94, 108
shell, Italian, 207
shell, ostrich egg, 221-2, 268, 271
shell: *Dentalium*, 377-8; *Spondylus*, 183, 189
silver, 93, 108, 113, 211, 237
stone, 108, 207
beaked jugs, 51, 52, 90, 100
Beakers: Bell: European, 285; Italian, 209; question of origin, 273; South-East European, 196, 197
burials, 267
chronology and, 284, 285-6
Corded, 285-6
Iberian, 267, 269-70
Wessex, 197, 282, 283, 284, 286
Beck, C.W., *et al.*, 28, 40, 277
Beck, H.C., 295, 302
and Stone, J.P.S., 302
Benac, A., 48, 54
Benoît, F., 52, 54
Bennyhoff, J.A., and Heizer, R.F., 29, 40
Bent, J.T., 91, 93, 103, 107, 112
Berciu, D., 142, 143, 149, 153, 177, 189
Berger, R., 314, 321, 322, 324, 329, 333
Bernabo Brea, L., 220, 228, 252
Bialor, P., 34, 40
Biancofiore, F., 236, 252
Binford, L.R., 2, 19, 27, 40
and Binford, S.R., 30, 40
Blance, B., 9, 19, 25, 40, 45, 51, 55, 252, 262, 263, 265, 267, 268, 269, 277
Blegen, C.W., 152, 177
et al., 111, 113, 114
Blinkenberg, C., 94, 113
boats: lead models of, 46, 56, 57, 92-3, 106, 108, 117, 119
representation of, on: frying pans, 45, 46, 92-3, 106; pottery, 56, 57, 92
Bodrogkeresztúr culture, 139, 142, 143, 199, 242
Bognar-Kutzian, I., 142, 177, 190
Bosanquet, R.C., 73, 77
Bossert, E-M. Fischer, 51, 55, 93, 98, 99, 111, 252
bowls: Aegean pottery: Early Helladic II open, 105, 126; Minoan footed, 105; with inturned, rolled rim, 89, 104
gold, 94-5
Italian pottery, 211, 214
silver, 94-5, 108, 117, 126
Sitagroi pottery, 357, 358
South-East European: footed, 146-7; types of, 148, 149, 150, 151, 165, 167
bracelets: copper, 161
lead, 107, 108, 118
silver, 93, 107, 117, 118, 211, 237
Spondylus shell, 47, 56, 60, 161, 188, 189

bracelets – *contd*
types of, 93
Branigan, K., 87, 114, 226, 229-31, 232, 236, 237, 252, 305, 308
Bray, W., 45, 50, 55, 267, 280, 339, 340
bristlecone pine calibration, 285, 286, 310, 312, 313, 321-2, 326, 344
see also calibration
Britain, British: axes, double, 289
axes, characterisation studies of Neolithic, 66
Beakers, 282, 283, 284
Middle Bronze Age, 284
transition to Neolithic, 25
see also Wessex
Brittany, Breton: Armorican Early Bronze Age, 283-4, 285, 290
graves, 283, 363
megalithic tombs, 262, 274, 275-6
Middle Bronze Age, 284
wealth of Early Bronze Age, 290
Wessex and, 283-4, 290
Britton, D., and Richards, E.E., 69, 77
Brown, D.F., 43, 102
Bucha, V., 313, 324, 344, 368
Buchner, G., 73, 77, 252
Bulgaria: Bulgarian sequence, 144-52
Chalcolithic of, 140-1, 148-9, 354-5
copper-mining in, 137
Early Bronze Age, 145, 149-50
metallurgy of, 137, 354
Troy parallels for, 150-2
Vesselinovo culture, development of, 146-8
see also Gumelnitsa culture, Karanovo, South-East Europe
burial conventions: Aegean: cist graves, 91, 94, 95; collective burial, 54, 224, 266, 267; Iberian relations and, 9, 24, 25, 44, 51-2, 53, 54, 262, 263, 266-7, 273-4, 353; Italian relations and, 203-4, 224-5; Minoan round tombs, 224, 264, 265, 266, 274-5, 279, 352; Mycenaean dromos, 54, 274; Mycenaean tholos, 263, 264, 265, 266, 274, 352; rock-cut tombs, 50, 90, 219, 224; rock shelters and caves, 224; round graves, 51, 54, 266-7; shaft graves, 224, 289, 290, 353, 367
Beaker, 267
Cycladic, 51, 90, 224, 265, 266-7, 274, 278
Egyptian, 263-4
European megalithic tombs: *see* megaliths
Iberian: Aegean relations and, 9, 24, 25, 44, 51-2, 53, 54, 262, 263, 266-7, 273-4, 352; Breton tombs and, 54, 262, 274, 275-6, 363; cave burials, 266; chronology and, 54, 262, 264, 267, 275-6, 352, 363; collective burial, 9, 51, 54, 262, 265, 266-7, 352; corbelled tombs, 263, 264, 270, 272, 274, 275, 279; cupola tombs, 270; megaliths, 9, 24, 25, 262, 266-7, 352; Passage Graves, 269, 270-1, 272, 274, 275, 351; rock-cut tombs, 45, 52, 53, 267, 269, 272, 278; round tombs, 51, 266, 272, 274, 278, 352; tholoi, 51-2, 54, 264, 265
burial conventions – *contd*
Italian: Aegean relations and, 203-4, 224-5; cemeteries, 206, 207-8, 209-10, 219, 225; collective burial, 204, 206, 207, 209, 214, 224, 225, 241; funerary sites, 205, 245-9; grave goods, 206-7, 208, 210, 214-15; natural caves, 205, 206, 207, 210, 214, 224, 241; rock-cut tombs, 45, 52, 53, 267, 269, 272, 278; single inhumation, 206, 207; trench graves, 205, 209, 211, 214, 224
Malta, rock-cut tombs, 225, 365
Sardinian, 50
Sicily: Aegean relations, 203-4; rock-cut tombs, 45, 50, 268, 279
Varna, 377-87
Wessex, barrow burials, 306-7
Burkitt, M.C., 71, 78
and Childe, V.G., 352, 368
Butler, J.J., and Van der Waals, J.D., 29, 40
Butmir culture, 43, 48
buttons: antimony, 209, 237
V-perforated 'tortoise', 269, 273

C

calibration: and chronology of Ancient Egypt, 322, 326, 327, 329-36, 345, 348
British prehistory and, 286, 287-8, 298
chart, 345-6
confidence region, 318-21
curves: Clark, R.M., 310, 317, 318; desirable properties of, 317, 329; forms of, 310, 317-18; kinks in, 310, 311, 318, 327, 328, 344, 367; Michael and Ralph, 310, 317-18; reliability of, 310, 321-2, 326, 345-6; Suess's, 310, 311, 317, 327, 329; Switsur's, 310, 317-18; Wendland and Donley, 310, 317
European prehistory and, 281, 285-8
evaluation of data, 329-33
function, 314-18, 322-3, 327-9
inverse calibration function, 315, 318-21
Malta and, 255, 256, 257
reliability of, 321-2, 326
simultaneity principle, 321-2
Cambi, L., 237, 252
Cann, J.R., and Renfrew, C., 51, 55, 252
et al., 162, 177
Capo Graziano culture, 220, 222, 228, 241
Case, H., and Apsimon, A., 2, 19
Caskey, J.L., 40, 111, 112, 222, 252, 277
and Caskey, E.G., 360, 368
Castelluccio culture, 220, 221, 228, 229, 235, 236-7, 348
Çatal Hüyük, 91, 103, 158, 160, 226, 365
Catling, H.W., *et al.*, 29, 40
Cavalier, M., 50, 55, 228, 252
Cernavoda-Ezero culture, 139, 142-3, 145, 149, 151, 152, 195, 199, 360
Chalandhriani, 9, 53, 89, 90, 91, 92, 95, 98, 99, 101, 105, 106, 126, 235, 266, 267
chamber tombs *see* burial conventions
Chapman, R.W., 262, 263, 304, 339, 340
characterisation of materials: and determination of sources, 24, 66
contrasted with style, 28

characterisation of materials – *contd*
defined, 66
of British Neolithic stone axes, 66
of obsidian, 28, 29, 32, 65-86
of *Spondylus* shell, 183-7
technical methods for, 22, 24, 25, 28-9, 66, 68-9
trade, trading patterns and, 17, 22, 28-9, 66
value of, 17, 23, 66
Charles, J.A., 87, 88, 101, 102-3, 130-6, 137, 154, 155, 354
chiefdoms: group-orientated, 304, 307
individualising, 304, 307
population increase and, 307-8
South-East European, 378, 382-3
Childe, V.G.,: as a moderate diffusionist, 5, 7-8, 9, 18, 26, 139-40, 203-4, 220, 264-5, 351, 352, 366
chronological tables, 343, 348, 349, 351-2, 354
concept of: cultural transmission, 44, 139-40; culture and culture areas, 14-15, 343; economic imperialism, 25, 26, 28; ethnic groups, 6, 15, 351; isochrons, 365; prehistory, 2-3, 18, 138, 139-40; role of the Danube, 44; social and economic processes, 8, 16-17
five propositions, 139-40, 342
influence of, 2, 9, 26
inventions made but once, 5, 26, 44, 49, 351
The Dawn of European Civilisation, 2, 26, 87, 139, 203-4, 342
views on: Aegean Early Bronze Age, 25, 87, 89, 289, 343, 351-2; collective burials, 9; European Bronze Age, 281, 282, 283, 286-7, 289; faience beads, 289, 294; Iberia, 9, 264-5, 267, 271, 351-2, 354; Indo-Europeans, 9, 15-16; Italy, 50, 203-4, 220, 233; Malta, 255; megaliths, 8, 264, 352; metallurgy, 9, 139, 149, 220, 233; South-East Europe, 138, 139-40, 143, 144, 149, 153, 158, 159, 163, 191, 265, 281, 282, 283; Vinča-Troy equation, 138, 191, 343, 354
works referred to, 19, 40, 55, 87, 112, 177, 252, 282, 368
Chiozza culture, 224, 225, 238, 243
Chotnica, 140, 148, 158, 159
chronology: absolute, 190, 341, 342
Aegean: and Iberia, 49, 52-3, 54, 216-19, 244, 245, 262, 267, 273, 275, 348, 350, 351-3; and Italy, 49, 216-19, 244, 245, 350, 351-3; and South-East Europe, 143, 144, 152, 153, 190, 191, 194, 195, 199, 200-1, 350, 354-63; Early Cycladic, 89-91; historical dates, 347; radiocarbon dating, 152, 153, 200-1, 203, 218-19, 243-4, 288, 343, 346
Anatolian, 218, 244, 348, 354
astronomical dating, 341-2
Balkan, 190, *see also* South-East Europe
Beaker, 284, 285-6
by cross-dating, 342-3, 348
by culture, 343
by relationships, 342
chronology – *contd*
by typology, 342
Childe's chronological tables, 343, 348, 349, 351-2, 354
contact and, 348, 350-1
conventional: basis for, 341-3; diffusionist theory and, 351, 352, 366; discrepancies between new and, 347, 359-63; logical structure of, 348-9; weaknesses of, 350-1
Cycladic, 87, 88, 89-91
disputes on, 1
Egyptian: historical, 326, 327, 331, 336, 341, 342, 345, 347, 348; tree-ring calibration and, 322, 326-7, 347, 348
European megaliths and, 262, 275-6, 367
Iberia: and the Aegean, 49, 52-3, 54, 216-19, 244, 245, 262, 267, 273, 275, 348, 350, 351-3; burial conventions and, 54, 262, 266, 267, 275-6, 352, 363; problems of, 49, 52-3, 54, 243, 245, 267, 268-9, 273; radiocarbon evidence, 262, 267, 273, 275
Italy: and the Aegean, 49, 216-19, 244, 245, 350, 351-3; calibrated dates and, 352; problems of, 348; radiocarbon evidence, 216-18, 243
Malta, 255-61, 348, 352, 365
metallurgy and, 364-6
Neolithic: and Early Bronze Age, 197; evidence and, 324, 343, 347;
new: and conventional, 347, 349-63; experimental tables, 346, 347; fault line between conventional and, 349-50; implications of, 363-6
relative, 16, 341, 342, 343, 348-9
Sardinia, 218, 352
seriation and, 16, 343
Sicily, 352
Sitagroi, 191, 192, 193, 198, 200-1, 361-3
South-East Europe, 138-9, 140, 142, 143-4, 152-3, 162, 191, 194, 195-6, 197, 199, 343, 348, 350, 353-4, 367, 377, 378-9, 380
stratigraphy and, 354, 355
thermoluminescence dating of pottery, 345, 363
Wessex: question of, 281-2, 285-8, 290, 305, 306, 347-8; radiocarbon dating and, 281-2, 285-8, 290, 305, 306, 347-8; relative, 283-5, 347-8
see also calibration, radiocarbon
civilisation: agricultural efficiency and, 36-7, 38
defined, 34-5
early development of Aegean, 34-9
irradiation of European barbarism by Oriental, 8, 26, 139, 282, 351
population increase and, 34-5, 36-7
religion and, 37
savagery, barbarism and, 3, 4, 28
settlement size and, 34-5, 36
similar stages of, 4-5, 26-7
Clark, J.G.D., 2, 16, 19, 23, 25, 29, 31, 40, 138, 140, 177, 294, 302, 343, 368
Clark, R.M., 310, 317, 318, 326, 380, 384
and Renfrew C., 257, 260, 308, 314, 317, 322, 323, 324, 330, 337

Clark, R.M. – *contd*
and Sowray, A., 317, 322, 324
Clarke, D.L., 2, 14, 17, 19, 284, 304
coal scuttles, 48, 104
Coghlan, H.H., 155, 171, 177
Coles, J.M., and Taylor, J., 306, 308
Collis, J.R., 339, 340
colonisation: Iberia: case against, 52-4; case for, 51-2; theory of, 9, 10, 25, 43, 44, 45, 51-4, 262, 263, 265-8, 276
Italy, 43, 203-4, 240, 241
nautical feasibility of, 45-7, 50, 51
communication: in the Aegean, 35, 38, 39
urbanisation and, 35, 38
Comsa, E., 149, 177
Conelle-Ortucchio group, 205, 211-12, 226, 232, 239, 248
contact: and culture process, 16-19
characterisation studies and, 25, 28-9, 66
culture and, 17, 22, 25
economic and social consequences of, 18, 22
inventions and, 18, 339
maritime, 45-7, 50, 51
trade and, 17, 22, 23, 27-8, 37, 38
trade as indicator and motive for, 23, 36
typological comparisons and, 66
West Mediterranean/Aegean, question of, 43-64
Copper Age: of Peninsular Italy, 202-54
of South-East Europe, 137-76
copper: characterisation studies of, 29
metallurgy *see* metallurgy
Cornaggia Castiglioni, O., *et al.*, 69, 73-4, 78, 222, 252
craft specialisation: metallurgy and, 37, 106, 242, 308, 382
urbanisation and, 35, 37, 106-7
Crete: Anatolian influence in, 89, 104
axe-adzes, 96
axes, shaft-hole, 97
burial conventions, 224
chronology, 89, 244, 348
daggers, 99, 100, 104, 123, 226
daggers, Koumasa silver, 230-1, 237
Early Bronze Age settlements in, 36, 37
Early Bronze 2 period, 88
gold finds from, 93
Italy and, 202
jugs, handled, 105
metal finds from, 88, 93, 127
Neolithic sites in, 35
obsidian trade, 104, 230
razors, 237
relations with Cyclades, 90
urbanisation in, 34, 37
use of lead in, 87, 92
use of silver in, 87, 231
see also Minoan, Mycenaean
culture: area: approach to archaeology, 16; Childe's concept of, 14-15, 343
as aggregate of systems, 27
change: culture-process model, 27-8, 140, 290-1; diffusionist model, 26; dynamics of, 15, 290-1, 308, 338; evolutionist model, 26-7; invasionist model, 25-6; trade and, 22, 23, 24
culture – *contd*
Childe's concept of, 14-15, 343
chronology by, 343
creep, 268
cultural causality and law, 26-7
evolution of, 9, 12
history, as an inductive science, 1
intensification and urbanisation, 36, 37, 38, 88
naming by, 16
people, language and, 14-16
process: contact and, 16-19; metallurgy and, 290; model of culture change, 27-8, 140, 290-1; social differentiation and, 290; South-East Europe and, 140; trade and, 22-42; urbanisation and, 35-8
sequence: Bulgarian, 144-52; Cycladic, 88, 89-91; Troad, 89
systems: economic systems and, 23-4, 27; articulation of subsystems within, 17, 22, 27, 338-9; trade as a subsystem of, 17, 23-4
Cunliffe, B.W., 339, 340
cups: ceramic and metal forms, 105
depas, 37, 38, 45, 90, 104, 105, 126, 128, 150, 159
gold: Aegean, 105, 126; Mycenaean, 289, 363; Rillaton, 289, 363
one-handled: Cycladic, 90; distribution within Aegean, 90, 104, 128; Italian, 207, 209, 210, 214, 227; Sicilian, 228; Sitagroi, 360, 375
silver: Aegean, 105; Cretan, 95
South-East European, 150, 159
Cyclades, Cycladic: arrowheads, 51, 225
axes: metal, 95-7, 109, 125, 232; stone, 51
Balkan relations, 45, 47-8, 87
burial conventions, 51, 90, 224, 265, 266-7, 274, 278
chronology, 87, 88, 89-91
contact with Aegean, 90, 128
contact with Iberia, question of, 9, 45, 51-4
contact with Italy, question of, 45, 50-1, 56, 63, 64
contact with West Mediterranean, question of, 43-64, 87
culture phases, 89-91, *see also* Grotta-Pelos, Keros-Syros, Phylakopi I
culture sequence, 88, 89-91
cups, one-handled, 90
daggers, 91, 97-101, 109-11, 121, 123, 124, 125, 233
Early Bronze Age settlements, 36
figurines, 36, 37, 45, 47-8, 50, 51, 53, 56, 58, 59, 60, 61, 62, 89, 90, 91-2, 94, 95, 104, 108-9, 117, 119, 120, 128, 149
fishing spears, 31, 225
fortifications, 51, 56, 62, 352
Malta and, 48-50, 56, 61
metallurgy, *see* metallurgy, Cycladic
Neolithic, 35, 51, 52
pottery, 50, 56, 64
shipping, 45-7
spirals, 48, 56, 59
trade, 88, 89, 104

D

dagger(s): adoption of the, 366
  Aegean, 52, 97-101, 109-11, 123, 232-6, 239-40
  Alcala, 52, 266
  Amorgos, 88, 85, 98-101, 106, 109-11, 121, 124, 125, 235, 236
  Anatolian, 98, 100, 103, 234-5, 236
  Beaker, 234-5
  bivalve mould for, 52
  Bronze Age, and social hierarchy, 307
  classification of Aegean, 98-125
  classification of Italian, 232-40
  Cretan, 99, 100, 104, 123, 226
  Cretan, Koumasa silver, 230-1, 237
  Cycladic, 91, 97-101, 109-11, 121, 123, 124, 125, 233
  Cypriot, 287
  gold, 380
  Iberian midrib, 52, 54, 56, 63, 266
  Italian, 50, 55, 63, 101, 207-42
  Levantine, 234, 236, 240
  Manika, 100, 106
  obsidian, 378
  Pelynt, 289, 353
  silver, 93, 230-1, 237
  simultaneous appearance of, 100
  South-East European, 234-5, 378, 380
  tin, 103
  tin bronze, 101
  trade in, 106
  Wessex, 283, 289, 353
Damon, P.E., *et al.*, 317, 320, 324, 336
Daniel, G.E., 2, 8, 19, 25, 41, 273, 280, 299, 302
  and Evans, J.D., 9, 19, 43, 202
Darwin, C., 2, 3, 9, 10
Deetz, J., 30, 41
defence, urbanisation and, 35, 39
depas cups, 37, 38, 45, 90, 104, 105, 126, 128, 150, 159
dendrochronological calibration *see* calibration
Deshayes, J., 95, 96, 97, 111, 154, 158, 177, 190, 358
Detev, P., 140, 142, 145, 146, 147, 148, 150, 177
de Vries, H., 312, 324
Dhimini culture, 194-5, 198, 199, 219
diadems: Cycladic silver, 93, 237
  gold, 379, 382
  Iberian, 237
  of sheet metal, 104
Diana culture, 219, 222, 225, 230, 238, 243
diffusion, diffusionist: challenge to hypothesis of, 294
  Elliot Smith's extreme diffusionism, 5, 25, 26, 263
  from higher centres, 6, 23, 26, 29, 263
  Iberia and, 9, 26, 262, 263, 265, *see also* colonisation
  invention made but once, 5, 26, 44, 49, 351
  irradiation of European barbarism by Oriental civilisation, 8, 26, 139, 282, 351
diffusion, diffusionist – *contd*
  megaliths and, 8, 25, 263-4
  migration or, 5-9, 26
  model based on Egypt, 25, 263-4
  model of culture change, 26, 264
  moderate diffusionism of Childe, 5, 7-8, 9, 18, 26, 139-40, 203-4, 220, 264-5, 351, 353, 366
  of influences, 6
  of metallurgy, 139
  rejection of assumptions of, 14
  stimulus, 265, 268
  theoretical aspect of, 265
  transatlantic problem, 5, 339
  typological method and, 14
  view of South-East Europe, 138, 139-40
  within the Aegean, 35, 88, 104-7
Dimitrov, D.P., 150, 177
Dixon, J.E., 41, 65
do Paço, A., 269, 277
Doran, J.E., 41
  and Hodson, F.R., 14, 19, 293, 294
Doumas, C., 87, 90, 93, 94, 98
Driehaus, J., 158, 177
duck vases, 50, 90, 100, 227
Dumitrescu, H., 159, 177
Dumitrescu, V., 137, 140, 177, 181
Dümmler, F., 93, 98, 112, 113
Durrani, S.A., *et al.*, 65

E

earrings, gold, 379, 382
economic: consequences of contact, 18, 22
  data, quantitative evaluation of, 30-4
  development, trade and, 22, 23-4, 27
  importance of trade, 24
  processes influencing metal industry, 8, 140
  significance of exchanges, 22
systems within cultures, 23-4, 27, 339
Edgar, C.C., 92, 112
Edwards, I.E.S., 314, 324, 329, 337
Egypt: beads, faience, 283, 294, 295, 296, 297, 298, 299, 300, 301, 302, 305
  chronology: historical chronology, 326, 327, 331, 336, 341, 342, 345, 347, 348; tree-ring calibration and, 326-37, 345, 348
  diffusion model based on, 25, 263-4
  flint objects from, 226
  Iberia and, 263-4, 271, 272
  mastaba, 263-4
  metallurgy of, 365
  obsidian artefacts from, 76-7
  pottery styles, 230
Ehrich, R.W., 2, 19, 111, 142, 177
El Argar culture, 237, 268, 269
Elliot Smith, G., 5, 19, 25, 26, 41, 263, 277
Emborio, 195, 199, 219
ethnic group, concept of, 6, 15, 351
European: Bell Beakers, 285
  Bronze Age: absolute chronology, 282; florescence of, 290-1; Mycenae and, 281, 282; radiocarbon dating, 283-4, 285-8; relative chronology, 282, 283-5
  burial conventions and the megaliths: *see* megaliths

European – *contd*
chronology: Bronze Age, 282-91; megaliths and, 262, 275-6, 367
Iron Age, 22, 338-9
metallurgy, 290-1, 339, 367
prehistory: and the 'New Archaeology', 2; Childe's contribution to, 2-3; contact and culture process, 16-19; culture, people and language, 14-16; deficiencies in, 17-18; evolution and monogenesis, 9-14; migration or diffusion, 5-9; problems in, 1-21; reassessment of approaches, 1-3; recent challenges to, 1-2; traditional structure of, 1, 17; volume of research on, 1
urbanisation in, 338-9
see also Iberia, Italy, South-East Europe
Eutresis culture, 89, 96, 97, 104, 111, 152, 195, 199, 244, 360, 366
Evans, A.J., 45, 55, 68, 78, 89, 113, 160, 177, 222, 255, 293, 294, 342
Evans, J., 10, 11, 12, 14, 20
Evans, J.D., 49, 54, 55, 221, 222, 255, 256, 260, 267, 277, 338, 340
and Renfrew, C., 30, 41, 189
evolution: and monogenesis, 9-14
biological, 3, 9-10, 14
convergent, 14
cultural, 9, 12, 14
evolutionist model of culture change, 26-7
multi-linear, 26-7, 35
organic, 3, 9-10, 14
parallel, 14
social, 3
exchanges: defined, 24-5
economic and social significance of, 22
of goods, and cross-dating, 342-3
prestige-goods chain, 183, 188-9
reciprocity, 22, 24, 29, 188
types of, 22
see also trade
Ezero, 137, 143, 145, 149, 150, 151, 195
culture, 139, 142-3, 196, 199, 234
Ezerovo, 143, 149, 151, 195

F

faience beads, 31, 65, 69, 221, 268, 283, 289-306, 353
Ferguson, C.W., 313, 324, 336, 344, 368
et al., 323, 324, 344, 368
Fergusson, J., 5, 6, 7, 8, 20
figurines: Aegean, 45, 49, 56, 58, 61, 352
bone, 47, 56, 140
Cycladic, 36, 37, 38, 45, 47-8, 50, 51, 53, 56, 58, 59, 60, 61, 62, 89, 90, 91-2, 94, 95, 104, 108-9, 117, 119, 120, 128, 149, 267
clay, 49, 56, 61, 223
fat, 49, 56, 61
fiddle, 49
flat, 53
folded-arm, 37, 38, 45, 47, 48, 49, 90, 92, 94, 95, 104, 105, 108-9, 117, 119, 120, 128, 149, 223
Iberian, 53, 263, 267, 270, 272, 352
lead, 91-2, 105, 107, 117
figurines – *contd*
Maltese, 49, 56, 61, 223
marble, 37, 38, 45, 47, 50, 56, 58, 62, 89, 90, 92, 94, 95, 104, 105, 108-9, 117, 119, 120, 149, 223
metal, 91-2, 105, 107
Minoan, 47, 56, 60
reclining, 49
Sardinian, 45, 50, 56, 62, 223
schematic, 47, 56, 60, 89, 105
seated, 47, 49, 56, 60, 61
shell, 94, 108, 120
silver, 105
Sitagroi schematic, 358, 360, 373
South-East European, 47-8, 56, 58, 60, 140, 142, 147, 148, 149, 194-5, 358
trade in, 90
fishing-spears: flint, 225; obsidian, 31
fission-track analysis, 28, 65
flint: arrowheads: Aegean, 225; Cycladic, 51, 225; Iberian, 53, 270, 271; Italian, 207, 209, 211, 212, 214, 216, 225
Campignian, 214
daggers, Italian, 207, 209, 211, 212, 214, 216, 226, 241-2
Egyptian flintwork, 226
fishing-spears, 225
geometric flints, 225-6
Grand Pressigny, 23
Polish banded, 23
spearheads, Aegean, 226
fortifications: Aegean, 51, 53-4, 56, 62, 90, 219, 229, 266, 352
Cycladic, 51, 56, 62, 352
Iberian: and the Aegean question, 9, 51, 53-4, 62, 262, 266, 351; at Los Millares, 9, 51, 53, 262, 351, 352; at Vila Nova de São Pedro, 51, 53, 56, 62, 262
Sicilian, 229
urbanisation and, 35, 36, 38, 106
Frankfort, H., 69, 78, 94
French, D.H., 142, 158, 178, 218, 355, 368
Friedmann, I., and Smith R.L., 67, 72, 78
Frierman, J., 175-6, 354
frying pans: decoration on, 90
metal prototype of, 105
of Syros, 45, 46, 56, 57, 90
ships on, 45, 46, 92-3, 106
spirals on, 48

G

Galbenu, D., 142, 161, 178
Galovic, R., 139, 142, 178
Galton, F., 26, 41
Garasanin, M.V., 48, 55, 139, 142, 143, 148, 150, 178, 181, 191, 198
Gaudo Group, 204, 205, 209-11, 224, 225, 226, 227, 229, 232, 236, 237, 239, 248
Gaul, J.H., 145, 161, 178
Gelfand, A.E., 14, 20
genetic affinity, and invention, 3, 5-6
Georgiades, A.N., 69, 75, 78, 113
Georgiev, G.I., 47, 55, 137, 138, 140, 142, 145, 146, 147, 149, 161, 162, 178, 377, 379, 380
and Angelov, N., 47, 55, 142, 161, 178, 360, 368

Georgiev, G.I. – *contd*
and Merpert, N.I., 137, 138, 143, 151, 178, 253
Gerloff, S., 281, 282, 306, 347
Ggantija phase, 219, 256, 259
Ghar Dalam phase, 74, 257, 259, 261
Gilman, A., 262, 263
Gimbutas, M., 15, 16, 20, 137, 138, 142, 143, 149, 163, 178, 180, 185, 190, 191, 294, 298, 302, 353-4, 355, 368, 379, 384
Giot, P.R., 262, 263
Glisic, J., 142, 178
gold: armlets, 378, 379, 387
beads, 113, 360, 379, 382
bowl, 94-5
cups: Aegean, 105, 126; Mycenaean, 289, 363; Rillaton, 289, 363
metallurgy: Aegean, 88, 93, 113, 219; South East European, 141, 159, 160, 377-80, 386-8
Wessex artefacts of, 283, 289, 294, 306, 308, 353
Gradeshnitsa, 185, 186, 188
graves *see* burial conventions
Grbic, M., 48, 55, 142, 148, 178
Grey Skorba phase, 49, 74, 259
Griffin, J.B., 339, 340
Grotta-Pelos culture, 89, 90, 94, 103, 105, 366
Guerrero, M.E., 52, 55, 277
Guido, M., 50, 55
Gumelnitsa (-Kodjadermen) culture, 139, 140, 142, 143, 145, 146, 148-9, 152, 158, 162, 175, 182, 188, 190, 192, 194, 227, 343, 350, 354, 355, 358, 359, 360, 372, 379, 381, 382

H

Haggett, P., 34, 41
halberds: English, 283
Italian copper, 207, 209, 211, 232-6
Haley, J.B, and Blegen, C.W., 25, 41
Hallam, B.R., *et al.*, 65, 202
Harding, A., 305, 308
and Warren, S.E., 293, 294, 305, 308
Harris, M., 16, 20
Harrison, R.J., *et al.*, 293, 294
Haselgrove, C., 339, 340
Hawkes, C.F.C., 1, 20, 305, 342, 347, 348, 351
Hayes, W.C., *et al.*, 342, 368
Heizer, R.F., 30, 41
Helbaek, H., 260, 261
Helladic cultures: chronology of, 195, 196, 199, 244
Early Helladic I, 89, 103, 152, 195, 196, 199
Early Helladic II, 88, 89, 90, 96, 97, 103, 105, 107, 152, 195, 196, 199, 224, 232, 244, 267
Early Helladic III, 89, 195, 196, 199, 221, 222, 228
Middle, 244
Helm, J., 15, 20
Herskovits, M.J., 29, 41
Heurtley, W.A., 298, 302
Higgs, E.S., 30
Higham, C.W., 30, 41
Hill, J.N., 30, 41
Hillebrand, J., 153, 178
Hodson, F.R., 2, 20
Hole, F., and Flannery, K.V., 30, 41, 159, 178
et al., 32, 41
Hood, M.S.F., 52, 55, 137, 138, 180, 280
Hooker, J.T., 31, 41
hooks, clay, 360, 376
Houtermans, J.C., 314, 317, 324, 330, 337
Hungary, 139, 196, 342
see also Baden culture, Bodrogkeresztúr, Tiszapolgar, Nagyrév, Pecica, Periam
Hutchinson, R.W., 46, 55

I

Iassa Tepe, 140, 146, 148, 164, 358
Iberia: Aegean question *see below*, burial conventions, chronology, colonisation, Cycladic, fortifications, metallurgy, pottery, tin trade, urbanisation
Alcalà: daggers, 52, 266; tombs, 274
Almerian culture, 51, 53, 266, 267, 271, 272, 348, 350, 351, 352
amber, 268
arrowheads: copper, 266; flint, 53, 270, 271
axes: flat copper, 266; stone, 51, 270
Beakers, 52-3, 267, 269, 270, 271, 272, 290
bone pins, 51, 53
burial conventions *see* burial conventions, Iberian
Chalcolithic, 25, 28, 53-4, 263, 264, 266, 269-73, 290
Childe's views on, 9, 264-5, 267, 271, 351-2, 354
chronology: Aegean relations and, 49, 52-3, 54, 216-19, 244, 245, 262, 267, 273, 275, 348, 350, 351-3; burial conventions and, 54, 262, 266, 267, 275-6, 352, 363; problems of, 49, 52-3, 54, 243, 245, 267, 268-9, 273; radiocarbon evidence, 262, 267, 273, 275
colonisation: case against, 52-4; case for, 51-2; theory of, 9, 10, 25, 43, 44, 45, 51-4, 262, 263, 265-8, 276
cultural regions, 270-1
culture, development of local, 272-3, 276
Cycladic relations, 9, 45, 51-4
daggers, midrib, 52, 54, 56, 63, 101, 266
diadems, 237
diffusionist theory and, 9, 26, 262, 263, 265-8
Egypt and, 263-4, 271, 272
El Argar culture, 237, 268, 269
faience beads, 268, 293
figurines, 53, 263, 267, 270, 272, 351, 352
fortifications: Aegean relations and, 9, 51, 53-4, 62, 262, 266, 351; at Los Millares, 9, 51, 52, 262, 351, 352; at Vila Nova de São Pedro, 51, 53, 56, 62, 262
Iberian development, 268-73
iconography, 51, 272
idols: bone, 270; stone, 51, 53, 270

Iberia – *contd*
ivory, 23, 263, 268, 271-2
Los Millares *see* Los Millares
Mesas de Asta, 51, 52, 267, 269
metallurgy: *see* metallurgy, Iberian
Mycenaean theory, 263, 264, 265
nautical contact, feasibility of, 51
Neolithic, 51, 266, 267, 269, 271, 272-3
North African influence, 268, 271-2
pottery: Aegean relations and, 51, 52, 53; grey wares, 268; Import Ware, 51, 52, 53, 56, 63, 266, 270; Impressed Ware, 51; painted ware, 51, 52, 53, 54, 270; pattern burnished ware, 51, 52, 54, 267, 270, 272; petrological examination of, 52, 266; red monochrome, 268; *Symbolkeramik*, 267, 268, 270, 273
stratigraphy, need for studies in, 269
tin: Aegean contact question, 53, 102, 239; sources of, 102, 231, 239, 268; use of, in Iberia, 53, 102, 268
urbanisation, 9, 39, 273, 338
Vila Nova de São Pedro *see* Vila Nova de São Pedro
idols: Aegean, 51, 53, 60
Iberian, 51, 53, 270
Indo-Europeans, 9, 15-16
innovation: contact and, 18, 339
diffusion of, 9
nature and circumstances of, 339-40, 342, 343
see also invention
invention(s): contact and, 18, 339
diffusion theory and, 14, 26
human inventiveness, 3-4
independent: of Aegean metallurgy, 37-8, 103-4, 365-6; of Iberian metallurgy, 26, 262, 266, 273, 276, 339, 352, 366; of Italian metallurgy, question of, 240; of South-East European metallurgy, 26, 137, 139, 140, 143, 152-62, 238, 239, 262, 339, 354; question of, 3-5
made but once, 5, 26, 44, 49, 351
stages of civilisation and, 4-5
Tyler's view, 18-19
views of 19th C. anthropologists, 3-4
Iron Age: British, 1, 2
European: oppida of, 338; studies on, 22
irrigation, 35-7
isochronic map, 364, 365-6
Italy: Aegean question *see below* burial conventions, chronology, colonisation, Cycladic, daggers, metallurgy, pottery
agriculture, 241
Apennine culture, 218, 220, 243
arrowheads, flint, 207, 209, 211, 212, 214, 216, 225
axes: axe-hammers, 226-7; flat copper, 207, 209, 212, 232, 241, 242; stone, 207, 212, 216, 226
beads, shell, 207
Beakers, 207, 209, 219
bone and shell artefacts, 207, 209, 211, 212, 214, 216
bonework, 228-9
burial conventions *see* burial conventions, Italian
Italy – *contd*
Childe's views on, 50, 203-4, 221, 233
chronology: Aegean relations and, 49 216-19, 244, 245, 350, 351-3; calibrated dates, 352; problem of, 348; radiocarbon evidence, 216-18, 243
colonisation, 43, 203-4, 240, 241
Copper Age: Aegean Early Bronze Age and, 219; assemblages, 205-16; direct Aegean contacts, 220-3; duration of, 218; innovations of, 223-9; of Peninsular Italy, 202-54; outline of, 205-16
Crete and, 202
cups, one-handled, 207, 209, 210, 214, 227
Cycladic relations, question of, 45, 50-1, 56, 63, 64, 106
daggers, 207-42
diffusion theory, 202, 203-4, 242
faience beads, 221-2
flint artefacts, 207, 209, 211, 212, 214, 216, 225-6, 242;
metallurgy *see* metallurgy, Italian
Mycenae and, 220, 229
Neolithic, 218, 220, 241, 242
pottery: Aegean relations and, 50, 56, 64, 227-8; bowls, 211, 214; continuity with Italian Neolithic, 227-8, 241; cups, 207, 209, 210, 214, 227; dark burnished ware, 206-7, 208, 210, 211, 214, 227; jugs, 207, 211, 227; Laterza, 202, 214-15, 218; multiple vessels, 210, 227; pattern burnish ware, 50, 54, 56, 64, 267
Proto-Apennine culture, 211, 214, 218, 220, 221
settlements, 206, 207, 209, 211, 212, 213, 214
sites, distribution of, 206, 207, 209, 211, 213, 214
stone artefacts, 207, 209, 211, 212, 214, 216, 226-7, 241, 242
tin, 231, 239
see also Conelle-Ortucchio, Gaudo, Macchia a Mare, Laterza, Remedello, Rinaldone
Ivanov, I.S., 378-84
ivory: combs, 263, 268, 271, 272
in Crete, 28, 36
in Cyclades, 94, 108, 120
in Iberia, 23, 263, 268, 271-2

J

jade, 28-9
jars: barrel-shaped, 358
footed, 89, 90
lugged, 228
South-East European, 143, 149
Jericho, obsidian trade, 51, 75-6
Jovanovic, B., 137, 138
Jugoslavia: Aegean relations with, 43, 45, 47-8
copper mining in, 137
spirals, 48, 56, 59
jugs: beaked, 51, 52, 90, 100
Cretan handled, 105
Italian, 207, 211, 227
South-East European, 143, 146-7, 148, 149, 150, 151, 158, 161

Junghans, S., *et al.*, 29, 41, 53, 55, 115

K

Kalicz, N., 47, 55, 143, 178
Kapros Grave D, 93-5
Karanovo: chronology, 194, 199
  culture, 146, 148, 152
  -Kremikovci culture, 145
  stratigraphical studies at, 137, 138, 142, 144, 145, 338
  I, 148, 162
  II, 381
  III, 145, 146, 193, 194, 358
  V, 148, 175, 195, 381, 383
  VI, 137, 148, 162, 175, 194, 195, 360, 380, 381, 383
  VII, 145, 150, 152, 163
Karbuna hoard, 142, 159
Kendall, D.G., 14, 20
Kephala, 51, 199, 267, 274
Keros-Syros culture, 46, 48, 88, 89-90, 91, 92, 93, 94, 96, 97, 98, 100, 103, 105, 232, 266-7
Kingery, W.D., and Frierman, J.D., 137, 138
Knossos, 68, 89, 160, 199, 219, 222
Kohl, G., 192, 198
  and Quitta, H., 138, 194
Kohler, E.L., and Ralph, E.K., 152, 178
Kossinna, G., 6, 15, 20, 26, 351, 367, 368
Kum Tepe, 89, 139, 146, 195
Kurgan cultures, 143, 149
Kunze, E., 46, 55, 112, 113
Kythnos hoard, 88, 95-7, 106, 121, 122

L

Lagozza culture, 219, 224, 225, 226, 227, 238, 243
Lake Van, obsidian from, 68, 76, 77
Lamb, W., 150, 178
lapis lazuli, 23, 28
Laterza: group, 205, 214-16, 221, 224, 225, 226, 229, 232, 235, 236, 237, 239, 248-9
  pottery, 202, 214-15, 218
lead: artefacts, 91-2, 107-8, 118
  boat models, 46, 56, 57, 92-3, 108, 117, 119
  bracelets, 107, 108, 118
  early working of, 91-3
  figurines, 91-2, 105, 107, 117
  ingots, 91, 118
  ores, 91
  rivets, 91
  role of, 88
  use of, in Aegean, 87, 91, 92
  use of, in Crete, 87, 92
  use of, in Cyclades, 88, 91-3, 107, 108
Lebena, 88, 89, 99, 104
Leeds, E.T., 6, 20, 43, 202, 262
Leisner, G. and V., 52, 53, 55, 262, 269, 271, 280
Leisner, V., and Schubart, H., 262, 263
Lerman, J.C., *et al.*, 312, 324
Lerna, 9, 53, 89, 90, 94, 99, 105, 106, 107, 127, 152, 199, 219, 221, 266, 267
Levkas, 88, 95, 99, 100, 111
Libby, W.F., 312, 326, 337
Lipari Islands: chronology, 216, 217, 219, 243
  copper working in, 238
  obsidian, 49, 65, 68, 70, 71, 72, 73, 74, 222
  pottery: Aegean similarities in, 228; matt-painted ware, 45
  question of Aegean contacts, 50, 220, 222, 228
  trade with Malta, 49
  see also Capo Graziano culture, Diana culture
liparite, 222, 230
Lloyd, S., and Mellaart, J., 158, 178
Los Millares: as a colony, 266
  chronology of, 269, 348, 350
  fortifications at, 9, 51, 53, 262, 351, 352
  metallurgy of, 102, 366
  midrib dagger, 52
  pottery, 52, 53
  township of, 9, 39
Lubbock, J., 4, 20
Lucas, A., 41, 76, 78, 300, 302

M

Macchia a Mare group, 205, 213-14, 224, 237, 239, 248
McKerrell, H., 281, 282, 293, 305, 308, 322, 325, 326, 330, 333, 337, 338, 340
  and Tylecots, R.F., 87
maceheads, 226, 227
Maier, R.A., 49, 55
Makkay, J., 137, 138, 190, 338, 340
Mallowan, M.E.L., 29, 41
Malta: Aegean relations and, 43, 44, 48-50, 56, 61, 223, 255, 259
  agriculture, 260-1
  Childe's views on, 255
  chronology, calibrated radiocarbon dating and, 218, 255-61, 348, 352, 365
  Copper Age, 220
  cultivated plants from, 260-1
  culture periods, duration of, 259
  culture sequence, 255, 256
  diffusionist view of, 259
  faience beads, association with, 221
  figurines, 49, 56, 61, 223
  Ggantija phase, 219, 256, 259
  Ghar Dalam phase, 74, 257, 259, 261
  Grey Skorba phase, 49, 74, 259
  obsidian used in, 69, 73-4, 75, 222
  Red Skorba phase, 74, 219, 257, 259
  rock-cut tombs, 225, 365
  society of, 255
  spirals of, 259, 265
  Tarxien cemetery culture, 220, 221, 222, 228, 255, 256, 257, 259
  Tarxien culture, 255, 257, 259
  temples of, 44, 49, 255, 259, 265, 365
  trade with Lipari, 49
  Zebbug culture, 225, 256, 257, 259
Manika: dagger, 100, 106
  finds from, 127
  tweezers, 93
Mann, L.McL., 300, 302

Margos, A., and Tontcheva, G., 143, 149, 178
Marinatos, S., 45, 46-7, 55, 113
Maritsa culture, 358, 359, 360
Marseilles, question of Aegean contact, 51, 52
Maxwell-Hyslop, R., 234, 236, 253
meat weights, 30-1
Mediterranean region, obsidian in: artefacts and sources in East, 75-6
  artefacts and sources in West, 73-5
  characterisation studies on, 73-7
  sources in or near, 67
megaliths: Breton, 262, 274, 275-6
  European, 2: and South America, 5; chronology and, 262, 275-6, 367; distribution of, and migration theory, 6-7; distribution of, 8; Egyptian hypothesis, 263-4; Gallery Graves, 274; independent development of, 262, 339, 363; Near Eastern origins, question of, 24, 25, 265; Passage Graves, 274, 275, 363; problem of, 273-4, 339, 353; radiocarbon dating and, 275, 352, 363
  Iberian, 9, 24, 25, 262, 266-7, 352
  see also burial conventions
Meighan, C.W., 30, 41
Mellaart, J., 47, 48, 55, 112, 139, 147, 151, 158, 160, 178, 191, 198, 218, 343, 354, 368
Melos: lead ores, 91
  obsidian from, 68, 69, 70, 73-4, 75, 77, 89, 104, 222
  obsidian trade with Cyclades, 89
  trade with Crete, 104
Merpert, N.I., 143, 150-1, 178
metallurgy: Aegean: catalogue of objects, 107-11; culture and, 105-7; earliest finds, 195, 238; gold, 88, 93, 113, 219; Iberia and, 9, 24, 26, 51, 52, 53, 262, 265, 266, 339, 351; important finds, 97, 127; Italy and, 229-39; origins of, 37-8, 103-4, 365-6; relation of metal to ceramic forms, 95, 105, 107; silver, 87, 93, 219; social contact and, 106, 107; spread of knowledge of, 88, 104, 106; tin, sources of, 102, 239; trade and, 37-8, 88, 104, 105-6, 107; urbanisation and, 106-7; warfare and, 106
  Anatolian, 103, 106, 266, 339, 354, 365
  culture process and, 290
  Cycladic: and the Aegean Early Bronze Age, 87-136; arsenical bronze, 101, 102-3; daggers and spearheads, 97-101, 109-11, 121, 123, 124, 125, 233; evidence for, 88, 93-5; Kapros Grave D, 93-5; Kythnos hoard, 95-7; lead, 88, 91-3, 107, 118; moulds, 101; recent studies on, 87; relation of metal to ceramic forms, 95; silver, 88, 93, 94-5, 231, 237; technology, 101-3; tin bronze, 101-2; tools, 95-7, 109, 125; trade, urbanisation and, 88
  diffusion of, 139
  economic processes influencing, 8, 140
  European, 6, 8, 26, 339, 367
  foci for early copper, 339
  Iberian: Aegean relations and, 9, 24, 26,
metallurgy, Iberian – *contd*
    51, 52, 53, 262, 265, 266, 339, 351; bivalve mould, 52, 53, 266; colonisation theory and, 9, 51; independent invention of, 26, 262, 266, 273, 276, 339, 352, 366; metal resources, question of, 9, 52, 102, 231; specialisation and, 273; trade, question of, 24, 26, 51, 53, 106, 231, 273; urbanisation and, 273
  independent invention of processes, 160, 365-6
  isochronic map for origins and development of, 364, 365-6
  Italian: absence of tin, 239; Aegean relations and, 229-32; antimony, 209, 216, 237-8, 239, 240, 242; arsenical bronze, 240; awls, 236, 242; axes, 207, 209, 212, 232, 238, 241, 242; casting, 229, 238-9, 240; copper artefacts, 207, 209, 211, 212, 213, 232-7; copper slag, 238; daggers *see* daggers; early, 202, 204, 229-32, 339, 366; independent invention of, 240; metal forms, 232-8; origins of, 238-40; possible Balkan links, 229; pre-Copper Age copper, 238-9, 240, 242; razors/scrapers, 236-7; silver, 207, 211, 229-31, 237, 239, 242; smelting, 229, 238-9, 240; sources of metal, 231, 237, 239; technology, 239
  of Thailand, 339
  of the Americas, 339
  social processes and structures, 8, 140, 307-8
  South-East European: alloying, question of, 153-4, 161; annealing, 154, 160; casting, 154, 155, 156-7, 158, 160, 161, 172; ceramic technology and, 137, 160, 161, 162; Chalcolithic, 140, 142; competence of craftsmen, 154, 156, 158; copper mining, 137; double-spiral pins, 142, 154, 158, 160; early use of metal, 139, 142, 195; evolution of, 161-2; gold, 377, 378-9, 380-1; independent origin of, 26, 137, 139, 140, 143, 153-62, 238, 239, 262, 339, 354, 377, 379, 381; isolation of, 159-60; metallurgical examination of copper axes, 171-4; metal types, 139, 140, 142, 153-4, 158-9, 162; moulds, 154-5; native ores, 155; smelting, 154, 155, 160, 162; Varna and social context of, 377-8
  trade and, 37-8, 88, 104, 105-6, 107, 307-8
  urbanisation and, 35, 36, 88, 106-7, 273
  wealth and, 38, 88, 290, 307
Michael, H.N., and Ralph, E.K., 310, 317-18, 325, 331, 337
migration: and innovation, 3
  arguments adduced for, 6-7, 263
  map of megalith-builders, 6, 7, 8
  model for culture change, 25-6
  or diffusion, 5-9
  origin of notion of prehistoric, 44, 263
  question of, in Aegean, 35
Mikov, V., 142, 145, 147, 149, 150, 158, 178
Milojčic, V., 137, 139, 142, 143, 152-3, 179, 181, 190, 191, 198, 218, 343, 348, 353, 355, 358, 360, 368

Minoan: chronology, 89, 195, 199, 244
Early Minoan I, 89, 103, 104, 366
Early Minoan II, 88, 89, 90, 103, 199, 232, 244
Early Minoan III, 89
figurines, 47, 56, 60
Late Bronze empire, 88
Middle Bronze Age, 244, 259
-Mycenaean civilisation, 35, 36, 38
round tombs, 224, 264, 265, 266, 274-5, 279, 352
seals, 94
settlements, destruction of, 26
Mochlos, 88, 92, 95, 97, 111, 224, 230
monogenesis: assumptions of, 14, 16
cladistic diagram explaining, 12
evolution and, 9-14
Montelius, O., 5, 6, 8, 12-13, 20, 111, 139, 202, 233, 253, 342, 351, 368
Monteoru culture, 196, 197
Morgan, L.H., 3, 20, 26
mother goddess symbolism, 51, 265, 267
Mycenae(an): amber, 24, 281, 285, 305, 353
and the European Bronze Age, 281, 282, 288, 289
burial conventions: dromos, 54, 274; Shaft Graves, 289, 290, 353, 367; tholoi, 263, 264, 265, 266, 274, 352
chronology, 288, 305, 350, 353-4, 367
empire, 88
faience beads, 221, 289, 293, 294, 295, 305-6, 353
gold cups, 289, 353
Iberian relations, 263, 264, 265
Italian relations, 220, 229
Late Bronze Age, 88
metal traders, question of, 281
pottery, 31
urbanisation, 34, 36
Wessex and: chronological problems, 305, 350, 353-4; question of links, 198, 289-90; without Mycenae, 281-92

N

Nagyrév culture, 196, 197, 198
Nandris, J.G., 65, 140, 179
natural selection: coinages and, 10-12
Darwin's theory, 9
ethnography and, 12
Navarro, J.M. de, 23, 41
Naxos, 89, 90, 91, 92-3, 94, 95, 96, 97, 108, 117, 119, 127, 266
Nemejcová-Pavukóvá, V., 149, 179
Nestor, I., 161, 179
Neuninger, H., and Pittioni, R., 301, 302
et al., 365, 368
Neustupny, E., 2, 20, 153, 179, 190, 194, 198, 281, 282, 310, 337, 345, 348, 354, 367, 368
neutron-activation analysis, 22, 28, 65, 202, 221, 293, 298
Newton, Sir Isaac, 341-2, 367-8
Newton, R.G., and Renfrew, C., 353, 369
and Spurrell, D.J., 295, 302
Nockolds, S.R., and Allen, R., 69, 78

O

obsidian: age of, 67
artefacts and sources, 73-6
characterisation of, 28, 65-73, 79-86
daggers, 378
dating and the hydration process, 67, 72
fishing spears, 31
groupings, 68, 72, 79-86
groups and subgroups, 31, 32, 68, 69, 70, 72, 79-86
'liparite', 222, 230
neutron-activation analysis, 202, 222
properties of: characterisation and, 68; conchoidal fracture, 66, 67
quantification studies, 31-4
sources of, 31-4, 49, 65-7, 79-86, 104, 222-3
trade: Aegean, 104, 183, 184; contact zones, 33, 34; fall-off in trade, 33-4; in South-East Europe, 161; Italy/Aegean question and, 222-3; mechanisms, 188; of 7th and 8th millennia B.C., 28, 29, 31-4, 35-6; patterns of, 29, 31-4, 37; supply zones, 33; volume of, 69, 105; with Jericho, 51, 75-6; with Malta, 49; with West Mediterranean, 222-3
used in: Aegean, 35-6, 69, 75-6, 183, 184; Balkans, 183, 184; Crete, 104, 222, 230; Cyclades, 89; Deh Luran area, 31-2; Egypt, 76-7; Malta, 69, 73-4, 75, 222; Zagros area, 31-4
Oppenheim, L., 29, 41
optical spectroscopy, 28, 65, 69, 293
ostrich egg shell; African, 23, 28
beads, 221-2, 268, 271
Otto, H., and Witter, W., 155, 179
oxygen isotope analysis, 183-9

P

Palmella points, 268, 269, 270
Pantellaria, obsidian from, 49, 68, 69, 70, 73, 74, 77, 222
Passek, T.S., 142, 179
Patay, P., *et al.*, 155, 179
Peacock, D.P.S.P., 22
Pecica culture, 298, 299
pectoral, Italian silver, 207, 216, 237
Peet, T.E., 222, 253
pendants of gold: Sesklo, 159, 238
South-East European, 159, 160
Periam culture, 196-7, 289
Perry, W.J., 5, 20
Petkov, N., 142, 149, 179
Petrie, W.M.F. (Sir Flinders), 14, 20, 343-4, 369
petrological examination, 28, 29, 52, 66, 68-9, 266
Phylakopi, 35, 36, 45, 89, 90, 91, 101, 106-7, 112, 118, 224, 266
I, 89, 97, 224
I culture, 90-1, 100
Second City of, 90-1
Piggott, S., 25, 41, 54, 274, 277, 283, 288, 289, 304, 308, 353, 369

pins: bone: Aegean, 51, 53, 268; bird-headed, 116, 268; crutch-headed, 211, 229; Iberian, 51, 53, 268; Italian, 229; vase-headed, 268
  bronze or copper: Aegean, 106, 116, 158, 237; Bohemian, 237; Camerton, 283, 287; crutch-headed, 237, 283, 287; 'Cypriote', knot-headed, 163, 287; double-spiral, 106, 142, 154, 158, 160, 266; South-East European, 142, 154, 158, 160; Wessex, 283, 287
  silver: Aegean, 93; crutch-headed, 207, 216, 229, 237, 239; Italian, 207, 216, 229, 237, 239; vase-headed, 93
Pittioni, R., 29, 42, 115, 179
Pitt-Rivers, A.L.F., 1, 9, 13, 14, 20
plaques: bossed bone, Italian, 217, 221, 222, 228, 236, 241
  clay: Iberian, 268; South-East European, 148, 164
  schist, Iberian, 53, 268, 270, 272
Plog, F.T., 17, 20
do Poço, A., and Sangmeister, E., 51, 52, 55
Polanyi, K., *et al.*, 22, 29, 42
Poliochni, 88, 90, 94, 97, 100, 101, 103, 106, 111, 150, 151, 228, 266
Pontine Islands, obsidian from, 222-3
population: increase and chiefdoms, 307-8
  size and civilisation, 34-5, 36-7, 38
Popovic, V., 25, 139, 148, 153, 179, 180
pottery: Aegean: and Iberia, 51, 52, 53; and Italy, 50, 56, 64, 227-8; dark-on-light painted ware, 89, 90; Early Bronze middle and last phases, 105, 107; Minyan ware, 26, 91; painted ware, 52, 107; pattern burnished ware, 56, 64, 267
  characterisation study of, 28, 29
  Cycladic, 50, 56, 64, 89
  Iberian: *see* Iberia, pottery
  Italian: *see* Italy, pottery
  Mycenaean, 31
  Sicilian, 228, 268
  Sitagroi: *see* Sitagroi, pottery
  South-East European, 142-67, 170, 175-6, 195, 355, 380
  styles and the invasionist model, 26
  thermoluminescence dating of, 345, 363
  trade and exchange of, 22
psychic unity, concept of, 4-5, 18-19
Puxeddu, C., 73, 78
pyxides, 89, 90

Q

quantification: of animal remains, 30-1
  of artefactual material, 30
  of imported material, 31-4
  of materials from economic standpoint, 25, 30-4
  of trade, 23, 24
  quantitative evaluation of economic data, 30-4
  social organisation and, 30
Quitta, H., 138, 152, 179, 192
  and Kohl, G., 194, 198

R

racial: arguments in prehistory, 6, 15, 18, 35
  group and ethnic group, 6, 15
  origins and invention, 3, 5-6
radiocarbon dating: accuracy and reliability of, 311
  assumptions underlying, 312-13, 314
  calendar and its calibration, 310-25
  calibration *see* calibration
  chronology and: Aegean, 152, 153, 200-1, 203, 218-19, 243-4, 288, 343, 346; Egypt, 326-37, 345, 348; European megaliths, 275, 353, 363; Iberia, 262, 267, 273, 275; implications for chronology, 2, 340, 343; Italy, 216-18, 243; Malta, 218, 255-61, 348, 353, 365; Sardinia, 218, 352; Sitagroi, 191, 192, 193, 198, 200-1, 354-63; South-East Europe, 137, 138, 139, 144, 152, 153, 162, 190, 200-1, 285; Wessex, 281-2, 283, 285-8, 290, 298, 305, 306, 347-8; West Mediterranean, 43, 47, 48, 49
  development of, 2
  errors in determination, 313-14, 323
  laboratories for, 311, 314, 323, 327, 344
  physical background of, 312-13
  radiocarbon and calendar years, 287, 288
  replicate determinations, 314, 323, 330
  role of the excavator, 323-4
  stratigraphy and, 323, 333
  time scales, 2, 43, 336
  use and limitations of, 17-18
Radmilli, A., 204, 249, 253
Red Skorba culture, 74, 219, 257, 259
religion: civilisation and centres of, 34-5, 37
  influence of, and the megaliths, 8
Remedello group, 205, 206-7, 224, 225, 226, 229, 232, 234, 235, 237, 239, 240, 243, 245-6
rhyta, 89, 104
Rinaldone group, 204, 205, 207-9, 219, 224, 226, 232, 234, 235, 236, 237, 239, 243, 246-7
Ripoli culture, 219, 224, 225, 226, 227, 243, 267
Robinson, W.S., and Brainerd, G.W., 14, 20
Rodden, R.J., 25, 42
Roman, P. and Morintz, S., 195, 198
Rowe, J.A., 26, 42
Rowe, J.H., 265, 267
Rumania, 140-1, 148-9, 285
  see also Gumelnitsa, Cernavoda, Salcutsa

S

Sabloff, J., and Lamberg-Karlovsky, C.C., 22, 23
Salcutsa culture, 139, 140, 142, 372
  see also Gumelnitsa
Saliagos, 30, 47, 51, 56, 60, 152, 199, 219, 226, 244
Sandars, N.K., 353, 369
Sangmeister, E., and Schubart, H., 262, 263
Santa Olalla, J.M., 53, 55
Sardinia: Aegean relations, 44, 45, 50, 106

Sardinia – *contd*
axe-adzes, 342
chronology, 218, 352
copper ingots, 102
figurines: clay, 223; marble, 45, 50, 56, 62, 223
fortification, 56, 62
obsidian of, 70, 72, 73, 222
silver artefacts, 237
Sasso-Fiorano culture, 224, 243
sauceboats: clay, 126
distribution of, 97, 104, 105
footed, 105
marble, 105
metal, 126
with 'Urfirnis' decoration, 90, 105, 152
savagery, 3, 4, 28, 39
Savory, H.N., 262, 263
Schachermeyr, F., 48, 55
Schaeffer, C.F.A., 163, 179
Schmidt, H., 143, 153, 179
Schubart, H., 262, 263, 293, 294
Seager, R.B., 46, 55
seals: Aegean, 35, 219
and social organisation, 36, 107
Cretan, 36
Cycladic, 94, 108, 120
greenstone, 94, 108, 120
Minoan, 94
Selkirk, A., 305, 309
Sergeev, T.P., 142, 179
seriation: and relative chronology, 16, 343
procedure of Petrie, 14, 343
typological, 14, 16
use of, 16, 34
Serra d'Alto culture, 225, 243
Sesklo, 34, 35, 99, 103, 159, 160, 226, 238, 380
Sestieri, P.C., 50, 55, 254
Shackleton, N., 183
Shawcross, W., 30, 42
Sherratt, A., 307, 309
ships: controversy over construction of, 45-6, 92
Cycladic shipping, 45-7, 56, 57, 92-3, 106
evidence of, 46-7, 50, 51, 92-3
feasibility of Aegean/West Mediterranean contacts, 46-7, 50, 51
lead models of, 46, 56, 57, 92-3, 108, 117, 119
represented on frying pans, 45, 46, 56, 57, 92-3
represented on pottery, 46, 56, 57, 92
Sicily: Aegean relations, 44, 45, 49-50, 203-4, 220
Castelluccio culture, 220, 221, 228, 229, 235, 236-7, 348
chronology, 352
Copper Age, 220
fortifications, 229
pottery, 228, 268
razors, 236-7
rock-cut tombs, 45, 50, 268, 279
silver, 8, 87-118, 201, 211, 216, 219, 231, 237, 239, 242
Siret, H. and L., 9, 20, 263, 351
L., 10, 20, 44, 55, 267, 269, 277, 351, 366, 369
Sitagroi: chronology, 191, 192, 193, 198, 200, 361-3
dates: and their context, 361-4; implications of, 194-8, 354-63; radiocarbon, 191, 192, 193, 198, 200-1, 354-63
evidence of, 354-63
excavations at, 190, 191, 355
figurines, 358, 360, 373
finds: Balkan-related, 356, 358-60, 372, 375; metal, 238, 360, 376; Troy-related, 356, 360-1, 376
location of, 199, 355
phases, 188-96, 219, 227, 244, 353-63, 370-6
pottery: bowls, 357, 360, 374; corded, 196; cups, 360, 374, 375; graphite painted ware, 192, 355, 356, 358, 359, 370, 371, 372; jar, barrel-shaped, 358; jug, 374; legged bowl, 357, 358; plain dark burnished, 191, 192, 357, 358; pot, two-handled, 372; shapes, 357, 358, 359, 360
Spondylus shell, 185, 186, 188
stratigraphy, 190, 191, 192, 193, 194, 195, 198, 338, 354, 355-6, 357, 363
Slater, E.A., 87, 88
Smith: C.S., 365, 369
H.S., 343, 349
M.A., 269, 280
W.C., 29, 42
Snodgrass, A.M., 2, 20, 31, 42, 281, 282, 326
social: archaeology, 304
change, factors in, 23, 304, 339
consequences of contact, 18, 22
context of South-East European metallurgy, 377-88
development and trade, 22
development of indigenous systems, 23, 339
evolution, 3
hierarchy, 304, 307
influence of metallurgy, 8, 140, 290, 307-8
organisation, 30, 35
ranking, 377-83
significance of exchanges, 22
stratification and urbanisation, 35, 37
structure, study of early, 16-17, 339
Wessex as a social question, 304-9
Sokal, R.R., and Sneath, P.H.A., 14, 21
South-East Europe: Aegean and, chronology, 143, 144, 152, 153, 190, 191, 195, 199, 200-1, 350, 354-63, 377-81; contact in Early Bronze Age, 142, 152, 153, 157, 197-8; figurines, 47-8; extent of influence, 137, 138-9, 140, 141, 143-4, 148, 149, 162; nautical contact, 45; Neolithic contacts, 139, 143, 149, 152, 153, 194-5; shaft-hole tools, 158; Troy parallels, 150-2; Vinča-Troy equation, 137, 138-9, 142, 191, 194, 198, 343, 350, 354, 367
agriculture, 142, 161, 162
altars, clay, 147, 148, 164
Anatolia and, 139, 143, 151, 162
axes: clay, 150, 151, 166; flat metal, 142, 158, 168; shaft-hole metal, 142, 154, 155-6, 158, 159, 160, 168, 170, 171-2, 365

South-East Europe – *contd*
axe-adzes, 154, 155-6, 157, 158, 159, 160, 168, 169, 172-3, 342
Bulgarian sequence, 144-52
Chalcolithic: period, 138, 139, 140-4, 148-9, 152, 191, 194, 354; metallurgy, 140, 142; theories on end of, 143
chronology, 138-9, 140, 142, 143-4, 152-3, 162, 191, 194, 195-6, 197, 199, 343, 348, 350, 354-63
Copper Age: autonomy of, 137-76; dating of, 138-9, 143-4, 152; map of sites, 140, 141; recent studies on, 137; wealth of, 290
culture: continuity of cultural development, 144, 146-7, 148, 381; cultures, 142, 144
Early Bronze Age, 139, 143-4, 149-50, 157, 163
figurines, 47-8, 56, 58, 60, 140, 142, 147, 148, 149, 194-5, 358, 382
metallurgy, *see* metallurgy, South-East European
Neolithic, 138-9, 152, 194-5, 354
ochre graves, 143, 150, 151, 152, 199
pottery, 142-67, 170, 175-6, 195, 355
radiocarbon dating, 137, 138, 139, 144, 152, 153, 162, 190, 200-1, 285
Sitagroi, radiocarbon and prehistory of, 190-201
stratigraphical evidence, 137, 138, 142, 144-52, 162
trade, 161-2
village settlements, 140, 142, 148, 161
spearheads, 88, 95, 97, 98, 207, 266
specialisation: metallurgy and, 37, 106, 242, 308
urbanisation and, 35, 37, 106-7
spirals, evidence of the, 47, 48, 56, 59, 259, 265
Spondylus shell, 23, 47, 56, 60, 161, 183-9, 207, 381-2
Srejovic, D., 139, 148, 179
Starčevo culture, 145, 148, 152
statistical: methods and cross-dating, 342-3
studies of obsidian, 31-4
Sterud, G., 2, 21
Steward, J.H., 26-7, 42
Stone, J.P.S., 221, 254, 295, 303
and Thomas, L.C., 31, 42, 65, 69, 78, 289, 293, 294, 296, 298, 299, 303
Stonehenge, 286, 298, 305, 307, 367
Stronach, D.B., 96, 98, 111, 235, 236, 254
Stuiver, M., and Suess, H.E., 152, 179
Suess, H.E., 152, 163, 179, 192, 198, 257, 260, 285, 286, 310, 311, 314, 317, 323, 325, 327, 330, 336, 337, 344, 369
Switsur, V.R., 310, 317-18, 320, 325
swords, 97-8, 100, 101, 111, 124
Symbolkeramik, 267, 268, 270, 272
Syros, 88, 89, 93, 237
see also Chalandhriani, Keros-Syros

T

Tarxien: cemetery culture, 220, 221, 222, 228, 255, 256, 257, 259
Tărtăria tablets, 152-3, 180-2
Taylour, W.D., 45, 55, 220, 254, 277
Tell Azmak, 140, 146, 147, 195
Tell Goljanio Delschevo, 185, 186, 187, 188
temples, Maltese, 44, 49, 255, 259, 265, 365
Thaspos culture, 229, 268, 279
Thermi, 89, 90, 92, 102, 103, 104, 111, 150, 151, 266
thermoluminescence dating of pottery, 345, 363
tholoi *see* burial conventions
Thomas, H.L., 2, 21, 43, 310, 311
tin: Aegean sources of, 101, 102, 135, 239
bronze, 101-2, 103, 130, 131, 132, 135-6, 240
Iberia and: Aegean contact question, 53, 102, 239; sources of, 102, 231, 239, 268; use of, 53, 102, 268
Italian, 231, 239
Mycenaean traders and, 281
trade in, 106, 239, 241
Tiryns culture, 221, 222, 228, 244
Tiszapolgar culture, 142, 161, 198, 199
Tite, M.S., 22, 23, 137, 138
Todorovic, J., and Cermanovic, A., 142, 148, 179, 181
tombs *see* burial conventions
trace-element analysis, 29, 33, 65, 69, 293, 301
trade: and contact, 17, 22, 23, 27-8, 37, 38
as a subsystem of culture, 17, 23-4
as indicator of and motive for contact, 23, 37
characterisation studies of, 66
cultural significance of, 24, 37
culture change and, 22, 23, 24, 25-8
culture process and, 22-42
defined, 24-5
economic development and, 22, 23-4, 27
economic importance of, 24
functions of, 27-8
importance of, 23
interregional Aegean, 34-9, 88-9
investigation of trading systems, 28-9
kinds of, 28
maritime, 45
mechanisms, 23, 24-5
metallurgy and, 24, 26, 37-8, 51, 53, 88, 106, 231, 273
obsidian, 28, 29, 31-4, 35-6, 49, 51, 75-6, 89, 104, 105, 161, 183, 184, 188, 222-3
prestige good, 183, 188-9
proof of, 24
qualitative studies of, 34-8
quantitative studies of, 23, 24, 31-4
recent studies in, 22-3
social development and, 22
Spondylus shell, 183-9
urbanisation and, 25, 34-9
see also exchange
tree-ring calibration *see* calibration
Tringham, R., 137, 138
Troad, 89, 98, 100, 102, 105, 123
Troy: chronology, 44, 195, 196, 244, 342
Cincinnati excavations, 89, 103
daggers, 98
figurine, lead, 92

Troy – *contd*
fortifications, 219, 266
parallels for Bulgarian sequence, 150-2
phases: I, 90, 103, 138-9, 140, 147, 150, 152, 196, 244, 360, 367; I-IV, and South-East Europe, 137, 196; II, 35, 88, 90, 94, 95, 102, 106, 150, 196, 219, 244, 360, 377-9
size of, 35, 36
stone tools, 227, 360
-Tordos, 143
-Vinča equation, 137, 138-9, 143, 191, 194, 198, 343, 350, 354, 367
Trump, D., 49, 55, 74, 78, 204, 207, 223, 249, 254, 255, 256, 257, 259, 260, 348, 369
Tsountas, C., 45, 46, 55, 91, 92, 101, 159, 160, 179, 254, 380, 384
tweezers, 93, 104, 106, 266
Tyler, E.B., 1, 3, 4, 18-19, 21, 339
typological: classification, 30
comparisons and contact, 66
method of Montelius, 12-13, 342
seriation, 14, 16

U

Übergangszeit, 196, 242
Unétice culture, 139, 163, 196, 197, 198, 281, 282, 287, 290, 298
urbanisation: Aegean, 27, 34-9, 106-7, 338
agricultural efficiency and, 36, 37, 38
centralisation and, 34
communications and, 35, 38
control of environment and, 37
culture intensification and, 36, 37, 38
culture process and, 35-6, 37-8
defined, 34-5
factors in, 38-9
fortifications and, 35, 36, 38, 106
Iberian, 9, 39, 273, 338
metallurgy and, 35, 36, 88, 106-7, 273
oppida of Iron Age, 338-9
population size and, 34-5, 36-7, 38
religion and, 37
settlement size and, 34-5, 36, 106
specialisation and, 35, 37, 106-7
trade and, 25, 34-9
transformation from village economy to, 35, 38-9
wealth and, 35, 38
Urnfield cultures, 16, 286, 301

V

Vajsova, H., 148, 179, 358, 360
Varna: and the social context of early metallurgy, 377-88
burial conventions, 377, 378, 379, 382, 387
chronology, 377, 378-9, 380
extent of site, 379
goldwork, 377, 379, 380, 386-8
pottery, 379, 380
significance of, 377, 378, 379, 380, 382-3
social ranking, 377, 378, 379, 382-3
wealth of, 378, 379, 383
Vesselinovo culture, 145, 146-8, 165, 192, 194, 357, 358
Vila Nova de São Pedro: as a colony, 266
bone pins, 51, 268
chronology, 269
fortifications, 51, 53, 56, 62, 262
Import Ware, 51, 52, 56, 63, 266
metallurgy, 51, 102
painted ware, 51, 52, 268
pottery, 51, 52-3
township of, 39
Vinča: chronology, 44, 48, 194, 357
culture, 142, 148, 164, 350, 357, 358
Early, 138-9
obsidian artefacts from, 77
phases: A-B, 148, 199; C-D, 142, 199; Pločnik, 142, 148, 194; *Spondylus* shell artefacts from, 185, 186, 188
Tordos, 148, 182, 194, 266
Troy-Vinča equation, 137, 138-9, 143, 191, 194, 198, 343, 350, 354, 367
Vlassa, N., 42, 152, 179, 180
Vučedol culture, 191, 196, 234
Vulpe, A., 158, 179

W

Wainwright, G.A., 76, 78
warfare, metallurgy and, 37, 106, 242, 366
wealth: metal as form of, 38
metallurgy and, 38, 88, 290, 307, 366
of Aegean Early Bronze period II, 88, 106-7, 219
of Amorgos, 95
of Cretan Early Bronze Age, 290
of South-East European Chalcolithic, 142-3
of Wessex, 290, 304, 306, 307
personal, and display, 307
Weinberg, S.S., 25, 35, 42, 49, 56, 111, 112, 148, 179, 193
Wendland, W.M., and Donley, D.S., 310, 317, 325
Wertime, T., 137, 138, 161, 179, 339, 340
Wessex: amber, 283, 289, 294, 306, 308, 353
and its contemporaries, 283-5
and the Beakers, 197, 282, 283, 284, 286
Armorican Early Bronze Age and, 283-4, 285, 290
as a social question, 304-9
barrow burials, 306-7
bone objects, 289
chiefdoms, 304, 307
chronology: question of, 163, 197, 198, 281-2, 285-8, 290, 305, 306, 347-8, 367; radiocarbon dating, 281-2, 285-8, 290, 305, 306, 347-8; relative, 283-5, 347-8
copper, 283, 289
culture: defined, 283; duration of, 306, 347-8; phase I, 283, 287-8, 347; phase II, 283, 287-8
faience beads, 281, 283, 289, 295, 296, 298, 301, 305, 306, 353
gold, 283, 289, 294, 306, 308, 353
Mycenae: and Wessex, 289-90, 305; contact question, 198, 350, 353-4; Wessex without, 281-92
Pelynt dagger, 289, 353

Wessex – *contd*
pins, 283, 287
Rillaton cup, 289, 353
trade function and, 28
Unétice and, 282, 283, 290
wealth of, 290, 304, 306, 307
West Mediterranean: Aegean and, 43-64, 350-3
nautical feasibilities, 45-7
obsidian artefacts and sources, 73-5
traditional approach to prehistory of, 43, 44-5, 49, 51-2
see also Iberia, Italy, Malta, Sardinia, Sicily
Westropp, M.H., 4-5, 21
Wheeler, Sir Mortimer, 338, 340
Whittle, E.H., and Arnaud, J.M., 262, 263
Willey, G.R., and Phillips, P., 26, 42
Willis, E.H., *et al*., 313, 325, 344, 369
Wilson, D., 2, 21
Wolters, P., 92, 94, 112, 113
Worsaae, J.J.A., 1, 5, 6-7, 21, 342, 369
writing, 34-5, 36, 38

Z

Zebbug culture, 225, 256, 257, 259
Zervos, C., 45, 46, 112, 113
Zies, E.G., 73, 78
Ziomecki, J., 47, 56
Zygouries, 88, 91, 99